The Practice in Proceedings in the Probate Courts of Massachusetts. With an Appendix of Uniform Forms and Rules Approved by the Supreme Judicial Court

You are holding a reproduction of an original work that is in the public domain in the United States of America, and possibly other countries. You may freely copy and distribute this work as no entity (individual or corporate) has a copyright on the body of the work. This book may contain prior copyright references, and library stamps (as most of these works were scanned from library copies). These have been scanned and retained as part of the historical artifact.

This book may have occasional imperfections such as missing or blurred pages, poor pictures, errant marks, etc. that were either part of the original artifact, or were introduced by the scanning process. We believe this work is culturally important, and despite the imperfections, have elected to bring it back into print as part of our continuing commitment to the preservation of printed works worldwide. We appreciate your understanding of the imperfections in the preservation process, and hope you enjoy this valuable book.

THE

PRACTICE IN PROCEEDINGS

IN

THE PROBATE COURTS

OF MASSACHUSETTS.

WITH AN

APPENDIX OF UNIFORM FORMS AND RULES
Approved by the Supreme Judicial Court

By WILLIAM L. SMITH,
Counsellor at Law.

SIXTH EDITION,

REVISED BY JOHN E. ABBOTT.

Adapted to the Revised Laws and embodying the
Probate Laws enacted in 1902

BOSTON.
LITTLE, BROWN, AND COMPANY.
1903.

T
Sm6865 p
1903

Entered according to Act of Congress, in the year 1863, by
LITTLE, BROWN, AND COMPANY,
In the Clerk's Office of the District Court of the District of Massachusetts

Entered according to Act of Congress, in the year 1876, by
LITTLE, BROWN, AND COMPANY,
In the Office of the Librarian of Congress, at Washington

Entered according to Act of Congress, in the year 1884, by
LITTLE, BROWN, AND COMPANY,
In the Office of the Librarian of Congress, at Washington.

Copyright, 1894, 1899, 1903, 1904,
BY LITTLE, BROWN, AND COMPANY

UNIVERSITY PRESS · JOHN WILSON
AND SON · CAMBRIDGE, U S A

PREFACE TO FIRST EDITION.

The design of this work is to present in a concise form the law and rules of practice regulating the proceedings in the probate courts. The leading cases in which questions of probate law have been considered and determined, have been carefully collected and cited. And the instructions as to the formal proceedings have been prepared with the view of practically aiding the correct and safe discharge of the responsible trusts to which they relate. The work is submitted to persons interested in the business of the probate courts, in the hope that it will, to some extent at least, supply a want that has been a subject of frequent remark.

W. L. S.

Springfield, Mass , Sept , 1863

PREFACE TO SIXTH EDITION.

The enactment of the Revised Laws made necessary a new edition of Smith's Probate Law. So far as concerns probate law and practice, the present edition includes the Revised Laws, the laws passed by the General Court in 1902, and the important decisions contained in Volumes 1 to 180, inclusive, of the Massachusetts Reports, together with a few cases which will appear in Volumes 181 and 182.

Radical changes have been made by the Revised Laws as to property rights of husbands and wives, and a statement of these changes will be found in the chapter relating to the Descent of Real Estate. Not only this subject, but also the subjects of Partition of Real Estate, Appeals, Survival of Actions, and the Collateral Inheritance and Succession Tax will be found to be much more fully treated in the present edition than in any former one.

Special attention is called to the case of Abbott *v.* Gaskins, 181 Mass. 501, in which the subject of the equity jurisdiction of the probate court is reviewed and carefully considered, and to the case of Bartlett v. Slater, 182 Mass. 208.

The editor trusts that the new index will prove to be a convenient guide to the contents of this edition.

JOHN E. ABBOTT.

Boston, Mass , January 10, 1903

CONTENTS.

	Page
TABLE OF CASES	xi
INDEX TO STATUTES	xxvii

CHAPTER I.

THE PROBATE COURTS — THEIR ORIGIN AND GENERAL JURISDICTION 1

CHAPTER II.

PROBATE OF WILLS 29
WHO MAY MAKE A WILL 30
THE FACTS TO BE PROVED IN SUPPORT OF THE WILL . . 31
    SECTION 1. As to the Signing by the Testator 31
    " 2. As to the Attestation by the Witnesses . . . 36
    " 3. As to the Competency of the Attesting Witnesses 39
    " 4. Execution of Codicils 42
    " 5. As to the Testator's Soundness of Mind . . . 44
    " 6. Wills Invalidated by Fraud and Undue Influence 55
    " 7. Revocation of Wills 59
    " 8. Formal Proceedings 70
    " 9. Proof of Wills made out of the State . . . 78
    " 10. Proof of Lost Wills 79
    " 11. Allowance of Wills proved out of the State . 81
    " 12. Proof of Nuncupative Wills 83

CHAPTER III

DEPOSIT, CUSTODY, AND PROCEEDINGS IN CASE OF CONCEALMENT OF WILLS 91

CHAPTER IV.

Appointment of Executors 94

CHAPTER V

Appointment of Administrators 102

CHAPTER VI

Appointment of Guardians 126

CHAPTER VII.

Appointment of Trustees — Trusts 144

CHAPTER VIII

Removal and Resignation of Executors and Others . . 159

CHAPTER IX

Inventories and the Collection of the Effects of Deceased Persons and Wards 168

CHAPTER X

Allowances to Widows, Minor Children, and Others . 177

CHAPTER XI

Sale of Personal Estate by Executors and Others — Sales and Investments by Guardians and Trustees — Temporary Investments by Executors . 184

CHAPTER XII

Notice of the Appointment of Executors, etc., and Payment of Debts and Legacies 192

CHAPTER XIII

Insolvent Estates of Deceased Persons 211

CHAPTER XIV

SALES OF LAND BY EXECUTORS, ADMINISTRATORS, AND GUARDIANS 239

CHAPTER XV

ACCOUNTS OF EXECUTORS, ADMINISTRATORS, GUARDIANS, AND TRUSTEES 279

CHAPTER XVI.

DESCENT AND DISTRIBUTION — ADVANCEMENTS 320

CHAPTER XVII.

PARTITION OF LANDS IN THE PROBATE COURT 374

CHAPTER XVIII

ASSIGNMENT OF DOWER AND OTHER LIFE-ESTATES . . 397
TABLE SHOWING THE PRESENT WORTH OF ESTATES IN DOWER 420

CHAPTER XIX.

PROBATE BONDS 428

CHAPTER XX.

SPECIFIC PERFORMANCE OF AGREEMENTS TO CONVEY LANDS — ARBITRATION AND COMPROMISE — SALE OF STANDING WOOD AND TIMBER — PURCHASE OF INTERESTS IN REAL ESTATE OF WARDS — SUPPORT OF MARRIED WOMEN LIVING APART FROM THEIR HUSBANDS — SUPPORT OF MINOR CHILDREN UNDER GUARDIANSHIP — SALE AND RELEASE OF A WIFE'S INTEREST IN LANDS WHEN THE HUSBAND IS UNDER GUARDIANSHIP — RELEASE OF CURTESY, DOWER, AND HOMESTEAD ESTATES BY GUARDIANS OF INSANE PERSONS — CONFIRMATION OF DEFECTIVE ACTS OF EXECUTORS AND OTHERS — CONTRIBUTION AMONG DEVISEES AND LEGATEES — WRITS OF HABEAS CORPUS 448

x CONTENTS.

CHAPTER XXI.

	Page
APPEALS FROM THE PROBATE COURT	463

CHAPTER XXII.

ADOPTION OF CHILDREN AND CHANGE OF NAME	479

CHAPTER XXIII.

MISCELLANEOUS PROVISIONS — SESSIONS OF THE PROBATE COURTS — JUDGES OF PROBATE — JUVENILE OFFENDERS — REGISTERED LAND — COMMITMENT OF INSANE PERSONS AND INEBRIATES — APPOINTMENT OF PROBATE COURT OFFICERS — ACTIONS BY AND AGAINST EXECUTORS AND ADMINISTRATORS — TRUSTEE PROCESS AGAINST EXECUTORS AND ADMINISTRATORS — ANNUAL RETURNS OF SHARES IN CORPORATIONS BY GUARDIANS — RIGHTS OF EXECUTORS TO VOTE AT CORPORATION MEETINGS — LIABILITY OF EXECUTORS FOR CORPORATION STOCK — RIGHT OF TRUSTEES OR GUARDIANS TO RELEASE DAMAGES FOR LAND TAKEN BY RAILWAY COMPANIES — EMBEZZLEMENT BY TRUSTEES, ETC. — CONCERNING THE INSANE — SPECIAL TRUST FUNDS FOR PARKS — FEES OF WITNESSES 488

CHAPTER XXIV

TAXATION OF COLLATERAL LEGACIES AND SUCCESSIONS	506

APPENDIX.

PROBATE RULES	527
EQUITY RULES	531
PROBATE FORMS	539

INDEXES	745

TABLE OF CASES CITED.

[THE FIGURES REFER TO THE PAGES]

A

Abbott v Abbott	423
v Bradstreet	16, 313
v Cottage City	505
v Foote	145, 312
v Gaskins	9, 80, 90, 158
Abercrombie v Sheldon	99, 195, 428
Adams v Adams	180, 182, 209, 210, 407
v Brackett	252
v Briggs Iron Co	394
v Field	32
v Leland	164
Ago v Conner	339
Aiken v Morse	195, 197, 218
Alden v Stebbins	197
Aldrich, Appellant	20
Alger v Colwell	98, 215, 433
Allen, Petitioner	253
v Ashley School Fund	244, 247
v Dean	162, 241
v Edwards	208, 360, 499
v Libbey	381, 388
Allendorff v Gaugengigl	404
Allis v Morton	135
Almy v Crapo	294
American Legion of Honor v Perry	289
Ames v Armstrong	429
v Jackson	198, 253, 297, 300
Ammidown v Kinsey	315
Andrees v Weller	53
Arms v Lyman	378
Arnold v Sabin	113, 116, 123, 176
Ashley, Appellant	362
Atherton v Corliss	31, 332, 407
Attorney-General v Barbour	145, 163, 164
v Brigham	197
v Garrison	161
Atwood v Atwood	403
Avery v. Pixley	62
Ayer v. Ayer	209
v Breed	467

B

Bacon, Appellant	19
Bacon v Bacon	47
v Gassett	363
v Pomeroy	220, 495
Baker v Baker	397
v Blood	11
v Dening	33
Balch v Shaw	514
v Stone	321, 322, 348
Baldwin v Parker	46, 76
v Standish	429
v Timmins	245, 396
Ballard v Carter	69
v Ives	351
Bamforth v Bamforth	276
Bancroft v Andrews	106, 251, 466
v Boston & Worcester Railroad Co	495
Bannatyne v Bannatyne	54
Baptist Church v Roberts	63
Bard v Wood	281
Barker v. Comins	47
Barnaby v Barnaby	419
Barnes v Boardman	387, 393
v Lynch	386, 393
Barney v Tourtellotte	453
Barry v Butlin	47
Bartlet v Harlow	393
Bartlett, Petitioner	16, 152, 505
Barton v Rice	362
v White	487
Bascom v Butterfield	213, 218
Bassett v Crafts	154
v Drew	113, 201
v Granger	203, 213, 307, 319
Batchelder, Petitioner	358
v Cambridge	120
Bates, Petitioner	411
Baxter v Abbott	46, 48, 49, 50, 74
Bayley v. Bayley	66, 76, 78
Beaman v Elliott	106
Bean v Farnan	449
Bemis v. Bemis	195

TABLE OF CASES CITED

[The figures refer to the Pages]

Bemis v Driscoll	422
v Leonard	248
v Stearns	361
Bennett v Brooks	36
v Kimball	158
v Overing	441, 442
v Russell	442, 444
v Sharp	76
v Sherrod	61 63
v Woodman	279, 441
Bent v Cobb	259
Beverstock v Brown	262
Bibb v Thomas	62
Bigelow v Bigelow	454
v Folger	219
v Gillott	66
v Hubbard	400
v Poole	362
Billings v Billings	163, 209
v Taylor	402
Blackinton v Blackinton	178, 356, 452
Blackler v Boott	208, 350
Blagge v Miles	351
Blan, Ex parte	186
Blake v Pegram	147, 281, 311, 311, 317
v Ward	315, 319, 440
Blanchard v Allen	195, 223, 236
Blaney v Blaney	252
Bliss v Lee	213
Blodgett v Moore	68
Blossom v. Blossom	403
v. Brightman	393
Bogle v. Bogle	165
Boldry v Parris	37
Bonnemort v Gill	99, 476
Booth v. Blundell	54
Borden v Jenks	149, 406
Bordman v Smith	227
Boston v Robbins	29, 450
Boston Bank v Minot	499
Boston Safe Deposit Co v Mixter 189, 239, 248, 254, 258, 264, 270, 275
Boulton v Beard	295
Bowditch v Banuelos	164
v Raymond	220
v Soltyk	16
Bowdlear v Bowdlear	350, 483
Bowdoin v Holland	104, 105
Bowen v Hoxie	350, 352, 460
Bowers v Hammond	222, 236
Bowker v Pierce	307, 311
Boyden v Mass Insurance Co	206, 208, 219, 221
Boylston v Carver	396
Boynton v Dyer	292, 293, 307, 308, 464

Boynton v P & S Railroad	288, 293
Bradford v Forbes	196
v Monks	115
Bradley v. Brigham	290
Bradstreet v Butterfield	144, 145
Brant v Wilson	66
Brazer v Clark	439
v Dean	130
Breed v Pratt	49, 53
Brettun v Fox	31, 339, 423
Brewster v Brewster	303
Bridge v. Bridge	296, 299, 317, 474, 475
Brierly v Equitable Aid Union	170
Briggs v. Barker	471
Brigham v Boston & Albany R R Co	254, 258
v Elwell	293, 294
v. Fayerweather	5
v Hunt	244
v Wheeler	131
Brimmer v Sohier	48
Bristol County Savings Bank v Woodward	221
Broadway National Bank v. Wood	231
Broderick v Broderick	38
Brooks v Barrett	49
v Brooks	445
v Jackson	294
v Lynde	207
v Rayner	196
v Rice	438
v. Tobin	165, 285, 438
v Whitmore	159, 430, 431, 435
Brow v Brightman	128
Brown v Anderson	297
v Baron	319
v Brown	44
v Corey	15
v Cushman	113
v Dean	495
v Greene	199
v Greenfield Life Association	171
v Howe	310
v Kelsey	291
v Kendall	494
v Lapham	404
v Pendergast	498, 499
v Thorndike	66
v Wells	88
Browne v Doolittle	5, 6, 72, 197, 204, 207, 212, 213, 215, 248, 266, 304, 318, 319, 355, 359, 366
Brownell v Briggs	323, 375, 454
Brush v Wilkins	67
Bryant v Allen	467

TABLE OF CASES CITED.

[The figures refer to the Pages.]

Bryce, *In re*	33	Child *v* Boston & Fairhaven Iron Works	496
Brydges *v* King	58	*v* Coffin	495
Buckley *v* Buckley	303	Childs *v* Jordan	170
v Frasier	324, 397, 483	Chilson *v* Adams	261
v Gerard	350, 351	Choate *v* Arrington	294, 442
Bucknam *v* Bucknam	451	*v* Jacobs 177, 203, 294, 440, 441	
v Phelps	216	*v* Thorndike 170, 289, 435	
Buffington *v* Fall River National Bank	407	Christopher *v* Christopher	67
Bulkeley *v* Noble	362	Church *v* Crocker	350
Bullard *v* Attorney-General	154, 155, 109, 436	*v* Savage	197, 267
		Clark *v* Clark	48
v Bullard	362	*v* Clay	281, 301
Burbank *v* Burbank	450	*v* Dunnevant	75
Burke *v* Burke	308	*v* Fisher	58
v Colbert	31, 324	*v* Garfield	306
Burns *v* United Workmen	171, 174	*v* Holbrook	201, 203
Burnside *v* Merrick	403	*v* Lancy	495
Burt *v* Ricker	186	*v* Tainter	240
Bush *v* Clark	180	*v* Wright	77, 79, 80
Butman *v* Porter	400	Clarke *v* Chapin	429
Buttrick *v* Tilton	325	*v* Cordis	138, 449
		v Schwarzenberg	171
		v Stanwood	231
C.		*v* Tufts	239, 242
Cady *v* Comey	499	Clarkson *v* De Peyster	292, 308
Caffrey *v* Darby	290	Cleveland *v* Quilty	12, 403
Callahan *v* Woodbridge	514, 522	Coates *v* Cheever	402
Capen *v* Duggan	499	Cobb *v* Kempton 160, 183, 201, 202, 243, 246, 312, 445	
v Skinner	470, 471		
Carlton *v* Carlton	42	*v* Muzzey	212, 298
Carpenter *v* Carpenter	289	*v* Newcomb	110
Carruth *v* Carruth	145, 146	*v* Rice	14
Carson *v* Carson	499	Cochran *v* Thorndike	324
Cassidy *v* Shimmin	174	Codman *v*. Brooks	322
Casson *v* Dade	37	*v* Krell	349
Cathaway *v* Bowles	356	Coffin *v* Cottle	6, 19
Catlin *v* Ware	300	Cole *v* Eaton	445
Caverly *v* Eastman	244	Colegrove *v* Robinson	213
Chadbourn *v* Chadbourn	449	Coleman *v* Hall	214
Chamberlin *v* Chamberlin	249	Coles *v* Trecothick	32
Chambers *v* Queen's Proctor	49	Collamore *v* Learned	479
Chandler *v* Ferris	57	Collier *v* Simpson	49
v R R Commissioners	181	Collins *v* Collins 98, 155, 168, 169, 200, 242, 201, 313	
v Simmons	134		
Chapin *v* Livermore	445	Colt *v* Learned	495
v Miner	15	Colwell *v* Alger	98, 108
v Waters, 98, 249, 288, 434, 489, 442		Commonwealth *v* Briggs	130
		v Fairbanks	18
Chase *v* Fitz	113, 496	*v* Keith	41
v Kittredge	36, 88, 73, 74	*v* Lines	42
v Lincoln	73	*v* Robinson	42
v Thompson	232, 366, 367	*v* Rogers	41
v Webster	179	*v* Wilson	49
Cheney *v* Webster	197, 200	Conant *v* Kendall	445
Cheney *v* Davis	289	*v* Kent	322
Cheshire National Bank *v* Jewett	172	*v* Little	397
		v Newton	439

TABLE OF CASES CITED

[The figures refer to the Pages]

Conant v Stratton	437, 442
Coney v Williams	433
Conkey v Dickinson	439
Conklin v Egerton's Administrator	239
Conly v Conly	496
Conner v Shepherd	413
Constantinides v. Walsh	199, 211, 324
Conto v Silvia	126
Converse v Converse	45
v Johnson	175, 197, 204, 212
v Wales	350
Cook v Horton	466
Cooke v Gibbs	497
Cooper v Robinson	258
Copeland v Sturtevant	425
Corcoran v Boston & Albany R R Co	496
Cote v Lawrence Manuf. Co	404
Cottle, Appellant	20
Coughlen's Case	54
Coverdale v Aldrich	240, 287
Cowden v Jacobson	340, 353, 476
Cowdrey v. Cowdrey	398, 424
Coye v Leach	358
Cravath v Plympton	495
Crippen v Dexter	66, 78, 83
Croade v Ingraham	413
Crocker v Cotting	374, 375
v Shaw	514
Crosbie v Macdonald	43
Crosby v Leavitt	101
Crouch v Eveleth	241
Crowninshield v. Crowninshield	47, 49
Cummings v Bird	496
v Bramhall	361, 363
v Cummings	318, 319, 348
v. Hodgdon	7, 463
v. Thompson	225
v Watson	294
Curley v. Squire	216
Curry v Spencer	511
Curtis v Bailey	281
Cushing v Burrell	209
v Field	212, 234
Cutter v Hamlen	495
Cutting v Tower	496
Cutto v Gilbert	64, 65
Cutts v Haskins	6
v Hodgdon	126

D

Daggett v White	155
Dale v. Hanover National Bank	177, 179, 180
Daley v. Francis	252, 471, 474, 475
Dallinger v Davis	195, 197
v. Richardson	5, 7
Dalton v Savage	320, 324, 330
Dan v Brown	62, 80
Dana v Wentworth	497
Dane v Dane Manuf Co	495
Daniels v. Pratt	289
Darley v Darley	58
D Arusment v Jones	119
Davis v. Calvert	49, 56
v Cowdin	319
v Davis	58, 79, 499
v Fsty	237
v French	296
v Sigourney	63, 79, 80
Davy v Smith	37
Dawes v Boylston	104, 105, 353
v Head	237, 440
v Shed	297, 433
v Winship	439
Dean v Dean's Heirs	78
Deane v Caldwell	220
Dearborn v Preston	377, 463
Deering v Adams	464
Defriez v Coffin	355, 436
Delafield v Parish	47
Delano v Bruerton	330, 483
Delay v Vinal	407
Demerritt v Randall	74
Demond v Boston	494
Dempsey v Lawson	65
Denholm v McKay	185, 257, 318
Derome v Vose	5, 7
Desper v Continental Water Meter Co	190
Dew v Clark	55
Dewey v Dewey	33, 34, 36, 38, 75
DeWitt v Harvey	395
Dexter v Brown	123
v Codman	149, 326, 466
v Cotting	72, 145, 156, 189, 248, 266, 436
v Inches	321
v Shepard	248
Dickey v Taft	175
Dickinson, Appellant	307
v Arms	297
v. Barber	48
v Durfee	259
Dietrick v Dietrick	56, 58
Dixon v Homer	145, 146
Dodd v Winship	317, 319, 465
Dodge v Breed	227
v March	58
Doe v Caperton	38, 74
v. Griffin	358

TABLE OF CASES CITED

[The figures refer to the Pages]

Doe v Harris	58, 62
v Lancashire	67
v Manifold	37
v Perks	62
Doherty v O'Callaghan	59, 474
Donovan v McCarty	36
Doole v Doole	452, 470, 472
Dorr v Wainwright	146, 291, 438
Downer, In re	61
Downing v Porter	465
Downs v Flanders	452
Doyle v Coburn	422
Drake v Green	161, 163
Draper v Baker	405
Drew v Carroll	388, 394
v Gordon	182, 183
Drinkwater v Drinkwater	240
Drummond v Parish	86
Drury v Natick	156
Dubé v Beaudry	134
Dublin v Chadbourn	5, 29
Dudley v Warner	80
Dunbar v Tainter	295
Duncan v Beard	74
Dunham v Dunham	433, 473, 474
Dunlap v Watson	292
Durant v Ashmore	79
Durfee v Durfee	80
Du Vivier v Hopkins	226
Dyer v Clark	403

E.

Eastham v Barrett	375, 377, 378, 379, 398, 424
Edds, Appellant	481
Eddy v Adams	200, 215
Edmunds v Rockwell	253
Edwards v Ela	299
Ela v Edwards	32, 33, 34, 39, 249
Eliot v Eliot	39
Eliott v Sparell	210
Elliot v Elliot	377, 378
Ellis v Boston, Hartford, & Erie R R	165
v Page	252
Ellsworth v Thayer	223
Elms v Elms	62
Emerson v Paine	222
v Thompson	297
Emery v. Batchelder	353
v Bidwell	499
v Burbank	89
v Hildreth	104
Emmons v Shaw	514
Essex v Brooks	9, 507, 522
Estes v Wilkes	193
Esty v Clark	353

Euston v Seymour	85
Evans' Appeal	60
Ewing v King	196

F.

Fales v Fales	381
Fall River v Riley	432
Fall River Whaling Co. v Borden	231
Fargo v. Miller	348
Farnum v Bascom	252
v Boutelle	221
Farrar v. Parker	467
Farwell v Steen	311
Faxon v Faxon	376
Fay v Haven	105, 292, 353, 433
v. Howe	307
v Hunt	484
v Muzzey	170, 287
v Rogers	441
v Taylor	250, 287, 437
v Valentine	438
v Vanderford	474
Felch v Hooper	190
Fellows v Smith	178
Fetherly v Waggoner	80
Field v Hanscomb	390
v Hitchcock	318
Finney v Barnes	192
Fisher v Metcalf	297
Fiske v Fiske	31, 332
v Pratt	474, 481
Fitts v Morse	363
Fletcher v Livingston	450
Flint v Valpey	213
Flintham's Appeal	200
Florey's Executors v Florey	59
Flynn v Flynn	327, 398, 400, 416
v Mass Benefit Association	171, 174
Foot v Dickinson	416
Forbes v Harrington	203, 431
v McHugh	96, 108, 169, 174, 279, 303, 436
Ford v Ford	61, 62
Forster v Forster	263
Forward v Forward	292, 295, 297
Foss v Hartwell	128
Foster's Appeal	80
Foster v Bailey	279
v Fifield	182, 287
v Leland	425
v Smith	324, 330
v Starkey	297
v Waterman	484
France v Andrews	357
Francis v Daley	251, 474

TABLE OF CASES CITED

[The figures refer to the Pages]

Franklin County Bank v Greenfield Bank 216
Freeland v Freeland 409
French v Hayward 226
Frothingham v Shaw 515
Fuller v Connelly 205, 212, 214, 215, 289, 432, 436, 498
  v Rust 398, 427
  v Wilbur 108

G

Gale v Nickerson 5, 30, 77, 174, 200, 317, 472, 473, 474
Gannon v Ruffin 206, 207
Garnett v Garnett 49, 136
Garvey v Garvey 160
Gaskill v Green 158
Gates v White 196, 505
Gay v Minot 19
George v George 36
Gerard v Buckley 376
Gerrish v Nason 35, 47
Gibbs v Taylor 498
Gibson, Appellant 182, 481
  v Farley 293
  v Gibson 53
Giles v Giles 62
Gilmore v. Hubbard 229
Glines v Weeks 204, 215, 218
Gloucester v Page 127
Glover v Hayden 58
Goddard v Whitney 323, 324
Goff v Kellogg 223
Goldthwait v Day 221, 234
Gombault v Public Administrator 54
Goodell v Goodell 257
Goods of Arthur White 84, 87
  Clarkes 33
  Frith 38
  Lay 86
  Main 118, 358
Goodwin v Jones 174
Goodyear Dental Vulcanite Co v Bacon 433
Gorden v Pearson 379
Gould v Camp 197
  v Lawrence 181, 454
  v Mansfield 88
  v Mather 240
  v Safford 86
Granger v Bassett 210, 304, 318
Graves v Goldthwait 393
Gray v Gray 476
  v Parke 130, 159, 160, 162, 167, 472

Gray v Sherman 42
Grayson v Atkinson 32
Green v Gaskill 9, 158
  v Hogan 152, 158, 196, 299, 407, 505
  v Russell 223
Greene v Borland 146
  v Brown 9
Greenleaf v Allen 212, 234
Greenough v Turner 423
  v Welles 239
Greenwood's Case 55
Greenwood v McGilvray 227, 234, 301
Gregg v Gregg 281
Gregson v Tuson 246, 251, 253, 258, 259
Greves v Shaw 520
Grinnell v Baxter 197, 298
Griswold v Chandler 299
Grow v Dobbins 196
Guckian v Riley 397, 427
Guptill v Ayer 216, 234, 500
Gurney v Waldron 128

H.

Haddock v Boston & Maine R R Co 29
Hagar v Wiswall 386
Hagerty v State 511
Hale v Hale 178, 179, 181, 471
  v Leatherbee 222
  v Munn 398
Hall v Cushing 495
  v Hall 33, 387, 390
  v Thayer 20
Hallowell's Estate 252
Hamilton v Hamilton 49
Hammond v Granger 146, 196, 201
Hancock v Hubbard 356, 440
Handy v State 76
Hannum v Day 244, 246
Haraden v Larrabee 210, 341
Harding v Larned 266, 306
  v Littlehale 170
  v Smith 220
  v Weld 70, 71, 126, 135
Hardy v Call 301
Harmon v Osgood 497, 499
Harrington v. Brown 104, 257
  v. Conolly 417
  v Harrington 248
Harris v Berrall 61
  v. Harris 244, 476
  v. Starkey 5, 12, 29, 476

TABLE OF CASES CITED

[The figures refer to the Pages.]

Harrison's Appeal	59
Hartwell v Rice	362, 363
Harvard College v Amory	307
v Gore	71
Harwood v Goodright	66
Hastings v Dickinson	409
v Mace	410
v Rider	45, 48
Hathorn v King	45, 48
Haven v. Foster	43, 181
Havens v Vandenburg	67
Haverhill Loan and Fund Association v Cronin	220, 221
Hawes v. Humphrey	69
Hayden v Barrett	341
Hays, In re	85
v Jackson	252
Hayward v Ellis	310
Healy v Reed	9, 158, 207
v Root	212
Heard v Drake	213
v Lodge	432
v Trull	466
Heath v Wells	253
Hemenway v Hemenway	210
Henry's Case	405
Henry v Estey	464
Hewes v Dehon	252
Hicks v Chapman	138
Higbee v Bacon	314
Higgins v Central New England & Western R R Co	495
Hildreth v Jones	404
v Marshall	213
Hill v Bacon	88
v Boston	144
v Davis	92
v Pike	397
Hitchcock v Shaw	40
Hix v Wittemore	54
Hoar v Marshall	499
Hodgdon v Cummings	476
Hogan v Grosvenor	33, 34, 38
Holbrook v Waters	499
Holden v Fletcher	195
Hollenpeck v McDonald	245
v Pixley	179, 180
Holmes v. Beal	248
v Moore	496
v Taber	210
v. Winchester	404, 422, 425
Holyoke v Haskins	6, 70
Hooker v Bancroft	174
v Olmstead	105, 221, 237, 291, 353, 438
Hooper, Petitioner	187
v Bradbury	144
v. Bradford	515, 522
Hooper v Shaw	514
Horton v Earle	353
Hosea v Jacobs	43
Houghton v Butler	496
Hovey v Dary	261
Howard's Will	76
Howard v Candish	414
v Priest	403
Howe v Berry	324
v Howe	507, 515, 517, 522, 523
v Lawrence	231
v Peabody	432
v. Watson	89
Howes v. Colburn	55, 73
Hubbard v Hubbard	84, 86
v Lloyd	291
Hudson v Hulbert	193, 253
v Lynn & Boston Railroad	495
Humes v Wood	251
Humphrey, Appellant	481
Hunnewell v Taylor	375
Hunt, Appellant	307
v Frost	257
v Hapgood	387
v Whitney	234
Hurley v O'Sullivan	350, 381
Hussey v Coffin	100
Hutchins v State Bank	30

I

Idley v Bowen	61, 79
Ingersol v Hopkins	68, 350
Inheritance Tax, Re	511
Ipswich Manufacturing Co v Story	294, 295
Irish v Smith	49
Ives v. Ashley	257

J.

Jackson v Betts	80
v Christman	76
v Kniffen	58
v Le Grange	73
v Luquere	73
v Van Deusen	38, 74
Jacobs v Jacobs	226
Jaques v Swasey	208, 363
Jauncey v Thorne	76
Jenkins v Dawes	40
v Stetson	83
v Wood	98, 108, 196, 242, 498

xviii   TABLE OF CASES CITED.

[The figures refer to the Pages.]

Jenks v Howland	6, 387	Knapp v Windsor	348
Jenner v Finch	37	Knight v Cunningham	196
Jenney v Wilcox	196	Knowlton v Johnson	356
Jennings v Pendergas	46	v Moore	508, 509
Jennison v Hapgood	184, 257, 287, 290, 291, 292, 295, 299, 300, 301, 315	Kochersperger v Drake	511
Jewett v Jewett	260		
v Phillips	231	**L.**	
v Turner	100		
Jochumsen v Suffolk Savings Bank	6, 119	Ladd's Will	60
Johnson's Will	79, 80	Ladd v Chase	352
Johnson v Ames	171, 234, 288	Lamb v Lamb	292
v Baker	299	Lamson v Knowles	8, 9, 355
v Home for Aged Women	252	v Schutt	242, 253
v Moore's Heirs	55	Landon v Howard	76
v Waterhouse	126	Langdon v Palmer	392
v Williams	31, 326	Lane v Moore	59, 67
Jones, Appellant	466	Larkins v Larkins	66
v Atchinson, Topeka & Santa Fé R R Co	146, 188	Larned v Bridge	239
		Larrabee v Tucker	322, 330
		Laughton v Atkins	64, 66
		Lavery v Egan	323, 325
v Brewer	398	Lawless v Reagan	138, 464, 465
v Murphy	63	Lazell v Lazell	422
v Richardson	98, 215, 363	Leathers v Greenacre	84, 86
v Simpson	56	Leavitt v Lamprey	399
v Treadwell	208, 360	v Leavitt	175
Judkins v Judkins	374	Le Breton v Fletcher	76
Julian v Boston, Clinton & Fitchburg R R Co	409	Lee, Appellant	251
		v Gay	352
		v Miller	423
		v Wells	20
		Leggate v Moulton	496
K.		Leland v Felton	170, 294
		Lemage v Goodban	65
Kaffenburg v Assner	470	Lenz v Prescott	356
Kavanaugh v Kavanaugh	187, 452	Leonard v Haworth	349
Kearns v Cuniff	415	v Leonard	413
Keith v Copeland	209	Lewis v Bolitho	464
Kendall v Gleason	349	v Lewis	60
Keniston v Mayhew	349	v Mason	48
Kennebel v Scrafton	68	Lincoln v Perry	323, 325, 355
Kenney's Case	466	Lisk v Lisk	177, 179
Kenney v Tucker	361	Litchfield v Cudworth	182, 257
Kent v Barker	351	Little v Chadwick	171, 288, 293
v Bothwell	174	v Conant	496
v Dunham	209, 210, 471	v Gibson	41
v Morrison	273, 408	v Little	54
Kimball v Perkins	306	Livermore v Bemis	308, 467, 471
v Story	353	v Haven	241
v Sumner	293	Livingston v Newkirk	252
v Tilton	88	Lobdell v Hayes	293
King v King	404	Loker v Gerald	400
Kingman v Soule	296	Lombard v Morse	128, 308
Kingsbury v Wilmarth	180	Long v Short	252
Kinliside v Harrison	76	Longford v Eyre	36
Kinne v Kinne	45	Look v Luce	198, 497

Loring v Alline	446	McGreevy v McGrath	94
v Bacon	431	McIntire v. Linehan	428
v Cunningham	170, 288	McKay v Kean	474
v Kendall	437, 438, 439	McKim v Aulbach	429
v Marsh	350	v Bartlett	231, 432
v Mass Horticultural Society	30	v Blake	307, 442, 435
		v Demmon	431
v Park	40	v Doane	5, 144, 203, 440
v Steineman	354, 356, 358	v Glover	433
Lovell v Minot	307	v Haley	168, 205, 433, 436, 498
Low v Bartlett	105		
Lowd v Brigham	377	v Harwood	433
Lowell, Appellant	156	v Hibbard	184, 307, 445
Lucas v Morse	15	v Mann	141, 169, 446
Luchterhand v Sears	449	v Morse	307, 445, 446
Lund v Woods	403	McLane v Curran	281, 310, 445
Luscomb v Ballard	296	McMahon v Gray	304, 393
Lyman v Coolidge	42	Mechanic's Savings Bank v Waite	354, 499
Lynch v Dodge	143		
Lynes v Hayden	448	Melanefy v Morrison	47
		Melia v Simmons	119
		Mence v Mence	66
		Mendell v Dunbar	37
M		Mercier v Chace	422, 424
		Merriam v Leonard	226
Macknet's Executors v Macknet	299	Merrill v Beckwith	190
		v Emery	408
Magoun v Illinois Trust & Savings Bank	510, 511	v New England Insurance Co	104
Mansfield v Pembroke	415	v Preston	320
Manson v Felton	297	Middlesex Bank v Minot	221
Marden v Boston	119, 357	Middleton v. Middleton	61
Marks v Sewall	394	Miles v Boyden	43
Marsh v French	380	Miller v Congdon	146, 210, 291
v McKenzie	182	v County Commissioners	375
Marshall v Mason	36	v Goodwin	449
Marston v Roe	67, 68	v Miller	57, 453
Martin v Clapp	176	v Smith	48
v Gage	466	Minot, Petitioner	350
Marvel v Babbitt	239	v Harris	349
v Phillips	496	v. Norcross	220, 435
Mason v Mason	400, 416	v Winthrop	512, 513, 517, 522
Mass General Hospital v Amory	146	Monk v Capen	424
		Moody v Shaw	520
Mathews v Mathews	324, 408	Mooers v White	44
Mattoon v Cowing	307, 445	Moore v Boston	288, 494
May v Bradlee	48, 59	v. Weaver	353
v May	310, 311	Moran v Hollings	496
v Skinner	187, 300, 302, 312, 476	Morey v American Loan and Trust Co	197
Maynard v Tyler	57	Moritz v Brough	59
McCabe v Bellows	405	Morrill v Morrill	390
v Fowler	289	v Wiseman	15
McCann v Randall	190	Morrissey v Mulhern	211
McConnell v Wildes	80	Morse v Hill	188
McDonald v Morton	188	v Mason	353
McFeely v Scott	7	v Natick	505
McGooch v McGooch	112	Morton v Hall	197

TABLE OF CASES CITED

[The figures refer to the Pages.]

Moses v Julian	20
Mount Hope Iron Co v Dearden	386, 390
Mulhall v Fallon	195
Mulhern v McDavitt	309
Mulligan v Newton	172
Munroe v Holmes	253, 297
v Luke	393
Murphy v Boston & Albany R R Co	496
v Walker	311
Murray v Wood	141, 169, 221, 446
Myer v Tighe	138

N

Nashua Savings Bank v Abbott	198
Nathan v Nathan	178
National Bank of Troy v Stanton	203
Needham v Ide	47, 48
Nelson v McGiffert	64
v Woodbury	223
Nettleton v. Dinehart	406
New England Hospital v Sohier	254
New England Trust Co v Eaton	316, 465
Newburyport v Creedon	199
Newcomb v Goss	214, 432
v Stebbins	293
v. Williams	160, 437, 444
v. Wing	440
Newell v. Homer	63, 80
v Peaslee	197, 201, 214, 319, 353, 359
v West	12, 179, 216, 223, 224, 303, 318, 434, 476
Newhall v Sadler	391
Newton v Cook	405
v Seaman's Friend Society	32, 77
Nicholes v Binns	54
Nichols, Appellant	188
Nickerson v Buck	15, 32, 33, 73, 74
v Chase	499
v Thatcher	415
Northampton v Smith	19, 464
Norton v Norton	244, 251
v. Sewall	113, 495
Nott v Sampson Manufacturing Co	259, 460
Noyes v Stone	328, 402
Nugent v Cloon	145
Nussear v Arnold	58
Nutt v Norton	67, 68
Nye v Taunton Branch R R Co	398

O.

O'Brien v Bailey	376
v Mahoney	374, 376, 379
O'Dee v. McCrate	176
Odiorne v Maxcy	431
O Donnell v Smith	134, 135
O'Gara v Neylon	332, 410
Ogden v Greenleaf	59
v Pattee	209
Onions v Tyrer	61
O'Reiley v Bevington	257
O'Rourke v Beard	352
Osborn v Cook	34
Osgood v Bliss	68
v Breed	15, 360
v Foster	170
v Osgood	452, 453
Ostrom v Curtis	217, 235
Overton v Overton	49

P

Paine v Fox	254
v Gill	434
v Hollister	178, 356, 409
v Moffitt	440
v Prentiss	353
v Stone	434
v Ulmer	494
Palmer v Mitchell	290
v Palmer	166, 250, 253, 294, 311
Parcher v Bussell	313, 315
Parker v Converse	145
v Kuckens	369
v Parker	5, 29, 399, 415, 466
v Sears	144
v Simpson	474, 495
v Townsend National Bank	230
Parkman v McCarthy	321, 324, 330, 341
Parks v Reilly	424
Parsons v Mills	223
v Spaulding	106
Pattee v Stetson	466
Patten v Poulton	79
Paul v Costello	470
v Paul	339, 423, 425
v Stone	195

TABLE OF CASES CITED

[The figures refer to the Pages]

Peabody v Norfolk	170
Pease v Allis	40
Peaslee v Peaslee	409
Peck v Metcalf	390
Peebles v Case	76
Pendleton v Pomeroy	308
Penhallow v. Dwight	172
Penniman v French	464
Perkins v Fellows	206, 221, 227, 301, 497
v. Finnegan	130, 102
v Stevens	41
Peters v Peters	5, 6 463
v Siders	350
Pettee v Wilmarth	178, 182, 471
Pettes v Brigham	35
Phelps v Palmer	375
v Phelps	407
Phillips v Allen	402
v Frye	295
Pickens v Davis	67
Picquet, Appellant	104, 430
Pierce v Gould	465, 466
v Keene	470
v Prescott	5, 12, 311, 354, 437
v Saxton	227
Pinkerton v Sargent	332
Pinney v McGregory	104, 107
Place v Washburn	453
Plimpton v Fuller	252
Plummer v Coler	510
Pollock v Learned	31, 209, 332
Pond v Pond	391
Poole v Munday	290, 314
v Richardson	48
Pope v Farnsworth	152
Potter v Baldwin	59
v Hazard	377, 392
v Wheeler	400
Powers v Codwise	40
Powow River National Bank v. Abbott	196
Pratt v Atwood	341
v Bates	150
v Felton	407
v Lamson	201
v Rice	43
Prentice v Dehon	196
Prentiss v Prentiss	350
Prescott v Durfee	104
v. Parker	437
v Pitts	439
v Read	305, 440
Prior v Talbot	291, 438
Pritchard v Norwood	123
Procter v. Newhall	393
Proctor v. Clark	182, 320, 427
Provis v Reed	58
Pryor v Coggin	62
Putnam v Story	240
Putney v Fletcher	160, 163, 171, 216, 221, 224, 239, 465 466
Pynchon v Lester	403

Q.

Quick v. Quick	80

R.

Ramsdill v Wentworth	350, 351
Ramsey v Humphrey	388
Rathbun v Colton	305
Raymond v Wagner	36, 37
Raynham v Wilmarth	399
Read v Hatch	496
Reed's Will	46
Reed v Dickerman	407
Reid v Borland	66
Reynolds v Reynolds	37
Rice v Bradford	514
v Freeland	375
v Parkman	263
v Smith	303
Rich v Gilkey	61
v Lord	375
v Tuckerman	195
Richards v Child	196
v Dutch	105
v Nightingale	213
v Richards	384, 392, 496
v Sweetland	160, 163, 171
Richardson v Bly	46
v Boynton	306
v Hazleton	12, 182, 434
v Oakman	441
Richmond's Appeal	57
Richmond, Petitioner	253, 298, 304
v Adams National Bank	128, 446
v Gray	266
Ricketson v Merrill	146, 291, 138
Riggs v Riggs	36, 37
Right v Price	36
Ripley v Collins	475
v Sampson	197, 205, 207, 405
Robbins v Bates	237
v. Haywood	293, 307
Robinson v. Bates	401
v Durfee	470, 471
v Hodge	433
v Hutchinson	49
v Millard	441, 445

TABLE OF CASES CITED

[The figures refer to the Pages.]

Robinson v. Ring	290
v. Robinson	195, 218
v. Simmons	324, 330, 405
Roger Williams National Bank v. Hall	231
Root v. Blake	448
v. Yeomans	305
Ross v. Ross	320, 484
Rotch v. Morgan	295
Russell v. Hoar	114
v. Russell	413
Ryan v. North End Savings Bank	308

S.

Sanford v. Marsh	311
Sargeant v. Fuller	401, 405
Sargent v. Sargent	209, 210
v. Sargent (108 Mass 420)	8, 9, 446
Savage v. Winchester	220, 221
Schiffelin v. Stewart	202, 298, 308
Scholey v. Rew	509
Schouler, Petitioner	145
Schultz v. Pulver	290
Scott v. Hancock	240, 415
v. Rand	163
v. Scott	61
Scrubly v. Fordham	61
Searle v. Chapman	405
Sears v. Putnam	353
v. Sears	375
v. Wills	226
Selectmen of Boston v. Boylston	176
Sever v. Russell	315
v. Sever	391
Sewall v. Raymond	251
v. Robbins	47, 66
v. Roberts	482
v. Wilmer	351
Shailer v. Bumstead	55, 58
Shannon v. Shannon	100
v. White	31
Shattuck v. Gragg	397
Shaw v. Paine	154
Sheafe v. O'Neil	300
Sherman v. Brewer	175
Shillaber v. Wyman	498
Shores v. Hooper	5, 29, 353, 359
Short v. Smith	66
Shumway v. Holbrook	30
Shurtleff v. Rile	306
Sigourney v. Sibley	20, 376
v. Wetherell	175, 295, 314
Silloway v. Brown	422, 423
Silverman v. Silverman	452
Simmons v. Almy	128
Simonds v. Simonds	88
Slack v. Slack	178, 475
Slattery v. Doyle	297
Slocomb v. Slocomb	78, 87
Sly v. Hunt	5
Small's Estate	512
Smith, Petitioner	321
v. Bradstreet	467
v. Dutton	318
v. Fenner	59
v. Haynes	467
v. Jewett	288
v. Philbrick	281
v. Rice	5, 6
v. Shaw	898
v. Sherman	113, 466, 496
v. Smith	48, 400, 453
v. Smith (175 Mass 483)	123, 190, 473
v. Wait	61
v. Wells	253
Snow v. Snow	322
Sowle v. Sowle	261
Sparhawk v. Russell	220
v. Sparhawk	40, 103
Spaulding v. Wakefield	288
Spelman v. Talbot	190, 226
Spooner v. Lovejoy	88
v. Spooner	197, 229
Sprague v. West	240
Spring v. Woodworth	138
Staigg v. Atkinson	149, 320, 326, 407
Stanwood v. Owen	219
State v. Alston	512
v. Ferris	511, 512
v. Hamlin	511
v. Price	79
v. Sawtelle	42
Stearns v. Brown	292
v. Fiske	111, 112
v. Stearns	293, 360, 375
Stebbins v. Lathrop	92, 117
v. Palmer	113, 465, 496
v. Smith	438
Steele v. Price	61
Stevens v. Cole	430, 440
v. Gage	289
v. Gaylord	105, 294, 295, 353
v. Palmer	354
v. Van Cleve	33, 45
Stewart v. Lispenard	45
v. Stewart	31
Stickney v. Hammond	64, 69
Stills v. Harmon	499
Stockbridge, Petitioner	206, 352

TABLE OF CASES CITED

[The figures refer to the Pages.]

Stone v Damon	40	Thompson v Thompson	55
v Littlefield	306	Thorndike v Hinckley	141, 221, 281
Stoughton v Leigh	402		
Stowe v Bowen	146	Thurston v. Maddocks	422
Strode v. Commonwealth	512	Tilden v. Tilden	33, 44
Strong v Moe	267, 309	Tirrel v Kenney	404, 423
Studley v Josselyn	250	Todd v Bradford	220
v Willis	203	v Sawyer	88
Sugden v St Leonards	63, 80	Toomey v McLean	404
Sullings v Richmond	356, 409	Towle v Bannister	216
v Sullings	409	v Lovet	494
Sullivan v Sullivan	40	v Swasey	332
Sumner v Crane	59, 76, 77	Townsend v Townsend	326, 332
v Parker	387	Trecothick v Austin	171, 288
v Williams	261, 296	Tumlestown v D'Alton	59
Sutton v Sutton	66	Trimmer v Jackson	35
Sutton Parish v. Cole	144	Tripp v Gifford	318
Swan v. Hammond	67, 68	Tucker v Fisk	5, 465, 467, 484
v Picquet	465	v Utley	495
Swasey v Jaques	9, 158, 348, 349, 463, 467	Tully v Tully	454
		Turnbull v Pomeroy	311
Sweeney v Muldoon	211	Tuttle v Robinson	289
Swett v Boardman	35	Tyler v Boyce	199
v Bussey	375	v Court of Registration	99
Swift, In re	511	v Odd Fellows' Association	128
Sykes v Meacham	196		
Symmes v Drew	414		

U.

United States v Perkins	510
Upham v Draper	308
Urann v Coates	311
Utica Insurance Co v. Lynch	293

T

Taft v Stevens	396
v Stow	198
Tainter v Clark	289
Talbot v Chamberlain	78, 83, 372
Tallman v Tallman	449
Tallon v Tallon	96, 200, 207
Tarbell v Forbes	80, 81
v Jewett	294, 295
v Parker	218, 240, 253, 259
v Tarbell	356, 409
Taylor v Blake	375
v Lewis	207
v Lovering	128
v Taylor	207, 304
Tenney v Poor	244, 246, 251
Terry v Foster	350
Thacher v Dunham	301
Thayer v Boston	71
v Finnegan	433
v Homer	160
v Keyes	440
v. Thayer	379, 386, 391
v Winchester	6, 98, 239, 242
Thomas v Le Baron	251, 261
Thompson, Ex parte	85, 86
v. Brown	307
v. McGaw	416

V.

Van Alst v Hunter	46
Vantine v Morse	499
Vaughan v Street Commissioners	120
Veazie v Marrett	200
Verdier v Verdier	75
Verry v McClellan	251
Very v Clarke	231
Vincent v Spooner	409

W

Wade v Lobdell	281, 314
Wainwright v Tuckerman	44
Wales v Coffin	423
v Willard	2, 6
Walker v Fuller	244, 248, 251, 252, 254, 259, 476
v. Hill	213

TABLE OF CASES CITED

[The figures refer to the Pages]

Walker v Lyman's Administrators	216
v Walker	268, 398
Wall v Provident Institution for Savings	169
Wallis v Bardwell	143
v Wallis	64, 80
Walsh v Wilson	403, 407
Walters v Nettleton	496
Waltham Bank v Wright	196, 297
Wamesit Power Co v Sterling Mills	395
Ward v Fuller	88
v. Gardner	379
v Ward	182
Warden v Richards	240
Wardwell v Wardwell	131
Ware v Merchants' National Bank	400
v Ware	49
Warner v Beach	67, 69, 70
v Warner's Estate	60
Warren v Para Rubber Shoe Co	495
Washburn v Hale	303
v Washburn	180
v White	482
Waterman v Hawkins	350
Waters v Stickney	12, 15, 77
Watson v King	357
v Watson	379, 397
Watts v Howard	302
Webster v Hale	209
v Vandeventer	164
v Webster	69
Webster Bank v Eldredge	154
Welch v Adams	105, 158, 209, 210, 238, 340, 353, 359
Weller v Weller	398, 414, 424
Wellington v Apthorp	88
Wellman v Lawrence	254
Wells v Child	99, 196, 437
Welsh v Welsh	170, 238
v Woodbury	320, 324, 380
Wemyss v White	145
Wendell v French	300, 301
Wentworth v Wentworth	178
Weston v Foster	375
Whall v Converse	348
Wheeler v Bent	61
v Bowen	499
v United States	42
Wheelock v Pierce	104
Whitaker v Green	418
Whitcomb v Taylor	276
White v British Museum	83
v Clapp	387, 391
v Cutler	401
White v Ditson	156, 202, 435, 439, 445
v Duggan	435
v New Bedford Waste Corporation	184
v Ripton	86
v Stanfield	210, 349
v Stinwood	434
v Story	414
v Swain	230, 235, 305
v Weatherbee	433, 437
v Willis	401
v Wilson	55, 160
Whithed v Mallory	401
Whitney v Closson	320
v Twombly	45
Wiggin v Swett	302, 317, 444, 466
Wilbor v Dyer	390
Wilbur v Hickey	241
Wilby v Phinney	220
Wilcox v Wilcox	16, 244, 403
Wild v Brewer	350
Wilder v Goss	350
v Thayer	349, 358
Wildbridge v Patterson	160
Wilkes v Rogers	309
Wilkins v Wainwright	205, 495
Willard v Briggs	454
v Lavender	15, 300, 436, 445
v Willard	377
Willcutt v Calnan	88
Willett v Blanford	290
Willey v Thompson	304
Williams v American Bank	222
v Robinson	47
v Spencer	47
v Williams	67, 178
Wilmarth v Bridges	397
Wilmerding, Re	510
Willwerth v Leonard	165
Wilson v Fosket	350
v Leishman	170
v Wilson	160, 163
v Wilson-Martin Fire Alarm Co	180
Wilton v Humphreys	77
Winchelsea v Wanchope	38
Winchester v Forster	88
v Holmes	404
Wineburgh v U S Steam & Street Railway Advertising Co	495
Wing v Wheeler	281
Winn v Santord	401
Winship v Bass	160, 163, 294, 295
Winslow v Goodwin	320
Winsor v Pratt	32

TABLE OF CASES CITED.   XXV
[The figures refer to the Pages]

Winthrop v Minot	375	Wright v Wright	33, 126, 182, 475
Wolcott v Wolcott	5		
Wood's Estate	209	Wyeth v Stone	484
Wood v Barstow	431	Wyman v Hooper	254, 257
v Stone	356	v Hubbard	292
v Washburn	433	v Symmes	40
Woodbury v Luddy	423		
v Obear	15, 48, 55, 58		
Woodward v Lincoln	424	**Y**	
Woodworth v Spring	130		
Worthington v. Klemm	34, 35	Yarrington v Robinson	498
Wright v Dunham	227	Yeackel v Litchfield	257
v Netherwood	67	Yeomans v. Brown	244, 246, 248

INDEX TO STATUTES.

Revised Statutes	Page		Page
c 69, § 8	145	c 156, § 34	14
General Statutes		§ 35	15
c 91,	322	§ 37	16
Public Statutes		§ 39	17
c 4, § 1	486	§ 40	17
c. 87, § 82	504	§ 45	26
§ 91	504	§ 47	27
c 110, § 11	486	c 158, § 4	19
c 124, § 3	324, 325	§ 5	21
c 125, § 4	341	§ 6	22
c 127, § 18	326	§ 7	22
§ 19	326	§ 8	22
§ 20	407	§ 9	23
§ 23	206	§ 10	23
c 132, § 5	168	§ 11	24
c 133, § 1	15	§ 12	24
§ 2	176	§ 13	24
§ 3	184	§ 14	24
§ 4	185	§ 15	25
c 134, § 15	251	§ 16	25
c 135, § 3	324, 325	§ 17	25
c 139, § 2	182	§ 19	25
§ 3	182	§ 20	25
c 141, § 27	9	§ 21	26
§ 28	10	§ 22	26
c 142, § 9	324	c 178, § 1	376
§ 14	10	Revised Laws	
c 143, § 2	428	c 3, § 5, cl 24	42
§ 14	89	c 8, § 5	16, 71, 192, 321
c 147, § 6	326	c 9, § 1	486
c 156, § 2	8	c 11, § 254	491
§ 3	10	§ 319	4
§ 4	7	c 12, § 23	296
§ 9	182	c 13, § 34	296
§ 22	11	c 14, § 8	502
§ 24	11	c. 15,	279, 420
§ 25	11	§ 1	500
§ 26	12	§ 2	209, 508
§ 27	12	§ 3	299, 514
§ 28	13	§ 4	204, 358, 517, 523
§ 30	13	§ 5	208, 304, 356, 517
§ 31	13	§ 6	208, 518
§ 32	14	§ 7	8, 208, 304, 518
§ 33	14	§ 8	242, 243, 518

			PAGE				PAGE
c	15, §	9	169, 518, 519	c	113, §	42	505
	§	10	17, 169, 519		§	48	505
	§	11	172, 519		§	55	232, 368
	§	12	516, 519, 520	c	116, §	18	96, 108, 129, 144, 153
	§	13	516, 520, 521				
	§	14	516, 521		§	30	502
	§	15	204, 356, 521	c	117, §	11	502
	§	16	173, 410, 521	c	118, §	61	428
	§	17	8, 522			73	171
	§	18	70, 113, 315, 522	c	124, §	1	328, 324
	§	19	280, 316, 522, 523	c	127, §	28	150, 276, 277
	§	20	280, 523		§	29	150, 276, 277
c	28, §	9	152		§	30	149, 150, 277
c	37, §	3	153		§	31	150, 277
	§	4	153	c	128,		492
	§	14	163, 164		§	85	396
c	44, §	4	491		§	92	492
c	48, §	17	147	c	129, §	1	245, 406
	§	18	147		§	2	406
	§	19	147	c.	131,		80, 243, 422
	§	25	148		§	8	339, 423
	§	108	148		§	9	423, 427
c	64, §	15	239		§	10	264, 338, 425, 427
c	74, §	6	89		§	11	377, 424
c	78, §	1	333		§	12	126
	§	5	152		§	13	426
	§	18	152	c	132, §	1	30, 327, 397
	§	26	334		§	2	327, 339
	§	27	334		§	3	328, 402
	§	28	334		§	4	328, 405
	§	29	334		§	5	400
c	81, §	9	199		§	6	409
	§	10	482		§	7	409
c	83, §	11	485		§	8	409
	§	29	129		§	9	340, 397, 411
	§	31	129		§	10	340, 413
	§	33	129		§	11	381, 411
c	86, §	10	8, 492		§	12	397
	§	12	492		§	13	332, 409
	§	52	487		§	14	415
	§	53	487	c	133, §	1	483
c	87, §	33	8, 492		§	2	322, 348, 349
	§	59	8, 493		§	3	341
	§	118	8		§	4	341
c	100, §	71	494, 496		§	5	341
	§	72	494, 495, 496		§	6	346
	§	73	494, 495, 496		§	7	321
	§	74	494, 496	c	134, §	3	243
	§	75	494, 496		§	11	151, 402, 451
	§	76	494, 496	c	135, §	1	30, 32, 116
	§	77	494, 496		§	2	40, 42
	§	78	494, 496		§	3	40
	§	79	494, 496		§	4	32, 42
c	109, §	17	502		§	5	82, 78
c	110, §	64	502		§	6	82
c	111, §	110	502		§	7	30, 32
c	113, §	25	232, 365, 368		§	8	60

INDEX TO STATUTES.   XXIX

		PAGE			PAGE
c 135, §	9	68	c 138, §	11	271
§	10	91	§	12	282, 368
§	11	91	§	13	283, 371
§	12	92	§	14	371
§	13	92	§	15	371
§	14	92	§	16	371
§	15	92, 93	§	17	283, 371
§	16	30, 31, 149	§	18	283, 371
§	16	332, 408	§	19	371
§	17	149	c 139, §	1	192
§	18	406, 407	§	2	193
§	19	349	§	3	193
§	20	352	§	4	193
§	21	206, 352	§	5	168, 169
§	22	87, 88	§	6	172, 173
§	23	88	§	8	95, 102, 143, 162, 194
§	24	88	§	9	102, 143, 163
§	25	352, 460	§	10	143, 162
§	26	461	§	11	150, 162, 163, 281
§	27	461	§	12	164
§	28	461	§	13	164
§	29	462	§	19	284
§	30	406, 462	c 140, §	1	177, 328 453
c. 136, §	1	71, 94	§	2	177 329
§	2	73	§	3	330, 355, 488
§	3	30, 119	§	4	360, 363
§	5	100	§	5	361
§	6	95, 199	§	6	361
§	9	96, 198	§	7	363
§	10	83	§	8	360
§	11	83	§	9	361
§	12	83	c 141, §	1	203, 204, 212
c 137, §	1	107	§	2	204, 212
§	2	107, 117	§	3	204, 212
§	3	106	§	4	204, 213
§	4	106	§	5	205, 215
§	5	105	§	6	303
§	6	103, 105	§	7	303, 474
§	7	103	§	9	197
§	8	103, 115	§	10	196, 197
§	9	104, 123, 472	§	11	197
§	10	123, 242	§	12	198
§	11	124	§	13	113, 201
§	12	124, 181, 472	§	14	202
§	13	15, 124, 299	§	15	202
§	14	124	§	16	202
§	15	124, 199	§	17	200
c 138, §	1	114	§	18	200
§	2	114	§	19	200
§	3	114	§	20	207, 359
§	4	114	§	21	359
§	5	122, 282	§	22	359
§	6	122	§	23	207, 208, 359
§	7	123	§	24	209
§	8	282	§	25	210
§	9	199	§	26	203
§	10	271	§	27	203

INDEX TO STATUTES.

			PAGE				PAGE
c 141,	§ 28	. . .	203	c 145,	§ 19	. . .	139
	§ 29		203		§ 20	. . .	8, 133
	§ 30		203		§ 21	.	133
	§ 31	. .	203		§ 22	. . .	159, 164
	§ 32	.	203		§ 23	. .	150, 277
c 142,	§ 1		211, 229		§ 24	. . .	277
	§ 2		216		§ 25	. . .	308
	§ 3		216, 218		§ 27	. . .	381, 397
	§ 4		216, 224		§ 28	. . .	8, 129, 455
	§ 5	. .	216		§ 29	. .	264, 309
	§ 7		219		§ 30	. .	183, 310
	§ 8	.	219		§ 31	. . .	183
	§ 9		216, 217		§ 32	. .	451
	§ 10	. . .	234		§ 33		332, 408
	§ 11		226		§ 35	. . .	187
	§ 12	.	226, 227, 229		§ 36	.	372
	§ 12	.	469, 478		§ 37	. . .	166
	§ 13	. .	469, 478		§ 38	. .	175
	§ 14	.	229, 478		§ 40	. .	8, 143
	§ 15	. .	227, 478		§ 41	.	143
	§ 16	. .	228, 478		§ 42	.	143, 162, 194
	§ 17	.	228, 478	c 146,	§ 1	. .	289
	§ 18		229		§ 2		245, 399
	§ 19	.	230		§ 3	.	. . 247
	§ 20		229		§ 4	.	230
	§ 21	.	231		§ 5		263
	§ 22	.	236		§ 6	.	. . 246
	§ 23		236		§ 7		246, 251, 264
	§ 24		233		§ 8	.	247
	§ 25		106, 233		§ 9	.	251, 256, 270
	§ 26	163, 230, 284, 437			§ 10	.	248
	§ 30	.	234		§ 11	. . .	266
	§ 31	.	236		§ 12	.	. 250
c 143,			83		§ 13	.	266
	§ 1		340, 353		§ 14	.	254, 266
	§ 2		353		§ 15		193, 255, 266
	§ 4		238		§ 16	. . .	256
	§ 5		238		§ 17	. .	244, 251, 254
c 144,			8, 341–346		§ 18	. . .	241, 243
c 145,	§ 1	.	126		§ 19		264
	§ 2	.	127, 132		§ 20	. . .	265
	§ 3		127, 132		§ 21	. .	266
	§ 4	.	126, 128, 132		§ 22	. . .	267
	§ 5		181		§ 23		265
	§ 6	.	133, 135		§ 24	. . .	265
	§ 7	133, 134, 135, 188			§ 25		270, 372
	§ 8		134		§ 26	.	273
	§ 9	.	136		§ 27		. 273
	§ 10		142		§ 28	.	273
	§ 11	.	137, 166		§ 29	. .	. 278
	§ 12	.	140		§ 30		. 268
	§ 13	. .	140		§ 31		271
	§ 14		140, 310		§ 32		. 271
	§ 15	. .	140		§ 33	.	263
	§ 16		138		§ 42	.	148, 194
	§ 17		138	c 147,	§ 1	. .	149
	§ 18	. .	142		§ 4	. . . .	144

		PAGE				PAGE
c. 147, §	5	115	c 149, §	17		432
§	6	115	§	19	162,	431
§	7	169	§	20		432
§	9	151	§	21		432
§	10	151	§	22		432
§	11	168	§	23		437
§	12	164	§	24	482,	441
§	13	152	§	25		280
§	14	154, 162, 194	§	26		412
§	15	188, 275	§	27		442
§	16	189, 275	§	29		445
§	17	190, 278	§	30		442
§	18	274	§	31		444
§	19	274	§	32		444
§	23	157	§	33		444
c. 148, §	1	8, 448	§	34		444
§	2	8, 240	§	35		446
§	3	187, 516	c 150, §	3		314
§	4	186, 272	§	4	172, 184,	302
§	5	278	§	5		256
§	6	277	§	6		294
§	7	271	§	7		185
§	8	254	§	9		185
§	9	181, 261, 330	§	10		185
§	10	249	§	11		320
§	11	260	§	12		299
§	13	449	§	14		299
§	14	450	§	15	300,	428
§	15	10, 89, 450	§	16		284
§	16	450	§	17		317
§	17	450	§	18		316
§	18	450	§	20	316,	365
§	19	258	§	22		313
§	20	259	§	23	282, 365,	367
§	21	249	§	24	206,	232
§	22	260	§	26	103, 232,	367
§	24	100, 460	§	27	314,	373
§	25	430	§	28	314,	373
§	26	104, 256	c 151	9		309
c 149, §	1	97, 120, 121, 141, 155, 169, 279, 280	§	20		8
§	2	97, 99, 120, 168, 169, 242	c 152, §	17		154
			§	24		400
§	3	99, 121, 129	c 153, §	1	30,	339
§	4	141, 156, 436	§	5		95
§	5	142	§	15	267,	456
§	6	156	§	16	269,	456
§	7	141, 156	§	17	267,	456
§	8	121, 159, 429	§	19	136, 140, 268, 269, 400, 457
§	9	428	§	20	137,	457
§	10	428, 429	§	21	137, 268, 401, 458
§	11	429	§	22	137, 268,	458
§	12	97	§	23	137, 269, 401, 458
§	13	258, 432	§	24	137,	458
§	14	159, 430	§	25		458
§	15	159, 431	§	31	6, 9,	463
§	16	159, 431	§	32	6, 9,	463

		PAGE				PAGE
c 153, § 33		128, 453, 454, 463	c 162, § 39			13, 14, 191
§ 34		453	§ 40			14, 27
§ 35		453	§ 41			14
§ 36		30, 339	§ 42			14
§ 37		6, 9, 463	§ 43			14, 175
c 154, § 1		479	§ 44			15, 300
§ 2		479, 480 481	§ 45			16, 72, 248
§ 3		480, 481	§ 45			266, 381
§ 4		481, 482	§ 46			16, 172
§ 5		482, 483	§ 47			16, 72
§ 6		482	§ 48			16, 17
§ 7		482, 483	§ 49			17
§ 8		483, 484	§ 50			93
§ 9		484	§ 55			26
§ 10		484	§ 56			26, 27
§ 11		484, 485	§ 57			27
§ 12		485	§ 58			27
§ 13		485, 486	§ 59			27
§ 14		486	§ 60			491
c 155, § 11		492	c 163, § 45			469
c 156, § 6		251	§ 53			194
c. 159 § 35		475	§ 82			505
c 160, § 21		208	§ 104			469
c 162, § 2		7	§ 105			469
§ 3		7, 102, 104, 107	§ 138			231
§ 4		9, 455	c 164, § 1			17
§ 5		9, 10, 158	§ 2			17, 18, 96, 119
§ 6		10	§ 3			18
§ 7		10, 158	§ 4			18
§ 8		463	§ 5			19
§ 9		468	§ 6			20
§ 10		6, 468	§ 7			20, 21
§ 11		6, 468	§ 8			21, 429
§ 12		468	§ 9			20, 21
§ 13		182, 470	§ 10			21, 22
§ 14		471	§ 11			22
§ 15		474	§ 12			22
§ 16		472	§ 13			22, 23
§ 17		472	§ 14			23
§ 18		6, 455, 464	§ 15			23
§ 19		453, 472	§ 16			23
§ 20		166, 472	§ 17			23, 24
§ 21		167	§ 18			24
§ 22		10, 11, 167	§ 19			24
§ 23		474	§ 20			24
§ 24		475	§ 21			24 25
§ 25		474	§ 22			25
§ 27		468	§ 23			25
§ 30		11, 28	§ 24			25
§ 31		11	§ 25			25, 26, 172
§ 32		11	§ 26			26
§ 33		12	§ 33			493
§ 34		12, 385, 112	§ 34			493
§ 35		12	§ 35			493
§ 36		12 13	c 165, § 56			284, 312
§ 37		13, 316	§ 60			284
§ 38		13, 165	§ 78			493

INDEX TO STATUTES. xxxiii

		PAGE			PAGE
c. 171, § 1	.	113, 494	c. 184, § 47	.	381, 388
§ 2	.	494	§ 48	. .	388
§ 14	.	384	§ 49	.	148, 388
§ 15	.	384	§ 50	. .	377
c. 172, § 1	. . .	113, 205, 494	§ 51	.	377
§ 2	. . .	205, 495	§ 52	.	382, 383
§ 3	. . .	496	§ 53	.	391
§ 4	.	296, 497	§ 54	.	380
§ 5	. .	497	§ 55	.	380
§ 6	. .	497	§ 56	.	390
§ 7	.	498	§ 57	.	392
§ 8	.	98, 498	§ 58	. . .	395
§ 9	. .	498	§ 59	.	395
§ 10	. . . .	499	c 185, § 1	. . .	406, 419
§ 11	. .	499	c. 189, § 20	.	499
c 173, § 5	.	186	§ 50	.	500
c 174, § 6	.	206	§ 51	.	500
§ 7	. .	206	§ 52	. .	500
c 175, § 20	.	89	§ 53	.	500
§ 23	. .	39	§ 54	.	501
c 178, § 1	.	243	§ 55	. . .	501
§ 55	. .	406	§ 56	.	501
c. 180, § 1	.	416	c 191, § 48	. . .	8
§ 2	. . .	417	§ 49	.	8
§ 3	. .	417	§ 50	.	8
§ 4	. .	417	§ 51	.	8
§ 5	. .	417	§ 52	.	8
§ 6	. .	417	§ 53	.	8
§ 7	.	418	c. 204, § 21	. .	505
§ 8	. .	418	§ 23	. 173, 385, 413	
§ 9	. . .	418	c 208, § 29	.	93
§ 10	. .	418	§ 48	.	503
§ 11		418, 419	MISCELLANEOUS STATUTES		
§ 12	.	419	1783, c 24	.	84
c 184, § 1	.	376, 395	c 36	.	108
§ 5	.	382	1856, c 173	.	4
§ 6	.	382	1858, c 93	. .	3
§ 12	. . .	377	1862, c 68	.	4
§ 13	. . .	385	1870, c 359	.	466
§ 22	. . .	377	1871, c 365	.	466
§ 29	. .	379	1873, c 314	. .	126
§ 31	. .	374, 379	1874, c 205	.	128
§ 32	. .	377	1884, c 131	. . .	15
§ 33	. .	387	c 141	. .	27
§ 34	. .	374	c 249	. . .	486
§ 35	. . .	381	1885, c 235	. . .	16
§ 36	. . .	383	c 255	.	322, 326
§ 37	. . .	384	c 276	.	325
§ 38	. . .	384	c 362	.	129
§ 39	. .	378	1887, c 290	.	323, 326
§ 40	. .	379	c 332, § 2	.	9
§ 41	.	386	1888, c 372	.	89
§ 42	.	391	1890, c 420, § 1	.	14, 27
§ 43	.	376	§ 2	. .	11, 28
§ 44	.	379, 382	c 117	. . . .	129
§ 45	.	395	1891, c 312	. . .	129
§ 46	.	377	c 415, § 1	. .	9, 10, 89

	PAGE
1891, c 415, § 2	12
§ 4	7
c. 425 . . 508, 512, 513	
1892, c 116	9
c 118	68
c 169	375
c. 337, § 1	19
§ 3	21
1893, c 151, § 1	24
c 372, § 1	11
c 469, § 2	23
c 469, § 3	23
1894, c 199	23
c 377, § 1	19
§ 3	21
1895, c 215	27
c 307	507
1897, c 147	16
1898, c 131	20, 21
c 234	24
1899, c 191, § 1	24
c 345, § 1	19
§ 3	21
1900, c 180	22
c 144, § 1	24
1901, c. 61	27

	PAGE
1901, c. 297	513
1902, c 160	91, 92
c 324	402
c 371 . 8, 9, 446	
c 473 315, 317, 513, 516, 517	
c 474 . . 126, 128	
c. 478 . . 378, 400, 456	
c 538 . . 10, 90, 158	
c 544	346

ACTS OF CONGRESS
July 6, 1797, 1 Stat at Large, c 11	507
July 1, 1862, c 119	507
June 30, 1864, c. 173 507, 508, 509	
July 14, 1870, c. 255	507
June 13, 1898, c 448 . 507, 508 509, 514	
April 12, 1902, c 500 .	507

ENGLISH STATUTES
31 Edward III c 11	108
21 Henry VIII c 5	108
29 Charles II c 3	84
4 William and Mary, c 3	84
25 George II c 6	40
1 Victoria, c 26, § 9	32

THE PROBATE COURTS.

CHAPTER I.

THE PROBATE COURTS THEIR ORIGIN AND GENERAL JURISDICTION.

THE colony charter, under which the English settlers of Massachusetts emigrated and organized, contained no particular provisions for the establishment of courts. It was framed for the regulation of a commercial and land corporation, rather than with a view to the establishment of a civil and political government. The colonists were strongly attached to the spirit of the English law, and adopted its leading maxims and its forms and modes of proceeding, so far as they were applicable and necessary to their peculiar condition and wants. The English probate jurisdiction, with which they were familiar, was confided to the ecclesiastical courts, whose jurisdiction was exclusive and entirely separate from the temporal courts; but there could be no ecclesiastical courts in the colony. There was no church establishment by means of which they could be organized on the English model, nor was such a system consistent with the religious sentiments and purposes of the people. Some new provision was therefore necessary for the exercise in the colony of the important powers given to the ecclesiastical courts in England; and as at that time there was no apparent necessity for the erection of a distinct probate court, the power of admitting wills to probate and of granting administration was given to the county courts, which were established under the general authority given by the charter to the governor and assistants to govern the company and their settlements. The county courts had jurisdiction in common law, probate, and equity, with an ultimate appeal to the governor and assistants. The earlier records exhibit probate decrees in the same pages with judgments in civil actions and sentences in criminal prosecutions. This provision, in the existing condition of the colony, was practically sufficient. Orders were passed from time to time, as experience suggested, to promote the convenient and prompt settlement of estates; but the probate jurisdiction remained with the county courts until the dissolution of the colony charter.

Under the province charter of William and Mary, granted in 1691, the courts were newly organized. The superior court of judicature, the court of common pleas, courts of general sessions, and of justices of the peace were established; but the charter which gave to the General Court authority to erect courts with civil and criminal jurisdiction ordained that the governor and council should " do, execute, and perform all that is necessary for the probate of wills, and granting administrations for, touching and concerning any interests or estate which any person or persons shall have within our said province or territory." Thus the probate jurisdiction was taken from the common-law courts, and in fact made independent of the legislative power. The provincial legislature passed an act erecting county courts of probate, but it was negatived by the king;[1] but under the authority vested in the governor and council by the charter, probate officers were appointed in the several counties, who were in effect surrogates, exercising a dele-

[1] Parsons, C. J., in Wales v. Willard, 2 Mass. 120.

gated authority, from whose decrees appeals were taken to the governor and council, who remained the supreme ordinary, or court of probate. This was the beginning of the probate courts as distinct tribunals.

The courts thus constituted continued to exercise probate jurisdiction until the formal establishment of the county probate courts under the State constitution. Statutes were enacted by the provincial legislature recognizing their jurisdiction, extending their powers and duties, and to some extent regulating their proceedings. The constitution of 1780 provided for the regulation of times and places of holding probate courts, and for appeals from the judges of probate to the governor and council until the legislature should make further provision. This system continued in actual operation until the passage of the act of 1784, by which the probate courts were first formally established. That statute provided for the holding of a court of probate within the several counties of the commonwealth, and for the appointment of judges and registers of probate, and transferred the appellate jurisdiction from the governor and council to the supreme judicial court, which was constituted the supreme court of probate. The same statute authorized the courts of probate to allow wills and grant administrations; to appoint guardians for minors and insane persons; to examine and allow the accounts of executors, administrators, and guardians; and to act in such other matters and things as they should have cognizance and jurisdiction of by the laws of the commonwealth.

The courts thus organized continued to exercise probate jurisdiction until the statute of 1858, c. 93, which abolished the office of judge of probate, and provided for the appointment in each county of a suitable person to be judge of probate and judge of the court of insolvency, and to be called the judge of probate and insolvency. The same statute provided for the election of registers of probate [1] and insolvency, to hold office for the term of five years, and transferred all the jurisdiction and authority then exercised by the judges of probate to the judges of probate and insolvency. The General Statutes of 1860 provided that judges of probate and insolvency should continue to hold their offices according to the tenor of their commissions, and that the judge and register of probate and insolvency in each county should continue to be judge and register of the probate court in such county.

By the statute of 1862, chapter 68, probate courts were made courts of record. The peculiar and appropriate jurisdiction of the probate court, embracing the probate of wills and granting administrations, and their incidents, is the same as that of the English ecclesiastical courts. Such was the jurisdiction first exercised by the governor and council, and their surrogates, under the province charter. But the powers of the probate court have been gradually increased by a series of state and provincial statutes, reaching back to the time of their separation from the common-law courts. Jurisdiction has been given to them of matters formerly within the exclusive cognizance of the courts of common law, and not analogous to any proceeding of the probate court as a court of ecclesiastical jurisdiction. These various statutes, based upon the suggestions of practical experience, and passed

[1] Registers of probate had been previously elected under St. of 1856, c 173. The Revised Laws provide that a register of probate and insolvency shall be elected in each county in 1903, and every fifth year thereafter. R. L. c. 11, § 319

with a view of promoting the prompt and economical disposition of the matters to which they relate, have resulted in establishing the large jurisdiction now exercised by the probate court.

This jurisdiction is separate and exclusive. By the separation of the probate and common-law jurisdictions under the provisions of the province charter, the separation between them became as well settled in this country as in England, and the same distinction has been substantially maintained The decrees of the probate court, upon subjects within its jurisdiction, are conclusive and final, unless appealed from.[1] They cannot be called in question in the common-law courts upon collateral proceedings [2] A writ of error will not lie to a judgment of the probate court;[3] nor will *certiorari* lie from the supreme court to the probate court.[4] None of the processes devised to reexamine the decisions of the common-law courts are applicable to the probate courts [5]

And as the proceedings of the probate courts are not according to the course of the common law and cannot be revised in a common-law court by a common-law process, its decrees, when the court exceeds its jurisdiction,

---

[1] Dublin v. Chadbourn, 16 Mass 433; Parker v Parker, 11 Cush. 519, 524, Shores v Hooper, 153 Mass. 228, 232.

[2] Pierce v. Prescott, 128 Mass 140 But see Brigham v Fayerweather, 140 Mass 411, 413 (explained in Sly v. Hunt, 159 Mass. 151), and Dallinger v. Richardson, 176 Mass 77

[3] Smith v Rice, 11 Mass. 507, 513. Derome v. Vose, 140 Mass. 575

[4] Peters v Peters, 8 Cush 529, 513, Browne v Doolittle, 151 Mass. 595, 600; and cases cited

[5] McKim v Doane, 137 Mass 199, Wolcott v Wolcott, 140 Mass. 194, Harris v. Starkey, 176 Mass. 445 For a discussion as to the jurisdiction of the probate court, see Gale v Nickerson, 144 Mass. 415, Tucker v. Fisk, 154 Mass 574

are necessarily void. Other erroneous and irregular judicial proceedings, which can be revised by a superior common-law court, are voidable only, and are good and valid until reversed. But the irregular decree of the probate court is a nullity, and may be set aside in any collateral proceeding by plea and proof.[1] The sure and convenient remedy, however, of any party aggrieved by a decree of the probate court is by appeal to the supreme court of probate in the manner provided by statute, except in the special cases where the appeal must be taken to the superior court.[2]

The supreme judicial court is constituted the supreme court of probate. This appellate jurisdiction is vested in the same court with that from the common-law courts (and that for a very wise reason, that there might not be conflicting decisions between two supreme courts administering the same laws), but in another and distinct capacity as if it were a distinct court.[3] It has a superintending

---

[1] Wales v. Willard, 2 Mass. 120; Cutts v. Haskins, 9 Mass. 543; Smith v. Rice, 11 Mass. 506, 513; Holyoke v. Haskins, 5 Pick. 20; Coffin v. Cottle, 9 Pick. 287; Jenks v. Howland, 3 Gray, 536; Jochumsen v. Suffolk Savings Bank, 3 Allen, 87; Thayer v. Winchester, 133 Mass. 447, and cases cited.

[2] *Post*, chap. xxi. A person aggrieved by an order, sentence, decree or denial of a probate court upon a petition brought under section 33 of chapter 153 of the Revised Laws, or upon a petition of a married woman concerning her separate estate, or upon a petition or application concerning the care, custody, education, and maintenance of minor children provided for by sections 31, 32, and 37 of said chapter, may appeal therefrom to the superior court in the manner provided in sections 10 and 11 of chapter 162 of the Revised Laws as to appeals to the supreme judicial court; and all proceedings on such appeals shall be the same, so far as practicable, as on appeals to the supreme judicial court. R. L. c. 162, § 18.

[3] Peters v. Peters, 8 Cush. 529. In the opinion in this case the subject of the jurisdiction of the probate courts is examined at length by Shaw, C. J. See Browne v. Doolittle, 151 Mass. 600.

and revisory power to re-examine and affirm or reverse all orders and decisions in probate, but as an appellate probate court.[1]

GENERAL STATUTE JURISDICTION.

The jurisdiction of the probate courts is incidentally considered in the following chapters in connection with the various subjects of which they have cognizance. Their general jurisdiction is thus defined by the following sections of chapter 162 of the Revised Laws:

"SECT. 2. The probate courts shall be courts of superior and general jurisdiction with reference to all cases and matters in which they have jurisdiction, and it shall not be necessary for any order, decree, sentence, warrant, writ, or process which may be made, issued, or pronounced by them to set out any adjudication or circumstances with greater particularity than would be required in other courts of superior and general jurisdiction, and the like presumption shall be made in favor of proceedings of the probate court as would be made in favor of proceedings of other courts of superior and general jurisdiction."[2]

"SECT 3. The probate court shall have jurisdiction of the probate of wills, of granting administration of the estates of persons who, at the time of their decease, were inhabitants of or resident in the county, and of persons who die out of the commonwealth leaving estate to be administered within the county, of the appointment of

[1] See note 5, p 5.

[2] It appears to have been assumed by the compilers of the Revised Laws that St 1891, c 415, § 4, which is embodied in R L c 162, § 2, superseded P S c 156, § 4. As to the effect of adjudication of probate court as to residence of a person, see McFeely v Scott 128 Mass. 16, Derome v Vose 140 Mass 575, Cummings v Hodgdon, 147 Mass. 21, Dallinger v Richardson, 176 Mass 77.

guardians to minors and others; of all matters relating to the estates of such deceased persons and wards; of petitions for the adoption of children, and for the change of names; and of such other matters as have been or may be placed within their jurisdiction." [1]

[1] P S c 156, § 2.

The probate court has jurisdiction also to commit insane persons and dipsomaniacs, R. L. c. 87, §§ 33, 59, to commit feeble-minded, R. L. c 87, § 118, to appoint receivers for property of absentees whose whereabouts are unknown and who have wives or minor children dependent upon them, to make orders for the care, management, and sale of such property, and, if such absentee does not appear and claim the unexpended balance of such property within fourteen years after the date of his disappearance or absconding as found and recorded by the court, to distribute the property as if the absentee had died intestate on the day fourteen years after said date, R L. c 144, to compel parents to support minor children under guardianship, R L c. 145, § 28, to determine all questions relative to the tax on collateral legacies and successions, R. L. c 15, § 17, to administer French spoliation claims, St 1902, c 371, to authorize the marriage of minors, R L. c 151, § 20, to hear and determine petitions alleging that a person is without due process of law deprived of his liberty or held in custody against his will, but not applying to a person convicted of crime and serving sentence therefor, R L c 191, §§ 48–53, to enforce specific performance (concurrently with the supreme judicial court and the superior court) of a written agreement for conveyance of real estate where the owner dies or is put under guardianship before making the conveyance, R L c 148, § 1; to authorize sale of real estate held in trust under a will, when, under the provisions of the will, such sale is dependent on consent of a person who has deceased R L c. 148, § 2, to appoint conservators of property of persons who are aged or mentally weak, R L c 145, § 40, to appoint temporary guardians in certain cases, R L c 145, § 20, and, except in the county of Suffolk, to commit juvenile offenders, R L c 86 § 10

The probate court has also jurisdiction to appoint an administrator for the purpose of collecting and receiving assets which, like the French spoliation claims, will not be general assets of the estate of the intestate, or liable for his debts, but will belong to particular persons, and the probate court has also jurisdiction of the settlement of the accounts of such administrator Sargent *v* Sargent, 168 Mass. 420, Lamson *v.*

"SECT 4. The probate court shall have exclusive original jurisdiction of petitions of married women relative to their separate estate, and of petitions or applications relative to the care, custody, education, and maintenance of minor children which is provided for by sections thirty-one, thirty-two, and thirty-seven of chapter one hundred and fifty-three" of the Revised Laws.[1]

"SECT 5. The probate court shall have jurisdiction in equity, concurrent with the supreme judicial court and with the superior court, of all cases and matters relative to the administration of the estates of deceased persons, to wills or to trusts which are created by will or other written instrument. Such jurisdiction may be exercised upon petition according to the usual course of proceedings in the probate court."[2]

Knowles, 170 Mass 205. To remove the doubt suggested by the court in Sargent v. Sargent, 168 Mass 420, 425, as to whether sureties on an administrator's bond in the ordinary form would be liable for the administrator's failure to distribute a French spoliation claim in accordance with the order of the probate court, St 1902, c. 371, was enacted.

The jurisdiction of the probate court to determine all questions relative to the tax on collateral legacies and successions does not take away the right of a legatee to sue at common law in the superior court for his legacy Essex v. Brooks, 164 Mass 79

For discussion of the law imposing tax on collateral legacies, etc , see chapter xxiv, *post.*

[1] St 1887, c 332, § 2

[2] P. S c 141, § 27; St 1891, c 415, § 1; St. 1892, c 116

Swasey v Jaques, 144 Mass 135. The supreme judicial court has no jurisdiction as a court of equity to compel a probate accounting Green v. Gaskill, 175 Mass 265, Greene v Brown, 180 Mass. 308.

The probate court has jurisdiction of a petition by one of the next of kin of a testator for instructions as to the construction of a will. Healy v Reed, 153 Mass 197

In Abbott v Gaskins, 181 Mass. (63 N. E Reporter, 933, decided May 23, 1902), it was held that the probate court does not have power

"Sect. 6 If a case is within the jurisdiction of the probate courts in two or more counties, the court which first takes cognizance thereof by the commencement of proceedings therein shall retain jurisdiction thereof, and shall exclude the jurisdiction of the probate courts of all other counties, and the administration or guardianship which is first granted shall extend to all the estate of the deceased or ward in the commonwealth." [1]

"Sect. 7. All matters of trust of which probate courts have jurisdiction, except those arising under wills, shall be within the jurisdiction of the probate court of any county in which any of the parties interested in the trust reside, or in which any of the land held in trust is situated, but such jurisdiction, when once assumed, shall exclude the probate court of any other county from taking jurisdiction of any matter subsequently arising in relation to the same trust." [2]

MISCELLANEOUS PROVISIONS RELATING TO PROBATE COURTS.

[Revised Laws, Chap 162, §§ 29-49]

"Sect. 22. The judges of the probate courts, or a majority of them, shall from time to time make rules for

to authorize the executors of a will to arbitrate or compromise controversies between persons claiming under the will and those claiming under the statutes regulating the descent and distribution of intestate estates. The power was claimed by the probate court under St 1891, c 415, § 1, now embodied in R L c 162, § 5 It is given exclusively to the supreme judicial court by P S c 142, § 14, now R L c 148, § 15, but the proceedings and decrees of the probate courts prior to June 28, 1902, authorizing and confirming such compromises, and the probate of wills to be executed in accordance with such compromises, are confirmed by St 1902, c 538, as if such proceedings and decrees had been originally made and entered in the supreme judicial court.

[1] P. S. c 156, § 3
[2] P S c. 141, § 28

regulating the practice and for conducting the business in their courts in all cases not expressly provided for by law, and shall prescribe forms, and, as soon as convenient after making or presenting them, shall submit a copy of their rules, forms, and course of proceedings to the supreme judicial court, may alter and amend them, and, from time to time, make such other rules and forms for regulating the proceedings in the probate courts as it considers necessary in order to secure regularity and uniformity." [1]

"Sect. 30. The supreme judicial court and the probate court shall make rules requiring notice of any hearing, motion, or other proceeding before said courts to be given to parties interested or to the attorney who has entered an appearance for them." [2]

"Sect. 31. Judges of the probate courts may transact business out of court at any time and place, if all parties who are entitled to notice assent thereto in writing or voluntarily appear, and in such cases, their decrees shall be entered as of such sessions of the court as the convenience of the parties may require." [3]

Sect. 32. Orders of notice and other official acts which are passed as of course, and which do not require a previous notice to an adverse party, may be issued and performed at any time." [4]

[1] P S c 156, § 22, St 1893, c 372, § 1.
When the rules require the last publication of a notice in probate proceedings to be two days at least before the return day, the probate court has no authority to order such publication to be one day at least before such day; and all proceedings based upon such a notice are invalid Baker v Blood, 128 Mass 543.
[2] St 1890, c 420, § 2
[3] P S c 156, § 24.
[4] Ibid § 25.

"Sect. 33. Probate courts shall have like power to enforce all orders, decrees, and sentences made by them in the exercise of any authority or jurisdiction which may be conferred upon them, and to punish contempt of their authority, as the supreme judicial court has in like cases."[1]

"Sect. 34. A warrant or commission for the appraisal of an estate, for examining the claims on insolvent estates, for the partition of land, or for the assignment of dower or curtesy or other interests in land, may be revoked by the court for sufficient cause, and a new commission may be issued or other appropriate proceedings taken."[2]

"Sect 35. Decrees and orders of the probate courts and of the judges thereof shall be made in writing, and the registers shall record in books which they shall keep for the purpose all such decrees and orders, all wills proved in the court, with the probate thereof, all letters testamentary and of administration, all warrants, returns, reports, accounts, and bonds, and all other acts and proceedings required to be recorded by the rules of the court or by the order of the judge."[3]

"Sect. 36 Each register shall keep a docket of all cases

[1] St 1891, c. 415, § 2.

[2] P S c 156, § 26

The power of the probate courts to revoke their own decrees is not limited to the proceedings specified in the statute. They have always exercised the power for the correction of errors arising from fraud or mistake. For a full examination of the authorities on this subject, see Waters v Stickney, 12 Allen, 1 See also Richardson v. Hazleton, 101 Mass 108, Pierce v Prescott, 128 Mass 145, Cleveland v. Quilty, ibid 578, Newell v. West, 149 Mass 520, Harris v. Starkey, 176 Mass 445; and cases cited The revocation may be made on a petition for a review of the decree, after notice to all persons interested. A decree may be revoked after the time allowed for an appeal from it has expired Cleveland v. Quilty, *supra*.

[3] P S c. 156, § 27.

and matters in the probate court of his county, and shall enter therein every case or matter by its appropriate title and number, brief memoranda of all proceedings had and papers filed therein, the dates of such proceedings or filing of such papers, and references to the places in which the proceedings or papers are recorded, if there is a record thereof. He shall also keep a separate alphabetical index of all such cases and matters, which shall refer both to said docket and to the files of the court. Such docket and index shall at all reasonable times be open to public inspection." [1]

"Sect. 37 Oaths which may be required in proceedings in probate courts may be administered by the judge or register in or out of court or by a justice of the peace, and, when administered out of court, a certificate thereof shall be returned and filed or recorded with the proceedings; but the judge may require any such oath to be taken before him in open court " [2]

"Sect. 38 If an executor, administrator, guardian, or trustee resigns his trust and neglects or refuses to deliver to his successor all the property held by him under his trust, the probate court may, upon the application of such successor of any person beneficially interested, order such delivery to be made, and shall have like powers for enforcing such order as are given to it by the provisions of section thirty-three." [3]

"Sect. 39. A probate court may, upon application of a person interested in an estate in process of settlement in such court, direct the temporary investment of any money belonging to such estate in securities to be approved by the judge; or it may authorize the money to be deposited in

[1] P. S c. 156, § 28   [2] Ibid § 30   [3] Ibid § 31.

any bank or institution in this commonwealth which is empowered to receive such deposits, upon such interest as such bank or institution may agree to pay."[1]

"SECT. 40 A duly authorized attorney-at-law may enter his appearance for the party represented by him in any proceeding in a probate court, and all processes and notices which may be served upon him shall have the same force and effect as if served upon the party whom he represents."[2]

"SECT 41 In proceedings in probate courts, the petitioner or the respondent may, at any time after the filing of the petition, file interrogatories in the register's office for the discovery of facts and documents material to the support or defence of the proceeding. Such interrogatories shall be answered under oath by the adverse party in the same manner and subject to the same restrictions and regulations as are provided by chapter one hundred and seventy-three relative to interrogatories in civil actions."[3]

"SECT. 42 If a party neglects or refuses to expunge, amend, or answer according to the requisitions of said chapter one hundred and seventy-three, the petition shall be dismissed or its prayer granted, or such other order or decree entered as may be required."[4]

"SECT 43. Upon complaint to a probate court by a person interested in the estate of a person deceased against a person who is suspected of having fraudulently received, concealed, embezzled, or conveyed away any property, real or personal, of the deceased, the court may cite such suspected person, although he is executor or administrator, to appear and be examined under oath upon the matter of

[1] P S c 156, § 32 [2] St 1890, c 420, § 1.
[3] P. S c 156, § 33 [4] Ibid § 34.

the complaint. If the person so cited refuses to appear and submit to examination, or to answer such interrogatories as may be lawfully propounded to him, the court may commit him to jail until he submits to the order of the court The interrogatories and answers shall be in writing, signed by the party examined, and shall be filed in the court." [1]

"Sect. 44. In cases which are contested before a probate court, or before the supreme court of probate, costs and expenses [2] in the discretion of the court may be awarded to either party, to be paid by the other party, or they may be awarded to either or both parties to be paid out of the estate which is the subject of the controversy, as justice and equity may require.[3] If costs are

[1] P S c 133, § 1.
[2] St 1884, c 131
[3] *General rule as to costs* Under the general rule, no costs are allowed in contested cases, in the probate court, or supreme court of probate When the contest is made upon frivolous pretences, or for reasons which the appellant knew or ought to have known were unfounded costs are allowed But when the case presents questions of law upon which the parties may not unreasonably differ, and upon which either may properly claim the instructions of the court, no costs are allowed Osgood v Breed, 12 Mass 536; Nickerson v Buck, 12 Cush 335, Woodbury v Obear, 7 Gray, 472. Waters v Stickney, 12 Allen, 17, Chapin v. Miner, 112 Mass. 271, and cases cited. Until the passage of St of 1884, c 131, counsel fees and other expenses were not allowed as costs, and taxable costs only were allowed Brown v Corey 134 Mass 249, Morrill v. Wiseman, ibid 252 note, Willard v Lavender, 147 Mass 15, and cases cited. St 1884, c. 131, amended P. S. c. 156, § 35, by inserting the words "and expenses" after the word "costs."

The probate court has no power to allow costs after a final decree has been entered in the controversy in which the costs accrued Lucas v Morse, 139 Mass 59

By R L c 137, § 13, special administrators by leave of the probate court may pay from the personal estate in their hands the ex-

awarded to be paid by one party to the other, execution may issue."

"SECT 45 The notice which may be required by law in any proceeding in a probate court may be dispensed with if all parties who are entitled thereto assent in writing to such proceedings or waive notice"[1]

"SECT 46 In appraisals of property, the judge or register may appoint only one appraiser if in his opinion the nature of the property makes it advisable so to do"[2]

"SECT. 47. Parties to probate proceedings may select the newspapers in which the notices which may be ordered upon their petitions shall be published, but the court may order the notice to be published in one other newspaper"[3]

"SECT. 48. A paper or instrument, discharging a claim or purporting to acknowledge the performance of a duty or the payment of money for which an executor, administrator, guardian, or trustee is chargeable or accountable

penses of the last sickness and funeral of the deceased, the expenses incurred by the executor named in the will of the deceased person in proving the same in the probate court, or in sustaining proof thereof in the supreme court, and also, after notice, such debts due from the deceased as the probate court may approve.

In suits brought by executors and trustees for instructions made necessary by some ambiguity or obscurity in a will, costs are allowed to be paid out of the estate Abbott v Bradstreet, 3 Allen, 587, Wilcox v Wilcox, 13 Allen 256, Bowditch v. Soltyk, 99 Mass. 136, Bartlett, Petitioner, 163 Mass 509, 522

[1] P S c 156, § 37
[2] St 1897, c 147
[3] St 1885, c 235, now embodied in R L. c. 8, § 5, cl. 13, provided that "any daily or weekly periodical devoted exclusively to legal news, which has been published in the Commonwealth for six consecutive months, shall be deemed a newspaper for the insertion of legal notices required by law, if the publication of such notice in such periodical is ordered by the court."

in a probate court, shall, upon the request of a party interested, be recorded in the registry of said court; and the registers of probate in their respective countries shall enter, record, index, and certify any original paper or instrument offered as aforesaid, and shall receive for such services the like compensation as registers of deeds would be entitled to demand for like services. Such compensation shall be paid by the person who leaves such paper or instrument for record, at the time of leaving it "[1]

" Sect. 49. The register of probate shall make without charge one certified copy of all wills proved, of inventories returned, of accounts settled, of partitions of land, of assignments of dower or curtesy, and of all orders and decrees of the court, and shall deliver such copies upon demand to the executor, administrator, guardian, widow, heir, or other party principally interested "[2]

A copy of the inventory and appraisal of every estate, any part of which is subject to the tax on collateral legacies and successions, or if the estate can be conveniently separated, a copy of the inventory and appraisal of such part, shall, within thirty days after it has been filed, be sent by the register of probate, by mail, to the treasurer and receiver-general without charge therefor.[3]

JUDGES OF THE PROBATE COURT.

[Revised Laws, c 164.]

" SECT. 1. There shall be one judge of probate and insolvency in each county except in the counties of Suffolk and Middlesex."

" SECT. 2 There shall be two judges of probate and in-

[1] P. S. c. 156, § 39   [2] Ibid § 40.   [3] R. L. c. 15, § 10

solvency for each of the counties of Suffolk and Middlesex. The senior judge shall be the first judge of probate and insolvency in each county, to whom, and to his successors, all bonds which are required by law to be given to the judge of the probate court or of the court of insolvency for said counties shall be made payable. The probate court and the court of insolvency for said counties may be held by one or both of the judges and, when so held, shall have and exercise all the powers and jurisdiction committed to the respective courts The judges shall so arrange the performance of their duties as to insure a prompt and punctual discharge thereof. Simultaneous sessions of the courts in said counties may be held if the public convenience requires Citations, orders of notice, and all other processes issued by the register of probate and insolvency for either of said counties shall bear teste of the first judge of said courts, respectively A deposit or investment which is made in the name of the judge of the probate court or the court of insolvency for either of said counties shall be made in the name of the first judge of the court, and shall be subject to the order of the court."

"Sect. 3. A judge of probate and insolvency, before entering upon the performance of his official duties, in addition to the oaths prescribed by the constitution, shall take and subscribe an oath that he will faithfully discharge said duties and that he will not, during his continuance in office, directly or indirectly, be interested in, or benefited by, the fees or emoluments which may arise in any suit or matter pending in either of the courts of which he is judge. Such oath shall be filed in the registry of probate of the county for which he is appointed "

"Sect. 4. The judges may perform each other's duties when they find it necessary or convenient."

STATUTE PROVISIONS AS TO JUDGES OF PROBATE. 19

"SECT. 5. If a judge of probate and insolvency is unable or fails from any cause to perform his duties or any part of them, or if, in his opinion, the court requires the assistance of another judge, or if there is a vacancy in the office of judge of probate and insolvency, his duties, or such of them as he may request, shall be performed in the same county by the judge of probate and insolvency of any other county who may be designated by the judge, or, in case of his failure so to designate, who may be designated by the register of probate and insolvency from time to time as may be necessary; but, unless objection is made by an interested party before the decree is made, any case may be heard and determined out of said county in the performance of such duties by such other judge, who may send his decree to the registry of probate for the county in which the case is pending. Two or more simultaneous sessions of the court may be held, the fact being so stated upon the record." [1]

[1] P. S c 158, § 4, St. 1892, c. 337, § 1, St 1894, c 377, § 1, St. 1899, c. 345, § 1

Coffin v Cottle. 9 Pick 287

A judge of probate has no jurisdiction over a will containing a devise of more than one hundred dollars in value to a person of whose will he has been appointed executor. Bacon, Appellant, 7 Gray 391

Where the judge was a debtor to the estate, though the debt was wholly secured by mortgage, it was *held* that he had no jurisdiction, and that the probate of the will before him was void. Gay v Minot, 3 Cush. 352

A bequest of money to trustees, to be devoted to the use and benefit of indigent persons in certain towns, does not make a judge of probate who is an inhabitant of one of those towns interested in the probate of the will which contains the bequest Northampton v Smith, 11 Met 390

Where the judge had a valid claim against the estate of a deceased person, but had determined in his own mind not to enforce his claim, and exercised jurisdiction over the estate by granting letters of administration, it was *held* that he was nevertheless interested as a creditor

"Sect. 6. The register of probate and insolvency shall certify on his records and to the auditor of the commonwealth the number of days and the dates upon which, and the occasion for which, the duties of the judge of probate and insolvency are performed by such judge of another county under the provisions of the preceding section."

"Sect 7. The judge who performs any duty under the provisions of section five shall, except as provided in the following section,[1] receive from the commonwealth, in addition to the amount otherwise allowed to him by law, fifteen dollars for each day that he performs such duties. Such compensation, so far as it is for services rendered for any cause, except for such interest as prevented the perform-

of the estate, and that the grant of administration was therefore void for want of jurisdiction, Sigourney v Sibley, 21 Pick. 101 ; and such void administration is not rendered valid by the circumstance that exception was not taken to his jurisdiction , ibid

The appointment of a special administrator on the estate in which the judge is interested is void Sigourney v Sibley, 22 Pick 507.

The fact that the judge had acted as the agent or attorney of a creditor, heir, or other person interested in an estate, although such action was illegal, does not make him interested so as to oust him of his jurisdiction Cottle, Appellant, 5 Pick 483

A judge cannot act in any matter in which a near relative or connection is one of the parties, and a brother-in-law or father-in-law is such a connection But he is not disqualified by the remote and contingent interest of a relative who is not a party to the proceeding Hall v. Thayer, 105 Mass 219, Aldrich, Appellant, 110 Mass 189

A judge who has written a will is disqualified to sit upon the probate of it; but, on appeal, it may be proved in the court above. Moses v Julian, 45 N. H 52

An adjudication by a judge, while absent from his county, upon a matter pending therein, is invalid, and the proceedings may be dismissed upon a petition in equity to the supreme court Lee v Wells, 15 Gray, 459. But this has not been the law since the enactment of St 1898, c 131 See R. L c. 164, § 9.

[1] This is evidently an error, as the "following section" relates only to bonds.

ance of his duties by the regular judge, shall, for any excess above three per cent of his salary, be deducted from the salary of the judge so assisted."[1]

"SECT. 8. Bonds which are required to be given to the judge shall be given, in case of vacancy in the office of judge, to the acting judge, and to his successors in office, and all business shall be done in his name or in the name of the probate court or the court of insolvency for the county in which the case or matter is pending; but bonds may be approved, and other acts, which are required to be done or certified by the judge, may be approved, done, or certified by the acting judge."[2]

"SECT. 9. The judge of probate and insolvency may, in cases in which a decree, order, or allowance can be made without a hearing, and in all cases after a hearing, make such decree, order, or allowance, and approve bonds, at any place in the commonwealth, with the same effect as if so made and approved in their respective counties; and if such judge, under the provisions of section five, acts in a county other than his own, such decrees, orders, or allowances may be signed, and bonds approved, outside of the county in which he may have been designated to act The provisions of this section shall not affect the validity of any decree, order, or allowance which was signed or bond which was approved prior to the third day of March in the year eighteen hundred and ninety-eight."[3]

REGISTERS OF THE PROBATE COURT.

"SECT. 10 Every register of probate and insolvency, before entering upon the performance of his official duties,

---

[1] St 1892, c. 337, § 3, St. 1894, c. 377, § 3; St 1899, c. 345, § 3
[2] P S c. 158, § 5.
[3] St. 1898, c 131.

in addition to the oaths prescribed by the constitution, shall take and subscribe an oath that he will faithfully discharge said duties, and that he will not, during his continuance in office, directly or indirectly, be interested in, or benefited by, the fees or emoluments which may arise in any suit or matter pending in either of the courts of which he is register Such oath shall be filed in the registry of probate of the county for which he is elected."[1]

" SECT. 11. He shall give bond to the treasurer and receiver-general for the faithful performance of his official duties in a sum not less than one thousand nor more than ten thousand dollars, as may be ordered by the judge, with one or more sureties who shall be approved by him."[2]

" SECT. 12. The register shall have the care and custody of all books, documents, and papers which appertain to the courts of which he is register, or which are deposited with the records of insolvency or filed in the registry of probate, and shall carefully preserve them and deliver them to his successor. He may, with the approval of the county commissioners and at the expense of the county, cause copies of the indexes, or new indexes, to the records which are in his custody, to be printed and to be sold at a price which shall be not less than the cost of paper, printing, and binding. He shall perform such other duties which appertain to his office as may be required by law or prescribed by the judge."[3]

" SECT. 13. He may at any time receive and place on file petitions and applications to the probate court or the court of insolvency, and may issue orders of notice and citations

[1] P. S. c. 158, § 6
[2] Ibid § 7
[3] Ibid § 8; St. 1900, c. 180.

in like manner and with like effect as if they were issued by the judge; but if the judge considers that such notice is insufficient, he may order further notice"[1]

" SECT. 14. He may issue process of attachment and of execution, and all other processes and all warrants, letters and licenses which may be necessary to carry into effect any order or decree of the courts, and they may run into any county and shall be executed and obeyed throughout the commonwealth. He may appoint appraisers to make any inventory which may be required to be returned to said courts."[2]

"SECT. 15. He shall furnish copies of records or other papers in his custody and shall collect therefor the fees provided by law."[3]

"SECT. 16. He shall, on the first Monday of January, April, July and October, in each year, account for and pay over to the treasurer and receiver-general all fees and compensation which have been received by him otherwise than by salary"[4]

" SECT. 17. The judges for the counties of Bristol, Essex, Franklin, Hampden, Hampshire, Middlesex, Norfolk, Suffolk, and Worcester may each appoint an assistant register of probate and insolvency for his county, who shall hold office for three years unless sooner removed by the judge. Such assistant register in Bristol, Hampden, and Hampshire may be a woman Before entering upon the performance of his duties, an assistant register shall take the oaths prescribed by the constitution, and shall give bond to the treasurer and receiver-general for the faithful

[1] P. S c 158, § 9.
[2] Ibid § 10, St 1894, c. 199.
[3] St. 1893, c 409, § 2.
[4] Ibid § 3

performance of his official duties, in a sum not less than five hundred nor more than five thousand dollars, as may be ordered by the judge, with one or more sureties who shall be approved by him." [1]

"Sect. 18. The register of probate and insolvency for the county of Suffolk may, subject to the approval of the judges of probate and insolvency for said county, appoint a clerk, and may remove him at his pleasure." [2]

"Sect. 19. The register shall forthwith report to the secretary of the commonwealth a vacancy in the office of assistant register, and the name, residence, and date of appointment of the person who may have been appointed to fill such vacancy." [3]

"Sect 20 An assistant register shall perform his duties under the direction of the register, and shall pay over to him all fees and amounts received as such assistant. He may authenticate papers and perform such other duties as are not performed by the register. In case of the absence, neglect, removal, resignation, or death of the register, the assistant may complete and attest any records remaining unfinished and may act as register until a new register is qualified or until the disability is removed." [4]

"Sect 21. The judges shall semi-annually inspect the doings of the registers of their courts, and see that the records and files are made up seasonably and kept in good order; and if the records are left incomplete for more than six consecutive months, such neglect, unless caused by

---

[1] P S c 158, § 11; St. 1893, c. 151, § 1; St. 1898, c. 234; St. 1899, c 191, § 1, St. 1900, c 144, § 1.

[2] P S c 158, § 12

[3] Ibid. § 13.

[4] Ibid § 14.

illness or casualty shall be adjudged a forfeiture of the bond of the register." [1]

"SECT. 22. In case of any neglect which causes a forfeiture of the bond of the register or assistant register, the judge shall forthwith give notice thereof in writing to the treasurer and receiver-general, who shall thereupon cause the bond to be put in suit; and the sum recovered in such suit shall be applied to the expense of making up the deficient records under the direction of the court in whose records the deficiency happens, and the surplus, if any, shall be carried into the account of such treasurer." [2]

"SECT. 23. The provisions of the two preceding sections shall not exempt registers or assistant registers from an action for any other breach of their bond, or from other liability for neglect or misconduct in their office " [3]

"SECT. 24. If upon the death, resignation, removal, or absence of the register, there is no assistant register, or if he also is absent, the judge shall appoint a temporary register, who shall act until a register is appointed, or elected and qualified, or until the disability is removed. Such temporary register shall be sworn before the judge, and a certificate thereof, with his appointment, shall be recorded with the proceedings of each court in which he acts." [4]

"SECT. 25. No judge, register, or assistant register of probate and insolvency, or any person who is employed in the registry of probate and insolvency in any county shall be interested in, or be benefited by, the fees or emoluments which may arise in any matter pending before the probate court or court of insolvency of such county;

[1] P. S. c. 158, § 15.   [2] Ibid. § 16
[3] Ibid § 17.   [4] Ibid. §§ 19, 20.

nor shall he act as counsel or attorney, either in or out of court, in any matter pending before said courts or in an appeal therefrom, nor shall he be appointed executor, administrator, guardian, commissioner, appraiser, or assignee of or upon an estate within the jurisdiction of such courts, nor shall he be interested in the fees or emoluments arising from any of said trusts, and no judge shall be retained or employed as counsel or attorney, either in or out of court, in any suit or matter which may depend on or in any way relate to a sentence, decision, warrant, order, or decree made or passed by him; nor for or against an executor, administrator, or guardian appointed within his jurisdiction, in any action or suit brought by or against the executor, administrator, or guardian as such; nor in any action or suit relating to the official conduct of such party; nor for or against a creditor, debtor, or assignee, in a cause or matter which arises out of or is connected with any proceedings before him; nor in an appeal in such cause or matter."[1]

"Sect 26. If a judge or register of probate desires to be appointed guardian of his minor child, who is an inhabitant of or resides in the same county, such appointment may be made, and all subsequent proceedings in regard thereto had, in the probate court of the most ancient adjoining county."[2]

SESSIONS OF THE COURTS.

[Revised Laws, c 162, §§ 55–59]

"Sect. 55. The judge of a probate court may keep order in court, and may punish any contempt of his authority"[3]

"Sect. 56. The probate court in each county shall always

[1] P. S. c. 158, § 21.   [2] Ibid § 22   [3] P S. c 156, § 45.

be open, except on the Lord's day and legal holidays, for all hearings, for matters in equity, for proceedings in contempt, and for making orders and decrees in all matters before them: but the times of all hearings shall be discretionary with the judges of said courts." [1]

"SECT. 57. The judge of a probate court may adjourn the court as occasion requires; and if he is absent at the time appointed for holding a court, the register shall adjourn it as he may consider necessary, or as the judge may order The register may also adjourn the court when there is a vacancy in the office of judge."

"SECT. 58. If the regular time for holding a probate court occurs on a legal holiday, or on the day of an annual state election, the court shall be held on the next secular day thereafter; on which day all notices, citations, orders, and other papers made returnable at said regular time, shall be returnable The proceedings thereon shall be of the same validity as if the notices, citations, orders, and other papers had been made so returnable." [2]

"SECT. 59. No court shall be held by adjournment or otherwise unless the register, assistant register, or a temporary register is present." [3]

ATTORNEYS AND PRACTICE IN PROBATE COURTS

A duly authorized attorney-at-law may enter his appearance as attorney for the party represented by him in any proceeding in a probate court, and all processes and notices which may be served upon him shall have the same force and effect as if served upon the party whom he represents.[4]

[1] St. 1895, c. 215; St 1901, c. 61
[2] St. 1884, c. 141
[3] P. S c 156, § 47
[4] R L. c 162, § 40; St. 1890, c. 420, § 1.

The supreme judicial court and the probate courts shall make rules requiring notice of any hearing, motion, or other proceeding before said courts to be given to parties interested or to the attorney who has entered an appearance for them.[1]

[1] R. L. c. 162, § 30; St. 1890, c 420, § 2

CHAPTER II.

PROBATE OF WILLS.

THE probate of a will is necessary to establish its due execution.[1] All questions as to the personal capacity of the testator, the signing of the will by him, and the attestation of the witnesses, must be determined by the probate court, or, on appeal, by the supreme court of probate. Such questions cannot be determined in the courts of common law,[2] and the decree of the probate court allowing or disallowing a will is conclusive,[3] unless appealed from;

[1] A will disposing of lands may be admitted to probate at any time after the death of the testator Haddock *v.* Boston & Maine R R, 146 Mass. 155

[2] Dublin *v* Chadbourn, 16 Mass 433, Parker *v* Parker, 11 Cush. 519, Boston *v* Robbins, 126 Mass. 388

[3] Shores *v* Hooper, 153 Mass 228, Harris *v.* Starkey, 176 Mass 445.

A decree allowing a will or adjudicating the intestacy of the estate of a deceased person in any court in this commonwealth having jurisdiction thereof shall, after two years from the rendition of such decree, or. if proceedings for a reversal thereof are had, after two years from the establishment of such decree, be final and conclusive in favor of purchasers for value, in good faith, without notice of any adverse claim, of any property, real or personal, from devisees, legatees, heirs, executors. administrators, or guardians, and in favor of executors, administrators, trustees, and guardians who have settled their accounts in due form, and have in good faith disposed of the assets of the estate in accordance with law, and also in favor of persons who have in good faith made payments to executors, administrators, trustees, or guardians If a subsequent decree reverses or qualifies the decree so originally rendered, heirs, devisees, legatees, and distributees shall be liable to a subsequent executor, administrator, or other person found entitled thereto, for any proceeds or assets of the estate received by them under the former decree, and in such case proceeds

it cannot be examined collaterally in any other court, except on a question of jurisdiction But until the will be admitted to probate, it is legally inoperative. Neither real nor personal estate will pass by it, for it cannot be used as evidence of title [1]

WHO MAY MAKE A WILL.

Every person of full age and sound mind may, by his last will in writing, signed by him or by a person in his presence and by his express direction, and attested and subscribed in his presence by three or more competent witnesses, dispose of his property, real and personal, except an estate tail, and except as provided in chapters one hundred and thirty-one, one hundred and thirty-two, and one hundred and thirty-five, and in section one of chapter one hundred and fifty-three of the Revised Laws. A married woman, in the same manner and with the same effect, may make a will [2]

of real estate shall be treated as real estate The provisions of this section shall not make an adjudication of the fact of death conclusive. R L c 136, § 3; Gale v Nickerson, 144 Mass 415

[1] R L c 135, § 7, Shumway v. Holbrook, 1 Pick. 114, Hutchins v State Bank, 12 Metcalf, 421, Loring v Mass Horticultural Society, 171 Mass 401

[2] R L c. 135, § 1.

If a court having jurisdiction has entered a decree that a married woman has been deserted by her husband, or is living apart from him for justifiable cause, she may convey her real property in the same manner and with the same effect as if she were sole; and the surviving husband shall not be entitled under the provisions of section 16 of chapter 135 of the Revised Laws to waive the provisions of a will made by her R L c 153, § 36.

A surviving husband, except as provided in R L c 153, § 36, or the widow of a deceased person, at any time within one year after the probate of the will of such deceased, may file in the registry of probate a writing signed by him or her waiving any provisions that may have been made by the will for him or her, or claiming such portion of the estate of the deceased as he or she would have taken if the deceased had died intestate, and he or she shall thereupon take the same

Since the Revised Laws went into effect a married woman has the same rights as her husband in regard to making a will and is subject to the same restrictions. Husband and wife are put on the same basis as to curtesy and dower and as to inheritance

The power to dispose of property by will depends wholly on statute. Brettun v. Fox, 100 Mass. 234, 235

THE FACTS TO BE PROVED IN SUPPORT OF THE WILL

The party seeking the probate of the will must prove affirmatively,

That the will was signed by the testator, or by some person in his presence and by his express direction;

That the will was attested and subscribed in the presence of the testator by three or more competent witnesses; and

That the testator, at the time when the will was executed, was of full age [1] and sound mind

All these facts must be proved. Proof of any one or more of them is not sufficient, unless all are established.

Section I.

AS TO THE SIGNING BY THE TESTATOR.

The statute provides that no will shall be effectual to pass or charge, or in any way to affect any estate, real or

portion of the property of the deceased as he or she would have taken if the deceased had died intestate R L c 135, § 16 Atherton v Corliss. 101 Mass 40, Pollock v Learned, 102 Mass 49, Shannon v White, 109 Mass 146, Burke v Colbert, 144 Mass 160, Johnson v. Williams, 152 Mass 415, Fiske v Fiske, 173 Mass 413

[1] Full age is reached on the day next preceding the anniversary of the person's birth. Thus, if he was born on the second day of January, 1870, he became of age on the first day of January, 1891, and as fractions of a day are not recognized by law, his full age was reached on the first instant of the latter day.

personal, unless it is in writing and signed by the testator, or by some person in his presence and by his express direction, and attested and subscribed in his presence by three or more competent witnesses.[1]

Questions as to the signing by the testator, and as to the attestation of the witnesses, have been frequently considered and determined by the courts.

It is not necessary that the testator's name be signed at the end of the will, though such is the common and advisable practice. Where a will commenced in the common form, "I, A. B., do make," etc., the whole will being in the testator's handwriting, it was held to be sufficiently signed, though there was no formal signature.[2] The signature, whatever may be its local position, must have been made with the intention of authenticating the entire instrument. One signature is sufficient, though the will be contained in several pages or sheets, and even when the testimonium clause referred to the preceding sheets as severally signed, and the will was in fact signed at the end only, the signing was held sufficient, it being evidently the testator's intention that his signature should apply to the whole.[3]

The testator may sign his will by making his "mark,"[4]

[1] R. L. c. 135, §§ 1, 7. To this rule exceptions are made by statute in the following cases. Wills made in conformity with the law existing at the time of their execution; wills made out of the state which are valid under the laws of the state or country in which they were made; and the nuncupative wills of soldiers and mariners. Ibid. §§ 4, 5, 6.

[2] Grayson v. Atkinson, 2 Ves. 454; Coles v. Trecothick, 9 Ves. 249; Adams v. Field, 21 Vt. 256.

[3] Winsor v. Pratt, 5 Moore, 484; Ela v. Edwards, 16 Gray, 91; Newton v. Seaman's Friend Society, 130 Mass. 91.

[4] Nickerson v. Buck, 12 Cush. 332. Under the English statute (1 Vict. c. 26, § 9), which requires the will to be signed by the testator or by some person in his presence and by his direction, and the sig-

and the fact that he was not able to write his name is not required to be proved.¹

The testator's name may be written by some other person, but it must be done in his presence and by his express direction; and the fact that the will was signed in that manner should be stated in the attestation clause. Where the testator's signature was made by another person guiding his hand, with his consent, and he afterwards acknowledged it, the signing was held to be the act of the testator, and sufficient.²

It is not essential that the very act of signing by the testator should be seen by the witnesses. The statute does not require him to sign in their presence. His acknowledgment that the name signed to the instrument is his, accompanied with a request that the person to whom the acknowledgment is made should attest it as a witness, is sufficient. The acknowledgment of his signature need not be in express words. His declaration that the instrument is his, his name being then signed to the paper, is enough; any form of expression implying that the will has been signed by him is sufficient.³ In the case of White v. The British Museum,⁴ where the will was entirely in the

nature to be made or acknowledged by the testator in the presence of witnesses, it was *held*, that a will signed by a mark, without the testator's name appearing, was sufficiently signed, the will being identified *aliunde*. In re Bryce, 2 Curteis, 325. Where the maiden name of the testatrix was written against her mark instead of her real name, by which she was described in the will, it being a clerical error, the will was admitted to probate. In the Goods of Clarkes, 1 Swa. & Tr. 22.

¹ Baker v. Dening, 8 Adol. & Ell. 94.
² Stevens v. Van Cleve, 4 Wash. C. C. 262.
³ Tilden v. Tilden, 13 Gray, 110; Nickerson v. Buck, 12 Cush. 332; Hogan v. Grosvenor, 10 Met. 54; Dewey v. Dewey, 1 Met. 349; Hall v. Hall, 17 Pick. 373; Ela v. Edwards, 16 Gray, 93.
⁴ 6 Bing. 310, and see Wright v. Wright, 7 Bing. 457.

testator's handwriting, the testator merely requested the witnesses to attest it; neither of them saw his signature, and only one of them knew what the instrument was; and the execution was held to be sufficient.[1] Tindal, C. J., said, "When we find the testator knew this instrument to be his will; that he produced it to the three persons, and asked them to sign the same, that he intended them to sign it as witnesses; that they subscribed their names in his presence, and returned the same identical instrument to him,—we think the testator did acknowledge in fact, though not in words, to the three witnesses, that the will was his." This acknowledgment need not be made to all the witnesses at the same time, but is sufficient if made separately to each witness at different times and places.[2]

No formal publication of the will by the testator is necessary. In a large majority of cases, the testator declares in the presence of the subscribing witnesses that the instrument executed by him is his will, and the fact that such a declaration was made is recited in the attestation clause and proved in the probate court. But such declaration is not necessary. There may exist very excellent reasons why the testator should not wish to disclose, and why the law should not require him to disclose, the fact that he has made a will at all,[3] either, as Swinburne

---

[1] It is not necessary to the validity of a will that it be read by or to the person executing it, it is sufficient if the court is satisfied, by competent evidence, that the contents of the will were known to or approved by the person executing it, at the time it was executed as a will. Worthington v. Klemm, 144 Mass. 167.

An instrument which contains a power of attorney *inter vivos* may also be a codicil to a will. Stewart v. Stewart, 177 Mass. 493.

[2] Hogan v. Grosvenor, 18 Met. 54. Dewey v. Dewey, 1 Met. 349, Ela v. Edwards, 16 Gray, 93.

[3] Osborn v. Cook, 11 Cush. 532.

says, " because the testator is afraid to offend such persons as do gape for greater bequests than either they have deserved, or the testator is willing to bestow upon them. (lest they, peradventure, understanding thereof would not suffer him to live in quiet) or else he should overmuch encourage others, to whom he meant to be more beneficial than they expected, (and so give them occasion to be more negligent husbands or stewards about their own affairs than otherwise they would have been if they had not expected such a benefit at the testator's hands or for some other considerations) "[1]

It must of course appear that the testator knew at the time he executed the instrument that it was his will Such knowledge, however, need not ordinarily be proved by direct evidence; it may be inferred from the testator's observance of the formalities of execution required by the statute. It will generally be presumed on proof of the execution that he knew the contents of the instrument.[2] But if the testator was incapable of reading from blindness, physical weakness, ignorance, or other cause, it is incumbent on the party offering the will for probate to meet such facts by evidence that the will was read to the testator previous to its execution, or that the contents were otherwise known to him.[3]

A will may be properly executed without a seal, none being required by statute.

---

[1] Swinburne, Pt 1, § 11 In Trimmer v Jackson (4 Burn's Eccl. Law, 9th ed 102), the witnesses were deceived by the execution, being led to believe that the instrument was a deed, not a will, and it was adjudged a sufficient execution

[2] Worthington v. Klemm, 144 Mass 107.

[3] Swett v Boardman, 1 Mass 262, Pettes v Brigham, 10 N H 514; 2 Greenl Ev. § 675 See Gerrish v Nason, 22 Maine, 438

The statute prohibiting the transaction of business on Sunday does not apply to the execution of wills, and a will executed on that day is valid.[1]

Section II.

AS TO THE ATTESTATION BY THE WITNESSES

The subscribing witnesses must subscribe the will in the presence of the testator.[2] The object of the rule is to enable him to have ocular evidence of the identity of the instrument which they attest. The mere corporal presence of the testator is not enough. He must be conscious of their act, and in a position where he can see it. If, therefore, after he has signed the will and before the witnesses have subscribed it, he falls into a state of insensibility, their attestation is not sufficient.[3] Nor will it be sufficient if they subscribe in a secret and clandestine manner, although in the same apartment.[4] It is not essential that the testator actually see the signing; it is enough if the situation of the respective parties be such that he may see it, and this is enough, even if the witnesses subscribe in another room.[5] Where the testator lay in bed, and the witnesses went with the will through a short passage into another room, and subscribed their names on a table in the middle of that room, both doors being open, so that the testator might have seen them

[1] Bennett v. Brooks, 9 Allen, 118; Donovan v. McCarty, 155 Mass. 543, 546, George v George, 47 N H 27

[2] See Chase v. Kittredge, 11 Allen, 49, Marshall v Mason, 176 Mass 216

[3] Right v Price, 1 Doug 241

[4] Longford v Eyre 1 P Wms. 740

[5] Dewey v Dewey, 1 Met 349, **Riggs v. Riggs**, 135 Mass 238, Raymond v. Wagner, 178 Mass 315.

subscribe if he would, though there was no proof that he did see their act, the attestation was held sufficient.[1] A blind man executing his will should be sensible of the presence of the witnesses through his remaining senses.[2]

On the other hand, though the witnesses are in the same room with the testator, it is not enough, if his view of the proceedings is necessarily obstructed. Where the testator was in bed in a room from one part of which he might, by inclining his head into the passage, have seen the witnesses subscribe the will, but could not see them in the position in which he actually was, the attestation was held not to be good.[3] The cause of the absence of

---

[1] Davy v. Smith, 3 Salk. 395. A testatrix signed in the presence of the witnesses who, twenty minutes afterwards, subscribed their names in an adjoining room. The door was open, but the testatrix was not aware that they were signing. *Held*, that the attestation was not sufficient. Jenner v. Ffinch, Law Rep. 5 P. D. 106. In Casson v. Dade (1 Bro. C. C. 99), the testatrix, being an invalid, executed the will when sitting in her carriage at the door of her attorney's office, the witnesses attending her; after having seen the execution they took the will into the office to subscribe their names, and the carriage was put back to the window, through which, it was sworn by a person in the carriage, the testatrix might have seen what passed. Lord Thurlow was of opinion that the will was well executed.

[2] Reynolds v. Reynolds, 1 Speers, S. C. 256.

[3] Doe v. Manifold, 1 M. & S. 294; Boldry v. Parris, 2 Cush. 433. See Riggs v. Riggs, 135 Mass. 238.

In Raymond v. Wagner, 178 Mass. 315, the attestation was held good, although two of the witnesses subscribed at a table in a room separated by a narrow entry from the room in which the testatrix was lying in bed. She could have seen them by raising herself slightly in bed, but it did not appear either that she raised herself or that she was able to raise herself. In Mendell v. Dunbar, 169 Mass. 74, it was held that the will was not properly attested, the testator, who was ill in bed, having signed in the presence of the witnesses, who then withdrew to another room, no part of which was visible from any part of the room where the testator remained, and they there subscribed as witnesses.

the witnesses is not material; the effect is the same, even if the absence was with the consent or request of the testator.[1] If the witness subscribes in the testator's absence it is not sufficient, even if he afterwards acknowledges his signature in the presence of the testator.[2] An attestation made in the testator's room is presumed to have been made in his presence until the contrary is shown; if not made in the same room it is presumed not to have been made in his presence until it is shown to have been otherwise.[3] And it will be presumed, in the absence of evidence to the contrary, that the witnesses subscribed in the most convenient part of the room, and the position of a table, probable to have been used, would be considered.[4]

It is not necessary to the due execution of the will that the attesting witnesses should subscribe in the presence of each other. A will attested by three witnesses, who separately and at different places subscribe their names, at the request of the testator, and in his presence, is well attested.[5]

An attesting witness may subscribe by making his "mark," but such manner of subscribing is never advisable and seldom necessary.[6]

No particular form of words is necessary in the attesta-

---

[1] Broderick v Broderick 1 P Wms 239
[2] Chase v Kittredge, 11 Allen, 49.
[3] 2 Greenl. Ev § 678
[4] Winchelsea v Wanchope, 3 Russ 444
[5] Hogan v Grosvenor, 10 Met 54, Dewey v Dewey, 1 Met. 349
[6] Chase v Kittredge, 11 Allen, 49, 59, Jackson v. Van Deusen, 5 Johns 144, Doe v. Caperton, 9 Carr & P 59. B, a witness, being unable to write, A, another witness, at his request, guided his hand Held, that B.'s subscription was sufficient In the Goods of Frith, 1 Swa & Trist 8

tion clause which the witnesses subscribe, nor need it state the fact that the witnesses subscribed it in the testator's presence, though the fact that they did so is required to be clearly proved.[1]

Section III.

AS TO THE COMPETENCY OF THE ATTESTING WITNESSES.

The object of the statute in requiring every will to be attested and subscribed in the testator's presence by three or more competent witnesses, is to surround the testator, at the time he executes his will, with disinterested persons, who may protect him from frauds that might otherwise be practised upon his infirmity or debility, and to ascertain and judge of his sanity.

Competent witnesses are persons who are not disqualified by reason of interest, crime, or deficiency of understanding.

Section 20 of chapter 175 of the Revised Laws provides that, except in certain cases there mentioned, "any person of sufficient understanding, although a party, may testify in any proceeding, civil or criminal, in court, or before a person who has authority to receive evidence." Section 23 of the same chapter provides that section 20 and the following two sections shall not apply to the attesting witnesses to a will or codicil. Their competency must therefore be determined by the rules previously in force.

It was formerly held that an attesting witness who took a beneficial devise or legacy under the will which he attested was not a competent witness to prove its execution; but as it was found that to allow a will to be wholly defeated on account of the existence of such an interest on the part of a witness was productive of inconvenience and

[1] Eliot v. Eliot, 10 Allen, 357; Ela v. Edwards, 16 Gray, 91.

injustice, a statute[1] was passed which restored the competency of such a witness by destroying his interest. The devise or legacy to the witness was made void, and he was admitted to testify The same rule is established in this state, by the statute which provides that "a beneficial device or legacy made in a will to a person who is a subscribing witness thereto, or to the husband or wife of such a person, shall be void unless there are three other competent subscribing witnesses to such will"[2]

A mere charge on the lands of the devisor for the payment of debts will not prevent his creditors from being competent witnesses to his will,[3] and a member of a corporation to which property is given by will, in trust for charitable uses, is a competent attesting witness[4] The executor named in a will is a competent subscribing witness[5] An heir at law who is disinherited is a competent witness in support of a will.[6] A wife is not a competent witness to her husband's will,[7] or to a will which contains a devise to him.[8]

A person who has been convicted of an infamous crime is not a competent witness, such a person being considered as having no regard for the obligations of an oath Certain crimes have been held to be infamous, and certain other offences have been held not to have a disqualifying

[1] 25 Geo II c. 6
[2] R. L c 135, § 3　　　　[3] Ibid § 2
[4] Loring v Park, 7 Gray, 42 A legacy to a town does not disqualify an inhabitant of and a taxpayer in the town from being an attesting witness to the will Hitchcock v Shaw, 160 Mass 140
[5] Wyman v Symmes, 10 Allen, 153, Sullivan v Sullivan, 106 Mass 474
[6] Sparhawk v. Sparhawk, 10 Allen, 155
[7] Pease v Allis, 110 Mass 157; Jenkins v. Dawes, 115 Mass 601, Powers v Codwise, 172 Mass 425.
[8] Sullivan v. Sullivan, *supra*.

effect. The precise rule does not clearly appear from the adjudicated cases. "The test appears to be whether or not the crime shows such depravity, or such a disposition to pervert public justice in the courts, as creates a violent presumption against the truthfulness of the offered witness, — the difficulty being in the application of this test."[1] It has been adjudged "that persons are rendered infamous, and therefore incompetent to testify, by having been convicted of forgery, perjury, subornation of perjury, suppression of testimony by bribery, conspiracy to procure the absence of a witness, or other conspiracy to accuse one of a crime, barratry,"[2] larceny,[3] and the receiving of stolen goods knowing them to have been stolen[4] But convictions for adultery,[5] for "deceit in the quality of provisions, deceits by false weights and measures, conspiracy to defraud by spreading false news,"[6] "the attempt, not amounting to a conspiracy, to procure the absence of a witness," and the keeping of gaming and bawdy houses, it seems, do not disqualify.[7] The full pardon of one convicted of an infamous crime restores his competency as a witness; but the mere remission of his sentence does not[8]

The statute provision that the will shall be attested by competent witnesses, refers to their competency at the time they subscribe. If, after the execution of the will, and before it is admitted to probate, any of the witnesses became infamous, insane, or otherwise disqualified, the will may be sustained by proof of the handwriting of those

[1] 1 Bishop, New Crim Law, § 971   [2] 1 Greenl Ev § 373.
[3] Commonwealth v. Keith, 8 Met 531
[4] Commonwealth v Rogers, 7 Met 500
[5] Little v. Gibson, 39 N. H , 505
[6] 1 Greenl Ev § 373   [7] 1 Bishop, New Crim Law, § 974
[8] Perkins v Stevens, 24 Pick 277

who are thus rendered incompetent to testify. If the witnesses are competent at the time they attest, their subsequent incompetency, from whatever cause it arises, will not prevent the probate and allowance of the will, if it is otherwise satisfactorily proved.[1] It has been claimed that a person under the age of fourteen years is presumed to be incompetent, from defect of understanding, to attest the execution of a will; but the competence of a child offered as a witness is to be determined by the court as a matter of fact in each case.[2]

Section 4 of chapter 135 of the Revised Laws provides that a will made and executed in conformity with the law existing at the time of its execution shall have the same effect as if made pursuant to the provisions of that chapter.

Section IV.

EXECUTION OF CODICILS.

A codicil is an addition or supplement to a will. By our statutes the term "will" is construed to include codicils.[3]

The formalities to be observed in the execution of codicils are the same as are required by statute in the execu-

---

[1] R. L. c. 135, § 2

[2] Carlton v Carlton, 40 N H. 14; State v Sawtelle, 66 N H 188, 502; Commonwealth v Lynes, 142 Mass 577, and Commonwealth v. Robinson, 165 Mass 426 In the last case cited, the witness who was allowed to testify was less than six years old at the time of the trial. In State v Sawtelle, supra, the testimony of Marion Sawtelle, a girl evidently less than fourteen years of age and who testified that she was eight years old, was admitted See also Wheeler v United States, 159 U S 523

[3] R L c 3, § 5, cl 24, Gray v Sherman, 5 Allen, 198; Lyman v Coolidge, 176 Mass 7, 9.

tion of wills. The codicil must be in writing, signed by the testator or by some person in his presence and by his express direction, and attested and subscribed in his presence by at least three competent witnesses. The attesting witnesses may be the same persons who subscribed the original will, or other competent witnesses. A will may have several codicils, and each must be separately executed

A codicil duly attested may communicate the efficacy of its attestation to an unattested will or previous codicil so as to render effectual any devise contained in such prior unattested paper, when the several instruments are written on the same paper. This may be the effect when the codicil does not refer in terms to the unattested instrument; and even when written on a separate paper if it expressly refers to the original instrument [1]

The effect of a codicil ratifying, confirming, and republishing a will is to give the same force to the will as if it had been written, executed, and published at the date of the codicil [2]

A codicil may have the effect of impliedly revoking the later in date of two wills by expressly referring to and recognizing the prior one as the actual will of the testator.[3] A codicil will refer to the latest of several wills if no express date is named.[4] A will revoked by implication, as by a change in the testator's circumstances, may be republished by a codicil duly attested.[5] So a will made

[1] 1 Jarm on Wills (6th Am ed), 104, 1 Underhill on Wills, § 216

[2] Brimmer v Sohier, 1 Cush. 118, Miles v. Boyden, 3 Pick 216; Haven v Forster, 14 Pick. 543; Pratt v. Rice, 7 Cush 212, Hosea v. Jacobs, 98 Mass 65

[3] Crosbie r. Macdonald, 4 Ves. 610. [4] Ibid.

[5] See 1 Williams Ex (6th Am. ed) 254, and cases there cited

by a person not of full age, or of unsound mind, or otherwise incapacitated, may be made effectual by a codicil republishing the same and duly executed after the disability is removed. And a will executed by a person under undue influence may be made valid by being confirmed and republished by a codicil subsequently executed, when the testator is free from such influence.[1] A codicil, by republishing a will, may give effect to a devise which would otherwise have been void on account of the devisee being a witness to the original will [2]

Section V.

AS TO THE TESTATOR'S SOUNDNESS OF MIND.

The right of disposing of property by will is limited by the statute to persons of sound mind, and the question raised by this restriction is the one presented for determination in a majority of the contested cases

To establish the testator's mental capacity it must appear that he possessed mind and memory sufficient to enable him to understand the nature and consequences of his testamentary act.

Mere ability to answer usual and familiar questions is not enough. The testator must have memory "A man

---

[1] See 1 Williams Ex (6th Am ed) 75

[2] Mooers ı White, 6 Johns Ch 375

An additional legacy, given by a codicil, is attended with the same incidents and qualities as the original legacy Tilden v Tilden, 13 Gray, 103 , Brown v Brown 137 Mass 541, and cases cited A second legacy given to a person by a codicil is to be treated as additional to the legacy in the original will, in the absence of anything signifying a different intention Wainwright v Tuckerman, 120 Mass 232, Bates, Petitioner, 151 Mass 252, 257.

in whom this faculty is wholly extinguished cannot be said to possess an understanding to any degree whatever, or for any purpose. But his memory may be very imperfect; it may be greatly impaired by age or disease, he may not be able at all times to recollect the names, the persons, or the families of those with whom he had been intimately acquainted, he may at times ask idle questions, and repeat those which had before been asked and answered, and yet his understanding be sufficiently sound for many of the ordinary transactions of life He may not have sufficient strength of memory and vigor of intellect to make and digest all the parts of a contract, and yet be competent to direct the disposition of his property by will. This is a subject which he may possibly have often thought of; and there is probably no person who has not arranged such a disposition in his mind before he committed it to writing. The question is not so much what was the degree of memory possessed by the testator, as this. Had he a disposing memory? Was he capable of recollecting the property he was about to bequeath, the manner of distributing it, and the objects of his bounty? To sum up the whole in its most simple and intelligible form, Were his mind and memory sufficiently sound to enable him to know and understand the business in which he was engaged at the time when he executed his will?"[1]

It is not necessary that the testator should be possessed of a mind naturally strong, to enable him to make a valid will.[2] Mere weakness of understanding is not an objec-

---

[1] Washington, J, in Stevens v Vancleve, 4 Wash C C 262; and see Hathorn v King. 8 Mass. 371; Hastings v Rider, 99 Mass 622; Converse v. Converse, 21 Vt 168, Kinne v. Kinne, 9 Conn 105, Stewart v Lispenard, 26 Wend 253.

[2] Whitney v. Twombly, 136 Mass. 145.

tion, for courts cannot measure the size of people's understandings and capacities "If a man," says Swinburne, "be of a mean understanding (neither of the wise sort or the foolish), but indifferent as it were betwixt a wise man and a fool, yea, though he rather incline to the foolish sort, so that for his dull capacity he might worthily be termed *grossum caput*, a dull pate, or a dunce, such a one is not prohibited from making his statement."[1]

In a large proportion of the cases in which the sanity of testators is made a question, the alleged want of capacity is in the decay of the faculties resulting from old age, or the effect of disease, or both combined. But neither extreme old age, nor debility of body, will affect the capacity to make a will, provided the testator possesses the sound mind necessary to the disposition of his property. The law looks only to the competency of his understanding.[2]

EVIDENCE ON QUESTIONS OF THE TESTATOR'S SANITY.

The legal presumption, in the absence of evidence to the contrary, is in favor of the testator's sanity.[3] It was

---

[1] Swinburne on Wills, Pt 2, § 4

[2] In Van Alst v Hunter (5 Johns Ch 148), the testator was more than ninety years old when he made his will. Chancellor Kent said. "It is one of the painful consequences of extreme old age that it ceases to excite interest, and is apt to be left solitary and neglected The control which the law still gives to a man over the disposal of his property is one of the most efficient means which he has in protracted life to command the attentions due to his infirmities" In Reed's Will (2 B Monr 79), the testator was eighty years old and physically helpless from palsy, and his will was sustained In Jennings v Pendergas (10 Md 346), a will made by a testatrix at the age of ninety-six was sustained

[3] Baxter v Abbott, 7 Gray, 71, Thomas, J, dissenting ; Baldwin v Parker, 99 Mass 84, Richardson v. Bly, 131 Mass —(63 N. E

formerly held that, the testator's sanity having been testified to by the attesting witnesses, the burden shifted, and was upon the party opposing the probate to show that the testator was not of sound mind, but the more recently decided cases hold that the burden of proving the sanity of the testator is upon him who offers the will for probate, and does not shift upon evidence of his sanity being given by the subscribing witnesses.[1]

The subscribing witnesses are regarded in law as persons placed near the testator at the time he executes his will, in order that no fraud may be practised upon him, and to judge of his capacity. They are supposed to have satisfied themselves as to the testator's mental condition, and are therefore permitted to give their opinions upon that point[2] They may be inquired of as to the grounds of their opinions on cross-examination, and other evidence is admissible to support or contradict them. Any person may testify as to the appearance of the testator, and to facts from which the state of his mind may be inferred, and medical experts may then be inquired of as to the conclusions they draw from the circumstances and symp-

Rep 3), Crowninshield v Crowninshield, 2 Gray, 524, so far as this case seems to hold that there is no legal presumption of the testator s sanity, is overruled by the later cases cited.

[1] Crowninshield v Crowninshield, 2 Gray, 524, Barker v. Comins, 110 Mass. 477, Bacon v. Bacon, 181 Mass — (62 N. E Rep 990), Williams v Robinson, 42 Vt 658, Gerrish v Nason, 22 M E 438, Delafield v Parish, 25 N Y 9, Barry v. Butlin, 1 Curt Eccl 638.

[2] Needham v Ide, 5 Pick 510, Williams v Spencer, 150 Mass 346, and cases cited; Melanefy v Morrison, 152 Mass 476; but their opinions as to whether the testator had sufficient strength of mind to comprehend a certain clause of the will are inadmissible Melanefy v Morrison, *supra* Declarations of a deceased witness that the testator was insane at the time of executing the will are inadmissible Sewall v Robbins, 139 Mass 164, and cases cited

toms proved to have existed.[1] The mere opinions of witnesses who are not experts have been held inadmissible;[2] but in Baxter v Abbott,[3] it was held that a physician who had practised many years in the testator's neighborhood, and had at times been his medical adviser, and who saw and conversed with him a short time before the making of the will, was competent to state his opinion of the testator's sanity, though he was not an expert on the particular subject of insanity.

The only witnesses who are competent to give in evidence their opinions as to the sanity of the testator are the witnesses to the will, a physician who has been his medical adviser, and persons qualified as experts in regard to mental diseases.[4]

Evidence of insanity both before and after the time of making the will is admissible.[5] The fact that the testator committed suicide soon after making his will may be proved, but is not conclusive evidence of insanity; for it is said his power of reasoning on other subjects may have

[1] Upon the trial of an issue of the testator's sanity, an expert, although he has heard all the evidence, is not to be asked, "Suppose all the facts stated by the witness to be true, was the testator laboring under an insane delusion, or was he of unsound mind?" But the facts upon which his opinion is asked should be put to him hypothetically Woodbury v Obear, 7 Gray, 467, Miller v Smith, 112 Mass. 475.

[2] Poole v. Richardson, 3 Mass 330; Needham v Ide, 5 Pick 510; Commonwealth v Fairbanks, 2 Allen, 511, Hastings v. Rider, 99 Mass. 624, Smith v Smith, 157 Mass 389, Clark v Clark, 168 Mass. 523, 525 In Hathorn v King, 8 Mass 371, attending physicians were first allowed to give their opinion.

[3] 7 Gray, 71 ; and see Hastings v. Rider, *supra;* Lewis v. Mason, 109 Mass 169

[4] May v Bradlee, 127 Mass 414, 421; Smith v. Smith, 157 Mass. 346, Clark v Clark, 168 Mass 523, 525.

[5] Dickinson v. Barber, 9 Mass 225.

EVIDENCE AS TO TESTATOR'S MENTAL CONDITION.   49

been wholly unimpaired.[1] The fact that he was under guardianship as an insane person is *prima facie* evidence of incapacity, but may be explained by other evidence.[2] The testator's declarations so near the time of making the will as to be a part of the *res gestæ* are admissible,[3] and the fact of his silence when the subject of his incapacity was talked of in his hearing has been allowed to be proved.[4] The fact that the will was written by the testator himself, and is sensible in its provisions, is the best evidence of his capacity,[5] but a will is not to be invalidated merely because its provisions are imprudent and unaccountable. General facts upon the subject of insanity, though contained in books of established reputation, are not admissible.[6] The attestation of a will is not evidence that the witness believed the testator to be sane.[7]

Evidence is admissible to show that the testator's family, either on his father's or mother's side, were subject to insanity, or that his parents or other near relatives were

[1] Brooks v Barrett, 7 Pick 97 A testator committed suicide on the day next after that on which he made his will, and the will was established. Chambers v Queen's Proctor, 2 Curteis, 415.

[2] Breed v Pratt, 18 Pick 115, Stone v Damon, 12 Mass 488, Crowninshield v Crowninshield, 2 Gray, 524, Garnett v Garnett, 114 Mass 381, Hamilton v. Hamilton, 10 R I 538

[3] 1 Greenl Ev § 108, Robinson v. Hutchinson, 26 Vt 38.

[4] Irish v Smith, 8 Serg & R 573

[5] Overton v. Overton, 7 B Mon. 61   See Davis v. Calvert, 5 Gill & Johns 269

[6] Commonwealth v Wilson, 1 Gray, 337 ; Ware v Ware, 8 Greenl. 42, Collier v Simpson, 5 Carr & P. 74

[7] Baxter v Abbott, 7 Gray, 71 On the trial of an appeal from the decree of the probate court allowing a will, it cannot be given in evidence against the will that one of the attesting witnesses who testified in the probate court to the testator's sanity, and has since deceased declared after the probate, that he wished to live to unsay what he had said, and that the testator was insane. Ibid

insane.¹ The fact is well established that a predisposition to insanity is frequently transmitted from parent to child through many generations. According to Esquirol, this hereditary taint is the most common of all the causes to which insanity can be referred, and other authorities assert that no other cause can be assigned for the disease in a majority of all the cases. The disease may not appear in a child who goes through life without being exposed to any exciting cause, but with such predisposition, insanity supervenes from very slight causes. Hereditary insanity is induced by the same exciting cause in the offspring as in the parent, and often appears about the same age and under the same form.²

Evidence of merely eccentric habits, together with the fact that the will contains directions that appear absurd, will not establish the fact of insanity,³ and it has been

¹ Baxter v. Abbott, 7 Gray, 81.
² " As we might suppose, children that are born before insanity manifests itself in the parents, are less subject to the disorder than those which are born afterwards. When one parent only is insane, there is less tendency for the predisposition to be transmitted than when both are affected, but according to Esquirol, this predisposition is much more readily transmitted through the female than through the male parent. Its transmission is also more strikingly remarked when it has been observed to exist in several generations of lineal ancestors, and, like other hereditary maladies, it appears to be subject to atavism; i.e., it may disappear in one generation, and reappear in the next. Further, the children of drunken parents, and of those who have been married late in life, are said to be more subject to insanity than those born under other circumstances." 2 Taylor's Med. Jur. (4th ed.) 505, and see 1 Beck's Med. Jur. 725, Ray's Med Jur (5th ed.) § 125.
³ A will was opposed because it bore intrinsic evidence of the testator's insanity. After making certain bequests, the testator directed his executors to cause some part of his bowels to be converted into fiddle-strings, that other parts should be sublimed into smelling-salts, and that the remainder of his body should be vitrified into lenses for

held that the life, opinions, and habits of a testator may be reviewed for the purpose of testing the allegations of insanity.[1] "Monomania is very liable to be confounded with eccentricity, but there is this difference between them: in monomania, there is obviously a change of character, — the individual is different to what he was; in eccentricity, such a difference is not marked, — he is, and always has been, singular in his ideas and actions. An eccentric man may be convinced that what he is doing is absurd, and contrary to the general rules of society, but he professes to set these at defiance. A true

---

optical purposes. He afterwards said, "The world may think this to be done in a spirit of singularity or whim." He had expressed a wish to have his body converted to purposes useful to mankind, and had consulted a physician in regard to chemical experiments to be made upon it. It appeared that he conducted his affairs with shrewdness and ability, and that he was treated by those with whom he dealt as a person of indisputable capacity. Sir Herbert Jenner, in giving judgment, held that insanity was not proved, that the facts merely amounted to eccentricity, and on this ground he pronounced for the validity of the will.

[1] J. W. G. made his will in England a few weeks before his death, in which he gave several legacies, and directed the remainder to be paid over to the Turkish ambassador for the poor of Constantinople, and also for the erection of a cenotaph in that city, inscribed with his name, and bearing a light perpetually burning therein. It appeared that he had lived long in the East, had studied the Koran a great deal, and was an avowed believer in Mahommedanism. The prerogative court, on the ground of this extraordinary bequest, which sounded to folly, and on parol evidence of the testator's wild and extravagant language, pronounced him of unsound mind; but it was *held*, reversing that decision, that as the insanity attributed to the deceased was not monomania, but general mental derangement, and as the proper mode of testing the allegation was to review the life, habits, and opinions of the testator, on such a review there was nothing absurd or irrational in the bequest, or anything in his conduct, at the date of the will, indicating derangement, and therefore the will was admitted to probate. 29 Eng. Law & Eq. 38.

monomaniac cannot be convinced of his error, and he thinks that his acts are consistent with reason and the general conduct of mankind In eccentricity, there is a will to do or not to do ; in real monomania, the controlling power of the will is lost Eccentric habits suddenly acquired are, however, presumptive of insanity."[1]

When the alleged want of capacity is in the weakness and prostration of physical disease, an inquiry into the character of the testator's malady will sometimes aid in determining the question of his soundness of mind. It is well established that different diseases, though equally fatal, exercise very unlike influences upon the mental faculties "Among the diseases which incapacitate an individual from making a valid will, or at least render his rationality doubtful, may be enumerated the following · lethargic and comatose affections. These suspend the action of the intellectual faculties; so also does an attack of apoplexy , and even if patients recover from its first effects, an imbecility of mind is often left which unfits an individual from the duty in question. Phrenitis, delirium tremens, and those inflammations which are accompanied with delirium, also impair the mind. Finally, in typhoid fevers, the low state which usually precedes death is one that may be considered as incapacitating the individual. On the other hand, there are many fatal diseases in which the patient preserves his mind to the last, and all dispositions of property made by him are of course valid. Of these, none is more striking than the clearness of intellect which sometimes attends the last stages of phthisis pulmonalis."[2]

[1] 2 Taylor's Med Jur (4th ed.), 551, 1 Clevenger Med Jur. of Insanity, 278, 344
[2] Beck's Med. Jur. (11th ed) 842.

Long-continued habits of intemperance may gradually impair the memory and other faculties, and produce a species of insanity which will render the person incapable of making a will. A person, however, who is habitually addicted to the use of intoxicating liquors, and at times violently excited, may make a valid will when he is free from the excitement of liquor. It has been held that if the testator's habits of intoxication are not such as to render him habitually incompetent for the transaction of business, it is necessary for the party objecting to his capacity on the ground of casual intoxication to prove its existence at the time the will was executed.[1] The question in these, as in all cases where unsoundness of mind is alleged, is whether the testator knew and understood the business in which he was engaged at the time he executed his will.

The testator's declarations to the effect that he was induced to sign his will when he was under the influence of intoxicating liquors, are not admissible evidence of the fact that he was so incapacitated.[2]

Lucid Intervals. — The party supporting the will may show that the testator, although insane at some period of his life, had recovered his reason, or that the will was made during a temporary cessation of the insanity.[3] Lunatics occasionally recover for a time, and are conscious of their acts. The lucid interval may be a few hours or minutes in duration, or it may continue for weeks, months, and even years. Evidence of a lucid interval is to be examined with great caution, especially in cases where the alleged interval was of brief duration. A mere dimi-

---

[1] Andrees v Weller, 2 Green, Ch 604
[2] Gibson v Gibson, 3 Jones (Mo), 227.
[3] Breed v Pratt, 18 Pick. 115.

nution in the violence of the disorder does not constitute a lucid interval. It need not, of course, appear that the predisposition to the disease had been extirpated, or that the testator had regained the same degree of intellectual ability that he possessed previous to his insanity; but it must appear that he was conscious of his acts, and able to understand their nature and consequences.[1] The fact that the will is a rational one and made in a rational manner, though not conclusive, is strong evidence that it was made in a lucid interval.[2]

In establishing the fact of a lucid interval, evidence has been admitted to show that the disposition of the testator's property made by his will was consistent with his intentions declared previous to his insanity.[3]

The rule that insanity proved to have existed at a particular time is presumed to continue, does not apply to temporary delirium connected with a violent disease.[4]

Partial Insanity — Monomania. — The objection has been raised in some cases that the testator, though of apparently sound mind upon general subjects, labored under an insane delusion in regard to particular matters, and that such delusions, operating upon his mind at the time he made his will, deprived him of his disposing capacity. Such delusions are said to be more commonly manifested in the testator's unaccountable antipathy to his children and near relatives, and unfounded suspicions of attempts by them on his life. But to defeat a will by evidence of an insane delusion merely, it has been held that the will must be

---

[1] Gombault v. Pub. Admr., 4 Bradf. (N. Y.) 226. Bannatyne v. Bannatyne, 14 Eng. Law & Eq. 581; 1 Jarm. on Wills (6th Am. ed.), 38.
[2] Nicholes v. Binns, 1 Swa. & Trist. 239.
[3] Coughlen's case, referred to in Booth v. Blundell, 19 Ves. 508.
[4] Hix v. Whittemore, 4 Met. 545; Little v. Little, 13 Gray, 266.

traced to, and shown to be the offspring of, such insane delusion.[1] The declarations of the testator, proceeding from partial insanity, are not admissible as evidence of the truth of his statements, but may properly be considered in connection with other facts in determining the general question as to his soundness of mind.[2]

It is within the discretion of the court to fix the limits of time before and after the making of the will within which evidence to show specific acts of unsoundness of mind on the part of the testator shall be confined. In Howes v. Colburn, 165 Mass. 385, this time was limited to a period from about eight years before the date of the will to about two and a half years after its date.

Section VI.

WILLS INVALIDATED BY FRAUD AND UNDUE INFLUENCE.

The testator, in order to make a valid will, must enjoy full liberty in the disposition of his estate. A will obtained

---

[1] In Greenwood's case, the testator, being sick and delirious, took some medicine from the hands of his brother, and imagined it was poison intended to kill him. He recovered, and returned to his profession, — that of a barrister, — but was never afterwards free from the morbid delusion. He disinherited his brother, who was his only next of kin. Two trials were had on the question of sustaining the will, with conflicting verdicts, and the result was a compromise. Stated by Lord Eldon in White v. Wilson, 13 Ves. 89.

A testator who, twenty-four years before his death, had a dangerous fever, during which he contracted a strong antipathy towards his brothers, which continued through his life, made his will shortly before his death, and disinherited them. There was no apparent cause for his antipathy. The will was set aside on the ground that his peculiar defect of intellect influenced his disposition of his estate. Johnson v. Moore's Heirs, 1 Little (Ky.), 371, and see Dew v. Clark, 3 Addams, 79; Thompson v. Thompson, 21 Barb. (N. Y.), 107.

[2] Woodbury v. Obear, 7 Gray, 467. For a full discussion of this point, see Shailer v. Bumstead, 99 Mass. 112.

by fraud is of course void,[1] and the effect is the same where the testator is constrained by fear, or where undue influence is used to control the disposition of his estate. An instrument executed under such circumstances is not the will of the testator, but is the dictation of another person. Any condition of things that restrains the testator from the free exercise of his own judgment, incapacitates him as a testator.

Objections of this class more frequently arise in cases where the testator was either of weak mind naturally, or was enfeebled by age or disease, and therefore liable to be controlled by influences which would not affect a person of strong mind and good health.[2] A person may be of sound mind and competent, if left to himself, to make a valid will, but he may be induced by the harassing importunities of those about him, and by the hope of quiet, to dispose of his property in a manner that his own healthy and unbiassed judgment would not approve. A will made under such circumstances is regarded as a result of coercion, and cannot be sustained.

The degree of undue influence which will invalidate a will must vary with the circumstances of each case. The importunity or threatening successfully employed to coerce one person will have no effect on another. The mental and physical condition of the testator, his natural strength or feebleness of mind, the power and disposition of the per-

[1] 1 Jarm. on Wills (6th Am ed), 36, 37, 1 Williams (7th Am ed), 53, Davis v Calvert, 5 Gill & Johns. 269, Dietrick v Dietrick, 5 Serg & R 207

[2] An alleged will which was wholly in the handwriting of the son of the testatrix, and mainly in his interest, and executed by her without the knowledge of the rest of the family when she was eighty-three years old, was disallowed, on the ground of undue influence, in Jones v. Simpson, 171 Mass. 474

son who seeks to control the testator, and the character of the influences brought to bear upon him, are to be considered. Honest suggestions and moderate persuasion do not amount to undue influence. After marriage, a husband or a wife may lawfully use persuasions to induce the other to make a favorable will.[1] To invalidate the will, it must appear that the ill-treatment, threats, violence, or persistent importunity, was such as to destroy the free agency of the testator.[2] In these cases, as in all others, the party offering the will for probate must prove the sanity of the testator; but if that fact is established, the burden of proving undue influence is upon the party alleging it.

It has been held that the harmony of the will with the testator's disposition and affections, and his declarations in regard to it when in health, are facts to be considered

[1] Maynard v. Tyler, 168 Mass. 107.
[2] Jarm. on Wills (6th Am. ed.) 36, 37; 1 Williams Ex. (7th Am. ed.), 55.

Any one has a right by fair argument or persuasion, or by virtuous influence, to induce another to make a will in his favor. Miller v. Miller, 5 Serg. & R. 267. 'Neither advice, nor argument, nor persuasion would vitiate a will made freely and from conviction, though such will might not have been made but for such advice or persuasion." Clayton, C. J., in Chandler v. Ferris, 1 Harr. 454. A testatrix whose property amounted to $27,000, who was eighty-three years of age, and had nephews and nieces, but no children, gave by her will about $5,000 in legacies to her nephews and nieces, and the residue to her confidential adviser and manager of her property, who lived in her house at the time the will was made, and until her death. On appeal from the probate of her will on the ground of her mental incapacity and his undue influence, it was *held*, that the burden of proof of the absence of undue influence rested upon the proponents of the will, and that in view of the character and extent of his confidential relations to the testatrix and the benefit received by him from the will, the jury would have been warranted in the inference, without any direct proof, that he took part in procuring the will from the testatrix. Richmond's Appeal, 59 Conn. 226.

in determining the question of undue influence.[1] If it appears that the will was written or procured to be written by a person largely benefited by its provisions, the circumstances under which it was made will be more strictly inquired into.[2] Evidence that the testator was of feeble mind, and believed in ghosts and supernatural influences, has some tendency to show that weakness of mind which would be easily imposed upon by the exertion of undue influence.[3] Subsequent declarations of the testator, to the effect that he had been forced to sign his will, are not competent evidence of the fact that force was used[4]

---

[1] Evidence having been introduced that the will was procured to be made by the undue influence of the residuary legatee, it was *held* that evidence was admissible, on the other side, that a large part of the property of the testatrix was inherited by her from her minor son, who died many years previous, and who was greatly attached to the residuary legatee, and had frequently expressed his intention, if he should attain the age of twenty-one years, to leave the bulk of his property to him, and that such intention was known to the testatrix Glover v Hayden, 4 Cush 580

For an examination of authorities as to the admissibility of the testator's declarations, see Shailer v Bumstead, 99 Mass 112

[2] Clarke v Fisher, 1 Paige, 171; Darley v Darley, 3 Bradf (N Y.) 481; Brydges v King, 1 Hagg 250, Dodge v March, 1 Hagg. 612

[3] Woodbury v. Obear, 7 Gray, 467. Evidence having been given that a devisee, who was accused of having made use of undue influence, had represented to the testator that the wife of one of his sons was an extravagant woman, who would waste anything that might be given to her husband, the opposers of the will were allowed to prove that her general behavior and character were good Dietrick v Dietrick 5 Serg & R. 207; and see Nussear v. Arnold, 13 Serg & R 323

When a subscribing witness, who is accused of having been an accomplice in a fraud upon the testator, is dead, evidence may be given of his general good character, Provis v Reed, 5 Bing. 435, but not if he is living, Doe v Harris, 7 Car, & P 330

[4] Ibid., Davis v. Davis. 123 Mass 590; Jackson v Kniffen,

When the will is presented for probate after the testator's death, the attorney who drafted it may testify as to the directions given to him by the testator, so that it may appear whether the instrument presented for probate is or is not the will of the alleged testator [1]

A will may be void in part and valid in part. It may be void as to such of its provisions as were procured by fraud or the exercise of undue influence, and valid so far as it was the free act of the testator. [2]

Section VII.

REVOCATION OF WILLS.

A will, executed in accordance with the requirements of the statute, is presumed to have existed until the death of the testator; but this presumption may be rebutted by proof of its revocation. The testator may revoke his will at his pleasure. The manner of revocation is pointed out by statute: —

"No will shall be revoked except by burning, tearing, cancelling or obliterating it with the intention of revoking it by the testator himself or by a person in his presence and by his direction; or by some other writing signed, attested, and subscribed in the same manner as a will, or by subsequent changes in the condition or circumstances

---

[2] Johns 31. Smith v. Fenner, 1 Gall (R I) 174, Moritz v Brough, 16 Serg & R 403 But such declarations are admissible to show a state of mind easily susceptible to undue influence. May v Bradlee, 127 Mass 414, Potter v Baldwin, 133 Mass. 427, Lane v Moore, 151 Mass 87

[1] Doherty v O'Callaghan, 157 Mass 90

[2] Trimlestown v D'Alton, 1 Dow & Cl 85 Harrison s Appeal, 48 Conn 202, Floiey's Executors v Florey, 24 Ala 241, Ogden v Greenleaf, 143 Mass. 349, Sumner v Crane, 155 Mass. 484.

of the testator from which a revocation is implied by law."[1]

The revocation of a will, therefore, may be either *express* or *implied.* It is expressly revoked by some act of destruction done upon it with the intention of revoking it; or by a new will or codicil intended as a substitute for it, or other writing, formally executed with the express intention of revocation.

EXPRESS REVOCATIONS.

The mere physical act of burning, tearing, cancelling,[2] or obliterating a will is not of itself sufficient to consti-

---

[1] R. L. c 135, § 8

[2] Cancelling, as the term was originally used, is the defacing of a written instrument by drawing cross lines diagonally over its face for the purpose of annulling it, but the testator may cancel his will by placing upon it any marks or writing that clearly exhibits his intention to annul the instrument. Evans' Appeal, 58 Penn 238.

A will covered the first page of the paper on which it was written, and part of the second. The testator, two years after the execution of the will, wrote the following words on the last half of the second page. "This will is hereby cancelled and annulled In full this 15th day of March, in the year 1859," and lower on the same page "In testimony whereof I here I have" There were no other marks of cancellation or defacement *Held* that the will was revoked by cancellation. Warner *v* Warner's Estate, 37 Vt. 356

But in 1884, the Supreme Court of Wisconsin, in Ladd's Will, 60 Wisc 187, decided that the words, "I revoke this will," written on the fourth page of the instrument, upon which no part of the will was written, were not a revocation of the will This case furnishes an elaborate discussion of the meaning of the word "cancellation," and considers critically the decision of the courts in the case of Evans' Appeal, 58 Penn 238, and Warner *v* Warner's Estate, 37 Vt. 356

When the word "obsolete" was written by the testator on the margin of his will, there being no other evidence of his intention, it was held that the will was not revoked Lewis *v* Lewis, 2 W & Serg 455.

An interlineation made by the testator's direction in the body

tute a revocation The act must be done *with the intention of revoking* If the testator inadvertently obliterates his will, it will remain in force, notwithstanding such obliteration [1] So, if he destroys it during a fit of insanity, or if it is destroyed by his consent, given after he has become *non compos*, [2] or if it is destroyed by another person without his knowledge, it is not revoked [3] Nor is the will revoked if its destruction by the testator is the effect on his mind of undue influence.[4]

Burning, tearing, etc., in a slight degree, with a declared intent to revoke, is a sufficient revocation. Where the testator gave his will "a rip" with his hands, "so as almost

of the will, after its execution, will not revoke the will, nor will it operate to change the provisions of the will Wheeler v Bent, 7 Pick 61

[1] A will was burnt by the testator on the supposition that he had substituted another for it, but which was not duly executed Probate of a copy of the first will granted. Scott v Scott, 1 Swa & Trist 258

[2] Idley v Bowen, 11 Wend 227; Ford v Ford, 7 Humph. 92, Scrubly v Fordham, 1 Add. 74 The testator to revoke a will, must be at the same time competent to make a will, or the act of revocation will be a nullity Smith v Wait, 4 Barb Sup Ct (N. Y) 28; *In re* Downer, 26 Eng Law & Eq 600. The burden of proving that the will was mutilated by the testator when of sound mind, is upon the party alleging the revocation Harris v Berrall, 1 Swa & Trist 153

[3] Onions v Tyler, 1 P Wms 345, Bennett v Sherrod, 3 Ired 303; Middleton v. Middleton, 19 Eng. Law & Eq. 340 The fact that a testator, who discovers such loss of his will, neglects to make another, has been held to furnish a presumption of his intention to revoke Steele v Price, 5 B. Mon. 68.

[4] Rich v Gilkey, 73 Maine, 595 Where the revocation proceeds from mistake, or from a false impression originating from deceit practised on the testator, it will be void, but where the testator merely expresses a doubt as to a fact, and upon that doubt revokes, the revocation would seem to be good 6 Cruise's Digest (Greenl ed), tit 38, c 6, § 26.

to tear a bit off," and then threw it on the fire, it was held to be a revocation, though the will fell from the fire and was preserved, slightly singed, by another person, without the testator's knowledge.[1] If the seal be torn from his will by the testator under the mistaken impression that it is an essential part of the execution of the instrument, the intention to revoke being clear, it would be a sufficient revocation.[2]

A mere declaration of an intention to revoke a will, not accompanied nor followed by any act in fulfilment of that intention, is of course insufficient.[3] And there may be a change of purpose that will prevent a revocation, even when the act of destruction is partly accomplished. A testator, under the impulse of passion against his devisee, tore his will twice through, when his arms were seized by a bystander, and he became pacified by the concessions of the devisee; he then fitted the pieces of the torn will together, and remarked, "It's a good job it is no worse." This was held to be no revocation.[4] The declarations of the testator, accompanying the act of revocation, are admissible in evidence to explain his intentions.[5]

[1] Bibb v. Thomas, 2 W Bl 1043, Doe v Harris 6 Ad & El. 209

[2] Avery v Pixley, 4 Mass 460. A testator, being ill in bed, called for his will, and one of the legatees named in the will deceived him by handing him an old letter in its stead Held, that if, from the rest of the testimony, the jury believed that the testator destroyed that letter, thinking it to be his will, such circumstances would amount to a revocation Pryor v Coggin, 17 Ga 444

[3] The mere direction to another by the testator to destroy his will is not sufficient, unless some act of destruction is thereupon done Giles v Giles, 1 Cam & Nor 174, Ford v. Ford, 7 Humph 92.

[4] Doe v Perks, 5 B & Ald 489, Elms v. Elms, 1 Swa & Trist 155.

[5] 1 Greenl Ev. § 273, Dan v Brown, 4 Cowen, 490.

It is to be observed that the statute requires the burning, tearing, cancelling, or obliterating to be by the testator himself, or by some person in his presence and by his direction. If, therefore, the testator requests a person who has the custody of his will to destroy it, and it is accordingly destroyed, such destruction, if not effected in the testator's presence, would not be a compliance with the terms of the statute.

If the will is found obliterated in the testator's possession, the presumption is that it was obliterated by him, and the burden of proving the contrary is on the party offering it for probate; but if it has been in the possession of one adversely interested, the presumption does not arise.[1] If the will is proved to have been in the testator's possession and cannot be found, it will be presumed that he destroyed it with the intention of revoking it;[2] but if it is traced out of his custody, the party asserting the revocation must show that it came again into such custody.

If the testator executes his will in duplicate, retaining one part and committing the other to the custody of another person, and then destroys one part, the inference generally is that he intended to revoke the will, but the strength of the presumption depends much on the circumstances. Thus, if he destroys the only copy in his possession, his intent to revoke is very strongly to be presumed; if he was possessed of both copies, and destroys but one, it is weaker; and if he alters one and then destroys it, retain-

---

[1] Baptist Church v. Roberts, 2 Barr, 10; Bennett v. Sheriod, 3 Ired. 303; Jones v. Murphy, 8 Watts & Serg. 275.

[2] Davis v. Sigourney, 8 Met. 488. Newell v. Homer, 120 Mass. 277. The oral declarations of the testator are admissible in evidence to rebut this presumption. Sugden v. St. Leonards, Law Rep. 1 P. D. 154.

ing the other entire, the presumption has been said still to hold, but weaker still, but the contrary also has been asserted.[1]

Cases have occurred where a will has been revoked and a codicil left entire, and the question has thereby been raised as to whether the revocation of the will has a revoking effect upon the codicil also If from its contents the codicil appears inseparably connected with the will, it will be held to be revoked; otherwise if it is independent of and unconnected with the will [2]

A will is also expressly revoked by a new will or codicil, inconsistent in its provisions with the original will, or plainly intended as a substitute for it, or by a writing which expressly declares an intention to revoke.[3] A subsequent will which makes a new disposition of the whole estate is a revocation of the first, without any words of revocation; but if the subsequent will contains no clause of revocation and makes no disposition of the estate inconsistent with the former will, it does not operate as a revocation, but both instruments remain in force [4]

---

[1] 2 Greenl Ev § 682

[2] Ibid , 1 Jarm on Wills (6th Am ed), 139 *et seq*

[3] If the new will contained a clause revoking the former will, and it has been lost, and cannot be admitted to probate for want of evidence of its other contents, it is a revocation, and may be set up in opposition to the probate of the earlier will Wallis *v.* Wallis, 114 Mass 510, Stickney *v* Hammond, 138 Mass 120, Nelson *v.* McGiffert, 3 Barb Ch 158

When the intention of the testator to revoke his will appears clearly from a subsequent will, it is a sufficient revocation, although such subsequent will is inoperative on account of the incapacity of the devisee to take under it. Laughton *v.* Atkins, 1 Pick. 545

[4] Cutto *v* Gilbert, 29 Eng Law & Eq 64, s c 9 Moore, P. C. 131 " The mere fact of making a subsequent testamentary paper does not work a total revocation of a prior one, unless the latter expressly, or in effect, revoke the former, or the two are incapable of standing together;

Where it appeared that the testator made a second will, *the contents of which were unknown*, it was held not to be a revocation of the first, because it did not appear either that it contained a revocatory clause or made a different disposition of the estate. And where it was found that the testator made a second will different from the first, *but it was not found in what the difference consisted*, it was held to be no revocation.[1] The burden is on the party offering the second will to show that it expressly revokes the former will, or has different contents; the mere words, " this is the last will of me," etc , are not sufficient for that purpose.[2]

If the subsequent instrument, whether it be a will or codicil, disposes of a part of the estate only, although it professes an intent to dispose of the whole, it is only a

---

for though it be a maxim, as Swinburne says above, that as no man can die with two testaments, yet any number of instruments, whatever be their relative date, or in whatever form they may be (so that they be all clearly testamentary), may be admitted to probate, as together containing the last will of the deceased. And if a subsequent testamentary paper be *partly* inconsistent with one of an earlier date, then such latter instrument will revoke the former, *as to those parts only where they are inconsistent.*" 1 Williams on Executors (7th Am. ed), 212

" The will of a man is the aggregate of his testamentary intentions, so far as they are manifested in writing, duly executed according to the statute. And as a will, if contained in one document, may be of several sheets, so it may consist of several independent papers, each so executed " By Sir J P Wilde, in Lemage *v.* Goodban, L. R 1 P. & D. 57, Dempsey *v.* Lawson, 2 P D 98

[1] 6 Cruise's Digest (Greenleaf), tit 38, c 6, §§ 11, 14, and cases there cited This rule is applied, even if it is found that the second will was stolen from the testator or destroyed by fraud. Ibid, note But when the second will is missing, parol evidence of its contents may be offered 2 Greenl Ev § 688 But such evidence must be strong and conclusive. Cutto *v* Gilbert, 29 Eng Law & Eq 64

[2] Cutto *v.* Gilbert, 29 Eng Law & Eq

revocation *pro tanto*, unless it contains words expressing the intention to revoke.[1]

A revocatory writing, intended for the express purpose of revoking a will, must be signed by the testator, or by some person in his presence and by his express direction, and attested and subscribed in his presence by three or more competent witnesses. The manner of execution is the same prescribed by statute for the execution of wills.[2] If such writing is made in another state or country, it may be executed in the manner prescribed for the execution of wills in such other state or country.[3] If the writing declares merely an intention to do some future act of revocation, it will not amount to a revocation; it must be a present actual revocation.[4]

The obliteration by a testator of a portion of his will, with the intention of revoking the obliterated portion only, is a valid revocation of the part erased. The other provisions of the will will not be revoked; and the instrument, the obliterated parts excepted, may be admitted to probate as the will of the testator.[5]

If a will which contains a clause revoking former wills is cancelled, an earlier will, which has not been destroyed,

---

[1] Brant v. Wilson, 8 Cowen, 56; Harwood v. Goodright, Cowp. 87.

[2] Reid v. Borland, 14 Mass 208; Laughton v. Atkins, 1 Pick. 542. An instrument containing a clause of revocation is not admissible in evidence to prove the revocation of a prior will until probated Laughton v Atkins, 1 Pick 535; Sewall v Robbins, 139 Mass 164 If probate of it is refused, it is inadmissible as evidence of revocation. Stickney v Hammond, 138 Mass 116

[3] Bayley v Bailey, 5 Cush 245, Crippen v Dexter, 13 Gray, 332.

[4] Brown v Thorndike, 15 Pick 388

[5] Bigelow v Gillott, 123 Mass. 102; Sutton v. Sutton, 2 Cowp 812, Larkins v Larkins, 3 B & P. 16, Short v Smith, 4 East, 418; Mence v Mence, 18 Ves 348.

will not be revived, unless there is affirmative evidence that the testator intended to revive the earlier will by such cancellation. His oral declarations are admissible in evidence for the purpose of showing his intention.[1]

Another class of revocations is that implied by law from changes occurring in the condition and circumstances of the testator subsequent to the execution of his will. Such revocations are founded on the reasonable presumption that his will would have been differently made under such different circumstances Under the common law the marriage of a man will not revoke his will; nor will his will made after marriage be revoked by the birth of a child; but the rule is established that the concurrence of marriage and the birth of a child, after the execution of the will, works an entire revocation;[2] and the rule applies to posthumous children.[3] It has been decided that parol evidence of the intention of the testator, that his will should stand unrevoked, is inadmissible to control the presumption resulting from marriage and the birth of children[4] The rule does not apply to cases where it appears that the changes in the testator's circumstances and obligations were anticipated and provided for by the will, as when the will makes provision for the future wife

[1] Pickens v Davis, 134 Mass 252, Lane v. Moore, 151 Mass 90. Cancellation of a will, with intent to revive a former will, will be effective without further republication of the earlier will. Williams v. Williams, 152 Mass 515

[2] Warner v. Beach, 4 Gray, 103, Brush v Wilkins, 4 Johns Ch 506; Havens v. Vandenburg, 1 Demo, 27, Swan v Hammond, 138 Mass. 46, Nutt v Norton, 142 Mass 242

[3] Doe v Lancashire, 5 T R 49. It is the same if the testator died without knowledge of the fact that his wife was pregnant Christopher v Christopher, 4 Bur 2182; or if the child died in the testator's lifetime. Wright v Netherwood, 2 Salk 593.

[4] Marston v. Roe, 8 Add. & El. 14, Doe v Lancashire, *supra*.

and issue,[1] but provision for the wife only has been held insufficient.[2] But by statute 1892, c. 118, which took effect July 1, 1892, (now embodied substantially in R. L. c 135, § 9), it was provided that "the marriage of any person shall act as the revocation of any will made by such person previous to such marriage, unless it shall appear from the will itself that the will was made in contemplation of such marriage, or unless and except so far as the will is made in exercise of a power of appointment, and the estate thereby appointed would not, in default of appointment, pass to the persons that would have been entitled to the same if it had been the testator's own estate and he or she had died without disposing of it by will."[3] The marriage of a single woman has been held to be an absolute revocation of her will,[4] even though her testamentary capacity was subsequently restored by the event of her surviving her husband,[5] but on this point doubts have been expressed, it being questioned whether her marriage worked a revocation, or merely a suspension.

An alteration in the estate of lands devised by the act of the devisor may operate as an implied revocation of his will A conveyance of the estate devised is a revocation of the devise, under such circumstances there is nothing left upon which the devise can operate. But the convey-

[1] Kennebel v Scrafton, 2 East, 530
[2] Marston v Roe, 8 Add & El 14.
[3] Ingersoll v Hopkins, 170 Mass 401
[4] Swan v Hammond, 138 Mass 47; Blodgett v Moore, 141 Mass 75. Nutt v Norton, 142 Mass 252 But a will may be effective as the execution of a power of appointment contained in an ante-nuptial agreement, notwithstanding a subsequent marriage, and such will, in so far as it is the execution of the power contained in the agreement, should be allowed; but such allowance will be a qualified or limited allowance Osgood v. Bliss, 141 Mass. 474.
[5] 1 Jarm on Wills (6th Am ed), 34, 57.

ance, to effect an entire revocation, must be of the whole estate devised If it is of but part of the estate, it is a revocation only to the extent of the conveyance.[1] The partition of an estate between tenants in common does not operate as a revocation of a prior devise made by one of the tenants of his share

Entire revocations by implication of law are limited to a very small number of cases. The statute does not intimate what changes in the condition and circumstances of the testator are intended to work a revocation, but leaves them to be decided by the general rules of law; and the reported cases furnish but little information as to the effect of changes in the testator's condition except as regards marriage and the birth of children, and alteration in the estate devised It has been held that revocation cannot be implied from the long-continued insanity of the testator from soon after the making of his will until his death,[2] nor from the large increase in value of his property subsequent to the making of his will, although such increase altogether changes the proportion between

---

[1] Hawes v Humphrey, 9 Pick 350, Ballard v Carter, 5 Pick 112; Webster v Webster, 105 Mass. 538.

For the rules as to revocation by alteration of estate, see 6 Cruise's Digest (Greenleaf's ed), tit 38, c 6, § 58 *et seq*

[2] Revocation of a will cannot be implied from the birth of a child to the testator, contemplated in the will, the death of the testator's wife, and of another child, leaving issue the testator's insanity for forty years, from soon after the making of his will till his death; and a fourfold increase in the value of his property, so as greatly to change the proportion between the specific legacies given to some children and the shares of other children who were made residuary legatees Warner v Beach, 4 Gray, 162

" It is not apparent that an entire revocation by implication of law results from any change of condition or circumstances, except that of a subsequent marriage " Swan v Hammond, 138 Mass. 47.

the specific legacies and the shares of the residuary legatees.[1]

Section VIII.

PROBATE OF WILLS — FORMAL PROCEEDINGS.

The will to be proved should be filed in the probate office of the county of which the deceased was an inhabitant, or in which he was resident at the time of his death.[2]

---

[1] Warner v. Beach, 4 Gray, 162. "Though the testament be made in time of sickness and peril of death, when the testator doth not hope for life, and afterwards he recover his health, yet is not the testament revoked by such recovery, or albeit the testator make his testament by reason of some great journey, yet it is not revoked by his return." Swinburne, Pt. 7, § 15.

For a general review of the decided cases upon the subject of implied revocations, see 1 Saunders (Williams), 278, note.

[2] If upon the decease of any person leaving an estate liable to a tax on collateral legacies and successions, a will disposing of such estate is not offered for probate, or an application for administration made within four months from the time of such decease, the proper probate court, upon application by the treasurer of the commonwealth, shall appoint an administrator. R. L. c. 15, § 18.

A person *non compos*, born in the county of Suffolk, removed, upon the death of her father, into the county of Middlesex, where she lived as part of her brother's family many years and until her death, being for the last years of her life under a guardian who provided for her support, whose residence was in Suffolk. *Held*, that her domicile at the time of her death was in Middlesex, and that letters of administration on her estate, granted by the judge of probate in Suffolk, were void for want of jurisdiction. Holyoke v. Haskins, 5 Pick. 20; Harding v. Weld, 128 Mass. 591.

Where a citizen, having lived many years at W., in the county of M., purchased and furnished a house at B., in the county of S., and afterwards with his family spent his summers at his house in W., where he continued to pay his taxes, and his winters in B., where he died, it was *held* that probate of his will might be taken in the county of M. Whether probate in the county of S. would not have been

PROBATE OF WILLS. 71

With the will there must be filed a petition, signed by the executor or other person who offers the will for probate, and addressed to the judge of the probate court, setting forth the place where the testator last dwelt, the date of his death, the fact that he left a will, and praying that the will be allowed. The full name of the widow of the deceased, if any, and the names, residences, and relationship of his heirs-at-law and next of kin should also be stated in the petition. If the next of kin are minors, the fact should be stated, and if they are under guardianship, the name and residence of the guardian should be given [1]

If the executor named in the will declines the trust, his declination in writing should be filed with the will.

NOTICE TO PERSONS INTERESTED.

Upon such petition, a citation is issued by the register of probate to the heirs-at-law of the deceased, and all persons interested in his estate, to appear at a day named and show cause, if any they have, why the will should not be allowed. The statute provides no form of serving the citation, nor does it provide in terms that any notice shall be given. The usual practice is to order notice to be given by publishing an attested copy of the citation in some newspaper printed in the county.[2] The person

valid likewise, *quære.* Harvard College *v* Gore, 5 Pick 370, Thayer *v* Boston, 124 Mass 145 See Harding *v.* Weld, 128 Mass. 590

[1] To the petition must be appended the certificate, under oath of the petitioner, that the statements made therein are true to the best of his knowledge and belief R L c 136, § 1

[2] Any daily or weekly periodical devoted exclusively to legal news, which has been published in the commonwealth for six consecutive months, shall be deemed a newspaper for the insertion of legal notices required by law, if the publication of such notice in such periodical is ordered by the court. R. L c 8, § 5, cl. 13.

presenting the will may designate the paper in which the citation shall be published, but if the judge deems the paper so designated insufficient to give due publicity, he may order the publication in one other newspaper.[1] The will is not required to be filed on a day when the probate court is held, but it may be filed and the citation issued on any day. The party offering the will for probate must serve the citation in accordance with its terms, and must make his return of the fact of service under oath, on or before the day fixed for the hearing

Formal notice is dispensed with when the heirs-at-law and all persons interested in the estate of the deceased assent to the granting of the petition or waive notice of the pendency of the petition, and the judge is satisfied that no person interested intends to object to the probate of the will Such assent or waiver must be in writing and signed by all the heirs-at-law, and should be annexed to the petition.[2]

THE HEARING — EVIDENCE OF THE SUBSCRIBING WITNESSES.

If it appears to the probate court, by the consent in writing of the heirs, or by other satisfactory evidence, that no person interested in the estate of a person deceased intends to object to the probate of an instrument purporting to be the will of such deceased person, the court may grant probate thereof upon the testimony of one only

---

[1] The same rule applies to the publication of other notices and citations issued by the probate courts R L c 162, § 47

[2] In any proceeding in a probate court the notice required by law may be dispensed with when all parties entitled thereto signify in writing their assent to such proceeding, or waive notice R L c 162, § 45 Dexter v Cotting, 149 Mass 96, Browne v Doolittle, 151 Mass 597.

of the subscribing witnesses, and the affidavit of such witness taken before the register of probate, may be received as evidence.[1] But if it does not so appear, all the subscribing witnesses, if they are within the state, must be produced at the time and place named in the citation. If there is a codicil to be proved, the witnesses who attested it must also be present. The subscribing witnesses, being considered in law as placed near the testator to ascertain and judge of his capacity, the party objecting to the probate of the will has a right to insist upon the testimony of all of them, if they can be produced.[2] Every clerk of a court of record and every justice of the peace may issue summonses to procure the attendance of the witnesses.

If it appears that a subscribing witness is dead, evidence is admissible to prove his handwriting.[3] If, having been competent at the time of his attestation, a witness has since become insane, or disqualified by reason of conviction of an infamous crime, or otherwise, his handwriting may be proved as if he were dead; but the fact of his incompetency must first be shown. If the witness cannot be found or resides out of the state, his handwriting may be proved, but it must first appear that a diligent search, satisfactory to the court under the circumstances, has

---

[1] R L c 136, § 2

[2] Chase v Lincoln, 3 Mass 236. There is no rule of law which requires that all of the attesting witnesses shall be examined at the outset. The order in which witnesses shall be called is a matter of discretion with the court, but all of the attesting witnesses should be called before the proponent of a will closes his case in chief. Howes v Colburn, 165 Mass 385.

[3] Nickerson v Buck, 12 Cush 332; Chase v Kittredge, 11 Allen, 52; Dean v Dean's Heirs, 1 Williams (Vt) 746, Jackson v Luquere, 5 Cowen, 221, Jackson v Le Grange, 19 Johns 386

been made for him. An indifferent inquiry, that leaves the matter in doubt, is not sufficient to let in secondary evidence of his attestation. In accounting for the absence of such a witness, answers to inquiries made of persons supposed to be able to give information of him may be given in evidence.[1] If an attesting witness who made his mark is dead, his mark must be proved to be his, and for this purpose evidence is admissible to show that the witness lived near the testator, that he could not write, and that no other person of the same name lived in the same neighborhood; and this evidence has been held sufficient to prove the attestation.[2] Proof of the handwriting of a deceased attesting witness is *prima facie* evidence that he duly and properly attested the will;[3] but the fact that he attested the will is not evidence that he believed the testator to be sane.[4] Where all the witnesses were dead, and no proof of their handwriting could be found, proof of the testator's handwriting was received as sufficient.[5]

[1] 1 Greenl. Ev. § 574.

[2] Doe v. Caperton, 9 Carr. & P. 59. In this case the will was attested by the signature of V. and the marks of Charles and Mary Drinkwater, and all were dead. V.'s handwriting was proved, and Mary Drinkwater testified: "I am the daughter of Charles and Mary Drinkwater, they are both dead; they lived near the testator; my mother could not write, and my father wrote his name only; no other Charles Drinkwater and no other Mary Drinkwater lived anywhere in that neighborhood." The evidence was held sufficient. In Jackson v. Van Dusen, the witness made his initials, which were proved. 5 Johns. 144.

[3] Nickerson v. Buck, 12 Cush. 332; Chase v. Kittredge, 11 Allen, 52.

[4] Baxter v. Abbott, 7 Gray, 71.

[5] Duncan v. Beard, 2 Nott & McCord, 400. Experts may testify to their opinion of the genuineness of the testator's signature, and may give their reasons for such opinion. Demerritt v. Randall, 116 Mass. 331.

It sometimes occurs. particularly where the will has been made many years before it is offered for probate, that an attesting witness does not retain a clear recollection of the circumstances attending the execution of the instrument, and in such cases less strictness of proof is sometimes required. In Dewey v. Dewey,[1] one of the witnesses testified that his name, which was upon the will, appeared to be his signature, but that he recollected nothing about it. One of the other witnesses testified that the first witness did subscribe in the testator's presence, and this was held sufficient. Dewey, J., said "The question is not whether this witness now recollects the circumstance of the attestation, and can state it as a matter within his memory. If this were requisite, the validity of a will would depend, not upon the fact whether it was duly executed, but whether the testator had been fortunate in securing witnesses of retentive memories. The real question is, whether the witness did in fact properly attest it."[2] In the absence of evidence to the contrary, it has been presumed from the fact of attestation that the requisites of the statute have been complied with.[3]

If a subscribing witness should deny the execution of the will, he may be contradicted as to that fact by another subscribing witness; and even if they should all swear that the will was not duly executed, the party offering the will would be allowed to go into circumstantial evidence to prove its due execution. But where the attesting

---

[1] 1 Met. 349

[2] Two of the three witnesses of a will nearly thirty years old were dead, and their signatures were proved, the third recognized his signature, but had no recollection of the transaction. The will was allowed. Verdier v. Verdier, 8 Rich (S. C.) 135.

[3] Clark v Dunnevant, 10 Leigh, 13.

witnesses so deny their attestation, the evidence, to give effect to the will, must be very clear [1] And where a witness has sworn that the testator was not of sound mind, his testimony has been successfully met by the evidence of other persons ; and wills have been established notwithstanding the adverse testimony of all the subscribing witnesses [2]

The due execution of the instrument and the testamentary capacity of the testator having been established by the party offering the will for probate, the burden is upon the persons opposing the probate to sustain their objections.[3] The rules observed as to the usual defences of fraud, undue influence, and revocation have been considered in previous sections of this chapter

No particular form of words is necessary to constitute a valid will. It may be admitted to probate, however inartificial it may be in expression, provided it bears the character and is executed according to the requisites of a will. A valid testamentary paper may be in the form of a deed or a letter.[4]

It is no objection to the validity of a will or codicil that it only appoints an executor.[5]

A codicil written on a separate paper, not known to the parties to be in existence at the time of the probate of

---

[1] See Jackson v Christman, 4 Wend 282; Handy v. The State, 7 Harr. & John 12

[2] See Peebles v. Case, 2 Bradf 226 , Jauncey v Thorne, 2 Barb Ch. 40 , Bennett v Sharp, 33 Eng Law & Eq 618. Kinbside v Harrison, 2 Phill 449 , Le Breton v Fletcher, 2 Hagg. 568 , Landon v Howard, 2 Addams, 215 ; Howard's Will 5 Monr 199

[3] Baldwin v Parker, 99 Mass 79 ; Beatty v. Fishel, 100 Mass. 449

[4] Bayley v Bailey, 5 Cush 260.

[5] Sumner v Crane, 155 Mass. 483.

PROBATE OF WILLS. 77

the will, may be subsequently admitted to probate. So may a codicil written on the back of the same leaf on which the will was written, if such codicil escaped attention at the time of the original probate [1]

If a will duly executed and witnessed incorporates in itself, by reference, any document or paper not so executed and witnessed, such document or paper, if it was in existence at the time of the execution of the will and is identified as the paper referred to therein, takes effect as part of the will, and is to be admitted to probate as such [2] And if by mistake such paper was not presented for probate with the will, it may be subsequently admitted to probate [3]

The burden is on the proponent to show that alterations or interlineations were made before the execution of the will [4]

Upon the allowance of the will, if no appeal is taken, and if there is an executor named in the will who is competent and willing to accept the trust, letters testamentary will issue to him upon his giving a sufficient bond for the faithful discharge of his trust. If there is no executor named in the will, or if the executor therein named declines the trust, or is incompetent, some suitable person will be appointed administrator with the will annexed [5]

---

[1] Waters v. Stickney, 12 Allen, 1; Gale v. Nickerson, 144 Mass. 416 A codicil may be allowed on appeal that was not offered below. Clark v. Wright, 3 Pick 67 ; Waters v. Stickney, 12 Allen, 1

[2] Newton v Seaman's Friend Society, 130 Mass 91

[3] Ibid It is no objection to the probate of a will that the testator agreed to make a different will, or that the will offered for probate revokes a will carrying out the agreement. Sumner v Crane, 155 Mass 483

[4] Wilton v Humphreys, 176 Mass. 253

[5] As to granting administration, see chap v.

Section IX.

PROOF OF WILLS MADE OUT OF THE STATE.

A will which is made out of this commonwealth and is valid according to the laws of the state or country in which it was made, may be proved and allowed in this commonwealth and shall thereupon have the same effect as if it had been executed according to the laws of this commonwealth.[1] This provision includes nuncupative wills.[2]

In such cases the same certainty of proof is required as when the will is made in this state, but the particular facts to be proved in support of the will must depend upon the requirements of the local laws of the state or country in which the will may have been executed.[3] It must be proved that all the formalities of execution made necessary by the local law, whatever they may be, were duly observed. The rules as to the testator's soundness of mind and the "presence" of the testator are of general application, and the formal proceedings in probate court are the same as in cases of wills made in this state.[4]

---

[1] R. L. c. 135, § 5

[2] Slocomb v Slocomb, 13 Allen, 38.

[3] Bayley v Bailey, 5 Cush 245 ; Crippen v Dexter, 13 Gray, 332.

[4] If an insane person, of sufficient mental capacity to change his domicile, in good faith removes his residence to another state pending proceedings here for the appointment of a guardian over him, and if his residence there continues until his death, and is assented to by his guardian after his appointment, he is such a resident of that state that its courts have jurisdiction of the original probate of his will. Talbot v. Chamberlain, 149 Mass. 57.

Section X.

PROOF OF LOST WILLS.

A will, proved to have been duly executed, which cannot be found after the testator's death, is presumed to have been destroyed by him with the intention of revoking it; but this presumption may be rebutted by evidence.[1] It may be that the will was destroyed by the testator in a fit of insanity, or that it was lost, or accidentally or fraudulently destroyed. Such accidental or fraudulent destruction will not deprive parties of their rights under its provisions, if they can produce the evidence necessary to establish the will.[2]

The fact that the will was made by the testator must be proved, and it must be shown that in its execution the provisions of the statute were complied with. If the fact of its destruction is not clearly proved, it must be shown, to the satisfaction of the court, that it has been lost. It must appear that an honest and diligent search has been unsuccessfully made for it in the place or places where it

---

[1] Davis v Sigourney, 8 Met. 487; Clark v Wright, 3 Pick 67, Idley v. Bowen, 11 Wend 227 "The presumption may be repelled, nor does it require evidence amounting to positive certainty, but only such as reasonably produces moral conviction" Sir John Nicholl, in Davis v. Davis, 2 Add. 226 The presumption may be rebutted by probable circumstances, among which declarations of unchanged affection and intention have much weight Patten v. Poulton, 1 Swa & Trist. 55

The declarations of the testator are admissible to show that he had no will, or had or had not destroyed it. Durant v Ashmore, 2 Rich 184; Johnson's Will, 40 Conn. 587, State v. Price, 5 B Monr 63

[2] A codicil destroyed without the testator's consent may be proved by parol and probated Clark v. Wright, 3 Pick. 67.

was most likely to be found, and then evidence may be admitted to prove its contents [1] If the contents are proved, it can be admitted to probate. But, in order to establish a will under such circumstances, the evidence of the contents must be strong, positive, and free from all doubt.[2]

[1] McConnell v. Wildes, 153 Mass 487, Jackson v Betts, 9 Cowen, 208, Dan v Brown, 4 Cowen, 483, Fetherly v Waggoner, 11 Wend. 599, Foster's Appeal, 87 Penn 67, Dudley v Wardner, 41 Vt 59

[2] Davis v Sigourney, 8 Met 487, Durfee v Durfee, ibid 490 note, Newell v Homer, 120 Mass. 277, Johnson s Will, 40 Conn 587. In Sugden v St Leonards, Law Rep 1 P D 154, the declarations of the testator, made both before and after the execution of his will, were held admissible to show its contents (Quick v Quick, 3 Swa & Trist 442, overruled.)

"When a will has been lost or destroyed, its contents may be proved by secondary evidence There may be a copy of the will, or a draft of it, or it may be proved by oral testimony Clark v. Wright, 3 Pick 67 Where a will is proved by oral testimony, it cannot be expected that any witness can testify to the exact words used, but what is required is the substance of its material provisions' Tarbell v. Forbes 177 Mass 238, 243, and cases cited.

It has been held in some cases that a lost will cannot be admitted to probate except upon proof of the whole contents Davis v Sigourney, 8 Met 486, Durfee v Durfee, ibid 490, Wallis v Wallis, 114 Mass 512 In other cases it has been held that when the contents are not completely proved, probate will be granted to the extent to which they are proved In Sugden v St Leonards, *supra*, decided in 1876, Cockburn, C. J, said 'As regards the only remaining question, namely, whether, assuming that we have not before us all the contents of the lost will, probate should be allowed of that which we have, so long as we are satisfied that we have the substantial parts of the will made out, I cannot bring myself to entertain a doubt If part of a will were accidentally burnt, or if a portion of it were torn out designedly by a wrong-doer, it would nevertheless, in my opinion, be the duty of a court of probate to give effect to the will of the testator as far as it could be ascertained It is not because some who would otherwise have benefited by the will, may thus fail to profit by the intended dispositions of the testator, that his will should be frustrated and fail of effect when his intentions remain clearly manifest. It

The party applying for the probate of a lost will should set forth in his petition all the material facts of the case, and should file with his petition a paper containing the contents of the will.

Section XI.

ALLOWANCE OF WILLS PROVED OUT OF THE STATE.

Any person interested in a will proved and allowed in any other of the United States or in a foreign country,

may be that in this will there were matters which Miss Sugden (the only witness to the contents) fails to remember, and I cannot but think that there must have been ultimate remainders which Miss Sugden no longer remembers,— indeed, she has herself said that there were other remainders that she does not recollect So far, therefore, we have the contents of the will before us in a defective form It may also be that there are some few legacies — there cannot be many — which she does not recollect They must be few, and they cannot have been of any material consequence But we have the substantial testamentary dispositions brought to our minds, and it would not be right to enable any wrong-doer or any accident — not putting it so high as an intentional wrong — which might happen to a will, and which would prevent the court which had to deal with it from being perfect master of its contents, to prevent the will from being carried into effect so far as the dispositions of the testator had become known I think there could not be a more mischievous consequence; and although it may be unfortunate that the will cannot be carried into execution to the full extent of the testamentary dispositions of the testator, I think that of two evils or two inconveniences it is far better, when the court can see its way to the essentially substantial dispositions made in a will, that it should give effect to them, although possibly some of the intentions of the testator may not be carried into effect "

Any substantial provision of a lost will, which is complete in itself and independent of the others, may, when proved, be admitted to probate, though other provisions cannot be proved, if the validity and operation of the part which is proved is not affected by those parts which cannot be proved 1 Underhill on Wills, § 278, cited with approval in Tarbell v. Forbes, 177 Mass 238, 244.

according to the laws of such state or country, or in a will which, according to the laws of the state or country where it was made, is valid without probate, may produce to the probate court in any county in which there is any estate, real or personal, on which said will may operate, a copy of such will and of the probate thereof, duly authenticated, or, if such will is valid without probate, a copy of the will or of the official record thereof duly authenticated by the proper officer having custody of such will or record in such state or country With the authenticated copy of the will should be presented a petition in writing, signed by the person presenting the will, setting forth the place of the testator's last residence, the facts that his will has been duly proved and allowed in such other state or country by the court having jurisdiction of the case, or that it is there valid without probate, that there is estate, real or personal, in the county in which the petition is presented upon which the will may operate, and praying that the will may be filed and recorded

Upon such petition, the statute requires the court to assign a time and place for a hearing and to cause notice to be given to all persons interested by publication in a newspaper three weeks successively, the first publication to be thirty days at least before the time assigned for the hearing

If at the hearing it appears from the copies, and such additional proof as to the authenticity and execution of the will as may be presented, that the instrument ought to be allowed in this commonwealth as the last will of the deceased, the court orders the copy to be filed and recorded, and the will has then the same effect as if it had been originally proved in the usual manner. After the will is so allowed and ordered to be recorded, the court grants letters testamentary, or letters of administration with the will annexed, as the circumstances of the case may require, and proceeds to the settlement of the estate that may be found in this state in the manner provided in chapter one hundred and forty-three of the Revised Laws.[1]

In cases of this kind no evidence of the execution of the will or of the sanity of the testator is required to be produced. The copy of the will, and of the decree of the court in which the will was originally proved, if properly authenticated, is conclusive, in the absence of any allegations of fraud, as to all the facts necessary to the establishment of the will, and as to the regularity of the proceedings and their conformity to the law of the state or country in which the will was originally proved.[2] The usual questions to be determined are, whether the record presented is duly authenticated, whether the court in which the will purports to have been proved had jurisdiction, and whether there is any real or personal estate in the county on which the will may operate.

Section XII.

PROOF OF NUNCUPATIVE WILLS.

A nuncupative will is a verbal disposition of the testator's *personal* estate, to take effect after his death. The statute provides that "a soldier in actual military service or a mariner at sea may dispose of his personal estate by a nuncupative will." The same provision was contained

[1] R. L. c. 136, §§ 10, 11, 12.
[2] Crippen v. Dexter, 13 Gray, 330; Talbot v. Chamberlain, 149 Mass. 57.

in the Revised Statutes (1836), and is the only provision relating to nuncupative wills in the statutes of this state. Previous to the enactment of the Revised Statutes any person, being in his last sickness, might dispose of his personal estate by a nuncupative will, and the manner of making and establishing such a will was prescribed at length by statute (1783, c 24). That statute, however, did not apply the term "nuncupative" to the testamentary dispositions of soldiers and mariners, but provided that they might dispose of their personal estate as they might have done before the passage of that act. The same exception was made in the provincial act, 4 W. & M. c 3, and the statute of frauds (29 Car. II. c. 3), which, particularly prescribing the manner of making and proving nuncupative wills, provided that soldiers and sailors might dispose of their personal property as they had previously done The distinction between nuncupative wills and the unwritten wills of soldiers and sailors was recognized at a very remote period. The unwritten wills of soldiers were denominated military wills, and other verbal testaments nuncupative wills.[1] The Revised Statutes of this state applied the term "nuncupative" to the wills of soldiers and mariners, but expressly reserved their previously existing rights as to their testamentary dispositions. It has been held accordingly in this commonwealth, and in other states where a similar provision of statute exists, that the rule governing the only unwritten wills now recognized, is the common law as it stood before the passage of the statute of frauds.[2] The wills of seamen

---

[1] Swinburne, Pt 1 §§ 12, 14

[2] In the Goods of Arthur White, 22 Law Rep (Boston) 110; Hubbard v Hubbard, 4 Selden, 196, Leathers v. Greenacre, 53 Maine, 561

have been held to come within the reason and the rule of military testaments.[1]

Although no form of words is needed to constitute a good nuncupative will, it is very necessary that the testator's declarations should plainly express his intentions. Swinburne says. "As for any precise form of words, none is required, neither is it material whether the testator do speak properly, or unproperly, so that his meaning do appear." "And although in written testaments it be also required that the words and sentences be such as thereby the testator's meaning may appear; yet more specially is it required in a nuncupative testament, for more supply may be made in written testaments than can be made in nuncupative testaments, concerning the testator's meaning."[2] Nuncupative wills may be made not only by the proper motions of the testator, but also in answer to the interrogation of other persons.[3]

---

[1] It has been held that the purser of a man-of-war is within this description, and that it includes the whole service, applying equally to superior officers up to the commander-in-chief as to a common seaman, being at sea. *In re* Hays, 2 Curt 338. And it has been held to apply to merchant seamen. Euston *v* Seymour, cited 2 Curt 339. A cook on board a merchant ship is a mariner. *Ex parte* Thompson, 4 Bradf. (N Y) 160.

[2] Part 4, § 29.

[3] Swinburne, Pt. 1, § 12. While in his last sickness, and about an hour before he died, being of sound mind, on being asked as to the disposition of his property, the testator said, in the presence of several witnesses, that he "wished his wife to have all his personal property." Beckwith, the mate of the vessel, then asked him if he wished her to have all his real property, and he replied, "Yes, all." He was then asked if he had no will, and he replied that he had had one, but it was destroyed. He was then asked by B what he should tell his wife, and he replied, "Tell her I loved her till the end." He was subsequently asked by B whom he wanted to settle his affairs, and he answered, "I want you to do it." He did not ask any one to bear witness that what he stated was his will. These conversations were

To prove a nuncupative will, it must appear that the testator was either a soldier in actual military service, or a mariner at sea, at the time when he made his testamentary declarations. The English courts have held that the privilege does not extend to soldiers quartered in barracks, either at home or abroad, but that the soldier must be engaged on an expedition at the time.[1] In behalf of seamen, however, the rule has been carried to the extreme limit of construction.[2] The substance of the testator's requests or instructions must be established, and it must be proved to the satisfaction of the court that the testator intended by his declarations to make a testamentary disposition of his property. It must appear, of course, that the testator was of sound mind.

No particular number of witnesses is required to establish a nuncupative will, but every fact necessary to support it should be proved by the most positive evidence.[3] The

proved by four witnesses It was held that they constituted a good nuncupative will, and that the evidence was sufficient to show that the testator intended to make B his executor Hubbard v Hubbard, 4 Selden, 196

[1] Drummond v. Parish, 3 Curteis, 522; White v. Ripton, ibid. 818. And see Leathers v Greenacre, 53 Maine, 561.

[2] A sailor, while the ship was in a foreign harbor, obtained leave to go on shore, where he was so injured by an accident that he did not return to the ship, but died of his injuries in a few days after the accident His nuncupative will was held to be the will of a seaman "at sea," though he was not on board the vessel at the time In the Goods of Lay, 2 Curteis, 375

A nuncupative will may be made by a mariner on a coasting vessel while she is on a voyage, and while lying at anchor in an arm of the sea where the tide ebbs and flows, a mile distant from the open sea and three miles from a settlement on shore Hubbard v Hubbard, 4 Selden, 196

[3] It may be established by the testimony of one witness Ex parte Thompson, 4 Bradf. 160, Gould v Safford, 39 Vt 498

In the probate court of Suffolk county, a nuncupative will was ad-

great danger of mistake, particularly in cases where the testator's declarations were not reduced to writing soon after they were made, and the obvious facilities for the fraudulent setting up of such wills, render it necessary that the evidence should be subjected to the closest scrutiny. Unless it is made morally certain that the declarations proved contain the true subject and import, at least, of the alleged nuncupation, and embody the testator's real testamentary intentions, the will cannot safely be allowed.

The person applying for the probate of a nuncupative will should set forth in his petition the material facts of the case, and the substance of the testamentary declarations of the testator. The usual notice must be given before any hearing upon the question of proving the will can be had. At the hearing, the will is reduced to writing in the form in which it may be established by the evidence, and is then admitted to probate.[1]

A nuncupative will executed in another state or country, according to the law of that state or country, which would not have been valid if made here, may be proved in this state, and have the same effect as if it had been executed according to the laws of this commonwealth.[2]

WHAT WILL PASS UNDER A WILL.

[Revised Laws, c 135]

"SECT. 22. A devise shall convey all the estate which the testator could lawfully devise in the lands mentioned,

mitted to probate on the testimony of one witness, who was also a legatee under the will; the court *held* that he was not an "attesting witness," and therefore not disqualified by reason of interest. In the Goods of Arthur White, 22 Law Reporter (Boston), 110

[1] The use is to prove it by witnesses, and then to write it Swinburne, Pt 1, § 12. "Being after his death proved by witnesses, and put in writing by the ordinary." Bac. Abr. Wills, D.

[2] Slocomb *v.* Slocomb, 13 Allen, 38

unless it clearly appears by the will that he intended to convey a less estate."[1]

"SECT. 23. An estate, right, or interest in lands acquired by a testator after the making of his will, shall pass thereby in like manner as if possessed by him at the time when he made his will, unless a different intention manifestly and clearly appears by the will"[2]

"SECT. 24. If a person devises lands of which he is not seised, but in which he has a right of entry, or if, after making a will, he is disseised of land devised thereby, such land shall nevertheless pass to the devisee in like manner as they would have descended to the testator's heirs if he had died intestate, and the devisee shall have the like remedy for the recovery of such land as such heirs might have had"[3]

AGREEMENTS TO MAKE WILLS OR GIVE LEGACIES.

Prior to May 17, 1888, it was well settled that a contract founded on a sufficient consideration to make a certain provision by will for a particular person was valid, and would be enforced.[4] But an oral promise to make a will of all the testator's property, real and personal, was held to be a contract for the sale of lands within the statute of frauds, and therefore invalid.[5]

Soon after the decision of the court in Wellington v.

[1] Willcutt v. Calnan, 98 Mass. 75, Spooner v Lovejoy, 108 Mass 529, Todd v Sawyer, 147 Mass 570, Simonds v Simonds, 168 Mass 144

[2] Winchester v. Forster, 3 Cush. 366, Hill v. Bacon, 106 Mass 578, Kimball v Tilton, 118 Mass 311

[3] Ward v Fuller, 15 Pick 185, Brown v. Wells, 12 Met 501

[4] Jenkins v Stetson, 9 Allen, 128, Wellington v. Apthorp, 145 Mass 69

[5] Gould v. Mansfield, 103 Mass 408.

Apthorp, the statute of 1888 (chapter 372) was passed, which provided that no agreement to make a will of either real or personal estate, and no agreement to give a legacy, or make a devise by will, shall be binding unless such agreement is in writing signed by the party whose executor or administrator is sought to be charged, or by some person by such party duly authorized[1] The act provided that nothing therein contained should in any way affect any agreement made prior to its passage, which was May 17, 1888. This act is now embodied in c. 74, § 6, of the Revised Laws.

COMPROMISES OF WILLS.

Under c. 148, § 15, of the Revised Laws, which embodies P S. c 143, § 14, the supreme judicial court has jurisdiction in equity to authorize the persons named as executors in an instrument purporting to be the last will of a person deceased, or the administrators with such will annexed, to adjust by arbitration or compromise any controversy between the persons who claim as devisees or legatees under such will and the persons entitled to the estate of the deceased under the statutes regulating the descent and distribution of intestate estates.

Under the broad equity powers granted by St. 1891, c. 415, § 1, some of the probate judges assumed that the probate court had concurrent jurisdiction with the supreme

---

[1] Emery v. Burbank, 163 Mass. 326. A letter written by direction of a woman eighty-five years old to her sister Ellen contained the words "Will you and Minnie come and stay with me as long as I live? I will pay all your expenses, and what property I have left will be yours, Ellen My expenses are very large, but all that I have shall be yours " It was held in Howe v. Watson, 179 Mass. 30 that this letter satisfied the requirements of St 1888, c 372.

judicial court for the purpose stated in the preceding paragraph, and in certain cases assumed to authorize such compromises of controversies arising under a will.

In Abbott v. Gaskins, 181 Mass (63 N E Rep. 953), it was held that the probate court did not have jurisdiction for this purpose. To confirm the proceedings and decrees of the probate courts in authorizing and confirming compromises of controversies under wills, St. 1902, c. 538, was passed.

CHAPTER III.

DEPOSIT, CUSTODY, AND PROCEEDINGS IN CASE OF CONCEALMENT OF WILLS

A WILL, when executed, if the testator sees fit, may be deposited in the registry of probate in the county where he lives, for safe keeping; and the register, upon being paid the fee of one dollar, is required to receive and keep it, and give a certificate of the deposit thereof. The will so deposited must be enclosed in a sealed wrapper, indorsed with the name of the testator, his place of residence, the day when, and the person by whom it is deposited, and may have indorsed thereon the name of the person to whom it is to be delivered after the testator's death.[1]

Such will, during the lifetime of the testator, can be delivered only to himself, or to some person authorized by him, by an order in writing duly proved by the oath of a subscribing witness,[2] after his death it will be delivered to the person named in the indorsement on the wrapper, if there is a person so named who demands it. In the mean time it cannot be opened or read. If not so demanded, it will be publicly opened at the first probate court held after notice of the testator's death. It will then be retained in the registry until it is offered for probate; or, if the jurisdiction of the case belongs to another court, it will be delivered to the executors or

[1] R. L. c 135, §§ 10, 11.   [2] St. 1902, c. 160.

other persons entitled to its custody to be presented for probate in such other court.[1]

The statute requires every person, other than the register of the probate court having the custody of a will, within thirty days after notice of the death of the testator, to deliver it into the probate court which has jurisdiction of the case, or to the executors named in the will; and if without reasonable cause an executor or other person neglects to so deliver a will, after being duly cited for that purpose, he may be committed to the jail by warrant of the court, there to be kept in close custody until he so delivers the will; and he will be further liable to any party aggrieved for the damage sustained by such neglect.[2] In order that such a citation may issue, a petition setting forth the facts should be presented to the court. Any person interested may petition.

Upon complaint under oath made to the probate court by a person claiming to be interested in the estate of a person deceased, against any one suspected of retaining, concealing, or conspiring with others to retain or conceal, any will or testamentary instrument of the deceased, the court may cite the suspected person to appear before it and be examined on oath upon the matter of the complaint. Upon such examination all interrogatories and answers must be in writing, signed by the party examined, and filed in the court[3] The citation may be served by an officer qualified to serve civil process, or by a private person. If by a private person, the fact that service was made as ordered must be proved by his

[1] R L c 135, §§ 12, 13, St. 1902, c 160
[2] R L c 135, § 14; Stebbins v Lathrop, 4 Pick. 33; Hill v. Davis, 4 Mass 137.
[3] R L c 135, § 15.

affidavit. The affidavit may be conveniently indorsed on the citation.

If the person cited refuses to appear and submit to examination, or to answer such interrogatories as are lawfully propounded to him, or to obey any lawful order, the judge may commit him to the jail, there to remain in close custody until he submits to the order of the court.[1]

On such complaint the judge in his discretion may award costs to be paid by either party, and may issue execution therefor.[2]

The will, after being admitted to probate, remains on the files of the probate office, except that, after the expiration of thirty days from the probate decree, upon the petition of the executor, or of any person interested in the estate of the testator, after such notice thereof as the court shall require and hearing had thereon, the court may permit the original will, if it appears to be necessary for the purpose, to be taken from the files and to be used in a foreign country, for the purpose of establishing the right or title of such executor or person to the estate of the testator in such country.[3]

---

[1] Whoever steals, or for any fraudulent purpose destroys, mutilates, or conceals a will, codicil or other testamentary instrument, shall be punished by imprisonment in the state prison not exceeding five years, or in the house of correction not exceeding two years R L c 208, § 29

[2] R L c 135, § 15.   [3] R. L c 162, § 50.

CHAPTER IV.

APPOINTMENT OF EXECUTORS.

An executor is the person to whom the testator has confided the trust of administering his estate according to his last will and testament.[1] He can derive his office only from a testamentary appointment confirmed by a decree of the probate court The appointment is generally made by express words contained in the will, but it may be made constructively by other than express words. The form of petition for the probate of a will in common use, made by the executor named in the will, prays that administration be granted to him, [2] and when the will has been proved and allowed, letters testamentary are issued to him, provided that he is legally competent for the office, and gives bond for the discharge of the trust as required by law.

Every non-resident executor, appointed by a probate court or the supreme judicial court, shall appoint in writing an agent residing in the commonwealth, upon whom service of legal process can be made. If such agent dies

---

[1] When a legacy lapses, or a bequest cannot be maintained, and such legacy or bequest is to be treated as intestate property, and to be distributed to the heirs at law, it is not necessary for the executor also to take out letters of administration on such intestate property; but he may distribute it as executor. McGreevy v McGrath, 152 Mass 24

[2] Facts alleged in the petition must be sworn to. R. L. c. 136, § 1.

or removes from the commonwealth, another agent must be appointed.[1] Such non-resident executor shall not be entitled to receive his letters of appointment until he has complied with the above requirement.[2] Service of any legal process upon such agent shall be of the same legal effect as if made upon his principal when in the commonwealth.[3]

WHO MAY BE EXECUTORS.

Any person may be nominated as executor, but all persons are not legally competent to act in that office. A minor or an infant *ventre sa mère* may be nominated in the will; but if at the time of proving the will the executor named therein is not of full age, administration with the will annexed is granted to some other person during his minority, unless there is another executor nominated in the will who accepts the trust, in which case such other executor administers until the minor arrives at full age; he can then, by giving bond, be admitted as joint executor.[4] If the executor named in the will is physically or mentally incapacitated, administration is granted to some other person. Any objection that would cause the removal of an executor is sufficient to prevent the confirmation of his appointment by the court.[5]

A married woman may be an executrix, administratrix, guardian, or trustee, and bind herself and the estate she represents, without any act or assent on the part of her husband.[6]

[1] R. L. c. 139, § 8.   [2] Ibid.
[3] Ibid.   [4] R. L. c. 136, § 6.
[5] As to removals, see *post*, chap. viii.
[6] R. L. c. 153, § 5.

The executor of an executor shall not, as such, administer on the estate of the first testator.[1]

A domestic trust company may be appointed executor of a will, codicil, or writing testamentary, or administrator with the will annexed.[2]

EXECUTORS TO GIVE BOND.

General Bond. — The executor, before letters testamentary are issued to him, is required to give bond with sufficient surety or sureties, in such sum as the judge of the probate court shall order, payable to the judge and his successor,[3] with condition to make and return to the probate court, within three months, a true inventory of all the testator's real and personal estate which at the time of making the inventory shall have come to the possession or knowledge of the executor;[4] to administer according to law and the will of the testator all his personal estate which may come to the possession of the executor, or of any person for him, and also the proceeds of any real

---

[1] R L c 136, § 9   Tallon *v* Tallon, 156 Mass 315

[2] R. L c 116, § 18

[3] In Suffolk and Middlesex, it is payable to the first judge of probate   R L c 164, § 2.

[4] An executor who fails to file an inventory and account is liable in an action brought by a judge of probate in behalf of the legatee, although the defendant offered to prove that all the assets mentioned in the inventory which was filed subsequently to the date of the writ were received more than three months after the filing of the bond, that no creditor had presented claims which had remained unpaid, that all the funeral expenses had been paid, that the testator at his decease was indebted to the executor in a sum greater than all the assets at any time in the hands of the executor, and that at no time had the executor funds with which to pay any portion of the legacy

In order to maintain an action for failure to file the requisite inventory and account, it is not necessary to show that any damage has been sustained beyond such omission   Forbes *v* McHugh, 152 Mass 412

estate that may be sold or mortgaged by the executor; to render upon oath a true account of his administration at least once a year until his trust is fulfilled, unless he is excused therefrom in any year by the court, and to render such account at such other times as the court may order.[1] When two or more persons are appointed executors, none can intermeddle or act as such but those who give bond.[2]

Bond when the Executor is Residuary Legatee. — If it appears to the judge that the bond above described is not necessary for the protection of any person interested in the estate, he may permit an executor, *who is residuary legatee,* instead of giving such bond, to give a bond with condition to pay all debts and legacies of the testator, and such sums as may be allowed by the probate court to the widow or minor children for necessaries; and in such case he is not required to return an inventory.[3]

An executor, therefore, who is residuary legatee may give a bond in the common form, which requires him to return an inventory of the estate: or he may be excused the labor and expense of making an inventory by giving bond to pay debts, legacies, and allowances. It is at his own option to give one or the other. The reason of this indulgence is that, as he is residuary legatee, no person can have an interest in procuring evidence of the assets except the creditors, legatees, and family of the deceased; and if he binds himself to pay all their claims, the amount of the assets is of no concern to any person except himself. But if he chooses to bind himself to pay the debts and legacies, he must abide by the consequences of his

---

[1] R. L. c. 149, § 1.
[2] Ibid § 12 As to bonds, generally, see *post*, chap xix.
[3] R. L. c. 149, § 2.

98   PROCEEDINGS IN THE PROBATE COURTS

election.[1] He must fulfil the condition of his bond, whether the assets are sufficient for the purpose or not. The condition of the bond is not to pay if there are assets, but to pay at all events. By giving such a bond he conclusively admits assets, and the admission will bind him and his sureties, even if the estate proves insolvent.[2] If, on the other hand, he gives a bond in the common form and returns an inventory, he will be responsible for the assets, but no further. When the executor knows that the estate is sufficient to meet all the claims against it, with the charges of administration and the allowances made to the widow and children of the testator, he may safely give a bond to pay the debts and legacies; but where there is any doubt whatever of the sufficiency of assets, he should give bond in the common form and return an inventory.[3]

[1] When an executor has given a bond to pay debts and legacies, a creditor of the estate may collect his debt, by attachment of the estate in the hands of the executor, by suit against the sureties on the bond, and by *scire facias* against the executor. R. L. c. 172, § 8 ; Jenkins *v* Wood, 140 Mass 66 ; Jenkins *v.* Wood, 144 Mass 238. It is no defence to an administrator *de bonis non* with the will annexed that the original executor, who was also the residuary legatee, gave a bond to pay debts and legacies. Collins *v* Collins, 140 Mass 502

[2] Colwell *v* Alger, 5 Gray, 67; Thayer *v* Winchester, 133 Mass. 449 ; Jenkins *v* Wood, 140 Mass 66. In a suit to recover a legacy, the plaintiff need not give any proof, except such bond, that the executor has assets in his hands. Jones *v.* Richardson, 5 Met. 247 , Chapin *v.* Waters, 110 Mass 200 ; Jenkins *v* Wood, 144 Mass 238

A bond to pay debts and legacies, given by an executor who is residuary legatee, who has thus been excused from returning an inventory within three months, cannot, after the expiration of a year and a half, be cancelled or surrendered by the probate court, or supreme court, even if no assets have come to the executor's hands. Alger *v* Colwell, 2 Gray, 404

[3] The giving of the bond to pay debts and legacies does not discharge the lien on the real estate of the testator for the payment of

An administrator with the will annexed gives a bond in like manner and with like condition as is required of an executor If such administrator is residuary legatee, the court may permit him to give a bond to pay debts and legacies, with like effect as though he was nominated executor in the will [1]

When no Sureties are required. — Executors are exempted from giving a surety or sureties on their bonds, when the testator has ordered or requested such exemption, or that no bond should be taken, or when all the persons interested in the estate who are of full age and legal capacity, other than creditors, certify to the court their consent thereto; but not until all creditors of the estate, and the guardian of any minor interested therein, have been notified, and had opportunity to show cause against the same.[2] The court, however, may, at or after the granting of letters testamentary, require bond with sufficient surety or sureties.[3]

Whenever an appointment of an executor, administrator,

his debts, except on such part as may be sold by the executor or administrator with the will annexed to a purchaser in good faith and for a valuable consideration, all estate not so sold may be taken on execution by any creditor not otherwise satisfied, in like manner as if a bond had been given in the other form R L c 140, § 2.

[1] R L. c. 149. § 2.

[2] Notice by publication in a newspaper is sufficient, although a minor who has no guardian is interested Wells t Child, 12 Allen, 330. A bond without surety approved by the probate court, without notice to creditors, is not such a bond as the statute requires, and the statute of limitations against executors will not be given to run from the filing of such a bond Abercrombie v. Sheldon, 8 Allen, 532

A general notice is ordinarily sufficient, even if it fails to reach some of the parties interested Bonnemort v. Gill, 167 Mass. 338, Tyler v Court of Registration, 175 Mass 71, 75.

[3] R L c. 149, § 3

guardian, or trustee is invalid by reason of any irregularity, or want of jurisdiction or authority of the court making the same, the person so appointed shall be held to account for all money, property, or assets which have come to his hands as executor, administrator, guardian, or trustee, or by reason of such appointment, in the same manner as if the appointment had been regular and valid ; and any bond given in pursuance of such appointment shall be held to be valid and binding, both on the principals and sureties, for that purpose.[1]

Payments made to or by such person as executor, administrator, guardian, or trustee, if in other respects properly made, may, with the approval of the probate court, be ratified and confirmed by the executor, administrator, guardian, or trustee, who may be afterwards legally appointed.[2]

If a person named as executor in a will has deceased or refuses to accept the trust, or after being duly cited for that purpose, neglects to appear and accept the same, or neglects for twenty days after probate of the will to give bond, letters testamentary are granted to the other executors if there are any competent and willing to accept the trust;[3] and if there are none, or if the executors are dead, or none are named in the will, administration of the

[1] R L c 148, § 24.
[2] Ibid
[3] R. L c 136, § 5. A person named in a will as executor who declines the trust, may recall his declination and be appointed executor prior to the appointment of an administrator with the will annexed Shannon v Shannon, 111 Mass 331.

A person named in a will as one of two executors and who has declined the trust cannot recall his declination and be appointed an executor after the granting of letters testamentary to the other executor. Jewett v. Turner, 172 Mass 496.

estate with the will annexed is granted to such persons as would have been entitled thereto if the deceased had died intestate; but after the expiration of the twenty days, and before letters testamentary or of administration are granted, the court may grant letters testamentary to any person appointed executor who gives the bond prescribed by law.

CHAPTER V.

APPOINTMENT OF ADMINISTRATORS

When a person dies, not having disposed of his property by will, he is said to die *intestate*, and the law prescribes the manner in which his estate may be settled, and the rights of all persons interested secured.[1]

IN WHAT CASES ADMINISTRATION IS GRANTED.

Administration may be granted by the probate court for each county of the estates of persons who at the time of their decease were inhabitants of or resident in such county.[2]

Every non-resident administrator appointed by a probate court or the supreme judicial court, shall appoint in writing an agent residing in the commonwealth upon whom service of legal process can be made. If such agent dies or removes from the commonwealth, another agent must be appointed. Such non-resident administrator shall not be entitled to receive his letters of appointment until he has complied with the above requirement.[3]

Administration de bonis non. — If a sole administrator dies before he completes the trust committed to him, or is removed by the court, or resigns, administration *de*

---

[1] An executor, if a portion of the estate is to be treated as intestate property, may administer it without taking out letters of administration. McGreevy v. McGrath, 152 Mass. 24.
[2] R. L. c. 162, § 3.
[3] R. L. c. 139, §§ 8, 9.

bonis non (of the estate not administered) will be granted, provided there is personal estate left unadministered to the amount of twenty dollars, or debts to that amount are remaining due from the estate.[1]

An administrator *de bonis non* may be appointed for the purpose of finally distributing sums of money which may have been deposited or invested by order of the probate court.[2]

Administration with the Will annexed. — In certain cases administration is granted of testate estates, where the testator omits to name an executor in his will, or where all of the executors named in the will are dead or incompetent, or refuse to accept the trust, or after being cited for that purpose neglect to accept the trust, or neglect for twenty days after probate of the will to give bond according to law,[3] or if the only executor is a minor.[4] In such cases administration with the will annexed is granted.

Administration de bonis non with the Will annexed — When a sole executor or administrator with the will annexed dies after entering upon the duties of his trust and before it is discharged, or is removed by the court, or resigns, administration *de bonis non* with the will annexed is granted, provided there is personal estate not administered to the amount of twenty dollars, or debts to that amount are remaining due from the estate, or that there is anything remaining to be performed in execution of the will, or if there is an order of distribution under section 26 of chapter 150, Rev. Laws, of money deposited or invested under authority of the probate court.[5]

[1] R. L. c 137, § 8.
[2] Ibid § 8
[3] Ibid. § 6
[4] Ibid. § 7.
[5] Ibid § 8

Special Administration — When by reason of delay in granting letters testamentary or of administration, or when for any other cause the judge of the probate court deems it expedient to do so, he may, at any time and place, and with or without notice to the parties interested, appoint a special administrator to collect and preserve the effects of the deceased.[1]

Ancillary Administration. — When a citizen of another state or country dies leaving estate to be administered in this state, administration of such estate may be granted here.[2] In such case, the administration granted here is treated as merely ancillary or auxiliary to the principal

---

[1] R. L. c. 137, § 9

[2] R. L. c. 162, § 3. A debt due the deceased from an inhabitant of this state is estate that may be administered here. Picquet, Appellant, 5 Pick 65. Emery v. Hildreth, 2 Gray, 231, Merrill v. New England Insurance Co, 103 Mass 248. So are articles of furniture and plate, though of small value, anything corresponding to *bona notabilia* in England would be sufficient for that purpose. Harrington v. Brown, 5 Pick 521, Pinney v. McGregory, 102 Mass 186. When a debtor takes up his residence in this state, after the death of the creditor in another state, administration on the creditor's estate will be granted in this state; and so when goods are brought into this state. Dawes v. Boylston, 9 Mass 337, Wheelock v. Pierce, 6 Cush 288, Pinney v. McGregory, *supra*, Prescott v. Durfee, 131 Mass 477. *Prima facie* evidence that a deceased non-resident had conveyed real estate in this state, in fraud of his creditors, is sufficient to warrant the grant of administration here. Bowdoin v. Holland, 10 Cush. 17. If the deceased left only real estate in this commonwealth, administration may be granted here, although his estate is solvent and an administrator has been appointed in the state where he resided. Prescott v. Durfee, 131 Mass 477. But if he left no estate in this state, administration cannot be granted here. Crosby v. Leavitt, 4 Allen, 410. Where administration has been granted in any county on the estate of a deceased non-resident, parol evidence is admissible to show that the deceased left estate within such county, although no such estate was included in the administrator's inventory. Harrington v. Brown, 5 Pick 519.

administration granted in the jurisdiction where the deceased dwelt. The appointment, however, of an administrator in the state where the deceased had his domicile is not a necessary prerequisite to the granting of such ancillary administration; but administration of the estate in this state may be granted, although no administrator has been appointed in the foreign state; and even if the deceased left a will, which has never been offered for probate in the place of his domicile.[1]

[1] Bowdoin v Holland, 10 Cush. 17 Executors of a foreign will have no right to act and dispose of the estate here until they have probated the will here, and letters testamentary have been issued to them. Welch v Adams, 152 Mass 83 If ancillary administration is taken out in another state upon the estate there of a deceased citizen of Massachusetts, a judgment there rendered establishing a claim against the estate is not binding here Low v Bartlett, 8 Allen, 259

The bond of an ancillary administrator is to return an inventory of the effects coming to his hands within this state Dawes v Boylston, 9 Mass 337 Such administrator is not obliged to account in the jurisdiction where the ancillary letters of administration were issued, for assets received elsewhere Fay v Haven, 3 Met. 114. Conversely, the bond of an administrator here does not cover the administration of assets collected by him in a foreign state under ancillary letters of administration Hooker v Olmstead, 6 Pick. 480. The duty of an ancillary administrator is to collect only the assets found within his jurisdiction, to appropriate so much of them to the payment of debts due citizens of that jurisdiction as would be authorized by the general solvency or insolvency of the estate, and to remit the balance to the place of principal administration Fay v Haven, *supra*, Richards v. Dutch, 8 Mass. 506. If the deceased had a domicile in a foreign state, his effects are to be distributed here according to the laws of that state, or transmitted thither for distribution by the administrator there. Stevens v. Gaylord, 11 Mass. 256. A foreign executor or administrator who takes out ancillary administration in this state, is not obliged to pay debts due the deceased's creditors here because he has assets in his hands collected in the foreign state, and this although he has paid all debts which the deceased owed elsewhere, and has a balance sufficient to pay all debts due here Fay v. Haven, *supra* An administrator appointed under the laws of another state cannot be recognized

WITHIN WHAT TIME ADMINISTRATION MUST BE APPLIED FOR.

Administration is not *originally* granted after the expiration of twenty years from the death of the testator or intestate,[1] except when any property or claim or right thereto remains undistributed, or thereafter accrues to the estate and remains to be administered In these excepted cases original administration may for cause be granted on such property; but such administration shall affect no other property.[2]

But if administration has once been granted, and left unfinished by the death, removal, or resignation of the executor or administrator, administration *de bonis non* may be granted after the expiration of twenty years. There is no statute limiting the time of granting administration of estates left unadministered by a former executor or administrator.[3]

IN WHAT COUNTY ADMINISTRATION MUST BE APPLIED FOR.

The petition for administration must be presented to the probate court of the county of which the deceased was an

---

in the courts of this state as the legal representative of the deceased. Beaman *v* Elliot, 10 Cush 172

[1] R L c 137, § 3

[2] Ibid § 4 Administration was granted when the only property to be affected thereby was a promissory note secured by a mortgage of land, and the land had been for more than twenty years in the adverse possession of the person opposing the petition for administration. Parsons *v.* Spaulding, 130 Mass 83

If a creditor who has failed to receive his dividend from an insolvent estate has deceased, an administrator may be appointed to receive and administer such dividend, although more than twenty years have elapsed since his death. R. L c. 142, § 25

[3] Bancroft *v* Andrews, 6 Cush. 493.

inhabitant or in which he was resident at the time of his death.[1]

If the deceased person died without the state, application must be made to the probate court of the county in which he left estate to be administered.[2]

TO WHOM ORIGINAL ADMINISTRATION IS GRANTED.

The statute [3] provides that —

"SECT. 1. Administration of the estate of a person deceased intestate shall be granted to one or more of the persons hereinafter mentioned, who shall, subject to the provisions of the following section, be entitled thereto as follows ·

"*First*, His widow or his next of kin, or the widow jointly with the next of kin, as the probate court may determine

"*Second*, If the deceased was a married woman, her husband, if he is competent and willing to undertake the trust, unless it is necessary or proper to appoint some other person.[4]

"*Third*, If all said persons are incompetent or evidently unsuitable for the discharge of the trust, or renounce the administration, or if, without sufficient cause, they neglect for thirty days after the death of the intestate to take administration of his estate, one or more of the principal creditors, after public notice upon the petition.

---

[1] R L c. 162, § 3   As to jurisdiction depending upon the question of residence, see page 70, notes.

[2] Pinney v. McGregory, 102 Mass 186

[3] R L c. 137, §§ 1, 2

[4] If the marriage was voidable, the husband will be entitled to administration, unless sentence of nullity was pronounced before her death   If it was void from the beginning, he is not entitled to administer.   1 Wms. Ex. (7th Am ed.) 491.

"*Fourth*, If there is no such creditor willing and competent to undertake the trust, any suitable persons.

"*Fifth*, If there is no widow, husband, or next of kin within this commonwealth, a public administrator in preference to creditors."

"SECT. 2. Administration of the estate of an intestate may be granted to one or more of his next of kin or any suitable person, if his widow and all his next of kin resident in the commonwealth, who are of full age and legal capacity, consent in writing thereto. Notice of the petition may be dispensed with as if all parties entitled thereto had signified their assent or waived notice."

The policy of granting administration to those most directly interested in the estate of the deceased has been long established. The statute 31 Edw. III, c. 11, which first took from the clergy their exclusive right to administer, provided that "the ordinaries shall depute of the next and most lawful friends of the dead person intestate to administer his goods:" and the statute 21 Henry VIII, c 5, provided that administration should be granted " to the widow of the deceased, or to the next of his kin, or to both, as by discretion of the same ordinary shall be thought good." This language of the statute Henry VIII was followed in our statute of 1783 (c 36), and still stands without material change

A domestic trust company may be appointed administrator.[1]

Who are Next of Kin. — In this state, the degrees of kindred are computed according to the rules of the civil law, which makes the deceased person the point from whence the degrees are numbered. Thus, a man's parents are related to him in the first degree, and so are his

[1] R. L. c. 116, § 18.

children   Both are equally near, but in granting administration the children, if competent, are preferred, they having a more direct interest in the estate. A grandson is in the same degree of kindred to the intestate as the intestate's brother, but is preferred for the same reason.

Kindred are lineal or collateral. Lineal consanguinity is that subsisting between persons who are all in a direct line of descent, one from the other, as between son, father, and grandfather; or father, son, and grandson, reckoning either upwards or downwards. Collateral kinsmen are those who are descended from one common ancestor, but not one from the other. A man and his cousins are collateral relations, they both descend from the same grandfather, but not lineally.

The next lineal kindred of an intestate are easily ascertained by counting either directly upwards or directly downwards to his nearest living relative. His father and son are both in the first degree; his grandfather and grandson both in the second. The nearness of a collateral kinsman to the intestate is ascertained by counting upwards to the common ancestor of both, and then following the branch downwards until the collateral kinsman is reached, reckoning one degree for each person. Thus, the intestate's brother is in the second degree; this is seen by counting upwards to their father, their common ancestor, one degree, and then downwards, collaterally, one degree, to the brother. The intestate's uncle is in the third degree, and so is his nephew. His cousin is in the fourth

Following this computation of kindred, and observing the preferences arising from interest, administration of the estate of an intestate will be granted to his next of kin in the following order: first, to children; second, if there are no children, to parents, third, if there are no children nor parents, to brothers and sisters, either of the whole or half blood, fourth, to grandparents, fifth, to nephews, nieces, uncles, aunts; sixth, to cousins. No distinction is made between kindred on the father's or mother's side. They are all in equal degree of kindred, and hence it may happen that there are persons equally related to the intestate and equally entitled to the administration, who are not related at all to each other

As to the Right of the Widow and Next of Kin to administer. — The statute does not give the widow an *exclusive* right to administer her husband's estate if there are next of kin who also claim the right, and are suitable persons. The right is first in the widow *and* next of kin, either or both, as the court may deem fit, and the personal suitableness of the widow and next of kin is to be considered in making the appointment If the widow is evidently unsuitable, the next of kin, if competent, is entitled to the sole administration. If the next of kin is unsuitable, she, if competent, may take administration alone If both are suitable, the court may grant administration to either, or jointly to both; and if both are unsuitable, the application of both will be refused.

And where there are several persons equally entitled to take administration as next of kin, and equally suitable, the probate court has power to appoint one or more of them.

If the widow and next of kin, as is often the case, renounce the administration, their renunciation does not give them a *right* to nominate a substitute.[1] There may be creditors whose right to administer under the statute

[1] Cobb v. Newcomb, 19 Pick. 337.

is prior to that of any such substitute. But where there are no creditors who are suitable, or if the creditors refuse, after being cited, to take the administration, any suitable person will generally be appointed on the recommendation of the widow and next of kin.

Nor will the renunciation of the next of kin, or the fact of their incompetency, give to other relatives of the intestate any *right* to administer. The preference made by the statute is of the *next* of kin, and if they decline, or are unsuitable, creditors are preferred to other kindred.

As to the Suitableness of the Widow or Next of Kin. — The question of suitableness must depend, in some measure, upon the facts of each case.[1] A person may be entirely suitable to administer when little more than some formal proceeding is necessary for the settlement of the estate, and may be unsuitable when the duties to be discharged are of a different character. The object of administration is to dispose of the estate of the intestate so as to secure the rights of creditors and make the best provision possible, under the circumstances, for the kin of the deceased. A person of unsound mind is of course unsuitable for such a trust, and so is a person whose

[1] It has been held that the widow may be set aside, if she has barred herself of all interest in her husband's personal estate by her marriage settlement, or has eloped from her husband, or has cohabited in his lifetime with another man, or lived separate from him. If she has been divorced, *a mensa et thoro*, she forfeits, it should seem, her right to administer. 1 Wms Ex. (7th Am ed) 496

Where, upon the application of the widow, it appeared that she was under the influence of a person who was indebted to the estate in a large amount, and who was charged with combining with the intestate in his lifetime to defraud his creditors and that such application was made at the request of such debtor and not to protect or subserve the interests of the widow, it was held that she was an unsuitable person to administer Stearns *v.* Fiske, 18 Pick. 24.

relation to the estate is such as to create the presumption that he would not administer with a due regard to the rights of those interested in the estate. The fact that one of several next of kin is also a creditor of the estate is rather adverse to, than in favor of, his being preferred. So, if he owes the estate, especially when the balance due has not been definitely ascertained. A man who is accustomed to business details is more suitable for the office of administrator than one who is not. Unsuitableness may be occasioned by physical debility, want of memory, or any infirmity which would prevent the efficient discharge of the duties required. In determining the question of suitableness, the relations of the applicant to the estate and to the other parties interested, the character of the duties which the condition of the estate will be likely to require of the administrator, and his personal fitness for those duties, are to be considered. A minor cannot administer.[1] A citizen of another state or country, if otherwise suitable, may be appointed to administer in this state.

The fact that one who is personally unsuitable is ready to give bond with sufficient sureties for the faithful discharge of his trust, does not make him suitable. The remedy of parties damaged by his official misconduct by action on his bond, may subject them to expense of litigation for which they can have no legal adequate remedy; and besides, an administrator, if so disposed, may prejudice the interests of parties concerned without being exposed to any action.[2]

As to the Right of Creditors to administer. — If the widow and next of kin are incompetent, or evidently

---
[1] McGooch v. McGooch, 4 Mass. 348.
[2] Stearns v. Fiske, 18 Pick. 27.

unsuitable, or if they neglect for thirty days after the intestate's death to take administration of his estate, the court grants administration to one or more of the principal creditors. This right is given to the creditor under such circumstances, in order that the collection of his claim may not be defeated for want of an administrator. The creditor applying must satisfy the court that he is a creditor, and this he may do by exhibiting his books of account or other evidences of debt. The amount of his claim seems not to be material,[1] but the claim must be one which by law survives.[2] The creditor cannot be appointed, however, until after the widow and next of kin have been cited, and had opportunity either to take or renounce the administration. The same considerations as to personal suitableness apply to a creditor who petitions for a grant of administration as to one next of kin. If the deceased left no widow, husband, or next of kin in this state, administration is granted to a public administrator in preference to creditors.[3]

[1] Arnold v Sabin, 1 Cush 525 In this case the claim of the creditor who was appointed was for fifty-eight cents.

[2] Smith v Sherman 4 Cush 408, Stebbins v. Palmer, 1 Pick 71 Norton v Sewall, 106 Mass 143, Chase v Fitz, 132 Mass 359, Brown v Cushman, 173 Mass 368.

As to survival of actions and the death and disabilities of parties, see R L c 171, and as to actions by and against executors and administrators, see R L c 172 For provision to protect the rights of a creditor whose cause of action does not accrue within two years after the giving of the administration bond, see R L c 141, § 13, and Bassett v Drew, 176 Mass 141

[3] If an application for administration is not made within four months from the time of the decease of the person leaving an estate liable to a tax on collateral legacies and successions, or a will disposing of such estate is not offered for probate, the treasurer of the commonwealth may make application for the appointment of an administrator. R L. c 15, § 18

As to the Right of Other Persons to administer. — The statute regulating the granting of administration further provides, —

"*Fourth*, If there is no such creditor willing and competent to undertake the trust, administration may be granted to such person as the court may deem fit.

"*Fifth*, If there is no widow, husband, or next of kin, within the commonwealth, administration shall be granted to a public administrator in preference to creditors."

When Administration is granted to a Public Administrator. — The statute provides for the appointment in each county of one or more public administrators, and makes it the duty of such administrator to administer upon the estate of any person who dies intestate within his county or dies elsewhere, leaving property in such county to be administered, and not leaving a known husband, widow, or heir in this state. But the administration will not be granted to the public administrator when the husband, widow, or any heir of the deceased claims in writing the right of administering, or requests the appointment of some other suitable person, if such husband, widow, heir, or other person accepts the trust and gives bond; and such husband, widow, heir, or other person may be appointed after letters of administration have been granted to a public administrator and before the final settlement of the estate. When the person so appointed gives the bond required by law, the power of the public administrator over the estate ceases.[1]

TO WHOM OTHER THAN ORIGINAL ADMINISTRATION IS GRANTED.

Neither the widow nor next of kin have a *right to claim* the grant of administration *de bonis non*.[2] The priority

[1] R L c. 138, §§ 1-4   [2] Russell *v* Hoar, 3 Met 190

of right to administer is regulated entirely by statute, and a distinction in this particular is made between original and other administration. It is provided, in case of the death, resignation, or removal of the original executor or administrator, without having fully administered the estate, that administration with the will annexed, or otherwise, as the case may require, may be granted to "some suitable person" to administer the estate not already administered.[1]

These provisions, while they do not exclude any person from the administration, give the probate court full discretion in the selection of the new administrator. In some cases where administration with the will annexed is granted, the next of kin may have no interest in the estate. They may take nothing under the provisions of the will, or their legacies may have been paid to them by the original executor. In such cases, the residuary legatee, or other person interested under the will, is entitled to administer, the general policy of the law in granting administration being to give the management of the property to the person who has the beneficial interest in it.

PROCEEDINGS IN PROBATE COURT. — PRACTICE.

The Petition. — The person claiming administration must apply by petition in writing to the probate court having jurisdiction of the case. The petition should set forth the fact of the death of the person whose estate is to be administered, the time of his death, the county of which he was last an inhabitant or in which he was resident, and the grounds on which the petitioner claims the right to administer. The petition should also state the name and residence of the widow, if any, of the deceased,

[1] R. L. c. 137, § 8.

and the names, residences, and degree of kindred of his next of kin. If the next of kin are minors, the fact should be stated. If the petition is by a creditor, the fact that the widow and next of kin have neglected for thirty days since the intestate's death to take administration should be stated There must be annexed to the petition the affidavit of the petitioner that the statements therein made are true to the best of his knowledge and belief.[1]

If the petition is for the appointment of a special administrator, the reasons for which letters testamentary or of administration are delayed, whether in consequence of a suit concerning the proof of a will or other cause, should be stated in the petition.

If the petitioner is a stranger to the estate, the reasons upon which he bases his application should be fully stated.

When a public administrator petitions, the fact that the deceased left no husband, widow, or heir in this state should be set forth.

If the petition is for other than original administration it should set forth the fact of the death, resignation, or removal of the executor or original administrator, and it should also appear from the petition that there is personal estate of the deceased remaining to be administered to the amount of twenty dollars, or that there are debts to that amount remaining due from the estate, or that something remains to be performed in execution of the will.

Notice to Persons interested. — The next step in the proceedings is the notification of all persons interested of the pendency of the petition This is absolutely necessary when the petitioner is a creditor or person other than the husband, widow, or next of kin of the deceased, unless all

[1] R L c 136, § 1.

persons having an equal or prior right to administer assent to the appointment of the petitioner, or renounce their right. The neglect of the widow and next of kin for thirty days after the intestate's death to take administration does not render their citation the less necessary, although a literal construction of the statute would seem to indicate otherwise.[1] The citation need not be personally served upon the widow and next of kin. It may be difficult in many cases to ascertain who are the next of kin, and if personal service was required, the proceedings would necessarily be attended with uncertainty and delay. The statute does not define the manner in which the citation shall be served, but leaves it to the discretion of the court. Ordinarily, publication of a general notice to all parties interested will be a sufficient citation. Any person interested in the estate may appear and show cause for or against the appointment of the person named in the petition.

If the person or persons whose right to administer is prior or equal to the petitioner's renounce administration in writing, the delay and expense of a citation may be avoided. But if the person having such prior claim comes into court and verbally declines to take administration, it is not enough. The renunciation, to be effectual, must be recorded, and should therefore be made in writing in all cases.[2]

[1] Arnold v. Sabin, 1 Cush. 525.
[2] Ibid., and see Stebbins v. Lathrop, 4 Pick. 44.

Administration of the estate of an intestate may be granted to one or more of his next of kin or any suitable person, when the widow of the deceased and all his next of kin resident in the commonwealth, who are of full age and legal capacity, consent in writing thereto. And the notice required by law may be dispensed with as if all parties entitled thereto had signified their assent or waived notice. R. L. c. 137, § 2.

As to Proof of the Death. — The questions usually raised in cases where the petitioner's appointment is contested relate to his suitableness for the trust, or to the priority of his right. It is not often that any doubt exists of the death of the person whose estate is the subject of the petition, but such cases occur where the long-continued absence of the person, without being heard of, renders his death probable, though the fact cannot be proved. After the lapse of seven years, without intelligence concerning him, the law presumes that he is dead, and administration is granted accordingly. It must appear, however, that he has not been heard from by persons who would have been likely to hear from him, if living, or that ineffectual search has been made for him. But though the presumption of death does not attach to the mere lapse of time, short of seven years, the fact of death may be found from a shorter period when other circumstances concur, as if the party sailed on a voyage which should long since have been accomplished, and the vessel has not been heard from. under such circumstances administration has been granted after the lapse of one year.[1]

The fact of the absence of the person without having been heard from for the period of seven years is only presumptive evidence of his death; and if administration is granted upon his estate, and it should subsequently appear that the supposed deceased person was, in fact, living at the time administration was granted, the pro-

[1] Administration was granted in January, 1858, on the estate of A., who sailed from Liverpool in January, 1857, for Valparaiso; the voyage should have been made in ten weeks, nothing had been heard of the ship. *Held*, that payment by the underwriters of the amount for which the ship was insured was very strong evidence in support of the petition for administration. In the Goods of Main, 1 Swa. & Trist. 11.

ceedings of the probate court will be held void for want of jurisdiction.[1]

Administrators, Bonds. — The appointment of the administrator or administrators is made complete by the approval of the bond required of them by statute. The bond must be with sufficient surety or sureties, in such sum as the judge of the probate court orders, payable to the judge[2] and his successors, and with condition, in the case of an original administrator, to make and return to the probate court within three months a true inventory of all the intestate's real and personal estate, which at the time of the making of such inventory shall have come

[1] Jochumsen *v.* Suffolk Savings Bank, 3 Allen, 87; Marden *v.* Boston, 155 Mass. 359; Meha *v.* Simmons, 45 Wis. 334; D'Arusment *v.* Jones, 4 Lea (Tenn.), 251.

A decree allowing a will or adjudicating the intestacy of the estate of a deceased person in any court in this commonwealth having jurisdiction thereof shall, after two years from the rendition of such decree, or, if proceedings for a reversal thereof are had, after two years from the establishment of such decree, be final and conclusive in favor of purchasers for value, in good faith, without notice of any adverse claim, of any property, real or personal, from devisees, legatees, heirs, executors, administrators, or guardians, and in favor of executors, administrators, trustees, and guardians, who have settled their accounts in due form, and have in good faith disposed of the assets of the estate in accordance with law, and also in favor of persons who have in good faith made payments to executors, administrators, trustees, or guardians. It is, however, provided that devisees, legatees, heirs, and distributees shall, in case of a subsequent decree reversing or qualifying the decree so originally rendered, be liable to a subsequent executor, administrator, or other person found entitled thereto, for any proceeds or assets of the estate received by them under the former decree, and in such case proceeds of real estate shall be treated as real estate. It is provided further that the provisions of section 3 of chapter 136 of the Revised Laws shall not make an adjudication of the fact of death conclusive. R. L. c. 136, § 3.

[2] In Suffolk and in Middlesex, the bond is payable to the first (senior) judge of probate. R. L. c. 161, § 2.

to the possession or knowledge of the administrator; to administer according to law all the personal estate of the deceased which may come to the possession of the administrator or of any person for him, and also the proceeds of any real estate that may be sold or mortgaged by the administrator; to render upon oath a true account of his administration at least once a year until his trust is fulfilled, unless he is excused therefrom in any year by the court, and at such other times as the court may order; to pay to such persons as the court may direct any balance remaining in his hands upon the settlement of his accounts, and to deliver his letters of administration into the probate court in case any will of the deceased is thereafter proved and allowed.[1] The condition of the bond required of an administrator *de bonis non* is the same as that of an administrator originally appointed.

Administrators with the will annexed, and administrators *de bonis non* with the will annexed, are required to give bond in like manner and with like condition as is required of an executor, and when such administrator is the residuary legatee under the will, the court may permit him to give a bond similar to that which may be given by an executor who is such legatee.[2]

An administrator of an estate, or an administrator with

---

[1] R. L. c 149, § 1 An executor or administrator must not only make a return of the property in his hands liable to taxation, but must in addition, in case of a partial or total distribution, give notice thereof to the assessors, stating the names and residences, and the amount paid to the several parties interested who are residents of this commonwealth, in order to discharge his duty and avoid taxation, if it is within three years of his appointment, for the amount last assessed to him Vaughan v Street Commissioners, 154 Mass 143 But see Batchelder v Cambridge, 176 Mass 384.

[2] R L c 149, § 2

the will annexed, shall be exempt from giving a surety or sureties on his bond, when all the persons interested in the estate, who are of full age and legal capacity, other than creditors, certify to the probate court their consent thereto; but not until all the creditors of the estate, and the guardian of any minor interested therein, have been notified and have had opportunity to show cause against the same; but such administrator shall in all cases give his own personal bond, with conditions as prescribed by law; provided, that the probate court may at or after the granting of letters of administration require a bond, with sufficient surety or sureties.[1]

Every administrator who neglects to give bond, with surety or sureties, when required by the probate court within such time as it directs, in accordance with this act, shall be considered to have declined or resigned the trust.[2]

The bond of a special administrator is conditioned to return an inventory within such time as the court shall order; to account on oath for all the estate of the deceased that shall be received by him as such special administrator, whenever required by the probate court; and to deliver the same to whoever shall be appointed executor or administrator of the deceased, or to such other person as shall be lawfully entitled to receive the same.[3]

A public administrator may give a separate bond for every estate which he is called upon to administer, or he may give a general bond for the faithful administration of all estates on which administration is granted to him as public administrator. His separate bond is the same as

[1] R L. c. 149, § 3.   [2] Ibid § 8   [3] Ibid. § 1

that required of other original administrators, with the further condition that if an executor or administrator is appointed as his successor in any case, to surrender his letters of administration into the probate court, with an account of his doings therein, and to pay over to his successor all property of the deceased not administered.[1] His general bond is conditioned to return into the probate court, within three months from the time letters of administration are granted to him on the estate of any person deceased, a true inventory of all the real and personal estate of such person which at the time of making such inventory shall have come to his possession or knowledge; to administer according to law all personal estate of every such person which may come to the possession of said administrator or of any person for him, and also the proceeds of any of the real estate of such person that may be sold by said administrator; to render upon oath a true account of his administration of every such estate at least once a year until the trust is fulfilled, unless he is excused therefrom in any year by the court, and at such other times as the court may order; to pay the balance of every such estate remaining in his hands upon the settlement of his accounts to such persons as the court may direct, and when such estate has been fully administered to deposit with the treasurer of the commonwealth the whole amount remaining in his hands; upon the appointment and qualification in any case of an executor or administrator as his successor, to surrender into the probate court his letters of administration in such case, with an account under oath of his doings therein and, upon a just settlement of such account, to pay over and deliver to such successor all sums of money remaining in his

[1] R L c 138, §§ 5, 6

hands, and all property, effects, and credits of the deceased not then administered.[1]

Upon the approval of the bond by the judge of the probate court, letters of administration issue to the person appointed, who may forthwith proceed in the execution of his trust unless an appeal is taken from the decree making the appointment.[2] But a *special* administrator may proceed, notwithstanding an appeal is taken, until it is otherwise ordered by the supreme court of probate.[3]

Authority of a Special Administrator. — It is the duty of a special administrator to collect all of the personal property of the deceased and to preserve it for the executor or administrator, and he may begin and maintain suits for that purpose. If he is appointed by reason of delay in granting letters testamentary, the court may authorize him to take charge of the real estate of the deceased or of any part of it, to collect the rents, to make necessary repairs, and to do all other things which the court may consider needful for the preservation of the property.[4] The court

---

[1] R. L. c. 138, § 7.

[2] When the decree of a judge of probate, appointing an administrator, is appealed from, the authority of such administrator is thereby suspended, and any further proceedings by him in that capacity are irregular. Arnold v. Sabin, 4 Cush. 47; Smith v. Smith, 175 Mass. 483.

On an appeal from a decree of the probate court granting letters of administration, the court may reverse the decree appointing the administrator, and affirm it as to the residue. Dexter v. Brown, 3 Mass. 32. If the sole heir and distributee of an estate free from debt, upon which no administration is taken out in his lifetime, takes possession of the entire property, believing that he has a right to do so, and transfers the property upon a good consideration, the transferee gains no title to the property legal or equitable, as against the administrator of the estate appointed after the distributee's death. Pritchard v. Norwood, 155 Mass. 539.

[3] R. L. c. 137, § 9.   [4] Ibid. § 10.

may also authorize him to sell any of the property in his chaige and to do anything else which in the opinion of the court may be required, so far as the court might authorize an administrator to do, except that a special administrator may be authorized to continue the business of the deceased for the benefit of his estate.[1] He may also pay such reasonable allowance as may be made by the court as an advancement for the support of the widow or children of the deceased;[2] and may, by leave of couit, pay from the personal property in his hands the expenses of the last sickness and funeral of the deceased, expense incurred by the executor named in the will of the deceased in proving the will in the probate couit or in sustaining pioof of it in the supreme judicial court, and also, after notice, such debts due from the deceased as the court may approve.[3]

The powers of the special administrator cease upon the gianting of letters testamentary or of administiation, and it is then his duty to deliver to the executor or administrator, or to such person as is otherwise lawfully authorized to receive it, all the estate of the deceased in his hands.[4]

A special administrator is not liable to an action by a creditor of the deceased, and the time of limitation for all actions against the estate begins to run only after the granting of letters testamentary or of administration in the usual form, in like manner and subject to the same conditions as if special administration had not been granted;[5] but if an appeal is taken from the decree of the probate court appointing an executor or administrator the

[1] R L c. 137, § 11. [2] Ibid § 12
[3] Ibid § 13. [4] Ibid § 14.
[5] Ibid. § 15.

time runs, if the decree is affirmed, from the time of affirmation if the bond has been filed, and, if not, from the date of the filing of the bond, if the decree is reversed, from the time when an appointment is finally made or affirmed and the bond is filed.

CHAPTER VI.

APPOINTMENT OF GUARDIANS.

THE probate court, when it appears necessary or convenient, may appoint guardians of minors and others who are inhabitants of or residents in the county, or who reside out of this commonwealth and have estate within the county.[1]

OF MINORS.

A father is the guardian by nature of his infant child; and on his death the mother;[2] the natural guardian has

---

[1] R. L. c. 145, § 1. A guardian of a minor residing in the town of West Roxbury, in the county of Norfolk, was appointed by the probate court of that county before the annexation of that town to the city of Boston and county of Suffolk by the St of 1873, c 314, and after such annexation resigned his guardianship, and his resignation was accepted by that court, but he still held in his hands the property of the minor, and the minor continued to reside in the same territory Held, that by § 3 of that statute the jurisdiction to appoint a new guardian of the minor was in the probate court of the county of Suffolk Harding v Weld, 128 Mass 587 See also Cutts v Hodgdon, 147 Mass 21

A judgment cannot properly be rendered in a civil action against an infant who has no probate guardian or guardian *ad litem*, although his parents in fact represent him at the trial and by the aid of counsel defend the action on his behalf. Johnson v. Waterhouse, 152 Mass. 585 See also Conto v Silvia, 170 Mass. 152.

[2] The mother of a bastard is its natural guardian while she is unmarried Wright v Wright, 2 Mass 109

By St 1902, c. 474, section 4 of chapter 145 of the Revised Laws was amended so as to put the father and the mother on an equality as to the custody of the person of a minor child and the care of his education

custody of the infant's person, but cannot act in matters relating to the infant's estate. If therefore an infant acquires property by inheritance or otherwise, the appointment of a guardian may be as necessary during the lifetime of the father as after his decease.

If the minor is under the age of fourteen years, the probate court may nominate and appoint his guardian.[1] If he is above that age, he may nominate his own guardian, but his choice is not conclusive upon the court. If in the opinion of the court the person nominated is not suitable for the trust, the court will reject him; and if the infant will not choose a proper person, the court will nominate and appoint a guardian. If the minor resides without the state, or if, after being cited, he neglects to nominate a suitable person, the court may appoint his guardian as if he were under the age of fourteen years.[2]

The nomination of a guardian by a minor above the age of fourteen years may be made before a justice of the peace, special commissioner, or a city or town clerk.[3]

The minor, for whom a guardian has been appointed, may, on his arrival at the age of fourteen years, nominate a new guardian; but such nomination does not, as of right, vacate the appointment previously made. His choice will be sanctioned or not, as the discretion of the court shall direct.

The guardian of a minor has the custody and tuition of

[1] A written agreement by the mother (herself an infant) of a boy less than fourteen years old, whose father is dead, to surrender all her rights of custody of the child to other persons, gives no such right to the child as to control the discretion of the probate court in subsequently appointing another person his guardian with the mother's assent. Gloucester v Page, 105 Mass. 231.

[2] R. L. c 145, § 2.

[3] Ibid. § 3

his ward, and the care and management of all his estate,[1] and, unless sooner discharged according to law, continues in office until the minor arrives at the age of twenty-one years. But the parents of the minor, if living, and in case of the death of either, the surviving parent, they being respectively competent to transact their own business, and fit persons for the trust, are entitled to the custody of the person of the minor and the care of his education,[2] but the probate court may order that the guardian shall have such custody, if, upon a hearing and after such notice to the parents or surviving parent as it may direct, it finds such parents or parent to be unfit to have such custody, or if it finds one of them unfit therefor, and the other files in court his or her consent in writing to such order.[3]

[1] The property of a person under guardianship may be taken on execution issued against him, it may therefore be attached on mesne process in all the usual modes, including trustee process. Guardians are not invested with the legal title of the ward's property, they have only the control and management of it, — a power not coupled with an interest. They can make no contract binding on his person or estate. Simmons v Almy 100 Mass 239, Lombard v Moise, 155 Mass 136. A guardian in suing for debts due his ward must sue in the name of the ward. Gurney v Waldron, 137 Mass 379, and cases cited, Tyler v Odd Fellows Association, 145 Mass 134; Richmond v Adams National Bank, 152 Mass 364. In a suit against an insane person under guardianship the writ should be served on the insane person and notice of the pendency of the action should be given to the guardian. Taylor v. Lovering, 171 Mass 303.

[2] R L c 145, § 4, as amended by St 1902, c 474. A father is not liable for the support of his minor child after the custody of the child has been given to the mother by a decree of the supreme judicial court under the statute of 1874, c 205. Brow v Brightman, 136 Mass 187, see also Foss v. Hartwell, 168 Mass. 66. St 1874, c 205, is now embodied, substantially, in R L c 153, § 33.

[3] R L c 145, § 4. The judge of probate of any county may appoint the Massachusetts Society for the Prevention of Cruelty to Children guardian of a minor under fourteen years of age resident therein, who is without a guardian, and is entirely abandoned, or treated with

The probate court, upon the application of a guardian entitled to the custody of his minor ward, may order either or both of the parents of the ward to contribute to the support and maintenance of such minor in such sums and at such times as it determines are just and reasonable.[1]

A domestic trust company may be appointed guardian, but such appointment shall apply to the estate and not to the person of the ward.[2]

Who are suitable for the Trust. — A guardian, having the control of the estate of his ward, should possess the qualifications necessary to its judicious management. The interests of the ward sometimes render necessary the sale of the estate, or portions of it, and a new investment of the proceeds; a proper discharge of the trust in such cases can be best promoted by the appointment of a guardian of business experience. In case of the death or unfitness of the minor's parents, the guardian has the custody and tuition of his ward, and he should therefore be a

gross and habitual cruelty by the parent or other person having the care or custody of him, or is illegally deprived of liberty Upon the complaint of the society that a child under five years of age has been abandoned in a public place, or in a vacant dwelling, a judge of any court within his jurisdiction may give the custody of such child for a period not exceeding thirty days to said society

In Hampden County the foregoing provisions shall be applicable to the Hampden County Children's Aid Association in like manner as to the Massachusetts Society for the Prevention of Cruelty to Children. R. L c 83, §§ 29, 31, 33

The Boston Children's Friend Society is empowered to become the guardian of minors, St 1885, c 362, also the Home for Destitute Catholic Children, St 1891, c 312, formerly known as the Association for the Protection of Destitute Roman Catholic Children, St. 1890, c. 117.

[1] R L c 145, § 28.
[2] R L. c. 116, § 18.

person not indifferent to the happiness of his ward, and competent to direct his education.[1]

It is advisable, when practicable, that the guardianship be given to some person whose natural affection for the ward will prompt him to the faithful discharge of his trust; for it often occurs that the minor's sole security is in the affection or the personal integrity of his guardian.[2] The sureties on a guardian's bond, though entirely sufficient at the time they sign it, may prove, when the minor arrives at full age, — perhaps at the end of ten or fifteen years, — to be bankrupt as well as their principal; and in such case, if the guardian is dishonest, the minor is without remedy. The court can, of course, order the guardian to file a bond with new sureties at any time, but it is sometimes the fact that the only person living who can be expected to interest himself in the welfare of the ward is the guardian who is wronging him, and thus the insufficiency of the bond may not be brought to the notice of the court until it is too late.

[1] Where both parents are dead, the guardian appointed in the courts of this state will have the exclusive right to the custody of the person of the child so long as the child continues within this jurisdiction; but the question of the proper custody of the child as between a domestic guardian and one appointed in the place of the domicile of the infant is to be decided by the supreme judicial court on *habeas corpus* or other proper process. Neither the domestic nor foreign guardian has an absolute right to the custody of the infant. In determining the question to whose custody the child shall be committed, his welfare and permanent good is the controlling consideration. Commonwealth v. Briggs, 16 Pick. 203; Woodworth v. Spring, 4 Allen, 321.

[2] Conduct of a guardian tending to alienate the affection of his infant ward from its mother, who is a person of good character, is a sufficient cause for his removal from the trust. Perkins v. Finnegan, 105 Mass. 501. Mere unsuitableness, without misconduct of any kind, is sufficient cause for the removal of a guardian. Gray v. Parke, 155 Mass. 433.

An administrator ought not, while he is engaged in the settlement of an estate, to be appointed guardian of a minor who is an heir to the same estate, unless there are decided personal reasons for the appointment. The two trusts are incompatible. It is the duty of the guardian to inspect the proceedings of the administrator, to examine his accounts, and to cause him to be cited if he is negligent in his administration. It is obvious that these essential duties might not be discharged when both the administration and guardianship were in the hands of the same person.

Testamentary Guardians. — A father, or, in case the father has died without exercising the power, a mother, may by his or her last will in writing appoint, subject to the approval of the probate court, a guardian for his or her child, whether born at the time of making the will, or afterwards, to continue during the minority of the child or a less time. Such testamentary guardian has the same powers, and performs the same duties with regard to the person and estate of the ward, as a guardian appointed by the probate court.[1] But a testator can appoint a guardian for his own children only. He cannot appoint guardians for other children, although he gives them his property.[2]

The Petition for the appointment of a minor under the age of fourteen years is usually made by the father or mother of the minor, if either of them is living; if they are not living, by some relative or friend of the minor. If the petition is by any person other than a parent, the assent of the parents, or the survivor of them, to

[1] R. L. c. 145, § 5
[2] Brigham *v.* Wheeler, 8 Met. 127; Wardwell *v.* Wardwell, 9 Allen, 518

the appointment prayed for should be indorsed on the petition. If both parents are dead, such assent may be given by the next of kin, or, if there are no known next of kin, by the persons who have the care of the minor. When such assent is expressed, the appointment prayed for is usually made at once; otherwise, a citation may be issued to parties interested before any appointment is made.[1] The petition should state the full name of the minor, the date of his birth, his residence, the full name and last place of residence of his father, and the ground upon which the petitioner claims the appointment

If the petition is for the appointment of some person other than a parent of the minor, and alleges the unfitness of the parents to have the custody of the child, the appointment prayed for cannot be made until after notice to the parents or surviving parent, and a hearing.[2]

If the minor is above the age of fourteen years, he may appear in court and nominate his guardian, or he may make his nomination before a justice of the peace, a special commissioner, or a city or town clerk.[3] In such cases, the petition may be made by the person nominated by the minor, and a certificate of the fact of the nomination should be indorsed on the petition by the justice, commissioner, or clerk before whom it is made. If the

[1] Publication of notice is not essential under the Pub. Sts c 139, §§ 2, 3, now embodied in R L c 145, §§ 2, 3, to the validity of an appointment by the probate court of a guardian for a minor under fourteen years of age. Notice may, of course, be ordered by the probate court, if deemed advisable in any case, and a guardian *ad litem* might properly be appointed to represent the minor, if that court thought it best, but neither is essential to the validity of the appointment. Gibson, Appellant, 154 Mass 378.

[2] R. L. c. 145, § 4.

[3] Ibid. § 3

minor neglects to nominate a guardian, any person interested may petition.

Temporary Guardians. — Upon the application of the mayor of a city, the selectmen of a town, the overseers of the poor of a city or town, or other person in interest, the judge of the probate court may, after giving due notice according to the rules of the probate court, appoint a temporary guardian of a minor, insane person, or spendthrift, and may, with or without notice, remove or discharge him or terminate the trust. If the court finds that the welfare of the minor requires the immediate appointment of a guardian of his person, such appointment may be made without notice. A temporary guardian shall continue in the execution of his duties, notwithstanding an appeal from the decree appointing him, until it is otherwise ordered by the supreme judicial court, or until his trust is otherwise legally terminated.[1] A temporary guardian, until his removal or the appointment of a permanent guardian, has the same powers and duties as a permanent guardian, and, in certain cases, is entitled to the sole custody and control of the ward.[2]

OF INSANE PERSONS AND SPENDTHRIFTS.

The probate court may appoint a guardian for an insane person, and for a person who so wastes his property by excessive drinking, gaming, idleness, or debauchery of any kind as to expose himself or his family to want or suffering, or any city or town to charge or expense for the support of himself or his family.[3]

The application for the appointment of a guardian of

---

[1] R. L. c. 145, § 20.   [2] Ibid. § 21.   [3] Ibid §§ 6, 7.

an insane person may be made by the relations or friends of such person, or by the mayor and aldermen or selectmen of the city or town of which such person is an inhabitant or resident

In the case of a spendthrift, the overseers of the poor of the city or town of which he is an inhabitant or resident, or upon which he is or may become chargeable, or a relation or relations of such spendthrift, may file a petition in the probate court, stating the facts and circumstances of the case and praying to have a guardian appointed In towns in which overseers of the poor are not chosen and in which selectmen act as overseers of the poor, the selectmen may file such petition. The capacity in which the complainants act should be stated in the petition.[1]

In all cases, notice of not less than fourteen days is given to the supposed insane person or spendthrift of the

---

[1] R L c 145, § 71 A copy of the petition for appointment of a guardian of a spendthrift, and of the order of notice thereon, may be recorded in the registry of deeds for the county or district in which any land of the supposed spendthrift is located, and if a guardian is appointed on such petition, all contracts, except for necessaries or relative to land, and all gifts, sales, or transfers of personal property, made by the spendthrift after an order of notice upon the petition has been issued by the probate court, and all contracts relative to and sales and conveyances of land made by the spendthrift after such record in the registry of deeds, for the county and district in which the land is located, and before the termination of the guardianship, will be void, even though the other party cannot be put *in statu quo* R L. c 145, § 8. Chandler *v* Simmons, 97 Mass 508; Dubé *v* Beaudry, 150 Mass 449; White *v.* New Bedford Waste Corporation, 178 Mass 20 An assignment will not, after the death of the assignor, be held to be invalid, because, nine years before the execution of the assignment, the assignor was placed under guardianship as a spendthrift, if the person appointed guardian did not accept the office, although the decree of the probate court appointing him has not been revoked. O Donnell *v* Smith, 142 Mass 505

time and place appointed for the hearing.[1] The notice must be served in the manner directed by the court, and no appointment can be made until after due service of the notice. If the insane person has previously been under guardianship, and the office of guardian has in any way become vacant, notice must be given to him before a new guardian can be appointed; and he is entitled to be heard upon the subject of the complaint in like manner as if he had not been under guardianship [2]

At the time and place named in the citation the complainants and the supposed insane person or spendthrift will be heard. Acts of the person complained of at or near the time of making the complaint may be proved for the purpose of showing the state of his mind and his manner of life, but not his acts at a remote period. If after a full hearing it appears that the person complained of is unable to take care of himself by reason of insanity, or is so wasteful of his property that a guardian is needed to protect his family or the public, a suitable person will be appointed.

The guardian appointed should not only be a suitable person in a general sense, but as far as is practicable should be fitted to discharge the duties rendered necessary by the particular condition and necessities of the ward. It is not enough, in every case, that the guardian is faithful and competent to manage the ward's estate to advantage; he should be a person capable of exercising a proper influence and judicious control over his ward. The permanent improvement and substantial welfare of the ward are the main objects of the guardianship; and the guardian who has the care and custody of his person should be

[1] R L c 145, §§ 6, 7
[2] Allis v. Morton, 4 Gray, 63. Harding v. Weld, 128 Mass 591, O'Donnell v. Smith, 142 Mass. 505.

personally fitted, by his relations to the ward and otherwise, to promote these objects [1] In many cases, the determination of the question of suitability may be influenced by the wishes of the ward, for a man may be so insane as to be a fit subject for guardianship, and yet have a sensible opinion and strong feeling as to the person to be placed over him, and the reasonable wishes of such a person should be consulted by the court.

When a guardian is appointed for an insane person or spendthrift, the court makes an allowance, to be paid by the guardian, for all reasonable expenses incurred by the ward in defending himself against the petition.[2] Such guardian has the care and custody of the person of his ward and the management of all his estate. The husband or wife of an insane person who desires to convey his or her real property absolutely or by mortgage, may file a petition in the probate court describing such real property, and praying that the dower of the wife, or an estate of homestead, or a tenancy by the curtesy at common law or by statute of the husband therein may be released, and stating the facts and reasons why the prayer of the petition should be granted The court may, after notice and a hearing, by a decree authorize the guardian of the insane person to make the release by joining in any deed or deeds, mortgage or mortgages, of the whole or a part of said real property, made within five years after said decree by the husband or wife of the insane person, or by a trustee for such husband or wife.[3] When a guardian of an insane husband or of an insane wife is authorized to release such

---

[1] A guardian may prosecute a divorce on behalf of his insane ward. Garnett *v.* Garnett, 114 Mass 379.

[2] R L c. 145, § 9.

[3] R. L c. 153, § 19.

tenancy by the curtesy of the husband, or dower of the wife, or an estate of homestead, and the court finds that part of the proceeds of the real property sold should be reserved for the use of the ward, it may order that a part of the proceeds, exclusive of any encumbrance existing on the property at time of sale, shall be paid over to the guardian and to be invested by the guardian for the benefit of the ward; such part of the proceeds not to exceed one-third of the net proceeds in case of release of curtesy or dower, nor to exceed eight hundred dollars in case of release of homestead; and in the last named case, the amount so paid to the guardian to be invested in a homestead and held by the guardian for the benefit of the insane wife, if she survives her husband, the rent or use of it to be enjoyed by the husband during his wife's life, and the homestead to be his, and to be conveyed to him by the guardian, if the husband survives the wife [1]

If the husband or wife of an insane person conveys real property in trust without power of revocation and makes a provision therein for the insane husband or wife which the probate court, after notice and a hearing, finds is sufficient in lieu of dower, the trustee may convey such real property free from all right of curtesy or dower, and if the court finds that the provision for husband or wife is sufficient in lieu of curtesy or dower, either in the whole or in particular portions of the real property of the husband or wife, the guardian will be authorized to release curtesy or dower in the whole or in such particular portions.[2] He may be discharged by the probate court on the application of the ward or otherwise, when it appears that such guardianship is no longer necessary.[3]

[1] R L c 153, §§ 20, 21, 22. [2] Ibid. §§ 23, 24
[3] R. L c. 145, § 11. A ward may appeal from a decree of the judge

OF PERSONS OUT OF THE STATE.

A guardian may be appointed for a minor, insane person, or spendthrift, residing out of this state, and having estate here, upon the petition of any friend of such person, or any one interested in his estate, in expectancy or otherwise. The application may be made to the probate court of any county in which there is any estate of such absent person;[1] and after such notice to all persons interested as the court shall order, and after a full hearing and examination, a guardian may be appointed. Such guardian has the same powers and duties with respect to any estate of the ward found within this state, and also with respect to the person of the ward if he comes to reside therein, as are prescribed for other guardians [2]

If a person who is a resident in another state is entitled to property of any description in this commonwealth, and is under the guardianship of a person who is also a resident in such other state, who produces to the probate court of the county in which such property or the principal part thereof is situated a full and complete and duly exempli-

of probate against his application to have the letters of guardianship revoked, and need not give bonds to prosecute the appeal McDonald v Morton, 1 Mass 543, Lawless v. Reagan, 128 Mass 594

In the absence of an express contract, no action can be sustained against a guardian to charge him personally with the support and education of his ward Spring v Woodworth, 4 Allen, 326, Hicks v Chapman, 10 Allen, 464 The appointment of a guardian to a spendthrift, under R L c 145, § 7, after the latter's purchase of goods, but before their delivery, does not affect his liability for the price Myer v Tighe, 151 Mass 354

[1] If the estate of the person liable to be put under guardianship consists in part of personal property held in trust for him, the probate court of the county where the trustee resides has jurisdiction to appoint the guardian Clarke v. Cordis, 4 Allen, 466.

[2] R L c 145, §§ 16, 17.

fied or authenticated transcript from the records of a court of competent jurisdiction in such other state, showing that he has there been appointed such guardian, and has given a bond and security in double the value of the property of such ward, then such transcript may be recorded in the probate court, and the guardian will be entitled to receive from the court letters of guardianship of the estate of the ward in this commonwealth which shall authorize him to care for and manage the real and personal property of such ward, to collect the rents and profits therefrom, and to demand, sue for, and recover any such property, and to remove any of the movable property or estate of such ward out of this commonwealth, if such removal will not conflict with the terms and limitations attending the right by which the ward holds the same. The court may also order any resident guardian, executor, or administrator, having any of the ward's estate, to deliver the same to any person who has so taken out letters of guardianship.[1]

OF MARRIED WOMEN.

The statutes allowing married women to hold property to their own use free from the control of their husbands rendered necessary some provisions for the care of the separate property of minor and insane married women. And it is now provided that, "if a married woman owns property, real or personal, a guardian may be appointed to her for the same causes, in the same manner, and with the same powers and duties, as if she were sole, except as hereinafter provided. But a guardian shall not be so appointed without such notice to the husband as the court may order

"Such guardian shall not have the care, custody, or education of his ward, except in case of the insanity of

[1] R. L c 145, § 19.

her husband, or in case of his abandoning her by absenting himself from the commonwealth and making no sufficient provision for her.

"Such guardian shall not apply the property of his ward to the maintenance of herself and her family while she is married, unless he is thereto authorized by the probate court on account of the inability of her husband suitably to maintain her or them, or for other cause which the court considers sufficient." [1]

And when a married woman is, by reason of insanity or infancy, incompetent to release her right of dower or right of homestead in her husband's lands, a guardian may be appointed for her in the same manner as if she were sole, with the powers and duties given to guardians of married women owning property, and the husband or any suitable person may be appointed.[2]

The guardian of an insane married woman may be authorized by the probate court to release his ward's dower interest or estate of homestead in any real estate of her husband which he desires to convey.[3]

The petition for the appointment of a guardian of a married woman should be in the general form prescribed for petitions for guardians of minors and insane persons, as the case may be, and should particularly state the reasons for which the proposed guardianship is necessary.

GUARDIANS' BONDS.

The guardian of a minor appointed by the probate court is required to give bond, with surety or sureties, to the judge of the probate court, in such sum as he shall order, with condition to make and return to the probate court at such time as it may order a true inventory of all the real

[1] R. L. c. 145, §§ 12-14. [2] Ibid § 15. [3] R L c. 153, § 19.

APPOINTMENT OF GUARDIANS. 141

and personal estate of the ward that at the time of the making of such inventory shall have come to the possession or knowledge of the guardian; to manage and dispose of all such estate according to law and for the best interests of the ward, and faithfully to discharge his trust in relation to such estate, and to the custody, education, and maintenance of the ward; to render upon oath, at least once a year until his trust is fulfilled, unless he is excused therefrom in any year by the court, a true account of the property in his hands, including the proceeds of all real estate sold or mortgaged by him, and of the management and disposition thereof, and also to render such account at such other times as the court may order; and, at the expiration of his trust, to settle his account in the probate court, or with the ward or his legal representatives, and to pay over and deliver all the estate remaining in his hands, or due from him on such settlement, to the person or persons lawfully entitled thereto.[1]

A testamentary guardian gives bond with the same condition as if appointed by the court, except that he is exempt from giving a surety or sureties on his bond, when the testator has ordered or requested such exemption, or that no bond should be required; but he must in all cases give his own personal bond; and the court may require him to give a bond with sureties at any time when it deems it proper, by reason of a change in the guardian's situation or circumstances, or for other sufficient cause. A testamentary guardian who neglects to give bond in accordance with law is considered to have declined or resigned the trust.[2]

[1] R L. c 149, § 1, cl 6; McKim v. Mann, 141 Mass 507, Murray v Wood, 114 Mass. 197, Thorndike v. Hinckley, 155 Mass. 266
[2] R. L c 149, §§ 4, 7.

When the custody of a minor is given to a guardian, for the reason that one or both of the parents are unfit to have such custody, the guardian may be allowed, in the discretion of the court, to give a bond without a surety; but the court may at any time, when it deems the protection of the ward's interests renders it necessary, require him to give a bond with sureties.[1]

The condition of the bond given by the guardian of an insane person or spendthrift is the same as that given by the guardian of a minor, except that the provisions relating to the education of the ward are omitted.[2]

The condition of the bond given by the guardian of a person without the commonwealth is the same as is required when the ward lives within the state, except that the provisions respecting the inventory, the disposal of the estate and effects, and the account to be rendered, are confined to such estate and effects as come to his hands in this state; and the provisions respecting the custody of the ward are not applicable, unless he comes to reside within this state.[3]

Upon the approval of his bond by the judge of the probate court, the guardian receives his letter of guardianship, and has full authority to proceed in the discharge of his trust.

Every non-resident guardian appointed by a probate court or the supreme judicial court shall appoint, in writing, an agent residing in the commonwealth upon whom service of legal process can be made. If such agent dies or removes from the commonwealth, another agent must be appointed. Such non-resident guardian shall not be

---

[1] R. L. c 149, § 5   [2] R. L c. 145, § 10.   [3] Ibid § 18.

APPOINTMENT OF GUARDIANS.

entitled to receive his letters of appointment until he has complied with the above requirement [1]

CONSERVATORS OF THE PROPERTY OF AGED PERSONS

If a person by reason of advanced age or mental weakness is unable properly to care for his property, the probate court of the county in which he resides may, upon his petition or upon the petition of one or more of his friends, appoint a conservator of his property. Upon the filing of such petition, the court shall appoint a time and place for a hearing, and shall cause at least fourteen days' notice thereof to be given to the person for whom a conservator is to be appointed, if he is not the petitioner. If at the hearing it appear that such person is incapable of properly caring for his property, a conservator shall be appointed who shall have the charge and management of such property subject to the direction of the court. Such conservator may be discharged by the probate court upon the application of the ward, or otherwise, when it appears that the conservatorship is no longer necessary.

Such conservator shall give such bond as is required of guardians of insane persons, and all provisions of law relative to the management, sale, or mortgage of the property of insane persons shall apply to such conservator. Non-resident conservators must appoint a resident agent in the same manner as required of non-resident executors and administrators.[2]

[1] R L c 146, § 42, and R L c 139, §§ 8, 9, 10 A ward is not liable for repairs put upon his dwelling-house by a person employed by the guardian to make them, even after the death of the guardian, although the repairs were necessary Wallis v. Bardwell, 126 Mass. 366 A spendthrift under guardianship cannot pass title to a promissory note by indorsement. Lynch v. Dodge, 130 Mass. 458.

[2] R. L. c. 145, §§ 40-42.

CHAPTER VII.

APPOINTMENT OF TRUSTEES — TRUSTS.

IN WHAT CASES TRUSTEES MAY BE APPOINTED.

If a testator has omitted in his will to appoint a trustee in this commonwealth, and if such appointment is necessary to carry into effect the provisions of the will, the probate court may, after notice to all persons interested, appoint a trustee, who shall have the same powers, rights, and duties, and the same title to the estate, as if he had been originally appointed by the testator.[1]

---

[1] R L c. 147, § 4; Hooper v Bradbury, 133 Mass 303

Trustees to whom real estate is devised with a power of sale, and who are exempt from giving bond, may legally execute the power without an appointment from the probate court Parker v Sears, 117 Mass 513

Certain domestic trust companies may be appointed trustees under any will or instrument creating a trust for the care and management of property R L c 116, § 18

A corporation may receive and hold property as trustee if the trust is consistent with the purposes of the original institution of the corporation. Sutton Parish v Cole, 3 Pick. 240, Hill v. Boston, 122 Mass 349.

The appointment of a trustee under a will by the probate court cannot be impeached for an irregularity in the proceedings not affecting the jurisdiction of that court in a suit in equity, but is to be regarded as a valid appointment McKim v. Doane, 137 Mass 195.

A decree appointing a trustee under a will made in a county other than that in which the will is admitted to probate, but in which part of the trust property is situated, is not void, and cannot be collaterally impeached Bradstreet v Butterfield, 129 Mass. 339 It is immate-

APPOINTMENT OF TRUSTEES.

And when a trustee under a written instrument declines, resigns, dies, or is removed before the objects of the trust are accomplished, and such instrument makes no adequate provision for supplying the vacancy, the supreme judicial court, the superior court, or the probate court, after notice to all persons interested, shall appoint a new trustee to act alone or jointly with the others, as the case may be [1] Such new trustee, upon giving the bond required, has the same powers, rights, and duties, whether as a sole or joint trustee, as if he had been originally appointed; and the trust estate vests in him in like manner as it had or would have vested in the trustee in whose place he is substituted; and the court may order such conveyances to be made by the former trustee or his representatives, or by the other remaining trustee, as may be proper or convenient to vest in him, either alone or jointly with the others, the trust estate.[2]

---

rial that the petition for the appointment of the trustee presented to and acted on by the court of one county was in form addressed to the court of another county Bradstreet *v* Butterfield, 129 Mass 339.

[1] H. devised property to H and R, their heirs and assigns, and the survivor of them, upon certain trusts R. died before the trusts were fully executed *Held*, that it was the duty of the probate court, under Rev Stats c 69, § 8 (R L c 147, § 5), the will being silent on the subject, to appoint a co-trustee to act with the survivor Dixon *v* Homer, 12 Cush 41, Attorney-General *v* Barbour, 121 Mass 574, Schouler, Petitioner, 134 Mass 426, Carruth *v* Carruth, 148 Mass 431, Dexter *v* Cotting, 149 Mass 95.

[2] R L c 147, § 6; Parker *v.* Converse, 5 Gray, 336; Dixon *v* Homer, 12 Cush 41, Nugent *v.* Cloon, 117 Mass. 219; Bradford *v* Monks, 132 Mass 405, Wemyss *v.* White, 159 Mass. 484 A trustee cannot withhold the income of a trust fund from the beneficiary's assignee, in order to repay to himself, by way of set-off, money lent by him to the beneficiary prior to his appointment as trustee. Abbott *v* Foote, 146 Mass 333.

If one trustee is appointed in place of two who have been removed,

If a tenant for life or for years and the remainderman or reversioner sustain damages in their property by the laying out, relocation, alteration, or discontinuance of, or by specific repairs on, a highway, or if the property is encumbered by a contingent remainder, executory devise, or power of appointment, entire damages, or an entire amount as indemnity, shall be assessed without apportionment thereof, and shall be paid to, or be recoverable by, any person whom the parties may appoint, and be held in trust by him for their benefit according to their respective interests. The trustee shall, from the income thereof, pay to the reversioner or remainderman the value of any annual rent or other payment which would, but for such damages, have been payable by the tenant, and the balance to the tenant during the period for which his estate was limited, and, upon its termination, he shall pay the principal to the reversioner or remainderman

the trust property is vested in him, and he has the right to prosecute suits to recover the same. Hammond v. Granger, 128 Mass 272, Greene v Borland, 4 Met 330

When a will creates two distinct trusts, and appoints but one trustee for their performance, the trustee may, if good reasons exist for doing so, accept one and refuse the other, and the probate court has power to appoint a new trustee to execute the trust which he has declined Carruth v Carruth, 148 Mass 431.

To validate the appointment of a sole trustee to succeed co-trustees, it seems that the consent of all the parties beneficially interested is necessary. Greene v Borland, 4 Met 330, Dixon v Homer, 12 Cush 41, and see Mass. Gen. Hospital v Amory, 12 Pick 445

An executor may be a trustee by the express terms of the will or by implication Dorr v. Wainwright, 13 Pick. 328, Miller v Congdon, 14 Gray, 114; Ricketson v Merrill, 148 Mass 76, Jones v. Atchison, etc R R Co, 150 Mass 304

A co-trustee is responsible only for his own acts, not for any defaults of his fellow trustees, in the absence of fraud Stowe v. Bowen, 99 Mass. 194 A surviving trustee will be responsible for any improper disposition of the trust property by him, although in the

The amount so to be placed in trust shall include only the damages assessed to the whole property when the value thereof is ascertained, and any damage special to a separate estate therein, and all interest or other earnings which accrue between the taking and the receipt by the trustee of the damages to the whole property, shall be awarded in the same proceedings separately.

If a person having an interest in such property is, by reason of legal disability, incapable of choosing a trustee, or is unascertained or not in being, or if the parties cannot agree upon a choice, the probate court of the county in which the property is situated shall, upon application of the county commissioners or of any persons interested or of any other person, in behalf of such persons, whether in being or not, as may by any possibility be or become interested in said property, appoint a trustee, who shall give to the judge of probate a bond with such sureties and in such sum as the judge may order, conditioned for the faithful performance of his duties.[1]

If it appears in any proceedings for the recovery of damages sustained as aforesaid that an interest in such property is unrepresented by reason of a contingency or other cause by which the owner thereof is unknown or cannot then be ascertained, a guardian *ad litem* may be appointed to represent such interest by the tribunal in which such proceedings are pending; or the judge of probate for the county in which such proceedings are pending may, upon petition of any party in interest, after such notice as he may order to all persons who, or whose issue unborn, are or may become interested

advantages of such disposition the deceased trustee shared. Blake v Pegram, 109 Mass 541.

[1] R. L. c. 48, §§ 17-19.

in such appointment, appoint a trustee, who, upon giving such bond as the judge of probate requires, shall represent such interest and shall receive, manage, and invest any money receivable on account thereof, for the benefit of the parties entitled thereto, and shall pay the principal and interest thereof to such parties when entitled thereto.[1]

A trustee may in like manner, and under the same conditions, be appointed in all cases where damages are sustained by taking land for public uses and in which provision is made that damages shall be assessed in the manner provided in the laying out of highways.[2]

Likewise, in case of partition of lands by sale or otherwise, if it appears that an estate for life or for years in any part of the land divided belongs to one person and the remainder to another person, the probate court of the county in which the proceedings are pending may, on petition of any party interested, appoint a trustee to receive, hold, manage, and invest any distributive share of the money arising from the partition, to which such persons may be entitled.[3]

A surviving husband or a widow who waives the provision made for him or her in the will of the deceased wife or husband thereby becomes entitled to such portion of the estate of the deceased person as he or she would have been entitled to if the deceased had died intestate; provided, however, that if the share of the real and personal estate to which he or she thus becomes entitled exceeds ten thousand dollars in value, he or she shall receive in addition to that amount only the income of the excess of said share above the sum of ten thousand dollars during his or her natural life, the personal property to be held in trust and

[1] R L c 48, § 25   [2] Ibid § 108.   [3] R. L. c. 184, § 49.

the real property vested in him or her for life; and except that, if the deceased leaves no kindred, the surviving husband or widow upon such waiver shall take the interest he or she would have taken if the deceased had died leaving kindred but no issue. In such case, upon application by any one interested, the probate court may appoint one or more trustees to receive, hold, and manage any personal estate to the income of which the surviving husband or widow is so entitled.[1]

If land is subject to a contingent remainder, executory devise, or power of appointment, the probate court for the county in which such land is situated may, upon the petition of any person who has an estate in possession, in such land, and after notice and other proceedings as provided in section 30 of chapter 127 of the Revised Laws, appoint one or more trustees, and authorize him or them to sell and convey such land or any part thereof in fee-simple, or to mortgage the same, if such sale and conveyance appear to the court to be necessary or expedient; and such conveyance or mortgage shall be valid and binding upon all persons.

If land is subject to a vested remainder or reversion, the probate court in which such land is situated may, upon the petition of any person who has either an estate in possession or the remainder or reversion in such land, and after the like notice and proceedings, appoint one or more trustees and authorize him or them to sell and convey such land, or any part thereof, in fee-simple, if such sale and conveyance appear to the court to be necessary or expe-

[1] R L c 135, §§ 16, 17; Borden v. Jenks, 140 Mass 563, Staigg v Atkinson, 144 Mass 570; Dexter v Codman, 148 Mass 422 Such trustees are subject to the provisions of chapter 147 of the Revised Laws, so far as the same are applicable.

dient, and such conveyance shall be valid and binding upon all persons.

Notice of the petition in any of the cases referred to in either of the two preceding paragraphs shall be given, in such manner as the court may order, to all persons who are or who may become interested in the land to which the petition relates, and to all persons whose issue, not in being, may become interested therein, and the court shall of its own motion in every case appoint a suitable person to appear and act therein as the next friend of all minors, persons not ascertained, and persons not in being, who are or may become interested in such land.[1] A decree, judgment, or an order made in the proceedings upon the petition, after such appointment, is conclusive upon all persons for whom such next friend was appointed[2]

Such trustee "shall give bond in such form and for such an amount as the court appointing him may order, and he shall receive and hold, invest, or apply the proceeds of any sale or mortgage made by him, for the benefit of the persons who would have been entitled to the real estate if such sale or mortgage had not been made, and the probate court of any county in which any part of such land is situated shall have jurisdiction of all matters thereafter arising in relation to such trust."[3]

When it appears that wood or timber, standing on land the use and improvement of which belongs, for life or otherwise, to a person other than the owner of the fee therein, has ceased to improve by growth, or ought for any cause to be cut, the supreme judicial court, or the probate court for the county in which the land lies, may appoint a trustee

[1] R L c 127, §§ 28, 29, 30; Pratt v Bates, 161 Mass 315.
[2] R L c. 127, § 30, and c 145, § 23.
[3] R. L. c 127, § 31

to sell and convey the wood or timber, to be cut and carried away within a time to be limited in the order of sale, and to hold and invest the proceeds thereof, after paying therefrom the expenses of such sale, and to pay over the income, above the taxes and other expenses of the trust, to the person entitled to such use and improvement while his right thereto continues, and thereafter to pay the principal sum to the owner of such land. Such sale, if authorized by a probate court, shall be made in the manner provided by law for the sale of real property by guardians; and if such sale is authorized by the supreme judicial court, the trustee shall give to such person as the court shall designate a bond for the use and benefit of the persons interested in the proceeds of the sale, with condition for the faithful discharge of the trust; and the court may remove the trustee and appoint another in his stead.[1]

If a trustee who derives his appointment or authority from a court which has no jurisdiction within this commonwealth, holds land in this commonwealth in trust for persons resident here, he shall, upon petition to the probate court in the county in which the land lies, and after notice, be required to take out letters of trust from said court; and upon his neglect or refusal so to do, the court shall declare such trust vacant, and shall appoint a new trustee, in whom the trust estate shall vest in like manner as if he had been originally appointed or authorized by said court.

"The notice to the trustee required by the preceding section may be given by serving on him a copy of the petition, and of the citation of the court issued thereon, fourteen days at least before the time fixed for the return of such citation, or by such other notice as the court may order."[2]

[1] R. L. c. 134, § 11.   [2] R. L. c. 147, §§ 9, 10.

No person succeeding to a trust as executor or administrator of a former trustee is required to accept such trust.[1]

Any cemetery corporation may take and hold funds upon trust to apply the income thereof to the improvement or embellishment of the cemetery, or to the care, preservation, or embellishment of any lot, or its appurtenances [2]

Any city or town is authorized to receive, hold, and apply any funds, moneys, or securities which may be deposited with the treasurer of such city or town for the preservation, care, improvement, or embellishing of any public or private burial place situated therein, or of burial lots located in the same, and may pass such ordinances or by-laws, not inconsistent with law, as may be necessary for said purpose, and may allow interest on such funds at a rate not exceeding six per cent a year.[3]

Any town or city shall also be authorized to take and hold in trust or otherwise any devise, grant, gift, or bequest that may be made for the purpose of laying out or improving any park or parks therein [4]

Churches or religious societies may appoint trustees, not exceeding five in number, who shall with their successors be a body corporate, for the purposes mentioned in section one of chapter thirty-seven of the Revised Laws, and shall be subject to all of the provisions of said chapter applicable thereto.

Incorporated and unincorporated religious societies and

---

[1] R. L c 147, § 13
A beneficiary may authorize his trustee to do what otherwise would be a breach of trust, or release and agree to hold him harmless for such an act after it is done. Pope *v* Farnsworth, 146 Mass 339.
[2] R. L c. 78, § 5, Green *v.* Hogan, 153 Mass 462.
[3] R. L c 78, § 18; Bartlett, Petitioner, 163 Mass. 513.
[4] R. L. c. 28, § 9

APPOINTMENT OF TRUSTEES.

churches may appoint trustees, not exceeding five, to hold and manage trust funds for their benefit, who shall hold their offices for three years and until others are appointed in their stead. At or before the time of the first appointment of such trustees, the society may establish regulations for their government which shall not be subject to alteration or amendment except by consent of all of the trustees in office and by a two-thirds vote of the church or society interested therein. Any funds held by the bodies corporate mentioned in the first and second sections of said chapter thirty-seven may be transferred to said trustees to be held in trust in like manner by them.[1]

Certain trust companies incorporated under the authority of this commonwealth may be appointed trustee under any will or instrument creating a trust for the care and management of property, under the same circumstances and in the same manner, and subject to the same control by the court having jurisdiction of the same, as in the case of a legally qualified person.[2]

FORMAL PROCEEDINGS.

A trustee appointed by will should petition the probate court for a confirmation of his appointment. The petition should state in general terms the nature of the trust, the manner in which it was created, and the willingness of the petitioner to accept the trust and give the bond required.

If the appointment is necessary in consequence of a vacancy in the office of trustee, the petition should set forth the fact, and state in what way the vacancy was occasioned, whether by the omission of the testator to

[1] R L c 37, §§ 4, 3   [2] R L. c 116, § 18.

make an appointment, or by the resignation or death of a former trustee, or otherwise

Any person interested in a trust estate may petition for the appointment of a trustee. A citation to parties interested will be ordered before an appointment is made, unless their written assent is given to the prayer of the petition.[1]

Every non-resident trustee, appointed by a probate court or the supreme judicial court, shall appoint, in writing, an agent residing in the commonwealth, upon whom service of legal process can be made. If such agent dies or removes from the commonwealth, another agent must be appointed. Such non-resident trustee shall not be entitled to receive his letters of appointment until he has complied with the above requirement.[2]

TRUSTEES' BONDS

Every trustee under a will, unless exempted, is required, before entering upon the duties of his trust, to give bond, with sufficient surety or sureties, to the judge of the probate court for the county in which the will is proved,[3]

---

[1] A testator appointed three trustees, and provided that, if a vacancy occurred in the number of trustees, the surviving or acting trustees should nominate a suitable person to be appointed by the judge of probate to fill the vacancy. A new trustee was so appointed without notice. Held, that the trustee was duly appointed, as in making the appointment the judge did not act officially, but under the will. Shaw v. Paine, 12 Allen, 293; Webster Bank v. Eldridge, 115 Mass. 424.

The regularity of the proceedings of the probate court as to notice in appointing a trustee cannot be questioned by the trustee or his sureties. Bassett v. Crafts, 129 Mass. 513.

[2] R. L. c. 147, § 14.

[3] Bullard v. Attorney-General, 153 Mass. 249.

in such sum as the court shall order, with condition to make and return to the probate court, at such time as it may order, a true inventory of all the real and personal estate belonging to him as trustee, which at the time of making such inventory shall have come to his possession or knowledge, to manage and dispose of all such estate, and faithfully to discharge his trust in relation thereto according to law and to the will of the testator; to render upon oath at least once a year until his trust is fulfilled, unless he is excused therefrom in any year by the court, a true account of the property in his hands and of the management and disposition thereof, and also to render such account at such other times as said court may order; at the expiration of his trust to settle his account in the probate court, and to pay over and deliver all the estate remaining in his hands, or due from him on such settlement, to the person or persons entitled thereto.[1]

Every trustee appointed by a probate court is required to give a bond similar to that given by trustees under wills The bond given by a trustee under a deed should be framed and conditioned in conformity to the terms of the deed.

Every trustee who neglects to give bond is considered to have declined or resigned the trust. If an executor of a will, who is also named therein as trustee, neglects to give bond as trustee, another person may be appointed to the trust.[2]

The statute provisions requiring trustees under a will to give bond have been held to be confined to private trusts of limited duration, and not to extend to a public

[1] R. L. c. 149, § 1. Collins v. Collins, 140 Mass. 507; Bullard v. Attorney-General, *supra*.
[2] Daggett v. White, 128 Mass 398

and permanent charity, the beneficiaries of which are indefinite, and a perpetual succession of trustees provided for in the will. Trustees for charitable trusts need not give bonds.[1]

A trustee under a will is exempt from giving a surety or sureties on his bond when the testator has ordered or requested such exemption, or that no bond should be required, and when all the persons beneficially interested [2] in the trust, who are of full age and legal capacity other than creditors, request such exemption, but not until the guardian of any minor interested therein, and such other persons as the court shall direct, have been notified, and have had opportunity to show cause against the same.[3] But the trustee is required to give his personal bond, and the court, at any time when it deems it proper, may require him to give a bond with sureties. If the trustee was not required to give bond by the laws in force at the time of his appointment, the court may at any time, by a special order, require him to give a bond with sureties. Any person interested in a trust estate may apply to the court by petition for an order requiring the trustee to furnish sureties; and if the trustee fails to comply with the order of the court, he will be removed, and a new trustee appointed in his stead.[4]

---

[1] Lowell, Appellant, 22 Pick. 215; Drury v. Natick, 10 Allen, 169; White v. Ditson, 140 Mass. 354

[2] This has been construed to mean such interested persons only as are in being and have a present vested interest in the estate, and not such as are not in being nor such as may become interested in the future Dexter v. Cotting, 149 Mass. 94

[3] R. L. c 149, § 4

[4] Ibid §§ 4, 6, 7; White v. Ditson, 140 Mass 354; Dexter v. Cotting, 149 Mass 94.

TERMINATION OF CERTAIN TRUSTS.

The statute provides that when it appears, upon petition or otherwise, to the probate court of the county where letters testamentary or of administration have been granted on the estate of a person deceased, that such person in his lifetime made a conveyance of his real estate in this state in trust for the benefit of his creditors, and the trustee certifies that all the debts secured thereby and due to persons other than himself have been paid, or otherwise adjusted to the satisfaction of the creditors so far as known, and that he desires to settle his trust account and terminate the trust, the court shall appoint a time and place for hearing all persons interested therein; notice of which shall be given by advertisement in some newspaper printed in the county or otherwise as the court may order. Upon such hearing the court may terminate the trust, so far as the creditors and persons claiming under them are concerned, and discharge such real estate therefrom, and may settle the trust account, and make any further order as to the disposition, distribution, or partition of the remaining trust estate, not inconsistent with the provisions of the original instrument creating the trust. This provision does not apply to any case where the instrument creating the trust does not bear date more than six years previous to the time appointed for the hearing; nor can it affect the operation of the insolvent laws.[1]

GENERAL EQUITY JURISDICTION.

The probate court has jurisdiction in equity, concurrent with the supreme judicial court and with the superior

[1] R. L. c. 147, § 23.

court, of all cases and matters relating to the administration of estates of deceased persons, to wills or to trusts created by will or other written instrument.[1]

But the probate court does not have power to authorize the executors of a will to arbitrate or compromise controversies between persons claiming under a will and those claiming under the statutes regulating the descent and distribution of intestate estates [2]

All matters of trust of which probate courts have jurisdiction, except those arising under wills, are within the jurisdiction of the probate court for any county in which any of the parties interested in the trust reside, or in which any of the land held in trust is situated; and such jurisdiction, when once assumed, excludes the probate court of any other county from taking jurisdiction of any matter subsequently arising in relation to the same trust [3]

---

[1] R L c 162, § 5, Swasey v Jaques, 144 Mass. 135, Welch v. Adams, 152 Mass 81; Healy v Reed, 153 Mass. 197, Green v Hogan, 153 Mass. 465, Bennett v Kimball, 175 Mass. 199, Green v Gaskill, ibid 265

[2] Abbott v. Gaskins, 181 Mass —— (63 N E Rep. 933); see also St. 1902, c 538

[3] R L c 162, § 7. Upon a petition for the appointment of a trustee of a fund, it cannot be said that necessarily and as matter of law, he is incompetent because he is a surety upon a bond of the *cestui que trust*, given by her as executrix of her husband, the former trustee, against whose estate, which far exceeds the trust fund in amount, and of which she is sole legatee, a claim appearing to be groundless is made by those ultimately entitled to the fund. Gaskill v Green, 152 Mass 256

CHAPTER VIII.

REMOVAL AND RESIGNATION OF EXECUTORS AND OTHERS.

If an executor, administrator, guardian, or trustee, who may be required by the probate court to give a new bond, does not comply with the order within the time fixed by the court, he will be removed, and some other person appointed in his stead;[1] and if he become insane, or otherwise incapable of discharging his trust, or is unsuitable therefor, he may be removed, notice having first been given to him and to all parties interested[2] If an administrator on his appointment fails to give a bond for the faithful performance of his duties when required, he will be considered as having declined the trust.[3]

An executor or other officer appointed by the probate court may be incapacitated by physical debility, want of memory, or any infirmity which prevents the efficient performance of his trust; and he may be evidently unsuitable because of his personal relations to the estate, either by reason of his being indebted to it, or of the interest he has under the will of his testator, or his situation as an heir at law, or because the prosecution of his individual claims against the estate would conflict with his official

---

[1] R. L. c. 149, §§ 14-16, Brooks v. Whitmore, 142 Mass 401
[2] R L c 139, § 11, c. 145, § 22; Gray v. Parke, 155 Mass 438.
[3] R L c 149, § 8

duties, or for other reasons. The statute does not enumerate any causes of unsuitability, but gives the court a broad discretion to include the various cases that may arise.[1]

The removal of executors and other trust officers is made upon the ground that their continuance in the trust would be a detriment to the interests of the heirs or other persons concerned. Mere personal objections, or the wish of the parties in interest to substitute another person whom they prefer, are not sufficient.[2] Such objections and preferences may properly be considered when an original appointment is to be made, or a vacancy is to be filled, but cannot affect the question of removing an officer who has been duly appointed and whose bond has been approved. The allegations of the petition asking for the removal must relate to matters of substance, and the burden is upon the petitioner to sustain the allegations in his petition.[3]

---

[1] See Winship v Bass, 12 Mass. 200, Wildridge v Patterson, 15 Mass. 148, Andrews v. Tucker, 7 Pick 250, Newcomb v. Williams, 9 Met 538, Thayer v Homer, 11 Met 104, Richards v Sweetland, 6 Cush 324; Hussey v Coffin, 1 Allen, 354; Putney v Fletcher, 148 Mass 247; Gray v Parke, 155 Mass 433, and cases cited

[2] Wilson v Wilson, 145 Mass 490

[3] A trustee under a will was directed to pay a certain sum to a *cestui*, "as by sickness or other misfortune he may need the same, any and all payments to be left entirely to the good judgment of the said trustee," any unexpended balance on the *cestui's* death was to go to the trustee and his heirs The trustee wrongfully refused to pay a part of the money to the beneficiary in time of sickness. It was *held* that he should be directed to pay the money to the beneficiary, but that he need not be removed   Garvey v Garvey, 150 Mass 185   An administrator who refuses to ask for a license to sell realty pending a petition to retain assets, is not removable   Cobb v Kempton, 154 Mass 266

When a trustee, directed by a decree to pay over a charitable fund to a particular object, at such times and in such sums as he in his

The fact that an administrator was an unsuitable person at the time of his appointment is not, of itself, sufficient to cause his removal. On a petition to remove him, the question as to the propriety of his appointment is not open. He cannot be removed except for cause existing at the time when the petition for his removal is heard.[1]

The relation existing between a guardian and his ward may require, for the proper discharge of its obligations, other than merely business qualifications; and the guardian may be unsuitable for the care and custody of the person of the ward, although no question be made of his integrity, disinterestedness, or general ability. The guardian of a person *non compos mentis* should be especially fitted for his trust, and in determining the question of personal suitableness, the peculiar condition, interests, and necessities of the ward must be considered. It is not enough, in every case, for the guardian to supply the material wants of his ward. It is his duty to make use of every available means to promote the ward's welfare, improvement, and happiness. With every disposition to discharge his obligations thoroughly and conscientiously, he may be, from various causes, incapable of exercising the beneficial influence over his ward that might be exerted by another. The continuance of the relation of guardian and ward under such circumstances might materially interfere with the permanent improvement and general welfare of the ward, and thus defeat the main object of the guardianship. Whenever, from any cause, the guardian becomes unable to perform

discretion may see fit, refuses to exercise such discretion because he does not approve of the disposal of the fund as decreed, he may and will be removed. Attorney-General *v.* Garrison, 101 Mass. 223.

[1] Drake *v.* Green, 10 Allen, 124.

an important and substantial part of the duties of his office, he is liable to be removed as "evidently unsuitable."[1]

If an executor, administrator, guardian, or trustee, removing from or residing out of the commonwealth, neglects to appoint in writing an agent here upon whom service of legal process against him can be made, he may be removed.[2] Nor will the letter of appointment be issued until an agent has been appointed.[3]

In case of the marriage of a woman who is an executrix, administratrix, guardian, or trustee, her sureties have the right, upon petition to the probate court in which her bond is filed, to be released from any further liability on the bond, beyond accounting for and paying over the money and property already in her hands by virtue of such trust, and if her sureties are so released, she will be required to furnish a new bond to the satisfaction of the court, or will be discharged from the trust.[4]

When an executor or administrator residing out of this state, having been duly cited by the probate court, neglects to render his accounts and settle the estate, he may be removed.[5] If the executor or administrator neglects to settle his accounts within six months after the return of the insolvent commissioners, or the final liquidation of the demands of the creditors, or within such further time as the court may allow, and thereby delays a decree of distri-

---

[1] See Perkins v Finnegan, 105 Mass 501; Gray v Parke, 155 Mass 438.

[2] R L c. 139, §§ 8, 9, 10, c 145, § 42, c. 147, § 14.

[3] R L c 139, § 8; c 145, § 42, c. 147, § 14.

[4] R L c 140, § 19

[5] R L c 139, § 11

The words "settlement of the estate," when applied to the estates of deceased persons, refer to the settlement of the probate account. Allen v. Dean, 148 Mass 594.

bution, such neglect shall be unfaithful administration, and he may be removed.[1]

Any unfaithful administration which will sustain an action on the bond of an executor or other officer appointed by the probate court, is sufficient cause for his removal.[2]

When there are two or more executors of a will, either of them may be removed for sufficient cause; and in such case the other executor or executors will proceed in the execution of the trust.[3]

A trustee may be removed on the application of the parties beneficially interested in the trust estate, if it appears that his removal is essential to their interests.[4]

A trustee who holds funds bequeathed to a city or town, for any charitable, religious, or educational purpose, may be removed by the probate court for neglect to make the annual exhibit of the condition of such funds as required by law, or for incapacity or unsuitability.[5]

The person applying for the removal of an executor or other officer should set forth in his petition the particular

---

[1] R. L. c 142, § 26

[2] It is no cause for the removal of an administrator that he declines to inventory, or commence proceedings to recover for the *benefit of the heirs*, certain real estate formerly belonging to the deceased, but which had been set off on an execution against him in his lifetime issued upon a judgment alleged by the heirs to have been recovered by the fraud of the plaintiff. Richards *v* Sweetland, 6 Cush 324, Drake *v* Green, 10 Allen, 124; Putney *v* Fletcher, 148 Mass. 247 But, otherwise, when creditors of an insolvent estate request the administrator to inventory real estate fraudulently conveyed by the intestate, offering to indemnify him, and he refuses Andrews *v* Tucker, 7 Pick 250

[3] Winship *v* Bass, 12 Mass 199, R L c 139, § 11

[4] R L c 147, § 11, Billings *v* Billings, 110 Mass. 225; Sparhawk *v* Sparhawk, 114 Mass 356, Scott *v* Rand, 118 Mass 215; Attorney General *v* Barbour, 121 Mass. 568; Wilson *v.* Wilson, 145 Mass 492

[5] R L c. 37, § 14.

fact of neglect or other maladministration which renders the removal proper. In all cases, the person whose removal is asked for is entitled to notice, and to an opportunity to show cause why the removal should be made. At the hearing, both the petitioner and the respondent may offer any evidence pertinent to the issue; and either party may appeal from the decree of the court making, or refusing to make, the removal.

The removal of a trustee who holds funds bequeathed to a city or town for a charitable, religious, or educational purpose, must be on the petition of five persons.[1] In all other cases any person interested in the trust estate may petition.

When an executor or administrator is removed, or letters of administration are revoked, all previous sales, whether of real or personal estate, made lawfully by him, and with good faith on the part of the purchaser, and all other lawful acts done by such executor or administrator, remain valid and effectual.[2]

Upon the request of an executor, administrator, guardian, or trustee, the probate court may, in its discretion, allow him to resign his trust.[3] The executor or other

---

[1] R. L. c. 37, § 14.

[2] R. L. c. 139, § 12.

[3] Ibid. § 13; c. 145, § 22; c. 147, § 12. The supreme judicial court has power under its general equity jurisdiction to allow a trustee to resign on his own application. Bowditch v. Banuelos, 1 Gray, 220; Attorney-General v. Barbour, 121 Mass. 573. If, pending an action brought by the trustees of a charity, one of the plaintiff trustees resigns the trust, such resignation will defeat the action. Adams v. Leland, 7 Pick. 62.

The abandonment of a trust by one of two trustees who are joint tenants does not vest his title in the remaining trustee, without deed or legal process. Webster v. Vandeventer, 6 Gray, 428.

But where in a conveyance to trustees it is provided that in case of

officer applying for leave to resign should present to the court, with his petition, a just and true account of his administration. Until his accounts are settled, after such notice to the parties interested as the circumstances of the case require, his request will not be allowed.

If an executor, administrator, guardian, or trustee who has resigned his trust neglects or refuses to deliver to his successor all the property held by him under his trust, the probate court may, upon the application of such successor or of any person beneficially interested, order such delivery to be made, and has like power and authority for enforcing its order and for punishing any contempt of such order as is vested in the supreme judicial court.[1]

If, after the granting of letters of administration as of an intestate estate, a will of the deceased is duly proved and allowed, the first administration will be revoked.[2]

The guardian of an insane person or spendthrift may be discharged by the probate court on the application

---

the death, resignation, or removal of one of the trustees, the premises shall vest in the survivors, on the resignation of one trustee it was *held* that the trust estate vested in the surviving trustees   Ellis *v.* Boston, Hartford & Erie R R. Co , 107 Mass 1

One who undertakes to act as trustee of a particular fund for another, from whom he received it without compensation, with no beneficial interest in the fund, and with no agreement to act for any specified length of time, is entitled to be discharged whenever the execution of the trust becomes inconvenient to him   Bogle *v* Bogle, 3 Allen, 158

The removal of a guardian by a decree of the supreme judicial court terminates the guardianship, and the sending the case back to the probate court for further proceedings does not qualify the terminating effect of the removal. Willwerth *v* Leonard, 156 Mass 277. No method is provided in which, after a guardianship has ceased for any cause, the decree on which it was based may be annulled (ibid)

[1] R L c. 162, § 38   See Brooks *v.* Tobin, 135 Mass 69.
[2] R. L. c. 137, § 5.

of the ward, or otherwise, when it appears that such guardianship is no longer necessary.[1] Such application of the ward may be resisted by the guardian; and all reasonable expenses incurred by him in good faith for the purpose of a proper inquiry into the condition of the ward, will be allowed to him in the settlement of his guardianship account.[2]

The marriage of a female under guardianship as a minor deprives her guardian of all right to her custody and education, but not of his right to her property.[3]

APPEALS FROM DECREES MAKING REMOVALS.

[Revised Laws, c 162.]

"Sect. 20. A decree of a probate court removing an executor, administrator, guardian, or trustee, shall have effect, notwithstanding an appeal from such decree, until otherwise ordered by a justice of the supreme court of probate, and a decree of a justice of the supreme court of probate upon appeal affirming such decree, or ordering such removal when the same has been refused by the probate court, shall have effect, notwithstanding an appeal therefrom to the full court, until otherwise ordered by the full court. The probate court may, in either such case, appoint a successor to the person removed, and the person removed shall thereupon deliver all the property held by him as such executor, administrator, guardian, or trustee to such successor, who shall proceed in the performance of his duties in like manner as if no appeal had been taken; but if the decree of removal is reversed by the supreme judicial court, the powers of such successor

---

[1] R. L c 145, § 11
[2] Palmer v Palmer, 1 Chandler (N H), 448
[3] R. L c. 145, § 37

shall thereupon cease, and he shall forthwith deliver to his predecessor in the trust, or to such person as the court may order, all property of the estate in his hands." [1]

"SECT. 21. A decree of a probate court made in pursuance of the provisions of the preceding section shall have effect, notwithstanding an appeal therefrom, until otherwise determined by the appellate court."

"SECT. 22. After an appeal has been claimed from an order or decree referred to in the two preceding sections, and before such appeal has been finally determined, a justice of the supreme court of probate may suspend or modify such order or decree during the pendency of such appeal."

[1] Gray v. Parke, 155 Mass 437.

CHAPTER IX.

INVENTORIES, AND THE COLLECTION OF THE EFFECTS OF DECEASED PERSONS AND WARDS

THE bonds of executors, administrators, guardians, and trustees contain a condition that the party giving the bond shall return into the probate court a true inventory of all the estate that shall come to his possession or knowledge.[1] Exceptions to this rule are made in favor of executors or administrators with the will annexed who are residuary legatees, who elect to give a bond for the payment of the debts and legacies, and run their own risk as to the sufficiency of assets;[2] and in favor of a trustee appointed in

---

[1] An executor who receives no assets and files no inventory within three months of his appointment commits a breach of his bond by failing to file an inventory within a reasonable time after assets come to his hands, although the Pub. Stats. c 132, § 5 (now R L c. 139, § 5), provide for one inventory only, and for including assets thereafter received in the executor's account Forbes v. McHugh, 152 Mass 412

To entitle an administrator to defend upon the ground of insufficiency of assets, there must be an inventory filed and a settlement of his account in the probate court McKim v. Haley, 173 Mass. 112.

An agreement which is signed by the testator's heirs at law authorizing and requesting the executrix, who was the testator's widow, "to proceed in the administration of the estate without taking or filing an inventory thereof, and without rendering any account of such administration in probate court," is revocable, and, having been revoked, does not operate to release the sureties on her bond. Fuller v Wilbur, 170 Mass. 506

[2] R L c 149, § 2 Colwell v Alger, 5 Gray, 67, Collins v. Collins, 140 Mass 505; Jenkins v. Wood, 144 Mass 238.

place of a former trustee who has deceased or has been removed, or has resigned, if the court deems an inventory unnecessary.¹ Every executor, except one who gives bond under the provisions of section two of chapter one hundred and forty-nine of the Revised Laws, and every administrator is required to return an inventory within three months after his appointment;² and every guardian and trustee within such time as the court may direct.³ In case an inventory is not filed of an estate, any part of which is subject to a tax on collateral legacies and successions, the executor, administrator, or trustee neglecting or refusing to file such inventory is liable to a penalty of not more than one thousand dollars, to be recovered by the treasurer of the commonwealth by appropriate proceedings against such executor, administrator, or trustee.⁴

¹ R L c 147, § 7
² R L c 139, § 5, Forbes v McHugh, 152 Mass. 413.
³ R L. c 149, § 1, cl 7; Collins v Collins, 140 Mass 505, Bullard v Atty-Gen, 153 Mass 251; R. L c 149, § 1, cl. 6; M'Kim v Mann, 141 Mass. 508, Murray v Wood, 144 Mass. 197. An inventory of every estate, any part of which may be subject to a tax on collateral legacies and successions, shall be filed by the executor, administrator, or trustee within three months from his appointment and qualification In case such executor, administrator, or trustee neglects or refuses to file such inventory, he shall be liable to a penalty of not more than one thousand dollars. A copy of such inventory shall be sent by the register of the probate court in which such inventory is filed to the treasurer of the commonwealth within thirty days after the same is filed. R L. c. 15, §§ 9, 10.
⁴ R L c 15, § 9

Assets. — An administrator can recover property for which the intestate could not sue. Wall v. Provident Institution for Savings, 6 Allen, 320

The administrator of the insolvent estate of a deceased person may maintain a bill in equity, filed within two years after giving bond, to recover for the benefit of creditors, even if all their claims are otherwise barred by the special statute of limitations, property conveyed

The inventory is equally an advantage to the executor, or other trust officer, and to the heirs, creditors, or other

by the intestate in his lifetime in fraud of them, which, when recovered, will constitute new assets. Welsh v Welsh, 105 Mass 229.

A testator who gave a bond to convey real estate, and took from the obligee an obligation to pay the purchase-money, executed a deed, but died before the day of payment The executor received the purchase-money and delivered the deed It was *held* that the executor was bound to account for the money. Loring t Cunningham, 9 Cush 87

Salary voted to a person after his decease, and paid to his executor, is assets of the estate, to be accounted for by the executor Ibid.

Manure taken from the barnyard of a homestead and piled upon the land, is part of the realty, and does not go to the administrator of the owner Fay v Muzzey, 13 Gray, 53

Debts due the testator from the executor named in the will, and from a firm of which he is a member, are to be treated and accounted for as assets, although he and the firm were insolvent at the time when he accepted the trust Leland v. Felton, 1 Allen, 531.

A legacy in money, on the death of the legatee, vests in his personal representatives, and not in his heirs-at-law. Osgood v Foster, 5 Allen, 560.

Right of property in a trade secret is personalty Peabody v. Norfolk, 98 Mass 452

A promissory note taken by a deputy-sheriff in satisfaction of an execution, on his death goes to the creditor, and not to the deputy's administrator Childs v. Jordan, 106 Mass 321

The liability of a surety on the bond of an administratrix, who is himself appointed administrator *de bonis non* of the estate on her removal, constitutes a debt due from him to the estate, and is assets in his hands Choate v Thorndike, 138 Mass 371.

The proceeds of the certificate of a member of a beneficiary association who has insured his life for his own benefit will go, after his death, to his executor or administrator. Harding v. Littlehale, 150 Mass. 100 But where the certificate has been assigned to secure payment of a valid claim larger than the fund payable under the certificate, the equitable right of the assignee to the fund, upon the member's death, will prevail over the legal title of the administrator. Brierly v. Equitable Aid Union, 170 Mass 218.

An action on a certificate under seal of a benefit association can be brought only by the administrator of the certificate holder, and *not* by

persons interested in the estate. It is the basis upon which he is to make his accounts It shows the amount for which he is chargeable, and limits his responsibility, unless there are assets not appraised that come to his hands On the other hand, the heirs or other persons interested have, in the record of the inventory, the best evidence that can be had under the circumstances of the value of the estate in the hands of the trustee; and it furnishes them with essential evidence in case it becomes necessary to institute proceedings against him, on account of any misappropriation of the property or other maladministration.

The inventory should include all the real estate,[1] and all

the beneficiaries named in the certificate Flynn v. Mass Benefit Association, 152 Mass. 288; Burns v. United Workmen, 153 Mass 173, Clarke v. Schwarzenberg, 162 Mass. 98 But see R. L. c. 118, § 73, and Brown v. Greenfield Life Association, 172 Mass 498.

[1] It is not the duty of an administrator, at the request and for the benefit of the heirs of his intestate, to inventory, or institute proceedings to recover, certain real estate which once belonged to the intestate, but which has been set off on an execution issued against him on a judgment obtained by fraud Richards v. Sweetland, 6 Cush 324. Otherwise, when the proceeds of land fraudulently conveyed are needed for the payment of debts due from the estate Andrews v. Tucker, 7 Pick 250, Putney v Fletcher 148 Mass. 248 If there was any specific personal property in the hands of the testator belonging to others, which he held in trust or otherwise, it is not assets in the hands of his executors, but is to be held by the executors as the testator himself held it But if the testator has money or other property in his hands belonging to others, whether in trust or otherwise, and it has no ear-mark, and is not distinguishable from the mass of his own property, the party owning it must come in as a general creditor, and it falls within the description of assets of the executor Trecothick v Austin 4 Mason, 29, Johnson v. Ames, 11 Pick 173; Little v Chadwick, 151 Mass. 111, and cases cited. Whenever any of the real estate of a decedent shall so pass to another person as to become subject to the collateral succession tax, the executor, administrator, or trustee of the decedent shall inform the treasurer of the common-

the goods, chattels, rights, and credits belonging to the estate appraised.[1] All notes and accounts due to the estate should be described in the inventory. The appraisers may find it difficult to appraise a note or account, except as its face indicates its value, and for this reason many administrators deem it unnecessary to include either notes or accounts in their inventory, and consider it sufficient to charge themselves with the proceeds of the debts collected in their accounts of administration. This course, if pursued in good faith, can work no wrong, but it does not fulfil all the purposes of the law requiring an inventory to be made. The administrator, moreover, cannot be prejudiced by the mention of notes and accounts in the inventory, even if they prove to be worthless; for if they remain uncollected without his fault, a credit, corresponding in amount with the appraised value of the worthless debt, will be allowed him in his account.[2]

Orders for the Appraisal of Estates are issued by the probate court. The appraisers must be three suitable, disinterested persons;[3] but the judge or register may appoint only one appraiser if in his opinion the nature of the property makes it advisable so to do.[4] No clerk or other person employed in the office of the probate court can be an appraiser in any case within the jurisdiction of the court.[5]

---

wealth of the fact within six months after he has assumed the duties of his trust, or if the fact is not known to him within that time, within one month from the time when the fact becomes known to him. R. L. c. 15, § 11.

[1] Corn or other product of the soil, raised annually by cultivation, and in a proper state to be gathered, is personal estate, and goes to the executor on the death of the owner. Penhallow v. Dwight, 7 Mass. 34; Mulligan v. Newton, 16 Gray, 212; Cheshire Nat. Bank v. Jewett, 119 Mass. 241.

[2] R. L. c. 150, § 4.
[3] R. L. c. 139, § 6.
[4] R. L. c. 162, § 46.
[5] R. L. c. 164, § 25.

The authority of appraisers appointed by the probate court extends to the appraisal of property situated in any part of the state [1] The order of appraisal is usually issued on the day when the executor or other officer is appointed. Any disinterested justice of the peace may appoint appraisers of any part of the estate which may be in his county.[2]

Oath of Appraisers. — Before proceeding to appraise the estate, the appraisers must be sworn to the faithful discharge of their duties. The oath may be administered by any justice of the peace, and a certificate thereof must be indorsed on the order by the justice who administers the oath.

Return of the Inventory — The value of each parcel of real estate and of each article of personal property should be separately stated in the inventory. The blanks attached to the orders of appraisal indicate the form in which the return is to be made

If the deceased had been a member of a copartnership, and both partnership estate and separate estate have come to the possession of the executor, such partnership estate should be separately appraised, and returned in a separate list

The estates of two or more minors under guardianship of the same person should be returned in separate schedules, if the minors are interested in different property, or have unequal interests in the same property.

---

[1] Appraisers may be appointed to appraise such property as may be subject to the legacy tax for the purposes of said tax upon the application of the treasurer of the commonwealth or any person interested in the property The return of such appraiser may be accepted by the court, and if accepted, it is binding upon the person by whom the tax is to be paid and upon the commonwealth   R. L c. 15, § 16.

[2] R L c 139, § 6 The fees for the services of appraisers of estates of deceased persons shall be such as the court having jurisdiction of the case may deem to be just and reasonable   R L. c 204, § 23

The inventory, when completed by the appraisers, is delivered to the executor or other person having charge of the estate appraised, who returns it to the probate office for record. He is required to make oath that it is a true and perfect inventory of all the estate that has come to his possession or knowledge. The oath may be administered by the judge or register of probate, in or out of court, or by any justice of the peace; and a certificate of the oath must be made on the inventory by the officer who administers it, and recorded with the inventory.

An administrator is bound to return only one inventory. If additional property comes to his hands, he is bound to account for it, but not to inventory it.[1]

COLLECTION OF THE EFFECTS.

It is not only the duty of the executor or administrator to point out to the appraisers the estate that has come to his possession or knowledge, but to take such measures as may be necessary for the collection of debts due the deceased, and for the recovery of any money, goods, effects, or other estate in the fraudulent possession of other persons.[2] The statute provides a process for the

[1] Hooker v. Bancroft, 4 Pick. 50. See Forbes v McHugh, 152 Mass 413, and cases cited

[2] Gale v. Nickerson, 151 Mass. 428, Flynn v. Mass. Benefit Association, 152 Mass 288, Burns v. Order of United Workmen, 153 Mass 173 An administrator who has received letters of administration under the authority of another state, cannot prosecute or defend an action in the courts of this commonwealth by virtue of such letters of administration. Goodwin v Jones, 3 Mass. 514, Cassidy v Shimmin, 122 Mass 412

Replevin can be maintained by an administrator in his own name for personal property belonging to the estate, and attached, after his appointment, as the property of a third person Kent v. Bothwell, 152 Mass 311

If the payee of a promissory note dies before his right of action

discovery of facts, by an examination in the probate court, which may be advantageously used as a preliminary step to the institution of a suit for the recovery of property fraudulently withheld from the estate. The statute provides that —

"Upon complaint to a probate court by a person interested in the estate of a person deceased against a person who is suspected of having fraudulently received, concealed, embezzled, or conveyed away any property, real or personal, of the deceased, the court may cite such suspected person, though he is executor or administrator, to appear and be examined under oath, upon the matter of the complaint If the person so cited refuses to appear and to submit to examination, or to answer such interrogatories as may be lawfully propounded to him, the court may commit him to jail until he submits to the order of the court. The interrogatories and answers shall be in writing, signed by the party examined, and shall be filed in court."[1]

Like proceedings may be had upon complaint of a guardian, ward, creditor, or other person interested in the estate of a ward, or having claims thereto in expectancy as heir or otherwise, against any one suspected of having fraudulently concealed, embezzled, or conveyed away any of the estate of the ward. The suspected person may be cited though he is the guardian.[2]

The authority given to the probate court by the above

upon it is barred by the statute of limitations, his administrator may sue upon the note within two years after the granting of letters of administration to him Converse *v.* Johnson, 146 Mass. 20.

[1] R. L c 162, § 43, Sigourney *v.* Wetherell, 6 Met 558, and cases cited; Leavitt *v* Leavitt, 135 Mass 194 Dickey *v.* Taft, 175 Mass 4

[2] R. L. c. 145, § 38; Leavitt *v.* Leavitt, *supra*; Sherman *v* Brewer, 11 Gray, 210

provisions extends only to an examination for the purpose of discovery. No other power is given. The examination is not to be controlled by other evidence, nor can relief be directly granted upon it by any decree of the probate court. The process can only result in a disclosure of facts to serve as the basis of other proceedings.[1]

If an executor or administrator unreasonably delays to raise money by collecting the debts and effects of the deceased, or by selling the real estate if necessary, or if he neglects to use in the payment of debts what money he has in his hands, and in consequence of such delay or neglect the estate of the deceased is taken on execution by his creditors, such delay or neglect shall be deemed to be unfaithful administration, and the executor or administrator shall be liable in an action on his bond for all damages occasioned thereby [2]

---

[1] Selectmen of Boston *v* Boylston, 4 Mass 322 The lapse of thirty years since the transactions inquired into, is no bar to such examination O'Dee *v* McCrate, 7 Greenl 467.

In a complaint to the judge of probate, for embezzlement of the estate of a person deceased, the complainant having described himself as "administrator and creditor,' and it appearing that he was not entitled to act as administrator, it was *held*, that the words "administrator and" were material, and could not be rejected as surplusage. Arnold *v* Sabin, 4 Cush 46; Wilson *v.* Leishman, 12 Met. 320

The court may permit the party cited to appear and be assisted by counsel in making answers to the interrogatories. Martin *v* Clapp, 99 Mass 470

[2] Pub Stats. c. 133, § 2 This section of the Public Statutes was omitted by the compilers of the Revised Laws as superfluous

CHAPTER X.

ALLOWANCES TO WIDOWS, MINOR CHILDREN, AND OTHERS

TO WIDOWS AND MINOR CHILDREN.

"The articles of apparel and the ornaments of the widow and minor children of a deceased person shall belong to them respectively. The widow may remain in the house of her husband for not more than six months next succeeding his death without being chargeable for rent.

"Such parts of the personal property of a deceased person as the probate court, having regard to all the circumstances of the case, may allow as necessaries to his widow, for herself and for his family under her care, or, if there is no widow, to his minor children, not exceeding one hundred dollars to any child, and also such provisions and other articles as are necessary for the reasonable sustenance of his family, and the use of his house and of the furniture therein, for six months next succeeding his death, shall not be taken as assets for the payment of debts, legacies, or charges of administration. After exhausting the personal property, real property may be sold to provide the amount of allowance decreed, in the same manner as it is sold for the payment of debts, if a decree authorizing such sale is made, upon the petition of any party in interest, within two years after the approval of the bond of the executor or administrator.[1]

---

[1] R L c 140, §§ 1, 2; Choate v Jacobs, 136 Mass 298; Dale v. Hanover Natl Bank. 155 Mass 141. Lisk v Lisk, ibid. 153

A widow has the right to expend money belonging to her husband's

The statute thus makes the apparel and ornaments of the widow and minor children of a deceased person their absolute property, and secures to them a home in his house for six months after his death, with such provisions and other articles as are necessary for their reasonable sustenance; and in addition to this statute allowance for the six months, the widow or minor children of the deceased, whether he was a housekeeper or not, are entitled to an allowance for necessaries, when their circumstances require it, from his personal estate. The power of the probate court to make allowances is not limited to intestate estates. An allowance may be granted, although provision was made for the widow by her husband's will in lieu of dower and accepted by her, and although the executor, being also residuary legatee, has given bond as such to pay the debts and legacies.[1] A marriage contract by which she released all claim to her husband's estate is no defence to her petition for an allowance[2] And the widow may have a second allowance at any time before the personal estate is exhausted.[3] A delay of over two years after the appointment

estate, which is in her possession at the time of his death, in the purchase of necessaries for her reasonable support within forty days after his death Fellows v. Smith, 130 Mass. 376

[1] Williams v Williams, 5 Gray, 24

A widow may be entitled to an allowance though she lived apart from her husband, rendering him no services and supporting herself, for several years previous to his death. Slack v. Slack, 123 Mass. 443.

[2] Blackinton v. Blackinton, 110 Mass. 461, Paine v Hollister, 139 Mass 145 Wentworth v Wentworth, 69 Maine, 247, Nathan v. Nathan, 166 Mass 294

[3] Hale v. Hale, 1 Gray, 518; Pettee v. Wilmarth, 5 Allen, 145 But after she has been paid the first allowance, and all the personal estate has been exhausted in the payment of debts and charges of administration, though within one year from the appointment of the administrator, no further allowance can be made to her, nor can she

of the administrator in filing a petition for a widow's allowance is not fatal to the widow's right[1]

The amount to be allowed the widow is determined by the court in its discretion.[2] There is no rule to regulate this discretion, and no rule could be framed to meet the great variety of circumstances upon which the allowance depends The amount is not ordinarily restricted to a sum merely sufficient for the necessaries of life, nor on the other hand is it to be increased to an extent inconsistent with the object of the allowance. The allowance is intended to furnish the widow, when she is left in distress by the decease of her husband, with necessaries for her support for a reasonable time, within which she can make arrangements for her own support.[3] It is not intended to furnish her with a capital for business purposes, or to establish a fund from which a permanent income may be derived. Any and all facts bearing upon the question of her necessities are to be considered, such as the amount of her separate property and means;[4] the fact that she is accustomed to earn her own support, or the contrary; that she is disabled by age, or otherwise; the number of her children and the fact of their tender age, etc.

The value of the estate, as shown by the inventory and

have leave to enter an appeal from the decree making the first allowance Hale v Hale, 1 Gray, 518.

[1] Lisk v Lisk, 155 Mass 153

[2] The question whether the allowance to the widow should have been made by the probate court, is not open in a hearing upon the administrator's account Newell v. West, 149 Mass. 521.

[3] The purpose of a widow's allowance is merely to provide for her necessities and those of her minor children for a short time, until they have an opportunity to adjust themselves to their new situation. Dale v Hanover Natl Bank, 155 Mass. 141, Lisk v. Lisk, ibid. 153, Chase v Webster, 168 Mass. 228.

[4] Hollenbeck v. Pixley, 3 Gray, 521.

by additional evidence, is to be regarded. It may be that the personal estate has been materially diminished by gifts made by the deceased, shortly before his death, to his heirs and others, while the new duties and obligations imposed upon the widow are not lessened by such diminution. In such case, the fact that such gifts have been made may be important to show the actual condition of the estate and of the family But facts as to the sum contributed by her on her marriage to her husband's estate. or as to the value of the services rendered to him and his family, while they may show that she is equitably entitled to a considerable share of his estate, do not bear upon the question actually at issue, the allowance not being made to correct an injustice, but to provide for her necessities.[1]

The whole of the personal estate may be given to the widow as an allowance, when the amount is not so great as to be extravagant[2] She is entitled to a reasonable allowance, even if the estate is insolvent;[3] and she is entitled to the amount of her allowance in priority to the payment of her husband's debts, expenses of his last sickness and funeral, and the charges of settling his estate.[4] An allowance may be made from the assets of a partnership in the hands of a surviving partner at the time of his death. although the assets are not sufficient to pay the partnership creditors in full[5]

Upon the petition of the widow or children, or either of

[1] Washburn v. Washburn, 10 Pick 374, Adams v Adams, 10 Met. 170, Hollenbeck v Pixley, 3 Gray, 525; Dale v. Hanover Natl. Bank, 155 Mass. 141.

[2] Brazer v Dean, 15 Mass 183, Bush v Clark, 127 Mass. 114.

[3] Dale v. Hanover Natl Bank, *supra*.

[4] Kingsbury v Wilmarth, 2 Allen, 310.

[5] Bush v Clark, *supra*

them, the probate court may, after notice to all parties interested, make a reasonable allowance out of the income of the estate, real or personal, in the hands of a *special* administrator appointed on account of the pendency of a suit concerning the probate of a will, as an advancement for their support, not exceeding such portion of the income of the estate as they would be entitled to whether the will is finally proved or not. An appeal from the decree concerning such allowance will not prevent the payment of the sum decreed if the petitioner gives bond to the special administrator, with sureties approved by the court, conditioned to repay the same if the decree is reversed.[1]

The allowance cannot be made from the proceeds of real estate sold for the payment of debts; for the surplus of such proceeds, if any, is required by statute to be treated as real estate, and disposed of among the same persons and in the same proportions as the real estate would have been if it had not been sold.[2] But since the Revised Laws took effect, the probate court may authorize the sale of real estate, after the personal property has been exhausted, to provide the amount of allowance decreed

The petition for an allowance to the widow or minor children sets forth the fact that there are personal assets belonging to the estate in question from which she or they are entitled to an allowance, and prays that an allowance may be decreed accordingly When the next of kin of the deceased are other than his minor children, notice of the

---

[1] R L c 137, § 12, Chandler *v.* R. R. Commissioners, 141 Mass. 211

' Support" includes not merely board, but everything necessary to proper maintenance Gould *v.* Lawrence, 160 Mass. 232.

[2] R L c. 148, § 9, Hale *v.* Hale, 1 Gray, 523, Haven *v* Foster, 9 Pick 130.

widow's petition is usually given to parties interested before a decree is made [1]

The widow, or any person aggrieved by the decree of the court upon her petition, may appeal to the supreme court of probate, [2] and the appeal, except when the allowance is made from the income of the estate in the hands of a special administrator, stays all proceedings under the decree until the matter is determined by the supreme court of probate.

The allowance to the widow for necessaries is not to be confounded with her distributive share of her husband's estate. That is a vested right of property which she takes by a title as high as that of a child or other next of kin; and it goes to her personal representative.[3] But the provision for necessities is temporary in its nature and personal in its character, and confers no absolute or contingent right of property which can survive her. If, therefore, an appeal is taken from a decree making an allowance, and she dies before the appeal is entered in the appellate court, all further proceedings are stayed; and the decree of the probate court, which was vacated by the appeal, cannot be revived.[4]

---

[1] If an allowance is made without notice to the parties interested, the supreme court of probate, in its discretion, will allow an appeal, after the expiration of thirty days, upon a petition filed under Pub. Stats. c 156, § 9 (now R L c 162, § 13), although by the statute no notice is required except in cases in which special administration is granted. Wright v. Wright, 13 Allen, 207.

[2] And the appellate court will not inquire into the probate discretion. Litchfield v. Cudworth, 15 Pick 23, Ward v. Ward, ibid 511

A probate judge has no authority to revoke a decree passed by himself, making an allowance to a widow out of her husband's estate, and to pass a new decree allowing her a less sum. Pettee v. Wilmarth, 5 Allen, 144, Marsh v. McKenzie, 99 Mass. 67, Richardson v. Hazelton, 101 Mass. 108

[3] Foster v. Fifield, 20 Pick 67; Proctor v. Clark, 154 Mass 49

[4] Adams v. Adams, 10 Met. 170; Drew v. Gordon, 13 Allen, 120.

A widow's claim for an allowance made to her may be enforced, after demand and refusal, by an action brought by her against the executor.[1]

ALLOWANCES TO WIVES OF INSANE PERSONS UNDER GUARDIANSHIP.

The statute provides that the probate court for the county in which the guardian of an insane person has been appointed, may make an allowance out of the estate of such insane person for the support of his wife, to be paid to her by the guardian during the continuance of the guardianship in such manner as the court shall direct.[2]

The allowance under this provision is not limited merely to necessaries for the wife. It is intended for her support, and the amount of the allowance must be proportioned to the condition and circumstances of the husband. It should be sufficient for her support in a manner consistent with the prudent use and management of his estate.

The order of the court fixing the amount of the allowance may also direct the guardian as to the time and manner of its payment to the wife

On the application of the guardian of an insane person, or of a child or the guardian of a child of an insane person, and after notice to all persons interested, the probate court may authorize and require the guardian of such insane person to apply such portion as the court may direct of the income of the ward, which is not required for his maintenance and support, to the maintenance and support of any child of the ward.[3]

[1] Drew v Gordon, 13 Allen, 120; Cobb v. Kempton, 154 Mass 269.
[2] R. L. c 145, § 31.
[3] Ibid. § 30.

CHAPTER XI.

SALE OF PERSONAL ESTATE BY EXECUTORS AND OTHERS — SALES AND INVESTMENTS BY GUARDIANS AND TRUSTEES — TEMPORARY INVESTMENTS BY EXECUTORS

The probate court, after the return of the inventory, on application made by an executor or administrator, or by any person interested in the estate, may order a part or the whole of the personal estate of the deceased to be sold by public auction or private sale, as shall be deemed most for the interest of all concerned.[1] The executor or administrator accounts for the property at a price for which it sells.

The personal property is generally sold by executors and administrators without any previous order of the court; and if they act in good faith and with sound discretion, the interests of no person concerned can be injuriously affected by such proceeding.[2] The subsequent approval of the court is practically equivalent to a previous order. The executor or administrator, however, makes a sale without first obtaining license at his own risk, and when it is probable that the property cannot be sold for its appraised value, he should apply to the court

[1] So provided by Pub Stats c 133, § 3, which was omitted as superfluous by the compilers of the Revised Laws, Jennison v Hapgood, 10 Pick 77

[2] R. L c 150, § 4 A trustee under a will filed in the probate court an inventory of certain shares of stock He afterwards misappropriated the stock It was *held* that he should be charged with the valuation in the inventory. McKim v Hibbard, 142 Mass. 422

for leave to make the sale, and thereby limit his responsibility to account.[1]

Mortgages of land and the debt secured thereby are personal estate in the hands of the executor or administrator, and so are lands taken on execution for a debt due the testator or intestate; and real estate so held in mortgage or taken on execution may be sold, subject to the right of redemption, at any time before the right of redemption is foreclosed, in the same manner as personal estate of a person deceased.[2]

The probate court upon petition of the executor or administrator, and after such notice thereof to the parties interested as the court may order, may, for the purpose of closing the settlement of an estate, license the executor or administrator to sell and assign any outstanding debts and claims which cannot be collected without inconvenient delay.[3] The petition for leave to make such sale or assignment should set forth the nature of the debt or claim to be sold, and the reasons for the proposed sale. The sale is required to be conducted in such manner as the court having regard, as far as it may be thought advisable or prudent, to the law in relation to sales of real estate by executors and administrators, shall order.[4] This provision

[1] Denholm v McKay, 148 Mass. 434.

[2] R. L c 150, §§ 7, 9, 10

[3] So provided in Pub Stats c 133, § 4, omitted as superfluous by the compilers of the Revised Laws.

[4] Suits for the recovery of debts or claims so sold and assigned are brought in the name of the purchasers The fact of the sale must be set forth in the writ or declaration, and the defendant may avail himself of any matter of defence of which he could have availed himself in a suit brought by the executor or administrator Costs are recovered by or against the plaintiff, and the executor or administrator is not liable therefor Such a suit, if brought upon a witnessed promissory note, is not barred by the general statute of limitations, if it

for the sale of debts and claims does not deprive executors and administrators of the right to transfer at pleasure deeds of mortgage, and the real estate conveyed and the debts secured thereby

Probate courts may authorize executors, administrators, guardians, and trustees to release and discharge, upon such terms and conditions as appear proper, any vested, contingent, or possible right or interest belonging to the persons or estates by them represented in or to any real or personal estate, whenever it appears to be for the benefit of the persons or estates. Notice of the application in such cases must be given as in cases of sale of real estate [1]

"An executor, administrator, guardian, or trustee duly appointed in another state or in a foreign country, and duly qualified and acting, who may be entitled to any personal property situated in this commonwealth, may file an authenticated copy of his appointment in the probate court for any county in which there is real property of his trust or, if there is no such real property, in any county in which there is personal property of his trust, and may upon petition to said court, after such notice to the treasurer and receiver-general, creditors, and all persons interested, as said court may order, be licensed to receive or sell by public or private sale upon such terms and to such person or persons as he shall think fit, or otherwise to dispose of, and to transfer and convey, shares in a corporation or other personal property, if the court finds that there is no execu-

could be maintained by the executor or administrator. R L c. 173, § 5.

An administrator of a mortgagee intestate may sell a mortgage not foreclosed without license from the probate court. Burt v Ricker, 6 Allen, 78. Before 1849 such a license was necessary *Ex parte* Blair, 13 Met 126

[1] R. L. c. 148, § 4.

tor, administrator, guardian, or trustee appointed in this commonwealth who is authorized so to receive and dispose of such shares or estate, and that such foreign executor, administrator, guardian, or trustee will be liable, upon and after such receipt or sale, to account for such shares or estate, or for the proceeds thereof, in the state or country in which he was appointed; and that no person resident in this commonwealth and interested as a creditor or otherwise objects to the granting of such license, or appears to be prejudiced thereby; but no such license shall be granted to a foreign executor or administrator until the expiration of six months after the death of his testator or intestate." [1]

SALES AND INVESTMENT BY GUARDIANS.

The probate court may, upon the application of a guardian, or of any person interested in the estate of a ward, and after notice to all other persons interested, authorize or require the guardian to sell and transfer any personal property held by him as guardian and to invest the proceeds thereof and all other moneys in his hands in such manner as may be most for the interest of all concerned. Said court may make such further order and give such directions as the case may require for the management, investment, and disposition of the estate in the hands of the guardian.[2]

SALES AND INVESTMENT OF ESTATES HELD IN TRUST

" If the sale and conveyance, transfer or exchange, of any real or personal property held in trust, or the partition of any such real property held in common and undivided,

---

[1] R. L. c. 148, § 3.
[2] R L c 145, § 35, Kavanaugh *v.* Kavanaugh, 146 Mass. 42, May *v.* Skinner, 149 Mass 380. The guardian of an insane person may be authorized to invest all the property of his ward in the purchase of an annuity on his life. Hooper, Petitioner, 120 Mass 102.

appears to be necessary or expedient, the supreme judicial court, the superior court, or the probate court, may, upon petition of a trustee or other party interested, after notice and other proceedings as hereinafter required, order such sale and conveyance, transfer, exchange, or partition to be made, and the investment, re-investment, and application of the proceeds of such sale in such manner as will best effect the objects of the trust [1]

"If the court, upon proceedings under the provisions of the preceding section, finds that the estate which is the subject of the petition may be held in trust for, or that a remainder or contingent interest therein may be limited over to, persons not ascertained or not in being, notice shall be given in such manner as the court may order to all persons who are or may become interested in such estate, and to all persons whose issue, not then in being, may become so interested; and the court shall of its own motion in every such case appoint a suitable person to appear and act therein as the next friend of all persons not ascertained or not in being, who are or may become interested in such

---

[1] R. L. c. 147, § 15, If a trustee conveys trust property to himself, the conveyance may be avoided by a part only of the *cestuis que trust*. Morse v. Hill, 136 Mass. 60.

An executor acting as trustee under a will has the power to sell the property held in trust. Jones v. Atchison, Topeka & Santa Fé Railroad, 150 Mass. 304

It is an improper investment of a trust fund for the trustee to buy of himself with it a mortgage of real estate which is worth much less than the amount of the fund so invested, and the facts that subsequently the *cestui que trust* authorized the trustee to bid off the mortgaged property for him at a sale of the same, and took a conveyance of it, cannot avail the trustee, if the *cestui que trust* acted solely on the false representations of the trustee as to the value of the property, and on learning the truth, promptly demanded that he should take back the property and account for the sum invested in the mortgage Nichols, Appellant, 157 Mass. 20.

estate, and, the provisions of sections twenty-three and twenty-four of chapter one hundred and forty-five" [of the Revised Laws, relative to appointment of guardian *ad litem* and next friend, and to the payment of the expenses and compensation of a guardian *ad litem* or next friend, including the compensation of his counsel] "which are not inconsistent herewith shall apply to such appointment. A conveyance or transfer made after such notice and proceeding shall be conclusive upon all persons for whom such guardian *ad litem* or next friend was appointed "[1] The trustee, when not himself the petitioner, must be made a party to the proceedings by notice.

Under these provisions of the statute, the trustee, in case of a difference of opinion between him and the persons interested in the estate in regard to the disposition to be made of the property in his hands, may protect himself by obtaining the direction of the court. And if the trustee should neglect to apply for the direction of the court, any person interested in the trust estate may make the application. It may happen that some particular disposition of the funds may be unsafe or improper, and such as the courts would not have sanctioned on a previous application, and yet it may not be such as to make the trustee liable as for misconduct in the discharge of his trust. In such a case, the loss or damage that would otherwise result may be prevented by an application to the court on the part of some person interested in the estate.

The application, whether made by the trustee or by a

[1] R. L. c. 147, § 16, Boston Safe Deposit & Trust Co *v* Mixter, 146 Mass 105; Dexter *v* Cotting, 149 Mass 95. A notice of a sale of a trust estate addressed to the "heirs at law, next of kin, and all other persons interested" is sufficient. Boston Safe Deposit & Trust Co *v* Mixter, *supra*.

person interested in the estate, should state all the facts of the particular case, and pray for the direction of the court.

If a person who is seised or possessed of real or personal property, or of an interest therein, upon a trust, express or implied, is under the age of twenty-one years, insane, out of the commonwealth, or not amenable to the process of any court therein which has equity powers, and when in the opinion of the supreme judicial court, the superior court, or of a probate court it is fit that a sale should be made of such property or of an interest therein, or that a conveyance or transfer should be made thereof in order to carry into effect the objects of the trust, the court may order such sale, conveyance, or transfer to be made, and may appoint a suitable person in the place of such trustee to sell, convey, or transfer the same in such manner as it may require. If a person so seised or possessed of an estate, or entitled thereto upon a trust, is within the jurisdiction of the court, he or his guardian may be ordered to make such conveyances as the court orders.[1]

TEMPORARY INVESTMENTS BY EXECUTORS AND ADMINISTRATORS

A probate court may, upon application of a person interested in an estate in process of settlement in such court, direct the temporary investment of the money belonging

[1] R L c 147, § 17; Felch v Hooper, 119 Mass 52 See McCann v. Randall, 147 Mass 98, Wilson v Wilson-Martin Fire Alarm Co, 151 Mass. 515

A foreign corporation having its usual place of business in this commonwealth is not within the purview of this statute Desper v Continental Water Meter Co., 137 Mass 252 Nor is a non-resident who has agreed to purchase land in this commonwealth and has not been served with process therein. Merrill v. Beckwith, 163 Mass 503.

to such estate in securities to be approved by the judge; or may authorize the same to be deposited in any bank or institution in the commonwealth which is empowered to receive such deposits, upon such interest as said bank or institution may agree to pay.[1]

[1] R. L. c. 162, § 39.

CHAPTER XII.

NOTICE OF THE APPOINTMENT OF EXECUTORS, ETC, AND PAYMENT OF DEBTS AND LEGACIES

THE statute provides that " an executor or administrator shall, within three months after giving bond for the discharge of his trust, cause notice of his appointment to be posted in two or more public places in the city or town in which the deceased last dwelt, or he may be required by the probate court to give notice by publication in some newspaper, or in such other manner as the court may order "[1] The letter testamentary or of administration, issued to the executor or administrator, directs the manner in which the notice is to be given in each case. A strict compliance with the terms of the order is necessary, in connection with the payment of debts, to protect the interests of the heirs or devisees as well as of the executor or administrator.[2] Unless the notice is given, the statute limiting the time with which suits may be brought against the executor or administrator will not apply.

The notice having been given, the statute provides a sure and convenient mode of perpetuating evidence of the fact.

[1] R L c. 139, § 1. Any daily or weekly periodical devoted exclusively to legal news which has been published in the commonwealth for six consecutive months, shall be deemed a newspaper for the insertion of legal notices required by law, if the publication of such notice in such periodical is ordered by the court. R. L c 8, § 5, cl 13.

[2] An executor's notice is sufficient, though signed by him as "administrator," and he describes himself therein as "duly appointed administrator." Finney v. Barnes, 97 Mass. 401.

An affidavit of the executor or administrator, or of the person employed by him to give such notice, being made before the judge or a justice of the peace, and filed and recorded with a copy of the notice in the probate office, is made evidence by statute of the time, place, and manner in which the notice was given.[1] The fact that notice was duly given may be proved whenever it becomes material by other evidence;[2] but questions as to the fact of notice may not be raised until after the lapse of several years, when it may be difficult and perhaps impossible for the executor or administrator to show his compliance with the order of the court by any of the ordinary means of proof. The affidavit should therefore be made and recorded in every case.[3]

If by accident or mistake notice is not given, or the evidence is not so perpetuated, the probate court, on the petition of the executor or administrator, may order such notice to be given at any time afterwards; in which case the periods of time limited for the commencement of actions against executors and administrators and for other purposes, which run from the time of their giving bond, shall run from the time of passing such order. And no such order will exempt the executor or administrator from any liability for damages incurred by reason of his omission to give notice within the three months.[4]

[1] R. L. c. 139, § 2, c. 146, § 15.
[2] Estes v. Wilkes, 16 Gray, 363. See Hudson v. Hulbert, 15 Pick. 423.
[3] The fact that the notice has been given as ordered may be proved by the affidavit of persons other than the executor or administrator, or the person employed by him to give such notice, by permission of the probate court upon satisfactory evidence that the notice was given as ordered. R. L. c. 139, § 2, c. 146, § 15.
[4] R. L. c. 139, §§ 3, 4.

In cases when executors, administrators, guardians, or trustees, or

If an executor, administrator, guardian, or trustee, at the time of his appointment resides out of the commonwealth, he is required to appoint in writing an agent residing here upon whom service of legal process against him as such executor can be made, and he will not be entitled to receive his letters of appointment as executor until he has appointed an agent. Such appointment must be in writing, and filed in the registry of probate; and in publishing notice of his own appointment the executor must state the name and address of his agent. If an executor removes from the commonwealth, he must appoint an agent in like manner; and if an agent dies or removes from the commonwealth before the final settlement of the estate, another like appointment must be made. The powers of an agent so appointed cannot be revoked until the final settlement of the estate, unless another like agent is appointed, and such appointment filed in the registry of probate. Neglect or refusal on the part of an executor to comply with these requirements may be deemed good cause for his removal, and the service of any legal process upon such agent shall be of the same legal effect as if made upon his principal when in the commonwealth.[1]

the persons employed by them to give notice of appointment, or notice of sale of real estate, have failed to file in the probate court affidavit of such notice, and such affidavit cannot be obtained, the probate court may, upon petition of any person interested in real estate, the title to which may be affected thereby, setting forth the particular failure complained of, and averring that the affidavit cannot now be obtained, order notice by publication to creditors of, and others interested in, the estate in the settlement of which the failure complained of occurred

Upon return of such notice, and after hearing, if the court is satisfied that notice was in fact given, it may make a decree that such notice was in fact given. R L c 148, § 26

[1] R. L. c. 139, § 8, c. 145, § 42, c. 147, § 14, c. 163, § 53.

PAYMENT OF DEBTS.

Limitation of Actions against Executors and Administrators — No executor or administrator, after having given notice of his appointment, as required by law, can be held to answer to the suit of any creditor of the deceased, unless it is commenced within two years from the time of his giving bond,[1] except when new assets come to his

[1] In computing the two years, the day on which the bond is given is to be excluded. Paul *v.* Stone, 112 Mass. 27

An executor is not liable as such, after the expiration of two years from the time of his giving bond, to an action on a covenant of warranty in a deed from his testator, although the covenant is not broken until after the expiration of two years; and although the executor is residuary legatee, and has given bond for the payment of debts and legacies, and takes the assets to himself without filing an inventory. Holden *v.* Fletcher, 6 Cush. 235.

A bond without surety approved by the probate court, without notice to creditors, is not such a bond as the statutes require, and the statute limitation will not apply. Abercrombie *v.* Sheldon, 8 Allen, 532.

A collector of taxes cannot maintain an action after the two years have expired. Rich *v.* Tuckerman 121 Mass 222; Dallinger *v.* Davis, 149 Mass. 63.

The operation of this statute is not suspended by the statute provisions relating to the insolvent estates of deceased persons. Aiken *v.* Morse, 104 Mass 277, Blanchard *v.* Allen, 116 Mass 447.

Leaving claims with the register of probate and his indorsement thereon that they were presented for allowance within two years from the filing of the administrator's bond, is equivalent to beginning suit, and avoids the bar of the statute of limitations. Robinson *v.* Robinson, 173 Mass 233.

An action on a decree of the probate court for the payment of a balance due from the estate of a deceased guardian to his ward is barred in two years from the appointment of the guardian's administrator, although the decree was not obtained until the two years had expired. Bemis *v.* Bemis, 13 Gray, 559

A creditor who recovers a judgment against an executor on an action brought within the two years, cannot bring an action upon the

hands after the expiration of the two years, in which case he is liable to an action if brought within one year after judgment after the expiration of the two years, although the executor has given bond to pay debts and legacies. Jenkins v. Wood, 134 Mass. 115. Nor will an action lie on such judgment against the executor personally. Jenkins v. Wood, 140 Mass. 66.

If the supreme judicial court, upon a bill in equity filed by a creditor whose claim has not been prosecuted within the two years, is of opinion that justice and equity require it, and that such creditor is not chargeable with culpable neglect in not prosecuting his claim within the time limited, it may give him judgment for the amount of his claim against the estate of the deceased person, but such judgment will not affect any payment or distribution made before the filing of such bill. R. L. c. 141, § 10; Knight v. Cunningham, 160 Mass. 580; Ewing v. King, 169 Mass. 97. Ignorance of the statute limitation will not relieve the creditor from the imputation of culpable neglect. Jenney v. Wilcox, 9 Allen, 245. The rights of creditors to collect their demands cannot be tried on a bill in equity brought by the executor to obtain the instructions of the court. Bradford v. Forbes, ibid 365. Where the creditor lived out of the state, and was assured by the executors that no further legal proceedings on her part were necessary, and she neglected to prosecute within the two years, it was *held* that the bill in equity could not be maintained. Wells v. Child, 12 Allen, 333. Nor is a creditor entitled to relief under R. L. c. 141, § 10, on the ground that he refrained from bringing suit at the suggestion of the administrator, relying on certain statements made in good faith by the administrator. Powow River National Bank v. Abbott, 179 Mass. 336. A creditor cannot maintain his bill on the ground that he is an alien residing in a foreign country, and never knew of the decease of the debtor or the appointment of the administrator until after the two years had expired. Sykes v. Meacham, 103 Mass. 285. And see Waltham Bank v. Wright, 8 Allen 121; Prentice v. Dehon, 10 Allen, 353; Richards v. Child, 98 Mass. 284; Spelman v. Talbot, 123 Mass. 489; Brooks v. Rayner, 127 Mass. 268; Grow v. Dobbins, 128 Mass. 271; Hammond v. Granger, 128 Mass. 275.

An executor who holds money under a will for the purpose of keeping a cemetery lot of the testator in a suitable condition, may be ordered by the judge of probate to deposit such money in a savings-bank, in perpetual trust, for the uses mentioned in the will. Gates v. White, 139 Mass. 353; Green v. Hogan, 153 Mass. 466.

A tax assessed on the personalty of a deceased person to his

the creditor has notice of the receipt of such new assets, and within two years after they are actually received.[1]

executor is the debt of the latter, and so an action to recover it is not barred by the lapse of two years from the notice of the executor's appointment Dallinger *i* Davis, 149 Mass 62.

If the payee of a note dies before his right of action on it is barred, his administrator may maintain an action on the note against the administrator of the maker of the note, although the action is not brought until more than two years after the plaintiff's appointment as administrator Converse *v.* Johnson, 146 Mass. 20

A decree of the probate court allowing distribution of all the personal estate of a deceased person before the end of the two years of administration is void as to creditors prosecuting their claims within this period, whether they have notice of it or not. Browne *v* Doolittle, 151 Mass 595, Newell *v* Peaslee, 151 Mass 601

A note given to a third person by a husband to secure the payment of money borrowed by him from his wife, although assigned to the wife during the husband's lifetime, is after his death a valid debt against his estate, and may be enforced Spooner *v* Spooner, 155 Mass 52

Where the intestate's shares in a corporation are valuable property, and liable to an assessment, it may be the duty of the administrator to pay the assessment. Ripley *v* Sampson, 10 Pick 371.

An administrator may not pay a note secured by mortgage given him by the intestate if it is more than six years overdue He is left to his rights as mortgagee Grinnell *v* Baxter, 17 Pick. 381

An administrator who, after representing the estate of his intestate insolvent, sells real estate pursuant to a license from the probate court, may apply the proceeds of such sale to the payment in full of a debt secured by mortgage on said real estate duly recorded, but previously unknown to him and the purchaser Church *v.* Savage, 7 Cush 440, Morton *v.* Hall, 118 Mass 511

An administrator who, by verbal agreement, has induced the creditors of an estate not to begin actions against the estate within two

---

[1] R L c 141, §§ 9. 10, 11, Attorney-General *v* Brigham, 142 Mass 249; Morey *v* American Loan and Trust Co , 149 Mass. 253 The avails of real estate sold by an administrator for payment of debts after the expiration of the two years are not new assets. Chenery *v* Webster, 8 Allen, 76; Alden *v* Stebbins, 99 Mass 616; Aiken *v.* Morse, 104 Mass 280, Gould *v.* Camp, 157 Mass 358.

And if an action seasonably commenced fails of a sufficient service or return by unavoidable accident, or when the writ in such action is abated or defeated for a defect in its form, or by a mistake in the form of the proceeding, or when after verdict for the plaintiff judgment is arrested; or if a judgment for the plaintiff is reversed on a writ of error, — the plaintiff may commence a new action for the same cause at any time within one year after the abatement or other determination of the original suit, or after the reversal of the judgment therein.[1]

years, cannot be required to set up the statute of frauds in personal actions against him on his promises. Ames v. Jackson, 115 Mass. 508.

A bill in equity, brought by a bank against the administrator of an estate represented insolvent, seeking to have the proceeds of a sale of a seat in the Boston Stock Exchange charged with an express trust by reason of an assignment of the seat as collateral for certain notes made by the intestate, is not barred by the short statute of limitations, although the bill was brought more than two years after the appointment of the administrator, and although the right of the plaintiff to bring suit upon the notes or to prove it as a debt of the intestate before the commissioners appointed when the estate was represented insolvent, is barred. Nashua Savings Bank v. Abbott, Administrator, 181 Mass —— (63 N E Rep 1058).

The claim of an executor, having the right to retain estate assets sufficient to pay a debt due him, is not subject to or barred by R. L. c 136, § 9, providing that no executor shall be held to answer any suit brought by a creditor of the testate unless commenced within two years from the giving of the executor's bond, though the estate is insolvent and the executor has failed to present his claim to the court, or though he has not filed a statement of his claim as required by

---

[1] R L c 141, § 12; Taft v. Stow, 174 Mass 171. In an action brought against an administrator in which judgment is recovered against him, two executions should be issued, one against the estate of his intestate for the damage only, and the other for the costs against the administrator personally. Look v. Luce, 136 Mass 249.

Special administrators are not liable to actions by any creditor of the deceased; and the time of limitation for all suits against the estate begins to run after the issue of letters testamentary or of administration in the usual form, in like manner as if such special administration had not been granted; but if an appeal is taken from the decree of the probate court appointing an executor or administrator, the time shall run in like manner and subject to the same conditions, if the decree is affirmed from the time of the affirmation if the bond has been filed, and if not, from the date of the filing of the bond; if the decree is reversed, from the time when an appointment is finally made or affirmed and the bond is filed.[1]

In the case of a public administrator who has given a general bond covering all estates on which administration is granted to him, the limitation begins to run, as to each estate, from the date of letters of administration.[2]

A new administrator appointed on the death, resignation, or removal of an executor or administrator, is liable to the actions of creditors for two years after

section 6 in case his claim is disputed. Brown *v.* Greene, 181 Mass —— (63 N E Rep. 2)

A debtor of the testator, when sued by the executor for the amount of the debt, cannot set off a debt due him from the testator which was not proved against the estate before the two years had expired. Tyler *v* Boyce, 135 Mass 559

The funeral expenses of a wife who has left property, when paid by her husband, constitute a preferred charge against her estate. Constantinides *v.* Walsh, 146 Mass. 281.

Any city or town which incurs expense for the support of a pauper having a settlement therein may recover the same against such person, his executors or administrators, in an action of contract for money paid, laid out, and expended for his use. R. L. c. 81, § 9, Newburyport *v* Creedon, 146 Mass 131

[1] R. L. c. 137, § 15, Smith *v* Smith, 175 Mass 483.
[2] R L. c. 138, § 9

he gives bond, unless the same were barred under the previous administration If he fails to give notice of his appointment in the manner prescribed for original administrators, he will have no benefit of the statute limitation. If assets come to his hands after the expiration of the two years, he is liable on account of such new assets in like manner as an original executor or administrator [1]

Every legatee may recover his legacy in an action at common law, and such action may be brought at any time against an executor or administrator with the will annexed for the recovery of a legacy.[2]

Proceeding when the Creditor's Right of Action accrues after the Two Years — A further exception to the rule limiting actions against executors and administrators to two years after giving bond is made by the statute in favor of a creditor whose right of action does not accrue within the two years A creditor holding such a claim should present a full statement of it in writing to the probate court, with a petition for an order requiring the executor or administrator to retain in his hands assets sufficient to satisfy it when it becomes due and payable. The claim may be presented at any time before the estate is fully administered If it appears on examination that

---

[1] R. L. c 141, §§ 17, 18, Eddy v Adams, 145 Mass. 489. The time within which an action may be commenced against the new administrator is not extended by his receiving property in settlement of a suit against a surety on the bond of his predecessor for a failure to account for estate which had been inventoried Veazie v. Marrett, 6 Allen, 372 ; Chenery v Webster, 8 Allen, 76

An action will he against the administrator *de bonis non* with the will annexed for a debt due from the testator, although the original executor, who was also the residuary trustee, gave a bond to pay debts and legacies Collins v Collins, 140 Mass 502

[2] R L c 141, § 19; Gale v Nickerson, 151 Mass 428; Tallon v. Tallon, 156 Mass 313.

the claim is, or may become, justly due from the estate, the court will order the executor to retain in his hands assets sufficient to meet it; or if a person interested in the estate offers to give bond to the alleged creditor, with sufficient surety or sureties, for the payment of the demand in case it is proved to be due, the court may order such bond to be taken, instead of requiring assets to be retained.[1] This proceeding applies to any claim arising out of a contract of the deceased, the right of action on which does not accrue within the two years[2] If the creditor fails to present his claim to the court, he cannot maintain an action against the heirs, next of kin, devisees, or legatees after the estate has been settled[3] The application to the court does not involve an inquiry into the amount of assets in the executor's hands, but is limited to the question whether the claim is, or may become, justly due from the estate.[4]

[1] R L c 141, § 13. This provision, so far as it relates to claims to become due, does not apply to or affect any estate which was not in process of settlement on the twenty-eighth day of February, 1879.

The statute does not compel the administrator to sell real estate to meet the liability when it shall accrue. Clark v Holbrook, 146 Mass. 366 A creditor of an estate upon which ancillary administration has been taken out here, is entitled to have assets retained to satisfy his claim when it shall accrue Newell v Peaslee, 151 Mass 601 A claim of a balance due a ward from a guardian deceased intestate, upon an account filed by him in his lifetime, which was not allowed by the probate court until more than six years after the taking out of administration on his estate, is within the statute Cobb v Kempton, 154 Mass 266

[2] The court may order the administrator of the estate of a deceased surety on a probate bond to retain assets to satisfy a claim of damages for a breach of the bond Hammond v. Granger, 128 Mass. 272

[3] Pratt v Lamson, 128 Mass. 528; Bassett v. Drew, 176 Mass. 141.

[4] Hammond v Granger, 131 Mass 351

The decision of the court upon the claim of the creditor is not conclusive against the executor or administrator, or other persons interested to oppose the allowance thereof, and they cannot be compelled to pay it, unless it is proved to be due in an action commenced within one year after it becomes payable, or, if an appeal is taken from the decision of the probate court, in an action commenced within one year after the final determination of the proceedings on the appeal.[1]

A creditor whose right of action accrues after the expiration of the two years, and whose claim could not legally be presented to the probate court, or whose claim, if presented, was not allowed, may, by action commenced within one year after his right of action accrues, recover his claim against the heirs and next of kin of the deceased, or his devisees or legatees, each of whom shall be liable to the creditor to an amount not exceeding the value of the real or personal property which he has received from the deceased. But if by the will of the deceased any part of his estate or any one or more of the devisees or legatees is made exclusively liable for the debt in exoneration of the residue of the estate or of other devisees or legatees, such provisions of the will shall be complied with, and the persons and estate so exempted shall be liable

[1] R. L. c 141, §§ 14, 15, 16; Cobb v Kempton, 154 Mass 270 The action is brought against the executor if he has been required to retain assets therefor, otherwise, on the bond given by the persons interested "If the action is brought on such bond, the plaintiff shall set forth his original cause of action against the deceased in like manner as would be required in a declaration for the same demand against the executor or administrator, and may allege the non-payment of the demand as a breach of the condition of the bond, and the defendant may answer any matter of defence that would be available in law against the demand if prosecuted in the usual manner against the executor or administrator." R L c. 141, § 16.

for only so much of the debt as cannot be recovered from those who are first chargeable therewith.[1]

When Executors, etc , may pay Debts without Personal Liability. — No executor or administrator can be held to answer to a suit of a creditor of the deceased, if commenced within one year after he gives bond, unless it is on a demand that would not be affected by the insolvency of the estate, or is brought after the estate has been represented insolvent for the purpose of ascertaining a contested claim [2] And if, within the year after giving notice of his appointment, he does not have notice of demands against the estate which will authorize him to represent it insolvent, he may proceed to pay the debts due, without any personal liability on that account to any creditor who has not given notice of his claim.

If he pays away the whole estate before notice of the demand of any other creditor, he is not required, in consequence of such notice, to represent the estate insolvent, but in an action against him he will be discharged upon proving such payments. If he pays away so much of the estate that the remainder is insufficient to pay a demand of which he afterwards has notice, he will be liable to pay on such demand only so much as may then remain. If there are two or more such demands, which together exceed the amount of assets remaining in his hands, he

---

[1] R. L c. 141, §§ 26-32; Bassett *v.* Granger, 136 Mass 176; McKim *v.* Doane, 137 Mass. 195 , Clark *v.* Holbrook, 146 Mass. 366; Forbes *v* Harrington, 171 Mass 386

[2] R L c. 141, § 1. This provision includes an executor who is also a residuary legatee, and has given bond to pay debts and legacies. The demands that " would not be affected by the insolvency of the estate " are such as are preferred by statute National Bank of Troy *v.* Stanton, 116 Mass. 439; Studley *v.* Willis, 134 Mass. 155.

may represent the estate insolvent; but creditors who have been previously paid are not liable to refund any part of the amount received by them.[1]

If it appears, upon the settlement of the account of an executor or administrator in the probate court, that the whole estate and effects which have come to his hands have been exhausted in paying the charges of administration and debts or claims entitled by law to a preference over the common creditors of the deceased, such settlement shall be a sufficient bar to any action brought against such executor or administrator by a creditor who is not

---

[1] R L c 141, §§ 1-4 ; Converse v. Johnson, 146 Mass 22, Browne v. Doolittle, 151 Mass. 595 As to the payment of debts when the estate is insolvent, see chap xiii More than two years after the notice of his appointment, and after the estate had been represented insolvent, the administrator found a bond executed to the intestate for the conveyance of land to him on payment of a certain sum A creditor who had not presented or proved his claim, and who had offered the administrator indemnity against costs, was held to have a right to a judicial determination whether an equity of redemption existed which was new assets. Glines v Weeks, 137 Mass. 547

Taxes on collateral legacies and successions shall be paid to the treasurer of the commonwealth by the executors, administrators, or trustees at the expiration of two years after the date of their giving bond, but whenever legacies or distributive shares shall be payable within two years, the taxes shall be payable at the time such legacies or shares are paid. But when the probate court has ordered funds to be retained to satisfy a claim of a creditor whose right of action does not accrue within two years, the payment of the tax may be suspended by an order of the court to await the disposition of the claim The taxes and interest that may accrue shall be a lien on the property until paid R L c 15, § 4 Whenever the legatee or devisee who has paid any such tax, afterwards refunds any portion of the property on which it was paid, or it is judicially determined that the whole or any part of the tax ought not to have been paid said tax or the due proportional part of it shall be paid back to him by the executor or trustee R L c. 15, § 15

entitled to such preference, although the estate has not been represented insolvent.[1]

All actions which would have survived if commenced by or against the original party in his lifetime may be commenced and prosecuted by and against his executors and administrators.

When an action of tort is commenced or prosecuted against the executor or administrator of the person originally liable, the plaintiff shall be entitled to recover only for the value of the goods taken, or for the damage actually sustained, without any vindictive or exemplary damages, or damages for any alleged outrage to the feelings of the injured party.[2]

In an action by or against an executor, administrator, or other person in a representative capacity, the defendant may set off a claim due to or from the testator, intestate, or person represented, respectively; but he shall not set off a claim due in his own right to or from the executor, administrator, or other person who sues or defends in a representative capacity, nor a claim which did not belong to him at the death of the testator or intestate.

When, upon such a set-off against an executor or administrator, a balance is found due to the defendant, the judgment therefor against the plaintiff shall be in the same

[1] R L c 141, § 5 The settlement in the probate court of an administrator's account, showing that he has exhausted all the estate of his intestate in paying the expenses of the last sickness, funeral, and administration, is a good defence to an action brought against the administrator on his bond, although the administrator has suffered a judgment to be recovered against him before such settlement of his account Fuller v Connelly, 142 Mass 227 But such defence is not available unless the administrator has filed an inventory and settled his account in the probate court McKim v Haley, 173 Mass 112

[2] R L. c 172, §§ 1, 2; Wilkins v. Wainwright, 173 Mass 212

form and have the same effect as if the suit had been originally commenced by the defendant.[1]

Police, district, and municipal courts may issue writs of *scire facias* against executors and administrators upon a suggestion of waste, after a judgment against them.[2]

PAYMENT OF LEGACIES.

The probate court has no jurisdiction of the questions to whom, or at what time, a legacy is to be paid. The executor pays the legacies under the authority given him by the will of the deceased.[3] The rule adopted by the courts, borrowed from the civil law, requires legacies to be paid, when the will prescribes no time for their payment, after the expiration of one year from the testator's death, it being presumed that the executor will be able to inform himself during the year of the sufficiency or insufficiency of the estate to meet the demands upon it; and the legatee may bring an action to recover his legacy after the expira-

[1] R L c 174, §§ 6, 7. If the defendant prevails, he may have an execution for costs against the executor *de bonis propriis*, although the estate of the plaintiff's testator has been represented insolvent Perkins v Fellows, 136 Mass 294 See Gannon v Ruffin, 151 Mass. 206, Boyden v Mass Life Insurance Co , 153 Mass 544.

[2] R L. c 160, § 21.

[3] When the legatee is a minor and has no guardian, or whenever the residence of a person named as a legatee is unknown, the court may direct that his legacy be deposited in some savings bank or other like institution, or invested in bank stock or other stocks. R. L. c 150, § 24

If the amount of a legacy has been deposited in a savings bank by order of the Court, on the representation that the residence of the legatee is unknown, and it afterwards appears that the legatee died before the testator and that his issue are entitled to it under the provisions of P S c. 127, § 23 (now R. L c 135, § 21), the probate court should order the amount to be paid to such issue Stockbridge, Petitioner, 145 Mass. 517.

tion of the year.[1] But if the executor or administrator within two years after having given bond for the discharge of his trust, is required by a legatee or next of kin to make payment, in whole or in part, of a legacy or distributive share, the probate court may require that such legatee or distributee shall first give bond to the executor or administrator, with surety or sureties to be approved by the court, and conditioned to repay the amount so to be paid, or so much thereof as may be necessary to satisfy any demands that may be afterwards recovered against the estate of the deceased, and to indemnify the executor or administrator against all loss or damage on account of such payment.[2]

A debt due to the estate of the deceased by a legatee or distributee of such estate is to be set off against and deducted from the legacy to such legatee or from the distributive share of such distributee.[3] The probate court

[1] Brooks v Lynde, 7 Allen, 64. A legatee of a fractional part of the residue of an estate in process of being administered in the probate court under a will, cannot in a suit at law recover of the administrator of the estate of the deceased executor under the will, the amount of the legacy before the amount of the residuum has been ascertained. Tallon v. Tallon, 156 Mass 313

[2] R. L. c. 141, § 20; Browne v. Doolittle, 151 Mass. 598. The probate court, pending a petition by a party interested, for instructions as to the construction of a will, may restrain the paying of legacies until the determination of the questions involved. Healy v. Reed, 153 Mass 197.

[3] R L c 141, § 23. Gannon v. Ruffin, 151 Mass. 204. See Taylor, v Taylor, 145 Mass 239. An agreement by an heir with an administrator that notes held by the latter may be deducted from the distributive share before the final settlement of the estate, will not amount to payment of the notes. Taylor v Lewis, 146 Mass 222. A gift by a parent to a child is not to be applied in satisfaction of a legacy to the child given by a will subsequently executed by the parent, in the absence of any understanding by the child that it should be so applied

hears and determines as to the validity and amount of any such debt, and may make all decrees and orders which may be necessary or proper to carry into effect such set-off or deduction [1]

Jaques v Swasey, 153 Mass 596   Administrators or executors cannot set off against or deduct from a devise or inherited share of real estate a debt due to the estate.   Jones v Treadwell, 169 Mass 430

[1] R. L. c 141, § 23   Blackler v Boott, 114 Mass. 24 , Boyden v. Mass Life Insurance Co , 153 Mass 544   A debt due from a legatee which is barred by the statute of limitations at the time of the testator's death, cannot be deducted from the legacy, unless the will clearly shows such an intention   Allen v Edwards, 136 Mass 138

An executor, administrator, or trustee holding property subject to the tax on collateral legacies and successions, shall deduct the tax or shall collect it from the legatee or person entitled to said property, and he shall not deliver property or a specific legacy subject to the tax to any person until he has collected the tax thereon   An executor or administrator shall collect taxes due upon land which is subject to said tax from the heirs or devisees entitled thereto and he may be authorized to sell said land if they refuse or neglect to pay said tax

When a legacy subject to the tax is charged upon or payable out of real estate, the heir or devisee, before paying it, shall deduct the tax therefrom and pay it to the executor, administrator, or trustee, and the tax shall remain a charge upon the real estate until it is paid, and the payment of it may be enforced by the executor, administrator, or trustee in the same manner as the payment of the legacy itself could be enforced

If any such legacy is given in money to any person for a limited period, the administrator, executor, or trustee shall retain the tax on the whole amount . but if it is not in money, he shall make application to the court having jurisdiction of his accounts to render an apportionment, if the case requires it, of the sum to be paid into his hands by the legatee on account of the tax, and for such further orders as the case may require   R. L c 15, §§ 5, 6, 7

When any person bequeaths or devises any property to father, mother, husband, wife, lineal descendant, brother, sister, an adopted child, the lineal descendant of any adopted child, the wife or widow of a son, or the husband of a daughter, during life or for a term of years, and the remainder to a collateral heir or to a stranger to the blood, the value of the prior estate shall, within three months after

Interest on Legacies — Interest is generally allowed to legatees after the expiration of one year from the death of the testator, and the rule applies when the will directs the legacy to be paid " as soon as possible," or " next after my lawful debts."[1] If the legacy is payable by the terms of the will at a specified time, it carries interest from that time.[2]

If an annuity, or the use, rent, income, or interest of property, real or personal, is given by will, deed, or other instrument to or in trust for the benefit of a person for life or until the happening of a contingency, such person shall be entitled to receive and enjoy the same from and after the death of the testator, unless it is otherwise provided in such will or instrument;[3] and if the income is not paid at the expiration of the year, to interest thereon from that time.[4] A person entitled to such annuity, rent, interest, or income, or his representative, shall have the same apportioned if his right or interest therein terminates between the days upon which it is payable, unless otherwise provided in such will or instrument; but no action shall be brought

the date of giving bond by the executor administrator, or trustee, be appraised and deducted from the appraised value of such property, and the remainder shall be subject to a tax of five per centum of its value Ibid § 2.

[1] Kent *v* Dunham, 106 Mass 586; Webster *v.* Hale, 8 Ves 410, Ogden *v.* Pattee, 119 Mass 82; Welch *v.* Adams, 152 Mass 74.

[2] The legatee is entitled to interest although the administrator had not, at the time the legacy was payable, assets available for the payment of debts and charges of administration of the estate Kent *v* Dunham, 106 Mass 586

[3] R L c 141, § 24, Pollock *v* Learned, 102 Mass 49; Sargent *v* Sargent, 103 Mass 297, Billings *v* Billings, 110 Mass 225; Cushing *v.* Burrell, 137 Mass 25, Keith *v* Copeland, 138 Mass. 304, Adams *v.* Adams, 139 Mass. 452.

[4] Ayer *v.* Ayer, 128 Mass 575

therefor until the expiration of the period for which the apportionment is made.[1]

When it is the duty of the executor, under the directions of the will, to invest and hold the amount of a legacy for a prescribed time, or until the happening of a contingent event, and he neglects to do so, the legatee may be entitled to compound interest.[2] A specific legacy carries with it all income or accessions that may accrue thereon after the death of the testator.

[1] R L c 141, § 25. Holmes v Taber, 9 Allen, 246 ; Granger v Bassett, 98 Mass. 462 ; Sargent v Sargent, 103 Mass 297 ; Haraden v Larrabee, 113 Mass 430. White v. Stanfield, 146 Mass 424, Hemenway v Hemenway, 171 Mass 42.

The words "annuity, rent, interest, or income" do not include undeclared dividends of corporations. Adams v. Adams, 139 Mass 452.

[2] Miller v Congdon, 14 Gray, 114 ; Eliott v. Spariell, 114 Mass 404, Kent v. Dunham, 106 Mass. 586, Welch v Adams, 152 Mass 86

CHAPTER XIII.

INSOLVENT ESTATES OF DECEASED PERSONS

WHEN the estate of a person deceased is insufficient to pay all his debts, it shall, after discharging the necessary expenses of his funeral and last sickness, and the charges of administration, be applied to the payment of his debts, which shall include equitable liabilities, in the following order : —

" *First*, Debts entitled to a preference under the laws of the United States ;

" *Second*, Public rates, taxes, and excise duties ;

" *Third*, Wages or compensation, to an amount not exceeding one hundred dollars, due to a clerk, servant, or operative for labor performed within one year next preceding the death of such deceased person, or for such labor so performed for the recovery of payment for which a judgment has been rendered ;

" *Fourth*, Debts due to all other persons.

" If there is not enough to pay all the debts of any class, the creditors of that class shall be paid ratably upon their respective debts ; and no payment shall be made to creditors of any class until all those of the preceding class or classes, of whose claims the executor or administrator has notice, have been fully paid." [1]

[1] R. L. c 142, § 1 ; Sweeney *v* Muldoon, 139 Mass. 307

A husband, having paid the funeral expenses of his wife, who has left property, may recover them of her executor. Constantides *v.* Walsh, 146 Mass. 281; Morrissey *v* Mulhern, 168 Mass. 412

THE REPRESENTATION OF INSOLVENCY.

If the estate is insolvent it is the duty of the executor or administrator to represent the fact to the probate court. His neglect to do so may make him personally liable to creditors of the deceased. He is allowed ample time to satisfy himself as to the condition of the estate. He is not held liable to answer to the suit of any creditor commenced within one year after he gives bond for the faithful discharge of his trust, unless the demand is one that would not be affected by the insolvency of the estate, or is brought after the estate has been represented insolvent for the purpose of ascertaining a contested claim.[1] If within one year after giving notice of his appointment he does not have notice of demands which will authorize him to represent the estate insolvent, he may proceed to pay the debts due from the estate, and he will not be personally liable to any creditor in consequence of payments made before notice of his demand. If he so pays away the whole of the estate before notice of the demand of any other creditor, he is not required in consequence of such notice to represent the estate insolvent, but may plead that he has fully administered, and be discharged on proving such payments.[2] Or if any effects remain, and

---

[1] R. L. c. 141, § 1, Greenleaf v. Allen, 127 Mass. 248; Converse v. Johnson, 146 Mass. 22; Browne v. Doolittle, 151 Mass. 595. But he is accountable for money paid on debts within the year, though without the knowledge that the estate was insolvent. Cobb v. Muzzey, 13 Gray, 57. In case the estate has been represented insolvent, the whole amount of the judgment against the administrator, including costs as well as debts, is to be certified to the judge of probate, and added to the list of claims reported by the commissioners of insolvency. Healy v. Root, 11 Pick. 389.

[2] R. L. c. 141, §§ 2, 3; Cushing v. Field, 9 Met. 180; Fuller v. Connelly, 142 Mass. 228; Browne v. Doolittle, *supra.* It is no bar to an

such remainder is insufficient to satisfy a demand of which he afterwards has notice, he is liable to pay only so much as may then remain; if there are two or more such demands, which together exceed the amount of assets remaining, he may then represent the estate insolvent, and pay over the amount in his hands to such persons as the court shall order, but creditors who have been previously paid cannot be required to refund any part of the amount received by them.[1]

action against an administrator, on a debt of his intestate, that he gave due notice of his appointment, and had no notice within a year thereafter of demands against the estate which would authorize him to represent it insolvent, and applied in payment of the debts of the deceased all the personal and a sufficient portion of the real estate to pay the debts then ascertained, and that the heirs at the same time sold all the residue of the real estate, and the administrator rendered his final account which was allowed. The statute applies only when the whole of the estate has been exhausted Hildreth ι Marshall, 7 Gray, 167, Bassett v. Granger, 136 Mass 174

[1] R. L c 141, § 4; Colegrove v. Robinson, 11 Met 238; Heard v Drake, 4 Gray, 516. This provision of the statute applies to payments made *after* the expiration of the year If the executor, *within* a year after giving notice of his appointment, pays a debt of his intestate, he may, if the estate afterwards proves insolvent, recover of the creditor the excess of the sum so paid over the amount awarded to the creditor by commissioners of insolvency Walker r Hill, 17 Mass 380; Bliss v Lee, 17 Pick 83; Heard v. Drake, 4 Gray, 514, Richards v. Nightingale, 9 Allen, 149 The administrator cannot recover unless he proves the insolvency of the estate by a commission of insolvency regularly issued, executed, and returned, and a dividend declared by the court Bascom v Butterfield, 1 Met 536, Flint v Valpey, 130 Mass 385. The general statute of limitations will begin to run against the claim of the administrator from the date when the dividend is ordered Richards v Nightingale, 9 Allen, 149. A decree of the probate court allowing distribution of all the personal estate of a deceased person before the end of the two years of administration, is void as to creditors prosecuting their claims within that period whether they have notice of it or not, and the administrator has no defence to actions by such creditors Browne v. Doolittle, 151 Mass 595, Newell v. Peaslee, 151 Mass. 601.

The executor or administrator is not to wait until the claims of creditors are proved at law before he makes his representation of insolvency. He may believe that there is a good defence against a claim that is presented to him; but if its recovery would cause insolvency, he should represent the estate insolvent. If he suffers judgment to be recovered against him before he represents the estate insolvent, he must pay the full amount of the judgment, without regard to the amount of assets in his hands.[1] And if, on demand made upon him to pay such judgment, or to show property of the deceased to be taken in execution, he neglects or refuses so to do, he and his sureties are liable on his administration bond to a suit by the judgment creditor, although the estate is in fact insolvent Having had full opportunity to ascertain the condition of the estate, and having allowed the claim to be prosecuted to final judgment without interfering by a representation of insolvency, the law will presume that he has the means in his hands to satisfy it.[2]

If it appears, upon the settlement of the account of an executor or administrator in the probate court, that the whole estate and effects which have come to his hands have been exhausted in paying the charges of administration and debts or claims entitled by law to a preference over the common creditors of the deceased, such settlement shall be a bar to an action brought against him by a creditor who is not entitled to such preference, although

---

[1] To a *scire facias* against an administrator to have execution of a former judgment recovered against him in that capacity, he may plead the insolvency of the estate of his intestate, as established since the recovery Coleman *v* Hall, 12 Mass 570; Fuller *v.* Connelly, 142 Mass 227

[2] Newcomb *v* Goss, 1 Met 333 But see Fuller *v* Connelly, 142 Mass. 230

the estate has not been represented insolvent.[1] But the executor or administrator who undertakes to pay the preferred claims without first making a representation of insolvency, must pay them strictly in the order prescribed by statute. The assets may not be sufficient to pay all the preferred debts, and in such case the several classes of creditors must be paid in their order. Taxes, for instance, cannot be paid until the two anterior classes of creditors have been fully satisfied, and if the assets are not sufficient to pay all the debts of any one class, the creditors of that class must be paid ratably. An executor who is residuary legatee, and who has given bond to pay the debts and legacies, cannot represent the estate insolvent, — the bond is a conclusive admission of sufficient assets.[2]

The representation of insolvency must be addressed to the probate court in the county in which the executor or administrator was appointed, and should set forth the amount of the indebtedness of the estate, so far as it can be ascertained (including the funeral expenses, charges of administration, and the allowance, if any, made to the widow or minor children), and the amount of the assets in the hands of the executor or administrator. There should also be filed a list of the claims against the estate, showing the name of each creditor and the sum claimed by each. If the evidence of the fact of insolvency is satisfactory, the court may appoint two or more fit persons to be commissioners to receive and examine the claims

[1] R. L. c. 141, § 5. Glines v Weeks, 137 Mass 551; Fuller v Connelly, 142 Mass 228; Eddy v. Adams, 145 Mass 490; Browne v Doolittle, 151 Mass. 597

[2] Alger v. Colwell, 2 Gray, 404; Jones v Richardson, 5 Met. 247.

of creditors, or may itself receive and examine the claims.[1]

TIME ALLOWED FOR PROOF OF CLAIMS.

If commissioners are appointed, six months after their appointment are allowed for the creditors to present and prove their claims. If the claims are examined by the court, six months after the order of the court directing the executor to give notice to creditors of the times and places of the examination are allowed. The court may in all cases, if it appears that a just and equitable distribution of the estate requires it, allow such further time, not exceeding eighteen months from the original appointment or order, as it may deem proper.[2] Such further time may be applied for by any creditor who has failed, after using due diligence, to present his claim for proof:[3] and the commission may be reopened for the purpose of correcting a mistake of the commissioners,[4] or for

---

[1] R L c. 142, §§ 2, 4, Curley v Squire, 141 Mass 509, 511, Newell v West, 149 Mass 528. Where a judge of probate had rejected a representation of insolvency made by an administrator, and upon a second application, which the administrator offered to support by legal evidence, again refused to receive it, giving his former decision as a reason for the second denial, and an appeal was taken, he was directed to receive the evidence, and thereupon to decree according to law and the justice of the case Bucknam v Phelps, 6 Mass 448. No appeal lies from a decree of the probate court appointing such commissioners. Putney v Fletcher, 140 Mass. 596.

The commissioners or, in case the court examines the claims, the executor or administrator, must notify the creditors of the times when and the places where their claims will be examined R. L c 142, §§ 3, 5

[2] R. L. c. 142, § 9, Guptill v Ayer, 149 Mass 50.

[3] Walker v Lyman's Administrators, 6 Pick 458, Towle v. Bannister, 16 Pick 255

[4] Towle v. Bannister 16 Pick. 254, Franklin County Bank v. Greenfield Bank, 138 Mass. 522.

other good cause. The application should fully set forth the facts of the case. The commission may be reopened at any time within the eighteen months, although the return of the commissioners may have been made to the probate court; and the party applying for such extension may appeal from a decree of the court denying the prayer of his petition. And in case of an appeal from the disallowance, in whole or in part, or from the allowance of a claim, further time may be allowed, not extending more than one month beyond the final decision of the appeal [1] And if a commissioner dies, resigns, or unreasonably neglects to make the return required by law, or is removed, a new commissioner may be appointed in his stead, and in such case the time for making proof of claims is extended six months from the appointment of the new commissioner. [2]

Such extensions of time, however, do not relieve a creditor from the obligation to commence the prosecution of his claim, either at law or before commissioners, within two years from the time when bond was given by the administrator. If proceedings are not commenced within that time, his claim will be barred, unless it can be proved as a contingent claim, or unless new assets come to the hands of the administrator after the decree of distribution, in which case his claim may be allowed and paid in the manner provided for contingent claims.[3] And even if there are new

---

[1] R L c. 142, § 9   [2] Ibid.

[3] The question whether further assets have come into the hands of an executor or administrator, so as to entitle a creditor to have the commission of insolvency opened, is not open to inquiry on an appeal from the decision of the commissioners allowing or disallowing the claim of a creditor Ostrom v. Curtis, 1 Cush. 461.

More than two years after his appointment, and after the estate had been represented insolvent, the administrator first discovered the existence of a bond executed to the intestate, by the terms of which the

assets, his claim will not be taken out of the statute of limitation for general purposes, but only in respect to the new assets.[1]

The commissioners cannot allow claims after the expiration of the time limited by statute or fixed by the court.[2]

PROOF OF CLAIMS

The warrant issued to the commissioners contains instructions for their formal proceedings. They must first be sworn to faithfully discharge the duties of their office The oath may be administered by any justice of the peace, and a certificate thereof should be made by him on the warrant, to be returned with their report. They are required to appoint convenient times and places for their meetings to receive and examine claims, and to give at least seven days' written notice of the time and place of each meeting, by mail or otherwise, to all known creditors of the deceased, and such other notice, by publishing in some newspaper or otherwise, as the court may order.[3] The executor or administrator is required to furnish them, fourteen days at least before their first meeting, the names and residences of all known creditors. The commissioners hold as

---

obligor was to reconvey land to the intestate on payment of a certain sum It was *held*, that the creditor had a right to the judicial determination of the question whether an equity of redemption existed which would be new assets. Glines *v*. Weeks, 137 Mass 547

[1] Aiken *v* Moise, 104 Mass 277, Tarbell *v* Parker, 106 Mass. 347, Glines *v* Weeks, 137 Mass 547 But leaving claims with the register of probate, and his indorsement thereon that they were presented for allowance within two years from the filing of the administrator's bond, is equivalent to bringing suit, and avoids the bar of the special statute of limitations Robinson *v* Robinson, 173 Mass. 233.

[2] Bascom *v* Butterfield, 1 Met. 536.

[3] R L. c 142, § 3

many meetings, within the six months, as are necessary for the complete discharge of the trust committed to them.

The commissioners or the court may require any claimant to make true answers, under oath, to all questions relating to his claim; and if he refuses to take such oath, or to answer fully all questions, they may disallow his claim. Either of the commissioners may administer such oath to the claimants and witnesses. The probate court may, except while an appeal is pending in the superior court or in the supreme judicial court from the allowance or the disallowance of a claim, upon the application of the executor or administrator, examine upon oath any person whose claim has been allowed, unless such allowance has been made by the supreme judicial court or by the superior court on appeal, may summon any person to give evidence relative to such claim, and, upon notice, alter or expunge a claim which it finds is founded wholly or partially in fraud, illegality, or mistake.[1]

The commissioners are to liquidate and balance all mutual demands subsisting between the deceased insolvent and his creditors. If the balance is found in favor of the creditor, it should be allowed by the commissioners, and included in their report; but if the balance is found to be against the creditor, it is not a subject of their report, which is to include claims against the estate only.[2]

[1] R L c 142, §§ 7, 8

[2] When the defendant in a suit brought by the administrator of an insolvent estate files in set-off a claim larger than that on which he is sued, he is entitled to judgment for the balance, and need not present his claim to the commissioners The judgment is to be presented to the judge of probate, and by him added to the claims allowed by the commissioners Bigelow v. Folger, 2 Met 255 In such suit the defendant may set off a note which falls due pending the suit, though not due when the action was commenced Ibid.; Boyden v Mass Life Insurance Co, 153 Mass. 548

Copartnership debts for which the deceased was liable may be proved against his estate [1]

A claim payable absolutely may be proved before its maturity,[2] and contingent liabilities which become absolute debts at any time before being presented to the commissioners may be allowed. [3]

---

[1] A stipulation in partnership articles that in case of the decease of either partner the business may be carried on for one year by the survivor for the mutual benefit of both parties, does not, in case of the death of one partner, justify the allowance against his insolvent estate of a debt contracted by the survivor within the year, with one who had notice of the death Stanwood v Owen, 14 Gray, 195, Bacon v. Pomeroy, 104 Mass 585. Payments made by the surviving partner while carrying on the partnership business pursuant to such stipulation, upon an account, some items of which were contracted before, and some after, the death of the other partner, must be applied to the discharge of the first items Ibid A surviving partner may prove a claim against the estate of his deceased partner. Sparhawk v Russell, 10 Met 307

[2] Haverhill Loan and Fund Association v. Cronin, 4 Allen, 141.

[3] A lessor is entitled to prove his claim for rent becoming payable by the terms of the lease before or after the death of the lessee, up to the time the claim is presented to the commissioners, but not for rent payable in the future. Deane v. Caldwell, 127 Mass. 242, Bowditch v. Raymond, 146 Mass. 114 And see Wilby v Phinney, 15 Mass 116, Harding v Smith, 11 Pick 478; Savage v Winchester, 15 Gray, 453

One having a right of action against the representative of a deceased sheriff whose estate is represented insolvent, for the misfeasance of the sheriff, must prosecute his claim before the commissioners and obtain a decree of the judge of probate in his favor in order to entitle him to a remedy on the bond given by the sheriff for the faithful performance of his duties, and he cannot maintain an action at law, except in the cases provided by the law respecting insolvent estates Todd v Bradford, 17 Mass 567.

An administrator *de bonis non* with the will annexed may prove before the commissioners of an insolvent estate of an intestate a claim for the amount received by the intestate as executor from the sale of real estate belonging to the estate of the testator and not accounted for Minot v Norcross, 143 Mass. 326

A ward after coming of age is not entitled to prove against the

When judgment is rendered against an estate which has been represented insolvent, and a certified copy from the probate court is filed in the clerk's office, execution will not be issued on the judgment, and it may be presented for allowance in the same manner as other claims of creditors.[1]

A creditor whose claim is secured, or partly secured, by mortgage or otherwise, cannot prove his full claim before the commissioners unless he first surrenders his security for the benefit of the estate. But he may be allowed the balance of his claim remaining after deducting the value of the security. Such value may be determined by agreement between the creditor and executor, or by a sale of the security, or it may be estimated by the commissioners [2]

---

estate in insolvency of his guardian a claim for the property which came into the hands of the guardian until the latter has settled his account in the probate court, or until a judgment has been obtained on his bond Murray v Wood, 144 Mass. 195. See Thorndike v Hinckley, 155 Mass 265.

[1] R. L c 142, § 32; Putney v. Fletcher, 148 Mass. 248, Goldthwait v Day, 149 Mass 187, Boyden v Mass Life Insurance Co., 153 Mass 548. But see Perkins v Fellows, 136 Mass. 294

[2] Farnum v Boutelle, 13 Met 159, Hooker v Olmstead, 6 Pick. 481, Middlesex Bank v. Minot, 4 Met 325; Haverhill Loan and Fund Association v Cronin, 4 Allen, 144; Bristol County Savings Bank v. Woodward, 137 Mass 412

But this rule does not apply to a case where the collateral security was furnished by a third person not primarily responsible for the debt A widow who has joined with her husband in a mortgage of her separate estate to secure his debt, which she has paid since his death for the purpose of exonerating her estate, may prove the amount before the commissioners And a creditor may prove his debt without first surrendering a mortgage of the separate estate of the debtor's wife, which he holds as security Savage v Winchester, 15 Gray, 453

For a full discussion of the subject of proof of a claim against an insolvent estate by a creditor holding security, and of the circum-

Interest is to be allowed on all claims expressly bearing interest, and upon claims not expressly bearing interest where there is evidence establishing the creditor's right to receive interest. Upon claims not bearing interest and not matured a rebate of interest is to be made The common practice is to compute this allowance and rebate of interest to the date of the death of the intestate Except in very rare cases, it is immaterial whether the interest stops at the death of the debtor or at a later day in the settlement of the estate, inasmuch as the proportion in which the assets are distributed among the creditors will be the same by either mode of computation. The main object is to fix upon some date to which the affairs of the deceased shall be adjusted. But cases have occurred where the assets have proved more than sufficient to pay the debts as they existed at the time of the death of the insolvent, but not sufficient to pay them with interest computed to the time of the decree of distribution. In such cases, and whenever the equitable distribution of the assets requires it, the court will add interest on the claims allowed to the time of distribution [1]

It is the duty of the executor or administrator to oppose the allowance of all claims improperly presented to the commissioners. If he is guilty of corrupt conduct in not

stances under which the creditor can prove for the whole amount of his claim, see Hale v Leatherbee, 175 Mass. 547.

P, the maker of a promissory note, gave E, after his indorsement thereof, a promissory note as collateral security, which was to apply to a renewal of the original note The original note was three times renewed, but before the last renewal note fell due P died. Although the bank which discounted this note had proved it against the insolvent estate of P, it was held that E could also prove the note given to him by P Emerson v Paine, 176 Mass 391.

[1] Williams v. American Bank, 4 Met 317; Bowers v Hammond, 139 Mass 360.

INSOLVENT ESTATES OF DECEASED PERSONS. 223

opposing the allowance of illegal claims, he will be liable to an action on his bond.[1] He should be present at the meetings of the commissioners, and should take an appeal from their decision whenever an appeal is necessary to protect the rights of persons interested in the estate.

The claim of an executor or administrator against the estate which he administers should be presented for allowance to the probate court, not to the commissioners.[2]

RETURN OF THE COMMISSIONERS.

At the expiration of the time limited for the proof of claims, the commissioners are required by law to make their returns to the probate court,[3] and performance of that duty may be compelled, on motion of any party interested, by the order of the court which appointed them.[4] Their return must give a list of all the claims presented to them, whether allowed or not, with the sum allowed on each, stated in separate classes, as follows first, debts entitled

[1] Parsons v Mills, 2 Mass 80

[2] Green v Russell, 132 Mass 536; Newell v. West, 149 Mass 528. An action cannot be brought on a claim disallowed by the commissioners before they have made their return Ellsworth v Thayer, 4 Pick 122, Goff v Kellogg, 18 Pick 256 An administrator who has resigned his trust is not to apply to the commissioners in insolvency to prove a debt due him personally from the estate when its amount may depend entirely upon the relation in which he stands to the estate, but must present his claim to the probate court Newell v West, supra

[3] It is the duty of the commissioners to make their own return to the probate court. It is no part of the official duty of the administrator to receive the report of the commissioners and carry or send it to the judge of probate, if he receives the report and undertakes to return it, this is merely a personal engagement, for the performance of which the sureties in his bond are not bound. Nelson v Woodbury, 1 Greenl 251

[4] Blanchard v Allen, 116 Mass 447

to a preference under the laws of the United States; second, public rates, taxes, and excise duties; third, preferred debts due to clerks, servants, or operatives for labor, fourth, debts due to all other persons. Debts proved against the deceased as a member of a partnership firm must be stated in a separate list.

If the claims are examined by the court, the register makes and certifies a list of all claims presented, with the amount allowed or disallowed on each claim.[1]

If the executor or administrator has settled his accounts in the probate court, the final distribution of the balance in his hands may be ordered after the expiration of thirty days from the return of the commissioners, and the settlement of the estate completed, unless there are contingent debts which could not be proved before the commissioners, or unless an appeal is taken from some decision of the commissioners or of the court.

PROVISIONS AS TO CONTINGENT CLAIMS.

The statute provides that "if at the expiration of the time allowed for the proof of claims a person is liable as a surety for the deceased, or has any other contingent claim against his estate which could not be proved as a debt within said time, the court upon proof of such facts shall, in ordering a dividend, leave in the hands of the executor or administrator a sum sufficient to pay to such contingent creditor a proportion equal to what is then to be paid to the other creditors. If such contingent debt becomes absolute within four years after the time of the giving of the executor's or administrator's bond, it may

[1] R L c 142, § 4; Putney v Fletcher, 140 Mass. 596, Newell v. West, 149 Mass. 528

be proved before the probate court, before the commissioners already appointed, or before others to be appointed for the purpose by the court. Upon the allowance of such claim the creditor shall be entitled to a dividend thereon equal to what has been paid to the other creditors, so far as the same can be paid without disturbing the former dividend ; and if the claim is not finally established, or if the dividend upon it does not exhaust the assets in the hands of the executor or administrator, the residue of the assets shall be divided among all creditors who have proved their debts. If there is a surplus after satisfying the claims of such creditors, with interest, it shall be distributed to the persons legally entitled thereto." [1]

These provisions of the statute apply only to cases where the claim is one that could not be proved as a debt under the commission. The surety on a promissory note made by the deceased which has been proved against the estate by the person holding it cannot have such a contingent claim. His claim against the estate could have been proved by him. He could have paid the holder, made the note his own property, and proved it as his own claim. Moreover, the holder who proved the note will take the entire dividend upon it, and the claim, so far as the insolvent estate is concerned, will be extinguished by the dividend paid to him. The surety cannot also take a dividend on the same debt. The statute refers to cases where the holder of the debt cannot, from some cause, prove his debt under the commission, or where the surety cannot make the debt his own by payment.[2]

[1] R L. c 142, §§ 27–29.
[2] Cummings *v* Thompson, 7 Met 132. The possible liability of surviving partners of a deceased insolvent to pay notes and obligations given by him in the name of the firm without their knowledge, for his

APPEALS FROM DECISIONS OF THE COMMISSIONERS.

The determination of the commissioners or of the probate court is not necessarily conclusive in any case. Any person whose claim is disallowed in whole or in part, and the executor or administrator, or any heir, legatee, devisee, or creditor of the insolvent estate who is dissatisfied with the allowance of a claim, may appeal from the decision of the commissioners or of the probate court, and the claim will thereupon be determined at common law in the county in which the probate or administration was granted. If the demand exceeds the sum of four thousand dollars in the county of Suffolk, or one thousand dollars in any other county, the appeal is taken either to the supreme judicial court or to the superior court; otherwise to the superior court.[1] The appeal must be claimed and notice thereof given at the registry of probate within thirty days after the return of the commissioners, or, when the court itself receives and examines the claims, within thirty days after the allowance or rejection of the claim.[2] If the appeal is by an executor or administrator, he must give notice thereof to the creditor within said thirty days. No reasons of appeal are required to be filed.[3] The appeal must be

private use, does not give them a contingent claim against the estate French v Hayward, 16 Gray, 512 And see Sears v. Wills, 7 Allen, 430, and Spelman v. Talbot, 123 Mass 489

[1] A claim against an insolvent estate of a deceased person pending in a state court on appeal from the decision of the commissioners appointed by the probate court cannot be removed to a United States court. Du Vivier v. Hopkins, 116 Mass 125.

[2] R L c 142, §§ 11, 12 When the time for proof of claims is extended, an appeal from a decision of the commissioners disallowing the claim of a creditor may be filed within thirty days after their final return, though such claim was presented and disallowed before the first return of the warrant. Merriam v Leonard, 6 Cush. 151

[3] Jacobs v Jacobs, 110 Mass. 229.

entered on the first Monday of the calendar month next succeeding the expiration of the thirty days.[1]

At the term of court at which the appeal is entered, the supposed creditor must file a statement in writing of his claim, setting forth briefly and distinctly all the material facts which would be necessary in a declaration for the same cause of action; and like proceedings are thereupon had in the pleadings, trial, and determination of the cause as in an action at law prosecuted in the usual manner, except that no execution is awarded against the executor or administrator for a debt found due to the claimant.[2] The appellate court has the same power as the probate court or the commissioners to examine the claimant, and the final judgment is conclusive, and the list of debts allowed by the commissioners will be altered if necessary to conform thereto.[3]

The party prevailing upon the appeal is entitled to costs, which, if recovered against the executor or administrator, may be allowed to him in his administration account.[4]

The statute provides that any person whose claim is disallowed by the commissioners, and who for other

---

[1] R L c 142, § 12

[2] But an execution against the executor for costs will nevertheless be awarded Greenwood v. McGilvray, 120 Mass. 516, Perkins v Fellows, 136 Mass 296

[3] R. L c. 142, § 13. The report of the commissioners on a claim is conclusive on either party who does not give notice of his dissatisfaction with it Boardman v. Smith, 4 Pick 212 See Wright v Dunham, 9 Pick. 37

[4] R L c 142, § 15; Pierce v Saxton, 14 Pick 274, Perkins v. Fellows, *supra* If the creditor, on appeal, does not recover a sum greater than that allowed by the commissioners, the executor shall recover his costs of suit against such creditor. Dodge v. Breed, 13 Mass 537

cause than his own neglect omits to claim or prosecute his appeal as above stated, may, by petitioning the supreme judicial court holden in any county, be allowed to claim and prosecute his appeal upon such terms as the court shall impose, if it appears that justice requires a further examination of his claim, but such petition must be presented within two years after the return of the commissioners, and within four years after the date of the administration bond.[1] The petition in such case should set forth particularly the nature of the claim and the cause of the petitioner's omission to seasonably claim and prosecute his appeal.

The allowance of such appeal shall not disturb any distribution ordered before notice of the petition or of the intention to present the same has been given in writing at the registry of probate, or to the executor or administrator, but the debts thus proved and allowed are paid only out of such assets as remain in or come to the hands of the executor or administrator after payment of the sums payable on such prior decree of distribution.[2] The party who intends to petition for leave to prosecute his appeal should therefore give immediate notice at the registry of probate, or to the executor, of his intention to present the same. The effect of such notice, if distribution has not already been ordered, may be to materially increase the amount of his dividend.

WAIVER OF APPEAL, AND ARBITRATION.

After the claiming of an appeal from a decision of the commissioners, the parties may waive a trial at law, and submit the claim to the determination of arbitrators to be agreed on between them and appointed accordingly by the

[1] R. L c 142, § 16.   [2] Ibid § 17.

probate court, and thereupon the appeal shall not be entered. The award of such arbitrators, if accepted by the court, shall be as conclusive as a judgment in a court of common law.[1]

The executor and the creditor, if they agree to submit the claim to arbitration, should join in a written representation of the fact to the court, and state therein the names of the arbitrators agreed upon. The arbitrators must notify the parties of the time and place fixed for the hearing, and after the hearing return to the court their award, with the rule and any papers issued therewith. They should also return a certificate of the costs of the arbitration.

The arbitrators have no power to award that the claimant is in fact indebted to the estate. They are to find only what amount, if any, is due from the estate to the claimant.[2]

DISTRIBUTION OF INSOLVENT ESTATES.

After the expiration of the time allowed by section 12 of chapter 142 of the Revised Laws for claiming appeals from the allowance or disallowance of a claim, the probate court decrees the distribution of the assets in the hands of the executor among the creditors whose claims have been allowed.[3] If before making the decree the court has notice of an appeal then claimed or pending, the decree may be suspended until the determination of the appeal, or a distribution may be ordered among the creditors whose debts are allowed, leaving in the hands of the executor or administrator a sum sufficient to pay the claimant whose demand is disputed a proportion equal to that of the other creditors.[4]

[1] R. L. c. 142, § 14.
[2] Gilmore v. Hubbard, 12 Cush. 220.
[3] Equitable liabilities shall be deemed to be debts provable against insolvent estates of deceased persons. R. L. c. 142, § 1.
[4] R. L. c 142, § 18. As to whether a decree of distribution can be

The court may, at any time before the expiration of the time allowed for claiming appeals, in its discretion order dividends paid to creditors whose claims have been allowed, whenever the court may deem it proper, leaving in the hands of the executor or administrator a sum sufficient to pay claims that may probably be proved a proportion equal to what is so paid to the other creditors.[1]

If the whole assets are not distributed upon the first decree, or if further assets come to the hands of the executor or administrator, the probate court will make such further decrees for distribution as the case requires.[2]

No final distribution can be made until the accounts of the executor or administrator are settled in the probate court, and the sum to be distributed thereby ascertained. His accounts should be settled at the earliest day practicable after the return of the commissioners or the list of claims allowed by the court is made, and he may be liable on his bond for neglect in this particular. The statute provides that if an executor or administrator neglects to render and settle his accounts in the probate court within six months after the final determination of the claims of creditors, or within such further time as the court may allow, and thereby delays a decree of distribution, such neglect may be deemed unfaithful administration; and he may be forthwith removed, and shall be liable in a suit on his bond for all damages occasioned by his default.[3] The return of the commissioners, without any appeal therefrom, is a final determination of the claims of creditors within

---

amended for error arising from mistake, see Parker *v.* Townsend National Bank, 121 Mass 565

[1] R. L. c 142, § 19
[2] Ibid § 20, White *v* Swain, 3 Pick 365
[3] R. L c 142, § 26.

the meaning of the statute, and the fact that contingent claims are presented against the estate is not material.[1]

In making the distribution, the preferred creditors, if the assets are sufficient, are paid in full, in the order required by statute. If there is not enough to pay all the debts of any one class, the creditors of that class are paid ratably upon their respective debts. The balance remaining after the payment of the preferred claims is distributed ratably among the other creditors. If the deceased had been a member of a copartnership, and died in possession of both separate and partnership estate, and was indebted as a partner as well as on private account, his partnership debts are payable from the partnership estate, and his separate debts from his separate estate. If there is a balance of the separate estate after the payment of his separate debts, it is added to the joint property for the payment of the joint creditors. If there is a balance of the joint property after the payment of the joint debts, it is divided among the separate estates of the partners according to their respective interests therein as it would have been if the partnership had been dissolved without insolvency; and the sum so appropriated to the separate estate of each partner is applied to the payment of his separate debts.[2]

[1] McKim v Bartlett, 129 Mass 226
[2] R. L c 142, § 21, c 163, § 138, Howe v. Lawrence, 9 Cush 553, Fall River Whaling Co v Borden, 10 Cush 458; Jewett v Phillips, 5 Allen, 120; Broadway Nat Bank v Wood, 165 Mass 312, Clarke v Stanwood, 166 Mass 379, Very v. Clarke, 177 Mass 52

The holder of a partnership note made payable to one partner and indorsed by him to the holder may prove it in insolvency against the estates both of the firm and of the indorsing partner before any dividend is declared on either. Roger Williams Nat Bank v Hall, 160 Mass 171

The order of distribution directs the executor or administrator to pay the balance in his hands to the persons named in the order, and specifies the sum to which each is entitled. He is also directed to give notice to each creditor of the amount of his dividend, and if any of the sums which he is ordered to pay remain for six months unclaimed, to deposit the same in a savings-bank or other like institution in the name of the judge of probate for the time being, to accumulate for the benefit of the person entitled thereto.[1]

When the executor or administrator has paid over or deposited the money in his hands as required by the decree of distribution, he may perpetuate the evidence thereof by presenting to the probate court, within one year after the decree was made, on account of such payments,

[1] When the person entitled to the money deposited satisfies the judge of his right to receive the same, the judge causes it to be paid over and transferred to him. R. L. c 150, § 23. The interest of a distributee in money ordered by the probate court to be paid to him, is equitable only; consequently unclaimed money deposited in the name of the judge of probate cannot be reached by trustee process as the property of the distributee. Chase v. Thompson, 153 Mass. 14.

When the residence of a legatee is unknown, or if he is a minor without a legal guardian, the legacy may be deposited in a savings-bank or like institution in the name of the judge of probate. R. L. c 150, § 24.

The limitation of the amount which savings-banks may receive for deposit does not apply to deposits made by direction of the probate court. R L c 113, § 25. Such deposits shall draw interest at the same rates as other deposits in the same bank, without regard to the amount deposited, and the probate court may order money so deposited and remaining unclaimed for more than five years to be paid into the state treasury. R L c 113, § 55.

The judge of probate may order money remaining unclaimed for twenty years to be paid to the residuary legatees, or if there are none, to the parties entitled; but a bond of indemnity will be required from the person to whom the money is paid. R. L. c 150, § 26.

which, being proved to the satisfaction of the court and verified by the oath of the party, is allowed as his final discharge. He may conveniently make such account by returning the original decree, with the receipts of the several creditors and the certificates of deposit annexed thereto, together with his own certificate that the several payments have been made as ordered.

After twenty years from the decree of distribution of an insolvent estate, the probate court, on application of any creditor whose claim was proved and allowed, and after notice of such application published for not less than two years on such days as the court shall direct, in one or more newspapers of the county, may order any unclaimed dividends with the interest received thereon, after deducting all expenses and charges of administration since the decree of distribution, to be distributed anew among the creditors who have received their dividends. If there is a surplus after satisfying the claims of such creditors with interest, it will be distributed to the heirs of the deceased. If a creditor who has failed to receive his dividend is deceased, administration may be granted on his estate, although more than twenty years have elapsed since his death, and his administrator may receive and administer the dividend.[1]

ACTIONS BY CREDITORS AFTER THE REPRESENTATION OF INSOLVENCY.

After the representation of insolvency and the appointment of commissioners, the law will not permit any of the assets of the estate to be taken from the executor or administrator by legal process to satisfy the demand of any creditor, until the question of insolvency is determined.

[1] R. L c 142, §§ 24, 25

No action can be maintained unless for a demand entitled to a preference, and which would not be affected by the insolvency of the estate, or unless the assets prove more than insufficient to pay all the debts allowed by the commissioners. If the estate is represented insolvent while an action is pending for any demand not entitled to such preference, the action can be discontinued without payment of costs; or, if the demand is disputed, the action may be tried and determined, and judgment rendered thereon, in the same manner and with the same effect as in the case of an appeal from the allowance or disallowance of the claim of a creditor; or the action may be continued without costs until it appears whether the estate is insolvent, and, if not insolvent, the plaintiff may prosecute the action as if no such representation had been made.[1]

RECOVERY OF CLAIMS NOT PROVED BEFORE THE COMMISSIONERS.

Every creditor of an insolvent estate who does not present his claim for allowance will be barred from recovering it, unless further assets come to the hands of the executor or administrator after the decree of distribution; in such case his claim may be proved and paid in the manner and with the limitations provided for contingent debts.[2] When such

---

[1] R. L. c. 142, § 30; Cushing v. Field, 9 Met 180; Johnson v. Ames, 6 Pick 330; Hunt v Whitney, 4 Mass 624, Greenwood v McGilvray, 120 Mass. 516, Greenleaf v Allen, 127 Mass. 248, Guptill v. Ayer, 149 Mass 50

[2] R L c 142, § 10; Guptill v Ayer, supra. The statute does not apply to a bill in equity brought by the administrator of a deceased partner whose estate is afterwards declared insolvent, against his surviving partner for an account, and the defendant is entitled to a decree if a balance is found in his favor Goldthwait v Day, 149 Mass 185

further assets come to the estate, the probate court, on application of such creditor, may open the commission. The creditor's petition must allege that further assets have come to the hands of the executor or administrator, and he must substantiate this allegation by proof. Without such proof the commission will not be opened. Either the creditor or executor may appeal from the decree of the probate court allowing or refusing the prayer of the petition.[1]

The claim of a creditor in whose favor the commission is reopened is not barred, in consequence of the lapse of time subsequent to the closing of the first commission, by any of the statutes of limitation. He may proceed by petition whenever there are new assets to be distributed. The executor or administrator is liable to account for all funds in his hands, though he may have received them more than twenty years after the decree of distribution was passed.[2]

If after the report of the commissioners the assets prove sufficient to pay all debts allowed, the executor or administrator pays them in full; and if any other debt is afterwards recovered against him, he is liable therefor only to the extent of the assets then remaining. If there are two or more such creditors, the assets, if insufficient to pay them in full, are divided between them in proportion to their debts. The executor or administrator, in an action brought against him on such demand, may prove the amount of assets in his hands, and thereupon judgment will be rendered in the usual form; but execution will not

---

[1] The decree if not appealed from is conclusive, and cannot be inquired into in a subsequent appeal from the subsequent decision of the commissioners allowing or disallowing the claim. Ostrom *v.* Curtis, 1 Cush. 461.

[2] Ibid., White *v.* Swain, 3 Pick. 365.

issue for more than the amount of such assets, and if there are two or more such judgments, the court will apportion the amount between them.[1]

If it is not ascertained, at the end of eighteen months after the granting of letters testamentary or of administration, whether an estate represented insolvent is or is not so in fact, any creditor whose claim has not been presented for proof may commence an action therefor against the executor or administrator, which may be continued without costs for the defendant until it appears whether the estate is insolvent.[2] If it appears solvent, the plaintiff may prosecute the action as if no such representation had been made. If it proves insolvent, he will have no remedy unless new assets come to the hands of the executor or administrator, in which case he may petition that the commission be opened, and if the commission is opened, he can prove his claim.

PROVISIONS AS TO INSOLVENT ESTATES OF DECEASED NON-RESIDENTS.

When an inhabitant of another state or country dies insolvent and leaves estate to be administered here, the estate found here is not to be transmitted to the foreign administrator until creditors who are citizens of this state have received their equitable dividends. If all the assets were transmitted to the foreign administrator, creditors in this state would be subjected to the expense of proving and collecting their demands abroad; and the pursuit of their claims in countries where the local law makes no provision for an equal distribution of the assets of a

[1] R. L. c. 142, §§ 22, 23; Bowers v. Hammond, 139 Mass. 363.
[2] R. L. c. 142, § 31. This provision does not suspend the special statute of limitations. Blanchard v. Allen, 116 Mass. 447.

deceased insolvent might be wholly fruitless. Under the provisions of our statute, citizens of this state cannot be put to the inconvenience of proving their claims abroad when there are assets here; nor, on the other hand, can the whole estate found here be expended in paying the claims of our citizens to the prejudice of foreign creditors; but the estate found here, as far as practicable, is to be so disposed of that all creditors of the deceased, here and elsewhere, may receive each an equal share in proportion to their respective debts.[1]

To this end, the statute provides that the assets shall not be sent to the foreign administrator until all creditors who are citizens of this state have received the just proportion that would be due to them if the whole estate of the deceased, wherever found, that is applicable to the payment of common creditors, were divided among all the creditors in proportion to their respective debts, without preferring any one species of debt to another,[2] in which case no creditor who is not a citizen of this state shall be paid out of the assets found here until all those who are citizens have received their just proportion

The statute further provides that if there is any residue remaining after such payment to the citizens of this state, it may be paid to any other creditors who have duly proved their debts, here, in proportion to the amount due to each of them, but no one shall receive more than would be due to him if the whole estate were divided ratably among all the creditors. The balance may be transmitted to the

---

[1] Dawes v Head, 3 Pick 128; Hooker v. Olmstead, 6 Pick. 481, Davis v Estey, 8 Pick. 475

[2] The local laws of some countries prefer debts on judgments, bonds, etc, to simple contract debts. Such preferences are not to be regarded in the distribution here.

foreign executor or administrator; or, if there is none, it shall, after the expiration of four years from the appointment of the administrator, be distributed ratably among all creditors, both citizens and others, who have proved their debts in this state.[1]

[1] R. L c 143, §§ 4, 5, Welch v Adams, 152 Mass. 76, 77.

The administrator of the insolvent estate of a deceased person may maintain a bill in equity, filed within two years after giving bond, to recover for the benefit of the creditors, even if all their claims are otherwise barred by the special statute of limitations, property conveyed by the intestate in his lifetime in fraud of them, which, when recovered, will constitute new assets. Welsh v. Welsh, 105 Mass. 229.

CHAPTER XIV.

SALES OF LAND BY EXECUTORS, ADMINISTRATORS, AND GUARDIANS.

SALES BY EXECUTORS AND ADMINISTRATORS.

WHEN the personal estate of a deceased person is insufficient to pay his debts and legacies with the charges of administration, his executor or administrator may sell his real estate for that purpose, having been first licensed therefor by the probate court, from which letters testamentary or of administration issued.[1]

---

[1] R. L. c 146, §§ 1, 4, Marvel v Babbitt, 143 Mass. 227; Boston Safe Deposit Co v. Mixter, 146 Mass 105, Putney v. Fletcher, 148 Mass. 218; Spooner v Spooner, 155 Mass 52.
Nothing in Rev. Laws, chap 64, shall extend to sales made by sheriffs, deputy sheriffs, constables, collectors of taxes, executors, administrators, guardians, assignees of insolvent debtors, or by any other person required by law to sell real or personal estate R L c 64, § 15 An executor who is residuary legatee and gives bond for the payment of debts and legacies acquires an absolute title in the estate devised, and may convey it without license. Clarke v. Tufts, 5 Pick 337; Thayer v Winchester, 133 Mass. 447. And an executor duly authorized thereto by the terms of the will may convey the lands of his testator without license. But when the executor, so empowered by the will, dies before making the conveyance, or renounces the office of executor, the power to sell does not devolve upon the administrator with the will annexed who succeeds him Such administrator can sell only by license of court. Tainter v Clark, 13 Met 220; Greenough v Welles, 10 Cush 571, Larned v Bridge, 17 Pick 339, Conklin v Edgerton's Administrator, 21 Wend 430 If the power to sell is given to two executors, one of whom resigns, the other may

The probate court may, upon the petition of an administrator, with the consent of all the parties interested exercise it singly. Gould v Mather, 104 Mass. 283; Warden v Richards, 11 Gray, 277.

If a will provides that, after the death of the testator's wife, who is the executrix, and to whom the use and income of his estate is given during her life, all the estate shall be converted into money, and does not in terms specify the person who shall do this, the power to sell the real estate is by necessary implication given to the administrator *de bonis non* with the will annexed. Putnam v Story, 132 Mass 205.

If the executor is authorized to sell lands for trust purposes, he does not, by renouncing the office of executor, lose the power to convey as trustee under the will. His sales and conveyances, made after the renunciation of his executorship and after his acceptance of the trust, are valid as against the devisees and their heirs. Clark v. Tainter, 7 Cush 567.

Where, under the provisions of a will, the sale of real estate by a trustee or executor is dependent upon the consent of a person who has deceased, the probate court having jurisdiction of the settlement of the estate may, in its discretion and if all parties interested assent, authorize the sale and conveyance of such real estate in like manner as if no such consent had been required. R L c 148, § 2. An administrator, being licensed to sell the estate of his intestate, may sell estate fraudulently conveyed by the deceased in whosesoever hands it may be. Drinkwater v Drinkwater, 4 Mass 354.

Where the intestate had only a power of appointment, in default of which the estate was to go to her heirs, and she made no appointment, it was *held* that she had no interest in the estate which could be sold by her administrator. Coverdale v Aldrich, 19 Pick 391.

Legatees under a will cannot maintain a bill in equity against the administrator with the will annexed of the testatrix who has obtained a license from the probate court to sell her real estate for the payment of legacies, to determine their rights. Sprague v West, 127 Mass 471.

A license to sell the real estate for the payment of debts will not be granted to the administrator where the only debt existing is secured by mortgage. Scott v. Hancock, 13 Mass 162.

When the debts are barred by the statute of limitations, a license to sell the real estate will be void. Tarbell v. Parker, 106 Mass 347.

A license to sell real estate in this commonwealth belonging to a deceased citizen of another state for the payment of debts will not be granted to the prejudice of the heirs when it appears that there was

or after notice, license him to sell the real property or any undivided interest therein belonging to the estate of the intestate, unless the appraisal shows that it exceeds fifteen hundred dollars in value, in such manner and upon such notice as the court orders, for the purpose of distribution; and the net proceeds of such sale, after deducting the expenses thereof and such amount as may be required for the payment of debts in consequence of a deficiency in personal property, shall, after two years from the filing of the administrator's bond, be distributed to the persons who would have been entitled to the real estate and in the proportions to which they would have been entitled, had it not been sold.[1]

As the legal title to real estate vests in the heirs or devisees immediately upon the death of the owner, the administrator, as such, has nothing to do with the lands of his intestate, except to see that they are appraised, until he is licensed to sell them for the payment of debts

a fund provided for the payment of debts in such other state, at least until it is shown that the creditors have used some diligence to obtain payment of such fund, and have met with some legal impediment. Livermore v. Haven, 23 Pick 116

The court cannot, on the petition of the administrator or executor, license a stranger to make the sale or conveyance Crouch v. Eveleth, 12 Mass 503

An estate of homestead is not exempt from a sale by the guardian of the owner, for the payment of his debts and for his support and maintenance, upon a license of the probate court Wilbur v Hickey, 8 Gray, 432. An executor who is authorized by will "to sell and make conveyance of personal and real estate either at public or private sale as the proper and convenient settlement of the estate may require," is empowered to sell the real estate only for the payment of debts, legacies, and the charges of administration, and not for the purpose of making partition or distribution among the devisees Allen v. Dean, 148 Mass 594.

[1] R. L. c. 146, § 18

and charges.[1] Nor has the executor, unless under an authority given him by the will of his testator.[2] When, therefore, lands are sold by executors and administrators, it is important for them to observe strictly the directions of the statute, from which alone they derive the power to make the conveyance. The probate court has no jurisdiction to grant a license to an executor who is also residuary legatee, and who has given a bond to pay debts and legacies.[3] Such a bond is a conclusive admission of assets, and takes the place of the property in providing a fund for the payment of debts and legacies. And the executor takes an absolute title in the land included in the residuary devise, and may convey it without license.[4]

Licenses to sell real estate are provided for by the statute only when the personal property is insufficient for the payment of debts, legacies, and charges of administration. The sale must be necessary for the payment of claims which can be enforced at law.[5] The convenience of parties

---

[1] Administrators, executors, and trustees may be licensed to sell real estate for the payment of the tax on collateral legacies and successions. R L c 15, § 8

[2] The court may authorize a special administrator, who is appointed by reason of delay in granting letters testamentary, to take charge of the real estate, collect the rents, make necessary repairs, and do all other things which it may deem needful for the preservation of the real estate and as a charge thereon R. L c 137, § 10

[3] Thayer v Winchester, 133 Mass. 447.

[4] Clarke v. Tufts, 5 Pick. 336 The giving of the bond for the payment of debts and legacies does not discharge the lien on the land for the payment of debts, except on such part as may be sold by the executor to one who purchases in good faith and for a valuable consideration All estate not so sold may be taken on execution by any creditor not otherwise satisfied, in like manner as if a bond had been given in the other form R L c 149, § 2; Collins v. Collins, 140 Mass 502. Jenkins v. Wood, 144 Mass 241.

[5] Lamson v Schutt, 4 Allen, 359. A petition for a license to sell real estate to meet a claim not accruing within two years from the

interested in the lands would be promoted, in some cases, by a sale of them by the administrator, although the proceeds are not needed for the payment of debts or legacies; but licenses cannot be granted under such circumstances except to public administrators (whose sales under license are considered in a subsequent part of this chapter), or when the appraised value of the real estate does not exceed the sum of fifteen hundred dollars,[1] or for the payment of the legacy and succession tax [2]

The Real Estate liable to be sold includes all lands of the deceased, and all rights of entry and of action, and all other rights and interests in lands which by law would descend to his heirs, or which would have been liable to attachment or execution by a creditor of the deceased in his lifetime;[3] but the title passed by any such sale is sub-

taking out of administration thereon will not lie pending a petition for the retention of assets to satisfy the claim   Cobb v Kempton, 154 Mass 266

[1] R L c 146, § 18
[2] R L c 15, § 8
[3] All land held in fee tail, except an estate tail in remainder, shall be liable for the debts of the tenant in tail, both in his lifetime and after his decease, as if held in fee simple; and if taken on execution, or sold by executors, administrators, or guardians, the creditor or purchaser shall hold such lands in fee simple   R L. c. 134, § 3.

All the lands of a debtor in possession, remainder, or reversion, all his rights of entry into lands and of redeeming mortgaged lands, and all such lands and rights which have been fraudulently conveyed by him with intent to defeat, delay, or defraud his creditors, or which have been purchased or directly or indirectly paid for by him but the record title thereto retained in the vendor or conveyed to a third person with intent to defeat, delay, or defraud the creditors of the debtor, or on a trust for him, express or implied, whereby he is entitled to a present conveyance, may, except as provided in chap 131 (relating to homesteads), be taken on execution for his debts.   R L c 178, § 1.

An executor or administrator licensed to sell lands fraudulently

ject to the right of dower of the wife or to the right of curtesy by the husband of the deceased, and no claim by entry or by action to lands fraudulently conveyed by

conveyed by the deceased, or fraudulently held by another person for him, or to which he had a right of entry or of action or a right to a conveyance, may, within one year after such license, sell the land without first obtaining possession thereof by entry or by action, or he may without a formal entry bring an action to obtain possession by virtue of such license, demanding the land as executor or administrator, and may sell the same within one year after possession is obtained R L. c 146, § 17; Yeomans *v* Brown, 8 Met 51, Allen *v* Ashley School Fund, 102 Mass 262, Hannum *v*. Day, 105 Mass 33, Walker *v* Fuller, 147 Mass 491 The case of Caverly *v* Eastman, 142 Mass 4, is interesting from its peculiar facts. But whether an administrator may prosecute a writ of entry brought by his intestate, *quære* Brigham *v*. Hunt, 152 Mass. 258 The executor may maintain a writ of entry to recover it without first selling the other real estate of his testator Tenney *v* Poor, 14 Gray, 500

Real estate conveyed by an intestate in his lifetime, without adequate consideration, and by way of gift, either in whole or in part, may be sold by his administrator to pay his debts, as estate conveyed by him with intent to defraud his creditors, if, at the time of the conveyance, he thereby rendered himself unable to pay his then existing creditors. Norton *v* Norton, 5 Cush 524, Allen *v* Trustees of Ashley School Fund, 102 Mass 262

The proceeds of a sale by an administrator of real estate conveyed by his intestate with a view to defraud creditors, though such conveyance was void at the time as against then existing creditors only, are applicable to the payment of all the creditors alike. Norton *v* Norton, *supra*

If an administrator receives payment of a note given for the purchase-money of an estate conveyed by his intestate to defraud creditors, he does not thereby ratify the conveyance, unless the payment is received with full knowledge of the facts, and the administrator is a party in interest, in which case it might be otherwise Ibid

The interest of a deceased partner in partnership real estate which is not required for the settlement of the affairs of the firm is to be treated as realty, and may be sold for the payment of legacies. Wilcox *v* Wilcox, 13 Allen, 252, Harris *v*. Harris, 153 Mass 439.

the deceased can be made, unless within five years after the decease of the grantor [1]

When land is demised for the term of one hundred years or more, the term, so long as fifty years thereof remain unexpired, is regarded by the statute as an estate in fee simple as to everything concerning the sale thereof by executors, administrators, and guardians, by license from any court [2]

The executor or administrator may sell lands held in mortgage, or taken in execution for a debt due the deceased, at any time before the right to redeem them is foreclosed, in the same manner as personal estate. The legal title to such lands is in him. He holds it in trust for the persons who would be entitled to the money if the mortgage or other debt had been paid But after the right of redemption is foreclosed, the executor should obtain license before making sale of the land, in the same manner as if the deceased had died seised of it. The license is not necessary to enable the executor to convey the legal title, which is already vested in him, but is intended solely to bind heirs and legatees, and make the title good against them as the owners of the beneficial interest [3]

The Petition for License to sell Real Estate must be presented by the executor or administrator to the probate court of the county in which letters testamentary or of administration issued. If there are two or more executors

---

[1] R L c 146, § 2.

[2] R. L c 129, § 1; Hollenbeck v McDonald, 112 Mass 247.

[3] An executor who, after foreclosing a mortgage held by his testator, sells and conveys the land without license of court, is not liable to an action on the covenant of good right to convey in his deed, if the legatees have received the purchase-money ; nor, it seems, if they have not Baldwin v Timmins, 3 Gray, 302

or administrators, all must join in the petition.[1] It may be presented as soon as the necessity of the proposed sale becomes apparent It must be in writing, and the statute requires to be set forth therein the value of the personal estate in the hands of the executor or administrator, the amount of the charges of administration, the amount of debts due from the deceased as nearly as they can be ascertained, and, in the case of a person dying testate, the amount of any legacies given in his will.[2] It is sufficient to state in the petition the gross amount of all the debts due, but the executor or administrator must file with his petition a list of the debts, so far as they can be ascertained, showing the name of each creditor and the sum due to each Such list of claims should be signed by the petitioner and sworn to.[3]

If it is necessary to sell only part of the real estate, the petitioner may also set forth the value, description, and condition of the estate, or of such part as he proposes to sell, and the court may direct what specific part shall be sold. If the estate is so situated that by a partial sale the residue of the estate, or of some specific piece or part thereof, would be greatly injured, the facts should be stated in the petition ; and the court may license a sale of the whole of the estate or of such part as may appear best.[4]

---

[1] Hannum v Day, 105 Mass 33 ; Cobb v. Kempton, 154 Mass. 270.

[2] R. L c 146, § 6.

[3] It is not necessary that the amount of the debts should have been previously ascertained by judgment against the executor, or by commission of insolvency Tenney v Pool, 14 Gray, 500

[4] R L. c 146, §§ 6, 7 , Yeomans v. Brown, 8 Met 58 , Gregson v. Tuson, 153 Mass. 328 A decree of the probate court, unappealed from, is conclusive of the question whether a part of the land sufficient

It is sometimes the case that the testator has made by will some disposition of his estate for the payment of his debts, or has given some directions which may vary the order in which the different parts of his estate shall be appropriated. Thus, though the personal property is first liable for payment of debts, the testator may expressly exempt it, or some portion of it, by making it the subject of a specific legacy, and may direct his debts to be paid out of other funds, or may leave other funds not exempted. Such specific legacies are not to be taken for the payment of debts, if there are other funds so first liable. The law will respect the testator's directions so far as is consistent with the rights of creditors. If the will contains a provision for the payment of debts, or which may require or induce the court to marshal the assets in a manner different from that which the law would otherwise provide, the executor shall set forth in the petition a copy of the will and the court shall marshal the assets accordingly, so far as can be done consistently with the rights of the creditors.[1] Undevised real property is first chargeable with the payment of debts or legacies in exoneration of the real estate devised, unless a different intention appears by the will.[2]

Notice to Parties interested. — The license will not be granted until notice of the petition, and of the time and place appointed for hearing the same, has been served either personally on all persons interested in the estate,[3]

to pay the debts may be sold without injuring the residue. Allen v. Trustees of the Ashley School Fund, 102 Mass 262.

[1] R L c 146, § 8.   [2] Ibid § 3

[3] When the executor petitions for license to sell land of which his testator was disseised at the time of his death, for the purpose of paying his debts, the disseisor in possession is not interested in the estate, within the meaning of the statute, and is not entitled to notice of the

at least fourteen days before the time appointed for the hearing, or by publication three weeks successively in some newspaper, as the court may order.[1] The petition may be filed in the probate office on any day, and the order issued by the register of probate. But if all persons interested signify their assent in writing to the sale, notice may be dispensed with.[2] The assent should be indorsed on the petition

The Necessity for the Proposed Sale. — The party applying for license to sell the real estate of his testator or intestate must prove the facts set forth in his petition. It must appear that a necessity exists for the sale he proposes to make If the personal assets are, in fact, sufficient for the payment of the debts and legacies, and he obtains a license by misrepresenting the condition of the

petition in order to render the license valid as against him. Yeomans v Brown, 8 Met 51 No notice need be given to persons who claim under a title derived independently of the deceased Walker v Fuller, 147 Mass. 491

The practice in the probate court is to order notice in the manner prescribed by statute, and it is not made the duty of the executor to obtain the appointment of guardians to all minors interested in the estate before he can obtain a license. Holmes v Beal, 9 Cush. 226

The wife of a devisee of real estate is not entitled to notice of a petititition of the devisor's administrator for license to sell it for the payment of debts, legacies, and charges of administration Harrington v Harrington, 13 Gray, 513

[1] R. L. c 146, § 10, Dexter v Shepard, 117 Mass. 480, Bemis v. Leonard, 118 Mass 502 A notice of a sale of a trust estate addressed to the "heirs at law, next of kin, and all other persons interested," is sufficient Boston Safe Deposit Co v Mixter, 146 Mass 100.

[2] R L c 162 § 15 Only persons in being who have a vested interest in the real estate are entitled to notice Dexter v Cotting, 149 Mass 92 But creditors of the estate are entitled to notice Browne v Doolittle, 151 Mass 595.

estate, a sale under a license so obtained is a breach of his bond for faithful administration.[1]

The averment and admission of the executor that a certain debt is due from the estate is not evidence to establish the fact. But any creditor of the deceased is a competent witness to prove his debt in support of the executor's petition.[2]

The adjudication of the probate court as to the existence of debts and charges is final, so far as it affects any title acquired by virtue of the license, but does not affect the right of the executor or administrator to contest the validity of such debts and charges [3]

Any person interested may appear and object to the granting of the license, and if it appears to the court that either the petition or the objection thereto is unreasonable, they may award costs to the prevailing party [4]

It may be that the heirs or devisees prefer to keep the estate entire and in their own hands, or the value of the property may be temporarily depressed, so that it cannot be sold immediately without a considerable sacrifice. If for these reasons, or for any reasons, the persons interested wish to stay proceedings under the petition and prevent the sale, they can effect that result by paying to the executor or administrator the amount of money needed for the payment of claims against the estate, and the money so received will be assets of the estate to be administered and accounted for ; and the executor or administrator will

---

[1] Chapin v Waters, 110 Mass 195 It is no defence that the sale was a pretence for the purpose of defeating a mortgage made by the devisee to defraud his creditors, or that the executor never received anything from the sale. Ibid

[2] Chamberlin v. Chamberlin, 4 Allen, 184 ; Ela v Edwards, 97 Mass 318.

[3] R L. c 148, § 21.   [4] Ibid § 10.

be liable on his bond for any failure to appropriate such assets to the payment of debts and legacies;[1] or any of the persons interested may give bond to the executor or administrator, in a sum and with sureties approved by the court, with condition to pay all legacies mentioned in the petition, all debts therein mentioned that shall eventually be found due from the estate, and charges of administration, so far as the personal estate may prove insufficient therefor If the money is so paid, or if such a bond is given, license to sell will not be granted.[2] The heirs may authorize the administrator to collect the rents and appropriate them to the payment of the debts, and thereby avoid the necessity for the sale.[3]

As to the License. — Upon the petition of an executor or administrator for a license to sell the real property of the deceased, the court may, if the petitioner so requests, authorize him to sell such property at public auction and to convey to the purchaser all the estate, right, title, and interest which the deceased had therein at the time of his death and which was then chargeable with the payment of his debts If the petitioner requests that such property may be sold by private sale, and the court, upon a hearing, finds that an advantageous offer for the purchase thereof has been made to the petitioner, and that the interests of all parties will be promoted by the acceptance of such offer,

---

[1] Fay v Taylor, 2 Gray, 154.

[2] R L c 146, § 12, Francis v. Daley, 150 Mass 385
The condition of the bond is not broken until it has been ascertained, by an account settled in court, that the personal estate is insufficient Studley v Josselyn, 5 Allen, 118

[3] But the occupation of the real estate by one of two administrators, who is also one of the heirs, without paying or charging himself with any rent, is not of itself a bar to granting the license to sell. Palmer v. Palmer, 13 Gray, 326.

it may authorize a conveyance by private sale in accordance with such offer or upon other terms; but such petitioner so authorized may nevertheless sell such property by public auction.¹ The court may license in terms the sale of the whole of the estate of the deceased, when the executor represents in his petition, and it appears to the court, that a sale of the whole is necessary,² or may license the sale of such part thereof as is deemed necessary and most for the interest of all concerned, or may direct what specific part shall be sold ³ The license is sufficient if it is in general terms, authorizing the sale of so much as will raise a certain sum; ⁴ but the license must concur with and be based upon the petition.⁵ If it is necessary, under the provisions of the will of the deceased, the court will marshal the assets, and the executor will appropriate the lands in the order specified by the court ⁶

[1] R L c 146 § 9; Walker v Fuller, 147 Mass 491
[2] R. L. c 146, § 7, Sewall v Raymond, 7 Met 454, Gregson v. Tuson, 153 Mass 329 Under a license to sell the whole, the reversion of land assigned to the widow as dower may be sold. Bancroft v. Andrews, 6 Cush 493, semble
[3] R L c 156, § 6, Gregson v Tuson, supra.
[4] Norton v Norton, 5 Cush. 524, Sewall v Raymond, 7 Met. 454
[5] On the petition for license to sell a specific portion of the estate for the payment of debts and charges, and after publication of notice to show cause why license should not be granted to sell "the whole of the real estate of said deceased," a license to sell "the whole of the real estate of said deceased" is irregular and void, and will not support an action by the administrator on the Pub Stats c. 134, § 15 (now R L. c 146, § 17), to recover the specific portion, as having been fraudulently conveyed by the deceased   Veiry v McClellan, 6 Gray, 535; Tenney v Poor, 14 Gray, 500; Gregson v. Tuson, supra, and cases cited

The executor may be licensed to sell land sufficient to pay a larger sum than the amount of debts and charges named in the petition Tenney v. Poor, 14 Gray, 500.

[6] See Humes v. Wood, 8 Pick. 478; Lee, Appellant, 18 Pick 285;

The general order of marshalling assets for the payment of debts is: 1. The personal estate not specifically bequeathed or otherwise exempted. 2. Lands appropriated in the will as a fund for the payment of debts. 3 Lands descended. 4 Lands specifically devised.[1] Specific legacies and devises are appropriated ratably to the payment of debts.[2]

License to sell for the payment of debts is not usually granted after the expiration of the period (two years) limited for the commencement of actions against executors and administrators who have given due notice of their appointment. The object and general effect of the statute making this limitation is to discharge the lien of creditors on the land at the expiration of the two years, thereby promoting the speedy settlement of estates, and establishing the titles of the heirs. If no claims exist but those against which the statute of limitations furnishes complete protection, the proceeds of the real estate are not needed for the payment of debts, and a license to sell cannot be granted. The question to be determined upon every application for a license is, whether the proposed sale

---

Adams v Brackett, 5 Met 280; Ellis v. Page, 7 Cush 161; Hewes v Dehon, 3 Gray, 205, Plimpton v. Fuller, 11 Allen, 139, Farnum v. Bascom, 122 Mass. 282; Johnson v. Home for Aged Women, 152 Mass 93, and cases cited

[1] Hays v. Jackson, 6 Mass. 149, Livingston v Newkirk, 3 Johns. Ch 312, Blaney v Blaney, 1 Cush 115, and cases cited

Any person interested may appeal from a decree granting a license to sell real estate, but on such an appeal the question of title, except so far as any doubt regarding it may affect the expediency of the sale, is not properly before the court. Walker v Fuller, 147 Mass 489. A sale during the time allowed for an appeal is invalid. Daley v Francis, 153 Mass 8

[2] Farnum v Bascom, 122 Mass. 282; Hallowell's Estate, 23 Penn. St 223; Long v. Short, 1 P Wms 403.

is necessary for the payment of claims against the estate [1] A license may be granted after the expiration of the two years, provided there are claims against the estate upon which the statute of limitations does not operate.[2] But the court will not grant a license after the two years have elapsed unless extraordinary circumstances render it proper, especially when the effect will be to disturb titles acquired under the presumption that all the debts had been paid.[3] But license to sell for the payment of legacies may be granted after the expiration of the two years.[4]

As to the Time of Sale.— No license to sell land con-

---

[1] Lamson *v* Schutt, 4 Allen, 359; Hudson *v* Hulburt, 15 Pick. 423; Heath *v* Wells, 5 Pick. 140, Tarbell *v* Parker, 106 Mass. 347. See also Gregson *v*. Tuson, 153 Mass 329

[2] Palmer *v* Palmer, 13 Gray, 326, Richmond, Petitioner, 2 Pick 567 License may be granted after the expiration of the two years if a sale is necessary for the payment of debts proved before commissioners within the two years Edmunds *v* Rockwell, 125 Mass 363.

[3] Where an executor has paid debts of his testator beyond the amount of the personal assets, within the time limited by statute, he cannot afterwards be licensed to sell lands to reimburse himself, unless the estate remains as it was at the death of the testator, and his application is made in a reasonable time after his payment of the debts Allen, Petitioner, 15 Mass 58

But where the land had neither been sold nor divided among the heirs, an administrator who had demands against his intestate and had made advances to the estate out of his own funds, but had rendered no account until after the time limiting the bringing of actions had expired, the delay having been occasioned in part by an attempt to collect a debt abroad, was licensed to sell Richmond, Petitioner, 2 Pick 567, and see Palmer *v* Palmer, 13 Gray, 326; Munroe *v* Holmes, 13 Allen, 109; Ames *v* Jackson, 115 Mass 511

[4] An executor died several years after his appointment without having paid the legacies given by the will No demand had ever been made upon him by the legatees. An administrator with the will annexed was licensed to sell real estate for the payment of the legacies eight years after the probate of the will. Smith *v*. Wells, 134 Mass 11.

tinues in force more than one year after it is granted, and sales must be made within the year,[1] except when a sale is made of land which was not in possession of the deceased at the time of his death, and is recovered by the executor or administrator. Land so recovered may be sold at any time within one year after possession is obtained.[2] But it is not essential that the deed be delivered within the year, provided all the other proceedings are regular.

Notice of the Time and Place of Sale must be given by notices posted thirty days at least before the sale, in some public place in the city or town in which the land lies, and in two adjoining cities or towns, if there are so many in the county, or, if the court granting the license so orders, by publishing the notice once in each of three successive weeks in a newspaper.[3] Such notice is essential to the validity of the sale. The form of the notice is not material, but the time and place fixed for the sale should be distinctly stated. An error in this particular may invalidate the sale.[4] The conditions of the sale are not necessarily to be stated;[5] but the notices should plainly identify the property,[6] and con-

---

[1] This provision is limited to sales by executors, administrators, or guardians, it does not extend to sales by trustees Boston Safe Deposit Co *v* Mixter, 146 Mass 105

[2] R L c 146, § 17; c. 148, § 8; Walker *v* Fuller, 147 Mass 491.

[3] R L c 146, § 14

[4] Where the sale was advertised to be on Friday, the 17th, whereas Friday was in fact the 16th, and the sale was made on the 16th, it was *held* void, although in the last publication, which was on the day of sale, the error was corrected Wellman *v* Lawrence, 15 Mass 226

Where the advertisement bore no date and recited the fact that license was granted "on the 5th day of April instant," and gave notice that the land would be sold "on the 22d day of said April," it was *held* that the notice was not so defective as to vacate the sale. Brigham *v* Boston & Albany R R Co, 102 Mass 14

[5] Paine *v* Fox, 16 Mass. 129 ,Wyman *v*. Hooper, 2 Gray, 141

[6] N. E. Hospital *v*. Sohier, 115 Mass. 50.

vey to the public all such information in regard to it as, in the judgment of the executor, is best calculated to promote the interests of the estate. It is important to executors, for their own protection, to preserve evidence of the fact that the notice was given as required by the terms of the license, and the statute provides a mode of perpetuating such evidence. An affidavit of the executor or administrator, or of the person employed by him to give such notice, filed and recorded with a copy of the notice in the registry of probate, or such affidavit made by any person and filed and recorded with such copy by permission of the court upon satisfactory evidence that the notice was given as ordered, shall be admitted as evidence of the time, place, and manner in which the notice was given.[1] The fact may be proved by other evidence;[2] but it may be difficult or impossible for the executor, after the lapse of years, in case a question is raised upon the covenants in his deed, to obtain such other evidence. In the absence of all evidence that such notice was given, there is no presumption within thirty years that it was given.[3] The affidavit, therefore, should be filed in all cases.

Where the affidavit of the notice of the sale of real estate has not been filed in the probate court, and such affidavit cannot be obtained, the probate court may, upon petition of any person interested in real estate, the title to which may be affected thereby, setting forth the particular failure complained of and averring that the affidavit cannot now be obtained, order notice by publication to creditors of, and

[1] R L c 146, § 15.

[2] The fact that notice has been given as ordered may be proved by the affidavit of persons other than the executor or administrator, or the person employed by him to give such notice, by permission of the probate court after satisfactory evidence. R. L. c. 146, § 15.

[3] Thomas v. Le Baron, 8 Met 355.

others interested in, the estate in settlement of which the failure complained of occurred.

Upon return of such notice and after hearing, if the court is satisfied that notice was in fact given, it may make a decree that such notice was in fact given [1]

Adjournment of the Sale. — If at the time appointed for the sale the executor or administrator deems it for the interest of all persons concerned that the sale be postponed, he may adjourn it for any time not exceeding fourteen days. Notice of such adjournment must be given by a public declaration at the time and place first appointed for making the sale; and if the adjournment is for more than one day, further notice of the sale must be given by posting or publishing, as time and circumstances may admit. [2]

The Sale must be by public auction, unless otherwise ordered, and must be conducted with a view to insure an unrestrained and honest competition among bidders, and thus to procure the highest price for the land. When it appears by the petition of an executor or administrator for a license to sell the real estate of the deceased, and upon a hearing on such petition, that an advantageous offer for the purchase thereof has been previously made to the petitioner, and that the interest of all parties concerned will be best promoted by an acceptance of such offer, the court having jurisdiction of such petition may authorize a sale and conveyance at private sale, in accordance with such offer, or upon such terms as may be adjudged best; but an executor or administrator so authorized to sell real estate at private sale may notwithstanding sell such estate by public auction if he deems it best so to do. [3] The executor or administra-

---

[1] R. L c. 148, § 26.   [2] R L c 146, § 16.
[3] Ibid § 9.

An agreement by an administrator or guardian to offer the real es-

tor making the sale cannot properly become the purchaser, directly or indirectly, though if it is purchased by him under color of a sale to some other person, the sale is not absolutely void; strangers to the property cannot call it in question, but it is voidable at the pleasure of the heirs of the deceased.[1] The heirs are not obliged to act jointly in avoiding the sale, but each one has an individual election[2] If the land is subsequently sold to a *bona fide* purchaser who had no notice that it had been bought at the administrator's sale for the administrator's benefit, such purchaser will hold it as against the heirs, though the sale might have been avoided by a suit against the first grantee, or one claiming under him, who had notice of the irregularity.[3] The same rule applies in cases of sales of land by guardians

The essential particulars to which the purchaser ought to look, in order to protect himself against suits by the heirs, are specified in the statute. He is not called upon to inform himself as to every particular connected with the administrator's or guardian's proceedings. He is not expected, for instance, to inquire whether or not the administrator obtained his license to sell by a false representation as to the condition of the estate. That is a matter in

---

tate of his intestate or ward for sale by auction, and to sell the same to a particular individual for an agreed price, provided no higher sum should be bid, is valid. But such an agreement to sell the estate at a fixed price, without regard to the biddings, is void Hunt v Frost, 4 Cush 54.

[1] Blood v Hayman, 13 Met 231; Jennison v. Hapgood, 7 Pick. 1; Harrington v Brown, 5 Pick 519, Wyman v Hooper, 2 Gray, 141; Robbins v Bates, 4 Cush. 104, Ives v. Ashley, 97 Mass 198; Denholm v McKay, 148 Mass 441 and cases cited See Yeackel v Litchfield, 13 Allen, 417; O'Reiley v Bevington, 155 Mass 72; Goodell v Goodell, 173 Mass 146.

[2] Litchfield v Cudworth, 15 Pick 23

[3] Blood v Hayman, 13 Met 231; Wyman v Hooper, 2 Gray, 141

which the heirs are directly concerned, and they have a remedy against an unfaithful administrator on his bond. The statute provides that no sale of real estate made by an executor, administrator, guardian, or trustee, or other person by license of court, and no title under such a sale, shall be avoided for the reason that the deed was not delivered within one year after the license, or on account of any irregularity in the proceedings, if it appears, —

First, That the license was granted by a court of competent jurisdiction;

Second, That the person licensed gave a bond which was approved by the judge of the probate court, if a bond was required upon the granting of the license,[1]

Third, That the notice of the time and place of sale was given according to the order of the court; and,

Fourth, That the property was sold by public auction in accordance with the notice, and is held by one who purchased it in good faith.[2] If, however, in any par-

---

[1] When a license or authority for the sale or mortgage of real estate is granted to an executor, administrator, guardian, or trustee, no special bond shall be required, but if the bond given by such executor, administrator, guardian, or trustee, upon his appointment, appears to the court to be insufficient, it shall, before granting such license or authority, require an additional bond containing the same conditions as are required in the bond to be given upon the appointment of such executor, administrator, guardian, or trustee R L. c 149, § 13

[2] R L. c 148, § 19. A sale by an executrix was held valid although she was described in the license, bond, and deed as "administratrix on the estate." Cooper *v* Robinson, 2 Cush 184, Brigham *v* Boston & Albany R R Co, 102 Mass 14, Gregson *v* Tuson, 153 Mass 326 The statute does not prohibit a trustee from making a sale after the lapse of a year from the granting of his license, except by public auction The word "trustee" seems to have been used in the statute inadvertently Boston Safe Deposit Co *v*. Mixter, 146 Mass. 105.

A license granted after the claims against the estate have become

ticular the purchaser is guilty of any collusion with the administrator, or has notice of any material defect in the proceedings, though it be in something into which he was not bound to inquire, he will not be protected by this provision of the statute [1]

"If the validity of a sale is drawn in question by a person who claims adversely to the title of the deceased or of the ward, or who claims under a title that is not derived from or through the deceased or the ward, the sale shall not be void on account of any irregularity in the proceedings, if the executor, administrator, guardian, or trustee was licensed to make the sale by a court of competent jurisdiction and executed and acknowledged in legal form a deed for the conveyance of the property." [2] The question at issue in such a suit is not whether the claimant's title is better than that of the administrator's vendee, but whether it is better than that of the deceased person or ward. If he shows a better title, he will recover, notwithstanding the conveyance by the administrator; but if he has not a better title than that of the deceased person or ward, it is no concern of his whether the land goes to the heirs or to the person who holds under the administrator. The particular proceedings of the administrator or guardian are therefore not material in such a suit [3]

---

barred by the special statute of limitations is void. Tarbell v Parker, 106 Mass 347. See also Gregson v Tuson, 153 Mass 326.

A guardian who acts as auctioneer in selling land of his ward is not authorized to sign a memorandum in writing, to take the sale out of the statute of frauds. Bent v Cobb, 9 Gray, 397

[1] Dickinson v Durfee, 139 Mass 232. Even where due notice is not given, a sale may be confirmed. Nott v Sampson Manufacturing Co, 142 Mass 479

[2] R. L. c 148, § 20. All objections in other respects are open. Walker v Fuller, 147 Mass 491

[3] Actions for the recovery of lands sold by executors and adminis-

Every person licensed to sell lands is required, upon application to the probate court by an heir, creditor, ward, or other person interested in the estate, to make answer upon oath to all matters touching his exercise and fulfilment of the license, as fully as he is liable to account and be examined relative to personal property. If, in relation to the exercise of such license or the sale under it, there is any neglect or misconduct in his proceedings by which a person interested in the estate suffers damage, such interested person may recover compensation therefor on the probate bond or otherwise as the case may require.[1]

The Deed — In his deed to the purchaser of the real estate, the executor, administrator, or guardian covenants with his grantee that, in making the sale, he was duly authorized by the court, that he has complied with the order of the court by giving the bond required by law, and by giving notice of the time and place of the sale; and that he has in all things observed the rules and directions of law relative thereto. The date of the decree of the court granting the license should also be stated in the deed.[2]

---

trators must be commenced within five years after the sale; and for lands sold by guardians, within five years after the termination of the guardianship, except that persons out of the estate or under legal disability to sue at the time when the right of action first accrues, may commence an action within five years after the removal of the disability or their return to the state. No entry, unless by judgment of law, can be made upon the land sold, with a view to avoid the sale, unless within the time of limitation. R. L. c. 148, § 22. A remainder-man, during the continuance of the life estate, is under legal disability within the meaning of the statute. Jewett *v* Jewett, 10 Gray, 31.

[1] R. L. c 148, § 11

[2] An administrator's deed is not rendered invalid by a misrecital

SALES OF LANDS BY EXECUTORS, ETC.   261

The executor or other person selling land under license is not required by any duty of his office to enter into a personal covenant for the absolute perfection of the title which he undertakes to convey, or for the validity of the conveyance beyond his own acts. He is at liberty to do so, if he chooses thus to excite the confidence of purchasers and enlarge the proceeds of the sale, and he may engage his own credit collaterally in the conveyance. But such covenant, although expressed to be made in his official capacity, is necessarily a personal covenant, for the breach of which he is personally liable.[1]

In every sale of the real estate of a deceased person or of a ward by an executor, administrator, or guardian, the surplus of the proceeds remaining on the final settlement of the accounts shall be considered as real estate, and shall be disposed of to the same persons and in the same proportions to whom and in which the real estate if not sold would have descended or been disposed of by the laws of this commonwealth.[2]

of the time when the license was granted, if it also contains a recital of other facts which show that the sale was made under the true license. Thomas v. LeBaron, 8 Met. 355. The deed need not state the reason for granting the license. Sowle v. Sowle, 10 Pick. 376.

[1] Sumner v. Williams, 8 Mass. 201; Chilson v. Adams, 6 Gray, 364. If there should be a surplus after a sale for the payment of debts, it is to be distributed like real estate. Hovey v. Dary, 154 Mass. 11. An administrator who recovers judgment as such, and levies execution on land, holds the legal estate in the land to the use of the heirs of his intestate, and if he sells and conveys it without having obtained license to do so, the conveyance can be avoided only by those for whose use he was seised, and if they receive the proceeds of the sale, they thereby confirm the sale. Thomas v. LeBaron, 10 Met. 403.

[2] R. L. c. 148, § 9; Hovey v. Dary, 154 Mass. 11. An administrator authorized by the probate court to sell real estate to pay the debts of the intestate under a license to sell " the whole of the estate, or

SALES BY FOREIGN EXECUTORS AND ADMINISTRATORS.

"An executor or administrator appointed in another state or in a foreign country on the estate of a person who was not at the time of his death a resident of this commonwealth and upon whose estate administration has not been granted in this commonwealth, duly qualified and acting, may file an authenticated copy of the record of his appointment and of his bond in the probate court for any county in which there is real property of the deceased, and such executor or administrator, after such notice to the treasurer and receiver-general, creditors, and all persons interested as the court may order, may be licensed to sell said real property or an undivided interest in real property in such manner and upon such notice as the court orders But such license shall not be granted unless the court finds that the whole of the real property of the deceased in this commonwealth does not exceed fifteen hundred dollars in value, that six months have expired since the death of the deceased, that the executor or administrator has given a sufficient bond and will be liable to account for the proceeds of the sale in the state or country in which he was appointed, and that no creditor or other person interested will be prejudiced thereby. The net proceeds of such sale, after deducting the expenses thereof, and after the payment and satisfaction of all

such part thereof as may appear to be most for the interest of all concerned," cannot be charged as trustee for money received from the sale before the sale has taken place, because if he should decide to sell only enough to pay the debts, the remainder would descend to the heirs, and would not be affected by the trustee process, while if the heirs should advance money to pay the debts, rather than to have their real estate sold, no sale would be likely to be made Beverstock v. Brown, 157 Mass 565

claims against said estate in this commonwealth, may be taken by said foreign executor or administrator out of this commonwealth to be accounted for in the court in which he received his appointment "[1]

Every foreign executor or administrator licensed to sell real estate must give notice of the time and place of sale, and otherwise proceed as is prescribed for an administrator appointed here when making such sale; and the evidence of such notice may be perpetuated in the same manner.[2]

SALES BY GUARDIANS.

For the Payment of Debts. — When the personal estate in the hands of a guardian is insufficient to pay all the debts of the ward, with the charges of managing his estate, the guardian may be licensed to sell the ward's real estate for that purpose, by the probate court for the county in which he is appointed, or by the supreme judicial court, or superior court in any county.[3] The guardian must proceed by petition, and the petition may be substantially in the same form as that of an executor or administrator who applies for leave to sell real estate for the payment of debts.[4] It must appear that a necessity exists for the sale proposed.

If it is represented in the petition and appears necessary to sell some part of the real estate of the ward, and that by such partial sale the residue of the estate, or of some specific piece or part thereof, would be greatly injured, the

---

[1] R L c 146, § 30.   [2] Ibid, § 33
[3] The legislature may license the sale of the real estate of minors notwithstanding they have delegated the same power to the judicial courts Rice v Parkman, 16 Mass 326; Forster v. Forster, 129 Mass. 564, and cases cited
[4] R L c 146, § 5.

court may license a sale of the whole of the estate, or of such part thereof as may appear best [1]

For Maintenance or Investment. — When the income of a ward's estate is insufficient to maintain him and his family, or when it appears that it would be for the benefit of a ward that his real estate or any part thereof, or any standing or growing wood thereon, should be sold, and the proceeds put out at interest or invested in some productive stock, his guardian may be licensed to sell the same.

When standing or growing wood is so sold, the guardian may grant to the purchaser the privilege of entering upon the land and cutting and carrying away such wood within such time as the guardian may allow. [2]

The guardian may be licensed to sell the ward's estate of homestead. [3]

A father is bound, to the extent of his ability, to support his minor child, but if the minor's property is sufficient for his maintenance and education in a more expensive manner than his father can reasonably afford, regard being had to the situation of the father's family, and to all the circumstances of the case, the expenses of the maintenance and education of such child may be defrayed out of his own property, in whole or in part, as shall be deemed reasonable by the probate court; and when necessary, his real estate may be sold for that purpose by the guardian under license. [4]

To obtain such license, the guardian must present to the court a petition setting forth the condition of the estate

---

[1] R. L. c. 146, § 7   As a general rule, executors, administrators, and guardians can be licensed to sell only at public auction. Boston Safe Deposit Co *v* Mixter, 116 Mass 105.

[2] R L c 146, § 19; Boston Safe Deposit Co *v.* Mixter, *supra*

[3] R L c. 131, § 10   [4] R L c 145, § 29.

and the facts and circumstances upon which his application is founded. If after a full examination, on the oath of the petitioner or otherwise, it appears either that it is necessary, or that it would be for the benefit of the ward, that the sale petitioned for should be made, the court may grant a license therefor, specifying therein whether the sale is to be made for the maintenance of the ward and his family, or that the proceeds may be put out and invested [1]

The property of a minor may be sold for the purpose of investing the proceeds upon the petition of the guardian or of any friend of the minor; and the court may authorize the guardian or any other suitable person to sell and convey the property. The statute provisions in relation to the licenses and sales on the petitions of guardians apply to licenses and sales on the petition of a friend of the minor, except that, upon a sale by a person other than the guardian, the proceeds are to be forthwith paid to the guardian upon his giving to the judge of probate a bond, with sufficient sureties, conditioned to account for such proceeds. If there is no guardian, the proceeds are required to be placed on interest or invested by the person authorized to sell the estate, in like manner as is required of a guardian. [2]

No license can be granted to a guardian until after notice, by public advertisement or otherwise, as the court shall order, to the next of kin of the ward, to all his heirs apparent or presumptive, and to all persons interested in the estate, but such notice may be dispensed with, if all persons interested signify in writing their assent to the sale. All who are next of kin, and heirs apparent or presumptive of the ward, are considered by the statute as

[1] R. L. c. 146, § 20.   [2] Ibid. §§ 23, 24.

interested in the estate, and may appear as such and answer to the petition of the guardian.[1]

No license to sell can be granted to the guardian of an insane person or spendthrift unless seven days' notice of the petition therefor has been given to the overseers of the poor of the place where the ward is an inhabitant or resides. The notice may be served upon any one of the overseers. This provision does not apply when the ward resides out of this state.[2]

Guardians are required to give notice of the time and place of sale, and otherwise proceed as prescribed in like cases for executors and administrators except when licensed to sell fractional shares at private sale; and the evidence of giving notice may be perpetuated in the same manner.[3]

If the sale is made for the maintenance of the ward and his family, the guardian is required to apply the proceeds, so far as necessary for that purpose, and to put out the residue at interest, or invest it in the best manner in his power, until the capital is wanted for such maintenance; in which case the capital may be used for that purpose in like manner as if it had been personal estate.[4]

If the estate is sold in order to put out on interest or

---

[1] R L c 146, § 11, c. 162, § 45, Dexter v Cotting, 149 Mass 92, Browne v Doolittle, 151 Mass 595.

[2] R L. c 146, § 13.

[3] Ibid §§ 14, 15 A sale of a minor's real estate by a guardian is void if no deed thereof is delivered or executed until the expiration of a year from the date of the license, and no money therefor has been paid to the guardian Richmond v Gray, 3 Allen, 25 The guardian of a spendthrift will be held responsible for all losses arising in consequence of the disregard of the terms of his license, and the ward's assent to his acts will not exonerate him Harding v. Larned, 4 Allen, 426

[4] R L c 146, § 21.

invest the proceeds, the guardian is required to make the investment according to his best judgment, or in pursuance of any order that may be made relating thereto by the court.[1] He has no right to apply the proceeds towards the support of the ward unless a necessity therefor arises after the granting of the license.[2]

When the guardian of a married man is licensed to sell real estate of his ward, the wife of the ward may join with the guardian in the conveyance, and thereby release her right of dower and the estate or right of homestead, in like manner as she might have done by joining in a conveyance made by her husband if he had been under no legal disability.[3]

If the wife so releases her right of dower or an estate of homestead, or so conveys her own estate, the proceeds of the sale may be so invested and disposed of as to secure to her, and to the minor children of the owner if it is an estate of homestead, the same rights in the principal and the income thereof as she or they would have had therein if it had not been sold. An agreement made between her and the guardian for securing and disposing of the proceeds, or of any part thereof, for the purpose aforesaid, if approved by the probate court for the county in which the guardian was appointed, or by the supreme court of probate upon appeal, or, in default of an agreement between her and the guardian approved as aforesaid, an order therefor made by the probate court shall be valid and binding on all persons interested in the granted property or in said proceeds, and may be enforced by the court or by an action at law.[4]

[1] R L c 146, § 22 [2] Strong v. Moe, 8 Allen, 125
[3] R. L. c. 153, § 15.
[4] Ibid § 17. A sale to the attorney of the guardian who recon-

If the guardian of an insane wife is authorized under the provisions of section 19 of chapter 153 of the Revised Laws to release the dower of his ward or an estate of homestead, and the probate court deems it proper that some portion of the proceeds of such real property, or of a sum loaned on mortgage thereof, should be reserved for the use of the ward, the court may order that in the case of dower, a certain sum not exceeding one-third of the net amount of such proceeds, exclusive of any encumbrance then existing on the estate, shall be paid over to such guardian to be invested and held by him for the benefit of the wife if she survives her husband, the income of such sum to be enjoyed by the husband during the life of his wife, or until otherwise ordered by the court upon good cause shown; and the principal to be his, and to be paid over to him, if he survives her; in case an estate of homestead is released, a certain sum, not exceeding eight hundred dollars, shall be set aside and paid over to such guardian to be invested in a homestead, and held by him for the benefit of his ward if she survives her husband; the rent or use thereof to be received and enjoyed by the husband during the life of his wife, or until otherwise ordered by the court upon good cause shown; and the homestead to be his. and to be conveyed to him to said guardian, if he survives her.[1]

The husband or wife of an insane person who desires to convey his or her real property, absolutely or by way of mortgage, may file a petition in the probate court describing such real property and praying that the dower of the wife or an estate of homestead or a tenancy by the curtesy at common law or by statute of the husband therein may

veyed to the guardian, and no money passed between them, may be voided by the persons interested. Walker v Walker, 101 Mass 169

[1] R L c. 153, §§ 21, 22

be released, setting forth the facts and reasons why the prayer of the petition should be granted. The court may, after notice and a hearing, by a decree authorize the guardian of the insane person to make such release by joining in any deed or deeds, mortgage or mortgages of the whole or a part of said real property which is or are made within five years after said decree either by the husband or wife of the insane person or by a trustee for such husband or wife.[1]

When the husband or wife of an insane person has conveyed real property in trust without a power of revocation, and makes a provision in such conveyance for the insane husband or wife, respectively, which the probate court, upon petition, after notice and a hearing, finds is sufficient in lieu of curtesy or dower, the trustee may convey such real property free from all right of curtesy or dower.[2]

When a guardian is licensed to sell the interest of the ward in any real estate of his wife, the wife may join with the guardian in the conveyance, and thereby sell and convey all her estate and interest in the granted property in like manner as she might have done by a conveyance thereof made jointly with her husband, if he had been under no legal disability.[3]

When a person under guardianship, having a guardian appointed within the commonwealth, removes or resides out of the commonwealth, such guardian may sell the real estate of his ward, and transfer and pay over the whole or any part of the proceeds, and the whole or any part of the ward's personal estate, to a guardian, trustee, or committee appointed by competent authority in the state or country within which the ward resides, upon such terms and in

[1] R. L. c. 153, § 19   [2] Ibid § 23.   [3] Ibid § 16.

such manner as the probate court for any county in which any such real or personal estate is found may decree upon petition filed therefor, and after notice given to all parties interested.[1]

SALE OF REAL ESTATE AT PRIVATE SALE.

When it appears, by the petition of the guardian for a license to sell the real estate of his ward, and upon the hearing thereon, that an advantageous offer has been previously made to the guardian for the purchase thereof, and that the interest of all parties concerned will be best promoted by an acceptance of such offer, the court may authorize the sale, at private sale in accordance with the offer, or upon such terms as may be adjudged best, with or without public notice. The guardian so licensed may sell at public auction, if he deems it best so to do[2]

SALES BY FOREIGN GUARDIANS

"If a minor, insane person, or spendthrift, who resides out of this commonwealth, is under guardianship in the state or country in which he resides, and has no guardian appointed in this commonwealth, the foreign guardian may file an authenticated copy of his appointment in the probate court for any county in which there is real property of the ward; after which, upon petition, he may be licensed to sell, mortgage, or lease the real property of the ward in any county, for the purposes, in the manner, and upon the terms provided in this chapter (R. L. c. 147) for a guardian appointed in this commonwealth, except as hereinafter provided.

"If the court finds that such foreign guardian has given

[1] R. L c. 146, § 25.
[2] Ibid § 9, Boston Safe Deposit Co v. Mixter, 146 Mass. 105.

bond with sufficient surety or sureties, in the state or county in which he was appointed, to account for the proceeds of such sale, mortgage, or lease, and if an authenticated copy of such bond is filed in said court, no further bond shall be required; otherwise, before such license is granted, he shall give bond, payable to the judge of said court and his successors, with sufficient surety or sureties, and with condition to account for and dispose of said proceeds according to law." [1]

All proceedings in probate courts respecting sales by a foreign executor, administrator, or guardian are had in the county in which an authenticated copy of his appointment is first filed. [2]

SALES BY PUBLIC ADMINISTRATORS.

Public administrators may be licensed to sell real estate for the payment of debts. The petition for such sale and the proceedings thereon, and under the license, are the same as are prescribed for other administrators. [3]

Sales by public administrators are not limited to cases where the sales are necessary for the payment of debts. The statute provides that after three years from the date of letters of administration to a public administrator, the probate court may, if it appears to be for the interest of all concerned, authorize the administrator to sell the real estate of the deceased, although such sale is not necessary for the payment of debts. In such case the public administrator proceeds in the same manner as is required of administrators when licensed to sell real estate for the payment of debts [4]

[1] R L. c 146, §§ 31, 32. [2] R L. c. 148, § 7.
[3] R. L c. 138, § 10. [4] R L c. 138, § 11.

RELEASE OF INTERESTS IN LAND BY EXECUTORS AND OTHERS

Executors, administrators, guardians, and trustees may be authorized by probate courts to release and discharge, upon such terms and conditions as may appear to be proper, a vested, contingent, or possible right or interest belonging to the persons or estates by them represented in or to real property, when such release or discharge appears to be for the benefit of such persons or estates.[1]

This provision does not apply to sales of the land itself, and has not any reference to sales of land by executors and administrators for the payment of debts and legacies, nor to sales by guardians for maintenance or investment. Leave to release the remote interests mentioned in the statute may be granted, when it appears to be for the benefit of the parties interested, whether the proceeds are necessary for the payment of debts and legacies or not. The person applying for leave to release such an interest should state in his petition the names and residences of all persons interested, and fully describe the nature of the interest to be released. The same notice of the petition must be given as is required in cases of sale for the payment of debts. When leave is granted, the court directs the manner in which the release shall be made.

MORTGAGE OF REAL ESTATE BY EXECUTORS AND ADMINISTRATORS.

The probate court having jurisdiction of the estate of a deceased person may, on petition and after notice to all persons interested, if upon a hearing it appears to be for the benefit of such estate, authorize an executor, adminis-

[1] R L c 148, § 4.

trator with the will annexed, or administrator to mortgage any real estate of the testator for the purpose of paying debts, legacies, or charges of administration, or for the purpose of paying an existing lien or mortgage on the estate of the testator, or it may authorize such executor or administrator to make an agreement for the extension or renewal of such an existing mortgage.

The petition must set forth a description of the estate to be mortgaged, the amount of money necessary to be raised, and the purposes for which the money is required. The decree of the court fixes the amount for which the mortgage may be given and the rate of interest to be paid, and may order the whole or any part of the money secured by the mortgage to be paid from time to time out of the income of the premises mortgaged.[1]

MORTGAGE OF REAL ESTATE BY GUARDIANS.

The probate court may, on the petition of a guardian, and if after due notice and hearing thereon it appears to be necessary or expedient, authorize the guardian to mortgage any real estate of his ward. The guardian must set forth in his petition a description of the estate to be mortgaged, and the amount of money necessary to be raised. The amount for which the mortgage is to be given is fixed by the decree of the court.[2]

MORTGAGE OF REAL ESTATE BY TRUSTEES.

The court having jurisdiction of a trust created by a written instrument may, on petition and after notice to

[1] R L c 146 §§ 26, 28
[2] Ibid §§ 27, 28   A guardian of a ward who has a life interest in the real estate, with an absolute and unrestricted right to convey the fee, can mortgage the estate in fee   Kent v Morrison, 153 Mass. 137.

all persons interested, if upon a hearing it appears to be for the benefit of the trust estate, authorize trustees to mortgage any real estate held by them in trust, for the purpose of paying sums assessed on their trust estate for betterments, or the expense of repairs and improvements on such estate made necessary by such betterments, or by the lawful taking of such estate or of a part thereof by a city or town, for the purpose of paying the expense of erecting, altering, completing, repairing, or improving a building on such estate; or for the purpose of paying the expense of other improvements of a permanent nature made or to be made upon such estate; or for the purpose of paying an existing lien or mortgage on such trust estate or on a part thereof, or it may authorize such trustees to make an agreement for the extension or renewal of such existing mortgage.[1]

The petition shall in such case set forth a description of the estate to be mortgaged, the amount of money necessary to be raised, and the purposes for which such money is required, and, if made to a probate court, shall be made in the county where the trustees were appointed, if the trust was created by will, or, if it was not so created, then in the county in which the estate or some part of the estate which is the subject of the petition is situated. The decree of the court upon such petition shall fix the amount for which the mortgage may be given, and the rate of interest which may be paid thereon, and may order the interest and the whole or any part of the money secured by the mortgage to be paid from time to time out of the income of the premises mortgaged.[2]

"If the sale and conveyance, transfer or exchange of any real or personal property held in trust, or the partition of

[1] R. L. c. 147, § 18.   [2] Ibid. § 19.

any such real property held in common and undivided, appears to be necessary or expedient, the supreme judicial court, the superior court, or the probate court, may, upon petition of a trustee or other party interested, after notice and other proceedings as hereinafter required, order such sale and conveyance, transfer, exchange, or partition to be made, and the investment, re-investment, and application of the proceeds of such sale in such manner as will best effect the objects of the trust." [1]

If it appears to the court, upon proceedings under the preceding section (R. L. c. 147, § 15), that the estate which is the subject of the petition may be held in trust for, or that a remainder or contingent interest therein may be limited over to, persons not ascertained or not in being, notice shall be given in such manner as the court may order to all persons who are or may become interested in such estate, and to all persons whose issue, not then in being, may become so interested ; and the court shall in every such case appoint a suitable person to appear and act therein as the next friend of all persons not ascertained or not in being, who are or may become interested in such estate, the cost of whose appearance, including the compensation of his counsel, shall be determined by the court, and paid, as it may order, either out of the trust estate or by the petitioner, in which latter case execution may issue therefor in the name of the next friend ; and a conveyance or transfer made after such notice and proceedings shall be conclusive upon all persons, whether in being or not in being, who are or may become interested in the trust, or to whom a remainder or contingent interest in the trust estate may be limited over. [2]

[1] R L c 147, § 15
[2] Ibid. § 16; Boston Safe Deposit Co. v Mixter, 146 Mass. 100.

SALE AND MORTGAGE OF ESTATES SUBJECT TO REMAINDERS

"If land is subject to a contingent remainder, executory devise, or power of appointment, the probate court for the county in which such land is situated, may, upon the petition of any person who has an estate in possession of such land, and after notice and other proceedings as hereinafter required, appoint one or more trustees, and authorize him or them to sell and convey such land or any part thereof in fee simple, if such sale and conveyance appears to the court to be necessary or expedient; or to mortgage the same, either with or without a power of sale, for such an amount, on such terms, and for such purposes as may seem to the court judicious or expedient, and such conveyance or mortgage shall be valid and binding upon all parties"[1]

"If land is subject to a vested remainder or reversion, the probate court for the county in which such land is situated may, upon the petition of any person who has either an estate in possession or the remainder or reversion in such land, and after notice and other proceedings as hereinafter required, appoint one or more trustees and authorize him or them to sell and convey such land or any part thereof, in fee simple, if such sale and conveyance appear to the court to be necessary or expedient, and such conveyance shall be valid and binding upon all persons"[2]

"Notice of a petition, under the provisions of the two preceding sections (R. L c. 127, §§ 28, 29), shall be given, in such manner as the court may order, to all persons who are or may become interested in the real estate to which the petition relates, and to all persons whose issue, not in

[1] R L c 127, § 28, Whitcomb v. Taylor, 122 Mass 243; Bamforth v Bamforth, 123 Mass 280
[2] R L. c 127, § 29

being, may become interested therein ; and the court shall of its own motion in every case appoint a suitable person to appear and act therein as the next friend of all minors, persons not ascertained, and persons not in being, who are or may become interested in such real estate : and the provisions of section twenty-three and twenty-four of chapter one hundred and forty-five (of the Rev Laws, as to appointment and compensation of guardian *ad litem* or next friend), which are not inconsistent herewith, shall apply in the case of such appointment." [1]

A trustee who is appointed under the provisions of section twenty-eight or twenty-nine shall give bond in such form and for such an amount as the court appointing him may order ; and he shall receive and hold, invest or apply, the proceeds of any sale or mortgage made by him, for the benefit of the persons who would have been entitled to the real estate if such sale or mortgage had not been made ; and the probate court of any county in which any part of such land is situated shall have jurisdiction of all matters thereafter arising in relation to such trust.[2]

A mortgage executed by an executor, administrator, guardian, or trustee, must set forth the fact that the same is executed by license of the court, and the date of such license. Every such mortgage may contain a power of sale.[3]

SALE OF LOTS IN CEMETERIES

Executors, administrators, guardians, and trustees may be authorized by probate courts, after notice to all persons interested or upon their assent thereto, to sell and convey or release, upon such terms and in such manner as said

[1] R L c. 127, § 30.   [2] Ibid. § 31.   [3] R L c. 148, § 6

courts may order, lots in cemeteries belonging to the persons or estates by them represented.[1]

APPOINTMENT OF TRUSTEE TO CONVEY.

When a person seised or possessed of real or personal estate, or of an interest therein, upon a trust, express or implied, is under the age of twenty-one years, insane, out of the commonwealth, or not amenable to the process of any court therein which has equity powers, and when in the opinion of the supreme judicial court, the superior court, or the probate court, it is fit that a sale should be made of such estate or of an interest therein, or that a conveyance or transfer should be made thereof in order to carry into effect the objects of the trust, the court may order such sale, conveyance, or transfer to be made, and may appoint some suitable person in the place of such trustee to sell, convey, or transfer the same in such manner as it may require. If a person, so seised or possessed of an estate, or entitled thereto upon a trust, is within the jurisdiction of the court, he or his guardian may be ordered to make such conveyances as the court orders.[2]

LEASES BY GUARDIAN OF WARD'S REAL PROPERTY.

The probate court may, upon the petition of a guardian, setting forth a description of the real property of his ward, the reason why it is necessary or expedient to give a written lease thereof and the length of the term, if after notice and a hearing it appears to be necessary or expedient, authorize such guardian to give a written lease of the real property of his ward, and the decree of the court shall fix the term and the amount for which it may be leased.[3]

[1] R. L. c 148, § 5   [2] R L. c. 147, § 17   [3] R L. c 146, § 29.

CHAPTER XV.

ACCOUNTS OF EXECUTORS, ADMINISTRATORS, GUARDIANS, AND TRUSTEES

EVERY executor, administrator, guardian, and every trustee who is required to give bond to the judge of a probate court, is required by law and by the condition of his bond to render an account relative to the estate in his hands at least once a year, and at such other times as shall be required by the court, until his trust is fulfilled ; but the court may, upon his application, excuse him from rendering an account in any year, if satisfied that it is not necessary or expedient that such account should be rendered [1]

No final settlement of the account of any executor, administrator, or trustee shall be allowed unless such account shows, and the judge of the probate court finds, that all taxes on collateral legacies and successions imposed by the provisions of chapter 15 of the Revised Laws upon any property or interest therein belonging to the estate to be settled by said account have been paid The treasurer of the commonwealth shall, within six months after the

---

[1] R L c 149, § 1 If an executor neglects to file an account within one year after his appointment, it is a breach of his bond, although a debt due from the testator to the executor and the burial expenses paid by him exceed in amount the assets, and no other claims are presented by creditors within two years Forbes v McHugh, 152 Mass. 412

The fact that the administrator is the executor and sole legatee of the estate under a will afterwards discovered, does not relieve him of the duty of making a proper settlement of his account as administrator. Bennett v Woodman, 116 Mass 518.

An administrator has the right to file and settle the account of his intestate as administrator *de bonis non* of an estate in the probate court before he can be called upon to deliver all of the assets in his hands belonging to the estate Foster v Bailey, 157 Mass 160

tax shall be due, sue in his own name for the recovery of all taxes unpaid, and shall also bring suit when the judge of probate shall certify to him that a final account of any executor, administrator, or trustee has been filed in such probate court, and that the final settlement of such estate is delayed because of the non-payment of such tax, and such certificate shall issue upon the application of any heir, legatee, or any person interested, provided, however, that the probate court may extend the time of payment of said tax whenever the circumstances require.[1]

Special administrators are held to account whenever required by the probate court.[2]

When property is held in trust under a written instrument or statute, and there is no adequate provision for an account of the management of the trust estate, the probate court in a county where land so held is situate, or where a person interested in the trust resides, may, on application of any person interested, require the trustee to render an account on oath; and the court first so applied to will thereafter have exclusive original jurisdiction therein.

An executor, administrator, guardian, or trustee whose appointment is invalid by reason of any irregularity or want of jurisdiction in the court appointing him, is held to account for all property that has come to his hands, and the bond given by him in pursuance of such appointment is valid and binding on him and his sureties. Payments made by or to him may, with the approval of the probate court, be ratified and confirmed by the executor, administrator, guardian, or trustee who may afterwards be legally appointed.[3]

It is the practice, to some extent, of executors and other trust officers appointed by the probate court to settle their accounts with the parties interested without rendering a final account to the court, and in a majority of cases no

[1] R L c 15, §§ 19, 20   [2] R. L. c 149, § 1, cl 3   [3] Ibid. § 25.

inconvenience results from that mode of proceeding. Such a settlement, however, between the administrator and the heirs, or between the guardian and his ward, is not a compliance with the condition of his bond; and he may be cited, on the petition of persons interested, to render his account in the probate court, notwithstanding such settlement. He may be held to account, although he produces the receipts of all the heirs acknowledging the payment of their distributive shares in full.[1] Such receipts are evidence for the consideration of the probate court in determining whether a further settlement shall be ordered or not; but they do not estop the heirs or the ward from calling on the administrator or the guardian to settle his accounts in court.

When one of two or more joint executors or administrators dies, or is removed before the administration is completed, the account is rendered by the other or others[2] When a sole executor or other trust officer dies, not having settled his account, it should be rendered by his executor or administrator;[3] and it has been held that it may be settled by the administrator of one of his sureties[4]

[1] Bard v Wood, 3 Met 74, Clark v Clay, 11 Foster (N H), 393; Wing v. Wheeler, 69 Maine, 282 Notwithstanding the settlement and receipt, the guardian is bound to answer on oath proper interrogatories respecting his account and the items thereof. and the ward may introduce evidence touching the execution and validity of the receipt Wade v Lobdell, 4 Cush 511, Blake v. Pegram, 101 Mass 592 A guardian who has furnished necessaries to his ward even if he had no property of the ward in his hands, cannot maintain an action at law against the ward until the guardianship has been discharged, and the amount due him ascertained by a settlement of his accounts in the probate court. Smith v Philbrick, 2 N H 395, McLane v Curran, 133 Mass 531; Thorndike v Hinckley, 155 Mass 265, and cases cited

[2] R L c. 139, § 11.

[3] The guardian's administrator may be cited for that purpose on petition of the ward Gregg v Gregg, 15 N. H. 190.

[4] Curtis v. Bailey, 1 Pick. 198.

PUBLIC ADMINISTRATORS.

Every public administrator shall upon the appointment and qualification of an executor or administrator as his successor, surrender into the probate court his letters of administration in such case, with an account under oath of his doings therein; and upon a just settlement of such account, shall pay over and deliver to his successor all sums of money remaining in his hands, and all property, effects, and credits of the deceased not then administered.[1]

Every public administrator who gives a general bond shall, at the probate court first held in his county after the first day of January in each year, render an account under oath of all balances of estates then remaining in his hands; and the court may at any time require additional sureties to be furnished upon such administrator's bond, or may require a new bond to be given.[2]

When an estate has been fully administered by a public administrator, he shall deposit the balance of such estate remaining in his hands with the treasurer of the commonwealth, who shall receive and hold it for the benefit of those who may have lawful claims thereon.[3]

The probate courts shall require every public administrator in their respective counties to render an account of his proceedings under any letters of administration at least once in each year until the trust has been fulfilled. And when, upon a final settlement of an estate, it appears that moneys remain in the hands of such administrator which by law should have been deposited with the treasurer of the commonwealth, the court shall certify that fact and a statement of the amount so withheld to said treasurer, who, unless such deposit is made within one month after the

[1] R. L. c 138, § 5. [2] Ibid § 8. [3] Ibid. § 12.

receipt of such notice, shall cause the bond of the administrator to be prosecuted for the recovery of such moneys.[1]

When a public administrator neglects to return an inventory, to settle an account, or to perform any other duty incumbent on him in relation to an estate, and there appears to be no heir entitled to such estate, the district attorney for the district within which the administrator received his letters shall, in behalf of the commonwealth, prosecute all suits and do all acts necessary and proper to insure a prompt and faithful administration of the estate and the payment of the proceeds thereof into the treasury of the commonwealth; and if no heir has, within two years after the granting of letters of administration, appeared and made claim in the probate court for his interest in such estate, it shall be presumed that there is no such heir, and the burden of proving his existence shall be upon the public administrator.[2]

If the total property of an intestate which has come into the possession or control of a public administrator is of a value less than twenty dollars, unless the same is the balance of an estate received from a prior public administrator, he shall forthwith reduce all such property into money, not taking administration thereon, and shall deposit such money, first deducting his reasonable expenses and charges, with the treasurer of the commonwealth, who shall receive and hold it for the benefit of any persons who may have legal claims thereon. Such claims may be presented to the auditor of the commonwealth within one year from such payment to the treasurer, and the auditor shall examine such claims and allow such as may be proved to his satisfaction, and upon the expiration of the year shall forthwith certify the same to the governor and council for payment of the whole of the claims or such proportion thereof as the funds will allow.[3]

Every public administrator, upon making such deposit,

[1] R. L. c. 138, § 13.   [2] Ibid § 17.   [3] Ibid § 18.

shall file with the treasurer a true and particular account, under oath, of all his dealings, receipts, payments, and charges on account of the property from which the money so deposited proceeds, including the name of the intestate, if known to him, and the treasurer shall thereupon deliver to him a receipt for such money. And such deposit shall exempt the public administrator making it from all responsibility for or on account of the money so deposited.[1]

CITATION TO RENDER ACCOUNT.

If the executor or other officer neglects or unreasonably delays the settlement of his account in the probate court, he may be cited for that purpose on the petition of any person interested in the estate concerning which the account is to be rendered. The petition should set forth the particulars in which the executor has been negligent, in accordance with the facts of the case Upon such petition, the court will issue a citation to the delinquent party, which must be served in the manner directed by its terms. If, after being cited, he neglects to appear or to render his account, leave will be granted to bring a suit on his bond; and he will be liable in like manner and to the same extent as an executor in his own wrong [2]

If an executor or administrator neglects to render and settle his accounts in the probate court within six months after the final determination of the claims of creditors, or within such further time as the court may allow, and thereby delays a decree of distribution, such neglect shall be deemed unfaithful administration; and he may be forthwith removed, and shall be liable in a suit on his bond for all damages occasioned by his default [3]

[1] R L c 139, § 19.   [2] R L c 150, § 16.
[3] R. L c 142, § 26. Auditors may be appointed by the judge of probate to examine accounts filed in the probate court R L c. 165, §§ 56, 60.

FORM OF ADMINISTRATION ACCOUNT.

In his account, the executor or administrator charges himself with the amount of assets that have come to his hands, and asks to be allowed for the amount of all debts paid by him, and the expenses of the administration. With the account, stated in this form, must be filed a schedule stating the names of all persons of whom he has received money, the sum received from each, and the time when each sum was received, and a second schedule, giving the several sums paid by him, the persons to whom, and the purpose for which each sum was paid. If the estate has been represented insolvent, the executor or administrator does not ask in his first account to be allowed any sum for the payment of debts owed by the deceased, he having no authority to pay the debts except under a decree of distribution issued by the court. He credits himself with the charges of administration, the amount of loss, if any, necessarily sustained by the estate in his hands, and with the amount of the allowance, if any, made by the court to the widow or minor children of the deceased. The balance, thus exhibited, remains in his hands until he is ordered by the court to distribute it among the creditors.[1]

If the deceased insolvent had been a member of a co-partnership and died in possession of both partnership estate and separate estate, and both partnership and separate claims are proved against his estate, the adminis-

[1] If an administrator who has received money belonging to the estate in another state under ancillary letters of administration accounts for it here, and a decree is rendered here that the amount so received is due the estate from the administrator, the decree will stand, unless appealed from. Brooks v. Tobin, 135 Mass. 69

trator should so state his account as to exhibit the amount of the partnership estate in his hands distinct from the separate estate. The expenses of administration in such case are to be deducted from the whole amount received by the executor, and the net proceeds of the joint stock are appropriated to pay the creditors of the firm, and the net proceeds of the separate estate to pay the separate creditors; the surplus, if any, of one fund being applied towards the liquidation of debts payable out of the other.

WITH WHAT THE EXECUTOR OR ADMINISTRATOR IS CHARGEABLE.

Every executor, administrator, guardian, and trustee shall be chargeable in his account with all the personal estate of the deceased which comes to his hands, and which is by law to be administered, although not included in the inventory; also with all proceeds of real estate sold or mortgaged, and with all interest, profit, and income that come to his hands from the personal estate of the deceased.[1]

The first item with which the executor or administrator charges himself in the schedule annexed to his first account is the value of the personal estate as shown by the inventory. He should charge himself with the full amount of the appraisal of the personal property, whether he has disposed of it for more or less than that amount.

If he has sold the personal estate for more than its appraised value, he next charges himself with the amount of the gain.

After thus accounting for the personal property inventoried, and for the gain, if any, on its sale, he charges

[1] R L c 150, § 5

himself with all proceeds of real estate sold by him, for the payment of debts and legacies, with the proceeds of any personal estate not included in the inventory, and with all interest, profit, and income that may have come to his hands from the personal estate of the deceased.[1]

[1] Manure taken from the barnyard of a homestead and piled on the land, though not broken up nor rotten, nor in a fit state for incorporation with the soil, is part of the realty, and is not chargeable to the administrator as personal estate Fay *v* Muzzey, 13 Gray, 53 But he is chargeable with the value of manure when it is personal property, although he has spread it in the usual course of good husbandry on the land of the deceased, and has sold the land for payment of debts Ibid

When the administrator of an insolvent estate sold real estate, under license of probate court, and the land sold was mortgaged, and the mortgage recorded, but was unknown to him or the purchaser at the time of the sale, it was *held* that he might apply the proceeds of the sale to the payment in full of the mortgage debt, and that he was chargeable in his account only for the balance of such proceeds. Church *v* Savage, 7 Cush 440

Money received by an administrator from the government of the United States, by means of a treaty with a foreign nation, as an indemnity for property taken from the intestate by such foreign nation, is assets in the administrator's hands Foster *v* Fifield, 20 Pick 67.

When personal property attached by trustee process was assigned by the owner subject to the attachment, and the attachment was dissolved by the owner's death, it was *held* that the property passed by the assignment, and was not assets in the administrator's hands. Coverdale *v.* Aldrich, 19 Pick 391

Where an executor sold lands of the testator, and became himself a purchaser with two others, under an agreement to share equally in the profits of resale, he was held to account for one-third part of such profits Jennison *v* Hapgood, 10 Pick 93

If, to prevent a sale of the real estate, the heirs furnish the executor or administrator with money sufficient for the payment of all claims against the estate and the expense of administration, and thereby render any sale of the real estate unnecessary the money so furnished by them is assets of the estate, to be accounted for by the administrator Fay *v.* Taylor, 2 Gray, 159

Money found, after the death of a testatrix, in a secret drawer of a chest belonging to her, does not pass by a specific bequest of the chest,

The executor or administrator is bound to exercise the same care and diligence in the management of the estate which men of intelligence and prudence employ in the conduct of their own affairs. He is not a guarantor, but he is held to account for a loss occasioned by his negligence. He may be liable for negligence even when he acts in good faith;[1] and he is chargeable with the value of property lost through his neglect, though it never came into his actual possession.[2] If property belonging to the

but is a portion of the residuum of the personal estate, for which the executor is bound to account. Smith *v.* Jewett, 3 Chandler (N. H.), 513.

If an executor receive money for a deed of real estate made by the testator, but not delivered until after his death, he is bound to account for it. Loring *v.* Cunningham, 9 Cush. 87.

Salary voted to a person after his decease, and paid to his executor, is assets of the estate, to be accounted for by the executor. Ibid.

The amount of land damages paid for land taken for a railroad, after the death of the intestate belongs to the heirs, and not to the administrator, although the estate is insolvent, and the whole estate is afterwards sold by the administrator under license, for the payment of debts. Boynton *v.* P. & S. Railroad, 4 Cush. 467. Otherwise, if actually taken before the intestate's death. Moore *v.* Boston, 8 Cush. 274; Chapin *v.* Waters, 116 Mass. 147.

If the testator had money or other property in his hands belonging to others, whether in trust or otherwise, and it has no ear-mark, and is not distinguishable from the mass of his property, the party owning it must come in as a general creditor of the estate, and the property is assets, to be accounted for by the executor. Trecothick *v.* Austin, 4 Mason 29. Johnson *v.* Ames, 11 Pick. 181, Little *v.* Chadwick, 151 Mass. 111, and cases cited.

[1] It is negligence for an executor to deliver a $1,000 United States bond worth $1,200 in the market at the time in payment of a legacy of $1,000 though the bond was appraised in the inventory at its face value. He must account for the premium and interest on it. Spaulding *v.* Wakefield, 53 Vt. 660.

[2] Two turkeys belonging to the intestate wandered away, after his death, to a neighbor's house, and there remained several months, when they were disposed of by the neighbor. They had never been in the administrator's possession, nor had he ever called for them. He was

ACCOUNTS OF EXECUTORS, ADMINISTRATORS, ETC   289

estate is stolen without his default or negligence, he is not chargeable.[1] He would not be liable for the loss of money ordered to charge himself with their value. Tuttle v Robinson, 33 N. H 104.

[1] Executors placed United States coupon bonds in the vault of a bank for safe keeping, and the bank was robbed by burglars They procured new bonds in place of those stolen by giving the government a bond of indemnity, and their agent, who was an employee in the treasury department, and was considered trustworthy, appropriated the bonds *Held*, that the executors were not liable for the loss caused by the burglary, nor for the dishonesty of their agent. Carpenter v Carpenter, 12 R I 544   See Stevens v Gage 55 N H. 175

An executor left securities in the custody of the testator's nephew to whom the testator had given them for safe keeping, and intrusted him with property of his own The nephew appropriated the bonds. *Held*, that the executor was not liable for the loss McCabe v Fowler, 84 N Y. 314

An executor who, before the death of his intestate, contracted with him for the purchase of real estate, entered into possession, and made payments on account of principal and interest of the purchase-money, has included in his inventory the amount of the agreed price and interest remaining unpaid, and to whom the heirs are ready to convey on payment thereof. is bound to charge himself with such amount in his administration account Chenery v Davis, 16 Gray, 89.

If a surety on the bond of the administrator who is removed for failure to account is himself appointed administrator *de bonis non* of the estate, his liability as surety is a debt due the estate with which he should charge himself, although the amount has not been ascertained Choate v Thorndike, 138 Mass 371.

If the executor of the will of a member of a beneficiary association receives from the association the amount due on a benefit certificate issued to the member, he takes it not as executor, but in trust to pay it over to the person entitled thereto American Legion of Honor v Perry, 140 Mass 580, Daniels v Pratt, 143 Mass 216

The settlement in the probate court of an administrator's account, showing that he has exhausted all the estate in paying the expenses of the late sickness, funeral, and administration, is a good defence to an action brought against the administrator on his bond, although he has suffered a judgment to be recovered against him before such settlement of his account Fuller v Connelly, 142 Mass 227

If the assets of a partnership are in the possession of one of the

deposited in his name as executor in a bank in good standing, but would be liable if the money was mingled with his own funds, and credited to him in his personal account. He may be charged with the amount of a debt due the estate if it remains uncollected through his neglect.[1] If, in his capacity as executor, he has received money not belonging to the estate, he must charge himself with it, unless he can show a liability to pay it over to one legally claiming it.[2]

If the executor or administrator continues the business in which the deceased was engaged at the time of his death, either at the request of the parties interested in the estate or under the directions of the will of his testator or the provisions of a copartnership agreement of the deceased, he must account for all profits of the business, and is not liable for losses.[3]

When an executor is by the express terms of the will of his testator, or by necessary implication, made a trustee of any part of the estate, he will be required to account for the trust fund in his capacity of executor, unless for greater convenience and with the assent of the probate court he opens a new account as trustee; in which event he must give a new bond as trustee, and transfer to his

partners at the time of his death, and are sold by his executor for less than their value, and the amount received is accounted for as assets of his estate, the surviving partners, on a bill in equity against the executor in his capacity as executor, are entitled to recover from the estate only their proportion of the amount actually received and interest, whatever rights they may have against the executor personally Bradley v Brigham, 144 Mass. 181

[1] Schultz v Pulver, 11 Wend 361; Caffrey v. Darby, 6 Ves 488; Robinson v Ring, 72 Me. 140

[2] Jennison v Hapgood, 10 Pick 104

[3] Poole v Munday, 103 Mass 174; Palmer v Mitchell, 2 My & K. 672, Willett v. Blandford, 1 Hare, 253

account as trustee the property to be held and administered by him in that character, before his liability as executor will terminate.[1] If he continues to hold the trust fund as executor, it is his duty to separate it from the mass of the testator's property and invest it in some secure and productive stock, or at interest on good security. And if in this respect he acts with strict fidelity and due diligence, he will not be responsible should any loss happen, either of principal or interest.[2] But the mere mental determination of an executor to appropriate property to himself as trustee is not such a setting apart as will cause a loss or depreciation of the trust fund to fall on the *cestui que trust;* the executor, in such case, must account for the entire trust fund, and the amount due from him must be stated by making annual rests, adding the interest each year to the principal.[3]

If an administrator appointed in this commonwealth collects funds in another state of debtors residing there, he must account for them here, unless he has taken out letters of ancillary administration in such other state; in that case, he will be held to account here only for the surplus remaining in his hands upon the settlement of the ancillary administration.[4] But money collected there of debtors residing here must be accounted for here.[5]

An ancillary administrator appointed in this commonwealth must account to the court by which he was so appointed for all assets received by him under his ancillary appointment, but not for assets received by him as

[1] Prior v Talbot. 10 Cush. 1, Ricketson v. Merrill, 148 Mass 76

[2] Dorr v Wainwright, 13 Pick 332, Brown v Kelsey, 2 Cush. 248; Hubbard v. Lloyd, 6 Cush 522

[3] Miller v Congdon, 14 Gray, 114; Collins v Collins, 140 Mass 507

[4] Hooker v Olmstead, 6 Pick. 481, Jennison v. Hapgood, 10 Pick 77.

[5] Ibid.

principal administrator in the place of the principal administration.[1]

When chargeable with Interest — An executor or administrator is not chargeable with interest on the money received by him in his official capacity unless he has made some profitable use of the money, or has been guilty of negligence in accounting for it.[2] An administrator is not expected to invest any part of the money belonging to the estate; nor is an executor, unless he is required to do so by the will of his testator. On the contrary, it is his duty to collect the assets and pay them over to the persons entitled to receive them as speedily as circumstances will allow. But if he has invested the money and received interest upon it, he must account for it, and the fact that he has received interest, or has made use of the money in his own business, may be inferred from a long delay in settling his accounts, or his neglect to pay over balances after demand made upon him.[3] But if the delay was without negligence on his part, he will not be chargeable with interest unless he has made profit of the funds[4] He is not to be charged with interest in any case from the date of his appointment, or of his receipt of the money. He is to be allowed a reasonable time to settle the estate, and the time proper to be allowed for that purpose must depend upon the circumstances of each case. No general rule would do justice in all cases[5] When the adminis-

---

[1] Fay v Haven, 3 Met 109

[2] Wyman v. Hubbard, 13 Mass 232, Stearns v Brown, 1 Pick. 530, Boynton v Dyer. 18 Pick 1, Dunlap v Watson, 124 Mass 305, White v Ditson, 140 Mass 351.

[3] Wyman v Hubbard, 13 Mass 232, Forward v Forward, 6 Allen, 494

[4] Lamb v Lamb, 11 Pick 374.

[5] See Clarkson v De Peyster, 2 Wend 77, Schiffelin v. Stewart, 1 Johns Ch. 620, Jennison v Hapgood, 10 Pick. 77.

trator employs the funds of the estate in trade, he is liable to be charged with compound interest,[1] and may be charged with the whole profits on the fund so employed [2]

Income of the Real Estate. — The administrator has no official authority to collect the rents of real estate belonging to the estate of his intestate; nor has the executor, unless authorized by the will of his testator. The real estate vests in the heirs or devisees immediately upon the death of the owner, and all rents that become due subsequent to his death belong to them. Even if the estate is insolvent, they are entitled to the rents and profits until the land is sold, by license of court, for the payment of debts.[3] But rents collected by the executor or administrator to be applied, by agreement with the parties interested, to the payment of claims against the estate, thereby rendering unnecessary a sale of the land, are personal assets, to be charged against the administrator in his account.[4]

If the real estate has been occupied by the executor or administrator, he may be required to account in the probate court to the heirs or devisees for the income thereof; and if the parties do not agree on the sum to be allowed, it will be determined by three disinterested per-

---

[1] Boynton v Dyer, 18 Pick 1, Robbins v Hayward, 1 Pick 52, note; Schiffelin v Stewart, 1 Johns Ch 620

[2] Utica Ins Co v. Lynch, 11 Paige, 520 If an executor mingles the assets of the estate with his own money, and afterwards fails, the parties entitled to the estate can come in and prove against the executor's estate only on an equality with his creditors. Little v. Chadwick, 151 Mass 109

[3] Gibson v. Farley, 16 Mass 280, Boynton v P & S Railroad, 4 Cush 469, Lobdell v. Hayes, 12 Gray, 237; Kimball v Sumner, 62 Me. 305

[4] Stearns v Stearns, 1 Pick 159, Newcomb v. Stebbins, 9 Met 514, Choate v. Jacobs, 136 Mass 299, Brigham v Elwell, 145 Mass. 522, and cases cited

sons, appointed by the court, whose award, when accepted by the court, will be final.[1] The executor may be required to account in like manner for rents collected by him.[2] The rents and income found to be due from the executor or administrator are not assets of the estate to be charged to him in his administration account, but belong to the heirs or devisees If the executor or administrator has an interest in the real estate as heir or devisee which entitles him to possession, he is not held to account for the income in the probate court.[3]

A *special* administrator, when authorized by the probate court to take charge of the real estate of his intestate, is chargeable with the rents

Debts due from the Executor or Administrator. — If the administrator is himself a debtor to the estate, the debt owed by him is regarded as assets of the estate, to be accounted for by him. He must charge himself with the amount of the debt, as if he had received it of any other person,[4] and he is bound to answer upon oath as to all

[1] R L c 150, § 6, Choate v Arrington, 116 Mass 552, Choate v Jacobs, 136 Mass 299, Brigham v Elwell, 145 Mass 522, Cummings v. Watson, 149 Mass. 263

[2] Brooks v Jackson, 125 Mass 307

[3] Palmer v Palmer, 13 Gray, 326, Almy v. Crapo, 100 Mass. 218, Cummings v Watson, *supra*

[4] Ipswich Manufacturing Co v. Story, 5 Met 310, Winship v Bass, 12 Mass 199, Stevens v. Gaylord, 11 Mass 266; Tarbell v Jewett, 129 Mass 457 Debts due to the estate of a testator from the executor named in his will and from a firm of which he is a member, are to be accounted for as assets, although he and his firm were insolvent at the time when he accepted the trust, and although he has never charged them in his account, and an account has been allowed in which they were not included, but were mentioned as notes which it had been impossible to collect, and although he has resigned his trust, and an administrator *de bonis non* has been appointed in his place Leland v. Felton, 1 Allen, 531.

facts tending to show that he was indebted to the deceased, even as to facts that take the claim out of the operation of the statute of limitations, though it may be apparently barred by that statute [1]

The old rule, that a testator by making a debtor his executor thereby releases his debt, has never been in force in this state. The debt is assets in the executor's hands for which he and his sureties are liable.[2]

WHAT IS ALLOWED TO THE EXECUTOR OR ADMINISTRATOR.

The executor or administrator of a solvent estate is allowed to credit himself in his account with all sums of money paid by him in satisfaction of legal demands against the estate, but not with money paid on demands for which the estate was not liable.[3]

---

[1] Sigourney v. Wetherell, 6 Met 553

[2] Ipswich Manufacturing Co v Story, 5 Met 313, Winship v Bass, 12 Mass 199; Stevens v Gaylord, 11 Mass 267, Tarbell v Jewett, 129 Mass. 457.

[3] An administrator will not be allowed the amount paid by him on a promissory note made by the intestate for which there was no legal consideration Phillips v. Frye, 14 Allen, 36.

If the property of a corporation upon a final settlement of its affairs is not sufficient to pay the debts and the administrator of a deceased member pays money as the intestate's contributory share to make good the deficit, — there being no legal obligation to make such payment, — he will not be allowed the amount so paid Ripley v Sampson, 10 Pick. 371

An executor has no authority to pay money to extinguish a claim of dower in land belonging to the estate of his testator. Forward v. Forward. 6 Allen, 494

An administrator is responsible for the misapplication of money paid in good faith and under the advice of counsel. Boulton v. Beard, 3 De G, M & G 608

Taxes paid by an administrator on lands in another state where he had not taken out administration were not allowed in his account. Jennison v Hapgood, 10 Pick 105. See Dunbar v Tainter, 7 Cush 574; Rotch v. Morgan, 105 Mass 426

The estate is not liable for money paid in pursuance of a promise, the consideration of which arises after the death of the testator or intestate. Upon such a promise the executor or administrator may be personally liable. Whether the amount is to be repaid to him from the estate is a question to be determined by the probate court, upon the settlement of his account.[1] It would be necessary for him to show, in support of his application for an allowance in such case, that the payment made by him was beneficial to the estate, or was made with the assent of the parties interested.

An administrator may pay assessments upon shares in banks and other corporations which he holds as part of the assets of the estate, and will be allowed in his account for such payments, provided the assessments were legally laid and the payments were necessary to redeem the shares from a lien created by the assessment, and were beneficial

[1] Kingman *v* Soule, 132 Mass 285, Luscomb *v* Ballard, 5 Gray, 403, Sumner *v.* Williams, 8 Mass 162 Davis *v* French, 20 Me 21

General expenses of administration incurred for the benefit of the whole estate are chargeable to capital, and not to income Bridge *v* Bridge 146 Mass 373.

When judgment for a return in an action of replevin is rendered against an executor or administrator, the goods returned by him shall not be considered as assets in his hands, and if they have been included in the inventory, it shall be a sufficient discharge for the executor or administrator to show that they have been returned in pursuance of such judgment. R L c. 172, § 4

Whenever personal property placed in the hands of a corporation or an individual as an accumulating fund for the future benefit of heirs or other persons has been duly assessed to such heirs or persons according to the provisions of clause 6, § 23, of chap 12 of the Revised Laws, and the persons so taxed neglect to pay the tax for one year after it has been committed to the collector the collector may, in his own name, maintain an action of contract therefor against said trustee, in like manner as for his own debt; and the amount thereof paid by said trustee may be allowed in his account as such trustee R. L. c. 13, § 34.

to the estate. And if he acted in good faith he would undoubtedly be protected, even if the shares should have subsequently fallen in value in his hands.[1]

The executor or administrator will not be allowed in his account for debts paid by him after they had become barred by the statute limiting the time (two years) within which suits can be brought against executors and administrators who have given legal notice of their appointment. The executor's promise to pay a claim so barred cannot affect the estate.[2]

But this limitation does not apply to debts due from the deceased to the executor or administrator, which may be allowed to him at any time in the settlement of his account, nor to advances made by him, in the course of administration, for the benefit of the estate.[3] Where the administrator, within the two years, assumed liabilities in the adjustment of debts due from the estate, he was allowed the sums paid by him with interest, although the payments were not made until after the expiration of the two years.[4]

It has been held in this state that an executor or administrator may revive by a new promise a claim barred by the *general* statute of limitations,[5] and that such new promise will bind the estate in his hands.[6] He cannot,

[1] Ripley v. Sampson, 10 Pick 371

[2] Brown v. Anderson, 13 Mass. 201; Dawes v. Shed, 15 Mass. 6, Emerson v. Thompson, 16 Mass 429; Waltham Bank v. Wright, 8 Allen, 121; Ames v. Jackson, 115 Mass 508, and cases cited

[3] Dickinson v. Arms, 8 Pick 394, Forward v. Forward, 6 Allen, 494, Munroe v. Holmes, 13 Allen, 109, Ames v. Jackson, *supra*.

[4] Ames v. Jackson, *supra*

[5] Foster v. Starkey, 12 Cush 324, Fisher v. Metcalf, 7 Allen, 209, Slattery v. Doyle, 180 Mass 27

[6] Manson v. Felton, 13 Pick 206, Emerson v. Thompson, 16 Mass 429, Foster v. Starkey, *supra*

however, revive a claim held by himself.[1] There seems to be no good reason for allowing an executor or administrator for payments made on debts barred by either statute of limitation.

If the estate has been represented insolvent, the executor is not allowed in his first account for the payment of debts, he having no authority to make such payments except under a decree of distribution issued by the court.[2] He credits himself only with the expenses of the last sickness and funeral of the deceased, charges of administration, the loss, if any, necessarily sustained by the estate in his hands, and with the amount of the allowances, if any, made by the court to the widow or minor children of the deceased. The balance thus exhibited remains in his hands until he is ordered by the court to distribute it among the creditors.

Funeral Charges and Expenses of the Last Sickness. — The executor or administrator is allowed in his account all reasonable sums paid for funeral expenses. The amount to be allowed for such expenses must depend, in some degree, upon the condition of the estate. If the funeral was under the direction of the family of the deceased, and the estate is solvent, the sum asked for such charges is usually allowed. but no extravagant expenses will be allowed as against the creditors of an insolvent estate.[3] All expenses of the last sickness of

---

[1] Richmond, petitioner, 2 Pick 567, Grinnell v. Baxter, 17 Pick. 383

[2] He is not allowed for sums paid on debts during the first year of his administration, though paid without knowledge that the estate was insolvent; nor for personal property applied by him to repairs and improvements of the real estate, though so applied in executing an agreement of the intestate Cobb v. Muzzey, 13 Gray, 57.

[3] A reasonable sum expended for a burial lot and for a monument

the deceased paid by the administrator are allowed in his account.[1]

Charges of Administration. — Executors and administrators are allowed their reasonable expenses incurred in the execution of their respective trusts, and such compensation for their services as the court in which their accounts are settled considers just and reasonable [2]

Under the head of expenses of administration are included all sums which have been paid by the executor

may be allowed as part of the funeral expenses R L c. 150, § 12. Such a provision in a will will not be void as a perpetuity. Green v. Hogan, 153 Mass. 466.

A demand for mourning furnished to the widow and family of the deceased is not a funeral expense Johnson v Baker, 2 Carr & Payne, 207, Griswold v Chandler, 5 N H 492, Macknet's Executors v. Macknet, 24 N J Eq 296 But see Wood's Estate, 1 Ashmead, and Flintham's Appeal, 11 Serg & R 16

[1] A testator at a distance from home during his last sickness sent for his wife and heirs, but died before they arrived The executor was allowed to charge in his account their expenses, which he had paid to them Jennison v Hapgood, 10 Pick 88 Whenever a decedent appoints one or more executors or trustees, and in lieu of their allowance makes a bequest or devise of property to them which would otherwise be liable to the tax on collateral legacies, or appoints them his residuary legatees, and said bequests, devises, or residuary legacies exceed what would be a reasonable compensation for their services, such excess shall be liable to such tax, and the probate court having jurisdiction of their accounts, upon the application of any one interested, or the treasurer of the commonwealth, shall fix such compensation. R. L. c 15, § 3

[2] R. L c 150, § 14, Edwards v Ela, 5 Allen, 87. When an executor's final account comes before the supreme court of probate on appeal, the compensation allowed him is subject to revision, as well as the other items Bridge v Bridge, 146 Mass. 377.

A special administrator by leave of the probate court may pay from the personal estate in his hands the expenses incurred by the executor named in the will of a deceased person in proving the same in the probate court, or in sustaining the proof thereof in the supreme court, and also, after notice, such debts due from the deceased as the probate court may approve. R L c. 137, § 13.

in the course of a faithful and prudent administration; such as the expense of appraising the estate, of collecting the effects and paying the debts, of attending the probate and other courts upon business of the estate, of advertising as required by law or any order of the court, and sums paid for legal and other necessary assistance.[1] The expenses of assigning dower, or making partition of land among the heirs or devisees, are not charges of administration, and are not allowed in the administration account.

It is no part of the duty of the executor or administrator to advance money for the payment of debts and necessary expenses; but if, not having cash assets in his hands, he makes advances for the benefit of the estate, he is entitled to interest on the money advanced.[2]

If judgment is rendered against an executor or administrator for costs in a suit commenced or prosecuted by him

---

[1] Administrator's charges for attending probate court at hearings in relation to estates connected with that of his intestate, for inquiring into and ascertaining the existence of property in another jurisdiction supposed to belong to the estate, and for taking legal advice in respect to such property, although it could be administered only in the other jurisdiction, allowed. Wendell v. French, 19 N H 205. In cases which are contested before a probate court or before the supreme court of probate, costs and expenses in the discretion of the court may be awarded to either party, to be paid by the other party, or they may be awarded to either or both parties, to be paid out of the estate which is the subject of the controversy, as justice and equity may require. If costs are awarded to be paid by one party to the other, execution may issue. R L c 162, § 44. But the probate court has no power under this statute to compel a guardian, on a petition by counsel, to pay for professional services rendered for the infant ward. Willard v. Lavender, 147 Mass 15.

Money paid with the approval of the judge of probate to any corporation duly authorized to act as surety of probate bonds, or to any person acting as surety of probate bonds, may be allowed in the discretion of the court as a charge against the estate. R. L. c 150, § 15.

[2] Jennison v Hapgood, 10 Pick 102; Ames v. Jackson, 115 Mass 508. See May v. Skinner, 152 Mass 328.

in that capacity, the estate in his hands cannot be taken in execution therefor, but execution is awarded against him as for his own debt, although the estate has been represented insolvent ; and the amount paid by him thereupon is allowed in his administration account, unless it appears to the probate court that the suit was commenced or prosecuted unnecessarily or without reasonable cause.[1] But such costs are not allowed in the administration account, until they have been actually paid by him. Their payment is a condition precedent to their allowance.[2]

Since the repeal of the statute allowing to executors and administrators stated commissions on the sums accounted for by them, there has been no rule common to all the probate courts in regard to their compensation. The executor or administrator usually credits himself in his account with such a sum as he considers himself entitled to receive, and the court, in its discretion, allows the sum asked for, or a less sum, regard being had to the character of the services rendered necessary by the condition of the estate, and actually performed [3]

[1] R. L c 172, § 6, Hardy v Call, 16 Mass 530; Greenwood v. McGilvray, 120 Mass 516, Perkins v Fellows, 136 Mass. 294.

[2] Thacher v Dunham, 5 Gray, 26

[3] Unfaithful administration will not deprive an executor of his right to compensation for his services so far as they have been beneficial to the estate. Jennison v. Hapgood, 10 Pick 112

When services not obviously alien to the administration have been rendered at the special request and advice of a party interested in the estate, he is estopped from objecting to the allowance of a just compensation for them in the settlement of the administrator's account. Wendell v. French, 19 N H 205

Upon a controversy between the administrator and the heirs, charges by him of time and money expended while endeavoring to effect a private settlement with them are not proper items of charge against the estate as expenses of administration. Clark v Clay, 11 Foster (N. H) 393 The executor was allowed a charge for trans-

An executor is sometimes entitled to credits in his account that he could not claim as administrator of an intestate estate. It being his duty to administer according to law and the will of his testator, he may be called upon, in order to carry out the provisions of the will, to perform services and incur expenses that would be irregular and unnecessary in a case of ordinary administration For all such services faithfully performed, and expenses properly incurred, he is entitled to be allowed.[1]

Loss on Sale of the Personal Estate. — The executor or administrator is not required to sustain any personal loss in consequence of the decrease or destruction, without his fault, of any part of the estate. If he has sold it for less than the appraised value, he will be allowed in his account for the loss, if it appears that the sale was expedient and for the interest of all concerned in the estate;[2] and he is entitled to be allowed for the amount of any debts inventoried as due to the deceased, if it appears to the court that they remain uncollected without his fault.

Allowances to the Widow and Minor Children. — The executor or administrator is allowed in his account for all sums paid by him, under order of the probate court, as allowances to the widow or minor children of the deceased; but if he pays money for their support without

ferring personalty to the special administrator. May v Skinner, 149 Mass 375

[1] Where an executor, to whom real estate is devised in trust, is authorized by the will to take down any part of the testator's buildings and to rebuild, to erect additional buildings, and to hire money for the purpose of bettering the trust estate, he may advance his own money for the like purposes, and charge it in his general administration account Watts v Howard, 7 Met. 478 And see Wiggin v Swett, 6 Met. 194.

[2] R L c 150, § 4.

ACCOUNTS OF EXECUTORS, ADMINISTRATORS, ETC. 303

being first authorized by the court, he makes the payment at his own risk.[1]

Debts due the Executor or Administrator from the Deceased. — If the executor or administrator is himself a creditor of the estate, he should procure the assent of the heirs, or other parties interested in the estate, to the allowance of his claim, before he presents his account to the probate court. If his claim is disputed by any person interested in the estate, he must file in the probate court a separate statement, setting forth distinctly and fully the nature and grounds of his claim; and it may then be submitted under an order of the court to one or more arbitrators, to be agreed on by the claimant and the party objecting. The court has like power to discharge the rule by which the claim is referred, and to reject and disallow the award, or to recommit it to the arbitrators, as may be exercised by the common law courts with regard to cases referred by a rule of those courts. The award of the arbitrators, if accepted by the probate court, is final and conclusive.

If the parties do not agree in the appointment of arbitrators, or if the award is not confirmed by the probate court, the court will decide on the claim; and if either party appeals from its decision to the supreme court of probate, either party or the court may have the claim submitted to a jury.[2]

If the claim of the executor or administrator results

[1] Washburn v. Hale, 10 Pick. 429 Brewster v. Brewster, 8 Mass. 131. The question whether an allowance to a widow from her husband's estate was properly made by the probate court is not open on a hearing on the administrator's account. Newell v West, 149 Mass 520.

[2] R L c 141, §§ 6, 7. Newell v West, 119 Mass 528; Forbes v. McHugh, 152 Mass. 413, Buckley v. Buckley, 157 Mass 536.

from a course of dealing, or involves mutual debts and credits, the balance only is the actual debt, and the whole account on both sides must be examined, in order to ascertain that balance; and, of course, all the items on both sides are put in issue.[1]

The executor or administrator is entitled to interest on his claim only for such a length of time, after taking administration, as is reasonably needed for the settlement of the estate.[2]

Distributive payments by an executor to residuary legatees are not allowed in his account rendered to the probate court. The settlement of the account determines the amount of residue subject to distribution, but not the rights or shares of those who are entitled.[3]

Before delivering any specific legacy or property subject to a succession tax to any person, the executor, administrator, or trustee shall deduct the tax therefrom. If such legacy is given in money to any person for a limited period, the tax on the whole amount shall be retained.[4]

It may be necessary for the executor or administrator to render more than one account of his administration of the estate committed to him. He is required to render an account at least once a year until his trust is fulfilled, unless he is excused therefrom in any year by the court, and at such other times as the court may order. If he receives assets, though they come to his hands more than

---

[1] Willey v Thompson, 9 Met 329

[2] Richmond, Petitioner, 2 Pick 567.

[3] Granger v Bassett, 98 Mass 462; Browne v. Doolittle, 151 Mass 596, and cases cited. An executor acting under the will, in setting off debts due the testator from the legatees on promissory notes bearing interest, is not entitled in his account to charge interest after the death of the testator. Taylor v Taylor, 145 Mass. 239.

[4] R. L. c 15, §§ 5, 7.

twenty years after the supposed final settlement and distribution of the estate, he is bound to account for them.[1] In stating any account after the first, he brings forward the balance of his last preceding account, and charges himself with the amount of all sums received by him not previously accounted for; and asks to be allowed for the amount of any additional payments made by him and expenses of administration. And he must annex schedules giving full details of such receipts and expenditures.

FORM OF GUARDIAN'S AND TRUSTEE'S ACCOUNTS.

The guardian or trustee presents his account in substantially the same form as that of an executor or administrator. He charges himself with the amount of the assets received by him, and asks to be allowed for the payments made by him and the charges of the trust. With the account must be filed a schedule stating the several sums received by him, the person of whom, and the time when, each sum was received, a second schedule containing a full statement of the payments and charges, and a third, stating particularly the manner in which any balance remaining in his hands is invested.

WITH WHAT THE GUARDIAN OR TRUSTEE IS CHARGEABLE

The guardian or trustee is required to charge himself with the value of the personal estate in his hands, according to the inventory, with the gain, if any, realized from its sale, with the rents and profits of the real estate;[2] with the proceeds of real estate sold or mortgaged by him;

[1] White v. Swain, 3 Pick 365, Prescott v Read, 8 Cush 365.
[2] Rathbun v Colton, 15 Pick. 471, Root v. Yeomans, 15 Pick. 488.

and with all sums received by him in his official capacity, from whatever source. He is bound to use the same degree of diligence in the recovery and preservation of the property of his ward or *cestui que trust* that is required of executors and administrators in the administration of the estates intrusted to them, and he is held responsible for any loss occasioned by his neglect.

He is held strictly to account for the interest arising from the trust fund. The general rule is that he is bound to take the same care of the trust fund as a discreet and prudent man would take of his own property, to manage it for the exclusive benefit of the ward or *cestui que trust*, and to make no profit or advantage out of it for himself; to keep it at all times, when practicable, profitably invested, and punctually to account for the income as well as the principal. If any of these duties are neglected, the loss resulting from the neglect must fall upon him, and not on the ward or *cestui que trust*. Hence, if through gross carelessness or ignorance he makes a bad investment, and thereby loses the whole or part of the trust fund, he will be held to replace it, and must charge himself with it in his account [1] But he is not liable for losses occasioned by bad investments, provided he acts in good faith and with sound discretion.[2] If he wholly

---

[1] Harding v Larned, 4 Allen, 426, Clark v Garfield, 8 Allen, 427; Richardson v Boynton, 12 Allen, 138; Kimball v Perkins, 130 Mass. 141. A guardian is liable to his ward for the rent of the ward's real estate which he has received, or which he might have received by the use of due diligence Shurtleff v Rile, 140 Mass 213 Where the trustee of an estate held in trust has been obliged to pay taxes upon an unproductive investment received by him from his predecessor, this expense is not to be deducted from the income of other productive investments, but is to be regarded as a charge upon the principal of the unproductive investment Stone v Littlefield, 151 Mass 485

[2] Kimball v. Perkins, 130 Mass 141. A loan by a guardian, upon

neglects to invest the trust funds, he is chargeable with the income that would have been derived from a proper investment,[1] and in cases of gross neglect, or if he employs the money in his own business, he is liable to be charged with compound interest.[2] He may not be chargeable with interest from the date of his appointment, or of his receipt of the money He is entitled to a reasonable

the promissory note of the borrower, payable in one year with interest, secured by a pledge of shares in a manufacturing corporation, the amount of the loan being about three-quarters of the par value of the shares, and less than three-quarters of their market value, was held to be an investment made with sound discretion, and although the borrower failed before the note became due, and the shares fell in value below the amount of the note, the guardian was held not to be responsible for the loss

And, the guardian having sold the shares and taken the purchaser's note for the price, with two indorsers, and the notes of another person secured by a mortgage on land, he was *held* to have exercised a sound discretion, and not to be responsible for a loss occasioned by the failure of all the parties to the notes, and a fall in the value of the mortgaged premises Lovell *v.* Minot, 20 Pick 116 And see Harvard College *v* Amory, 9 Pick 459, Thompson *v.* Brown, 4 Johns. Ch. 628, Bowker *v.* Pierce, 130 Mass. 262, Hunt, Appellant, 141 Mass 515, McKim *v* Hibbard, 142 Mass 422; Dickinson, Appellant, 152 Mass. 184

[1] Mattoon *v.* Cowing, 13 Gray, 387; McKim *v* Morse, 130 Mass. 439

[2] Boynton *v* Dyer, 18 Pick. 1 Where the guardian had received rents and income from stocks, and had rendered no account for many years, it was ordered that an account should be settled, with a rest for every year, and the balance thus struck carried forward, to be again on interest whenever the sum should be so large that a trustee acting faithfully and discreetly would have put it in a productive state, and $500 was held to be such a sum. Robbins *v* Hayward, 1 Pick 528, note

Simple interest only was allowed on a note due on demand from the guardian to the ward, the note being so small that it was not a sufficient object to make a new investment with the interest Fay *v.* Howe, 1 Pick 527. See Bassett *v.* Granger, 140 Mass. 183, McKim *v.* Blake, 139 Mass. 593.

time in which to make the investment, and the length of time that will be deemed reasonable for that purpose must depend upon the condition of the property at the time he received it, his opportunity of making investments, or other circumstances controlling his proceedings.[1]

If the guardian is also executor of the will in which a legacy is given to his ward, he cannot charge himself in his guardianship account with the amount of the legacy until, by the terms of the will, it becomes payable; until that time he must account for it as executor. This distinction, while it does not affect his personal liability, may be of importance to his sureties.[2]

The guardian shall settle all accounts of his ward, and sue for and receive all debts due to him, or, with the approbation of the probate court, may compound for the same, and give a discharge to the debtor on receiving a fair dividend of his estate.[3]

---

[1] In Boynton v. Dyer, 18 Pick 1, one year was deemed a reasonable time; in Clarkson v. De Peyster, 2 Wend 77, six months were held sufficient, and in Schieffelin v. Stewart, 1 Johns Ch 620, two years were allowed

[2] Livermore v Bemis 2 Allen, 394. A *cestui que trust* cannot maintain an action for money had and received against the trustee, under a testamentary trust, although a balance appears by his accounts to be due, if the trust is still open and there has not been a final settlement of his accounts in the probate court. Upham v Draper, 157 Mass. 292

[3] R. L. c. 145, § 25. A guardian has no title to his ward's property and cannot maintain a bill in equity in his own name to avoid a conveyance or transfer by the ward of his property. Lombard v Morse, 155 Mass. 136

A guardian has no authority to withdraw from a bank funds due to his ward as administrator of an estate. Ryan v. North End Savings Bank, 168 Mass 215

A suit may be brought in the name of an infant as well by his guardian as by his next friend. Burke v. Burke, 170 Mass 499

WHAT IS ALLOWED TO THE GUARDIAN OR TRUSTEE

The guardian is allowed to credit himself with all sums properly paid by him for the support and education of his ward. He may expend a part or the whole of the income of the ward's estate for these purposes, as occasion requires, and if the income is not sufficient, the principal, but such expenses must be consistent with a prudent management of the estate. If the ward is a minor, and has a father living, the expense of his maintenance and education is to be paid by the father, unless the ward's property is sufficient to support him in a manner more expensive than his father can reasonably afford; in which case the expense of the maintenance and education of the minor may be defrayed out of his own property, in whole or in part, as the probate court deems reasonable.[1] If the ward is a married woman, the guardian cannot expend her estate for the support of herself and her family, unless authorized by the court on account of the inability

---

[1] R. L c 145, § 29, Strong *v.* Moe, 8 Allen, 125. A husband who receives into his family the children of his wife by a former marriage stands to them *in loco parentis*, and in the absence of express contract or of circumstances showing a different arrangement, has a right to their services, and is liable for their support and education. And where, for seven years, he has lived in a house belonging to his wife and her three children by a former marriage, has been appointed guardian of the children, and kept them in the house with himself and their mother, has no property of his own, has earned only enough during the time to support the united family, and has sold the real estate of his wards by leave of court, he is not to be charged in his account with any previous rent thereof or credited with taxes paid thereon, or for the board and clothing of his wards, but may be allowed a reasonable amount paid for the expense of one of his wards at a boarding-school Mulhern *v.* McDavitt, 16 Gray, 404. See Wilkes *v.* Rogers, 6 Johns. 566.

of the husband suitably to maintain her and them, or for other cause which the court deems reasonable.[1]

The probate court, on the application of the guardian of an insane person, or of a child, or the guardian of a child of an insane person, and after notice to all other persons interested, may authorize and require the guardian of the insane person to apply such portion as the court may direct of the income of the ward which is not required for his maintenance and support, to the maintenance and support of his children.[2]

In all cases, the amounts to be allowed to the guardian in his account of his ward's expenses will be determined with reference to the condition and circumstances of the ward.[3]

A claim for damages for a tort by a guardian against his ward cannot be allowed in his account.[4]

If the guardian has advanced his own money for the payment of debts and expenses of his ward, under circumstances that render that course of proceeding proper, he is entitled to interest on the money so advanced.[5]

---

[1] R. L. c 145, § 14.

[2] Ibid. § 30

[3] The guardian (of an insane person) is appointed for the welfare, comfort, and security of the ward, and not for the increase of the estate in his hands by accumulations from the income, in order to enlarge the wealth of remote or collateral relatives who may ultimately succeed to the inheritance It is no part of his duty to diminish the reasonable comforts of his ward, or to prevent him from enjoying such luxuries, or indulging such tastes, as would be allowable and proper in the case of a man similarly situated in other respects, but in the full possession of his faculties. Ames, J , in May v May, 109 Mass 256

[4] Brown v. Howe, 9 Gray, 84 Nor will an action of contract for necessaries lie. McLane v. Curran, 133 Mass. 532.

[5] Hayward v Ellis, 13 Pick 272

ACCOUNTS OF EXECUTORS, ADMINISTRATORS, ETC. 311

Guardians and trustees are allowed for all necessary expenses incurred in the execution of their respective trusts, and such compensation for their services as the court may consider just and reasonable [1]

[1] Urann v Coates, 117 Mass 41, Turnbull v Pomeroy, 140 Mass. 117 Where the guardian of an insane person continued the ward's business with advantage to the estate and with the concurrence of all the parties interested, and erected a building for the use of the business on land of the ward s wife, he was not allowed in his account for the cost of the building, but was allowed rent for it Murphy v Walker, 131 Mass. 341.

Expenses of the guardian incurred in resisting, in good faith, the ward's application for a revocation of the guardianship, were allowed in his account. Palmer v. Palmer, 1 Chandler (N H), 418

A guardian who is also trustee is not allowed full compensation in each capacity for the same service. Blake v. Pegram, 101 Mass 592

A trustee or guardian is not allowed in his account for any part of the expenses of a controversy occasioned in a great measure by his own fault. Blake v. Pegram, 109 Mass. 541; Urann v Coates, 117 Mass. 44.

He is not allowed compensation for changing investments of his ward's property, or making repairs thereon, in the form of commissions on the amounts invested or expended. May v May, 109 Mass 252

An agreement made by a trustee with his *cestui que trust* as to the amount of compensation he shall receive is not invalid if the *cestui que trust* is *sui juris* and competent to act, and no fraud is practised or advantage taken, and such agreement is to be considered in determining the amount of the trustee's charges Bowker v Pierce, 130 Mass 262

A guardian who charges himself in his account with a large surplus of his ward's income and interest thereon, but refuses to disclose what use he has made of it, is presumed to have derived profits from its use sufficient to compensate him for the care of it, and is not entitled to other compensation Blake v Pegram, 109 Mass. 541, Pierce v Prescott, 128 Mass 140.

A trustee is not allowed compensation for taking charge of a trust fund while he himself is a borrower of it. Farwell v Steen, 46 Vt 678.

A trustee cannot withhold the income of a trust fund from the

If the same person is guardian of two or more wards, although they may be equally interested in the property in his hands, he should render a separate account of his guardianship of each, and is bound to account whenever either of them arrives at full age.

ALLOWANCE OF PROBATE ACCOUNTS

The executor or administrator will avoid some delay and expense if, before presenting his account to the probate court, he submits it to the heirs or other parties interested, and obtains their assent in writing to its allowance. Such assent may be conveniently indorsed on the account. If they do not so express their assent, the court, before proceeding to pass upon the account, will order such notice to be given to them as the circumstances of the case require. After the account has been filed, the judge, before approving the same, may appoint one or more auditors to hear the parties interested, examine their vouchers and the evidence, and report upon the same, which report shall be *prima facie* evidence upon such matters as are expressly referred to the auditors.[1]

If an account has been filed in the probate court and if

beneficiary's assignee in order to repay to himself by way of set-off money lent by him to the beneficiary prior to his appointment as trustee, nor will a decree of the probate court that the trustee is so entitled be good in the absence of personal notice to the assignee or the beneficiary Abbott *v* Foote, 146 Mass. 333. A guardian was not allowed a charge in his account for superintending the building of a stable for his ward May *v* Skinner, 149 Mass. 375

A decree of the probate court showing a balance due from a guardian to his ward upon the expiration of the guardianship, and the refusal of the guardian or his representative to pay it over in accordance with such decree, creates a debt in favor of the ward, for which he may sue in his own name. Cobb *v* Kempton, 154 Mass. 266.

[1] R L. c 165, § 56.

the court finds that the items of said account should be finally determined and adjudicated, or if the accountant after two years from a former adjudication or from his appointment desires such determination and adjudication, notice of such proposed action shall be given to all parties as it may order. If the interest of a person unborn, unascertained, or legally incompetent to act in his own behalf, is not represented except by the accountant, the court shall appoint a competent and disinterested person to act as guardian *ad litem* or next friend for such person, and to represent his interest in the case.[1] The person so appointed shall make oath to perform his duty faithfully and impartially, and shall be entitled to such reasonable compensation for his services as the court may allow.

When all living parties who are interested as beneficiaries in a trust created by will proved and allowed in this commonwealth reside out of the commonwealth, the probate court having jurisdiction of the trust may, on application of the parties in interest, or of the executor, administrator, or trustee, and if it deems it just and expedient, authorize the executor, administrator, or trustee to pay over the fund to a trustee appointed by the proper court in any other state or country, provided all the *cestuis que trustent* who are living, and the executor, administrator, or trustee signify their consent, and the court is satisfied that the laws of such other state or country secure the due performance of said trust; and upon such payment shown to the satisfaction of said probate court, the executor, adminis-

---

[1] R. L. c. 150, § 22. Abbott *v.* Bradstreet, 3 Allen, 587; Collins *v.* Collins, 140 Mass. 502. The decree of the court of probate allowing the final account of an administrator cannot be impeached in an action at law against the administrator for services rendered the deceased. Parcher *v.* Bussell, 11 Cush. 107.

trator, or trustee appointed here may be discharged from further responsibility by decree of said court.[1]

When there are contingent interests in such trust fund, whether the persons who may be entitled thereto are in being or not, and where any of the *cestuis que trustent* are minors, the court, before making an order or decree in the premises, shall cause such interests and minors to be properly represented by guardians *ad litem* or otherwise at its discretion.[2]

Any person interested in the estate may appear and object to the allowance of the account, either that the administrator or other trustee has not charged himself with all the assets of the estate, or that he has credited himself with sums that ought not to have been paid from the estate, or that he claims a larger sum for compensation than he is justly entitled to receive, or because of any overcharge or omission in his account.[3] The executor or guardian is not only required to make oath to the correctness of his account, but to answer specifically all questions concerning it.[4] And the party at whose instance interrogatories have been proposed to him touching his account, has a right to offer evidence to disprove his answers.[5]

The court, upon the hearing, may order the accountant to charge himself with sums not included in his account, if it appears that he has received them in his official capacity, and may disallow any of the items with which

---

[1] R L c 150, § 27.   [2] Ibid. § 28.

[3] If the administration, in a particular transaction, has not been strictly according to law, the administrator cannot be charged with mal-administration in respect to such transaction by persons at whose request he acted therein Poole *v* Munday, 103 Mass 174

[4] R L. c 150, § 3 , Sigourney *v* Wetherell, 6 Met 553; Wade *v.* Lobdell, 4 Cush. 510; Blake *v.* Pegram, 101 Mass. 592.

[5] Higbee *v* Bacon, 8 Pick 484.

ACCOUNTS OF EXECUTORS, ADMINISTRATORS, ETC 315

he credits himself; and the decree of the court allowing the account, as it may be finally adjusted, is conclusive, unless appealed from [1] The supreme court will not, as a court of chancery, resettle an administration account alleged to have been fraudulently settled in the probate court, [2] nor can the decree of the probate court, duly allowing the final account of an administrator, be impeached in an action at law against him upon a claim against the deceased [3] The person aggrieved by the decree can take his objections to the supreme court of probate only by appeal. If the proceedings in the probate court were such that they may be treated as a nullity on account of fraud, the administrator may be cited to account anew.

The accounts of two or more joint executors, administrators, guardians, or trustees may be allowed by the pro-

[1] It is made the duty of the treasurer of the commonwealth to bring suit for the recovery of all legacy and succession taxes not paid, when the judge certifies to him that the final account of any executor, administrator, or trustee has been filed in the court, and that the final settlement of the estate is delayed by reason of the non-payment of such tax And the judge is required to issue the certificate upon the application of any heir, legatee, or person at interest. The time for payment of the legacy tax may be extended by the probate court whenever the circumstances of the case may require. R L c. 15, § 18 See also St 1902, c 473. If the administrator of the estate of a deceased partner in a firm has made a settlement with the surviving partners, and his account, including the amount received from such settlement, has been allowed by the probate court, that court has no jurisdiction to open the account, upon the petition of the successor of such administrator to which the surviving partners only are made respondents, on the ground that the settlement was induced by the fraud of the surviving partners. Blake v Ward, 137 Mass. 94.

[2] Jennison v Hapgood, 7 Pick 1; Sever v Russell. 4 Cush 513; Ammidown v. Kinsey, 144 Mass. 587

[3] Parcher v Bussell, 11 Cush. 107.

bate court upon the oath of one of them.[1] The oath may be administered by the judge or register in or out of court, or by a justice of the peace ; but the judge may require the oath to be taken before him in open court [2]

No final settlement of an account of any executor, administrator, or trustee shall be allowed unless such account shows, and the judge finds, that the legacy and succession tax has been paid. A proper voucher for such payment is the receipt of the treasurer of the commonwealth.[3]

WHEN SETTLED ACCOUNTS MAY BE OPENED

When an account of an executor, administrator, or trustee is settled in the absence of a person adversely interested, and without notice to him, such account may be opened on the application of such person at any time within six months after the settlement thereof, and upon the settlement of an account all former accounts of the

[1] R L c 150, § 18.

[2] R L c 162, § 37. The probate court, in passing upon the allowance of the account of a trustee under a will, may determine whether a trustee has accounted to the parties entitled to the income of the trust fund for the whole of the income. New England Trust Co v. Eaton, 140 Mass 532 When an executor, administrator, guardian, or trustee has paid or delivered over to the persons entitled thereto the money or other property in his hands, as required by a decree of a probate court, he may perpetuate the evidence thereof by presenting to said court, within one year after the decree is made, an account of such payments or of the delivery over of such property ; which account being proved to the satisfaction of the court, and verified by the oath of the party, shall be allowed as his final discharge, and ordered to be recorded. Such discharge shall forever exonerate the party and his sureties from all liability under such decree, unless his account is impeached for fraud or manifest error R L c. 150, § 20

[3] R L c 15, § 19 But where there has been or shall be a devise. descent or bequest, to collateral relatives or strangers to the blood, liable to collateral inheritance tax, to take effect in possession or come

same accountant may be so far opened as to correct a mistake or error therein;[1] except that a matter in dispute, which has been previously heard and determined by the court, shall not without leave of the court be again brought in question by any of the parties to such dispute.[2]

To avail himself of the exception provided by the above section, the administrator should take care that any matter heard and determined should be so stated as to appear in the decree of the court allowing his account. If his account is disputed, he should call upon the party objecting to specify in writing the items to which he objects His account being then settled, the entire proceedings

into actual enjoyment after the expiration of one or more life estates or a term of years, the tax on such property shall not be payable nor interest begin to run thereon until the person or persons entitled thereto shall come into actual possession of such property, and the tax thereon shall be assessed upon the value of the property at the time when the right of possession accrues to the person entitled thereto as aforesaid, and such person or persons shall pay the tax upon coming into possession of such property The executor or administrator of the decedent's estate may settle his account in the probate court without being liable for said tax, provided, that such person or persons may pay the tax at any time prior to their coming into possession, and in such cases the tax shall be assessed on the value of the estate at the time of the payment of the tax, after deducting the value of the life estate or estate for years; and provided further, that the tax on real estate shall remain a lien on the real estate on which the same is chargeable, until it is paid. St. 1902, c. 473.

[1] Wiggin v Swett, 6 Met 194. See Blake v. Pegram, 101 Mass. 592. Gale v Nickerson, 144 Mass 415, Dodd v Winship 144 Mass 461

[2] R L. c 150, § 17. A former account may be opened, although an appeal was taken from its allowance in the probate court, and determined in the supreme court of probate   Blake v Pegram, 109 Mass 541   Bridge v Bridge, 146 Mass. 377, and cases cited

Former accounts may be opened although the persons by whom they were rendered have ceased to represent the estate. Blake v Pegram, 109 Mass 541.

The right to open former accounts is limited to accounts rendered

will appear upon the records of the court, and no doubt can afterwards arise as to the particular items disputed and determined.[1] Even then, by leave of the court, the account may be opened, though undoubtedly the court would be cautious in exercising such a power in regard to a subject once controverted and once judicially settled.[2]

Where an account has been settled for many years, the heirs or other parties concerned acquiescing in the settlement, it will not be opened on their application unless good cause is shown for the delay; but the administrator or other trust officer may be cited at any time to account for assets not included in his settled accounts.[3]

in the settlement of the same estate. Granger *v.* Bassett, 98 Mass 462 Such acquiescence and delay on the part of the guardian as would bar him from holding the executors liable for selling the assets of the estate for less than their value, will not deprive the minor wards of their right to have the accounts of the executors opened to correct any errors therein Denholm *v* McKay, 148 Mass 434, Tripp *v* Gifford, 155 Mass 108.

Though an executor has resigned or has been removed, he must still account as executor; he will still be obliged to submit to an examination, and to answer all questions in relation to his accounts Newell *v.* West, 149 Mass 528

[1] Cummings *v* Cummings, 123 Mass. 271, Ibid., 128 Mass 532.

[2] Field *v* Hitchcock, 14 Pick 405, Smith *v* Dutton, 4 Shepley, 308, Browne *v.* Doolittle, 151 Mass 600, and cases cited.

[3] An administrator settled his first account in 1818, and a second account in 1822; but in 1825, on the petition of the residuary legatee, a re-hearing was had in the probate court, and the administrator was ordered to credit the estate with an additional sum. From this decree the legatee appealed, on the ground that a larger sum should be credited, but failed to prosecute the appeal, and it was dismissed. The legatee thereupon demanded payment of the administrator of the sum so ordered to be credited, and upon his refusal to pay brought an action against him, in which judgment was rendered, in 1835, in favor of the administrator, on the ground that the decree had been vacated by the appeal. In 1836 the legatee filed a petition in the probate court for a second re-hearing, on the ground that the account

had been settled fraudulently, but the petition was dismissed by that court in 1837, on appeal, it was ordered that unless the respondent should pay to the legatee the amount he had been ordered to credit the estate in 1825, with interest from the time of the demand and costs, the prayer of the petition should be granted. Davis v Cowdin, 20 Pick 510; Cummings v Cummings, 128 Mass. 532, Blake v Ward, 137 Mass 94   See Bassett v. Granger, 103 Mass. 177.

If a trustee under a will, through inadvertence, errs in stating, in an account filed by him, that a certain sum paid to a *cestui que trust* was part of the income, instead of a part of the principal of a trust fund, the probate court, on an appeal to the supreme court of probate, may grant the trustee leave to reopen the account and correct the error, if it is material   Dodd v Winship, 144 Mass 461   See Browne v Doolittle, 151 Mass 596 ; Newell v Peaslee, 151 Mass 601

An executor who, in his first account, erroneously charges himself with the rents of real estate to which he was himself entitled as residuary devisee, is not estopped from showing the mistake and having it corrected.   Brown v. Baron, 162 Mass. 56.

CHAPTER XVI.

DESCENT AND DISTRIBUTION — ADVANCEMENTS

DESCENT, or hereditary succession, is the title whereby a person, on the death of his ancestor, acquires his estate by right of representation, as his heir.[1]

DESCENT OF REAL ESTATE. — GENERAL RULES.

When a person dies seised of land, tenements, or hereditaments, or of any right thereto, or entitled to any interest therein, in fee-simple or for the life of another,[2] not having lawfully devised the same, they shall descend, subject

---

[1] The status of any person with the inherent capacity of succession or inheritance, is to be ascertained by the law of the domicile which creates the status. Ross v Ross, 129 Mass 243 ; Merrill v Preston, 135 Mass 456, Proctor v Clark, 154 Mass. 45

[2] This description of the real estate is so framed as to include, not only lands of which the ancestor was actually seised, but also remainders and reversions, and the right to lands of which he had been disseised or in any other way ousted Com Rep 1834, note to c 61

Contingent interests, both in real and personal estate, are transmissible like vested interests Winslow v Goodwin, 7 Met 363; Dalton v Savage, 9 Met 28 , Welsh v Woodbury, 144 Mass 515, and cases cited

Real estate held by an executor or administrator in mortgage, or on execution for a debt due to the deceased, is considered personal assets in his hands, and if not sold by him or redeemed does not descend to the heirs as real estate, but is assigned and distributed to the same persons and in the same proportions as if it had been part of the personal estate of the deceased R L c 150, § 11.

to his debts and to the rights of the husband or wife and minor children of the deceased as provided in chapters 131, 132, and 140 of the Revised Laws, in manner following.[1] —

"*First*, In equal shares to his children and to the issue[2] of any deceased child by right of representation, and if there is no surviving child of the intestate, then to all his other lineal descendants. If all such descendants are in the same degree of kindred to the intestate, they shall share the estate equally; otherwise, they shall take according to the right of representation.

"*Second*, If he leaves no issue, then in equal shares to his father and mother.

"*Third*, If he leaves no issue nor mother, then to his father.

"*Fourth*, If he leaves no issue nor father, then to his mother.

"*Fifth*, If he leaves no issue and no father or mother, then to his brothers and sisters and to the issue of any deceased brother or sister by right of representation, and if there is no surviving brother or sister of the intestate, then to all the issue of his deceased brothers and sisters. If all such issue are in the same degree of kindred to the

---

[1] R L c 133, § 7, Dexter *v* Inches, 147 Mass 326, Smith, Petitioner, 156 Mass. 408

The real estate of an intestate, in default of children or surviving brothers or sisters, will be distributed among the nearest descendants or issue in equal degree of kindred to the intestate *per capita*, and to those in more remote degree, *per stirpes*. Balch *v.* Stone, 149 Mass. 39 If an illegitimate intestate leaves no relatives except a brother and sister of his mother, and children of her deceased brothers his personal estate will go to the uncle and aunt, to the exclusion of his cousins Parkman *v.* McCarthy, 149 Mass 502

[2] The word "issue," as applied to the descent of estates, includes all the lawful lineal descendants of the ancestor. R. L. c. 8, § 5, cl. 7.

intestate, they shall share the estate equally, otherwise, they shall take according to the right of representation.[1]

"*Sixth*, If he leaves no issue, and no father, mother, brother, or sister, and no issue of any deceased brother or sister, then to his next of kin in equal degree; except that when there are two or more collateral kindred in equal degree, but claiming through different ancestors, those who claim through the nearest ancestor shall be preferred to those claiming through an ancestor who is more remote.[2]

"*Seventh*, If an intestate leaves no kindred and no widow or husband, his or her estate shall escheat to the commonwealth."

The degrees of kindred are computed according to the rules of the civil law; and the kindred of the half blood inherit equally with those of the whole blood in the same degree.[3]

RIGHTS OF A SURVIVING HUSBAND IN THE PROPERTY OF HIS DECEASED WIFE AND RIGHTS OF A WIFE IN THE PROPERTY OF HER DECEASED HUSBAND.

a. *Under the Public Statutes.*

The Revised Laws make radical changes in regard to the rights of a surviving husband in the property of his deceased wife and in regard to the rights of a wife in the

---

[1] Conant v Kent, 130 Mass 178

[2] Snow v Snow, 111 Mass 389, Balch v Stone, 149 Mass. 39

"Next of kin," under 26 U S Sts at Large, pp 862. 908, relating to payment of French Spoliation Claims, are not to be determined as of the time of the testator's death, but as of the date of the passage of the act Codman v Brooks, 167 Mass 499

[3] Larrabee v. Tucker, 116 Mass 562, R L c 133, § 2

For the provisions of law under which the estates of persons deceased prior to Oct 1, 1876, descend, see Gen Stats. c 91

DESCENT AND DISTRIBUTION UNDER PUBLIC STATUTES 323

property of her deceased husband Before stating the provisions of the Revised Laws on this subject, it will be well, for the purpose of comparison and reference, to summarize those provisions of the Public Statutes in which the principal changes have been made

The law which was superseded when the Revised Laws took effect on the first day of January, 1902, provided as follows: —

" When a man and his wife are seised in her right, and when a married woman is seised to her sole and separate use, of an estate of inheritance in lands, and they have had issue born alive which might have inherited such estate, the husband shall on the death of the wife hold the lands for his life as a tenant thereof by the curtesy. If they have had no such issue, he shall hold one half of such lands for his life. If she dies and leaves no issue living, he shall take her real estate in fee to an amount not exceeding five thousand dollars in value, and shall also have an estate by the curtesy or other life interest, as before provided, in her other real estate. If she dies intestate and leaves no kindred, he shall take the whole of her real estate in fee.[1] "

[1] P. S c. 124, § 1, as amended by St 1885, c 255, and St 1887, c 290 A husband is entitled to his curtesy in an estate tail of which his wife was seised Goddard v. Whitney, 140 Mass. 101

By a will, real estate was given to four children for life, " and when they shall respectively decease, to their respective heirs," etc One of the children was a married woman who died intestate It was *held*, that her husband was her heir, and not her three brothers Lavery v Egan, 143 Mass. 389. See also Lincoln v Perry, 149 Mass. 374, Brownell v Briggs, 173 Mass. 531.

A married woman died leaving a husband, but no issue She made a will, to which her husband did not assent, by which she gave him a pecuniary legacy, and added these words " Which is to be in full settlement of all his demands upon my estate," and devised the rest of

The Public Statutes as amended also provided that, if a married woman died possessed of personal property not lawfully disposed of by will, and leaving issue, her husband should be entitled, after payment of her debts, funeral expenses, and charges of administration, to one half of the residue; and to the whole of such residue if she left no issue.[1]

As to the surviving wife the Public Statutes provided, in regard to real estate of her deceased husband, as follows. —

"A wife shall be entitled to her dower at common law in the lands of her deceased husband When her husband dies intestate" (and when he dies testate and she waives the provisions of his will)[2] "and leaves no issue living,

---

her estate to others *Held*, that the husband was not entitled, under P S c 124, c 1, to one half of his wife's lands for his life Burke v Colbert, 144 Mass 160

P. S c. 124, § 3, gave to a husband a fee in his wife's lands to an amount not exceeding five thousand dollars in value, when they had had no children Howe v Berry, 168 Mass. 418

[1] P S c 135, § 3, Goddard v. Whitney, 140 Mass 101, Constantinides v Walsh, 146 Mass 282, Parkman v McCarthy, 149 Mass. 504, Robinson v Simmons, 156 Mass 126.

[2] The surplus of proceeds of land sold by an executor or administrator, remaining on the settlement of his accounts, is considered *real estate*, and is disposed of to the same persons and in the same proportions as the land would descend if not sold P. S. c 142 § 9.

The statute extends to contingent as well as to vested interests Dalton v Savage, 9 Met 37, Welsh v Woodbury, 144 Mass. 545, and cases cited

Where a will does not dispose of the whole estate of a testator, property not disposed of therein passes to the next of kin and heirs at law as intestate property. Foster v. Smith, 156 Mass 379

Cochran v. Thorndike, 133 Mass 46, Mathews v. Mathews, 141 Mass 511

A child by adoption is "issue" within the meaning of P S c. 124, § 3 Buckley v. Frasier, 153 Mass 525.

she shall take his real estate in fee to an amount not exceeding five thousand dollars in value, and shall also be entitled during her life to one-half of the other real estate of which he died seized ; or, if she files her election therefor within six months after the date of letters of administration on his estate, she may have, instead of such life estate, her dower in his real estate other than that taken by her in fee. If her husband dies intestate and leaves no kindred, she shall take the whole of his real estate in fee."[1] A wife shall also be entitled to remain in the house of her husband for forty days after his death without being chargeable with rent.

If the husband died possessed of personal property not lawfully disposed of by will, and leaving issue, the widow was entitled, after payment of any allowances to her and to minor children, the debts of the deceased, funeral expenses, and charges of administration, to one-third of the residue ; and, if the husband left no issue, the widow was entitled to the whole of the residue to the amount of five thousand dollars and to one-half of the excess of the residue above ten thousand dollars ; and if the husband left no kindred, she was entitled to the whole of the residue [2]

A widow could waive the provisions of her husband's will and she would then be entitled to dower in his real estate and to the same share of his personal property as she would have received if he had died intestate, except

[1] P. S. c. 124, § 3 ; Staigg v Atkinson, 144 Mass 570, Buttrick v. Tilton, 155 Mass. 463

Although the husband and wife have separated by mutual agreement, she will still retain her right to share in his estate on his decease Whitney v Closson, 138 Mass. 49.

A husband is the statutory heir of his wife Lavery v. Egan, 143 Mass. 389 , Lincoln v. Perry, 149 Mass 368.

[2] P S. c 135, § 3, as amended by St. 1885, c. 276.

that, if she would thus become entitled to an amount exceeding ten thousand dollars, she would receive only the income during her life of the excess above ten thousand dollars.[1]

Without her husband's written consent, the will of a married woman could not deprive him of his tenancy by the curtesy in her real estate, or of the right to the use for his life of one-half of her real estate, if they had had no issue born alive, or of more than one-half of her personal property, or of her real estate not exceeding five thousand dollars in value when no issue survived her, except that a married woman deserted by her husband or living apart from him for a justifiable cause, when the fact of such desertion or living apart had been established by the decree of a court having jurisdiction of the parties, could by will or by deed dispose of her real estate without her husband's consent.[2]

b Under the Revised Laws.

"A husband shall, upon the death of his wife, hold one-third of her land for his life. Such estate shall be known as his tenancy by curtesy, and the provisions of law applicable to dower shall be applicable to curtesy. A wife shall, upon the death of her husband, hold her dower at common law in her deceased husband's land. Such estate shall be known as her tenancy by dower. But in order to be entitled to such curtesy or dower the surviving husband or wife shall file his or her election and claim therefor in the registry of probate within one year after the date of

[1] P. S. c 127, §§ 18, 19. Staigg v Atkinson, 144 Mass 570; Dexter v Codman, 148 Mass 422, Townsend v Townsend, 156 Mass 455

[2] P S c 147, § 6 ; St 1885, c 255 ; St. 1887, c 290, Johnson v Williams, 152 Mass 414

the approval of the bond of the executor or administrator of the deceased, and shall thereupon hold instead of the interest in real property given in section three of chapter one hundred and forty, curtesy or dower, respectively; otherwise such estate shall be held to be waived. Such curtesy and dower may be assigned by the probate court in the same manner as dower is now assigned, and the tenant by curtesy or dower shall be entitled to the possession and profits of one undivided third of the real estate of the deceased from her or his death until the assignment of curtesy or dower, and to all remedies therefor which the heirs of the deceased have in the residue of the estate. Rights of curtesy which exist when this chapter takes effect may be claimed and held in the manner above provided, but in such case the husband shall take no other interest in the real or personal property of his wife, and, except as preserved herein, curtesy at common law is abolished."[1]

"If a deed of land is made to a married woman, who, at the time of its execution, mortgages such land to the grantor to secure the payment of the whole or a part of the purchase-money, or to a third person to obtain the whole or a part of such purchase-money, her seisin shall not give her husband an estate by the curtesy as against such mortgagee."[2]

---

[1] R. L. c. 132, § 1. A widow's right to have dower assigned to her out of the lands of her deceased husband, cannot be attached or taken on execution in an action at law. McMahon v. Gray, 150 Mass. 289.

When land is taken by right of eminent domain the wife of the person whose land is so taken is not entitled, by reason of her inchoate right of dower, to have a portion of the proceeds set apart by a court in equity for her benefit in case she survives her husband. Flynn v. Flynn, 171 Mass. 312.

[2] R. L. c. 132, § 2.

"A widow shall not be entitled to dower in wild land of which her husband dies seised, except wood lots or other land used with his farm or dwelling-house, nor in such land which is conveyed by him although it is afterward cleared." [1]

"If, upon a mortgage made by a husband, his wife has released her right of dower, or if a husband is seised of land subject to a mortgage which is valid and effectual as against his wife, she shall nevertheless be entitled to dower in the land mortgaged as against every person except the mortgagee and those claiming under him. If the heir or other person who claims under the husband redeems the mortgage, the widow shall either repay such part of the money which was paid by the person so redeeming as shall be equal to the proportion which her interest in the land mortgaged bears to the whole value thereof, or, at her election, she shall be entitled to dower according to the value of the estate after deducting the money paid for redemption." [2]

"The articles of apparel and the ornaments of the widow and minor children of a deceased person shall belong to them respectively The widow may remain in the house of her husband for not more than six months next succeeding his death without being chargeable for rent" [3]

"Such parts of the personal property of a deceased person as the probate court, having regard to all the circumstances of the case, may allow as necessaries to his widow for herself and for his family under her care or, if there is

---

[1] R. L c 132, § 3. A widow who does not live upon the dower estate has no right to cut the wood thereon for sale. Noyes v Stone, 163 Mass 490

[2] R. L. c 132, § 4   [3] R L c 140, § 1

no widow, to his minor children, not exceeding one hundred dollars to any child, and also such provisions and other articles as are necessary for the reasonable sustenance of his family, and the use of his house and of the furniture therein, for six months next succeeding his death, shall not be taken as assets for the payment of debts, legacies, or charges of administration. After exhausting the personal property, real property may be sold to provide the amount of allowance decreed, in the same manner as it is sold for the payment of debts, if a decree authorizing such sale is made, upon the petition of any party in interest, within two years after the approval of the bond of the executor or administrator."[1]

"If a person dies possessed of property not lawfully disposed of by will, it shall be distributed as follows: —

"First, The personal property remaining after said allowances shall be applied to the payment of the debts of the deceased and the charges of his last sickness and funeral and of the settlement of his estate.

"Second, The residue of the personal property shall be distributed among the persons and in the proportions prescribed for the descent of real property in chapter one hundred and thirty-three, except as otherwise provided herein.

"Third, If the deceased leaves no issue, the surviving husband or widow shall take five thousand dollars and one-half of the remaining personal property and one-half of the remaining real property. If the personal property is insufficient to pay said five thousand dollars, the deficiency shall, upon the petition of any party in interest, be paid from the sale or mortgage, in the manner provided for the payment of debts or legacies, of any interest of the

[1] R. L. c. 140, § 2. See page 177 *et seq*, *ante*.

deceased in real property which he could have conveyed at the time of his death.

"If the deceased leaves issue, a surviving husband or widow shall take one-third of the remaining personal property and one-third of the remaining real property.

"If the deceased leaves no kindred, a surviving husband or widow shall take the whole of the remaining real and personal property.

"If the deceased leaves no husband, widow, or kindred, the whole of the remaining personal property shall escheat to the commonwealth"[1]

"The surviving husband, except as provided in section thirty-six of chapter one hundred and fifty-three" (which authorizes a wife deserted by her husband or living apart from him for a justifiable cause to convey her real property by deed or will without his consent), "or the widow of a deceased person, at any time within one year after the probate of the will of such deceased, may file in the registry of probate a writing signed by him or by her, waiving any provisions that may have been made in it for him or for

---

[1] R L c 140, § 3, Parkman v. McCarthy, 149 Mass 504; Robinson v. Simmons, 156 Mass. 126.

The surplus of proceeds of land sold by an executor or administrator, remaining on settlement of his accounts, is considered real estate and is disposed of to the same persons and in the same proportions as the land would descend if not sold   R L. c 148 § 9

The statute extends to contingent as well as to vested interests Dalton v. Savage, 9 Met 37; Welsh v. Woodbury, 144 Mass 545

Where a will does not dispose of the whole estate of a testator, property not disposed of therein passes to the next of kin and heirs at law as intestate property. Foster v. Smith, 156 Mass 379

Children of the half blood inherit equally with those of the whole blood. Larrabee v Tucker, 116 Mass 562   An adopted child who is at the same time the grandson of the adopting father cannot inherit the property of his grandfather in a twofold capacity, as his son and as his grandson   Delano v Bruerton, 148 Mass 619.

DESCENT AND DISTRIBUTION UNDER THE REVISED LAWS. 331

her, or claiming such portion of the estate of the deceased as he or she would have taken if the deceased had died intestate, and he or she shall thereupon take the same portion of the property of the deceased, real and personal, that he or she would have taken if the deceased had died intestate; except that if he or she would thus take real and personal property to an amount exceeding ten thousand dollars in value, he or she shall receive in addition to that amount only the income during his or her life of the excess of his or her share of such estate above that amount, the personal property to be held in trust and the real property vested in him or her for life, from the death of the deceased; and except that if the deceased leaves no kindred, he or she upon such waiver shall take the interest he or she would have taken if the deceased had died leaving kindred but no issue. If the real and personal property of the deceased which the surviving husband or widow takes under the foregoing provisions exceeds ten thousand dollars in value, the ten thousand dollars above given absolutely shall be paid out of that part of the personal property in which the husband or widow is interested, and if such part is insufficient the deficiency shall, upon the petition of any person interested, be paid from the sale or mortgage in fee, in the manner provided for the payment of debts or legacies, of that part of the real property in which he or she is interested. Such sale or mortgage may be made either before or after such part is set off from the other real property of the deceased for the life of the husband or widow.

"If, after probate of such will, legal proceedings have been instituted wherein its validity or effect is drawn in question, the probate court may, within said one year, on petition and after such notice as it may order, extend the time for filing the aforesaid claim and waiver until the expiration of six months from the termination of such legal proceedings."[1]

"No surviving husband or widow of a deceased person shall make claim for an interest in the estate of such deceased or begin an action or other proceeding for the recovery thereof, unless such claim or action is made or begun within twenty years after the decease of the wife or husband, or after he or she has ceased to occupy, or to receive the profits of, his or her share of such real estate, except that if at the time of such decease the surviving husband or widow is absent from the commonwealth, under twenty-one years of age, insane or imprisoned, he or she may make such claim or begin such action or proceeding at any time within twenty years after such disability ceases."[2]

"Lots in cemeteries incorporated under the provisions

---

[1] R. L. c. 135, § 16 A widow filed her waiver and died before the probate of her husband's will. *Held*, that the waiver was sufficient and that her share of the estate passed to her representatives. Atherton *v.* Corliss, 101 Mass. 40.

The privilege of waiver is a personal right which, if the widow is insane, neither she nor her guardian can exercise. Pinkerton *v.* Sargent, 102 Mass. 568. But see R. L. c. 145, § 33.

The income of the excess of the share above $10,000 is to be computed from the time of the death of the testator. Pollock *v.* Learned, 102 Mass. 49; Towle *v.* Swasey, 106 Mass. 106.

For a case in which a widow waived the provisions of her husband's will and the meaning of the word "family," used in the will, was construed, see Townsend *v.* Townsend, 156 Mass. 454.

A widow who has waived the provisions of her husband's will cannot avail herself of a provision for her in the will which operates as an appointment of property under a trust deed. Fiske *v.* Fiske 173 Mass. 413.

A widow who has not waived the provisions of her husband's will, by which he has given the entire estate to her, is not entitled to dower in land which in his lifetime was seised on an execution against him and set off to his creditors in full satisfaction of the judgment. Barnard *v.* Fall River Savings Bank, 135 Mass. 326.

[2] R. L. c. 132, § 13; O'Gara *v.* Neylon, 161 Mass. 140.

of section one of chapter seventy-eight of the Revised Laws, tombs in public cemeteries, and lots and tombs in public cemeteries in towns, shall be held indivisible, and upon the decease of a proprietor of such lot the title thereto shall vest in his heirs at law or devisees subject to the following limitations and conditions If he leaves a widow and children, they shall have the possession, care, and control of said lot or tomb in common during her life. If he leaves a widow and no children, she shall have such possession, care, and control during her life If he leaves children and no widow, they shall have in common the possession, care, and control of such lots or tombs during their joint lives, and the survivor of them during his life. The persons in possession, care, and control of such lots or tombs may erect a monument and make other permanent improvements thereon. The widow shall have a right of permanent interment for her own body in such lot or tomb, but it may be removed therefrom to some other family lot or tomb with the consent of her heirs. If two or more persons are entitled to the possession, care, and control of such lot or tomb, they shall designate in writing to the clerk of the corporation, or, if it is a tomb or lot in a public cemetery, to the board of cemetery commissioners, if any, or to the city or town clerk, which of their number shall represent the lot; and, in default of such designation, the board of trustees or directors of the corporation, the board of cemetery commissioners, if any, or the board of health if such lots or tombs are in public cemeteries in cities or towns, shall enter of record which of said persons shall represent the lot during such default. The widow may at any time release her right in such lot, but no conveyance or devise by any other person shall deprive her of such right."

"Before entering of record the name of any person to represent such lot or tomb, the board of cemetery commissioners, if any, or the board of health of a town, shall hear the parties entitled to the control thereof at such time and place as it shall have previously appointed by a notice published in a newspaper, if any, of the town, otherwise, by posting a copy in a public place therein."

"A wife shall be entitled to a right of interment for her own body in any burial lot or tomb of which her husband was seised during coverture, which right shall be exempt from the operation of the laws regulating conveyance, descent, and devise, but which may be released by her in the same manner as dower."

"A husband shall have the same rights in the tomb or burial lot of his wife as a wife has in that of her husband, and may assert or release the same in the same manner as she may assert or release her rights."[1]

SUMMARY OF CHANGES MADE BY THE REVISED LAWS AS TO THE RIGHTS OF A SURVIVING HUSBAND IN THE PROPERTY OF HIS DECEASED WIFE AND AS TO THE RIGHTS OF A WIFE IN THE PROPERTY OF HER DECEASED HUSBAND.

a. As to the Surviving Husband.

Curtesy at common law is abolished, and, in place of it, the husband may, upon the death of his wife, hold one-third of her land for his life, provided he files his election and claim therefor in the registry of probate within one year after the date of the approval of the bond of the executor or administrator of his wife. This estate is termed his tenancy by curtesy. If he does not file such an election and claim for curtesy, then under the provisions of

[1] R. L. c. 78, §§ 26-29 inclusive.

section three of chapter one hundred and forty of the Revised Laws, if his wife dies intestate and leaves no issue, the surviving husband, after payment of debts of the wife and the charges of her last sickness and funeral and of the settlement of her estate, is entitled to five thousand dollars and one-half of the remaining personal property and one-half of the remaining real property, in fee; and if the personal property is insufficient to pay the five thousand dollars, the deficiency is to be paid from the sale or mortgage, in the manner provided for the payment of debts or legacies, of any interest of the deceased wife in real property which she could have conveyed at the time of her death If the deceased wife dies intestate and leaves issue, the surviving husband takes one-third of the personal property remaining after the payments of debts, etc, and one-third of the remaining real property.

If the wife leaves a will, the surviving husband, at any time within one year after the probate of the will, may file in the registry of probate a writing signed by him waiving any provisions that may have been made in the will for him, or claiming such portion of the estate of his wife as he would have taken if she had died intestate, and he will thereupon take the same share of her property, real and personal, that he would have taken if she had died intestate; except that if he would thus take real and personal property to an amount exceeding ten thousand dollars in value he will receive only the income during his life of the excess above ten thousand dollars, the personal property to be held in trust and the real property to be vested in him for life, from the death of the wife; and except that if the wife leaves no kindred he will take, upon such waiver, the interest he would have taken if she had died leaving kindred but no issue. If the real and personal property of the wife which the surviving husband would take, upon such waiver, exceeds ten thousand dollars in value, the ten thousand dollars given absolutely is to be paid out of the personal property in which the husband is interested, and if such part is insufficient the deficiency is to be paid from the sale or mortgage of that part of the real property in which the husband is interested.

b. *As to the Surviving Wife.*

The surviving wife is entitled to dower at common law in the real property of her husband, provided she files her election and claim therefor in the registry of probate within one year after the date of the approval of the bond of the executor or administrator of her husband. If she does not file such election and claim, and if her husband dies intestate, the surviving wife, after the payment of such allowance as may be made by the probate court to her, including such provisions and other articles as are necessary for the reasonable sustenance of the family of the husband and the use of his house and of the furniture therein for six months next succeeding his death, and after payment of his debts, and the charges of his last sickness and funeral and of the settlement of his estate, is entitled to five thousand dollars and one-half of the remaining personal property and to one-half of the remaining real property, if her husband leaves no issue; and to one-third of the remaining personal property and one-third of the remaining real property, if he leaves issue. If the personal property is insufficient to pay said five thousand dollars, the deficiency shall be paid from the sale or mortgage, in the manner provided for the payments or debts or legacies, of any interest of the husband in real property which he could have conveyed at the time of his death.

The surviving wife can waive the provisions of her husband's will in the same manner and with the same effect, in all respects, as above stated in regard to the waiver by a surviving husband of the provisions of the will of his deceased wife.

From this brief summary it will be seen that husband and wife are placed on an equality by the Revised Laws, excepting that certain allowances may be made to her by the probate court for the temporary support of herself and her children and that she is given the use of her husband's house and of the furniture therein for six months next succeeding his death, free of charge for rent. For nearly seven hundred years prior to the date when the Revised Laws took effect, a widow had been entitled to the use of her husband's house free of rent for a period of forty days. This is now extended to six months. The dower right must now be claimed, even when the husband dies intestate, and the right of dower is superior to the claims of creditors, except where it has been released. If dower is not claimed, the widow, if her husband dies intestate and without issue, is entitled to property to the value of five thousand dollars and to one-half of the remaining personal property, and one-half of the remaining real property, absolutely; and if the personal property is not sufficient to pay the five thousand dollars, real estate may be sold or mortgaged to make up any deficiency; and if there are issue, the widow takes absolutely one-third of the personal property and one-third of the real property This distribution is after payment of the debts, etc. ; but, in place of the use and income for life of one-third of the real estate, the widow is given one-third of the remaining real estate absolutely. If the personal property does not amount to five thousand dollars in value, after payment of the debts and charges, the deficiency is made up by the sale or mortgage of real estate, where there are no issue, and in many cases this would be greatly for the advantage of the widow

The practical result of the changes made by the Revised Laws is that a widow whose husband dies intestate and leaves issue takes absolutely one-third of all of her husband's property, after the payment of his debts and the charges of administration, and, if the husband does not leave issue, the widow will receive, after the payment of debts and charges of administration, five thousand dollars and one-half of all of the remaining property, both real and personal, and this she will hold absolutely The Revised Laws also provide that real estate may be sold for the purpose of paying any allowance made to the widow by the probate court Under the former law the allowance could only be made out of the personal property.

Notwithstanding the very liberal provisions of the Revised Laws, if the husband left much real estate and was heavily in debt it might be advisable for the widow to claim her dower

HOMESTEAD ESTATES OF WIDOWS AND MINOR CHILDREN.

The estate of homestead existing at the death of a householder continues for the benefit of his widow and minor children, and shall be held and enjoyed by them, if one of them or a purchaser under the provisions of section ten of chapter 131 of the Revised Laws occupies the premises, until the youngest child is twenty-one years of age, and until the marriage or death of the widow. But all the right, title, and interest of the deceased in the premises in which such estate exists, except the estate of homestead thus continued, is subject to the laws relating to devise, descent, dower, and sale for the payment of debts and legacies.[1]

"The real and personal property of a woman shall upon her marriage remain her separate property, and a married woman may receive, receipt for, hold, manage, and dispose of property, real and personal, in the same manner as if she were sole. But no conveyance by a married woman of real property shall, except, as provided in section thirty-six" [of chapter 153 of Revised Laws, which section authorizes a married woman who has been deserted by her husband or is living apart from him for justifiable cause to convey her real property as if she were sole], "extinguish or impair her husband's tenancy by the curtesy by statute or his rights to curtesy when this chapter" [chapter 153] "takes effect in such property unless he joins in the conveyance or otherwise releases his said rights"[2]

If a deed of land is made to a married woman, who at the time of its execution mortgages such land to the grantor to secure the payment of the whole or a part of the purchase-money, or to a third party to obtain the whole or a part of such purchase-money, her seisin shall not give her husband an estate by the curtesy as against such mortgagee.[3]

If a widow is entitled by the provisions of law, by deed of jointure, or under the will of her husband, to an undivided interest in his real estate either for life or during widowhood, and her right is not disputed by his heirs or devisees, such interest may be assigned to her, in whatever counties the lands lie, by the probate court for the

---

[1] R L c. 131, § 8 An estate of homestead cannot be affected by the will of the householder Brettun *v* Fox, 100 Mass 234 The right depends upon occupancy. Paul *v* Paul, 136 Mass. 286.

[2] R L c. 153, § 1 ; Ago *v* Conner, 167 Mass 390

[3] R. L c. 132, § 2.

county in which the estate of her husband is settled. Such assignment may be made upon her petition, or, if she does not petition therefor within one year from the decease of her husband, upon petition by an heir or devisee of her husband, by any person having an estate in the land subject to such interest, or by the guardian of any such heir, devisee, or person.[1]

Upon such petition the court shall issue a warrant to three discreet and disinterested persons, who shall be sworn to perform their duty faithfully and impartially according to their best skill and judgment, and who shall set off the widow's interest by metes and bounds if it can be so done without damage to the whole estate. But if the estate out of which a widow's interest is to be assigned consists of a mill or other tenement which cannot be divided without damage to the whole, such interest may be assigned out of the rents or profits thereof, to be held and received by the widow as a tenant in common with the other owners of the estate [2]

ESTATES OF DECEASED NON-RESIDENTS.

"If administration is taken in this commonwealth on the estate of a person who was an inhabitant of any other state or country, his estate found here shall, after payment of his debts, be disposed of according to his last will, if he left any duly executed according to law; otherwise, his real estate shall descend according to the laws of this commonwealth, and his personal property shall be distributed and disposed of according to the laws of the state or country of which he was an inhabitant."[3]

[1] R L c 132, § 9 [2] Ibid. § 10.
[3] R. L. c 148, § 1; Welch v Adams, 152 Mass. 76, Cowden v. Jacobson, 165 Mass. 240

AS TO ILLEGITIMATE CHILDREN.

An illegitimate child is the heir of his mother and of any maternal ancestor, and the lawful issue of an illegitimate person takes by descent any estate which such person would have taken if living.

If an illegitimate child dies intestate and without issue, who may lawfully inherit his estate, his estate descends to his mother, or, in case she is not living, to the persons who would have been entitled thereto by inheritance through his mother if he had been a legitimate child

An illegitimate child whose parents have intermarried, and whose father has acknowledged him as his child, is deemed legitimate.[1]

SETTLEMENT OF ESTATES OF ABSENTEES.

"If a resident of the commonwealth having property therein has disappeared, absconded, or is absent therefrom and has left no agent therein and his whereabouts are unknown; or if such resident, who has a wife or minor child dependent upon him wholly or partly for support, has disappeared without making sufficient provision for such support and his whereabouts are unknown, or if it is known that they are without the commonwealth; or if

---

[1] R L c. 133, §§ 3, 4, 5; Parkman v McCarthy, 149 Mass 502.

A bastard and his issue cannot inherit from his mother's collateral kindred Pratt v Atwood, 108 Mass. 40, Haraden v. Larrabee, 113 Mass 430

In Hayden v. Barrett, 172 Mass. 472, it was held that an illegitimate child was the "heir by blood" of his mother within the meaning of a will construed in that case

Pub Sts c 125, § 4, and St 1882, c. 132 (now embodied in R L c 133, § 4), do not apply to the distribution of the estate of a child of an illegitimate child theretofore deceased Sanford v Marsh, 180 Mass 210.

abandoned property of a person who is not a resident of the commonwealth is found therein and no agent therein is authorized to take care thereof, a person who would be entitled to administer upon the estate of such resident if he were dead, or such wife, or a person in behalf of such wife or minor child, or if abandoned property belongs to such non-resident any suitable person, may file a petition, under oath, in the probate court for the county in which any such property is located or found, stating the name, age, occupation, and last known residence or address of such absentee or of such non-resident, the date and circumstances of the disappearance and the names and residence of the family of such absentee and of other persons of whom inquiry may be made, and containing a schedule of his property, real and personal, so far as known, and its location within the commonwealth, and praying that such property may be taken possession of and a receiver thereof appointed under the provisions of this chapter."

"The court may thereupon issue a warrant directed to the sheriff or his deputy, which may run into and be served in any county, commanding him to take possession of the property named in said schedule, and hold the same subject to the order of the court, and make return of said warrant as soon as may be with his doings thereon with a schedule of the property taken possession of by virtue thereof. The officer shall post a copy of the warrant upon each parcel of land named in the schedule and cause so much of the warrant as relates to land to be recorded in the registry of deeds for the county and district in which the land is located He shall receive such fees for serving the warrant as the court allows, but not more than those established by law for similar service upon a writ of attachment. If the petition is dismissed, said fees and the cost of publishing and serving the notice hereinafter provided shall be paid by the petitioner. If a receiver is appointed said fees and cost shall be paid by the receiver and allowed in his account."

"Upon the return of such warrant, the court may issue a notice which shall recite the substance of the petition, warrant, and officer's return, and shall be addressed to such absentee or non-resident and to all persons who claim an interest in said property, and to all whom it may concern, citing them to appear at a time and place named and show cause why a receiver of the property named in the officer's schedule should not be appointed and said property held and disposed of under the provisions of this chapter."

"The return of said notice shall be not less than thirty nor more than sixty days after its date. The court shall order said notice to be published in one or more newspapers within the commonwealth, once in each of three successive weeks, and to be posted in two or more conspicuous places in the city or town in which the absentee last resided or was known to have been either temporarily or permanently, and upon each parcel of land named in the officer's schedule, and a copy to be mailed to the last known address of such absentee or non-resident. The court may order other and further notice to be given within or without the commonwealth."

"The absentee or non-resident and any person who claims an interest in any of the property may appear and show cause why the prayer of the petition should not be granted. The court may after hearing dismiss the petition and order the property in possession of the officer to be returned to the person entitled thereto, or it may appoint a receiver of the property which is in the possession of the officer and named in his schedule. If a receiver is appointed the court shall find and record the date of the disappearance or absconding of the absentee, and such receiver shall give bond to the judge of probate and his successors in office in such sum and with such condition as the court orders, with a company named in section sixty-one of chapter one hundred and eighteen and approved by the court as surety thereon"

"After the filing and approval of such bond the court may order the sheriff or his deputy to transfer and deliver to such receiver the possession of the property under the aforesaid warrant, and the receiver shall file in the registry of probate a schedule of the property received by him."

"Such receiver upon petition filed by him may be authorized and directed to take possession of any additional property within the commonwealth which belongs to such absentee, or of any additional abandoned property which belongs to such non-resident, and to demand and collect all debts due such absentee from any person within the commonwealth, and hold the same as if it had been transferred and delivered to him by the officer."

"The court may make orders for the care, custody, leasing, and investing of said property and its proceeds If any of said property consists of live animals or is perishable or cannot be kept without great or disproportionate expense, the court may, at any time after the return of the warrant, order such property to be sold at public or private sale After the appointment of a receiver, upon his petition and after notice, the court may order all or part of said property, including the rights of the absentee or of the non-resident in land, to be sold at public or private sale to supply money for payments authorized by this chapter or for re-investment approved by the court."

"The court may order said property or its proceeds acquired by mortgage, lease, or sale to be applied in payment of charges incurred or that may be incurred in the support and maintenance of the absentee's wife and minor children, and to the discharge of such debts as may be proved against said absentee."

"The receiver shall be allowed such compensation and such disbursements as the court orders to be paid out of said property or its proceeds. If such absentee appears within fourteen years after the date of the disappearance and absconding as found and recorded by the court, the receiver shall account to him for, deliver, and pay over the unexpended balance of said property. If, within said fourteen years, an administrator, executor, assignee in insolvency, or trustee in bankruptcy of said absentee is appointed, such receiver shall account for, deliver, and pay over to him the unexpended balance of said property. If said absentee does not appear and claim said property within said fourteen years, all the right, title, and interest of said absentee in said property, real or personal, or the proceeds thereof, shall be barred, and no action, suit, or petition in any form shall be commenced by said absentee after the expiration of said fourteen years for or on account of said property or its proceeds."

"If, at the expiration of said fourteen years, said property has not been accounted for, delivered, or paid over under the provisions of the preceding section, the court shall order the distribution of the unexpended balance thereof to the persons to whom, and in the shares and proportions in which, it would have been distributed if said absentee had died intestate on the day fourteen years after the date of the disappearance or absconding as found and recorded by the court."

"If such receiver of the property of an absentee is not appointed within thirteen years after the date found by the court under the provisions of section five, the time limited for accounting for, or fixed for distributing, said property or its proceeds, or for barring actions relative thereto, shall be one year after the date of the appointment of the receiver instead of the fourteen years provided in the two preceding sections. If within fourteen years after the date of the appointment of such receiver of the property of a non-resident, said non-resident or an administrator, executor, assignee in insolvency, or trustee in bankruptcy, of said non-resident does not appear and claim said property or its proceeds, all the right, title, and interest of said non-resident in and to said property, real or personal, or the proceeds thereof, shall be barred, and no action, suit, or petition in any form shall be begun by said non-resident after the expiration of said fourteen years for or on account of said property or its proceeds; and the remainder thereof shall be distributed as provided in section eleven, as if said non-resident had died intestate on the day fourteen years after the date of the appointment of the receiver."[1]

RIGHT OF REPRESENTATION.

Inheritance or succession "by right of representation" is the taking by the descendants of a deceased heir of the same share or right in the estate of another person as their parent would have taken if living[2] If the an-

[1] R L c 144, as amended by St. 1902, c. 544.
[2] R L. c. 133, § 6.

cestor leaves children, and there is no living issue of any deceased child, they will share his estate equally; if he leaves grandchildren only, they will take it in equal shares; and if he has no children or grandchildren living at the time of his death, his great-grandchildren, if any, being his lineal descendants, and all of an equal degree of consanguinity to him, will take the inheritance equally

But when the lineal descendants of the ancestor, living at the time of his death, are not of an equal degree of consanguinity to him, — as, for instance, when he leaves one son and two or more grandchildren who are the children of a deceased son, — the rule of representation applies. The son, in such case, takes half the estate, and the children of the deceased son represent their father, and, together, take the other half, which is the same share that their father would have taken if living Or suppose the ancestor leaves B, his only surviving son, and D and E, grandsons by his deceased son, C, and F and G, great-grandsons by H, a daughter of C, H being also dead. Here would be lineal descendants living in three different degrees of consanguinity; namely, a son, two grandsons, and two great-grandsons; B, the son, would take the half estate; D and E, two of the three children of C, would take two-thirds of the other half; and F and G would take the remaining third of the second half; and all would hold as tenants in common.

AS TO THE NEXT OF KIN.

The "next of kin," to whom the estate descends when the intestate leaves no issue, and no father, mother, brother, or sister, are to be ascertained by reference to the rules of the civil law, according to which the degrees of kindred are computed.[1] According to those rules, the father of the intestate stands in the first degree, his grandfather in the second, his great-grandfather in the third, etc. The child of the intestate is also in the first degree, his grandchild in the second, his great-grandchild in the third, the rule of computation being the same both in the ascending and descending lines The degree of kindred in which a collateral kinsman stands is calculated by counting upwards from the intestate to the common ancestor of both, and then downwards to such collateral relative, reckoning one degree for each person. Thus, the intestate and his cousin are related in the fourth degree; the intestate's father being in the first degree, his grandfather, their common ancestor, in the second, his uncle, counting downwards from the common ancestor, in the third, his uncle's son (his cousin), in the fourth The intestate's brother stands in the second degree, his nieces and nephews in the third.[2]

The statute makes no distinction between ascendants and descendants, and none between kindred on the father's and on the mother's side;[3] but when there are two or more collateral kindred in equal degree, those claiming through the nearest ancestor are preferred to those claiming through an ancestor more remote. The intestate's nephew, for instance, is preferred to the intestate's uncle, though both are in the same degree of kindred. The

[1] R L. c 133, § 2. For the meaning of the term "blood relations," see Cummings v. Cummings, 146 Mass. 507. See also Whall v. Converse, 146 Mass 345.

[2] Swasey v Jaques, 114 Mass 135 ; Fargo v Miller, 150 Mass 225.

[3] The next of kin of a deceased intestate, being her paternal grandmother and her maternal grandfather and grandmother, are each entitled to a third part of the intestate's estate. Knapp v Windsor, 6 Cush 156; Balch v. Stone, 149 Mass. 42.

common ancestor of the intestate and his uncle is the intestate's grandfather, while the nephew claims through the intestate's father, the nearer ancestor.[1]

Kindred of the half blood inherit equally with those of the whole blood in the same degree.[2]

ISSUE OF THE TESTATOR NOT PROVIDED FOR IN HIS WILL.

"If a testator omits to provide in his will for any of his children or for the issue of a deceased child, they shall take the same share of his estate that they would have taken if he had died intestate, unless they have been provided for by the testator in his lifetime, or unless it appears that the omission was intentional, and not occasioned by accident or mistake."[3]

That the omission was intentional, and not occasioned by accident or mistake, may be manifest from the will

---

[1] Minot v Harris, 132 Mass 528

[2] R. L. c. 133, § 2. "Heirs at law" means next of kin. White v. Stanfield, 146 Mass 424, Kendall v Gleason, 152 Mass 457.

The words "nearest of kin" mean nearest blood relations. Swasey v Jaques, 144 Mass 135, Keniston v Mayhew, 169 Mass 169, Leonard v Haworth, 171 Mass 500

If the grantor in a declaration of trust, as well as the trustee, life tenant, and the remainderman whose "heirs at law" are to take their shares in a certain contingency, are all domiciled in this state at the time of its execution here, and provision is made for the apppointment here of a successor in case of the trustee's death, such "heirs at law" are to be determined by the law of this commonwealth Codman v. Krell, 152 Mass 214

[3] R L c 135, § 19

If the testator gives his daughter an annuity by will, and she dies in his lifetime, her issue born before the making of the will do not take any part of his estate, although the will contains no specific provision for such issue. Wilder v Thayer, 97 Mass. 439

Where the omission was occasioned by the testator's mistake as to the legal effect of the will and its provisions, the children were allowed to share in the estate. Ignorance of the testator and oversight of the

350   PROCEEDINGS IN THE PROBATE COURTS.

itself.[1] It has been held that the fact that the child was named in the will, though no legacy was given to him, was sufficient to show that he was not forgotten by the testator, and that the omission to provide for him was intentional. And where the testator devised estate to the children of his daughter, describing them as such, but giving her no legacy, the same rule was applied[2] The fact that the omission was designed may also be shown by parol evidence.[3] Evidence of declarations of the tes-

scribe are alike grounds of relief   Ramsdill v Wentworth, 101 Mass. 125   But see Hurley v O'Sullivan, 137 Mass. 86

A testator gave a legacy to a child not his own, and afterwards adopted her   Held, that she was not entitled to share in his estate as if he had died intestate   Bowdlear v Bowdlear, 112 Mass. 184.

A testatrix gave all her estate to her husband, and had a child born a month after the will was made   It was found that the omission to provide for the child was intentional   Peters v Siders, 126 Mass. 135

A child of a testator, born after his death, cannot, in any proper sense of the term, be deemed provided for in his will by a general devise of a reversion to the heirs of the testator   Waterman v Hawkins, 63 Maine, 156; Bowen v Hoxie, 137 Mass 527

The opinion of Judge Clifford in Loring v Marsh, 2 Clifford 311, contains a review of all the then existing statutes and decisions upon this subject

There is no omission to provide by will for children, if there should be any living at the testator's decease, if, after a bequest to his wife, whom he knew to be pregnant at the time of making the will, he gave the rest of his property to a trustee to pay the whole income to her during life and the reversion to those who at the time of her death would be his heirs-at-law by blood   Minot, Petitioner, 164 Mass. 38.

[1] Prentiss v Prentiss, 11 Allen, 47.

[2] Terry v Foster, 1 Mass 146, Church v Crocker, 3 Mass 17, Wild v Brewer, 2 Mass. 570; Wilder v. Goss, 14 Mass. 357.

[3] Ramsdill v Wentworth, 101 Mass 125, Buckley v Gerard, 123 Mass. 8; Ingersoll v Hopkins, 170 Mass 403

Oral evidence that a testatrix who devised all her estate to her husband was a woman of great intelligence and capacity, and very fond of her children, who were of tender age and never separated from her,

tator is admissible to show that the omission was intentional.[1] The burden of proof is upon the party opposing the claim of the child to show that the omission was intentional.[2] The statute applies to children born after the making of the will, and before the death of the father;[3] but it has been held not to apply to cases where the testator omits to provide for an illegitimate child.[4] Nor does it apply to cases where the testator has a power of appointment over the estate to dispose of the inheritance, but only to cases where it is the testator's own estate in fee.[5]

A child for whom the testator has unintentionally omitted to provide may cause his share of the personal estate to be ascertained by applying to the probate court for a decree of distribution. His share or proportion of the real estate, if certain and not disputed by parties interested, may also be assigned to him by the probate court,[6] if his share is disputed and uncertain, he must

---

that she had great affection for her husband and the most perfect confidence in him, and that he was very devoted to her, is admissible and will justify a finding that her omission to provide in her will for her children was intentional and not occasioned by accident or mistake although no declaration of the intention of the testatrix appears Buckley v. Gerard, 123 Mass 8

[1] Wilson v Fosket, 6 Met 400 , Converse v. Wales, 4 Allen, 512

[2] Ramsdill v Wentworth, 106 Mass. 320

[3] A testator gave a small legacy to each of his children, living at the date of his will, by name (all of whom died before him without issue), and the residue of his property to his wife, and afterwards had other children born to him. Held, that evidence of his having said to his wife, since the birth of his younger children, "You will have all there is," was not sufficient to show an intent to omit to provide for them in his will, and that they were entitled to the same share of his estate as if he had died intestate Bancroft v Ives, 3 Gray, 367.

[4] Kent v Barker, 2 Gray, 535.

[5] Sewall v. Wilmer, 132 Mass 131 , Blagge v. Miles, 1 Story, 426

[6] See post, chap. xvii., on Partition.

apply to the common law courts for an assignment of his share of the real estate.

POSTHUMOUS CHILDREN.

"If a child of the testator, born after his father's death, has no provision made for him by his father in his will or otherwise, he shall take the same share of his father's estate which he would have taken if his father had died intestate"[1] Devisees and legatees are required to contribute equally, in proportion to the value of what they respectively receive under the will, to the share of a posthumous child or a child omitted in the will of his parent, unless there is some provision in the will requiring a different apportionment, in order to give effect to the intention of the testator as to that part of his estate which passes by his will.[2]

ISSUE OF DEVISEE OR LEGATEE DYING IN THE TESTATOR'S LIFETIME

"If a devise or legacy is made to a child or other relation of the testator, who dies before the testator, but leaves issue surviving the testator, such issue shall, unless a different disposition is made or required by the will, take the same estate which the person whose issue they are would have taken if he had survived the testator"[3]

---

[1] R L c 135, § 20; Bowen v Hoxie, 137 Mass. 527.
[2] R. L. c 135, § 25, Bowen v Hoxie, *supra*
[3] R L c. 135, § 21 Stockbridge, Petitioner, 145 Mass 519; O'Rourke v Beard, 151 Mass 9, Ladd v. Chase, 155 Mass 417; Lee v Gay, 155 Mass 423

A testator by his will bequeathed the residue of his estate to A. and B, the latter being the testator's brother-in-law, " to be equally divided between them, share and share alike, to them and their heirs

SETTLEMENT OF ESTATES OF NON-RESIDENTS.

"If administration is taken in this commonwealth upon the estate of a person who was an inhabitant of another state or country, his estate found here shall, after payment of his debts, be disposed of according to his will, if he left any duly executed according to law; otherwise his real property shall descend according to the laws of this commonwealth, and his personal property shall be distributed and disposed of according to the laws of the state or country of which he was an inhabitant."

"After the payment of all debts for which such estate is liable in this commonwealth, the residue of the personal property may be distributed and disposed of, as provided in the preceding section, by the probate court; or, in the discretion of the court, it may be transmitted to the executor or administrator, if any, in the state or country of which the deceased was an inhabitant, to be there disposed of according to the laws thereof."[1]

and assigns" B died in the testator's lifetime, and it was held that the legacy to him lapsed Horton v Earle, 162 Mass. 448.

A wife is not a "relation" within the meaning of the statute. Esty v Clark, 101 Mass. 36. Nor is a stepson. Nor is a brother-in-law. Horton v Earle, supra Only relations by blood are intended Kimball v Story, 108 Mass 382

In the case of a bequest of an annuity for life, the issue of the legatee, born before the making of the will, do not take any share in the estate Wilder v Thayer, 97 Mass 439. See Morse v Mason, 11 Allen, 36, Sears v Putnam, 102 Mass. 10, Moore v Weaver, 16 Gray, 305, Paine v Prentiss, 5 Met 396

[1] R L c 143, §§ 1, 2, Dawes v. Boylston 9 Mass 337; Stevens v. Gaylord, 11 Mass 256, Hooker v Olmstead, 6 Pick 481, Fay v. Haven, 3 Met 109, Emery v Batchelder 132 Mass 452, Newell v. Peaslee, 151 Mass. 603, Welch v Adams, 152 Mass 77; Cowden v. Jacobson, 165 Mass 240 As to distribution of insolvent estates of non residents, see page 236

The distribution of intestate estates is within the peculiar and exclusive jurisdiction of the probate courts [1] The administrator, or any of the distributees, on application to the probate court, can obtain a decree of distribution specifying the names of persons who are entitled to share in the estate, and the amount to which each is entitled. In the great majority of cases of persons dying intestate, the heirs and distributees will be the children, parents, brothers, and sisters, or other near connections, all of whom may be known to the administrator; and in such cases the administrator is practically safe in paying to each distributee the amount to which he is entitled, and taking his receipt therefor, without first obtaining a decree of distribution. But when the heirs or any of them are residing out of the commonwealth, or when the administrator has doubts as to who is entitled to share in the estate, or as to the proportions of the several heirs, he should apply to the court for a decree of distribution And a decree, made after such notice as the court may order, settles the facts as to who are entitled, and what kin are living, and will protect an administrator, acting in good faith, in conforming to it;[2] and he is held by his bond to distribute the estate as the court may order

[1] The heirs and next of kin of an intestate, after conveying to other persons all their interest in his real and personal estate, are not entitled, against the wish of their grantee, to a decree for the assignment and distribution of real estate held by the administrator under his foreclosure of a mortgage thereof to the intestate Stevens *v* Palmer, 15 Gray, 505

A distributive share in a minor intestate's estate is attachable by trustee process as soon as the administrator thereof has given bond and received letters of administration, although the minor's guardian still holds the personal estate, and his final account has not been filed or allowed. Mechanics' Savings Bank *v* Waite, 150 Mass 234

[2] Loring *v* Steineman, 1 Met. 204; Pierce *v*. Prescott, 128 Mass.

A decree of distribution may also be necessary to enable the next of kin to bring a suit on the bond of an unfaithful administrator for the recovery of his distributive share of the estate.

THE PETITION FOR DISTRIBUTION.

The petition for a decree of distribution should state the names and residences of each of the supposed distributees, the degree of kindred in which each of them stands to the intestate, the balance in the hands of the administrator for distribution, the amount of any advancement made by the intestate in his lifetime to either of the heirs, and whether such advancement was made from the real or personal estate, or both. The petition may be made by the administrator, or any party interested in the distribution.

Upon such petition, such notice must be given as will be most likely to reach the parties interested.[1] The supreme court of probate, in the case of an English subject dying in this commonwealth, has ordered notice to be published in a London newspaper. The order, what-

---

140; Shores v Hooper, 153 Mass. 232; Defriez v Coffin, 155 Mass. 203; Lamson v Knowles, 170 Mass. 297.

A testator gave a share of his estate, consisting of personalty here, and land in another state, to his brother's wife, who was domiciled there, "to have and to hold the same to her during her life, and at her decease to her heirs at law and their heirs and assigns forever." It was *held*, that as to the personalty which remained at her death, it should go to her heirs at law according to the statutes of distribution then in force in Massachusetts. Lincoln v Perry, 149 Mass. 368.

[1] Under the provision that notice may be dispensed with when all the "parties entitled thereto" give their assent in writing or waive notice, creditors of the estate are entitled to notice. Browne v. Doolittle, 151 Mass. 595.

ever may be its terms, must be complied with by the petitioner, before a decree of distribution can issue.[1]

THE DISTRIBUTION.

A decree of distribution expressed in the general terms used by the statute to designate the heirs at law is not sufficient. It is for the court to ascertain who are the existing individuals entitled, under the statute, to share in the estate, to decree distribution to them by name, and determine the amount due to each.[2] If all the parties

---

[1] An action will not lie against an administrator for a distributive share of the estate before a decree of distribution. Cathaway v. Bowles, 136 Mass. 54.

[2] Loring v Steineman, 1 Met. 204. The court will not order a distributive share to be paid to a person to whom the heir has assigned it, the investigation of such an assignment is not within the jurisdiction of the probate court Knowlton v. Johnson, 46 Me. 489; Wood v Stone, 2 Chandler (N H), 572 Nor will the court order the share of an heir to be paid to the other heirs on the ground that he is indebted to them Hancock v. Hubbard, 19 Pick 167 See Lenz v. Prescott, 144 Mass 515

The widow's distributive share may be assigned to her, although by an ante-nuptial agreement she released all claims on her husband's estate Sullings v. Richmond, 5 Allen, 187; Blackinton v Blackinton, 110 Mass 461 But the agreement will be enforced in equity Tarbell v Tarbell, 10 Allen, 278; Paine v Hollister, 139 Mass 144

An executor, administrator, or trustee, having in charge any property subject to a tax on collateral successions, shall deduct the tax therefrom, or shall collect the tax from the person entitled to the property, and he shall not deliver property or a specific legacy subject to the tax to any person until he has collected the tax R L c 15, § 5

Whenever the devisee, legatee, or heir, who has paid any such tax, afterwards refunds any portion of the property on which it was paid, or it is judicially determined that the whole or any part of such tax ought not to have been paid, the tax or the due proportional part of it shall be paid back to him by the executor, administrator, or trustee. Ibid § 15

appear upon notice, or are known to be living, these questions are easily determined A more difficult question sometimes arises when a descendant or next of kin of the intestate is absent from the state and cannot be found. Whether such person shall be included in the distribution, as he is entitled to be if living, must be determined by the rules of evidence and presumptions of facts from circumstances which are resorted to by all tribunals in determining questions of fact The possibility of mistake cannot prevent the distribution, and the distribution when made must be of the entire estate If such absent heir left his usual home for temporary purposes of business or pleasure, and has not been heard from or known to be living for the term of seven years, the presumption of life ceases and that of his death arises. It must appear that he has not been heard of by those persons who would be likely to hear of him, or that search has been ineffectually made for such a person.[1] This presumption of death may be rebutted by counter-evidence Where other circumstances concurred, the fact of death has been found, without direct evidence, from the lapse of a shorter period than seven years; as, when the party sailed in a vessel which had not been heard from for a much longer time than was necessary for the accomplishment of the voyage;[2] but the presumption of law does not attach to the mere lapse of time short of seven years.

If such person was unmarried at the time he went abroad, there is no presumption of his subsequent marriage; and if the fact of his marriage is proved, there is no presumption that he left issue. These are facts to be

[1] France v Andrews, 15 Adol & E. 756; Marden v. Boston, 155 Mass 359

[2] Watson v. King, 1 Stark. 97

proved, and the burden of proof of the affirmative is on the party who avers it.[1]

Under some circumstances, it is impossible to ascertain with certainty what persons are entitled to inherit an estate, as when several near relatives perish by shipwreck or other common disaster.[2] In the absence of all evidence of the particular circumstances of the calamity, it is presumed that all perished together, and that therefore neither could transmit rights to the other. Thus, where a father and his only child perished at sea, there being no evidence showing which survived, it was decided that his estate should go to his nephews and nieces, his heirs at law, and not to her uncles and aunts, who would have taken it if she had survived her father and the estate had vested in her.[3] It would be reasonable and proper to hold that one of middle age and in the full vigor of life would ordinarily survive a mere infant or a person well stricken in years. And evidence of circumstances, however slight, attending the disaster, is important, as from slight circumstances inferences of fact materially affecting the question may be drawn.

The time when distribution can be properly made must depend upon the circumstances of each case. If all the persons entitled to shares are known, the distribution may be made at any time after the debts are paid.[4] But as the administrator is liable to the actions of creditors for two years after he gives bond, the payment of any distributive

[1] Loring v. Steineman, 1 Met. 211; Doe v. Griffin, 15 East, 293; In the Goods of Main, 1 Swa. & Trist. 11.

[2] Batchelder, Petitioner, 147 Mass. 465.

[3] Coye v. Leach, 8 Met. 371.

[4] If legacies or distributive shares are paid within two years, the legacy tax thereon is payable at the time the same are paid. R. L. c. 15, § 4.

share during the continuance of such liability may be attended with risk, unless the distributee first gives bond, as the court may require him to do, for the protection of the administrator.[1]

The court, after notice to all persons interested, may, subject to the rights of creditors, order a partial distribution, when it can be made without detriment to the estate.[2]

If by the provisions of a will a legacy is to be distributed in whole or in part among the heirs or next of kin of any person, or among persons of a certain class, the probate court, upon the application of any person interested, after notice, may order distribution to be made among such persons as according to the will seem to be entitled to the legacy.[3]

A debt due to the estate from an heir or distributee is set off against and deducted from his share of the estate. The probate court determines as to the validity and amount of the debt, and may make all decrees and orders which may be necessary or proper to carry into effect such set-off or deduction; but this shall not prejudice any remedy of an executor or administrator for the recovery of such debt nor affect the liability of the legatee or distributee for the excess of his indebtedness over the amount of his share in or claim upon the estate to which he is indebted.[4]

[1] R L c 141, § 20. A decree allowing distribution of all the personal estate before the end of the two years of administration is void as to creditors prosecuting their claims within that period. Browne v Doolittle, 151 Mass 595. See Newell v Peaslee, 151 Mass. 601

[2] R. L c 141, § 21, Browne v Doolittle, *supra*, Welch v. Adams, 152 Mass 85, Shores v Hooper, 153 Mass 233

[3] R L c 141, § 22

[4] Ibid § 23: Blackler v Boott, 114 Mass. 24

A debt due from a legatee which at the death of the testator was barred by the statute of limitations cannot be deducted from the

ADVANCEMENTS.

The subject of advancements is necessarily to be considered in connection with the descent and distribution of intestate estates. Advancements may be made of real or personal estate, and to any child or other lineal descendant. They are usually made with a view of establishing a son in business, or on the event of marriage. If the advancement is equal to, or exceeds, the amount in value of the share which the child would have taken in the estate, if no advancement had been made, such child will be excluded from any share in the distribution; if it is less in amount, such child will be entitled to sufficient in the distribution to make up his full share, and no more. If he dies before the intestate, leaving issue, the amount of his advancement is regarded as so much received by his representatives towards their share of the estate, in like manner as if the advancement had been directly to them.[1] He is not required to refund any part of the advancement, although it exceeds his share,[2] and interest is not to be computed on it.[3]

If the advancement is made in real estate, its value is considered as part of the real estate to be divided; if in personal estate, as part of the personal estate; and if in either case it exceeds the share of real or personal estate, respectively, that would have come to the heir so advanced, he does not refund any part of it, but receives so much

---

legacy, unless the language of the will clearly expresses such an intention. Allen v. Edwards, 136 Mass. 138.

This statute relates only to personal estate. Jones v. Treadwell, 169 Mass. 430.

[1] R. L. c. 140, § 8.
[2] Ibid § 4; Stearns v. Stearns, 1 Pick. 161.
[3] Osgood v. Breed, 17 Mass. 356.

less out of the other part of the estate as will make his whole share equal to those of the other heirs who are in the same degree with him.[1]

Questions concerning advancements are determined by the probate court, and the judgment of the court is conclusive, unless appealed from. Questions as to advancements of personal property are settled by the decree of distribution, and of real estate by the decree of partition.[2]

EVIDENCE OF ADVANCEMENTS.

The advancement must be proved to have been intended as such, chargeable on the child's share of the estate, otherwise, it will be deemed an absolute gift or a loan, as the case may be. The statute prescribes what shall be the requisite evidence of an advancement: "Gifts and grants shall be held to have been made as advancements, if they are expressed in the gift or grant to be so made, or if charged in writing as such by the intestate, or acknowledged in writing as such by the party receiving them."[3] It is not expressly provided that an advance-

---

[1] R. L. c. 140, § 5; Bemis *v*. Stearns, 16 Mass. 200.

[2] The probate court in which the estate of a deceased person is settled may hear and determine all questions of advancements arising in relation to such estate, or such questions may be heard and determined upon a petition for partition either in the superior court or the probate court, but when such a question arises upon a petition for partition, the court may suspend proceedings until the question has been decided in the probate court in which the estate of the deceased is settled. R. L. c. 140, § 9. When a child in consideration of a sum paid him by his father, by way of advancement, releases his claim to his share of the inheritance, although the sum so paid was much less than his share of his father's estate at his death would have been worth, it shall bar him of his share. Kenney *v*. Tucker, 8 Mass. 142.

[3] R. L. c. 140, § 6; Cummings *v.* Bramhall, 120 Mass. 552.

ment shall not be proved in any other manner, but that is undoubtedly the meaning of the statute. It has accordingly been held that where a note was given by a son for money received by him of his father, oral testimony was inadmissible to prove that the money so received was an advancement.[1] Various sums of money, charged by the parent in the usual way of keeping accounts, have been held not to be an advancement.[2] And where land was conveyed by the father to the son, there being nothing in the deed to show the fact, it was held not to be an advancement.[3] The execution of a will merges all prior advance-

---

[1] Barton v. Rice, 22 Pick. 508.
[2] Ashley, Appellant, 4 Pick. 21.
[3] Bullard v. Bullard, 5 Pick. 527. A written acknowledgment, signed by husband and wife, in these words, "Received of J. S. $300, it being a part of my wife's portion," and found among the notes of J. S. after his decease, is sufficient proof of an advancement to the wife. So of an acknowledgment in writing by a husband, whose wife is insane, of a gift from her father for her support, "as a part of her portion out of her father's estate," preserved by the father in a bundle of letters relating to her support at an insane asylum. A book of accounts kept by the deceased, with three leaves cut out, together with evidence of his declarations that he had made charges in his book, as advancements to his children, are not competent evidence of such advancements. Hartwell v. Rice, 1 Gray, 587.

Where a child gave a receipt for articles delivered, promising to return them if called for, and the parent wrote in the receipt that they were to answer as a part of the child's portion, it was held to be an advancement. So of the words, "articles that I let my daughter N. have," in a book containing memoranda by a parent of advancements to his other children. Bulkeley v. Noble, 2 Pick. 337.

Entries in book left by the intestate, showing "the moneys I have advanced to my children severally, and to which I shall give credit to any or each of them as they may pay me from time to time," show loans of the children, not advancements. Bigelow v. Poole, 10 Gray, 104.

Children agreed in writing that sums of money received by them from their father should be treated as advancements in the settlement of his estate, the agreement having been made in the lifetime of the

ments,[1] unless a different provision is made in the will, it being deemed that the testator graduated the amount of his legacies with reference to them, but the execution of a will which is afterwards revoked cannot operate as a merger.[2]

VALUE OF ADVANCEMENTS.

The statute prescribes the manner in which the value of advancements shall be ascertained. "If the value of an advancement is expressed in the conveyance, in the charge thereof made by the intestate, or in the acknowledgment by the party receiving it, such value shall be adopted in the division and distribution of the estate; otherwise it shall be determined according to the value when the property was given."[3]

THE WIDOW'S SHARE WHEN ADVANCEMENTS HAVE BEEN MADE.

The widow is entitled only to her share in the residue after deducting the value of the advancement.[4]

DISTRIBUTION WHEN ADVANCEMENTS HAVE BEEN MADE.

To ascertain the share to which each heir is entitled, in a case where advancements have been made: first, if there is a widow, deduct from the sum to be distributed one-third for her share; to the remainder add the advance-

---

father, and without his knowledge. *Held*, that the agreement was not sufficient to establish an advancement. Fitts v Morse, 103 Mass. 164. And see Bacon v Gassett, 13 Allen, 334, Cummings v Bramhall, 120 Mass 553.

[1] Jones v. Richardson, 5 Met. 247, Jaques v. Swasey, 153 Mass 596.
[2] Hartwell v Rice, 1 Gray, 587
[3] R. L c. 140, § 7   [4] Ibid § 4.

ment of each heir who has received *less than a full share*,[1] and divide the sum by the number of such heirs. The quotient will be the amount of a full share of the estate. Each heir who has had no advancement will be entitled to a full share, and each of the others to a full share less the amount of his advancement. Thus, suppose the administrator's final account shows a balance in his hands of $9,000; that the intestate left a widow, four children, A, B, C, and D, and two grandchildren, sons of E, a deceased son of the intestate, and that A has been advanced $2,000, C $1,000, D $800, and E $400. —

Amount to be distributed	$9,000
Deduct widow's share, one-third	3,000
	$6,000
Add A's advancement	2,000
" C's "	1,000
" D's "	800
" E's "	400
There being five shares	5)10,200
Amount of a full share	$2,040
A will take	40
B, having had no advancement, will take a full share	2,040
C will take	1,040
D " "	1,240
The two grandsons together will take	1,640
	$6,000

[1] To find whether either of the heirs has received more than a full share, add *all* the advancements to the remainder, and divide the amount by the number of *all* the heirs; if the quotient be less than the advancement made to any heir, such heir and the amount of his advancement must be altogether omitted in the computation.

PERPETUATION OF EVIDENCE OF PAYMENTS UNDER THE DECREE OF DISTRIBUTION. — DISCHARGE OF EXECUTOR, ETC

The decree of distribution contains the names of all the persons entitled to share in the personal estate of the deceased, and specifies the amount to which each is entitled. The administrator is directed to give written notice, by mail or otherwise, to each of the persons named in the decree of the amount due him or her, and if any sum remains for six months unclaimed, the executor, administrator, guardian, or trustee, who was ordered to pay the same, may deposit it in a savings-bank or other like institution, or invest it in bank stocks or other stocks, as the probate court may direct, to accumulate for the benefit of the person entitled thereto. The deposit or investment is made in the name of the judge of the probate court for the time being, and subject to the order of the judge and his successors in office. The person who makes such deposit or investment is required to file in the probate court a memorandum thereof, with the original certificates, deposit book of the bank, or other evidences of title thereto, which shall be allowed as a sufficient voucher for such payment. When the person entitled to the money deposited or invested satisfies the judge of his right to receive it, the judge shall cause it to be paid over and transferred to him.[1]

[1] R. L. c 150, § 23

The limitation of the amount any one person can deposit in a savings-bank and receive interest thereon does not apply to such deposits. R. L c 113, § 25.

The interest of a distributee is equitable only in money ordered by the probate court to be paid to him, and upon his refusal to receive it, deposited prematurely by the administrator in a trust company, which in its certificate of deposit acknowledges the receipt of the money for

When an executor, administrator, guardian, or trustee has paid or delivered to the persons entitled thereto the money or other property in his hands, as required by a decree of the probate court, he may perpetuate the evidence thereof by presenting to the probate court, within one year after the decree is made, an account of such payments or the delivery of such property; which being proved to the satisfaction of the court, and verified by the oath of the accountant, shall be allowed as his final discharge. Such discharge will forever exonerate the accountant and his sureties from all liability under the decree, unless his account is impeached for fraud or manifest error.[1]

The administrator may conveniently render his account of payments and deposits made under a decree of distribution by returning to the court the original decree, with the receipts of the several distributees and certificates of deposit or deposit books, and his own certificate of the fact that the terms of the order have been complied with. In a majority of cases, the administrator is practically safe in taking receipts from the persons to whom he makes payments, without rendering a further account; but it is only by rendering such an account that he can obtain a formal discharge from liability under the decree.

When the person entitled to a sum of money deposited in a savings-bank by the administrator under a decree of distribution satisfies the judge of his right to receive the same, the judge will cause it to be paid over to him.

the distributee and promises to pay the amount to the judge of probate or his assigns; and the fund so deposited cannot be reached by trustee process as the property of the distributee. Chase v. Thompson, 153 Mass. 14.

[1] R. L c. 150, § 20, Browne v Doolittle, 151 Mass. 596.

The person so entitled to the money should make a petition in writing to the court showing the grounds of his claim, and, if the money is ordered to be paid to him, should procure an attested copy of the order for presentation at the bank.[1]

FINAL DISTRIBUTION OF SUMS OF MONEY DEPOSITED OR INVESTED BY ORDER OF PROBATE COURTS.

" The probate court may, upon the petition of any person interested and after public notice, order all money or the proceeds thereof deposited or invested by its authority and which shall have remained unclaimed for a period of twenty years from the date of such deposit or investment, to be paid to the residuary legatee, if any, of the testator to whose estate the money belonged, or, if such residuary legatee is dead, to his heirs who are living at the time of such distribution: and if no such residuary legatee or any of his heirs be then living, or if the deceased person died intestate, said money and the proceeds thereof shall be disposed of and distributed among the persons entitled thereto and in the manner provided by chapter one hundred and forty. The court shall first require from the person or persons to whom such sums shall be ordered to be paid, a sufficient bond of indemnity with two sufficient sureties to be approved by the judge of probate, with condition to repay to the person or persons for whose benefit such deposit or investment was originally made, or to the personal representatives of such person or persons, all sums paid over by the order of the court under the provisions of this section."[2]

---

[1] R. L. c. 150, § 23, Chase v. Thompson, 153 Mass. 15.
[2] R. L c 150, § 26.

The provisions of section 25 of chapter 113 of the Revised Laws, limiting the amount of deposits which a savings-bank or institution for savings can receive from one person to one thousand dollars, and limiting the sum on which interest may be allowed to sixteen hundred dollars (made up of the principal of one thousand dollars and accumulated interest thereon), do not apply to deposits made in the name of a judge of probate or by order of court.[1]

"The probate court, court of insolvency, or other court, respectively, shall, upon the application of any person interested or of the attorney-general, and after public notice, order and decree that all sums of money heretofore or hereafter deposited with such corporation" (a savings-bank or institution for savings), "by authority of any of said courts or of a judge thereof, and which shall have remained unclaimed for a period of more than five years from the date of such deposit, with the increase and proceeds thereof, to be paid to the treasurer and receiver-general, to be held and used by him according to law, subject for fifteen years only to be repaid to the person having and establishing a lawful right thereto, with interest at the rate of three per cent per annum from the time it is so paid to said treasurer to the time it is paid over by him to such person."[2]

BALANCES IN THE HANDS OF PUBLIC ADMINISTRATORS.

"When an estate has been fully administered by a public administrator, he shall deposit the balance of such estate remaining in his hands with the treasurer and receiver-general, who shall receive and hold it for the benefit of those who may have lawful claims thereon."[3]

---

[1] R L c 113, § 25.   [2] Ibid § 55.
[3] R L c. 138, § 12. The probate court has authority to order a

"The probate courts shall require every public administrator in their respective counties to render an account of his proceedings under any letters of administration at least once in each year until the trust has been fulfilled. And when, upon a final settlement of an estate, it appears that moneys remain in the hands of such administrator, which by law should have been deposited with the treasurer of the commonwealth, the court shall certify that fact and a statement of the amount so withheld to said treasurer, who, unless such deposit is made within one month after the receipt of such notice, shall cause the bond of the administrator to be prosecuted for the recovery of such moneys."

"If, at any time within six years after a public administrator has made deposit with the treasurer of the balance of an estate remaining in his hands, any person applies to the probate court which granted letters of administration on said estate and makes it appear that he is legally entitled by the will of the deceased or otherwise to the administration of said estate, the court shall grant administration thereof, or, upon probate of such will, shall grant letters testamentary to such applicant, or at his request to some other suitable person; but before granting such administration, the court shall order personal notice of the application to be served, at least fourteen days before the hearing, upon a public administrator of the county, who shall appear in behalf of the commonwealth."

"After the expiration of thirty days from the appointment of an executor or administrator as provided in the

public administrator to distribute the balance of an estate among the next of kin of the intestate. Parker *v.* Kuckens, 7 Allen, 509.

preceding section, if no appeal is claimed by any person interested, the treasurer shall pay over to such executor or administrator all money deposited in the treasury to the credit of such estate, to be administered in like manner as the estates of other deceased persons."

"Upon the death, resignation, or removal of a public administrator, the probate court shall issue a warrant to some other public administrator in the same county, on his application therefor, requiring him to examine the accounts of such late public administrator touching the estates on which he has taken out letters of administration, and to return into the probate court a statement of all of such estates that are not fully administered, and of the balance of each estate that remained in the hands of such public administrator at the time of his death, resignation, or removal. And thereupon the court shall issue to the public administrator making the return, upon his giving the requisite bond, letters of administration upon such of said estates as are not already administered, although the personal estate remaining may not amount to twenty dollars."

"When a public administrator neglects to return an inventory, to settle an account, or to perform any other duty incumbent on him in relation to an estate, and there appears to be no heir entitled to such estate, the district-attorney for the district within which the administrator received his letters shall, in behalf of the commonwealth, prosecute all suits and do all acts necessary and proper to insure a prompt and faithful administration of the estate, and the payment of the proceeds thereof into the treasury of the commonwealth, and if no heir has, within two years after the granting of letters of administration, appeared and made claim in the probate court for his interest in such estate, it shall be presumed that there is no such heir, and the burden of proving his existence shall be upon the public administrator."

"When the total property of an intestate which has come into the possession or control of a public administrator is of a value less than twenty dollars (unless the same is the balance of an estate received from a prior public administrator), he shall forthwith reduce all such property into money, not taking administration thereon, and shall deposit such money, first deducting his reasonable expenses and charges, with the treasurer of the commonwealth, who shall receive and hold it for the benefit of any persons who may have legal claims thereon. Such claims may be presented to the auditor of the commonwealth within one year from such payment to the treasurer and receiver-general, and the auditor shall examine such claims and allow such as may be proved to his satisfaction, and upon the expiration of the year shall forthwith certify the same to the governor and council for payment of the whole of the claims, or such proportion thereof as the funds will allow."

"A public administrator, upon making such deposit, shall file with the treasurer and receiver-general a true and particular account, under oath, of all his dealings, receipts, payments, and charges on account of the property from which the money so deposited proceeds, including the name of the intestate, if known to him, and the treasurer and receiver-general shall thereupon deliver to him a receipt for such money. Such deposit shall exempt the public administrator making it from all responsibility for or on account of the money so deposited."[1]

[1] R. L. c. 138, §§ 13-19.

PAYMENTS TO GUARDIANS AND TRUSTEES APPOINTED IN OTHER STATES.

"A guardian appointed within the commonwealth, whose ward removes from or resides out of the commonwealth, may sell the real property of his ward, and transfer and pay over the whole or any part of the proceeds and the whole or any part of the ward's personal property to a guardian, trustee, or committee appointed by competent authority in the state or country in which the ward resides, upon such terms and in such manner as the probate court by which he was appointed may, after notice to all parties interested, decree upon petition filed therefor"[1]

"An executor, administrator, or trustee, who has in his hands personal property belonging to a person under guardianship residing out of this commonwealth and having no guardian appointed therein, may pay over and transfer the whole or any part of such personal property to a guardian, trustee, or committee appointed by competent authority in the state or country in which such person resides, upon the terms and in the manner required by the provisions of section twenty-five of chapter one hundred and forty-six."[2]

"If all living parties who are interested as beneficiaries in a trust created by will which is proved and allowed in this commonwealth reside out of this commonwealth, the probate court which has jurisdiction of the trust may, upon petition of the parties in interest, or of the executor, administrator, or trustee, if it considers it just and expedient, authorize the executor, administrator, or trustee to pay over the fund to a trustee appointed by the proper court

[1] R L c 146, § 25; Talbot v. Chamberlain, 149 Mass. 61.
[2] R. L. c. 145, § 36.

in any other state or country, if all the beneficiaries who are living and the executor, administrator, or trustee signify their consent, and the court is satisfied that the laws of such other state or country secure the due performance of said trust; and upon such payment, shown to the satisfaction of said probate court, the executor, administrator, or trustee appointed here may be discharged from further responsibility by decree of said court."

"If there are contingent interests in such trust fund, whether the persons who may be entitled thereto are in being or not, or if any of the beneficiaries are minors, the court, before making an order or decree, shall cause such interests and minors to be properly represented by guardians *ad litem* or otherwise at its discretion."[1]

[1] R. L. c. 150, §§ 27, 28.

CHAPTER XVII.

PARTITION OF LANDS IN THE PROBATE COURT.

The probate court in which the estate of a deceased person is in course of settlement or has been settled may, upon petition of any party interested, make partition of all the land of such deceased person lying within the commonwealth, among his heirs or devisees and all persons holding under them by conveyance or otherwise; and the probate court has concurrent jurisdiction with the superior court of petitions for partition of lands held by joint tenants or tenants in common, if the shares do not appear to be in dispute or uncertain.[1]

---

[1] R. L. c 184, §§ 34 31. Partition is a matter of right, and neither mere inconvenience nor the fact that the land is subject to a right of way is sufficient to prevent it Crocker v. Cotting, 170 Mass 68, 70 No man can be held to a tenancy in common of land without his own consent. O'Brien v Mahoney, 179 Mass 200.

Partition may be made in the probate court between heirs even where the estate of the ancestor is in course of settlement and where there is a pending claim of one of the heirs against the estate which, if allowed in full, is greater than the inventoried value of the real and personal property of the estate. O'Brien v Mahoney, supra

Cases where Petition for Partition can be maintained

Persons entitled to life estates in land as tenants in common can have partition, but such partition will not affect rights of remaindermen. Judkins v. Judkins. 109 Mass. 181.

The owner of an undivided share in land may maintain a petition for partition, although persons not ascertained are entitled to a con-

As early as 1693, the provincial legislature of Massachusetts provided that "all persons holding any lands,
tingent remainder in other shares, and although petitioner's share is subject to an overdue mortgage. Taylor v Blake, 109 Mass 513

Property subject to easements may be partitioned Weston v. Foster, 7 Met 297, Crocker v Cotting, 170 Mass 68.

Under statutes giving to a widow an absolute title in fee simple to an undivided part of the lands of which her husband died seized, she is a tenant in common with the other heirs and entitled to partition. Sears v. Sears, 121 Mass 267, Eastham v. Barrett, 152 Mass 56; Brownell v Briggs, 173 Mass 529, 531

A mortgagor not in possession, under a mortgage of an undivided half of a parcel of land, may maintain a petition for partition Rich v Loid, 18 Pick 322

Cases where Petition for Partition cannot be maintained.

Partition cannot be had on petition of all of the co-tenants. Swett v Bussey, 7 Mass 503, Winthrop v. Minot, 9 Cush 405.

Proceedings for partition cannot be instituted in the probate court pending a petition for partition begun by some of the heirs and an action by the widow of the intestate for the recovery of her dower in the supreme court Stearns v Stearns, 16 Mass 167, Miller v County Commissioners, 119 Mass 485 [St. 1892, c 169, provided that the supreme judicial court should no longer have original jurisdiction of petitions for partition, writs of entry, or other real actions]

Buildings owned in common but standing on land to which the petitioners do not claim title, are not the subject of partition. Rice v. Freeland, 12 Cush 170

A tenant in common of two parcels of land in different proportions, of one parcel as co-tenant with one person and of the other as co-tenant with the same person and others, cannot have judgment for partition of both parcels on one petition Hunnewell v Taylor, 3 Gray, 111

A judgment creditor who has levied his execution on real estate held by his debtor in common with third persons, cannot maintain a petition for partition until after the expiration of the year within which the debtor may redeem. Phelps v Palmer, 15 Gray, 499.

A partition cannot be granted, although all the parties in interest desire it, where by a codicil to a will the legal estate in the lands is vested in the executors with authority, in order to avoid the expense and labor of a partition among the testator's devisees, to sell the real estate and to divide the net proceeds of sales among the devisees

tenements, or hereditaments as co parceners, joint tenants, or tenants in common, may be compelled by writ of partition at common law to divide the same"

Writs of partition, recognized by Pub. Sts. c 178, § 1, although abolished in England in 1834 and superseded in Massachusetts in practice by petitions for partition, could still be used in this commonwealth until they were abolished by Rev. Laws, c. 184, § 1 O'Brien v. Mahoney, 179 Mass. 200.

The proceedings for partition among heirs and devisees and all persons holding under them, must be in the probate court of the same county in which letters testamentary or of administration were regularly granted. No other probate court can have jurisdiction; and if the grant of administration was void for want of jurisdiction, the court in which such void administration was granted has no power to order partition.[1]

No partition shall be made by the probate court if it finds that the shares of the respective parties are in dispute, or are uncertain by reason of depending upon the construction or effect of a devise or other conveyance, or upon other questions which the court considers should be determined by another tribunal.[2] When it appears, by adverse claim or otherwise, that the shares are in dispute

---

according to the respective interests devised to them in the original will Gerard v Buckley, 137 Mass 475

A petition for partition of land cannot be maintained if the mortgagee of the land has entered for condition broken and is in actual possession of the premises at the time of the filing of the petition O'Brien v. Bailey, 163 Mass. 325

For a case where a contingent life estate prevented partition, see Faxon v. Faxon, 174 Mass 509

[1] Sigourney v Sibley, 21 Pick. 101.
[2] R L. c. 184, § 43

or uncertain, the court may order the case to be removed to the superior court, and the statute provides that it shall be so removed at the request of any party in interest [1] But if the court has properly assumed jurisdiction and issued a warrant to commissioners, it may retain its jurisdiction, although it subsequently appears that the shares or proportions of the parties are uncertain.[2]

Partitions may be made notwithstanding the existence of a lease of the whole or a part of the estate to be divided ; but the partition cannot prejudice the right of a lessee Partitions may be made notwithstanding any of the tenants in common may be, alone or jointly with others, trustee, attorney, or guardian of any other tenant [3] No partition shall be defeated by the payment by any party to it of any mortgage, lien, tax, or other incumbrance when the other parties have a right to redeem. But in such case the interlocutory decree shall determine the terms of redemption from a contribution on account of such payment. Final judgment for partition shall not be entered till the terms of the interlocutory judgment have been complied with.[4]

When an estate or right of homestead exists in property in which other parties have an interest, the party entitled to the homestead, or any other party interested, may upon petition have partition thereof like tenants in common.[5]

[1] R L c 184, § 32. It is the duty of the probate court to make the partition if there is no real uncertainty as to the shares or proportions of the parties, although one of the parties may insist that there is a dispute or controversy concerning them Dearborn *v.* Preston, 7 Allen, 192; Elliot *v* Elliot, 137 Mass. 116, Eastham *v.* Barrett, 152 Mass 57, Lowd *v* Brigham, 154 Mass 108
[2] R. L c 184, § 46 ; Potter *v* Hazard, 11 Allen, 187.
[3] R. L c 184, §§ 50, 51; Willard *v.* Willard, 145 U. S 116.
[4] R. L. c. 184, §§ 12, 22.   [5] R L. c. 131, § 11.

When a widow is entitled to an undivided interest in lands owned by her husband as tenant in common, the probate court may empower commissioners to make partition of the lands so owned in common, and then to assign to the widow her interest in the portion set off to the estate of her husband.[1]

The wife of a man who is under guardianship may join with the guardian, and the guardian of a woman may join with her husband, in making partition of her real estate, held in joint tenancy or in common, and they may make any release or other conveyance necessary or proper for that purpose, in like manner as the parties might do if neither of them was under legal disability.[2]

The statute requires that the partition, when made on the application of an heir, shall be made of all the estate that descended from the ancestor, and which any party interested, whether the applicant or others, requires to have included in the partition; and when made on the application of a devisee, it shall be made of all the estate held by the applicant jointly or in common with others holding under the testator, which he or any other devisee requires to have included. The same rule applies when the application is made by any person holding under an heir or devisee.[3]

Upon such partition the court may set off to the petitioner his share and leave the residue of the land for the persons entitled thereto, subject to a future partition; or it may set off to the persons entitled to said residue their respective shares therein. If two or more of such persons

---

[1] R. L. c 132, § 11, Elliot v. Elliot, 137 Mass 116; Eastham v Barrett, 152 Mass 57

[2] R. L. c 153, § 18. See also St 1902, c 478

[3] Arms v. Lyman, 5 Pick. 210, R. L c. 184, § 39.

consent to hold their shares undivided, such shares may be so set off.[1]

When a part of the real estate of the deceased lies in common and undivided with that of another person, the court may, before making partition among those claiming under the deceased, cause the real estate of the deceased to be divided and set off from the part held by such co-tenant.[2]

A widow's right to dower is no bar to a partition among tenants in common.[3]

If a person to or for whom a share has been assigned is evicted by a person who at the time of the partition had a title older and better than those who were parties to the action for partition, the person so evicted may have a new partition of the residue, as if partition had not been made.[4]

If, after a first partition, improvements have been made on a part of the land which by a new partition is taken from the share of the party who made the improvements, he shall be entitled to compensation therefor, which shall be determined and awarded by the commissioners and paid by the party to whom such part of the land shall be assigned on the new partition, and the court may issue an execution therefor.

[1] R. L. c. 184, § 40; Gordon v. Pearson, 1 Mass. 328; Thayer v. Thayer, 7 Pick. 209.

The survivor takes a vested inheritable fee defined by its value until duly set out or assigned, which descends like other real estate. Eastham v. Barrett, 152 Mass. 56.

Estates in remainder are not within the purview of these statutes Watson v. Watson, 150 Mass. 85

[2] R. L. c. 184, § 44   [3] Ward v. Gardner, 112 Mass. 42

[4] R. L. c. 184, § 29. The provisions of this section apply also to partitions made in the probate court under R. L. c. 184, § 31 O'Brien v. Mahoney, 179 Mass 200.

A person who holds land under a partition made under the provisions of chapter 184 of the Revised Laws shall, in case of an eviction, be entitled to compensation for improvements made thereon.[1]

PRELIMINARY PROCEEDINGS IN PROBATE COURT.

Proceedings for partition in the probate court are commenced by petition signed by one or more of the parties interested in the real estate. The petitioner should state the proportion which his share bears to the whole estate, and whether he claims as heir, devisee, or tenant in common, or otherwise. The names and residences of all the other parties interested should be stated, and if any of them are married women, the names of their husbands; if any are minors, the fact should appear, and the names and residences of the guardians, if any, should be stated.

A petition for partition of all the real estate of a person whose estate is in course of settlement in the probate court, need not contain a description of the premises to be divided, except where a part of the real estate lies in common and undivided with that of another person.[2] If any part of the land of the deceased lies in common with that of another person, a description of such land should be annexed to the petition, and the share of the deceased therein, and the names of the co-tenants should be stated. If there are any advancements made by the deceased to be considered in making the partition, the several sums advanced and the names of the persons who received them should be fully stated.[3]

---

[1] R. L. c 184, §§ 54, 55

[2] Marsh v French, 159 Mass. 469.

[3] On a petition for partition, if the petitioner's right to recover depends upon the trial of the issue whether his omission from his

When a widow is entitled to an undivided interest in lands owned by her husband as tenant in common, and does not apply for partition within one year from the decease of her husband, the heir or devisee of the husband, or any person having an estate in the lands subject to her interest, may petition.[1]

A guardian may petition for the partition of his ward's real estate, except where he has an interest adverse to that of the ward in the estate to be divided.[2]

Notice of the petition is required to be given to all the parties interested to appear and show cause against it. The citation may be issued by the register of probate on any day when the petition is filed in the probate office. The notice must be served fourteen days at least before the time appointed for the hearing on the parties personally, if they can be found within the commonwealth, and, if not, it must be published once in each of three successive weeks, before such hearing, in such newspaper or newspapers as the court shall order. But such notice may be dispensed with when all the parties in interest signify in writing their assent to the partition or waive notice.[3]

father's will was intentional, he is entitled to open and close Hurley v. O'Sullivan, 137 Mass. 86

A tenant in fee simple of land subject to the estate to which the widow of an intestate without issue is entitled in an undivided half thereof, may maintain a petition for partition against the widow as to so much of his interest as he has in possession, and the court may, under R. L. c. 184, § 47, order the land to be sold. Allen v. Libbey, 140 Mass. 82

A person not named in the petition to entitle himself to appear and answer, after a trial upon the merits and the verdict of a jury, must first show that he has some title or interest in the land. Fales v. Fales, 148 Mass. 42.

[1] R. L. c. 132, § 11.   [2] R. L. c. 145, § 27.
[3] R. L. c. 184, § 35; R. L. c. 162, § 45.

If a part of the land of the deceased lies in common and undivided with that of another person, the probate court may, before making partition among those claiming under the deceased, cause the land of the deceased to be set off from the part held by such co-tenant. A notice of the intended partition containing a description of the land to be divided, with a statement of the share claimed to belong to the estate of the deceased, and of the time and place appointed for a hearing, shall be served by delivering to the co-tenant an attested copy, or by leaving such copy at the place of his abode in this commonwealth fourteen days at least before the time appointed for the hearing [1]

All persons who would be bound by the partition are entitled to notice, whether they have an estate of inheritance, for life or years, in possession, remainder, or reversion, and whether vested or contingent, and if the petitioner holds an estate for life or years, the person entitled to the remainder or reversion is entitled to notice as one of the parties interested. In cases in which remainders or estates are devised or limited to, or in trust for, persons not in being at the time of the application for partition, notice must be given to the persons who may be parents of such persons, setting forth the origin and nature of the remainder or interest so devised or limited The notice may be given personally or by publication, or in such other manner as the court may order, as provided in sections 5 and 6 of chapter 184 of the Revised Laws [2]

At the time named in the order of notice, any person interested may appear and be heard upon the petition. The statute requires that the court shall appoint a disinterested person to act for any heir, devisee, or other person interested in the land, who is absent from the common-

[1] R L c 184, § 44.   [2] Ibid. § 52.

wealth, in all things relative to the partition, and that, if any infant or insane person is interested in the land, and has no guardian within the commonwealth, it shall appoint a guardian *ad litem*.[1] And in cases in which remainders or estates are devised or limited to, or in trust for, persons not in being at the time of the application for partition, the court appoints a suitable person to act as the next friend of such persons in all proceedings touching the partition, the cost of whose appearance and services, including compensation of his counsel to be determined by the court, shall be paid by the persons who apply for partition, and execution may be issued therefor in the name of the person appointed.[2]

In cases where it appears that any part of the lands to be divided belongs to persons having different interests, so that an estate for life or for a term of years belongs to one person, and the remainders are devised or limited to other persons, the court may appoint a trustee to receive and invest any distributive share of the money arising from such partition to which such persons may be entitled, the annual income to be paid over to the person in whom was the estate for life or term of years, and the principal, after the termination of such estate, to the persons to whom such remainders were devised or limited, when they can be ascertained and are entitled thereto.[3]

If, upon the hearing, it appears that the partition prayed for should be made, the court appoints three or five disinterested persons as commissioners to make the division. If the land to be divided lies in different counties, the judge may, if he thinks fit, issue a separate warrant and appoint different commissioners for each county; and the partition in such case is made in each county in like

[1] R. L. c. 184, § 36.   [2] Ibid § 52.   [3] Ibid § 49.

manner as if there were no other land to be divided, or the entire land may be divided by the same commissioners.[1] The warrant states the name of each heir or devisee, and the share of the estate to which each is entitled If there are any advancements made by the deceased to be considered in making the partition, the names of the persons who received the advancements and the sum received by each should also be stated in the warrant or in a paper appended thereto.

If upon the death of any of several plaintiffs or petitioners in a suit for partition the interest of the deceased party passes to the surviving plaintiffs or petitioners, or to any person admitted to join them in the suit, it shall be prosecuted in the manner provided respecting real actions; but if the interest of the deceased party passes to a person not so admitted as a plaintiff or petitioner, such person may, by order of the court, be made a defendant or respondent, and the same proceedings may be had against him as would have been necessary to make him an original defendant or respondent.

If upon the death of any of several defendants or respondents the interest of the deceased party passes to the surviving defendants or respondents, the suit may proceed against them without any new process; but if the interest of the deceased party passes to any other person, that person may be made a defendant or respondent in the manner prescribed in the preceding section.[2]

PROCEEDINGS OF THE COMMISSIONERS.

Before proceeding to make the partition, the commissioners must make oath that they will faithfully and

[1] R L c 184, §§ 37, 38
[2] R L c 171, §§ 14, 15, Richards v Richards, 136 Mass. 126.

impartially execute their duties, and a certificate of their oath should be made on the warrant by the justice who administers it.[1]

The commissioners are required to give sufficient notice of the time and place appointed by them for making the partition to all persons interested who are known and are within the state, and to the agent of any absent heir or devisee appointed by the court. The notice should be in writing and signed by the commissioners, and served upon each of the persons interested, by giving him a copy thereof, or leaving a copy at his place of abode, and a return, stating the manner in which the service was made, should be indorsed by the officer or other person making it, upon the original notice. If the service was made by a person other than an officer qualified to serve civil process, the return should be accompanied by his affidavit.

All the commissioners are required to meet for the performance of any of their duties, but the acts of a majority of them are valid.[2]

At the time and place appointed for making the partition, the commissioners proceed to appraise all the estate

---

[1] A warrant or commission for the appraisal of an estate, for examining the claims on insolvent estates, for the partition of land, or for the assignment of dower or curtesy or other interests in land, may be revoked by the court for sufficient cause, and a new commission may be issued or other appropriate proceedings taken   R L c 162, § 34

The court shall determine the compensation of private persons who perform service required by law, or in the execution of legal process, if no other provision therefor is made   R. L. c. 204, § 23. This statute applies to fees of appraisers of estates of deceased persons, of commissioners for making partition of real estate, and to fees of many other persons appointed to perform service required by law or in the execution of legal process.

[2] R L. c. 184, § 13

to be divided, and, after hearing the parties who may be present, to make the partition among the persons entitled thereto, regard being had to the value of the advancements, if any, made by the deceased in his lifetime [1] The petitioner's share is not alone to be set off, but the share of each person interested is to be assigned to him, unless two or more of the parties consent to hold their shares together and undivided. And the partition must embrace the entire estate when either of the parties interested requires it. If there are several parcels of land, the commissioners are not obliged to set off to each heir a portion of every parcel, but they may assign to one, or more, or all, an entire parcel each, as the situation of the land may make it advisable [2]

If a part of the land cannot be divided without great inconvenience to the owners or is of greater value than the share of any party, or if all the land cannot be divided without such inconvenience, the whole or any part thereof may be set off to any one or more of the parties, upon payment by him or them to any one or more of the others of such sums of money as the commissioners may award to make the partition just and equal.[3]

---

[1] As to advancements, see page 360

[2] Hagar v Wiswall, 10 Pick 152, Barnes v. Lynch, 151 Mass 510, 513 The commissioners may assign to the petitioner all the right in a passageway theretofore appurtenant to the whole estate "to become exclusively appurtenant to the share set off to the petitioner," the way being upon other land of the petitioner, and the parcel set off to the respondent being separated from it by that set off to the petitioner Mount Hope Iron Co v Dearden, 140 Mass 430

[3] R L c 184, § 41, Thayer v. Thayer, 7 Pick 209 When heirs agree that the commissioners shall assign the greater part to the eldest son, on his paying them such sums of money as the commissioners shall award to make the partition just and equal, and the estate is so assigned, and they receive the money awarded to them, they thereby

If a party dies during the pendency of the petition, the share or proportion belonging to him may be assigned in his name to his estate, to be held and disposed of in the same manner as if the partition had been made prior to his decease.[1]

SALE OF LAND THAT CANNOT BE ADVANTAGEOUSLY DIVIDED

In any case of partition the court may, at the time of appointing commissioners, or subsequently by agreement of parties, or at any time after notice to all persons interested, order the commissioners to make sale and conveyance of the whole or any part of the land that cannot be advantageously divided, upon such terms and conditions and with such securities for the proceeds of such sale as the court may order, and to distribute and pay over the proceeds of the sale in such manner as to make the partition just and equal. If the court orders such sale before the commissioners are appointed, it may appoint one

waive their strict legal rights, and cannot afterwards, when the rights of others are affected avoid the division by showing that the estate might have been divided among them all without great prejudice to the whole. White v Clapp, 8 Met 365, Jenks v Howland, 3 Gray, 536, and cases cited

A conveyance by one tenant in common of land purporting to give a good title in severalty to a particular portion of it, cannot affect the right of the other tenants in common to have partition of the estate Barnes v Boardman, 157 Mass 479

[1] R. L. c 184, § 33 The commissioners may permit the parties to state their preferences and to give their reasons for any particular division of the land, but are not required to hear experts or other witnesses as to the effect thereof upon the parties, or upon adjoining property owned by them in severalty, nor are they bound by admissions made by the parties Hall v Hall, 152 Mass 136

The judge of probate has no authority to settle lands assigned for dower, after the widow's term has expired, on one or more of the next of kin to the exclusion of the others. Hunt v Hapgood, 4 Mass 117, Sumner v. Parker, 7 Mass. 79

commissioner to make such sale, conveyance, and division of its proceeds. The sale is made by public auction, after like notice as is required for the sale of lands by executors and administrators, and the evidence thereof may be perpetuated in like manner by returns filed with the register of probate. The conveyance is made by the commissioners, and is conclusive against all parties to the proceedings for partition, and against those claiming by, through, or under them. The statute provisions for the protection of purchasers at sales by executors or administrators apply to sales by the commissioners [1] A distributive share of the money arising from the sale remaining unpaid at the time of confirming the proceedings, or of establishing the partition, is deposited in such savings-banks or other like institutions as the court may direct, in like manner as distributive shares remaining unclaimed in the hands of administrators are deposited [2]

Prior to 1870, on an application for partition of lands there was no power to order a sale.

RETURN OF THE COMMISSIONERS, AND PROCEEDINGS THEREON.

The return of the commissioners should fully set forth their proceedings under the warrant. The fact that they gave notice to parties interested of the time and place of making the partition should appear in their report, and the fact that the persons notified were present, or not, should be stated. The original notice to parties, with the

[1] For these provisions, see R. L. c 148, § 19
[2] R L c 184, §§ 47, 48, Allen v Libbey, 140 Mass 84; Drew v Carroll, 154 Mass 184 A sale may be ordered by the court after the commissioners have made their report. Ramsey v Humphrey, 162 Mass. 385

return of the person who made the service, should be annexed to the report. Their appraisal of the several parcels of real estate should be stated in words at length, and the share assigned to each heir or devisee should be described by metes and bounds. When a piece of land of more value than one equal share of the estate is given to one of the heirs, the fact that it could not be divided without great inconvenience to the owners should be stated, in terms, in the return, and the sums of money to be paid by such heir to the other owners should be stated. The commissioners should also present with their report a statement of the expenses, including their own compensation, of making the partition The warrant under which they acted must be returned with their report.

If the report of the commissioners is satisfactory to all the persons interested, they should certify their approval thereof in writing before it is presented to the court; and if either of the parties is entitled to a sum of money, to be paid by one or more of the other parties, under an award of the commissioners, some delay and expense may be avoided if his certificate of the fact that the money has been paid or secured to his satisfaction is returned with the report; unless the parties interested express their assent to the establishment of the partition as made by the commissioners, notice to them will be ordered before any decree is made upon the report

If the commissioners were ordered to sell the land, their report should state the amount received from the sale, the names of the persons among whom the proceeds were distributed, and the sum paid to each, they should file with their report the receipts of the persons to whom the money was paid, and an affidavit that notice of the time and place of the sale was given as ordered by the court, together with a copy of such notice.

Any party interested may appear and object to the report of the commissioners In all cases, the court may, for any sufficient reason, set aside the return, and commit the case anew to the same or other commissioners.[1] Any mistake, neglect, or misconduct on the part of the commissioners, by which an injustice is done to either party interested, would, of course, be sufficient reason for setting aside the return And it is a valid objection that the division made by them is unequal or inconvenient [2]

---

[1] R. L. c 184, § 56; Hall v Hall, 152 Mass 136 The respondent in a petition for partition of land who does not object to an interlocutory judgment for partition, cannot, at a hearing upon the motion to confirm the commissioners' report, set up want of title in the petitioner as a bar to the petition. Mount Hope Iron Co v Dearden, 110 Mass 430

Upon the question of setting aside the return of the commissioners, parol evidence of their proceedings not appearing in the return is competent so far as it tends to show mistakes of law made by the commissioners which materially affect the equality or justice of the distribution Hall v. Hall, *supra*.

If the warrant to the commissioners describes the boundary line of one of the lots as "running by" a lane, their return is not irregular because it includes land to the centre of the lane as part of the premises Hall v Hall, *supra*

[2] But as the committee is appointed by the court, and persons selected on whose integrity and judgment the court thinks it can safely rely, and against whom neither party can raise any objection, great confidence is placed by the court in the report of the committee, and it will not be held to be any objection to a report that witnesses can be found who will testify that the division is, in their opinion, unjust or inconvenient To induce the court to set aside the report, the inequality or inconvenience must be clearly and distinctly pointed out, and shown to the court by clear and direct evidence It is much more safe to rely upon the judgment of an impartial committee than upon the opinion of witnesses selected by the parties — RICHARDSON, C J , in Morrill v Morrill, 5 N H 329 See Peck v Metcalf, 8 R I 386 , Field v. Hanscomb, 15 Maine, 365 , Wilbur v Dyer, 39 Maine, 169.

The partition cannot be confirmed by a decree of the court until all sums of money awarded by the commissioners to make the partition equal are paid to the persons entitled thereto, or secured to their satisfaction or that of the court. A decree without such payment or security is erroneous, and is not a bar to a subsequent partition on the petition of the party to whom the money was awarded.[1]

The partition is made complete by a decree of the court accepting the report of the commissioners and assigning to each of the parties interested a share of the land in severalty.

Expenses of the Partition. — The expenses and charges of the proceedings shall be allowed by the court and paid by all the parties interested in the partition in proportion to their respective interests, and the court may issue execution therefor.[2]

---

[1] R. L. c. 184, § 53; Jenks v. Howland, 3 Gray, 536; Thayer v. Thayer, 7 Pick 209; Newhall v. Sadler, 16 Mass 122.

An informal decree of the probate court confirming the return of the commissioners cannot afterwards be invalidated for want of a more formal and technical decree of division White v Clapp, 8 Met. 365.

A proceeding in the probate court pursuant to an agreement between tenants in common for partition of the estate, although incompetent to effect the partition, was held equivalent to a license from each of the tenants that each might enter and occupy the part assigned to him by such intended partition until the commencement of legal process for partition, which was held to be a revocation of such license Pond v Pond, 14 Mass 403.

By an appeal from a decree of the probate court accepting the return of the commissioners for the division of an estate, the return is open to every objection that could lawfully have been made to its acceptance in the court below Sever v. Sever, 8 Mass 132.

[2] R L c 184, § 42. The commissioners are entitled to compensation for their services and expenses if they acted faithfully and impartially, although their return is not accepted, or their charges

Record of the Partition. — The return of the commissioners, when accepted by the court, remains in the registry of probate, but the statute requires that a copy thereof, certified by the register, shall be recorded in the registry of deeds for each of the several counties or districts where the lands lie.[1]

UPON WHOM THE PARTITION IS BINDING.

The partition, when finally confirmed and established, is conclusive on all the heirs and devisees of the deceased, and all persons claiming under them; and on all other persons interested in the premises who appeared and answered in the case, or assented in writing to the proposed partition, or upon whom notice of the petition was served, personally or by publication, or who waived notice, or for whom an agent was appointed, and upon all persons claiming under them. All other persons may pursue their legal remedies for recovering the land, or any part thereof,

---

allowed by the probate court, and may maintain an action therefor against the petitioner for the partition. And the petitioner or other party to the proceedings who has paid the expenses of making the partition is entitled to contribution from all the other parties in interest, and may maintain actions therefor and obtain the execution provided for by the statute. Potter *v.* Hazard, 11 Allen, 187; Langdon *v.* Palmer, 133 Mass. 413.

Judgment was rendered upon the report of the commissioners on a petition for partition of land that their report be accepted and that "partition be made," and it was further ordered that "the case be continued *nisi* upon the question of costs." Before any adjudication on this question the petitioner died, and his administrator was admitted by the court to prosecute the case. It was *held*, that the administrator was erroneously admitted to prosecute and that costs could not be awarded against the respondent. Richards *v.* Richards, 136 Mass. 126.

[1] R. L. c. 184, § 57.

and for obtaining partition of the same, as if the proceedings in the probate court had not been had.[1]

While a partition, when finally confirmed and established, is conclusive on a person having a mortgage, attachment, or other lien on the share of a part owner, so far as relates to the partition and the assignment of the shares, the lien will remain in full force upon the part assigned to or left for such part owner.

It is well settled, however, that a conveyance by metes and bounds of any separate parcel by one co-tenant, or of a share of any separate parcel, is voidable by his co-tenants and is available only by way of estoppel against the grantor and his heirs. To allow and give legal effect to such alienation of the interest of a tenant in common in a part of the land held in common, without the consent of the other co-tenants, would be to create to their injury new tenancies in common in parcels of the land held in common.[2] The reason for the rule is well stated by Chief

---

[1] R L c 184, § 45; Procter v. Newhall, 17 Mass 81; Rice v Smith, 14 Mass 431; Munroe v Luke, 19 Pick. 39, and cases cited.

An execution against one holding lands in joint tenancy, or tenancy in common, cannot be extended by metes and bounds on a part of the lands so holden Bartlet v Harlow, 12 Mass. 348.

A levy of execution on the undivided interest of a tenant in common in a part of the land held in common is invalid Blossom v. Brightman, 21 Pick 283

[2] Bartlet v. Harlow, 12 Mass 348; Blossom v Brightman, 21 Pick 283, Graves v Goldthwait, 153 Mass 268; Barnes v. Lynch, 151 Mass 510; Barnes v. Boardman, 157 Mass 479

A mortgage made by a tenant in common of an undivided interest in a specified parcel of the land held in common is invalid as against his co-tenants; and the mortgagee cannot object to the decree of a probate court affirming the report of commissioners appointed to make partition, by which the commissioners, without regard to the mortgage, set off the land mortgaged to the co-tenants other than the mortgagor and awarded a certain sum of money to the mortgagor to make

Justice Shaw in Adams v Briggs Iron Company, 7 Cush. 361, 369· "The ground upon which this doctrine is established is, that a tenant in common of an entire estate is entitled, on partition, to have his property assigned in one entire parcel, according to his aliquot part. The respective co-tenants may convey their shares to one or many grantees, as they please, so it be of the entire estate; because, whether there be one or many co-tenants, each may still have partition, which is inseparably incident to an estate in common, and have it in one parcel and of the like kind and quality with the estate which he holds in common. I have a moiety; my co-tenant has a moiety. He may convey a quarter of the whole estate to one, an eighth to another, a sixteenth to another, and so on indefinitely, letting in other co-tenants with me. But all being seized of aliquot parts, in the same estate, and of like kind and quality, my right to partition is not disturbed by the number of co-tenants. But if he could convey his aliquot part in specified parcels of the estate, he might diminish the value of my right, if not render it worthless."

DIVISION OF WATER RIGHTS.

Joint tenants or tenants in common of a mill privilege, water right, or other incorporeal hereditament, may be compelled to divide the same, either by suit in equity in the superior court or in the manner provided in chapter

---

the partition just and equal, nor can the mortgagee demand that the sum so awarded be paid or secured to the mortgagee. Marks v Sewall, 120 Mass 174.

If a member of an Indian tribe mortgages the undivided interest acquired by him in all of its undivided lands, and subsequently partition is duly had of such lands, the mortgage lien will attach to the portion assigned to the mortgagor Drew v Carroll, 154 Mass 181.

184 of the Revised Laws for the partition of land. In the latter case the commissioners appointed to make partition are required to set forth in their return the best method of setting off to the several parties their respective shares, and thereupon the court may make all such orders and decrees as might be made in equity.

In like manner partition may be made of the water of a natural stream, not navigable, the banks of which are owned by different riparian proprietors.[1]

PARTITION OF LANDS HELD BY AN EXECUTOR OR ADMINISTRATOR IN MORTGAGE OR ON EXECUTION.

Real property which is held by an executor or administrator in mortgage, or taken on execution by him, may, at any time before the right of redemption is foreclosed, be sold subject to such right, in the same manner as personal property of a person deceased; and after such right has been foreclosed, it may be sold in the same manner as real property of which the deceased died seised.

If land so held by an executor or administrator in mortgage or on execution is not redeemed or sold as provided in the preceding paragraph, the statute requires that it shall be assigned and distributed to the same persons and in the same proportions as if it had been part of the personal property of the deceased; and if upon such distribution the property comes to two or more persons, the probate court may cause partition to be made between them in like manner as if it had been real property held by the deceased in his lifetime.[2]

[1] R L c 184, §§ 58, 59; DeWitt v Harvey, 4 Gray, 486; Wamesit Power Co v Sterling Mills, 158 Mass 435

[2] An executor or administrator to whom land is set off on execution takes an estate in such land in trust therein, and neither the legal

PARTITION OF REGISTERED LAND.

In all proceedings for partition of registered land, or for the assignment in fee of registered land claimed by husband or wife by statutory right, after the entry of the final judgment or decree of partition and the acceptance of the report of the commissioners, a copy of the judgment or decree and of the return of the commissioners, certified by the clerk or register, as the case may be, must be filed and registered; and thereupon, if the land is set off to the owners in severalty, any owner will be entitled to have a certificate of the share set off to him in severalty, and to receive an owner's duplicate certificate therefor. If the land is ordered to be sold, the purchaser or his assigns will be entitled to have a certificate of title issued to him or them upon presenting the deed of the commissioners for registration.[1]

estate nor the possession vests in the heirs or legatees until the land is apportioned and distributed in the probate court, or until a final settlement of the estate. Boylston v Carver, 4 Mass 597; Baldwin v. Timmins, 3 Gray, 302

A mortgagee's title to real estate vests, on his decease, in his executor or administrator, and a quitclaim deed from an heir, made before a decree of distribution though before the foreclosure of the mortgage, will not give the grantee a sufficient title to sustain a writ of entry It is only by a decree of the probate court that the title of the administrator or executor is terminated, and such decree for the assignment and distribution of the estate is necessary to determine in whom and in what proportions the estate shall vest. Taft v Stevens, 3 Gray, 504

[1] R L c. 128, § 85.

CHAPTER XVIII.

ASSIGNMENT OF DOWER AND OTHER LIFE-ESTATES.

WHEN THE PROBATE COURT MAY ASSIGN DOWER.

A WIFE is entitled to her dower at common law in the lands of her deceased husband, provided she files her election and claim therefor in the registry of probate within one year after the date of the approval of the bond of the executor or administrator of her husband; and if her right is not disputed by his heirs or devisees, it may be assigned to her, in whatever counties the lands lie, by the probate court for the county in which the estate of the husband is settled.[1]

[1] R. L c 132, §§ 1, 9; Buckley v Frasier, 153 Mass 526. A widow is not dowable of a remainder of which her husband died seised Wilmarth v Bridges, 113 Mass 407; Watson v Watson, 150 Mass 84; Hill v. Pike, 174 Mass. 582 Nor of a reversion Baker v Baker, 167 Mass 575 A widow may assign her right of dower with the right to have the dower assigned to her for the benefit of her assignee Guckian v Riley, 135 Mass. 73.

Dower may be assigned by the heirs, without any order of court and without a deed, it not being a conveyance of title The widow holds her estate by law, and not by contract, and requires nothing but to have her part distinguished from the rest of the land Conant v Little, 1 Pick 189; Shattuck v Gragg, 23 Pick 88. A guardian may assign dower in his ward's estate to any widow entitled thereto. R. L. c 145, § 27

The widow may occupy the land jointly with the heirs, or may receive her share of the rents and profits, so long as the heirs do not object, without having her interest assigned. R. L c 132, § 12.

A widow's right to have dower assigned to her cannot be attached

THE ESTATE OF DOWER

Dower at common law exists where a man is seised of an estate of inheritance and dies in the lifetime of his wife. In that case she is entitled to be endowed for her natural life of all the lands of which her husband was seised, either in deed or in law, at any time during the coverture, and of which any issue that she might have had might by possibility have been heir.[1] Her right is so protected by law that no act of the husband can deprive her of it. And she is entitled to her dower, though her husband dies insolvent.[2] She is also entitled to dower in

or taken on execution in an action of law The remedy of her creditor is by a bill in equity. McMahon v Gray, 150 Mass 289

A widow before her dower is assigned to her has no estate in the lands of her deceased husband Smith v Shaw, 150 Mass. 297, Flynn v Flynn, 171 Mass 312. See Eastham v Barrett, 152 Mass. 56

An assignment of dower by the probate court against common right in all the lands of which the husband died seised, and duly accepted and enjoyed by her, is conclusive that dower was set out in all his real estate. Fuller v Rust 153 Mass 46.

A widow is not dowable of lands of which her deceased husband had only a momentary seisin. Pendleton v Pomeroy, 4 Allen, 510.

A guardian may assign dower. Jones v Brewer, 1 Pick 314

A widow having an estate of homestead is entitled to have her dower assigned to her out of the whole of the real estate of her deceased husband, and then to have her estate of homestead set off to her from the remainder of the estate Cowdrey v Cowdrey, 131 Mass. 186, Weller v Weller, 131 Mass 446

The purchase by a railroad corporation of land necessary for station purposes does not extinguish an existing inchoate right of dower therein Nye v Taunton Branch R R Co, 113 Mass 277

[1] 4 Kent, Com 37, Hale v Munn, 4 Gray, 132

[2] Dower at common law is the life estate of a wife in one-third of all the legal estates of inheritance of which her husband is seised at any time during coverture of a sole, beneficial, and immediate seisin, and which any issue of theirs might directly inherit It has three stages, namely (1) Its inchoate stage, extending from the time of

real property sold by an executor or administrator for payment of debts, legacies, etc.[1]

To establish a claim to dower at common law, it must be shown that there was a marriage, and a seisin by the husband at some time during the coverture, and that the husband is dead. Without the concurrence of these three circumstances no title to dower can be consummated. To enable the probate court to assign dower, it must further appear that the husband was seised at the time of his death.[2]

Dower attaches to all marriages not absolutely void and existing at the death of the husband. Though the marriage was voidable, if it was not annulled by decree during the husband's lifetime, the widow will take her dower. Dower belongs to a marriage within the age of consent, though the husband dies within that age.[3]

the marriage or the acquisition of the property in question to the time of the husband's death ; (2) Its consummate stage, extending from the death of the husband ; and (3) Its assigned stage, extending from the time it is set off to the widow. Am & Eng. Encyclopædia of Law, 1st ed , vol v p. 885.

In dower against the alienee of her husband, a widow is to recover her dower as the tenements were at the time of the alienation by the husband , but against the heir she is to have dower in improvements made by him after the descent Catlin v. Ware, 9 Mass. 218 ; Parker v Parker, 17 Pick 240

Where two widows entitled to dower in the same land the one having the elder title released it to the tenant without having it set off to her, it was *held* that the other widow was entitled to dower only in two-thirds of the land. Leavitt v Lamprey, 13 Pick 382

When a sale by a guardian of the ward's land, in which the guardian herself has a right of dower, is avoided by the ward because made to the guardian herself, the right of dower revives Walker v. Walker, 101 Mass. 169

[1] R L c. 146, § 2.
[2] Sheafe v O'Neil, 9 Mass 9 ; Raynham v. Wilmarth, 13 Met. 415
[3] But if the parties separate during such nonage, and do not afterwards cohabit, the marriage will be void without a decree of divorce or other legal process. R. L. c. 151, § 9

After a divorce, a wife is not entitled to dower in the land of her husband, unless, after a decree of divorce *nisi* granted upon the libel of the wife, the husband dies before such decree is made absolute, except that if the divorce was for the cause of adultery committed by the husband, or because of his sentence to confinement at hard labor, she is entitled to dower in the same manner as if he were dead.[1]

A married woman may bar her right of dower in an estate conveyed by her husband or by operation of law by joining in the deed conveying the same, and therein releasing her right to dower, or by releasing the same by a subsequent deed executed either separately or jointly with her husband. Her dower may also be released in the manner provided in chapter one hundred and fifty-three.[2]

If the guardian of an insane wife is authorized, under the provisions of section 19 of chapter 153 of the Revised Laws, to release the dower of his ward, and the probate court finds that a portion of the proceeds of such real prop-

[1] R. L c 152, § 24, Smith *v* Smith, 13 Mass 231; Loker *v* Gerald, 157 Mass 42.

[2] R L c 132, § 5, Mason *v.* Mason, 140 Mass 63.

St. 1902, c. 478, provides that the signature of any married woman under the age of twenty-one years, affixed by her to any instrument relating to the conveyance of land of her husband, shall have the same effect as if she were over that age

While a wife may bar her right of dower by releasing the same in a deed executed by her husband, or by a subsequent deed executed either separately or jointly with her husband, yet she cannot convey her inchoate right of dower to a person to whom her husband has not conveyed the land Such a deed is void. Flynn *v* Flynn, 171 Mass. 312, 314.

A husband conveyed an undivided moiety, in which also his wife released her right to dower, partition was afterwards made by deed It was *held* that the wife was dowable only in the moiety assigned to her husband in the partition. Potter *v.* Wheeler, 13 Mass 504.

ASSIGNMENT OF DOWER AND OTHER LIFE-ESTATES. 401

erty, or of a sum loaned on mortgage thereof, should be reserved for the use of such ward, it may order that a certain portion, not exceeding one-third of the net amount of the proceeds or sum actually realized from such sale or mortgage, exclusive of any encumbrance then existing on the property, shall be set aside and paid over to such guardian, who shall invest and hold it for the benefit of the wife during her life if she survives her husband. The income of such portion shall be received and enjoyed by the husband during the life of his wife, or until otherwise ordered by the court for cause. If he survives her, the principal shall, upon her decease, be paid over to him; but if he does not survive her, to his heirs, executors, or administrators.[1]

When the husband of an insane woman has conveyed real estate in trust without a power of revocation, and in such conveyance provision is made for his wife, which the probate court, upon petition, after notice and a hearing, finds is sufficient in lieu of dower therein, the trustee in such conveyance may convey such real property free from all right of dower.[2]

OF WHAT LANDS THE WIDOW IS DOWABLE

As to Wild Lands. — A widow is not entitled under the statute to dower in wild lands of which her husband died

---

[1] R. L. c 153, § 21

[2] Ibid § 23. A wife may contract with her husband to release dower Winn v. Sanford, 148 Mass 39.

A widow is not entitled to dower in lands conveyed away by her husband before his marriage, although such conveyance was fraudulent and void as against his creditors Whithed v Mallory, 4 Cush. 138 But if the fraudulent conveyance of the land was made during coverture, she is entitled to her dower, even though she joined in the conveyance with her husband to release it Robinson v. Bates, 3 Met. 10

seised, except wood-lots or other land used with the farm or dwelling-house.¹ Her right in such land is limited to wood and timber used and consumed on the estate, and for purposes connected with its proper use, occupation, and enjoyment.²

Mines and Quarries. — A widow is entitled to dower in such mines and quarries as were actually opened and used during the lifetime of the husband, whether he continued to work them to the period of his death or not.³ A bed of iron ore of considerable extent is regarded as opened, although the openings which had been wrought by the husband had been partially filled up and abandoned, and other openings into the same bed had been made by the heirs.⁴ The tenant in dower may work an open mine or quarry for her own benefit, but it is waste for her to open and work it.

Lands of Tenants in Common. — A widow is entitled to dower in lands owned by her husband as tenant in common

---

[1] R. L. c. 132, § 3

[2] White v. Cutler, 17 Pick. 248; White v Willis, 7 Pick. 143; Noyes v Stone, 163 Mass 490 See Phillips v. Allen, 7 Allen, 115. When it appears that the wood and timber have ceased to improve by growth, or for any cause ought to be cut, the probate court may appoint a trustee and authorize him to sell it, invest the proceeds, and pay to the widow the income thereof during her life, and at her death to pay the principal sum to the owner of the land. R. L. c. 134, § 11.

[3] Stoughton v. Leigh, 1 Taunt. 402

[4] Coates v. Cheever, 1 Cowen, 460 A husband died seised of four acres of land consisting of a slate quarry, mostly below the surface of the ground, but partially above ground One quarter of an acre of the quarry had been dug over, and the practice was to take a section of ten or twelve feet square on the surface, and go down to a certain depth, and then begin on the surface again *Held*, that not only that portion of the quarry which had been actually dug, but the whole extent owned by the husband, must be considered as opened, and so the widow was entitled to dower in the same. Billings v. Taylor, 10 Pick. 460

with other persons [1] But land purchased by partners, with partnership funds, for partnership purposes, is considered in equity as partnership stock. Though conveyed to them as tenants in common, it vests in them and their respective heirs in trust for the purposes of the partnership, and is to be applied, if necessary, towards payment of the partnership debts If so required for the payment of debts, the widows of partners are not entitled to dower in such land.[2]

If the land, though purchased with partnership funds, was purchased in such a manner as to preclude such implied trust, the widow will be entitled to her dower therein. This may be the case when there is an express agreement at the time of the purchase that the property is to be held by the partners separately for their separate use, or a similar provision in the articles of copartnership, or where the price of the purchase is charged to the partners respectively, in their several accounts with the firm.[3]

Lands encumbered by Mortgage. — A widow is not entitled to dower at common law in estates of which her husband is only equitably seised But the statute extends her right of dower to equities of redemption of mortgaged estates.[4] If she has released her right of dower upon a

---

[1] Pynchon v. Lester, 6 Gray, 314 ; Blossom v Blossom, 9 Allen, 254

[2] Dyer v. Clark, 5 Met 562; Howard v Priest, ibid 582; Burnside v. Merrick, 4 Met. 537, Wilcox v Wilcox, 13 Allen, 252.

[3] Dyer v Clark, 5 Met 579 But where land was conveyed by a deed absolute on its face, the widow of the grantee was allowed dower therein, although the conveyance was in fact on an oral agreement that on the repayment of a certain loan the land should be reconveyed, and the grantee never entered under his deed or claimed possession of the estate Atwood v Atwood, 22 Pick 283

[4] Lund v Woods, 11 Met 566; Walsh v Wilson, 130 Mass 124.

A wife joined with her husband as grantor in a mortgage of land " in order to release her rights under the homestead exemption act."

mortgage made by her husband, or if he is seised of land subject to a mortgage which is valid and effectual as against her, she is nevertheless entitled to dower in the mortgaged premises as against every person except the mortgagee and those claiming under him. If the heir or other person claiming under the husband redeems the mortgage, the widow can either repay such part of the money paid by him as is equal to the proportion which her interest in the mortgaged premises bears to the whole

The deed contained full covenants of seisin and warranty. It was *held*, that she did not thereby bar her right of dower in the land, although the estate at the time the mortgage was given was of less value than eight hundred dollars. Tiriel *v* Kenney, 137 Mass. 30. See Allendorff *v* Gaugengigl, 146 Mass. 542 ; Toomey *v* McLean, 105 Mass. 122 ; Sargeant *v* Fuller, ibid. 119 ; Brown *v* Lapham, 3 Cush. 551 ; Hildreth *v* Jones, 13 Mass. 525.

An heir of real estate liable to sale for payment of debts of the deceased, and subject to a mortgage for payment of one of them, who gives bond to the executor conditioned to pay all the debts, and in fulfilling that condition takes to himself an assignment of the mortgage, cannot by virtue of the mortgage title and by foreclosure defeat estates of dower and homestead previously assigned to the widow in the mortgaged premises with his assent. King *v* King, 100 Mass. 224.

If a wife releases dower in her husband's land at his request in consideration of an oral agreement by him to convey to her other land, and he neglects to do so and becomes insolvent, she cannot maintain a bill in equity against his assignees in insolvency to compel such conveyance, nor to make reimbursement to her for the value of the dower out of her husband's estate. Winchester *v* Holmes, 138 Mass. 540. And if within six months of the commencement of the insolvency proceedings the husband conveys land to her through a third person, and she had reasonable cause to believe him insolvent, his assignees may avoid the conveyance. Holmes *v.* Winchester, 135 Mass. 299.

Had the agreement on the husband's part been to convey to her personalty, the wife would have been protected. Holmes *v* Winchester, 133 Mass. 140.

value thereof, or she can, at her election, take dower only according to the value of the estate after deducting the money paid for redemption.[1]

Applications for dower in mortgaged lands are not usually made to the probate court, although that court may assign dower in such lands when all the parties interested consent. The legal estate is in the mortgagee, but as the mortgage is intended only as security for a debt, it is considered as between the mortgagor and all the world, except the mortgagee and his assigns, only as a pledge and an encumbrance, the mortgagor still remaining the owner of the estate. If, therefore, the heirs or devisees do not dispute the widow's claim, and the mortgagee consents, the probate court may assign dower in the whole estate mortgaged, and the assignment will be valid, although the widow joined her husband in the mortgage deed for the purpose of relinquishing her dower.[2]

Leased Lands. — When land is demised for the term of one hundred years or more, the term, so long as fifty years thereof remain unexpired, is regarded by the statute as an estate in fee-simple as to everything concerning the right of dower or of curtesy therein. When curtesy or dower is assigned out of such land, the husband or widow and his or her assigns are held to pay to the owner of the unex-

---

[1] R. L. c. 132, § 4. Newton v. Cook, 4 Gray, 46. If the mortgage is paid out of the personal property by the administrators, the widow will be entitled to her dower in the whole land without liability for contribution. Robinson v. Simmons, 156 Mass. 126. See Sargeant v. Fuller, 105 Mass. 119.

To redeem land from a mortgage made by her husband and herself, a widow cannot maintain a bill in equity without offering to pay the whole amount due on the mortgage. McCabe v. Bellows, 7 Gray, 148. See Searle v. Chapman, 121 Mass. 19.

[2] Henry's Case, 4 Cush. 257; Draper v. Baker, 12 Cush. 288.

pired residue of the term one-third of the rent reserved in the lease under which the wife or husband held the term.[1]

If a tenant in dower, by the curtesy, or for life or years, commits or suffers waste on the premises, the person having the next immediate estate of inheritance may have an action of waste against such tenant, wherein he shall recover the place wasted and the amount of the damage. An heir may bring such action for waste done in the time of his ancestor.[2]

When the estate of a devisee under a will is taken for the tenancy by the curtesy of the husband, or for the dower of the widow of the testator, all the other devisees and legatees shall contribute their respective proportions of the loss to the person from whom the estate is so taken, so that the loss may fall equally upon all the devisees and legatees in proportion to the value of property received by them under the will; but no devisee or legatee shall be held to contribute who is exempted therefrom by the provisions of the will.[3]

A widow is entitled to dower in land taken on execution from her husband or taken on execution upon a judgment against his executor or administrator.[4]

DOWER WHEN THE WIDOW WAIVES THE PROVISIONS MADE FOR HER BY WILL

A widow is not entitled to her dower in addition to the provisions of her husband's will, unless such plainly appears by the will to have been the intention of the testator.[5]

---

[1] R L c 129, §§ 1, 2.   [2] R. L c 185, § 1.
[3] R. L c 135, § 30.   [4] R. L. c 178, § 55.
[5] R L c 135, § 18, Borden v Jenks, 140 Mass 563. A widow who has not waived the provisions of her husband's will by which he

At common law, a devise or bequest to the wife of a testator was presumed to be in addition to her dower, unless it was clearly the testator's intention that it should be in lieu of dower; but under the statute the widow takes the provision made for her in the will in lieu of dower, unless it plainly appears by the will that the testator intended such provision to be in addition to her dower. If the testator's intention is left in doubt, she cannot take dower unless she first waives the provision made for her in the will. The inadequacy of the provision merely will not justify the inference that it was intended to be in addition to dower.[1]

has given his entire estate to her, is not entitled to dower in land which, in his lifetime, was seized on an execution against him and set off to his creditor in full satisfaction of the judgment. Barnard v. Fall River Savings Bank, 135 Mass. 326.

P. S. c. 127, § 20, now embodied in R. L. c. 135, § 18, applies only to lands within the Commonwealth. Staigg v. Atkinson, 144 Mass. 564.

It seems that a claim for improvements made by the tenant of premises in which dower is claimed, for the purpose of keeping the house in tenable condition, not having been pleaded or suggested of record before the appointment of commissioners to set out the dower, is not open to the tenant at the hearing upon the demandant's motion for the confirmation of the commissioners' report. Walsh v. Wilson, 131 Mass. 535.

[1] Reed v. Dickerman, 12 Pick. 146; Pratt v. Felton, 4 Cush. 174; Buffinton v. Fall River National Bank, 113 Mass. 246. See Atherton v. Corliss, 101 Mass. 40.

Where a testator devised specific parts of his real estate to his wife in fee, and bequeathed to her all his personal property, and ordered that the other part of his real estate should be disposed of as the law directs, and the wife accepted the devise and bequest made to her, it was *held*, that she was not entitled to dower in such other part of the real estate. Adams v. Adams, 5 Met. 278. See Phelps v. Phelps, 20 Pick. 556; Delay v. Vinal, 1 Met. 57.

When a widow died soon after her husband, without expressly waiving the provision for her in his will in lieu of dower, her accept-

The widow may make her election to take her dower effectual by filing in the probate office, in writing, at any time within one year after the probate of the will, her waiver of the provisions therein made for her, or her claim to such portion of her husband's estate as she would have been entitled to it if he had died intestate.[1] When any legal proceeding is instituted, wherein the validity or effect of the will is drawn in question, the probate court may, within one year after probate of the will, on petition of the widow and after notice, authorize her to file her waiver within six months after the final determination of such proceeding.[2] If she is insane or a minor, her guardian may make the waiver.[3] If she makes no such waiver, she cannot take dower, unless it plainly appears from the will that the testator intended that she should have such provisions in addition to her dower.

DOWER BARRED BY JOINTURE OR PECUNIARY PROVISION.

A woman may be barred of her dower by a jointure settled on her, with her assent, before her marriage; provided such jointure consist of a freehold estate in lands for the life of the wife at least, to take effect in possession or profit immediately on the death of the husband; her

---

ance of the provision in the will was presumed, it being more beneficial to her than her right of dower Merrill v Emery, 10 Pick. 507

[1] A widow within six months after the probate of her husband's will filed in the probate court a writing signed by her, stating that she waived the provision made for her by the will, " and hereby gives notice that she will claim her dower in the real estate of the deceased and so much of the personal estate as she may be entitled to by law " *Held* that this was an election by her to take dower in her husband's estate and that she was not entitled to one half of said estate for life Mathews v Mathews, 141 Mass 511

[2] R L c. 135, § 16

[3] R L c 145, § 33, Kent v. Morrison, 153 Mass 140.

ASSIGNMENT OF DOWER AND OTHER LIFE-ESTATES 409

assent to such jointure being expressed, if she is of full age, by her becoming a party to the conveyance by which it is settled, and, if she is under age, by her joining with her father or guardian in such conveyance. Any pecuniary provision made for the benefit of an intended wife, and in lieu of dower, if so assented to, will bar her right of dower in her husband's lands.[1]

If such jointure or pecuniary provision is made before the marriage, and without the assent of the intended wife, or if it is made after marriage, it will bar her dower, unless within six months after the death of her husband she makes her election to waive such provision and be endowed of his lands. If the husband dies while absent from his wife, she may make her election within six months after notice of his death, and in all cases she has six months for that purpose, after she has notice of the existence of such jointure or provision.[2]

---

[1] R L c 132, §§ 6, 7; Vincent v. Spooner, 2 Cush. 467, Sullings v Richmond, 5 Allen, 187, Tarbell v Tarbell, 10 Allen, 278 The widow is not bound by an ante-nuptial contract if there was a failure to perform it on the part of her husband. Sullings v Sullings, 9 Allen, 234. See Butman v Porter, 100 Mass. 337; Freeland v Freeland, 128 Mass 509, Paine v Hollister, 139 Mass. 144.

If the wife's assent was procured by fraud to an ante-nuptial contract by way of jointure, such a contract cannot be ratified by her during coverture, and may be avoided by her. Peaslee v. Peaslee, 117 Mass 171.

A jointure must be a freehold estate. Hastings v Dickinson, 7 Mass 153

A widow who has received personal property under the will of one to whom her husband had conveyed land of which he was seised during coverture, without her joining in the conveyance, is not barred of her dower in such land   Julian v Boston, Clinton, &c. R R, 128 Mass 555.

[2] R L c 132, § 8, Bigelow v Hubbard, 97 Mass. 195, Peaslee v Peaslee, *supra*.

No provision is made by statute as to the manner in which the widow may signify her election in such cases, but she can make her election effectual by commencing proceedings for the recovery of her dower, by petition or otherwise, within the six months.

LIMITATION OF CLAIM FOR INTEREST IN REALTY.

A widow is not entitled to make claim for an interest in the real estate of her deceased husband or to begin an action or other proceeding for the recovery thereof unless the same is made or commenced within twenty years after the decease of the husband or after she has ceased to occupy, or to receive the profits, of her share of such real estate; except that if at the time of the husband's death the widow is absent from the state, under twenty-one years of age, insane, or imprisoned, she may make such claim or commence proceedings at any time within twenty years after such disability ceases.[1]

PROCEEDINGS IN PROBATE COURT.

The petition for the assignment of dower or other interest in land must be presented to the probate court in

[1] R L c 132, § 13. But a widow who for more than twenty years after her husband's death has occupied, with his heirs, lands of which he died seised, and of which she was dowable, or has without their objection received the rents and profits of such land, may bring a petition for the assignment of her dower whenever the heirs seek to hold their shares of the rents and profits in severalty. Hastings v Mace, 157 Mass. 499.

Where a widow has not continued to occupy with the heirs of her deceased husband land of which he died seised, or to receive her share of the rents and profits thereof, her right of dower is not saved by the fact that she occupied the land and received the rents and profits for several years, if her writ is not brought when she ceases to occupy the land or to receive the rents and profits, and not until more than twenty years after her husband's death. O'Gara v. Neylon, 161 Mass 140.

which the estate of the husband is settled, and should set forth the facts that the husband died seised of certain lands in this commonwealth, that the petitioner is entitled to dower or to an undivided interest in such land, and that her right is not disputed by the heirs or devisees. The names and residences of all persons interested in the lands must be stated in the petition. If any of the persons interested are married women, the names of their husbands should be given, and if any are minors, the names and residences of their guardians.

If the widow omits to petition within one year from the death of her husband, the petition may be made by the heirs or devisees of her husband, or any of them, or by any person having any estate in the lands subject to dower or to such interest, or by the guardian of any such heirs, devisees, or persons [1]

The petition may be filed in the probate office on any day, and a citation thereon issued by the register.

If any part of the land in which the widow claims an undivided interest was owned by the husband in common with any other person, a description of such land should be annexed to the petition, and the proportion owned by the husband, and the names for the co-tenants, must be stated. The petition may be made by the widow or by any person entitled to petition for assignment of her interest [2] The citation issued in such cases must be served on each of the co-tenants, together with a copy of the description of the land annexed to the petition

If upon the hearing it appears that the right of the widow is not disputed by the heirs or devisees, the court issues a warrant to three discreet and disinterested persons, authorizing them to set off her interest, and empow-

[1] R. L. c 132, § 9   [2] Ibid. § 11.

ering them, if the circumstances of the case require it, first to make partition of any land owned by the husband as tenant in common.[1]

PROCEEDINGS OF THE COMMISSIONERS.

Before proceeding to set off the interest of the widow, or to make partition, the commissioners must be sworn to perform their duty faithfully and impartially according to their best skill and judgment. The oath may be administered by any justice of the peace, and a certificate thereof should be made upon the warrant.

If partition is to be made before the dower can be assigned, the commissioners must give notice, as in other cases of partition, of the time and place appointed for that purpose to all persons interested who are known and are within the state, that they may be present if they see fit.

If the commissioners are to assign dower only, and there is no partition to be made, they are not required by statute to give notice to parties interested, but it is advisable to give such notice in all cases of assignments of interests in real estate.

In making the assignment, all the lands of which the husband died seised are first to be appraised by the commissioners at their present value. The authority of the commissioners extends to all lands of which the husband died seised within the commonwealth. The lands should be appraised with reference to the amount of annual income they produce; it not being the object of the law to

[1] Any warrant or commission for the appraisement of an estate, for examining the claims on insolvent estates, for the partition of real estate, or for the assignment of dower or other interests in real estate, may be revoked by the court for sufficient cause, and the court may thereupon issue a new commission or proceed otherwise as the circumstances of the case shall require. R. L c 162, § 34.

ASSIGNMENT OF DOWER AND OTHER LIFE-ESTATES. 413

assign the widow one-third of the land in quantity, but to give her such a part as will yield her one-third of its entire income.[1]

The part assigned to the widow must be set off by metes and bounds, where it can be done without damage to the whole estate. But where the estate consists of a mill or other tenement which cannot be divided without damage to the whole, the interest of the widow may be assigned out of the rents or profits thereof, to be had and received by the widow as a tenant in common with the other owners of the estate.[2] The widow in such case may have either an alternate occupancy of the whole estate, or her share of the rents and profits. The ancient rule gave her every third toll-dish for her dower in a mill, or the use of the whole mill every third month or year. It is not material in what way the result is reached, provided the right of the parties are plainly defined and established.[3] Assignments of this kind are usually made by agreement between the parties; a proper spirit of accommodation will enable them to reach an adjustment more satisfactory to themselves than any action of the commissioners is likely to prove.

---

[1] Conner v. Shepherd, 15 Mass. 167; Leonard v. Leonard, 4 Mass. 533. The fees for the services of appraisers of estates of deceased persons, appraisers of real estate taken on execution, persons appointed under legal process for assigning dower or making partition of real estate, when no express provision is made for the compensation therefor, shall be such as the court having jurisdiction of the case may deem to be just and reasonable. R. L. c. 204, § 23.

[2] R. L. c. 132, § 10. But a covenant to pay the widow money by way of rent in consideration of her forbearing to exercise her right to dower, is a personal covenant, and cannot run with the land so as to bind the assignee of the (so-called) lessee. Croade v. Ingraham, 13 Pick. 33.

[3] Russell v. Russell, 15 Gray, 159. The assignment of her dower

If the entire estate in which the widow's interest is claimed consists of a dwelling-house, certain rooms in the house, with the right of using the stairways, halls, etc., may be set off to the widow. But the part of the premises so assigned to her must be sufficient for her substantial enjoyment of her share of the estate.[1] It seems that at common law the widow is not compelled to take dower so assigned, but may claim a rent issuing out of the estate.[2] But the practice has the sanction of long usage in this state.

The return of the commissioners to the probate court should give a detailed report of their proceedings under the warrant directed to them. The fact that notice was given to persons interested, and the manner in which it was given, should be stated. If the parties notified were present at the time and place appointed for making the partition or assignment, the fact should appear in the return. The sums at which the several parcels of land belonging to the estate were appraised should be expressed in words at length; and if the dower is set off by metes and bounds, the boundaries should be so described as to leave no uncertainty as to the portion assigned.

The assent of all parties in interest to the assignment as to a widow of a person who acquired a homestead which existed at his death of certain specific rooms in the house, and certain specific parcels of land, with rights of way over other parts of the house and over parts of the remaining land, does not make her a tenant in common of the servient estate with the heir at law of the deceased, so as to bar her of an estate of homestead in the premises. Weller *v* Weller, 131 Mass. 146

[1] In Howard *v* Candish, Palmer, 264, the sheriff assigned to the widow a third part of each chamber, and chalked out her part, this was held to be an idle and malicious assignment, and the sheriff was committed to prison. Symmes *v* Drew, 21 Pick. 278.

[2] White *v*. Story, 2 Hill (N. Y.), 543; Park on Dower, 254.

ASSIGNMENT OF DOWER AND OTHER LIFE-ESTATES

made by the commissioners should be indorsed on the return; otherwise a citation will issue to them before final action is had. The assignment of dower is made complete by the confirmation by the court[1] of the return of the commissioners, and its record in the probate office. In cases where the husband was a co-tenant, and partition was made previous to the assignment of dower, the return should also be recorded in the registry of deeds for the county in which the land lies.

WHEN WIDOWS MAY BE ENDOWED ANEW.

" If a woman is lawfully evicted of land which has been assigned to her as dower or settled upon her as jointure, or is deprived of the provision made for her by will or otherwise in lieu of dower, she may be endowed anew in like manner as if such assignment, jointure, or other provision had not been made;"[2] as when she has been endowed of lands mortgaged by her husband before his marriage, and has been evicted by the mortgage.[3]

A widow is "deprived of the provision made for her by will," within the meaning of the statute, when all her hus-

[1] The confirmation relates back to the time of the assignment. Parker v. Parker, 17 Pick. 236. Mansfield v. Pembroke, 5 Pick. 449. A judgment of the probate court made after May 1, confirming the report of commissioners filed before that date, assigning a parcel of land to a widow for life, in lieu of dower, does not relate back to the date of the assignment so as to make her liable to the remainderman for taxes assessed on May 1, and paid by him. Kearns v. Cunniff, 138 Mass. 434.

A dowress in occupation of land may in an action of trespass against a stranger put in evidence, on the question of her possession, probate proceedings setting off the land to her which, whether valid or invalid, have never been doubted. Nickerson v. Thacher, 146 Mass. 609.

[2] R. L. c 132, § 14

[3] Scott v. Hancock, 13 Mass. 168.

band's estate is taken for the payment of his debts; as, where the husband gave his wife by will the whole of his estate, on condition that she should pay his debts and legacies, and the estate proved to be insolvent She is entitled, in such case, to her dower, although she may not have formally waived the provision made for her by will, the provision made for her having wholly failed. But before dower can be assigned to her, it must be ascertained that the whole estate, estimating its value without the encumbrance of the widow's dower, is not sufficient to discharge the liabilities.[1] And it is no objection, in such case, to an application for an assignment of dower, that a previous application had been made and refused before there was sufficient evidence that the widow would be deprived of the provision made by the will, and that she did not appeal from the decree of refusal.[2]

WRIT OF DOWER.

[Revised Laws, c 180]

"SECT. 1. A woman entitled to dower, if it is not set out to her by the heir or other tenant of the freehold, to her satisfaction according to law or assigned to her by the probate court, may recover the same by writ of dower as hereinafter provided"

[1] Thompson v McGaw, 1 Met 66

[2] Thompson v McGaw, 1 Met. 66. After a tenant in dower has assigned her estate, she is not liable to the assignees of the reversion for waste committed by her assignee. Foot v Dickinson, 2 Met 611

A conveyance by a married woman during her husband's lifetime of her inchoate right of dower is void as to any party other than he who holds the land in which the right might otherwise be asserted, and does not estop her from maintaining a writ of dower against the grantee, even although he has not been repaid the sum paid by him as the consideration for the conveyance. Mason v Mason, 140 Mass 63; Flynn v Flynn, 171 Mass 312, 314

"SECT. 2. She shall demand her dower of the person seised of the freehold at the time when she makes such demand, unless such person is unknown to her or absent from the commonwealth. She shall not commence her action therefor before the expiration of one month, nor after the expiration of one year, from such demand; but she may make a new demand and commence an action thereon."

"SECT. 3 A demand of dower shall be sufficient if it is in writing, signed by the widow or by her agent or attorney, containing a general description of the land in which the dower is claimed, and is given to the tenant of the freehold or left at his last and usual place of abode."

"SECT. 4. If the demandant recovers judgment for her dower, she shall in the same action recover damages for its detention, which shall be assessed by a jury under the direction of the court, unless the parties file in court a written agreement that the damages shall be assessed by the commissioners as hereinafter provided."[1]

"SECT. 5. If the court finds that the demandant is entitled to her dower, it shall award the interlocutory judgment therefor and issue its warrant to three disinterested commissioners to set out said dower equally and impartially, and as conveniently as may be, and, if an agreement has been filed as provided in the preceding section, to award damages for its detention."

"SECT 6. Said commissioners, before entering upon their duties, shall be sworn faithfully and impartially to execute the warrant, a certificate of which oath shall be made on the warrant by the person who administers it. They shall give notice to the parties of the time and place appointed for setting out the dower, and all of the commissioners shall

[1] Harrington v Conolly, 116 Mass. 69.

meet for the performance of any of their duties, but a majority may act."

"Sect. 7. The commissioners shall make and sign a report of their doings, with any damages assessed by them, and return it with their warrant to the court from which said warrant was issued If their report is confirmed, judgment shall be rendered that the assignment of dower shall be firm and effectual during the life of the demandant, and for the damages as assessed by said commissioners."

"Sect. 8 A party aggrieved by a judgment rendered under the provisions of section five, or upon a report of the commissioners under the provisions of the preceding section, may appeal therefrom in any matter of law apparent upon the record to the supreme judicial court; but an appeal from the judgment rendered under the provisions of the preceding section, shall not draw in question the interlocutory judgment"

"Sect. 9. When final judgment has been recovered by the demandant, execution shall issue thereon for possession and for costs, and, if the judgment is for damages also, for damages."

"Sect. 10. The action shall be brought against the person who is tenant of the freehold at the time when it is commenced If the demand was not made on him, he shall be liable only for the time during which he held the land; but if the demandant recovers her dower and damages in the writ of dower, she may thereafter recover in an action of tort against the prior tenant of the freehold, on whom her demand was made, the rents and profits for the time during which he held the land after the demand"[1]

"Sect. 11. If the land cannot be divided without damage

[1] Whitaker v. Green, 129 Mass. 417

to the whole, the dower may be assigned out of the rents or profits, which shall be received by the demandant as tenant in common with the other owners."

"SECT. 12. The provisions of chapter one hundred and thirty-two relative to the land out of which dower may be claimed and the manner in which it may be barred, and those of section one of chapter one hundred and eighty-five relative to the liability of the tenant for waste, shall apply to proceedings under this chapter."[1]

PRESENT VALUE OF DOWER ESTATES.

As the table of mortality and rate of interest to be employed in valuing dowers is not fixed by law, the values according to two tables and rates are given, and those which they exhibit may be regarded as fixing the maximum and minimum limits of the fair valuation of such an estate when the life on which it depends is not actually impaired or diseased. If the life is unquestionably sound, the figures should be based on the Healthy Districts table, especially if the age of the person is advanced.

The table on the following pages is prepared so that the value of a life estate or dower may be computed simply by finding the present age of the person on whose life it depends in the left or right hand column, and copying the value figures on the same line of an estate of $100, from the appropriate column and multiplying them by the ratio of the value of the estate in question to 100.[2] For example: —

[1] R L c. 180, §§ 1-12
[2] In determining the value of an annuity on real estate for the purpose of imposing a tax on collateral legacies and successions, the so-called "Actuaries' Combined Experienced Tables" are to be used R. L. c 15, § 16.

TABLE

Showing at ages 15 to 98 the Present Value of a Life Estate of $100, under the Collateral Succession Law [Chapter 15 of Revised Laws]. Also the Present Value of a Widow's Dower in an Estate of $100 according to two Tables of Mortality and Rates of Interest.

Prepared by WALTER C. WRIGHT, Actuary of the New England Mutual Life Insurance Co.

Present Age.	Value of Life estate. Combined Experience 4 per cent.*	Value of Dower. Combined Experience. 4 per cent.	Value of Dower. Combined Experience. 6 per cent.	English Life Healthy Districts. Females. 4 per cent.	English Life Healthy Districts. Females. 6 per cent.	Present Age.
15	75.99	25.33	28.30	25.64	28.48	15
16	75.58	25.19	28.20	25.48	28.36	16
17	75.16	25.05	28.11	25.33	28.24	17
18	74.72	24.91	28.01	25.19	28.12	18
19	74.27	24.76	27.90	25.04	28.02	19
20	73.80	24.60	27.79	24.91	27.92	20
21	73.32	24.44	27.67	24.76	27.82	21
22	72.82	24.28	27.55	24.63	27.72	22
23	72.30	24.10	27.42	24.48	27.62	23
24	71.76	23.92	27.29	24.33	27.52	24
25	71.21	23.74	27.15	24.19	27.42	25
26	70.64	23.55	27.01	24.04	27.32	26
27	70.05	23.35	26.85	23.86	27.20	27
28	69.44	23.15	26.69	23.72	27.08	28
29	68.81	22.94	26.53	23.56	26.96	29
30	68.16	22.72	26.35	23.39	26.84	30
31	67.49	22.50	26.17	23.20	26.70	31
32	66.79	22.26	25.98	23.01	26.56	32
33	66.08	22.03	25.79	22.83	26.42	33
34	65.34	21.78	25.58	22.63	26.26	34
35	64.58	21.53	25.36	22.41	26.10	35
36	63.79	21.26	25.14	22.20	25.92	36
37	62.98	20.99	24.90	21.99	25.74	37
38	62.14	20.71	24.65	21.75	25.56	38
39	61.27	20.42	24.39	21.51	25.36	39
40	60.37	20.12	24.12	21.27	25.16	40
41	59.44	19.81	23.84	21.00	24.92	41
42	58.48	19.49	23.54	20.73	24.70	42
43	57.50	19.17	23.22	20.45	24.46	43
44	56.48	18.83	22.90	20.16	24.20	44
45	55.43	18.48	22.56	19.87	23.92	45
46	54.36	18.12	22.20	19.55	23.64	46
47	53.27	17.76	21.85	19.23	23.34	47
48	52.16	17.39	21.47	18.89	23.02	48
49	51.03	17.01	21.09	18.55	22.68	49
50	49.88	16.63	20.70	18.19	22.34	50
51	48.72	16.24	20.30	17.81	21.98	51
52	47.54	15.85	19.88	17.43	21.58	52
53	46.34	15.45	19.46	17.04	21.18	53
54	45.13	15.04	19.03	16.61	20.76	54

* Of Life Estate of $100.00, or of an Annuity of $4.00.

ASSIGNMENT OF DOWER AND OTHER LIFE-ESTATES.

Present Age.	Value of Life estate. Combined Experience 4 per cent.*	Value of Dower. Combined Experience. 4 per cent.	Value of Dower. Combined Experience. 6 per cent.	Value of Dower. English Life Healthy Districts. Females. 4 per cent.	Value of Dower. English Life Healthy Districts. Females. 6 per cent.	Present Age.
55	43.91	14.64	18.59	16.19	20.30	55
56	42.68	14.23	18.14	15.75	19.84	56
57	41.44	13.81	17.69	15.28	19.34	57
58	40.18	13.39	17.22	14.83	18.82	58
59	38.92	12.97	16.75	14.37	18.32	59
60	37.66	12.55	16.27	13.92	17.82	60
61	36.39	12.13	15.79	13.48	17.34	61
62	35.12	11.71	15.30	13.03	16.82	62
63	33.86	11.29	14.81	12.59	16.32	63
64	32.60	10.87	14.31	12.15	15.82	64
65	31.34	10.45	13.82	11.71	15.30	65
66	30.10	10.03	13.32	11.27	14.80	66
67	28.87	9.62	12.83	10.83	14.28	67
68	27.65	9.22	12.33	10.40	13.76	68
69	26.45	8.82	11.84	9.96	13.24	69
70	25.27	8.42	11.36	9.55	12.72	70
71	24.10	8.03	10.87	9.12	12.22	71
72	22.96	7.65	10.40	8.71	11.70	72
73	21.84	7.28	9.92	8.29	11.20	73
74	20.74	6.91	9.46	7.91	10.70	74
75	19.66	6.55	9.00	7.51	10.22	75
76	18.60	6.20	8.55	7.13	9.74	76
77	17.58	5.86	8.10	6.76	9.26	77
78	16.57	5.52	7.66	6.40	8.80	78
79	15.60	5.20	7.24	6.05	8.36	79
80	14.64	4.88	6.82	5.72	7.92	80
81	13.72	4.57	6.41	5.40	7.50	81
82	12.81	4.27	6.00	5.09	7.10	82
83	11.92	3.97	5.61	4.80	6.70	83
84	11.04	3.68	5.21	4.52	6.32	84
85	10.18	3.39	4.82	4.25	5.96	85
86	9.31	3.10	4.42	3.99	5.62	86
87	8.46	2.82	4.03	3.75	5.28	87
88	7.60	2.53	3.63	3.52	4.96	88
89	6.76	2.25	3.24	3.29	4.68	89
90	5.94	1.98	2.86	3.09	4.38	90
91	5.14	1.71	2.48	2.89	4.12	91
92	4.36	1.45	2.11	2.71	3.86	92
93	3.62	1.21	1.76	2.53	3.62	93
94	2.95	.98	1.43	2.36	3.38	94
95	2.34	.78	1.14	2.21	3.18	95
96	1.85	.62	.90	2.07	2.96	96
97	1.47	.49	.72	1.93	2.78	97
98	.96	.32	.47	1.80	2.60	98

* Of Life Estate of $100.00, or of an Annuity of $4.00.

Suppose a widow whose age is 30 is entitled to dower in an estate worth $6,000 opposite the number 30, representing the age, is the sum $22.72 (see Combined Experience column at four per cent); multiply that sum by 60 (the number of hundreds in 6,000), and the product is $1,363.20, which is the present value of her dower at four per cent according to the Combined Experience tables. At the same per cent, according to the English Healthy Districts table, it is $1,403.40.

ESTATES OF HOMESTEAD.

Every householder having a family may have an estate of homestead, to the extent in value of eight hundred dollars,[1] in the farm or lot of land and buildings thereon, owned or rightly possessed by lease or otherwise and occupied by him as a residence, and such estate is exempt from attachment, levy on execution, and sale for the payment of his debts or legacies, and from the laws of conveyance, descent, and devise except as provided in chapter 131 of the Revised Laws.[2] To create such estate of homestead, the fact that it is designed to be held as a homestead

---

[1] The householder's estate of homestead, once acquired, is not defeated by the death or removal of his wife and children from the premises, or by her obtaining a divorce from bed and board and a decree giving her the custody of the children, if he continues to reside thereon. She cannot by her separate act deprive him of such estate. Doyle v Coburn, 6 Allen, 71; Silloway v Brown, 12 Allen, 30

[2] No estate of homestead exists in land held in common and undivided. Thurston v Maddocks, 6 Allen, 427; Silloway v Brown, 12 Allen, 30; Bemis v Driscoll, 101 Mass. 418, Holmes v. Winchester, 138 Mass 542, and cases cited.

The estate is not necessarily limited to that part of a dwellinghouse occupied by the family, but may exist in the whole of a house, some rooms of which are to let to tenants. Mercier v Chace, 11 Allen, 194. It may exist in a country hotel. Lazell v Lazell, 8 Allen, 575.

must be set forth in the deed by which the property is acquired that it is designed to be held as a homestead; or, after the title has been acquired, such design must be declared by writing duly signed, sealed, acknowledged, and recorded in the registry of deeds for the county or district in which the property is situated. The acquisition of a new estate of homestead will defeat and discharge any such previous estate.

The right of homestead may be released by a deed in which the wife of the householder joins for the purpose of releasing it,[1] but if it exists at the time of his death, it "shall continue for the benefit of his widow and minor children, and be held and enjoyed by them, if some one of them occupies the premises, until the youngest child is twenty-one years of age, and until the marriage or death of the widow."[2] And the estate may be set off to the parties entitled thereto by metes and bounds, in the same manner that dower may be set off to a widow.[3]

[1] A wife does not "join in a deed of conveyance" of a homestead by simply inserting her name in the final clause of the deed, and signing and sealing it. Greenough v. Turner, 11 Gray, 332. See Wales v Coffin, 13 Allen, 213, Tirrell v Kenney, 137 Mass 30.

An estate of homestead cannot be lost by mere abandonment until a new homestead is acquired elsewhere Woodbury v. Luddy, 14 Allen, 1, Abbott v. Abbott, 97 Mass 136

[2] R. L c 131, § 8 The right of possession and enjoyment will be in such only of the parties who have title as remain in occupation of the premises Abbott v Abbott, 97 Mass 136; Paul v. Paul, 136 Mass 287 The use of a room in the house by the widow, for the purpose of storing furniture, is a sufficient occupation Brettun v. Fox, 100 Mass. 234.

The estate is not defeated by the death of the wife and the removal of the children, if the householder continues it as his home Silloway v Brown, 12 Allen, 30.

The estate must also be actually occupied as a residence Lee v. Miller, 11 Allen, 37.

[3] R L c 131, § 9.

424   PROCEEDINGS IN THE PROBATE COURTS.

When an estate of homestead exists in property in which other parties have an interest, the party entitled to the homestead, or any other party interested in such property, may have partition thereof like tenants in common.[1]

The widow takes her homestead estate in addition to her dower. The dower may be assigned to her out of the whole real estate of her husband, and the estate of homestead from the estate remaining after the assignment of dower.[2]

The probate court has no jurisdiction to set out an estate of homestead, if the right to it is disputed by the heirs or devisees.[3]

The widow, and the guardian of the minor children, when he has obtained a license therefor from the probate court as in the case of sales of real estate of minors, may join in a sale of such estate of homestead; or, if there is no widow entitled to such rights therein, the guardian upon such license may make sale thereof, and the widow may make such sale if there are no minor children. The purchaser shall have the right to enjoy and possess the premises for the full time that the widow and children or either of them might have continued to hold and enjoy the same if no sale had been made. The probate

[1] R. L. c 131, § 11.
[2] Cowdrey v Cowdrey, 131 Mass 186, Weller v Weller, ibid 446; Mercier v Chace, 11 Allen, 194, Monk v Capen, 5 Allen, 146.
[3] Woodward v Lincoln, 9 Allen, 239 A widow who has acquired a right of homestead in premises worth less than eight hundred dollars, and is in the occupation thereof at the time of her husband's death, may continue such occupation, and avail herself of her right of homestead as a defence against one who claims title under her husband, although her homestead has not been set out to her by the court. Parks v. Reilly, 5 Allen, 77 See Eastham v Barrett, 152 Mass 56

court may apportion the proceeds of the sale among the parties entitled thereto.[1]

RIGHT OF HOMESTEAD OF INSOLVENT DEBTORS

When the property of a debtor is assigned under the laws in relation to insolvent debtors, and such debtor claims, and it appears to the court wherein the proceedings in insolvency are pending that he is entitled to hold a part thereof as a homestead, and that the property in which such estate of homestead exists is of greater value than eight hundred dollars, the court shall cause the property to be appraised by three impartial and discreet men, one of whom shall be appointed by the insolvent, one by the assignee, and the third by the court; or in case either the assignee or insolvent neglects to appoint, the court shall appoint for him. The persons so appointed shall be duly sworn faithfully and impartially to appraise the property, and shall proceed to appraise and set off an estate of homestead in the same to the insolvent debtor in the manner prescribed in case of a judgment debtor; and the residue shall vest in and be disposed of by the assignee in the same manner as property not exempt by law from levy on execution. The appraisers shall be entitled to the same fees, to be paid out of the estate in

---

[1] R. L. c 131, § 10. A widow who left an estate in which she had a right of homestead which she did not know of, was held to have lost her right of homestead. Paul *v.* Paul, 136 Mass 286, Foster *v* Leland, 141 Mass 187. Where an estate of homestead has been acquired in land of greater value than the limit of the homestead exemption, and the surplus has been alienated by sale or transfer according to law, the owner of the residue may maintain a writ of entry to recover the land subject to the right of homestead. Copeland *v* Sturtevant, 156 Mass 114. An estate of homestead does not exist in lands held in common and undivided. Holmes *v* Winchester, 138 Mass 542.

insolvency, as are allowed to appraisers of real estate seized upon execution.

If a judgment creditor requires an execution to be levied on property claimed by the debtor to be as a homestead exempt from such levy, and if the officer holding such execution is of opinion that the premises are of greater value than eight hundred dollars, appraisers shall be appointed to appraise the property in the manner provided by law for an appraisal in the case of the levy of an execution on real estate. If in the judgment of the appraisers the premises are of greater value than eight hundred dollars, they shall set off to the judgment debtor so much of the premises, including the dwelling-house in whole or in part, as shall appear to them to be of the value of eight hundred dollars; and the residue of the property shall be levied upon and disposed of in like manner as real estate not exempt from levy on execution; and if the property levied on is subject to a mortgage, it may be set off or sold subject to the mortgage and to the estate of homestead in like manner as land subject to a mortgage only.[1]

ASSIGNMENT OF OTHER ESTATES FOR LIFE.

When a widow is entitled by the provisions of law, by deed of jointure, or under the will of her husband, to an undivided interest in his real estate, either for life or during widowhood, if her right is not disputed by his heirs or devisees, such interest may be assigned to her, in whatever counties the lands lie, by the probate court for the county in which the estate of her husband is settled The assignment may be made upon her petition, or, if she

[1] R. L. c 131, §§ 12, 13

does not petition within one year from the death of her husband, upon petition by an heir or devisee of her husband by any person having an estate in the lands subject to such interest, or by the guardian of such heir, devisee, or person The interest of the widow is set off by metes and bounds, when it can be so done without damage to the whole estate But when the estate consists of a mill or other tenement which cannot be divided without damage to the whole, her interest may be assigned out of the rents or profits to be received by the widow as a tenant in common with the other owners of the estate.[1]

[1] R L c 132, §§ 9, 10 , Guckian v Riley, 135 Mass 73 , Fuller v. Rust, 153 Mass 50, Proctor v Clark, 154 Mass 50.

CHAPTER XIX.

PROBATE BONDS

AS TO BONDS GENERALLY.[1]

THE sureties in every bond given to the judge of the probate court must, except as provided in section sixty-one of chapter one hundred and eighteen of the Revised Laws (authorizing the acceptance as surety of a qualified foreign fidelity insurance company), be inhabitants of this commonwealth, and such as the judge or register approves,[2] and no bond required to be given to the judge, or filed in the probate office, is sufficient, unless examined and ap-

---

[1] As to the conditions of bonds given to the judge of probate, in the course of proceedings in the probate court, see the chapters referring to the several proceedings in which bonds are required.

[2] R. L. c 149, § 9

The money paid to fidelity insurance companies or to any person acting as surety on an official bond may be allowed as a charge against the estate R L c 150, § 15.

A bond without surety, given by an administrator and approved by the judge of probate without notice to creditors, is not such a bond as the statutes of this commonwealth require. Abercrombie v Sheldon, 8 Allen, 532.

A probate bond in the ordinary form of a trustee's bond filed in the registry of probate, satisfactory to the beneficiaries and accepted orally by the judge of probate, but never approved by him in writing as required by P S c. 143, § 2 (now R L c. 149, § 10), is valid at common law, and the sureties are liable upon it in a suit brought in the name of the judge. Whether such bond is invalid as a statutory bond, *quære* McIntire v. Linehan, 178 Mass. 263.

proved by the judge or by the register, and his approval thereof under his official signature is written thereon.[1]

Whenever bonds are required to be given to the judge of a probate court by two or more persons acting jointly as executors, administrators, trustees, or otherwise, such persons may give either separate or joint bonds [2]

All bonds given to the probate court must be in such sum as the judge shall order, and made payable to the judge and his successors in office; in cases where the office is vacant, to the acting judge and his successors.[3]

---

[1] R L. c. 149, § 10. An executor or administrator shall, when exempt from giving a surety, give his own personal bond, with conditions as prescribed by law; but the probate court may at or after granting of letters testamentary or letters of administration require a bond, with sufficient surety or sureties

Every executor or administrator who neglects to give bond, with surety or sureties, when required by the probate court within such time as it orders, shall be found to have declined or resigned the trust R L. c 149, §§ 3, 8.

An executor's bond which is signed by two sureties who are inhabitants of this commonwealth, and by a third person who is an inhabitant of another state, if approved by the probate court, is sufficient to qualify him to act The additional surety may add to, but cannot impair, the value of the contract Clarke v Chapin, 7 Allen, 425.

An executor's bond, approved by the judge, in which the sureties are each bound in half the sum in which the principal is bound, is not for that cause void, but is binding on the obligors, and sufficient to give effect to the executor's appointment, and to render his acts as such valid; but it seems that the supreme court, on an appeal from the decree of the judge of probate approving a bond in that form, would not countenance such a departure from the usual course of proceeding Baldwin v Standish, 7 Cush 207.

[2] R. L. c. 149, § 11. An executor who gives a separate bond is not liable for a loss caused, without negligence on his part, by the default of his co-executor McKim v Aulbach, 130 Mass 481 See Ames v. Armstrong, 106 Mass. 15

[3] R. L. c. 164, § 8 Any bond given by an executor, administrator, guardian, or trustee whose appointment is invalid by reason of an irregularity or of want of jurisdiction or authority in the court

In practice, particularly when the sureties reside at a distance from the place of holding the probate court, bonds are executed in anticipation of the probate of the will, or other decree requiring a bond to be given, and are held in readiness to be offered for approval whenever the decree is passed. When this course is followed, care should be taken by the party offering the bond that the instrument be unexceptionable, both as to the penal sum and the sufficiency of the sureties. The amount of the penalty of the bond should be proportioned to the extent of the interest to be protected, regard being had to the situation of the estate and to all the circumstances of the case [1] In a majority of cases, the sum named in the bond should be double the value of the property which the bond is intended to secure; and the executor, administrator, or trustee must certify on the back of the bond the value of the real estate and of the best personal property, to the best of his knowledge and belief.

WHEN NEW BONDS MAY BE REQUIRED.

When the sureties or the penal sum in a bond given to the probate court are insufficient, the supreme judicial court, or the probate court, after notice to the principal in the bond, may require a new bond with such surety or sureties, and in such penal sum, as the court shall direct [2]

---

making such appointment, shall be held valid and binding both on the principals and the sureties. R. L c. 148, § 25.

[1] In an application by a foreigner for ancillary letters of administration, for the purpose of collecting a debt, a bond was taken by the supreme court of probate in $5,000, which amount was less than that of the debt to be collected, it appearing that the heirs and foreign creditors were secured under the laws of the intestate's domicile, and that there were probably no creditors in the United States Picquet, Appellant, 5 Pick 65.

[2] R. L c 149, § 14, Brooks v. Whitmore, 142 Mass. 401. The

PROBATE BONDS.

Any surety may, upon his petition to the supreme judicial court, or the probate court, be discharged from all further responsibility, if the court, after due notice to all persons interested, deems it reasonable and proper; and the principal will thereupon be required to give a new bond.[1]

If the principal does not give such new bond within such time as is ordered by the court, he shall be removed from his trust, and some other person appointed in his stead.[2]

In case of the marriage of a woman who is executrix, administratrix, guardian, or trustee, her sureties have the right, on petition to the probate court in which her bond is filed, to be released from any further liability on her bond, beyond accounting for and paying over the money or property already in her hands, and if her sureties are so released, she will be required to give a new bond to the satisfaction of the court.[3]

---

guardian of a minor who had given bond in the form required by law, having represented to the judge of probate that, since his appointment, his ward had received a legacy exceeding in amount the penalty of the bond, and having suggested that the judge should make such order in the premises as to law and justice might appertain, the judge ordered him to file a new bond in a larger sum, and the guardian filed a new bond accordingly, with a new surety. Held, that both bonds were valid, that the sureties were to be deemed co-sureties, and that, being sureties in different sums, they were, as between themselves, compellable to contribute in proportion to the different penalties of their respective bonds. Loring v. Bacon, 3 Cush. 465; Brooks v. Whitmore, 139 Mass. 358; Forbes v. Harrington, 171 Mass. 389.

[1] R. L. c. 149, § 15, Brooks v. Whitmore, 142 Mass. 401. If, without the assent or knowledge of a surety, his co-surety is discharged from all further responsibility, and a new bond is given by the principal and approved by the court, the first-named surety is also discharged from liability for further acts of the principal, although the new bond recites that it is in addition to the first bond. McKim v. Demmon, 130 Mass. 404.

[2] R. L. c. 149, § 16.   [3] R. L. c. 149, § 19.

432   PROCEEDINGS IN THE PROBATE COURTS.

When an executor, administrator, guardian, or trustee is licensed to sell real estate, and the bond given by him at the time of his appointment appears to the court to be insufficient, he may be required to give an additional bond.[1]

When a new bond is so required, the sureties in the prior bond are liable for all breaches of the condition committed before the new bond is approved by the judge.[2]

SUITS ON BONDS OF EXECUTORS AND ADMINISTRATORS.

Suits on probate bonds are brought in the name of the judge of the probate court,[3] and, except in certain classes of cases specified by the statute,[4] are brought only on

[1] R L c 149, § 13 As to the removal of executors and others for failing to file a new bond when ordered, see chap viii.

[2] Ibid. § 17 ; McKim v Bartlett, 129 Mass. 226 , McKim v. Blake, 132 Mass 343

[3] When the judge is obligor as principal or surety in a bond given to a former judge of the court, suit may be brought upon the bond in the name of the judge mentioned therein, his executors or administrators. R L c 149, § 24

[4] Ibid §§ 20-22 , Fall River v. Riley, 138 Mass. 338; Fuller v. Connelly, 142 Mass 230

If an administrator suffers judgment to be recovered against him before he represents the estate insolvent, he must pay the full amount of the judgment, even if the estate is insolvent, and he and his sureties are liable to a suit by the judgment creditor on the bond. Newcomb v Goss, 1 Met 333 This decision, however, is questioned in Fuller v. Connelly, 142 Mass 230

If a probate bond is altered by the judge of probate without the consent of the sureties, they will be no longer bound by it Howe v. Peabody, 2 Gray, 556

In an action on a bond against an administrator and his sureties for a refusal to pay a judgment recorded against him, such judgment, if not obtained by fraud or collusion, is conclusive on the sureties, in regard to all matters of defence affecting the merits of the claim as between the parties to the judgment Heard v. Lodge, 20 Pick. 53 ;

leave granted by the court. There are three cases, and only three, in which a person can sue the bond of an

White *v* Weatherbee, 126 Mass 452 ; McKim *v.* Glover, 167 Mass. 280 ; McKim *v.* Haley, 173 Mass 114

But the sureties are not liable on a judgment obtained on a demand which was barred by the special statute of limitations Dawes *v* Shed, 15 Mass 6 ; Robinson *v* Hodge, 117 Mass 222

If the payment of a legacy is charged upon land devised to a person who is also the executor of the will, and the legatee joins in a mortgage of the land given by the devisee to secure a sum of money borrowed for the latter's personal use, and the mortgagee afterwards sells the land under a power contained in the mortgage, and applies the proceeds of the sale to the payment of the mortgage debt, the legatee loses his right to proceed against the land to enforce payment of his legacy, and an action therefor cannot be maintained for his benefit against a surety on the executor's bond Thayer *v.* Finnegan, 134 Mass 62

The failure of an executor who as sole legatee under the will, there being no creditors, is the only person interested in the disposition of the estate, to file an inventory and render an account within the prescribed time, is a technical breach of his bond. McKim *v.* Harwood, 129 Mass 75

A bond given by an executor upon the probate of a will in the probate court is not vacated, but only suspended in its operation by a subsequent appeal from the probate of the will , and upon an affirmance of the same, no new bond need be given by the executor Dunham *v* Dunham, 16 Gray, 577

A bond to pay debts and legacies given by an executor and residuary legatee cannot after the expiration of a year and a half be cancelled or surrendered by the judge of probate. Alger *v* Colwell, 2 Gray, 404

Where an administration bond was not executed by the administrator, the sureties were *held* not to be liable Wood *v* Washburn, 2 Pick 24 ; Goodyear Dental Vulcanite Co *v.* Bacon, 151 Mass 460

If an administrator of an estate represented to be insolvent neglects to render and settle his account in the probate court within the time prescribed, he and his sureties are liable to nominal damages at least, in a suit on his bond, although he was not cited by the judge of probate to render an account Fay *v.* Haven, 3 Met. 109 ; Coney *v* Williams, 9 Mass 114

The question whether an account settled in the probate court by

executor or administrator for his own benefit, without first obtaining authority from the probate court. 1st.

an administrator was fraudulent, cannot be tried in an action on the administration bond for not settling a true account Paine v. Stone, 10 Pick 75.

A devisee of real estate which is taken from him by a title paramount to the testator's, has his remedy for the value of his estate upon the bond of the executor being also the residuary legatee for the payment of debts and legacies, and this without a previous demand upon, or action against, the executor Paine v Gill, 13 Mass 365

If during the lifetime of a devisee the real estate devised to him is unlawfully sold by the executor, his heirs are not entitled to an execution in a suit brought in the name of the judge of probate on the bond of the executor, but it must be applied for and issue to the administrator Chapin v Waters, 116 Mass 140.

If the decree of a judge of probate granting leave to bring an action on an administrator's bond bears date prior to the time of bringing the action, evidence is not admissible at the trial to show that the decree, although actually made at the date stated, was not reduced to writing till after action brought Richardson v Hazelton, 101 Mass. 108 See Newell v West, 149 Mass 531

A previous demand on a surety in a bond is not necessary in order to maintain an action upon it against him. Wood v Barstow, 10 Pick. 368

An action on an administration bond brought for the benefit of a creditor of an heir who levied on land which descended to the heir, but whose levy was defeated through the fault of the administrator, cannot be sustained, such creditor having no direct interest in the bond Fay v. Hunt, 5 Pick 398

If a judge of probate grants leave to bring an action on a probate bond for the benefit of an individual upon his filing a bond to indemnify the judge against the costs of the suit, and the action is brought before such bond is filed, the judge may afterwards receive such bond, and it will relate back to the commencement of the action White v. Stanwood, 4 Pick 380

Sureties are liable for the amount of any chattels which have come to the administrator's hands as well before as after the execution of the bond and granting of administration. Odiorne v Maxcy, 13 Mass 177

If a surety on a probate bond of the administrator of an estate who is removed for failure to account, is himself appointed administrator

When the claim is by a creditor who has recovered judgment against the executors or administrators, and they de bonis non of the estate, his liability on the bond constitutes a debt from him to the estate, which is assets in his hands. Choate v Thorndike, 138 Mass 371

The surviving surety of a bond of a trustee under a will was on his petition discharged, the decree reciting that the trustee had filed " a new and sufficient bond " In fact the second bond was approved on the same day that the discharge was granted, but before the granting of the discharge, and the second bond was approved as " an additional bond " *Held*, that the second bond was to be treated as a "new bond," and that the sureties on it were not discharged by the discharge of the surety on the first bond Brooks v Whitmore, 139 Mass 356

A surety is chargeable with a sum received by the trustee as part of the income of the trust fund which he has not paid over to the *cestui que trust*, but which he has applied to make up a deficiency in the investment of capital McKim v. Blake, 139 Mass. 593

A person who executes as surety a probate bond in blank and intrusts it to his principal to be filled in, and delivered to the obligee, is bound by the instrument as delivered White v Duggan, 140 Mass. 18. Under the condition of an executor's bond, the sureties on the bond are not liable for the proceeds of real estate sold by the executor by authority of the will and not needed for the payment of expenses, debts, or specific legacies. White v Ditson, 140 Mass 351. See Minot v. Norcross, 143 Mass 334

A trustee under a will gave a probate bond with A and B as sureties A died, and D, who was a surety on another bond for the same principal as trustee of another estate, supposed that he was a co-surety with A on the first bond, and petitioned the probate court to be discharged, and he was discharged accordingly. The trustee then gave another bond in the same penal sum as the other, with B and C as sureties, which was approved by the judge of probate as " a new bond " The judge and parties all acted under the same apprehension as D *Held*, that both bonds were valid, and that the sureties on each bond after a breach thereof were liable in proportion to the several liabilities assumed by them. Brooks v. Whitmore, 142 Mass. 399

The settlement in the probate court of an administrator's account, showing that he has exhausted all the estate of his intestate in paying

have neglected upon demand made by him to pay the same or to show sufficient goods or estate of the deceased

the expenses of the last sickness, funeral, and administration, is a good defence to an action brought against the administrator upon his bond although the administrator has suffered a judgment to be recovered against him before such settlement of his account. Fuller v. Connelly, 142 Mass 227. But to entitle an administrator to depend upon the ground of insufficiency of assets, there must be an inventory filed and a settlement of his account in the probate court. McKim v. Haley, 173 Mass 112, 114

The proper proceeding to compel a guardian to pay legal counsel for professional services rendered for an infant ward is by action against the ward or on the guardian's bond. Willard v. Lavender, 147 Mass 15

An executor who receives no assets and files no inventory within three months of his appointment, commits a breach of his bond by failing to file an inventory within a reasonable time after assets come to his hands If an executor neglects to file an account within one year after his appointment, it is a breach of his bond, although a debt due to the executor from the testator and the burial expenses paid by him exceed in amount the assets, and no claims are presented by creditors within two years Forbes v McHugh, 152 Mass 412

The provision in the Public Statutes that a trustee of an estate may be exempted from giving sureties on his bond at the request of " all the persons beneficially interested " therein, refers to such interested persons only as are in being and have a vested interest in the estate Dexter v Cotting, 149 Mass. 92. See R L c. 149, § 4

The questions whether trustees under a will shall give bonds to the judge of probate and perform the other duties of trustees who are obliged to give such bonds are primarily for the probate court Bullard v. Attorney-General, 153 Mass. 249

After verdict in an action on a probate bond for the penal sum thereof, it is discretionary with the court upon a hearing in equity to fix the amount for which execution shall be awarded, or to submit the question to a jury Defriez v Coffin, 155 Mass 203.

If after the passing of a decree in the probate court exempting an executor from giving sureties on his bond he files a bond without any surety dated on the day when the will was first presented for probate, bearing the approval of the judge of probate written thereon in due form, but dated and actually written on the day of the date of the bond, this will be a sufficient bond, and the statute of limitations will

to be taken on execution for that purpose. 2d When the estate is insolvent, and the amount due the creditor has been ascertained by a decree of distribution 3d. By a person next of kin whose distributive share of the personal estate has been ascertained by a decree of the probate court. In each case, the person bringing the action must first have made an ineffectual demand upon the executor or administrator. These, it will be seen, are cases in which the right of the claimant has been liquidated and ascertained by matter of record, amounting to a conclusive judgment between the parties, and nothing remains but payment.[1]

In all other cases, the party aggrieved by the failure of the executor or administrator to perform his duty, must obtain leave of the probate court before bringing an action on the bond.[2] This is the course to be pursued by a legatee when the executor neglects to pay his legacy;[3]

begin to run in favor of the executor on the day when it is filed. Wells v. Child, 12 Allen, 330

[1] Loring v Kendall, 1 Gray, 316; Newcomb v. Williams, 9 Met 536, Barton v. White, 21 Pick 60; Pierce v. Prescott, 128 Mass. 141.

The administrator of the next of kin may bring an action on the bond without obtaining leave of the court. White v Weatherbee, 126 Mass. 450

If an executor or administrator neglects to render and settle his accounts in the probate court within six months after the final determination of the claims of creditors, or within such further time as the court may allow, and thereby delays a decree of distribution, such neglect shall be deemed unfaithful administration; and he may be forthwith removed, and shall be liable in a suit on his bond for all damages occasioned by his default R L c 112, § 26

[2] R L c 149, § 23.

[3] Newcomb v Williams, 9 Met 525; Fay v. Taylor, 2 Gray, 158, Conant v Stratton, 107 Mass 474 A legatee's right of action arises only after demand upon the executor for payment of the legacy. Prescott v Parker, 14 Mass 429

and by a creditor, or one next of kin (whose claim or share has not been ascertained by a judgment or decree), or other person aggrieved by any maladministration.[1]

[1] For the failure of the administrator to account within one year, no action lies on the probate bond, after the allowance by the judge of probate, at the request of the parties in interest, of an account subsequently rendered by him. Loring v. Kendall, 1 Gray, 305.

Where a creditor gives up his securities against an estate, on a personal promise by the executor to pay his debt, it seems that he thereby loses his remedy on the executor's bond, given to pay debts and legacies. Stebbins v. Smith, 4 Pick. 97.

If an executor be also appointed trustee in the will, but gives bond only as executor, he is chargeable in that capacity for the property in his hands, until he has given bond as trustee, and charged himself with the property as trustee. Prior v. Talbot, 10 Cush. 1; Ricketson v. Merrill, 148 Mass. 82.

Where a general legacy is given to one for life, with remainder over, and no special trustee is appointed to manage the same, the executor is liable on his bond, if he does not renounce the trust, for any default in reference to such legacy. Dorr v. Wainwright, 13 Pick. 328; Brooks v. Rice, 131 Mass. 408.

An administrator's bond given here does not cover proceedings under letters of ancillary administration taken out in another state. Hooker v. Olmstead, 6 Pick. 481.

In his inventory filed in the probate court, a guardian included assets received by him in another state under ancillary letters of guardianship, and by a decree of the probate court here there was found to be due from him a certain sum. He resigned as guardian in this commonwealth, and his resignation was accepted, and he had not received his discharge as guardian in the other state. *Held*, that so long as the decree of the probate court remained in force, there was a breach of the condition of the bond, that at the expiration of his trust he should pay over all the estate to the persons lawfully entitled thereto. Brooks v. Tobin, 135 Mass. 69.

A bond given by an administrator, on being licensed to sell so much only of his intestate's real estate as is sufficient for the payment of debts and charges, is not a probate bond, and an action upon it cannot be commenced originally in the supreme judicial court. Fay v. Valentine, 8 Pick. 526.

A bond given by a person who is simply a trustee under an oral

These are cases in which the maladministration may have been alike injurious to all the creditors, next of kin, or appointment is not a valid probate bond, and the sureties are not estopped from setting up that defence by a recital in the bond that such person had been "duly appointed trustee." Conant *v* Newton, 126 Mass 105.

A probate bond is not provable in bankruptcy against one of the sureties before a breach of condition of the bond, nor, it seems, before judgment in an action brought for such breach Loring *v.* Kendall, 1 Gray, 305.

When a testator devised an annuity to his widow, and authorized his executor to sell lands sufficient to raise a fund, the interest of which should be equal to the annuity, the executor's neglect to raise said fund was held to be a breach of his bond. Prescott *v* Pitts, 9 Mass 376.

When the same person is executor of a will and guardian of a minor to whom a legacy is given by the will, he holds the amount of the legacy in his capacity of executor, and not as guardian, until he settles an account of his administration in the probate court, crediting himself as executor with the legacy, and charging himself therewith as guardian Until such account is allowed by the probate court, an action cannot be maintained against him and his sureties, on his guardianship bond, for neglect to pay the legacy, but an action may be maintained against him and his sureties on the bond given by him as executor. Conkey *v* Dickinson, 13 Met 51, White *v* Ditson, 140 Mass. 354

A suit on the administrator's bond can be maintained for the benefit of the heirs, for waste in suffering property to be sold at a disadvantage and loss, on execution. Brazer *v.* Clark, 5 Pick. 96; Dawes *v.* Winship, ibid. 97, note

Where an executor sold real estate under a license obtained by his misrepresentations as to the condition of the estate in his hands, it was *held* that such sale was a breach of his bond Chapin *v* Waters, 110 Mass 195

A devisee of real estate, having only a contingent interest therein, or a present interest defeasible upon a condition subsequent, is not entitled to bring an action on the administration bond. Stevens *v.* Cole, 7 Cush 467 Whether a devisee of real estate is a person interested in the estate of a testator, and entitled as such to bring an action on the administration bond, *quære* Ibid

A refusal by an administrator to comply with a decree of the pro-

legatees. No one of them is exclusively entitled to prosecute an action, and the statute therefore authorizes the probate court to designate some one of the persons interested to bring an action for the benefit of all.[1]

An action may be brought on a probate bond at any time within twenty years after the breach of the condition relied on as a cause of action.[2]

Any person interested in the estate may petition for leave to sue the bond.[3] The petition should state clearly all the facts necessary for the consideration of the court, or proper to be notified to the adverse party. Upon the

bate court in itself void, is not a breach of his bond Hancock v. Hubbard, 19 Pick 167; Dawes v Head, 3 Pick 128

The failure of an administrator to pay to the widow of his intestate an allowance ordered to be paid by a decree of the probate court, is a breach of his bond The failure to pay the heirs of his intestate on demand rents of real estate received by him before any decree of the probate court is not a breach If a decree of the probate court reforming the account of an administrator has been affirmed by the supreme judicial court on appeal, and the case remitted to the probate court for further proceedings, that court may authorize the bringing of an action on the administrator's bond, although the certificate of the decision of the supreme court has not then been filed in the probate court, and in the action on the bond neither the administrator nor his sureties are entitled to contest the validity of the order authorizing the action Choate v. Jacobs, 136 Mass 298.

A right of action against a trustee under a will on his bond arises upon a demand by his successor for the trust fund, and his refusal to pay over the same If a right of action against such trustee and the sureties on his bond has been barred by the failure of his successor to sue within the time limited by statute, such bar cannot be removed and a new right of action created by a new demand upon the first trustee for the trust fund made by the second trustee after a reappointment as such McKim v Doane, 137 Mass 195

[1] Newcomb v Wing, 3 Pick 168, Paine v Moffit, 11 Pick 496

[2] Prescott v Read, 8 Cush. 365, Thayer v Keyes, 136 Mass. 104.

[3] The father of an infant interested in the estate having himself no adverse interest therein, may petition, as next friend of the infant, for leave to sue the bond Stevens v Cole, 7 Cush 467

petition, a citation usually issues to the administrator and his sureties, and the petitioner must see that the citation is served in the manner required by its terms.[1]

The petitioner must be prepared, at the time fixed for the hearing, to show that the administrator has so failed to perform his duty as to render proper a suit on his bond. The leave to bring the action can only be granted by a decree in writing.[2] An appeal lies from a decree of the probate court refusing leave to sue the bond, but the signers of the bond cannot appeal from a decree allowing a suit,[3] nor contest the validity of the decree in the action.[4]

When the judge is obligor, as principal or surety, in a bond given to a former judge of the court, the register of the probate court for the county in which such bond was given may authorize a suit thereon, in like manner and upon the same conditions as the court may in other cases [5]

---

[1] Leave may be granted to a legatee to bring an action on a probate bond, without notice to the obligors of the application for such leave, or previously summoning the principal obligor to render an account, and ordering distribution thereon Richardson v Oakman, 15 Gray, 57, Bennett v. Woodman, 116 Mass 519.

Upon a special bond given by an administrator licensed to sell more real estate than is necessary for the payment of debts, to account for the surplus proceeds, an action will lie after neglect for an unreasonable time to render such an account in the probate court, although he has not been cited to do so Bennett v. Overing, 16 Gray, 267

The sureties on a general bond given by an executor who has also given a special bond on being licensed to sell real estate for payment of debts and legacies, are not liable for the neglect of the executor to pay to the residuary legatees entitled thereto the balance of the proceeds of the sale, although the executor charges himself in his general account with the whole of such balance. Robinson v Millard, 133 Mass. 236.

[2] Fay v Rogers, 2 Gray, 175   [3] Ibid

[4] Bennett v Woodman, 116 Mass. 518; Choate v. Jacobs, 136 Mass. 297

[5] R L c. 149, § 24.

Every suit on an administration bond must be brought in the superior court, held for the county in which the bond was taken.[1] The writ must be indorsed by the persons for whose benefit or at whose request the action is brought, or by their attorney, and the indorsers are liable for the costs of suit. If the principal in the bond is resident within the commonwealth at the commencement of the action, and is not made a defendant therein, or is not served with process, the court may, at the request of any of the sureties, continue or postpone the action so long as may be necessary to summon or bring in the principal.[2] If the action is brought by a judgment creditor, or by a creditor or a distributee, the amount of whose claim or share has been established by a decree of distribution, there must be a further indorsement specifying that it is brought for the use or benefit of such creditor or next of kin;[3] and execution, if he obtains judgment, will be awarded for his own use. In every other case the recovery is of all damages occasioned by the default of the delinquent administrator, not the especial damage sustained by any one person. The suit is for the benefit of all persons interested. One judgment is rendered for the entire penalty, and execution is awarded in the name of the judge of probate as the rights of the parties interested require.[4]

When it appears that the condition of the bond of an executor or administrator has been broken, the court upon a hearing in equity shall award execution in the name of the plaintiff as follows: —

[1] R. L. c. 149, § 30 [2] Ibid. § 27.
[3] Ibid § 26, Bennett v. Russell, 2 Allen, 537
[4] Bennett v Overing, 16 Gray, 267, Conant v Stratton, 107 Mass. 474; Chapin v. Waters, 110 Mass 195, Choate v. Arrington, 116 Mass 552

First, If the action is brought for the benefit of a creditor, execution shall be awarded for the use of the creditor for the amount due to him upon the judgment that he has recovered, or upon the decree of distribution in his favor.

Second, if the action is brought for the benefit of a person who is next of kin, execution shall be awarded for the use of such person for the amount due to him according to the decree of the probate court.

Third, If the action is brought for a breach of the condition in not accounting for the estate as required by law, execution shall be awarded, without expressing that it is for the use of any person, for the full value of all the estate of the deceased that has come to the hands of the executor or administrator, and for which he does not satisfactorily account, and for all damages occasioned by his neglect or maladministration.

Fourth, If the action is brought for any other breach of the condition of the bond, execution shall be awarded for such amount and for the use of such person or persons, or without expressing it to be for the use of any particular person, as the court determines.

Fifth, If there are two or more persons for whose use execution is to be awarded as provided in this section, a separate execution shall be issued for the sum due to each of them.

Sixth, The execution shall include the costs of suit, as well as the debt or damages; and if there is more than one execution, the costs shall be equally divided between them. When an execution awarded under the preceding section is expressed to be for the use of a particular person, such person shall be considered as the judgment creditor, and may cause the execution to be levied in his name and for his benefit, as if the action had been brought and the judgment recovered in his name.[1]

The money received on such execution is assets of the estate to be administered, and goes into the hands of the rightful executor or administrator for that purpose. Generally, maladministration which constitutes a breach of his bond will disqualify an administrator and cause his removal. But if there were two or more executors, and separate bonds were given, there may be a co-executor not implicated, in which case the money is paid to him And it may be that the breach of the bond was of such a nature as not to implicate the integrity of the executor, as when the suit was brought to settle some question of right, in which case he may charge himself with the amount of the judgment recovered, and settle the estate. But when the breath of the bond is followed, as is generally the case, by the removal of the executor or administrator, and there is no co-executor not implicated, the money recovered on the execution is paid to the administrator appointed in his stead, to be administered according to law[2] In case the awards of execution do not exhaust the whole penalty, the judgment for the residue stands for any other breach, which may at any time afterwards occur, to be sued for by *scire facias*, either for the benefit of a party entitled to claim in his own right, or by the judge of the probate court as trustee for others.[3]

---

[1] R L c 149. §§ 31, 32.

[2] Ibid § 33; Newcomb *v* Williams, 9 Met 538, Wiggin *v.* Swett, 6 Met 198 The entry of judgment may be suspended until opportunity has been afforded for an application to the probate court for the removal of the administrator. Bennett *v.* Russell, 2 Allen, 537

[3] R L c. 149, § 34.

SUITS UPON BONDS OF TRUSTEES AND GUARDIANS.

Bonds given by trustees may be put in suit by order of the probate court for the use and benefit of any person interested in the trust estate, and bonds given by guardians for the use and benefit of the ward or any person interested in the estate.[1] The proceedings in either case

[1] R L c 149, § 29, White v. Ditson, 140 Mass 357, McKim v Hibbard, 142 Mass 422

A guardian, licensed to sell real estate for the purpose of investment, did not duly invest the proceeds, but charged himself with such proceeds, and with interest thereon from year to year, in his general guardianship account, which was allowed by the court, and expended sums equal to such interest for the support of his ward *Held*, that he was responsible for such proceeds upon the special bond given by him on obtaining the license, but not for the interest thereon upon his general bond Mattoon v. Cowing, 13 Gray, 387, McKim v Morse, 130 Mass 439 See Robinson v Millard, 133 Mass. 236

A guardian is responsible on his general bond for money due from him to his ward at the time of his appointment, and for the rent of real estate occupied by the guardian before that time Mattoon v. Cowing, 13 Gray, 387

The sureties on a guardian's bond are not discharged from liability by the fact that the guardian's account is not settled until more than two years after his death, and after the right of action against his administrator is barred by the statute of limitations Chapin r. Livermore, 13 Gray, 561, Cobb v Kempton, 154 Mass. 266. Nor in money had and received

A bill in equity for the recovery of a debt due from the ward cannot be sustained against the guardian, the remedy is by action on the bond. Conant v Kendall, 21 Pick. 36 The guardian is not liable, in an action of assumpsit, to one who has furnished necessaries for the ward, but only in an action on his bond Cole v Eaton, 8 Cush 587

The remedy of a ward against the guardian to account for money received from the sale of real estate by order of court, is likewise by a suit on the bond, not an action for money had and received. Brooks v Brooks, 11 Cush. 18 See McLane v. Curran, 133 Mass 531, Willard v Lavender, 147 Mass 15.

A surety on a special bond given by a guardian upon obtaining a license to sell his ward's real estate for maintenance, is liable for a

are conducted in like manner as suits on the bonds of executors and administrators, but no suit can be maintained unless it is brought by leave of the probate court.

Action against sureties in a guardian's bond are limited to four years from the time the guardian is discharged, except that if at the time of the discharge the person entitled to bring the action is out of the state, it may be commenced at any time within four years after his return [1] By the term "discharged" in the statute is intended any mode by which the guardianship is effectually determined, either by the removal, resignation, or death of the guardian, the arrival of a minor ward at full age, or otherwise.[2] The limitation applies as well to bonds given by guardians on obtaining license to sell real estate, as to the general guardianship bond

BONDS OF ADMINISTRATORS OF FRENCH SPOLIATION AWARDS

In Sargent *v.* Sargent, 168 Mass 420, 426, the opinion of the court suggested a doubt as to the liability of sureties on an administrator's bond in the ordinary form for a failure by the administrator to distribute French spoliation awards according to the order of the probate court. To remove this doubt, St. 1902, c. 371, was enacted

failure by the guardian to invest the proceeds of the sale not needed for maintenance. McKim *v* Morse, 130 Mass 439.

A ward after coming of age is not entitled to prove against the estate in insolvency of his guardian a claim for the property which came into the hands of the guardian until the latter has settled his account in the probate court, or until a judgment has been obtained upon his bond. Murray *v* Wood, 144 Mass 195

[1] R. L c. 149, § 35 The death of the ward is a discharge of the guardian McKim *v.* Mann, 141 Mass. 507; Richmond *v.* Adams National Bank, 152 Mass 364

[2] Loring *v.* Alline, 9 Cush 68

This statute gives to the probate court exclusive original jurisdiction of all matters relating to the administration of moneys appropriated by the congress of the United States on account of French spoliations, and provides that every bond given after the passage of the act by any administrator engaged in the administration of French spoliation awards shall contain a condition substantially as follows: "To administer according to law and the orders of the probate court all French spoliation awards which shall come to his possession as such administrator." The statute also prescribes the form of approval by the judge or register of such bonds.

CHAPTER XX.

SPECIFIC PERFORMANCE OF AGREEMENTS TO CONVEY LANDS — ARBITRATION AND COMPROMISE — SALE OF STANDING WOOD AND TIMBER — RELEASE OF INTERESTS IN REAL ESTATE OF WARDS. — SUPPORT OF MARRIED WOMEN LIVING APART FROM THEIR HUSBANDS — CONTRIBUTION BETWEEN DEVISEES AND LEGATEES.

CONVEYANCES OF LANDS BY EXECUTORS, ADMINISTRATORS, AND GUARDIANS UNDER CONTRACTS. — SPECIFIC PERFORMANCE.

"IF a person who has entered into a written agreement for the conveyance of real property dies or is put under guardianship before making such conveyance, the probate court shall have jurisdiction concurrent with the supreme judicial court and the superior court to enforce a specific performance of such agreement, and, upon a petition therefor by any person interested in the conveyance, shall, after notice, if upon the hearing it appears that the deceased, were he living, or the ward, were he not under guardianship, would be required to make the conveyance, order the executor or administrator or the guardian to make the same, which conveyance shall have like force and effect as if made by the person who agreed to convey."[1]

[1] R. L. c. 148, § 1; Root v. Blake, 14 Pick. 271.
The jurisdiction given by this statute to the probate court is concurrent with that of the supreme judicial court, and the superior court, and is governed by the same rules. Lynes v. Hayden, 119 Mass. 482.
If the petition for specific performance is dismissed by the probate

ADJUSTMENT OF DEMANDS BY ARBITRATION OR COMPROMISE

Probate courts may authorize executors, administrators, guardians, and trustees to adjust, by arbitration or compromise, any demands in favor of or against the estates by them represented.[1] The executor or other officer who is desirous of so adjusting a claim should present a petition to the court setting forth the nature of the demand, and representing that it can be adjusted by arbitration or compromise, and that the interests of the estate represented by him will be promoted thereby. Any adjustment by arbitration or compromise, without leave of the court first obtained, would be at the risk of the executor or other person making it, and might give rise to questions upon the settlement of his accounts in the probate court.[2]

court, the petitioner cannot bring a new petition in the supreme judicial court His remedy is by appeal Luchterhand v Sears, 108 Mass 552.

The court has jurisdiction to decree specific performance by the representatives of a deceased husband of a written agreement made by him with his intended wife before marriage, in consideration of her past service to him and of the contemplated marriage, to convey land to her, reserving a life-estate therein to himself Miller v. Goodwin, 8 Gray, 542.

[1] R L c 148, § 13.

[2] Chadbourn v Chadbourn, 9 Allen, 173; Blake v Ward, 137 Mass. 94 See Tallman v. Tallman, 5 Cush. 325; Clarke v. Cordis, 4 Allen, 466; Ware v Merchants' National Bank, 151 Mass. 445.

If an administrator submits to arbitration a demand against the estate of his intestate, the award will be binding on him. Bean v. Farnam, 6 Pick 269

An award on a submission by a guardian, that the ward and infant heir shall pay an annuity to the widow in lieu of dower, is voidable, not void Barnaby v Barnaby, 1 Pick 221.

If land held by two persons as trustees is taken by a city for a

Controversies between different claimants to an estate in the hands of executors, administrators, guardians, and trustees, and between the persons claiming as devisees or legatees under a will and the persons entitled to the estate of the deceased under the statutes regulating the descent and distribution of intestate estates, may be settled by arbitration or compromise in the supreme judicial court.[1]

SALE OF STANDING WOOD AND TIMBER

"If the supreme judicial court or the probate court for the county in which the land lies finds that wood or timber, standing on land the use and improvement of which belongs, for life or otherwise, to a person other than the owner of the fee therein, has ceased to improve by growth, or ought for any cause to be cut, it may appoint a trustee to sell and convey said wood or timber, to be cut and carried away within a time to be limited in the order of sale, to hold and invest the proceeds thereof after paying therefrom the expenses of such sale, to pay over the income, above the taxes and other expenses of the trust, to the person entitled to such use and improvement while his right thereto continues, and thereafter to pay the

---

highway, an arbitration entered into between a lessee and one of the trustees only, in accordance with which the city pays a sum of money to the lessee, is void Boston v Robbins, 126 Mass. 384

[1] R L c 148, §§ 14-18 On a bill in equity under the statute to establish a compromise of a charitable devise for the benefit of a town, the attorney-general alone can represent those beneficially interested, and the inhabitants of the town cannot intervene by petition to oppose the compromise, or appeal from a decree settling its terms Burbank v Burbank, 152 Mass 254

A purchaser of standing wood and timber, after severing the trees from the land, has an irrevocable license to enter and remove them. Fletcher v Livingston, 153 Mass 388.

principal of the fund to the owner of such land If wood or timber has been cut as aforesaid, no more thereof shall be cut on such land by the person entitled to such use and improvement without permission from said court. Such sale, if authorized by a probate court, shall be made in the manner provided by law for the sale of real property by guardians; and if such sale is so authorized by the supreme judicial court, the trustees shall give to such person as the court shall designate a bond, for the use and benefit of the persons interested in the proceeds of the sale, with condition for the faithful discharge of the trust, and the court may from time to time remove the trustee, and appoint another in his stead."[1]

PURCHASE OF INTERESTS IN REAL ESTATE OF WARDS.

Probate courts, after notice to all persons interested, may authorize guardians to obtain by purchase the release and conveyance of a right of dower or of curtesy, homestead, life-estate, estate for years, or other interest, vested or contingent, held or owned by any person in or to any real property of their wards, and to make any contract concerning such rights or interests which may be necessary to effect such purchase.[2]

PROTECTION AND SUPPORT OF MARRIED WOMEN LIVING APART FROM THEIR HUSBANDS

When a husband fails, without just cause, to furnish suitable support for his wife, or has deserted her, or when the wife, for justifiable cause, is actually living apart from her husband, the probate court may, by its order on the petition of the wife, or, if she is insane, on

[1] R. L. c. 134, § 11   [2] R L. c. 145, § 32.

the petition of her guardian or next friend, prohibit the husband from imposing any restraint on her personal liberty for such time as the court shall in such order direct, or until the further order of the court thereon; and the court may, upon the application of the husband or wife or of her guardian, make such further order as it deems expedient concerning the support of the wife, and the care, custody, and maintenance of the minor children of the parties, and may determine with which of their parents the children or any of them shall remain; and may, from time to time, afterwards, on a similar application, revise and alter such order, or make a new order or decree, as the circumstances of the parents or the benefit of the children may require. The petition may be brought in the county in which either of the parties lives,[1] except

[1] A decree for the separate maintenance of a wife will be valid, even though the husband resides out of the State, if notice is served upon him. Blackinton v. Blackinton, 141 Mass. 435; Osgood v. Osgood, 153 Mass. 39.

It is no bar to an action under the statute that the wife has contracted for a valuable consideration, to release her husband from all claim by her on him for support, and to indemnify him from any such claim. Silverman v. Silverman, 140 Mass. 560.

A decree that the husband pay a sum in gross for all support of his wife in the future cannot be entered without the consent of all parties. Doole v. Doole, 144 Mass. 278.

On a petition brought under this statute the probate court cannot make a decree against the guardian of a spendthrift husband. Kavanaugh v. Kavanaugh, 146 Mass. 40.

If an attachment of a husband's real estate is made on a wife's petition for separate maintenance, the probate court to enforce the payment of an allowance to her for her support may issue successive executions until the property attached is exhausted, and the attachment will continue until that time. Downs v. Flanders, 150 Mass. 93.

An attachment of property of a husband by his wife, who is living apart from him, made less than four months prior to the first publica-

that, if the petitioner has left the county in which the parties have lived together and the respondent still lives therein, the petition must be brought in that county.

Upon the petition an attachment of the husband's property may be made as upon a libel for divorce, and the court may require the husband to pay into court for the use of the wife such sum of money as may enable her to maintain her petition. The court has power to enforce its decrees in the same manner as decrees are enforced in equity; and its decrees will have effect, notwithstanding an appeal, until otherwise ordered by the superior court.[1]

tion of notice of the filing of a petition in involuntary proceedings in insolvency against, will be dissolved by such proceedings. Place v. Washburn, 163 Mass 530

A decree of the probate court on a wife's petition for separate maintenance, adjudging that she is living apart from her husband for justifiable cause, is, while it remains in force, a bar to a libel for a divorce on the ground of desertion Miller v Miller, 150 Mass 111

A decree of the probate court that a wife is living apart from her husband for justifiable cause is not competent evidence in an action against the husband by a third person for the board of his wife and child, that the wife was living apart from him for justifiable cause, although the same cause which was the basis of the decree continued during all the time such board was furnished Barney v. Tourtellotte, 138 Mass 106.

The probate court has authority to order the respondent to appear by publication of notice, and to determine the length of time which shall elapse between the last publication and the return day. Osgood v. Osgood, 153 Mass. 38.

A wife who is actually living apart from her husband for justifiable cause can maintain a petition for separate support. even though at the time of her filing her petition he had no notice, express or implied, that she was so living. Smith v Smith, 154 Mass 262.

[1] R. L. c. 153, §§ 33-35, c. 162, § 19

The statute, so far as it provides that, when a wife is living apart from her husband for justifiable cause and he fails to support her, the court may make such order as it deems expedient for her support and for the maintenance of the minor children, is constitutional although

The court in which a libel for divorce is pending may, without entering a decree of divorce, cause the libel to be continued on the docket from time to time, and during such continuance may make orders and decrees relative to a temporary separation of the parties, the separate maintenance of the wife, and the custody and support of the minor children. Such orders and decrees may be changed or annulled as the court may determine, and shall, while they are in force, supersede any order or decree of the probate court under the provisions of section thirty-three of chapter one hundred and fifty-three, and may suspend the right of said court to act under the provisions of said section.[1]

SUPPORT OF MINOR CHILDREN UNDER GUARDIANSHIP.

The probate court may, upon the petition of a guardian entitled to the custody of his minor ward, during the life-

it makes no provision for a trial by jury Bigelow v. Bigelow, 120 Mass. 320.

The court has power to make an order for the separate support of a wife while living in the same house with her husband and performing some of the duties of a wife; and the statute is constitutional. Bucknam v Bucknam, 176 Mass 229

The probate court may properly require a man to contribute to his wife's support, although his only means of complying with the order is derived from a pension granted him by the United States. Tully v Tully, 159 Mass 91.

"Support" includes not merely board, but everything necessary to proper maintenance Gould v. Lawrence, 160 Mass 232.

A court of equity cannot decide whether a wife is living apart from her husband for justifiable cause; and a wife who has filed in the probate court a petition for separate maintenance, upon which no order for such maintenance has been granted, cannot maintain a bill in equity to reach property alleged to belong to the husband, and to hold it until such an order shall be entered Willard v Briggs, 161 Mass. 58; Brownell v. Briggs, 173 Mass. 529, 532.

[1] R L c 152, § 17

time of either or both of his parents, and after notice to all parties interested, order and require the said parents, or either of them, to contribute to the support and maintenance of such minor in such sums and at such times as it determines are just and reasonable. Such parent or parents may be required to give a bond conditioned to comply with such order and payable to the judge of said court and his successors in such sum and with such sureties as the court orders. The court may from time to time, upon application of either party, revise or alter such order or make such new order or decree as the circumstances of the parents or the benefit of the minor may require.[1]

The probate court has exclusive original jurisdiction of the petitions of married women concerning their separate estate, and of the petitions or applications concerning the care, custody, education, and maintenance of minor children.[2]

Appeals from the probate court, on petitions for separate support brought under section 33 of Rev Laws, c. 153, and petitions of married women concerning their separate estate, and petitions concerning the care, custody, education, and maintenance of minor children shall be taken to the superior court And such appeals, and the proceedings thereon, shall, so far as practicable, be the same as on appeals to the supreme judicial court.[3]

SALE AND RELEASE OF A WIFE'S INTEREST IN LANDS WHEN THE HUSBAND IS UNDER GUARDIANSHIP.

If the guardian of a married man is licensed to sell his ward's real estate, the wife of the ward may join with the guardian in the conveyance for the purpose of releasing her right of dower and the estate or right of homestead, in like

[1] R. L c 145, § 28.   [2] R L c 162, § 4.   [3] Ibid § 18.

manner as she might have done by joining in a conveyance thereof made by her husband if he had been under no legal disability.[1] If such guardian is licensed to sell the ward's interest in real estate of his wife, she may join with the guardian in the conveyance, and thereby convey her estate in the granted premises If the wife so releases her right of dower or an estate of homestead, or so conveys her own estate, the proceeds of the sale may be so invested and disposed of as to secure to the wife and to the minor children of the owner, if it is an estate of homestead, the same rights in the principal and the income thereof that she or they would have had therein if it had not been sold. An agreement between her and the guardian for securing and disposing of the proceeds or of any part thereof for the purpose aforesaid, if approved by the probate court for the county in which the guardian was appointed, or by the supreme court of probate upon appeal, or, in default of an agreement between her and the guardian approved as aforesaid, an order therefor made by the probate court is valid and binding on all persons interested in the granted property or in said proceeds, and may be enforced by the court or by an action at law.[2]

RELEASE OF CURTESY, DOWER, AND HOMESTEAD ESTATES BY GUARDIANS OF INSANE PERSONS

"The husband or wife of an insane person who desires to convey his or her real property absolutely or by mortgage may file a petition in the probate court describing such real

[1] The signature of any married woman under the age of twenty-one years, affixed by her to any instrument relating to the conveyance of land of her husband, shall have the same effect as if she were over that age St 1902, c 478.
[2] R. L. c 153, §§ 15–17.

property, and praying that the dower of the wife or an estate of homestead or a tenancy by the curtesy at common law or by statute of the husband therein may be released, and stating the facts and reasons why the prayer of the petition should be granted. The court may, after notice and a hearing, by a decree authorize the guardian of the insane person to make the release by joining in any deed or deeds, mortgage or mortgages of the whole or a part of such real property, to be made within five years after the decree by the husband or wife of the insane person or by a trustee for such husband or wife." [1]

" If the guardian of an insane husband is authorized under the provisions of the preceding section to release such tenancy by the curtesy and the probate court finds that a portion of the proceeds of such real property, or of an amount loaned on mortgage thereof, should be reserved for the use of such ward, it may order that a certain portion, not exceeding one-third of the net amount if it is in respect of the tenancy by the curtesy by statute, of the proceeds or amount actually realized from such sale or mortgage, exclusive of any encumbrance then existing on the property, shall be set aside and paid over to such guardian, who shall invest and hold it for the benefit of the husband during his life, if he survives his wife. The income of such portion shall be received and enjoyed by the wife during the life of her husband, or until otherwise ordered by the court for cause. If she survives him the principal shall upon his decease be paid over to her, but if she does not survive him, to her heirs, executors, or administrators." [2]

" If the guardian of an insane wife is authorized under the provisions of section nineteen to release the dower of

---

[1] R L c 153, § 19 [2] Ibid § 20

his ward, and the probate court finds that a portion of the proceeds of such real property, or of an amount loaned on mortgage thereof, should be reserved for the use of such ward, it may order that a certain portion, not exceeding one-third of the net amount of the proceeds or amount actually realized from such sale or mortgage, exclusive of any encumbrance then existing on the property, shall be set aside and paid over to such guardian, who shall invest and hold it for the benefit of the wife during her life if she survives her husband. The income of such portion shall be received and enjoyed by the husband during the life of his wife, or until otherwise ordered by the court for cause. If he survives her the principal shall, upon her decease, be paid over to him, but if he does not survive her, to his heirs, executors, or administrators "[1]

"If the guardian of an insane wife is authorized under the provisions of section nineteen to release an estate of homestead, and the probate court finds that a portion of the proceeds of the real property sold, or of an amount loaned on mortgage thereof, should be reserved for the use of the ward, it may order that a certain portion, not exceeding eight hundred dollars, shall be set aside and paid over to such guardian, to be invested in a homestead, and held by him for the benefit of his ward, if she survives her husband; the rent or use thereof to be received and enjoyed by the husband during the life of his wife, or until otherwise ordered by the court for cause; and the homestead to be his, and to be conveyed to him by said guardian, if he survives her."[2]

"If the husband or wife of an insane person conveys real property in trust without a power of revocation, and makes a provision therein for the insane husband or wife,

[1] R. L. c 153, § 21   [2] Ibid § 22.

respectively, which the probate court, upon petition, after notice and a hearing, finds is sufficient in lieu of curtesy or dower, the trustee may convey such real property free from all right of curtesy or dower." [1]

"The court, under the provisions of the preceding section, may find that the provision for the husband or wife is sufficient in lieu of curtesy or dowry either in the whole or in particular portions of the real property of the husband or wife, and thereupon the guardian of such insane husband or wife may be authorized to release the curtesy or dower in the whole or in particular portions thereof" [2]

"Proceedings in the probate court under the provisions of the six preceding sections shall, if the husband or wife of such insane person is an inhabitant of this commonwealth, be in the county in which he or she resides; otherwise in a county in which any of his or her real property is situated, and a certified copy of all final orders and decrees in such proceedings shall be recorded in the registry of deeds in every county or district in which such real property is situated." [3]

CONFIRMATION OF DEFECTIVE ACTS OR PROCEEDINGS OF PROBATE COURTS, OR OF PERSONS ACTING UNDER APPOINTMENT FROM PROBATE COURTS

"If the authority or validity of an act or proceeding of the probate court, or of a person acting as executor, administrator, guardian, or trustee, is drawn in question by reason of an alleged irregularity, defective notice, or want of authority, any party interested in or affected by such act or proceeding may apply to the probate court having jurisdiction of the subject-matter relative to which

[1] R. L. c. 153, § 23.   [2] Ibid. § 24.   [3] Ibid. § 25.

the act or proceeding has been had, and the court, after notice to all parties interested, and to the persons who may be the parents of such parties not in being, with power to appoint a guardian or next friend to represent the interests of any person unborn or unascertained, may hear and determine the matter and confirm the act or proceeding, in whole or in part, and may authorize and empower the executor, administrator, guardian, or trustee, or any successor or other person who may be legally appointed to act in the same capacity, to ratify and confirm such act or proceeding, and to execute and deliver such deeds, releases, conveyances, and other instruments as may be found necessary for that purpose, but no act or proceeding shall be ratified or confirmed which the court might not have passed or authorized in the first instance upon due proceedings."[1]

CONTRIBUTION AMONG DEVISEES AND LEGATEES.

"If a posthumous child, or a child or the issue of a child omitted in the will, takes under the provisions of section nineteen or twenty a portion of the estate of a testator, such portion shall be taken from all the devisees and legatees in proportion to and not exceeding the value of what they respectively receive under such will, unless in consequence of a specific devise or legacy or of some other provision of the will a different apportionment is found necessary in order to give effect to the testator's intention relative to that part of his estate which passes by his will."[2]

[1] R L c 148, § 24; Nott v Sampson Mfg. Co., 142 Mass 481
[2] R L c 135, § 25 For a case in which it was held that the share of a posthumous child should be taken from the residuary bequest in a will, see Bowen v Hoxie, 137 Mass. 527.

"If property which is given by will is taken from a devisee or legatee for the payment of the debts of the testator, all the other devisees and legatees shall, subject to the provisions of the following section, contribute their respective proportions of the loss to the person from whom such property is taken, so that the loss may fall on all the devisees and legatees in proportion to and not exceeding the value of the property received by each."[1]

"If the testator, by making a specific devise or bequest, has virtually exempted a devisee or legatee from liability to contribute with the others for the payment of the debts, or if by any other provisions in his will he has prescribed or required an appropriation of his estate different from that prescribed in the preceding section, his property shall be appropriated and applied in conformity with the provisions of the will, so far as such appropriation and application can be made without affecting the liability of his whole estate for the payment of his debts."[2]

"If a posthumous child, or a child or the issue of a child omitted in the will, takes under the provisions of section nineteen or twenty a portion of the estate of a testator, such portion of the estate shall, for the purposes of the two preceding sections, be considered as if it had been devised or bequeathed to such child or other descendant; and he shall contribute with the devisees and legatees, and be entitled to claim contribution from them, as before provided."[3]

"If a person who is liable to contribute according to the provisions of the three preceding sections is insolvent or unable to pay his just proportion of the contribution required, the other persons so liable to contribute shall be severally liable for the loss occasioned by such insol-

[1] R L c 135, § 26   [2] Ibid § 27   [3] Ibid § 28

vency, each one in proportion to and not exceeding the value of the property received by him from the estate of the deceased; and if a person who is so liable dies without having paid his proportion, his executors and administrators shall be liable therefor in like manner as if it had been his own debt and to the extent to which he would have been liable if living."[1]

"If the estate of a devisee under a will is taken for the tenancy by the curtesy of the husband, or for the dower of the widow, of the testator, all the other devisees and legatees shall contribute their respective proportions of the loss to the person from whom the estate is so taken, so that the loss may fall upon all the devisees and legatees in proportion to and not exceeding the value of property received by them under the will; but no devisee or legatee shall contribute if exempted therefrom by the provisions of the will."[2]

WRITS OF HABEAS CORPUS.

Any court which has jurisdiction of libels for divorce or for nullity of marriage, of petitions for separate support or maintenance, or of any other proceeding in which the care and custody of any child or children is drawn in question, may issue a writ of habeas corpus when necessary in order to bring before it such child or children. The writ may be made returnable forthwith before the court by which it is issued, and, upon its return, said court may make any appropriate order or decree relative to the child or children who may thus be brought before it.[3]

[1] R. L c 135, § 29.   [2] Ibid § 30   [3] St 1902, c 324.

CHAPTER XXI.

APPEALS FROM THE PROBATE COURT.

THE supreme judicial court is also the supreme court of probate, and has appellate jurisdiction of all matters determinable by the probate courts, and by the probate judges, except as otherwise expressly provided. The statute provides that "a person who is aggrieved by an order, sentence, decree, or denial of a probate court or of a judge of such court may, except as otherwise provided, appeal therefrom to the supreme judicial court."[1]

This provision of the statute applies to all decrees or orders of the probate court except appeals from decrees or orders on petition of married women for separate support brought under section 33, chapter 153, of the Revised Laws, and petitions of married women concerning their separate estates, provided for by sections 31 and 32 of said chapter, and petitions concerning the care, custody, education, and maintenance of minor children, provided for by section 37 of said chapter, are to be taken to the superior court, and all proceedings thereon shall, so far as practica-

---

[1] R. L. c. 162, §§ 8, 9 ; Swasey v. Jaques, 144 Mass. 135. Objection to the jurisdiction of the probate court can be taken only by way of appeal. Cummings v. Hodgdon, 147 Mass. 21.

An appeal lies from the decision of a judge of probate dismissing a petition for partition. Dearborn v. Preston, 7 Allen, 192.

The supreme court has no authority to issue a writ of certiorari to the probate court, or to annul or reverse a decree of that court otherwise than by appeal. Peters v. Peters, 8 Cush. 529.

ble, be the same as on appeals to the supreme judicial court.[1]

WHO ARE ENTITLED TO APPEAL.

The right to appeal depends upon the relations of the appellant to the subject-matter of the decree or other order. It is not limited to the parties directly connected with the proceeding in question, but is given to "any *person* aggrieved." Mere dissatisfaction with the decree gives no right to an appeal from it. But a person is aggrieved within the meaning of the statute whenever his rights are concluded or in any way affected by it.[2] He

---

[1] R. L. c. 162, § 18.

[2] One claiming property of a deceased person under a gift *causa mortis* is not affected by decrees of the probate court charging the administrator with the property and ordering it to be distributed to the next of kin, and cannot appeal from such decrees, though he appeared and produced witnesses in that court. Lewis *v.* Bolitho, 6 Gray, 137.

A testator bequeathed money to trustees to be managed as an accumulating fund for sixty years, and then to be paid to the town of N. or its agents, for the purpose of purchasing land within the town for a model farm. *Held*, that the town could appeal from a decree respecting the testator's will. Northampton *v.* Smith, 11 Met. 390.

From a decree of the probate court appointing a guardian to a minor child, the trustees of a fund bequeathed for the benefit of such child have no authority to appeal. Deering *v.* Adams, 34 Maine, 41.

A creditor of the estate of a deceased person cannot appeal from a decree refusing the petition of the administrator for leave to sell real estate of the deceased for the payment of debts. Henry *v.* Estey, 13 Gray, 336.

The stepmother of minor children whose parents are both dead cannot appeal from a decree appointing a guardian for the children. Lawless *v.* Reagan, 128 Mass. 592. Nor can the uncle and next friend of a *non compos* appeal from an allowance of the guardian's account, without showing himself to be heir or creditor. Penniman *v.* French, 2 Mass. 140; Boynton *v.* Dyer, 18 Pick. 4.

The creditor of a deceased person may appeal from the granting of

may be aggrieved when the rights and interests to be affected are those which he has in a representative administration Stebbins *v* Palmer, 1 Pick. 71. But a debtor cannot appeal. Swan *v* Picquet, 3 Pick. 443

The party appealing must have some pecuniary interest or some personal right which is immediately or remotely affected or concluded by the decree appealed from. Lawless *v* Reagan, 128 Mass. 592

A trustee may appeal from a decree refusing him leave to reopen his account and correct an error therein Dodd *v*. Winship, 144 Mass. 461.

If an appeal from a decree of the probate court appointing a person administrator of an estate, upon his petition alleging that he was next of kin, fails because the appellant does not prove that he is a party entitled to appeal, and is dismissed upon that ground only, the decree stands as if not appealed from; and it is within the power of the probate court, upon the petition of a public administrator, to revoke and annul that decree Cleveland *v* Quilty. 128 Mass 578.

A creditor cannot appeal from a decree appointing commissioners to receive and examine claims of creditors against the estate of a deceased person which has been represented insolvent, although the decree is made without notice to the creditors Putney *v* Fletcher, 140 Mass 596.

One entitled to a share in the reversion of a trust fund to be accounted for, can appeal from a decree allowing the executor's final account. Pierce *v* Gould, 143 Mass 234

The next of kin of an adopting parent who but for the adoption would be his heirs at law, may appeal from a decree dismissing a petition to revoke a decree of adoption on the ground of fraud practised on the court. Tucker *v* Fisk, 151 Mass. 574

An appeal from a decree of the judge of probate allowing the account of an executor, should be made by the executor or administrator of a residuary legatee where such a one is named in the will, and not by one entitled to a distributive share of the estate of such residuary legatee Downing *v* Porter, 9 Mass. 386.

The probate court, in passing upon the allowance of the account of a trustee under a will, may determine whether the trustee has accounted to the parties entitled to the income of the trust fund for the whole of the income ; and the question of the correctness of this determination is open on appeal New England Trust Co. *v* Eaton, 140 Mass 532

No appeal lies from a decree of the probate court ordering that the

capacity; an administrator *de bonis non* may appeal from the decree allowing the administration account of the original executor or administrator,[1] and an administrator appointed in another state, on the estate of a person there deceased, may appeal from the decree of a probate court in this state appointing an administrator here[2] One who has purchased lands of the heirs or devisees may be so interested as to appeal from a decree respecting the estate of the testator or intestate;[3]

account of an administrator be not allowed, because he has not charged himself with the amount due on a certain mortgage, but not ascertaining that amount, nor settling the account. Cook *v.* Horton, 129 Mass 527

In cases where there is a right of appeal from the probate court, the matter in controversy should be judicially heard and considered in the court below, and a *pro forma* judgment merely should not be entered. Parker *v.* Parker, 118 Mass 110, Heard *v.* Trull, 175 Mass. 239

The right of appeal to the superior court given to any boy convicted and sentenced by a judge of the probate court, extends to convictions and sentences by the judges of the probate court under the statutes of 1870, c. 359, and 1871, c 365 Kenney's Case, 108 Mass. 492

There can be no appeal from the action of the judge of probate authorizing an action to be brought in his name on an administration bond, for no decree by him is necessary Jones, Appellant, 8 Pick. 121 See Putney *v* Fletcher, 140 Mass 596, and cases cited

A widow of a testator has a right of appeal from the allowance of the will of her husband Dexter *v* Codman, 148 Mass 421. But on an appeal by one claiming to be the widow of a testator, the appellant, if the claim is disputed, must show to a reasonable certainty that she is the widow; otherwise the appeal will be dismissed for want of jurisdiction Pattee *v* Stetson, 170 Mass. 93.

[1] Wiggin *v* Swett, 6 Met 194 See Pierce *v* Gould, 143 Mass. 234

[2] Smith *v.* Sherman, 4 Cush 408; Martin *v* Gage, 147 Mass 204

[3] A purchaser of the reversionary interest in land of a deceased insolvent assigned to his widow as dower, may appeal from the decree of the probate court appointing an administrator *de bonis non* Bancroft *v* Andrews, 6 Cush 493

M died seised of land, one half of which descended to his daughter

and so may a creditor of the heir or devisee under some circumstances.[1]

MANNER OF ENTERING THE APPEAL.

Notice of the appeal must be filed in the registry of probate, and the appeal must be entered in the supreme judicial court within thirty days after the act appealed from. Upon the entry of the appeal, the appellant shall file a statement of his objections to the act appealed from A copy of such notice and of so much of the record of the

---

S, she married B, who survived her, and became tenant by the curtesy of said half of the land B conveyed his interest to C *Held*, that C could appeal from a decree allowing an account which showed a balance due to M's administrator, the land being liable to be sold to satisfy such balance Bryant *v* Allen, 6 N H 116.

Where a guardian was licensed to sell real estate of his ward, and the next of kin of the ward appealed on the ground that he, and not the ward, was the owner of the land, it was *held* that the question of title could not be settled in a probate court, and that the appeal could not be entertained Ayer *v.* Breed, 110 Mass 548

[1] When a will, by which the testator's land was devised, was allowed by the probate court, it was *held* that a creditor of one of the heirs at law of the testator was not entitled, merely as such, to appeal from the decree. Otherwise, if the creditor has attached such land at the time of the decree, and appeal claimed in an action against the heir. Smith *v.* Bradstreet, 16 Pick 264

The surety in a guardian's bond may appeal from a decree allowing the account of his principal Livermore *v* Bemis, 2 Allen, 394 And see Fairai *v.* Parker, 3 Allen, 556

If there is property of a testator not devised or bequeathed, his heir or next of kin may appeal from the allowance of the executor's account. Smith *v* Haynes, 111 Mass. 346.

A person aggrieved by the decree of the probate court on a petition by the executor of a will for instructions as to the construction of a will, may appeal Swasey *v* Jacques, 144 Mass 138; Green *v* Hogan 143 Mass. 462.

An appeal lies from a decree of the probate court dismissing a petition to revoke a decree of adoption on the ground of fraud practised on the court. Tucker *v.* Fisk, 154 Mass 574

probate court as relates to the appeal must be filed in the supreme judicial court upon the entry of the appeal, or as soon as may be thereafter

Notice of the entry of the appeal in the supreme judicial court must be given to all parties adversely interested who have entered appearances in the probate court, and it will be sufficient to serve the notice in the manner provided by the rules of court for the service of notices; but the court may order such further notice to be given as it may think fit

A person appealing from decrees settling different accounts of an executor, administrator, guardian, or trustee, may unite his appeals in one notice of appeal, and enter the same as one appeal in the supreme judicial court; and if an appeal shall be taken by any other person from any of the decrees, or from a decree made at the same time or previously, and settling any other account of such executor, administrator, guardian, or trustee, such appeal may be entered in the supreme judicial court as part of the matter comprised in the appeal previously entered. The court may deal with such different accounts upon appeal as if they formed one continuous account, and may give effect to any alteration that it may make in any account by altering the balance of the last account without altering the balance of any previous account.[1]

The supreme judicial court or the superior court may at any time, in its discretion and upon terms, consolidate any separate appeals from the probate court pending therein, respectively, and may thereafter deal with such consolidated appeals together or otherwise, as justice may require [2]

The party appealing is not required by statute to

[1] R L c 162, §§ 10-12.   [2] Ibid § 27

recognize or give any bond for the prosecution of his appeal.

An appeal from the decision of commissioners or of the probate court upon a claim against estates of deceased persons represented insolvent, must be claimed and notice thereof given within thirty days after the return of the commissioners or, when the court receives and examines the claims, within thirty days after the allowance or rejection of the claim; and the appeal must be entered either in the supreme judicial court (where it can be entered if the claim exceeds four thousand dollars in Suffolk County or one thousand dollars in any other county), or in the superior court, on the first Monday of the calendar month next succeeding the expiration of said thirty days

An appeal from the decision of a court of insolvency upon a claim against an estate in insolvency or upon the question of granting a discharge must be claimed and notice thereof given within ten days after the decision appealed from; and the appeal must be entered in the superior court for the county at the return day next after the expiration of fourteen days from the time of claiming it

Upon the entry of an appeal by a creditor, he must file a statement of his claim substantially as in a declaration in an action at law. Upon an appeal from a decision granting or refusing a discharge to an insolvent debtor, the superior court, upon written demand filed with the clerk by the debtor, the assignee, or a creditor, frames issues of fact to be tried by a jury; but if no such demand is made, the appeal is heard and determined by the court.[1]

[1] R L c 142, §§ 12, 13, c 163, §§ 45, 104, 105
No appeal lies to the superior court from a decree of the court of insolvency annulling a discharge granted to an insolvent debtor.

Proceedings when Appeal is omitted to be taken in Season. — The statute provides that if a person aggrieved omits to claim or prosecute his appeal, without default on his part, the supreme court of probate, or superior court in cases where it is provided by law that appeals shall be taken to the superior court,[1] if it appears that justice requires a revision of the case, may, on the petition of the party aggrieved and upon terms, allow an appeal to be entered and prosecuted. Such petition may be entered in the clerk's office at any time, and the order of notice thereon may be made returnable at a rule day [2] A copy of the record, attested by the register of probate, should be filed with the petition. Such appeal cannot be allowed without due notice to the party adversely interested, nor unless the petition therefor is filed within one year after passing the decree or order complained of, except that if the petitioner was without the United States at the time of passing the decree or order, he may file his

Pierce v. Keene, 173 Mass. 431. Nor from a decree making an allowance to an insolvent debtor. Kaffenburg v. Assuer, 163 Mass 295

One of two assignees in insolvency may appeal from an order granting the discharge of an insolvent debtor, where the refusal of his coassignee to join in the appeal appears of record Paul v Costello, 177 Mass 580

[1] Capen v Skinner, 139 Mass. 190

The entry should be made at the term at which leave is granted, and if not made until the second term held in the county after the leave is granted, it will be too late Robinson v Durfee, 7 Allen, 242

If the probate court upon the petition of a wife for separate support enters a decree by consent of both parties that the husband pay to the wife a sum in gross as the whole sum to which she is entitled by way of separate support, and the husband pays such sum to the wife, who gives a receipt for it and never offers to return it, she thereby waives her right to appeal from the decree upon the ground that the sum awarded is insufficient Doole v. Doole, 144 Mass. 278

[2] R L c 162, § 13

petition at any time within three months after his return, and within two years after the act complained of.[1] The appeal should be entered at the term at which leave is granted.[2]

EFFECT OF THE APPEAL

After an appeal is claimed and notice given at the probate office, all proceedings in pursuance of the act appealed from are stayed, except as otherwise expressly provided, until the determination thereof by the supreme court of

---

[1] R. L. c. 162, § 14, Capen v. Skinner, 139 Mass. 190, Briggs v. Barker, 145 Mass. 287, Daley v. Francis, 153 Mass 10. This provision does not authorize the entry of an appeal when the decree of the court below has been executed. After a widow has received the amount of an allowance, no appeal can be taken by her, nor allowed on her petition, from the decree making the allowance Hale v. Hale, 1 Gray, 522 See Pettee v Wilmarth, 5 Allen, 144

An heir at law who has notice of an appeal taken by another heir at law from the probate of a will and takes no steps towards prosecuting that appeal, cannot, after the expiration of thirty days, though within a year, from the decree, and after it has been affirmed by the supreme court, by consent of the first appellee, obtain leave to make a new appeal, under this statute, or to have the decree of affirmance set aside. Such heir might have petitioned to become a party to the appeal, or to enter an appeal in his own behalf, and then have prosecuted it to a final result, although the first appellant had withdrawn his appeal. Kent v. Dunham, 14 Gray, 279. See Livermore v Bemis, 2 Allen, 394; Jacobs v Jacobs, 110 Mass 229

[2] Robinson v Durfee, 7 Allen, 242 If an appellant who claims his appeal seasonably, gives due notice thereof, and duly files and serves upon the adverse party his reasons of appeal, omits through accident and mistake to enter his appeal in the appellate court, he is not entitled to maintain a petition to the appellate court for leave to enter the appeal, filed more than a year after the decree of the probate court was rendered Briggs v Barker, 115 Mass 287

The late entry of a probate appeal with the appellee's written consent during the time in which an entry is authorized to be made upon petition and notice, confers the same jurisdiction as if it had been seasonably entered. Daley v. Francis, 153 Mass 8

probate; but if, upon such appeal, such act is affirmed, it will thereafter be of full force and validity.[1] But if the appellant in writing waives his appeal before the entry thereof, proceedings may be had in the probate court as if no appeal had been taken

There is a great difference between the effect of an appeal from the decision of a probate court and an appeal from the judgment of other courts. An appeal from the

[1] R L c 162, § 16; Gale v Nickerson, 144 Mass 416. But in case of an appeal from a decree appointing a special administrator, he nevertheless proceeds in the execution of his duties until it is otherwise ordered by the supreme court of probate And an appeal from a decree making an allowance to the widow or children of the deceased, from the real or personal property in the hands of a special administrator, will not prevent the payment of the allowance if the petitioner gives bond to the special administrator, with sureties approved by the court, and conditioned to repay the same, if the decree is reversed R L c 137, §§ 9, 12

And a decree of the probate court or of a single justice of the supreme court of probate removing an executor, administrator, guardian, or trustee, and a decree of the probate court on petition of a wife who is living apart from her husband, for support, will have effect, notwithstanding an appeal, until otherwise ordered by the supreme court R L c 162, §§ 19, 20 After an appeal has been claimed from an order or decree referred to in the two preceding sections, and before such appeal has been finally determined, a justice of the supreme court of probate may suspend or modify such order or decree during the pendency of such appeal. Ibid § 22; Doole v Doole, 144 Mass. 280; Gray v Parke, 155 Mass. 437.

And an appeal from a final or interlocutory order or decree in equity of a probate court which is made in the exercise of any jurisdiction in equity conferred upon it, shall not suspend or stay proceedings under such order or decree pending the appeal But the probate court, or a justice of the supreme judicial court, in case of appeal, may stay all proceedings under such order or decree pending the appeal, and may make such orders as shall be necessary or proper to protect the rights of persons interested, pending the appeal , or may vary or discharge upon motion any such order of the probate court for a stay of proceedings, or for protection of any such rights. R L. c. 162, § 17.

judgment of other courts removes the cause itself to the appellate court, vacates the judgment of the lower court, and the appellate court renders judgment therein and enforces the judgment by it own process

The order or decree of the probate court is not vacated by an appeal, but is suspended ; and, upon being affirmed by the supreme court, it takes effect and operates as a decree of the probate court, and any intermediate action which may have been had under the decree is valid.

For example, when a will has been allowed by a decree of the probate court and the executor has given bond, and, upon appeal, the decree allowing the will is affirmed by the supreme court, the bond continues in force as if no appeal had been taken ; the authority of the executor being merely suspended during the pendency of the appeal; and, upon filing in the probate court a certified copy of the affirmance by the supreme court of the decree of the probate court, the executor can proceed in the discharge of his duties without giving a new bond and without other formalities.[1] Of course such certified copy of a decree of a single justice of the supreme court should not be filed until after the time has expired for appeal to the full court, unless appeal is waived.

THE PROCEEDINGS IN THE APPELLATE COURT.

Appeals and petitions for appeal are entered on a docket in the appellate court with cases in equity, and have the

[1] Dunham *v.* Dunham, 16 Gray, 577; Gale *v* Nickerson, 144 Mass 416.

But in case of an appeal from the decree of the probate court allowing a will, the two years within which an executor shall be held to answer to the suit of a creditor of the deceased begin to run from the date when the decree of the probate court is affirmed Smith *v.* Smith, 175 Mass 483

same rights as to hearing and determination as such cases.

The supreme judicial court may, upon appeal, reverse or affirm, in whole or in part, any decree or order of the probate court, and may enter such decree thereon as the probate court ought to have entered, may remand the case for further proceedings, or make any other order therein, as law and justice may require.

The supreme judicial court, upon request of a party to a probate matter pending therein, may in its discretion frame issues of fact to be tried by a jury and direct them to be tried in the supreme judicial court or in the superior court in the county in which the matter is pending or upon the request of all parties, in any other county.[1]

The appeal gives no jurisdiction to the appellate court to proceed in the settlement of an estate, but only to reconsider the order appealed from; and its judgment is carried into effect by the probate court, whose jurisdiction over the cause and the parties is not taken away by the appeal.[2]

A justice either of the supreme judicial court or of the superior court, or the full court, may, if necessary, hear

---

[1] R L c 162, §§ 15, 23, 25 Bridge v. Bridge, 146 Mass 377; Francis v Daley, 150 Mass. 383, Daley v Francis, 153 Mass 10

When a debt claimed by an executor or administrator as a debt due to him from the deceased is disputed on an appeal, either party or the court may have the claim submitted to a jury. R L. c. 141, § 7

In probate cases the framing of issues in the supreme court of probate rests in the discretion of the presiding justice, and his decision discharging an issue after a trial thereon before him will not be disturbed, in the absence of anything to show that he was wrong Fay v Vanderford, 154 Mass 498, Fiske v Pratt, 157 Mass 83; Doherty v. O'Callaghan, ibid. 90; McKay v Kean, 167 Mass 524, Parker v Simpson, 180 Mass. 234

[2] Dunham v Dunham, 16 Gray, 578, Gale v Nickerson, 144 Mass 416.

and determine cases pending in a county other than that in which such justice or court is sitting [1]

An appeal lies from the decision of a single judge of the supreme court of probate to the full court in matter of fact as well as of law.[2]

COMPLAINT FOR AFFIRMATION OF DECREE

If the appellant fails to enter and prosecute his appeal, the supreme court of probate may, upon the complaint of any person interested, affirm the former decree or order, or make such other order as law and justice require. Such complaint must be in writing, and should set forth the fact that the appeal was taken, and that the appellant has failed to enter and prosecute it, and pray for an affirmation of the decree and for an allowance of costs. With the complaint must also be filed a copy of the decree appealed from, and of the papers in the case attested by the register of probate.

If the appellant fails to enter his appeal within the time allowed by law, the probate court from which the appeal was taken may, upon petition of any person interested, and upon such notice to the appellant as the court shall order, dismiss the appeal and affirm the decree or order appealed from; and further proceedings may then be had in the probate court as if no appeal had been taken.[3]

[1] R. L. c 159, § 35, Ripley v Collins, 162 Mass 450
[2] Wright v Wright, 13 Allen, 207; Slack v Slack, 123 Mass 443
[3] R L c 162, § 24, Daley v Francis, 153 Mass. 10

If a master on an appeal from a decree allowing an executor's account declines to revise the compensation allowed to the executor, his report will be recommitted if the appellant so desires Bridge v. Bridge, 146 Mass. 373

On an appeal by one only of the persons interested in real estate from a decree of the probate court granting a license to sell it, the question of title, except so far as any doubt regarding it may affect

APPEALS FROM ALLOWANCE OF CLAIMS AGAINST INSOLVENT ESTATES OF DECEASED PERSONS.

Such appeal shall be claimed and notice thereof given at the registry of probate within thirty days after the

the expediency of the sale is not properly before the court, and if there is no waiver of the objection, cannot be determined. Walker v Fuller, 147 Mass 489

The date of a decree of the probate court, as recited therein, cannot be controlled by other evidence upon an appeal from the decree, but the party aggrieved should apply to that court to correct the error, if any. Newell v West, 149 Mass 520

An appeal in a probate matter from the final decree of a single justice of the supreme judicial court is thereupon pending before the full court, which upon a waiver of the appeal will affirm such decree. Gray v Gray, 150 Mass 56

In appeals to the full court from a decree of a single justice of the supreme judicial court in a probate appeal, his decision will not be reversed as to matters of fact, unless it clearly appears to be erroneous. Hodgdon v Cummings, 151 Mass. 293

Items of date later than a probate account are not to be brought before the supreme court of probate on an appeal in the first instance from a decree disallowing certain items in a guardian's account. May v Skinner, 152 Mass. 328.

On an appeal from a decree that an interest in real estate was personal property, and charging the executor with it, when the reason of appeal filed was that the executor was not charged to the full value of such interest, the executor was allowed to show that he was not chargeable with such interest to all. Harris v. Harris. 153 Mass 439

On the trial of a probate appeal, the appellant is restricted to the matters stated in the reasons of appeal filed in the case. Cowden v Jacobson, 165 Mass 241

A decree of distribution of the probate court can, on appeal, be revised after the executor has distributed the estate as ordered by the probate court, so as to enable one entitled to share in the estate, but who was omitted by mistake in the order of distribution and who is not chargeable with laches, to recover his share from those to whom the estate was distributed. Harris v. Starkey. 176 Mass. 445

As to rights of the legal representatives of an appellant dying while appeal is pending, see Bonnemort v. Gill, 167 Mass 338

return of the commissioners, or when the court itself receives and examines the claims, within thirty days after the allowance or rejection of the claim. If the appeal is by an executor or administrator, he shall give notice thereof to the creditor within said thirty days. The appeal shall be entered on the first Monday of the calendar month next succeeding the expiration of said thirty days.

Upon the entry of the appeal the supposed creditor shall file a statement in writing of his claim, setting forth briefly and distinctly all the material facts which would be necessary in a declaration for the same cause of action; and like proceedings shall be had in the pleadings, trial, and determination of the cause, as in an action at law; but no execution shall be awarded against the executor or administrator for a debt found due to the claimant. The appellate court shall have the same power as the probate court or the commissioners to examine the claimant, and the final judgment shall be conclusive, and the list of debts allowed shall be altered, if necessary, to conform thereto

After the claiming of such appeal, the parties may waive a trial at law and submit the claim to the determination of arbitrators to be agreed on by the parties and appointed by the probate court, and thereupon the appeal shall not be entered. The award of such arbitrators, if accepted by the court, shall be as conclusive as a judgment in a court of common law

The party prevailing upon such appeal shall be entitled to costs, which, if recovered against the executor or administrator, may be allowed to him in his administration account.

If a person whose claim has been disallowed by the commissioners or by the probate court, omits for other cause than his own neglect, to claim or prosecute his appeal as before provided, the supreme judicial court in any county, may, upon his petition therefor filed within two years after the return of the commissioners, and within four years after the date' of the administration bond, allow him upon terms to enter and prosecute his appeal.

The allowance of such appeal and the judgment thereon shall not disturb any distribution ordered before notice of the petition, or of the intention to present the same, has been given in writing at the registry of probate or to the executor or administrator; but any debt thus proved and allowed shall be paid only out of such assets as remain in or come to the hands of the executor or administrator after payment of the sums payable on such prior decree of distribution.[1]

[1] R. L c 142, §§ 12-17.

CHAPTER XXII.

ADOPTION OF CHILDREN AND CHANGE OF NAME

ADOPTION.

[Revised Laws, c 154]

"SECT. 1. A person of full age may petition the probate court in the county in which he resides for leave to adopt as his child another person younger than himself, unless such other person is his or her wife, husband, brother, sister, uncle, or aunt, either of the whole or half blood. If the petitioner has a husband or wife living, who is competent to join in the petition, such husband or wife shall join therein, and upon adoption the child shall in law be the child of both. If a person who is not an inhabitant of this commonwealth desires to adopt a child who resides here, the petition may be made to the probate court in the county in which the child resides."[1]

"SECT. 2. A decree for such adoption shall not be made, except as hereinafter provided, without the written

[1] At the trial of petitions to set aside decrees of adoption of two nieces and a nephew, the adopting parent being seventy years old and the adopted children being respectively forty-three, thirty-nine, and twenty-five years old, requests for rulings that it is not competent under the adoption law "for a person in the senile age of life to adopt persons in the prime and vigor of life," or "for an adoption to be made for the purpose of operating simply as and to take the place of a last will and testament," were rightly refused, although the court found that an important purpose of the adopting parent was to make the adopted persons his heirs at law. Collamore v. Learned, 171 Mass 99.

consent of the child, if it is above the age of fourteen years; of her husband, if she is a married woman; of the lawful parents, or surviving parent; of the parent having the lawful custody of the child, if the parents are divorced or are living separately, of the guardian of the child, if any; of the mother only of the child, if illegitimate; or of the person substituted for any of the above-named by the provisions of this chapter. A person whose consent is hereby required shall not thereby be debarred from being the adopting parent. If the child has been previously adopted, the consent of the previous adopting parent shall also be required."

"SECT. 3. The consent of the persons named in the preceding section, other than the child or her husband, if any, shall not be required if the person to be adopted is of full age, nor shall the consent of any such person other than the child be required if such person is adjudged by the court hearing the petition to be hopelessly insane, or is imprisoned in the state prison or in a house of correction in this commonwealth under sentence for a term of which more than three years remain unexpired at the date of the petition; or if he has wilfully deserted and neglected to provide proper care and maintenance for such child for two years last preceding the date of the petition, or if he has suffered such child to be supported for more than two years continuously, prior to the petition, by an incorporated charitable institution or as a pauper by a city or town or by the commonwealth, or if he has been sentenced to imprisonment for drunkenness upon a third conviction within one year and neglects to provide proper care and maintenance for such child; or if such person has been convicted of being a common night-walker, or a lewd, wanton, and lascivious person, and neglects to provide proper care and maintenance for such child. A giving up in writing of a child, for the purpose of adoption, to an incorporated charitable institution, shall operate as a consent to any adoption subsequently approved by such institution Notice of the petition shall be given to the state board of charity, if the child is supported as a pauper by a city or town or by the commonwealth "

"SECT. 4. If the written consent required by the provisions of the two preceding sections is not submitted to the court with the petition, the court shall order notice by personal service on the parties of a copy of the petition and order thereon, or, if they are not found within this commonwealth, by publication of the petition and order once in each of three successive weeks in such newspaper as the court orders, the last publication to be seven days at least before the time appointed for the hearing, and the court may require additional notice and consent."[1]

"SECT 5. If, after such notice, a person whose consent is required does not appear and object to the adoption, the court may act upon the petition without his consent, sub-

[1] Notice of a petition for the adoption of a child is necessary in all cases where the written consent required by section 2 is not submitted to the court with the petition, even if a case is presented by the petition, which, if proved to exist, would authorize the judge of probate to decree the adoption without consent. Humphrey, Appellant, 137 Mass 84

The probate court may decree the adoption of a child whose parents are unknown and are not brought within any of the exceptions of § 3, and who has no guardian, and who has not been given up in writing, for the purpose of adoption, to a charitable institution incorporated by law; and the probate court, after the notice required by § 4 has been given, may appoint a guardian *ad litem* for such child, with power to give or withhold consent to such adoption Edds, Appellant, 137 Mass. 346

Notice to the father of an illegitimate minor of an application for its adoption is not required Gibson, Appellant, 154 Mass 378.

ject to his right of appeal, or it may appoint a guardian *ad litem*, with power to give or withhold consent." [1]

"SECT. 6. If the court is satisfied of the identity and relations of the persons, and that the petitioner is of sufficient ability to bring up the child and provide suitable support and education for it, and that the child should be adopted, it shall make a decree, by which, except as regards succession to property, all rights, duties, and other legal consequences of the natural relation of child and parent shall thereafter exist between the child and the petitioner and his kindred, and shall, except as regards marriage, incest, or cohabitation, terminate between the person so adopted and his natural parents and kindred or any previous adopting parent; but such decree shall not place the adopting parent or adopted child in any relation to any person, except each other, different from that before existing as regards marriage, rape, incest, or other sexual crime committed by either or both. The court may also decree such change of name as the petitioner may request. If the person so adopted is of adult age, he shall not be freed by such decree from the obligations imposed by the provisions of section ten of chapter eighty-one." [2]

"SECT. 7. A person who is adopted in accordance with the provisions of this chapter shall take the same share of the property which the adopting parent could dispose of by

---

[1] If the parents of the child to be adopted are dead, and the probate court, on the petition of the guardian of the child for leave to adopt it, which is assented to by the petitioner as guardian, makes a decree in accordance with the prayer of the petition, the fact that no guardian *ad litem* was appointed, even if such appointment should have been made, does not make the decree void, but voidable only. Sewall *v.* Roberts, 115 Mass. 262.

[2] An adopted child acquires the settlement of its father by adoption. Washburn *v.* White, 140 Mass. 568.

will as he would have taken if born to such parent in lawful wedlock, and he shall stand in regard to the legal descendants, but to no other of the kindred of such adopting parent, in the same position as if so born to him. If the person adopted dies intestate, his property, acquired by himself or by gift or inheritance from his adopting parent, or from the kindred of such parent, shall be distributed according to the provisions of chapters one hundred and thirty-three and one hundred and forty among the persons who would have been his kindred if he had been born to his adopting parent in lawful wedlock; and property received by gift or inheritance from his natural parents or kindred shall be distributed in the same manner as if no act of adoption had taken place. The apportionment and distribution shall be ascertained by the court. A person shall not by adoption lose his right to inherit from his natural parents or kindred." [1]

" SECT. 8. The word *child*, or its equivalent, in a grant, trust-settlement, entail, devise, or bequest, shall include a child adopted by the settlor, grantor, or testator, unless the contrary plainly appears by the terms of the instru-

---

[1] An adopted child who is at the same time the grandchild of the adopting father cannot inherit the property of his grandfather in a twofold capacity as his son and as his grandson. Delano v. Bruerton, 148 Mass. 619.

A child by adoption is "issue" within R. L. c. 140, § 3. The general intent of the statute is to place the adopted child in relation to the adopting parents, so far as their property is concerned, in the same position that he would be if their natural child. Buckley v. Frasier, 153 Mass. 525.

A child who has been adopted by and has taken the name of the testator is not entitled to the same share of his estate as if he had died intestate, when by the will made before the adoption special provision is made for her by the name she then bore. Bowdlear v. Bowdlear, 112 Mass. 184.

ment, but if the settlor, grantor, or testator is not himself the adopting parent, the child by adoption shall not have, under such instrument, the rights of a child born in lawful wedlock to the adopting parent, unless it plainly appears to have been the intention of the settlor, grantor, or testator to include an adopted child." [1]

"Sect. 9. An inhabitant of another state, adopted as a child in accordance with the laws thereof, shall upon proof of such fact be entitled in this commonwealth to the same rights of succession to property as he would have had in the state in which he was adopted, except so far as such rights are in conflict with the provision of this chapter." [2]

"Sect. 10. If the child has been previously adopted, all the legal consequences of the former decree shall, upon a subsequent adoption, determine, except so far as any interest in property may have vested in the adopted child, and a decree to that effect shall be entered upon the records of the court."

"Sect. 11. The supreme judicial court may allow a parent who, upon a petition for adoption, had no personal notice of the proceedings before the decree, to appeal therefrom at any time within one year after actual notice thereof, if he first makes oath that he was not, at the time of filing such petition, undergoing imprisonment as speci-

[1] Wyeth v. Stone, 144 Mass 441.
The next of kin of an adopting parent who but for his adoption would be the heirs at law, may petition the probate court to annul the decree of adoption on the ground of fraud. Tucker v. Fisk, 154 Mass 574, Fiske v. Pratt, 157 Mass 83.

[2] Even though the wife of the adopting person has given no formal consent to the adoption, as is required by the statutes of this commonwealth. Ross v. Ross, 129 Mass. 243. See Foster v. Waterman, 124 Mass 592.

ADOPTION OF CHILDREN AND CHANGE OF NAME 485

fied in section three or that, if so imprisoned, he has since been pardoned on the ground of innocence or has had his sentence reversed."

["Whoever receives an infant under two years of age for adoption or for giving it a home, or for procuring a home or adoption for it, shall, before receiving the same, ascertain its name, age, and birthplace, and the name and residence of its parent or parents, and shall keep a record of the same and of the date of such reception. He shall forthwith upon the reception of said infant give notice in writing thereof to the state board of charity, and upon request of said board shall give information and render the reports concerning such infant required by it; and within two days after its discharge shall give notice in writing to said board of the discharge and disposal of such infant. Said state board may investigate the case, and, at any time previous to a decree of adoption, take any such infant into its custody, if in the judgment of said board the public interest and the protection of the infant so require."] [1]

CHANGE OF NAMES.

"SECT. 12. A petition for the change of name of a person may be heard by the probate court in the county in which the petitioner resides. No change of the name of a person, except upon the adoption of a child under the provisions of this chapter or upon the marriage or divorce of a woman, shall be lawful unless made by said court for a sufficient reason consistent with the public interests and satisfactory to it."

"SECT. 13 The court shall, before decreeing a change of name, require public notice of the petition to be given,

[1] R. L. c 83, § 11.

and any person may be heard thereon. It shall also require public notice to be given of the change decreed, and on return of proof thereof may grant a certificate, under the seal of the court, of the name which the person is to bear, and which shall thereafter be his legal name."

"SECT 14. Each register of probate shall annually in the month of December make a return to the secretary of the commonwealth of all changes of names made in the court of which he is register"

The secretary of the commonwealth shall at the close of each session of the general court collate and cause to be printed in one volume a list of the changes of names returned during the preceding year by the probate courts [1]

The secretary of the commonwealth was required by acts of 1884, c 249, to collate and cause to be printed in one volume all the special acts of this commonwealth heretofore passed authorizing changes of names of persons, and all the returns of changes of names heretofore published by virtue of the fourteenth section of the one hundred and tenth chapter of the General Statutes and the first section of the fourth chapter of the Public Statutes.

A child shall not be indentured, adopted, or placed in charge of any person from a state institution until notice of the application therefor has been given to the state board of charity, and until its report in writing, made after investigation into the propriety thereof, has been filed with such institution. All applications for the release or discharge of any children so indentured or placed in charge shall in like manner be given to the state board

[1] R. L. c 9, § 1.

for its report. The state board of charity shall seek out suitable persons who are willing to adopt, take charge of, educate, and maintain children arrested for offences, committed to a state institution, abandoned or neglected, and give notice thereof to the institutions, boards, officers or persons having authority so to dispose of said children.[1]

[1] R. L. c. 86, §§ 52, 53

CHAPTER XXIII.

MISCELLANEOUS PROVISIONS

SESSIONS OF THE PROBATE COURTS.

PROBATE courts shall be held in each year at the times and within the cities and towns hereinafter mentioned, in such places therein as the several judges shall from time to time appoint. Sufficient notice of such appointments shall be given by the judges, as often as changes take place, by advertisement in a newspaper or by posting the notice in public places:

For the county of Barnstable, at Barnstable, on the second Tuesday of January, February, March, May, June, July, August, September, November, and December, and on the first Tuesday of April and October.

For the county of Berkshire, at Pittsfield, on the first Tuesday of January, February, March, April, May, June, September, October, and December, on the third Tuesday of July, and on the Wednesday next after the first Monday of November; at Lee, on the Wednesday next after the first Tuesday of January, April, and October, and on the Wednesday next after the third Tuesday of July, at Adams, on the Thursday next after the first Tuesday of January and October, on the Wednesday next after the first Tuesday of March, and on the Thursday next after the third Tuesday of July; and at Great Barrington, on the Wednesday next after the first Tuesday of February, May, September, and December.

For the county of Bristol, at Fall River, on the first Friday of January, April, July, and October, on the third Friday of February, May, and November, and on the second Friday of September; at New Bedford on the first Friday of February, May, August, and November, and on the third Friday of March, June, and September; and at Taunton, on the first Friday of March, June, September, and December, and on the third Friday of January, April, October, and December.

For the county of Dukes County, at Edgartown, on the third Monday of January and July, and on the first Monday of March and December; at Vineyard Haven, on the third Monday of April, and on the first Monday of September; and at West Tisbury, on the first Monday of June, and on the third Monday of October.

For the county of Essex, at Salem, on the first Monday of each month and on the third Monday of each month except August, at Lawrence, on the second Monday of January, March, May, June, July, September, and November; at Haverhill, on the second Monday of April and October; at Newburyport, on the fourth Monday of January, March, May, June, July, September, and November; and at Gloucester, on the fourth Monday of April and October.

For the county of Franklin, at Greenfield, on the first Tuesday of each month except November, and on the third Tuesday of February, March, and December; at Orange, on the third Tuesday of January, April, July, and October; at Shelburne Falls, on the third Tuesday of May and November; at Northfield, on the third Tuesday of September, and at Conway, on the third Tuesday of June.

For the county of Hampden, at Springfield, on the first Wednesday of each month except August; at Holyoke, on the third Wednesday of January, March, June, and October; at Palmer, on the second Wednesday of February, May, and September, and the fourth Wednesday of November; and at Westfield, on the third Wednesday of February, May, September, and December

For the county of Hampshire, at Northampton, on the first Tuesday of each month; at Amherst, on the second Tuesday of January, March, June, August, and November; at Belchertown, on the second Tuesday of May and October, at Williamsburg, on the third Tuesday of May and October; and at Ware, on the second Tuesday of February, September, and December, and on the third Tuesday of June.

For the county of Middlesex, at Cambridge, on the first, second, and fourth Tuesday of each month, except August, and at Lowell, on the third Tuesday of each month, except August.

For the county of Nantucket, at Nantucket, on the Thursday next after the second Tuesday of each month.

For the county of Norfolk, at Dedham, on the first and third Wednesday, at Quincy, on the second Wednesday, and at Brookline, on the fourth Wednesday of each month except August. The county commissioners of the county of Norfolk may provide, furnish, and maintain suitable rooms and accommodations in the city of Boston for the use of the probate court for the county of Norfolk, for the hearing and trial of such contested cases in said court as the parties thereto or their counsel may desire to have heard and tried in the city of Boston

For the county of Plymouth, at Plymouth, on the second Monday of each month except August, and at Brockton, on the fourth Monday of each month except July.

MISCELLANEOUS PROVISIONS.

For the county of Suffolk, at Boston, on each Thursday except the first, second, fourth, and fifth Thursdays of August.

For the county of Worcester, at Worcester, on the first, second, third, and fifth Tuesday of each month except August, at Fitchburg, on the fourth Tuesday of each month except August.[1]

MISCELLANEOUS PROVISIONS CONCERNING JUDGES OF PROBATE.

In each county, except Suffolk and Nantucket, the judge and register of the probate court, and the clerk of the courts, shall be a board of examiners, and if two of said offices are held by the said person in any county, the sheriff shall be a member of the board.[2]

Judges of probate may, in case of a disagreement, determine the amount to be paid to a town of less than ten thousand inhabitants by the trustees or managers of an institution containing more than six inmates for the tuition in the public schools of a child between the ages of five and fifteen years, not theretofore resident in the town, and who is an inmate of such institution.[3]

Juvenile Offenders.

Boys under fifteen years of age may be committed to the Lyman school by police, district, and municipal courts and trial justices, and, except in the county of Suffolk, by judges of probate. Girls under seventeen years of age may be committed to the industrial school by said courts, judges, and justices, except as aforesaid, and, except in the county of Suffolk, by commissioners, appointed as provided in chapter 86, section 13, of the Revised Laws.

[1] R. L. c. 162, § 60.   [2] R L c. 11, § 254   [3] R L. c 44, § 4.

Judges of probate, except in the county of Suffolk, may receive complaints, issue warrants, and hear cases against juvenile offenders at such times or places, in or out of their respective counties, as convenience may require. The judge of probate may act in such case for the judge of any other county, whether absent or not, if so requested [1]

Judges of probate also have jurisdiction of complaints by parents, guardians, selectmen, or overseers of the poor for misconduct or neglect of the master, and by the master for gross misbehavior of one bound as an apprentice or servant.[2]

Registered Land.

The provisions of chapter 128 of the Revised Laws do not in any way affect or impair the jurisdiction of the probate court to license an executor or administrator or guardian to sell or mortgage registered land for any purpose for which a license may be granted in the case of unregistered land. The purchaser or mortgagee who takes a deed which is executed in pursuance of such license shall be entitled to a new certificate of title, or memorandum of registration.[3]

Commitment of Insane Persons and Inebriates.

A judge of the probate court may, within his county, commit to an insane hospital any insane person then residing or being in said county, who, in his opinion, is a proper subject for its treatment or custody.[4] Such judge may also commit to the Massachusetts hospital for dipsomaniacs and inebriates any male, or to a state insane hospital any male

---

[1] R L c 86, §§ 10, 12. [2] R L. c 155, § 11
[3] R. L c. 128, § 92. [4] R L. c. 87, § 33.

or female, who is addicted or subject to dipsomania or inebriety either in public or private.[1]

Appointment of Probate Court Officers.

The judges of probate for the county of Suffolk shall appoint an officer to attend the sessions of the probate court and court of insolvency, and may at any time, for a cause which they consider sufficient, remove him, and may fill any vacancy caused by removal or otherwise. Such officer shall give bond in the sum of one thousand dollars for the faithful performance of his duties, payable to the treasurer of the county of Suffolk, with sufficient sureties, who shall be approved by a judge of said court. Such officer may serve the orders, precepts, and processes issued by said courts or by a judge thereof

In addition to the officers whom the sheriff of the county of Middlesex is authorized by section 73 of chapter 165 to appoint, he may appoint, subject to the approval of the judges of probate and insolvency for said county, an officer who shall serve as a permanent court officer for attendance at the session of the probate court. Such officer shall serve the orders, precepts, and processes issued by said probate court or by either judge thereof.

The judges of probate and insolvency for the county of Middlesex may appoint a messenger for the courts of probate and insolvency of said county, may at any time remove him for a cause which is by them considered sufficient, and may fill a vacancy caused by a removal or otherwise. Said messenger shall wait upon said courts and perform such duties as the judges may direct.[2]

[1] R L c 87, § 59.   [2] R L c 164, §§ 33–35

[Revised Laws, c 172]

Actions by and against Executors and Administrators.

" SECT. 1. An action which would have survived if commenced by or against the original party in his lifetime may be commenced and prosecuted by or against his executor or administrator " [1]

[1] In addition to the actions which survive by the common law, the following also survive actions of replevin, tort for assault, battery, imprisonment, or other damage to the person, for goods taken and carried away or converted, or for damage to real or personal property, and actions against sheriffs for the misconduct or negligence of themselves or their deputies. R L c 171, § 1 If a person or corporation by his or its negligence, or by the gross negligence of his or its agents or servants while engaged in his or its business, causes the death of a person who is in the exercise of due care, and not in his or its employment or service, he or it shall be liable in damages in the sum of not less than five hundred, nor more than five thousand dollars to be assessed with reference to the degree of his or its culpability or of that of his or its agents or servants, to be recovered in an action of tort, commenced within one year after the injury which caused the death, by the executor or administrator of the deceased, one-half thereof for the use of the widow, and one half to the use of the children of the deceased, or, if there are no children, the whole to the use of the widow, or, if there is no widow, the whole to the use of the next of kin R. L c 171, § 2

For the provisions of law as to recovery of damages for injury resulting in death of an employee, with or without conscious suffering, see R L c 106, §§ 71-78, Cote *v* Lawrence Manuf. Co., 178 Mass. 295 These sections of the Revised Laws do not apply to injuries caused to domestic servants or farm laborers by fellow employees. R L c 106, § 79

Actions which survive.

For conversion of title deeds during lifetime Towle *v* Lovet, 6 Mass 394 Against sheriff for default of deputy in not returning execution. Paine *v* Ulmer, 7 Mass 317 For assault and battery Brown *v*. Kendall, 6 Cush 292 For taking land by eminent domain. Moore *v*. Boston, 8 Cush. 274. Against city for highway defect Demond *v*. Boston, 7 Gray, 544 For injuries causing insensibility and,

ACTIONS BY AND AGAINST EXECUTORS, ETC. 495

"SECT. 2. If an action of tort is commenced or prosecuted against the executor or administrator of the person shortly afterwards, death, but (except where action is brought by widow or next of kin, under provisions of R L c. 106, § 73, on account of injury resulting in instantaneous death of an employee or in his death without conscious suffering, or by the legal representatives under provisions of R. L c 106, § 72, on account of injury resulting in death not instantaneous of an employee, or in his death preceded by conscious suffering), only nominal damages can be recovered in the absence of conscious suffering Bancroft v Boston & Worcester Railroad Co , 11 Allen, 34, Mulchahey v Washburn Car Wheel Co., 145 Mass. 281 Against an apothecary for negligently selling a deadly poison. Norton v Sewall, 106 Mass 143. For mill-owner's obstruction of flowage by dam Brown v. Dean, 123 Mass 254. Against two severally liable, and also against two jointly liable, if one dies Colt v. Learned, 133 Mass 409, Tucker v Utley, 168 Mass. 415. For deceit in letting infected dwelling-house Cutter v. Hamlen, 147 Mass 471. For death of one domiciled in Massachusetts and killed in a railroad accident in Connecticut, and an administrator appointed in Massachusetts may sue there to recover damages under a Connecticut statute Higgins v Central New England & Western Railroad Co , 155 Mass 176 see also Mulhall v Fallon, 176 Mass. 266, 268. By corporation for fraudulent misconduct of its deceased president Warren v Para Rubber Shoe Co , 166 Mass 97 Against officer of a corporation for misappropriation of corporate property. Winebuigh v. United States Steam & Street Railway Advertising Co , 173 Mass 60 For injury to person and property from assault by dogs. Wilkins v Wainwright, 173 Mass 212 For redemption of land from tax sale Clark v. Lancy, 178 Mass. 460. For assault on account of ejecting in an improper manner an obnoxious passenger from a street railway car Hudson v Lynn & Boston Railroad, 178 Mass 64 In equity to rescind and set aside a contract procured by the fraud and undue influence of defendant by reason of which defendant's mother conveyed to him substantially all of her property. Parker v. Simpson, 180 Mass. 334, 343.

Actions which do not survive

Against assignee of a bankrupt. Hall v. Cushing, 8 Mass. 521. Against deputy for negligent levy. Cravath v Plympton, 13 Mass 453 For stockholder's liability for corporate debts Child v. Coffin, 17 Mass 64; Ripley v Sampson, 10 Pick. 371; Dane v Dane Manuf. Co , 14 Gray, 488, Bacon v Pomeroy, 104 Mass. 577 (For history

originally liable, the plaintiff shall be entitled to recover only for the value of the goods taken, or for the damage actually sustained, without vindictive or exemplary damages, or damages for any alleged outrage to the feelings of the injured party."

"SECT. 3. If the executor or administrator of a trustee, carrier, depositary, or other person who claimed only a special property in goods which he held for the use and benefit of another recovers such goods, or damages for the

of the law relative to liability of stockholders in Massachusetts corporations, see Child v. Boston & Fairhaven Iron Works, 137 Mass 516, 517.) For breach of promise when no special damage is shown, or where averment of special damage is insufficient Stebbins v Palmer, 1 Pick 71; Smith v Sherman, 4 Cush 408, Chase v. Fitz, 132 Mass 359 Of debt for cutting and carrying off trees Little v Conant, 2 Pick 527 For diverting water-course Holmes v Moore, 5 Pick 257. For fraudulent recommendation of trader. Read v Hatch, 19 Pick 47 For libel, even though causing loss of a valuable office. Walters v Nettleton, 5 Cush. 544; Cummings v. Bird. 115 Mass 346. For malicious prosecution Nettleton v Dinehart, 5 Cush 543, Conly v Conly, 121 Mass 550 For deceit in sale of poisoned grain Cutting v Tower, 14 Gray, 183 For fraud in getting verdict set aside. Leggate v. Moulton, 115 Mass 552 For fraudulent representations, inducing disposal of land Leggate v Moulton, *supra*. For injuries causing instant death, (except when action is brought under Employers' Liability Act, now R L c 106, §§ 71-79) Moran v Hollings, 125 Mass 93 Against railroad company for injury to brakeman falling from train, if evidence fails to show how he fell, what he was doing, whether death was instantaneous, or whether there was conscious suffering Corcoran v. Boston & Albany Railroad Co., 133 Mass. 507, Murphy v. Same, 167 Mass 64 In equity for false representations of a trustee, unless his personal representatives received an estate benefited by his fraud, or unless he held a fiduciary relation to the person defrauded Houghton v Butler, 166 Mass 547 For enforcing the agreement of a deceased person to manage the business of manufacturing a patented article and to advance all funds requisite, but to look to the business for repayment Marvel v Phillips, 162 Mass 399.

An administrator cannot, on death of his intestate, be made a party to a petition for partition Richards v. Richards, 136 Mass 126.

taking or detention thereof, in an action of replevin or tort, the goods or money recovered shall not be assets in his hands, but shall, after deducting the costs and expenses of the action, be paid over and delivered to the person for whose use and benefit they were so held or claimed by the deceased person."

"SECT. 4. If judgment for a return in an action of replevin is rendered against an executor or administrator, the property returned by him shall not be assets in his hands; and if it has been included in the inventory, the executor or administrator shall be allowed therefor in his account if he shows that it has been returned in pursuance of such judgment."

"SECT 5. Writs of attachments and executions against executors or administrators for debts due from the deceased testator or intestate shall run only against the goods and estate of the deceased in their hands, and not against their bodies, goods, or estate." [1]

"SECT. 6 If a judgment for costs is rendered against an executor or administrator in an action commenced by or against him or in an action commenced by or against the testator or intestate, wherein the executor or administrator has appeared and taken upon himself the prosecution or defence, he shall be personally liable for the costs, and the execution shall be awarded against his body, goods, and estate, as if it were for his own debt. Costs paid by him shall be allowed in his account unless the probate court determines that the action was prosecuted or defended without reasonable cause." [2]

[1] Cooke v Gibbs, 3 Mass 193; Dana v. Wentworth, 111 Mass 291, Harmon v Osgood, 151 Mass. 501

[2] Look v. Luce, 136 Mass 249, 140 Mass. 461, Perkins v. Fellows, 136 Mass. 294

"SECT. 7. If the judgment is for debt or damages and costs, an execution for the debt or damages shall be awarded against the goods and estate of the deceased in the hands of the executor or administrator, and another execution for the costs against the goods, estate, and body of the executor or administrator, as if it were for his own debt."[1]

"SECT. 8. Upon the return unsatisfied of an execution against an executor or administrator for a debt due from the estate of the deceased, the court may, upon a suggestion by the creditor of waste, issue a writ of *scire facias* against the executor or administrator. If the defendant does not appear and show sufficient cause to the contrary, he shall be found guilty of waste and shall be personally liable for the amount thereof, if it can be ascertained, otherwise for the amount due on the original judgment, with interest from the time when it was rendered, and judgment and execution shall be awarded as for his own debt."[2]

"SECT. 9. If an executor or administrator dies or is removed from office during the pendency of an action to which he is a party, the suit may be prosecuted by or against the administrator *de bonis non* in like manner as if commenced by or against such last administrator;[3] and the provisions of the preceding chapter relative to the appearance or citation of an administrator and relative to a non-suit or default shall apply to such administrator *de bonis non.*"

---

[1] Yarrington *v* Robinson, 141 Mass. 450 ; Gibbs *v.* Taylor, 143 Mass 187, McKim *v* Haley, 173 Mass 112

[2] Shillaber *v.* Wyman, 15 Mass 322; Jenkins *v.* Wood, 134 Mass. 117, 140 Mass 66, 144 Mass. 238 , Fuller *v* Connelly, 142 Mass 230.

[3] Brown *v.* Pendergast, 7 Allen, 427.

"SECT. 10. If an executor or administrator dies or is removed after judgment has been rendered either for or against him, the court may issue a writ of *scire facias* in favor of or against the administrator *de bonis non*, and a new execution may be issued in like manner as it may be done in favor of or against an original executor or administrator, in case of the death of his testator or intestate after a judgment rendered for or against him; except that a judgment against the first executor or administrator for costs for which he was personally liable shall be enforced only against his executor or administrator and not against the administrator *de bonis non.*"

"SECT. 11. If a judgment is rendered for or against an executor or administrator, a writ of error may be brought thereon by or against an administrator *de bonis non* in like manner as it might have been brought by or against the executor or administrator who was party to the judgment." [1]

[Revised Laws, c 189]

Trustee Process against Executors and Administrators.

"SECT. 20. Debts, legacies, goods, effects, or credits due from or in the hands of an executor or administrator as such, may be attached in his hands by the trustee process." [2]

[1] Brown v. Pendergast, 7 Allen, 427.
[2] Holbrook v. Waters, 19 Pick 354; Wheeler v Bowen 20 Pick 563; Hoar v. Marshall, 2 Gray, 251. Boston Bank v Minot, 3 Met 507, Cady v Comey, 10 Met 459; Davis v Davis, 2 Cush 111, Stills v Harmon, 7 Cush 406, Carson v Carson, 6 Allen, 397, Vantine v. Morse, 104 Mass 275, Nickerson v Chase, 122 Mass 296, Capen v Duggan, 136 Mass 501; Allen v Edwards, 136 Mass. 138; Emery v. Bidwell, 140 Mass. 271; Mechanics' Savings Bank v Waite, 150 Mass. 234, Harmon v Osgood, 151 Mass 501

"Sect. 50. If a person who is summoned as trustee in his own right dies before the judgment recovered by the plaintiff has been fully satisfied, the goods, effects, and credits in his hands at the time of the attachment shall remain bound thereby, and his executor or administrator shall be liable therefor as if the writ had been originally served on him."

"Sect 51. If a person who is so summoned dies before judgment in the original action, his executor or administrator may appear voluntarily, or may be cited to appear as in other cases. The further proceedings shall then be conducted in the same manner as if the executor or administrator had been originally summoned as a trustee, except that the examination of the deceased, if any has been filed, shall have the same effect as if he was living."

"Sect. 52 If the executor or administrator does not appear, the plaintiff, instead of suggesting the death of the trustee, may take judgment against him by default or otherwise as if he were living, and the executor or administrator shall pay upon the execution the amount which the deceased would have been liable to pay to the defendant, and shall be thereby discharged for the amount so paid If he does not voluntarily pay the amount in his hands, the plaintiff may proceed against him by a writ of *scire facias.*"[1]

"Sect 53. If a person who is summoned as trustee dies after judgment in the original action, his executor or administrator may pay upon the execution the amount which the deceased would have been liable to pay were he living, and he shall be discharged from all further demands on account thereof in the manner before mentioned. If he refuses to make such payment, the plaintiff may proceed against him by a writ of *scire facias*"

[1] Guptill *v.* Ayer, 149 Mass. 51.

"SECT. 54. If a person, against whom as trustee execution issues, is not living at the expiration of thirty days after final judgment in the trustee process, a demand, for the purpose of holding the attachment, may be made upon the executor or administrator of such deceased person at any time within thirty days after his appointment, and shall have the same effect as if made within thirty days after the judgment."

"SECT. 55 If an executor or administrator as such is adjudged a trustee, the execution shall not be served on his own goods or estate nor on his person, and he shall be liable for the amount in his hands only in like manner and to the same extent as he would have been liable to the defendant if there had been no trustee process."

"SECT. 56. If, after final judgment against an executor or administrator for a sum certain due from him as trustee, he neglects to pay the same, the original plaintiff in the trustee process shall have the same remedy for recovering the amount, either upon a suggestion of waste or by a suit on the administration bond, as the defendant in the trustee process would have had upon a judgment recovered by himself for the same demand against the executor or administrator"

Annual Returns of Shares in Corporations by Guardians.

A guardian who holds, or whose ward holds, shares of stock in any corporation, including banks located in the commonwealth liable to taxation, and an executor, administrator, trustee, or other person who holds in trust any such stock, shall annually, between the first and tenth day of May, return under oath to said commissioner the names and residences, on the first day of that month, of themselves and of all such wards or other persons to whom any portion of the income from such stock is payable, the number of shares of stock so held, and the name and location of the corporation.[1]

Rights of Executors to Vote at Corporation Meetings.

An executor, administrator, guardian, conservator, or trustee shall represent the shares of his trust at all meetings of the corporation, and may vote as a stockholder.[2]

Liability of Executors for Corporation Stock.

The estates and funds in the hands of executors, administrators, guardians, conservators, or trustees shall be liable to no greater extent than the testator, intestate, ward, or person interested in the trust fund would have been, if living and competent to act and hold stock in his own name.[3]

Right of Trustees or Guardians to release Damages for Land taken by Railway Companies.

When the lands or other property of a person under guardianship, or lands held in trust, are taken for the use of a railroad, the guardian or trustee may release all damages, in like manner as if the same were held in his own right.[4]

EMBEZZLEMENT BY TRUSTEES, ETC.

A trustee under an express trust created by a deed, will, or other instrument in writing, or a guardian, executor, or administrator, or any person upon or to whom such a

---

[1] R. L c 14, § 8. [2] R. L. c 109, § 17.
[3] R L c 110, § 64 As to liability of stockholders of trust companies and of mortgage loan and investment companies, see R. L. c 116, § 30; c. 117, § 11.
[4] R L c. 111, § 110.

trust has devolved or come, who embezzles or fraudulently converts or appropriates money, goods, or property held or possessed by him for the use or benefit, either wholly or partially, of some other person or for a public or charitable purpose, to or for his own use or benefit or the use or benefit of any person other than such person as aforesaid, or for any purpose other than such public or charitable purpose as aforesaid, or who otherwise fraudulently disposes of or destroys such property, shall be guilty of larcency, and shall be punished by imprisonment in the state prison for not more than ten years or by a fine of not more than two thousand dollars and imprisonment in jail for not more than two years [1]

Privileges and Discharge of Persons committed to Insane Hospitals.

An attorney at law, regularly retained by or on behalf of any person committed to an insane hospital, asylum, or receptacle for the insane, shall be admitted to visit his client at all reasonable times, if, in the opinion of the superintending officer of such hospital, asylum, or receptacle, such visit would not be injurious to such person, or if a justice of the supreme judicial court, or of the superior court, or a judge of probate in any county first orders in writing that such visits be allowed.

Two of the trustees of a state insane hospital, on application in writing or of their own motion, or a justice of the supreme judicial court in any county, or the judge of probate for the county in which the hospital is situated or in which the patient had his residence at the time of his commitment or admission, on such application, and after such notice as the said trustees or judge may consider

[1] R. L. c 208, § 48.

reasonable and proper, may discharge any person confined therein, if it appears that he is not insane, or if insane, will be sufficiently provided for by himself, his guardian, relatives, or friends, or by the city or town liable for his support, or that his confinement therein is not longer necessary for the safety of the public or his own welfare.[1]

Special Trust Funds for Parks, Cemeteries, etc.

Any savings bank or institution for savings may receive on deposit to any amount funds in trust for the purpose of setting out shade-trees in streets and parks, and improving the same; for purchasing land for parks, and improving the same; for maintaining cemeteries or cemetery lots; or for erecting and maintaining drinking fountains in public places. Such funds shall be placed on interest in such corporation, and the interest and dividends arising therefrom shall be paid semi-annually to such city, town, or cemetery authorities as may be designated by the donors of said funds, or by the will of the person bequeathing the same, and shall be expended by such authorities within their respective cities, towns, or cemeteries for any or all of said purposes as may be specified by such donors or such will. No part of the principal of such funds shall be withdrawn or expended, and the same shall be exempt from attachment or levy on execution.

A judge of probate, after notice and a hearing, may authorize an executor, administrator, or trustee holding money or other personal property for any of the purposes above mentioned, to deposit such moneys or the avails arising from such personal property, in any such corporation designated by the judge, to be held by it in the manner and for the uses and purposes above mentioned, and upon

[1] Pub. Stats. c. 87, §§ 82, 91.

the trusts upon which said executor, administrator, or trustee held the same; and upon the deposit of such money and its receipt and acceptance by such corporation, the executor, administrator, or trustee shall be discharged from further care and responsibility therefor.[1]

Fees of Witnesses in Probate Courts.

The fees for attending as a witness in a civil case in the probate court or court of insolvency, or to persons, except the debtor, who are examined under the provisions of section 82 of chapter 163 of the Revised Laws as to the dealings and property of an insolvent debtor, unless fraudulent conduct is charged and proved against them, are one dollar and fifty cents a day; for attendance in a criminal case, one dollar and twenty-five cents a day, for attending on any other occasion for which no express provision is made, fifty cents a day; and in all cases five cents a mile for travel out and home. Each witness must certify in writing the amount of his travel and attendance [2]

[1] R. L. c. 113, §§ 42, 43; Gates v. White, 139 Mass 353, Abbott v. Cottage City, 143 Mass 525, Green v Hogan, 153 Mass. 462, Bartlett, Petitioner, 163 Mass 507, 513; Morse v. Natick, 176 Mass. 510, 513

[2] R. L. c. 204, § 21.

CHAPTER XXIV.

TAXATION OF COLLATERAL LEGACIES AND SUCCESSIONS.

[Revised Laws, c 15]

"SECT 1. All property within the jurisdiction of the commonwealth, corporeal or incorporeal, and any interest therein, whether belonging to inhabitants of the commonwealth or not, which shall pass by will, or by the laws regulating intestate succession, or by deed, grant, sale, or gift, made or intended to take effect in possession or enjoyment after the death of the grantor, to any person, absolutely or in trust, except to or for the use of the father, mother, husband, wife, lineal descendant, brother, sister, adopted child, the lineal descendant of any adopted child, the wife or widow of a son, or the husband of a daughter, of a decedent, or to or for the use of charitable, educational, or religious societies or institutions, the property of which is by law exempt from taxation, or to a city or town for public purposes, shall be subject to a tax of five per cent of its value, for the use of the commonwealth; and administrators, executors, and trustees, and any such grantees under a conveyance made during the grantor's life, shall be liable for such taxes, with interest, until the same have been paid;[1] but no bequest, devise, or distributive share of

---

[1] DEFINITION AND HISTORY OF INHERITANCE AND SUCCESSION TAXES

The inheritance, legacy, or succession tax may be defined as an excise or bonus imposed by the state or government upon the privilege of taking or receiving the property of a decedent by devise, descent,

an estate, unless its value exceeds five hundred dollars, shall be subject to the provisions of this chapter." [1]

or distribution, whether such property passes to lineal or collateral heirs or to strangers to the blood The right to impose the tax rests upon the constitutional power of the government or state, as a sovereign, to change or to repeal the laws governing the transmission of property by will or descent The public contribution which death duties exact is predicated on the passing of property as the result of death, as distinct from a tax on property disassociated from its transmission or receipt by will or as the result of intestacy. Such taxes were known to the Roman law and were the ancient law of the continent of Europe. In England inheritance and legacy taxes are described under the term "Death Duties" In Hanson's Death Duties, p 1, it is said "Historically, probate duty is the oldest form of death duty, having been established in 1694" This probate duty was a fixed tax, dependent on the amount of the personal estate, and payable by means of stamp duties on the grant of letters of probate In 1780 this tax was supplemented by what became known as a legacy tax

Legacy and succession taxes have been imposed by various acts of the Congress of the United States. The earliest act of Congress imposing a legacy tax was that of July 6, 1797, 1 Stat at Large, c 11, which continued in force until June 30, 1802 The next act imposing a legacy tax was the act of July 1, 1862, c. 119, which was followed by the act of June 30, 1864 The act last cited was repealed by the act of July 11, 1870, which took effect October 1, 1870 Legacy and succession taxes were again imposed by Congress by the "War Revenue Act," so called, passed during the war with Spain, and being the act of June 13, 1898 c. 448, which was repealed, so far as these taxes are concerned, by the act of April 12, 1902, c 500, which took effect July 1, 1902, except as to collection of and lien for any taxes unpaid

---

[1] The exemption of bequests not exceeding five hundred dollars and of bequests to towns for any public purpose was first made by St 1895, c 307 Before the passage of this statute, it was decided in Essex v Brooks, 164 Mass 79, that a legacy to a town for the establishing and maintaining of a public library was not subject to the tax

The exemption of bequests not exceeding five hundred dollars does not apply to legacies to which persons became entitled before St. 1895, c. 307, took effect. Howe v Howe, 179 Mass 546

"SECT 2 If a person bequeaths or devises property to or for the use of a father, mother, husband, wife, lineal

when the repealing act took effect The act of June 13, 1898, was substantially a re-enactment of the provisions of the act of June 30, 1864 so far as it relates to legacy and succession taxes, and it imposed a tax both on property passing to lineal heirs and also on property passing to collateral heirs and others, the tax being a graded one and increasing in proportion to the value of the property and to the remoteness of the relationship to the decedent, all legacies or property passing by will or by law to a husband or wife, and all legacies or distributive shares of personal property not exceeding $10,000 in value passing to other persons, being exempt from the tax. In Knowlton v. Moore, 178 U. S. 41, it was held that the amount of each particular legacy or distributive share, and not the sum of the whole personal estate of a decedent, was the amount on which the tax is imposed and by which the rate is measured

A law imposing legacy and inheritance taxes was first enacted in the United States in Pennsylvania in 1826. This was followed by the enactment of similar laws in Maryland in 1844; Delaware, 1869, West Virginia, 1887, Connecticut, New Jersey, Ohio, Maine, and Massachusetts, 1891, Tennessee in 1891 and repealed in 1893, and in California, Colorado, Minnesota, and other States.

The first act passed in Massachusetts which imposed a tax on collateral inheritances and successions was chapter 425 of the acts of 1891.

Pennsylvania received from this tax in 1892 over $1,110,000, and New York received in the same year over $1,786,000 New York imposes a small tax on property passing to direct heirs other than husband or wife, and a larger tax on property passing to others The Illinois law is similar to that of New York in this respect

Massachusetts has received from the collateral inheritance and succession tax, exclusive of interest, the following amounts for the years named, to wit· 1892, $13,854, 1893, $59,419; 1894, $239,368, 1895, $419,177; 1896, $275,573, 1897, $501,360, 1898, $563,672; 1899, $478,758; 1900, $397,939, 1901, $506,093 In 1901 the expense of collection, including the compensation of appraisers, charges of the various registers of probate and the salary of the legacy tax clerk, was $2,316 There was also received in 1901 for interest $8,043

It is strongly urged that the laws imposing taxes on personal property should be repealed, except as to the taxes imposed on corporations, and that a small excise should be laid on property of a decedent

descendant, brother, sister, an adopted child, the lineal descendant of an adopted child, the wife or widow of a

passing to all persons other than the husband or the wife, and that such an excise would not be burdensome, that it would be equitable, and that it would yield as much as is now derived from the existing system, or lack of system, or taxing personal property in Massachusetts

An excellent history of inheritance and legacy taxes can be found in the second edition of Dos Passos on Inheritance Tax Law, and also in Hanson's Death Duties and Dowell's History of Taxation, vol 3.

CONSTITUTIONALITY OF THE TAX

a Under Acts of Congress

In Scholey v. Rew, 23 Wall. 331, the act of June 30, 1864, was held to be constitutional and valid, and a similar decision was made in the case of Knowlton v Moore, 178 U S 41, as to sections 29 and 30 of act of June 13, 1898, being the sections imposing a legacy and succession tax and providing for its collection. The case last cited is a very carefully considered one, and the opinion of the court contains an elaborate review of the authorities. In this case it was held that the taxes upon legacies and distributive shares of personal property imposed by the "War Revenue Act" are imposed upon the transmission or receipt of such inheritances and legacies and not upon the property itself, that the direct taxes which must be apportioned under U S Constitution, Art 1, § 10, do not include the tax on the transmission or receipt of legacies or distributive shares of personal property imposed by said act, as that tax is a duty or excise, as distinguished from a tax on property; that the uniformity required by U. S Constitution, Art 1, § 9, providing that "duties, imposts, and excises shall be uniform throughout the United States," is not an intrinsic uniformity relating to the inherent character of the tax as respects its operation on individuals, but is merely a geographical uniformity requiring the same plan and the same method to be operative throughout the United States, that a difference between the testamentary and intestacy laws of the States does not prevent the geographical uniformity of the "War Revenue Act," under which the primary right of taxation upon legacies and distributive shares depends upon the degree of relationship or want of relationship to the deceased, since the rate is the same wherever the degree of relationship or want of relationship is the same, so that the rule is uniform, although there may be different con-

son, or the husband of a daughter, for life or for a term of years, with the remainder to a collateral heir or to a

ditions among the States as to the objects upon which the tax is levied; and that the progressive rate feature of the act, by which the rates are graded in accordance with the amounts of the legacies or distributive shares and progressively increased as those amounts increase, cannot be held unconstitutional on the ground that it is repugnant to fundamental principles of equality and justice, but that the question whether a progressive tax is more just and equal than a proportional one is, in the absence of constitutional limitation, a legislative, and not a judicial, question. This case cites with approval the opinion delivered by Mr. Justice Brown in United States v Perkins, 163 U S 625, in which he said "The tax is not upon the property itself, but upon the right to dispose of it, and it is not until it has yielded its contribution to the State that it becomes the property of the legatee" The case of United States v Perkins involved the question whether property bequeathed to the United States was subject to a succession tax, and it was held that it was In Plummer v Coler, 178 U S 115, it was decided that, under the inheritance tax laws of a State, a tax may validly be imposed on a legacy consisting of U S. bonds issued under a statute declaring them to be exempt from taxation in any form This case quotes with approval from the opinion of the court in Magoun v. Illinois Trust & Savings Bank, 470 U. S 283, the following "The constitutionality of the (inheritance) taxes has been declared, and the principle upon which they are based explained, in United States v Perkins, 163 U S. 625" (and in sundry other cases cited) "It is not necessary to review these cases, or to state at length the reasoning by which they are supported They are based on two principles · 1. An inheritance tax is not one on property but one on the succession 2 The right to take property by devise or descent is the creature of the law, and not a natural right — a privilege, and therefore the authority which confers it may impose conditions on it. From these principles it is deduced that the states may tax the privilege, discriminate between relatives and between these and strangers, and grant exemptions, and are not precluded from this power by the provisions of the respective state constitutions requiring uniformity and equality of taxation."

b. *Under Laws of States other than Massachusetts*

In California it was decided in *Re* Wilmerding, 117 Cal 281, that the requirement of the California constitution that all property shall

stranger to the blood, the value of such particular estate shall, within three months after the appointment of the

be taxed according to its value does not applied to the tax imposed by the California collateral inheritance tax act of 1893, as such tax is upon the right of succession and not upon property, and that the discrimination made by the act in favor of surviving brothers and sisters and against the children of deceased brothers and sisters does not render the act invalid as class legislation.

In Colorado the validity of the inheritance tax act was sustained in *Re* Inheritance Tax, 23 Col 442.

In Illinois it was held in Kochersperger *v* Drake, 167 Ill 122, that a statute creating classes of property of deceased persons for the purpose of a succession tax, although it exempts some classes from taxation and provides different rates for other classes but is uniform as to all property in the same class, does not violate the Ill Constitution of 1870, Art 9, requiring property to be taxed according to its value In Magoun *v* Ill Trust & Savings Bank, 170 U. S 283, it was held that the legacy and inheritance tax law of Illinois was constitutional, that exemptions from a statute taxing inheritances do not render its operation unequal within the meaning of the 14th Amendment to the Constitution of the United States, and that a collateral inheritance law which does not impose a uniform rate, but classifies legacies to strangers to the blood and imposes higher rates on the larger sums, is not in violation of the rule of equality of the 14th Amendment The case of Curry *v* Spencer, 61 N. H. 624, which held the New Hampshire inheritance tax law to be in violation of the constitution of that State, is characterized by the U. S Supreme Court in the Magoun case as "extreme"

In Maine the inheritance tax law of that State was held to be constitutional in an able opinion in the case of State *v.* Hamlin, 86 Me. 495 For a very valuable note to this case, see 41 Am State Rep. pp 580, 581, 582.

In New York the carefully considered case of *In re* Swift, 137 N Y 77, holds that the New York collateral tax act of 1885, as amended, is constitutional.

In Ohio, it was decided in State *v* Ferris, 53 Ohio St 314 (decided in 1895), that the law imposing an inheritance tax was unconstitutional simply because of the exemption of estates of $20,000 and under and because, in cases where the estate exceeded $20,000, the entire estate was taxed without any exemption, and this was held to be in violation of the Ohio bill of rights But in Hagerty *v* State, 55 Ohio St 613,

executor, administrator, or trustee, be appraised in the manner provided in section sixteen and deducted from the

(decided in 1897), the act of April 20, 1894, amending the act imposing a collateral inheritance tax, was held to be constitutional, the exemption features having been omitted in this later act which had been decided to be unconstitutional in State v. Ferris. This later Ohio law exempted property of the value of $200, which exemption is expressly authorized by the Ohio constitution in the levying of taxes upon property, and imposed a uniform tax of five per cent upon the value of all property in excess of that amount passing to collateral heirs or to strangers to the blood.

In Pennsylvania, in the case of Strode v. Commonwealth, 52 Pa. St. 181 (decided in 1866), the appellate court affirmed the judgment of the lower court and affirmed its opinion, in which it was said: "What is called a 'collateral inheritance tax' is a bonus exacted from the collateral kindred and others as the condition on which they may be admitted to take the estate left by a deceased relative or testator. The estate does not belong to them except as a right to it is conferred by the state. Independent of government no such right could exist. The death of the owner would necessarily terminate his control over it, and it would pass to the first who might obtain possession. The right of the owner to transfer it to another after death, or of kindred to succeed, is the result of municipal regulation and must consequently be enjoyed subject to such conditions as the state sees fit to impose. And we see the state continually imposing new conditions, sometimes enlarging at others restraining, the privilege, and sometimes again entirely taking it away by changing the parties who are to succeed." In Small's Estate, 151 Pa. St. 1, (decided in 1892), construing the act of May 6, 1887, it was held that the interest of a non-resident partner in a limited partnership association located in Pennsylvania was subject to the inheritance tax.

In Tennessee the inheritance law then in force in that state was held to be constitutional in the well-considered case of State v. Alston, 94 Tenn. 674 (decided in 1895).

c. *Under the Law of Massachusetts*

The original act imposing a tax on collateral legacies and successions was St. 1891, c. 425. In Minot v. Winthrop, 162 Mass. 113, this act was held to be constitutional; that the tax imposed by it was an excise; and that this excise was reasonable and was not unequal. The first section of this act contained a proviso that no estate should be sub-

appraised value of such property, and the remainder shall be subject to a tax of five per cent of its value"[1]

ject to the tax imposed by the act unless the value of the estate, after the payment of all debts, exceeded $10,000. This proviso was repealed by St. 1901, c. 297. As to this exemption the court say in Minot v. Winthrop. "The statutes of the different states and nations which have levied taxes on devises, legacies, and inheritances have usually made exemptions, and these have sometimes related to the value of the estates, and sometimes to the value of the property received by the heirs, devisees, legatees, or distributees. The exemption in the statute under consideration is certainly large as an exemption of estates, but it is peculiarly within the discretion of the legislature to determine what exemptions should be made in apportioning the burdens of taxation among those who can best bear them, and we are not satisfied that this exemption is so clearly unreasonable as to require us to declare the statute void." The court also say in this case "We are of opinion that the privilege of transmitting or receiving by will or descent property on the death of the owner, is a commodity within the meaning of this word in the constitution, and that an excise may be laid upon it. Although St. 1891, c. 425, in form imposes a tax upon the property which passes in the manner described in the first section, yet the tax plainly is not meant to be a substitute for the annual tax upon estates, or to be an additional tax of that nature; the statute can only take effect by regarding the tax as an excise, and the statute should be so construed as to take effect, if such a construction reasonably can be given to it. We see no difficulty in doing this, and are of opinion that the statute was intended to impose a tax in the nature of an excise." The opinion in Minot v. Winthrop was written by Chief Justice Field, and is elaborate, exhaustive, and able.

Decisions Construing the Massachusetts Law

In Minot v. Winthrop, 162 Mass. 113 it was held that the exemption of "charitable, educational, or religious societies or institutions, the property of which is exempt by law from taxation," is confined to societies and institutions the property of which is exempt from

---

[1] St. 1902, c. 473, provides as follows —

"In all cases where there has been or shall be a devise, descent, or bequest to collateral relatives or strangers to the blood, liable to col-

"SECT 3 If a testator gives, bequeaths, or devises to his executors or trustees any property otherwise liable to said taxation by the law of Massachusetts. To same effect is Rice v. Bradford, 180 Mass 515, in which a legacy to Bowdoin College was held to be subject to the tax

The donor of a power of appointment, rather than the donee, must be regarded as the decedent whose estate is subject to taxation. Emmons v. Shaw, 171 Mass. 410

The executor of a foreign will proved in Massachusetts is liable to pay the collateral inheritance tax upon the following property of the testator within the jurisdiction of this commonwealth real estate, cash on hand, bonds of railroad companies, of cities without the commonwealth, of other states and of the United States Callahan v. Woodbridge, 171 Mass. 595

For the purpose of determining on what amount the tax is to be computed, expenses of administration must be deducted, as the tax is to be paid only on the amount which passes to the successor or successors Callahan v Woodbridge, *supra*.

A legacy tax paid to the United States under the War Revenue Act of 1898 is to be deducted before paying the Massachusetts succession tax Hooper v Shaw, 176 Mass 190

A corporation organized under the laws of Massachusetts for the purpose of administering a fund given to be applied to charitable purposes is not subject to the collateral inheritance tax, and it is immaterial that a portion of the fund was given to charitable institutions without the state. Balch v. Shaw, 174 Mass 144

Property was conveyed prior to St 1891, c 425, by a married woman to a trustee to pay her the income for life and the principal after her death to such persons as she should appoint by will. She died in 1895, leaving a will by which she appointed the property to persons not exempt under the statute. *Held*, that the property was subject to the tax Crocker v. Shaw, 174 Mass 266.

Property of a resident of Salem, in the hands of his agents in New York, consisting of bonds and stocks of foreign corporations, a certificate of indebtedness of a foreign corporation, bonds secured by mortgage of real estate in New Hampshire, the makers of the bonds

---

lateral inheritance tax, to take effect in possession or come into actual enjoyment after the expiration of one or more life estates or a term of years, the tax on such property shall not be payable nor interest begin

tax, in lieu of their compensation, the value thereof in excess of reasonable compensation, as determined by the

and mortgages living in New York, and of cash on deposit in a savings bank and with individuals in Brooklyn, was held in Frothingham v Shaw, 175 Mass 59, to be subject to the Massachusetts collateral inheritance tax, there having been no administration in New York and the Massachusetts executor having taken possession of the property.

The value of the property subject to the tax is to be determined as of the date of the death of the testator or intestate, and the income subsequently accruing is not subject to the tax. Hooper v. Bradford, 178 Mass. 95, Howe v. Howe, 179 Mass 546.

---

to run thereon until the person or persons entitled thereto shall come into actual possession of such property, and the tax thereon shall be assessed upon the value of the property at the time when the right of possession accrues to the person entitled thereto as aforesaid, and such person or persons shall pay the tax upon coming into possession of such property The executor or administrator of the decedent's estate may settle his account in the probate court without being liable for said tax *provided*, that such person or persons may pay the tax at any time prior to their coming into possession, and in such cases the tax shall be assessed on the value of the estate at the time of the payment of the tax, after deducting the value of the life estate or estates for years; and *provided, further*, that the tax on real estate shall remain a lien on the real estate on which the same is chargeable until it is paid "

In reply to a communication from the treasurer and receiver-general, inquiring, first, whether this statute of 1902 applies to the estates of non-resident decedents, and, second, whether the statute applies to estates of resident decedents where the intervening life estate is taxable, the attorney-general of the commonwealth gave his opinion under date of August 26, 1902, in which he says·—

"The first question is not free from difficulty. The statute does not in terms distinguish between the estates of resident and non-resident decedents, and there is much force in the contention that no such distinction was contemplated by the legislature in its enactment. It will result, however, if the act is construed to include the estates of non-resident decedents, that the existing law relating to the taxation of collateral legacies and successions, will become practically inoperative or at least ineffective in every case where personal property of a non-resident decedent, which may be within the jurisdiction of the

probate court upon the application of any interested party or of the treasurer and receiver-general, shall nevertheless be subject to the provisions of this chapter."

commonwealth, vests in or comes into the actual possession of a collateral relative or stranger to the blood liable to the collateral inheritance tax, after the expiration of one or more life estates, and both the property and the legatee in whom it vests are beyond the limits of the commonwealth

In view of what I deem to be the purpose of the statute, I cannot believe that the legislature intended by implication to effect so radical a change in the existing law The undoubted object of St. 1902, c 473, was not to disturb the ultimate liability of taxable persons and its enforcement, as at present fixed under the collateral inheritance tax law, but to revise or amend the law only so far as relates to the time when such liability shall, in certain cases, accrue. Upon this construction of the statute, I am forced to take the view that it does not serve to postpone the time when the tax shall be due and payable, where there has been a devise, descent, or bequest, consisting of property in this commonwealth belonging to a non-resident, which vests or takes effect in possession in the future, and that your first question must be answered in the negative

This conclusion receives confirmation from the language of the act itself The statute provides that "The executor or administrator of the decedent's estate may settle his account in the probate court without being liable for said tax," a provision which can only apply to the estates of resident decedents, since the executor or administrator of a non-resident decedent is not required to file an account in the probate court of this commonwealth, but may receive the property of the decedent which may be within the jurisdiction of the commonwealth, upon the allowance by the court of the petition required by R L. c 148, § 3 (see R L c 15, §§ 12, 13, and 14), if it appears that such executor or administrator is, in the State where he is appointed, liable for the property so received This language, therefore, supports the conclusion that the provisions of St 1902, c 473, can only apply to estates the executors or administrators of which are compelled to file an account in the probate courts of this commonwealth.

To your second question, I am of the opinion that I must reply in the affirmative Neither the purpose nor the language of the act can be construed to warrant a distinction between an intervening life estate which is taxable and one which is not taxable. The statute clearly postpones the time when the tax shall become due upon a tax-

"Sect. 4. Taxes imposed by the provisions of this chapter shall be payable to the treasurer and receiver-general by the executors, administrators, or trustees, at the expiration of two years after the date of their giving bond; but if legacies or distributive shares are paid within the two years, the taxes thereon shall be payable at the same time. If the probate court acting under the provisions of section thirteen of chapter one hundred and forty-one has ordered the executor or administrator to retain funds to satisfy a claim of a creditor, the payment of the tax may be suspended by the court to await the disposition of such claim. If the taxes are not paid when due, interest shall be charged and collected from the time the same became payable; and said taxes and interest shall be and remain a lien on the property subject to the taxes until the same are paid."

"Sect. 5. An executor, administrator, or trustee holding property subject to said tax shall deduct the tax therefrom

---

able remainder to the time when such remainder vests in the remainderman, without reference to the character of the life estate which precedes it."

In Minot v Winthrop, 162 Mass 113, decided before the passage of St. 1902, c. 473, where a testatrix had given the income of the sum of ten thousand dollars to her husband and, on his death, the principal to his daughter, who was not the daughter of the testatrix, it was held that, although the legacy to the husband was exempt from the tax, the tax should be computed on the daughter's interest and deducted from the principal and paid over to the treasurer of the commonwealth at the expiration of two years from the date of the giving of bond by the executor, or when the legacy was paid, if paid within the two years It was also held in Minot v Winthrop that the tax on an annuity was to be paid out of the annuity as soon as the annuity became payable, and at the time when payments on account of it are made, even though the effect might be that the first payment or payments on account of the annuity might be exhausted by the tax See also Howe v Howe, 179 Mass 546.

or collect it from the legatee or person entitled to said property, and he shall not deliver property or a specific legacy subject to said tax until he has collected the tax thereon An executor or administrator shall collect taxes due upon land which is subject to tax under the provisions hereof from the heirs or devisees entitled thereto, and he may be authorized to sell said land according to the provisions of section eight if they refuse or neglect to pay said tax."

"SECT 6. If a legacy subject to said tax is charged upon or payable out of real estate, the heir or devisee, before paying it, shall deduct said tax therefrom and pay it to the executor, administrator, or trustee, and the tax shall remain a charge upon said real estate until it is paid. Payment thereof may be enforced by the executor, administrator, or trustee in the same manner as the payment of the legacy itself could be enforced."

"SECT. 7. If a pecuniary legacy is given to any person for a limited period, the executor, administrator, or trustee shall retain the tax on the whole amount; but if it is not in money, he shall apply to the probate court having jurisdiction of his accounts to make an apportionment, if the case requires it, of the sum to be paid into his hands by such legatee on account of said tax, and for such further orders as the case may require."

"SECT. 8. The probate court may authorize executors, administrators, and trustees to sell the real estate of a decedent for the payment of said tax in the same manner as it may authorize them to sell real estate for the payment of debts."

"SECT. 9. An inventory of every estate, any part of which may be subject to a tax under the provisions of this chapter, shall be filed by the executor, administrator, or trustee within three months after his appointment. If he neglects or refuses to file such inventory, he shall be liable to a penalty of not more than one thousand dollars, which shall be recovered by the treasurer and receiver-general; and the register of probate shall notify the treasurer and receiver-general of any such neglect or refusal within thirty days after the expiration of the said three months."

"SECT. 10. A copy of the inventory and appraisal of every estate, any part of which is subject to a tax under the provisions of this chapter or, if the estate can be conveniently separated, a copy of the inventory and appraisal of such part, shall within thirty days after it has been filed be sent by the register of probate, by mail, to the treasurer and receiver-general without charge therefor. A refusal or neglect by the register of probate so to send a copy of such inventory and appraisal shall be a breach of his official bond."

"SECT. 11. If real estate of a decedent so passes to another person as to become subject to said tax, his executor, administrator, or trustee shall inform the treasurer and receiver-general thereof within six months after his appointment, or, if the fact is not known to him within that time, then within one month after the fact becomes known to him."

"SECT. 12. If a foreign executor, administrator, or trustee assigns or transfers any stock or obligation in any national bank located in this commonwealth, or in any corporation organized under the laws of this commonwealth, owned by a deceased non-resident at the time of his death and liable to a tax under the provisions of this chapter, the tax shall be paid to the treasurer and receiver-general at the time of such assignment or transfer, and if it is not paid when due such executor, administrator, or trustee shall be personally liable therefor until it is paid. A bank located in this commonwealth or a corporation organized under the laws of this commonwealth which shall record a transfer of any share of its stock or of its obligations made by a foreign executor, administrator, or trustee, or issue a new certificate for a share of its stock or of the transfer of an obligation at the instance of a foreign executor, administrator, or trustee, before all taxes imposed thereon by the provisions of this chapter have been paid, shall be liable for such tax in an action of contract, brought by the treasurer and receiver-general." [1]

"SECT. 13 Securities or assets belonging to the estate of a deceased non-resident shall not be delivered or transferred to a foreign executor, administrator, or legal representative of said decedent, unless such executor, administrator, or legal representative has been licensed to receive such securities or assets under the provisions of section three of chapter one hundred and forty-eight, without serving notice upon the treasurer and receiver-general of the time and place of such intended delivery or transfer seven days at least before the time of such delivery or transfer. The treasurer and receiver-general, either personally or by representative, may examine such securities or assets at the time of such delivery or transfer. Failure to serve such

---

[1] The fact that shares of stock in corporations organized under the laws of this commonwealth, and of national banking corporations located here, belonging to a resident of another state, the certificates of which are there at the time of his death, are transferred there by the executor of his will under authority of his appointment in that state before he is appointed executor here, does not exempt such shares from the collateral inheritance tax here. Greves v Shaw, 173 Mass. 205. Stock of the Boston & Albany R R Co, a corporation having its franchises from Massachusetts and also from New York, belonging to the estate of a deceased non-resident, is subject to the tax. Moody v. Shaw, 173 Mass. 375.

notice or to allow such examination shall render the person or corporation making the delivery or transfer liable in an action of contract brought by the treasurer and receiver-general to the payment of the tax due upon said securities or assets."

"SECT. 14. The treasurer and receiver-general shall be made a party to all petitions by foreign executors, administrators, or trustees brought under the provisions of section three of chapter one hundred and forty-eight, and no decree shall be made upon any such petition unless it appears that notice of such petition has been served on the treasurer and receiver-general fourteen days at least before the return day of such petition."

"SECT. 15. If a person who has paid such tax afterward refunds a portion of the property on which it was paid or if it is judicially determined that the whole or any part of such tax ought not to have been paid, said tax, or the due proportion thereof, shall be repaid to him by the executor, administrator, or trustee."

"SECT. 16. Said tax shall be assessed upon the actual value of said property as found by the probate court. Upon the application of the treasurer and receiver-general or of any party interested in the succession, the probate court shall appoint three disinterested appraisers who, first being sworn, shall appraise such property at its actual market value and shall make return thereof to said court. Such return, when accepted by said court, shall be final. The fees of said appraisers, as determined by the judge of said court, shall be paid by the treasurer and receiver-general. The value of an annuity or life estate shall be determined by the 'ACTUARIES' COMBINED EXPERIENCE TABLES,' at four per cent compound interest." [1]

[1] The value of the property subject to the tax is to be determined

"SECT. 17. The probate court having jurisdiction of the settlement of the estate of the decedent shall, subject to appeal as in other cases, hear and determine all questions relative to said tax affecting any devise, legacy, or inheritance, and the treasurer and receiver-general shall represent the commonwealth in any such proceedings."[1]

"SECT. 18. If, upon the decease of a person leaving an estate liable to a tax under the provisions of this chapter, a will disposing of such estate is not offered for probate, or an application for administration made within four months after such decease, the proper probate court, upon application by the treasurer and receiver-general, shall appoint an administrator."

"SECT. 19. No final account of an executor, administrator, or trustee shall be allowed by the probate court unless such account shows, and the judge of said court finds, that all taxes imposed by the provisions of this chapter upon any property or interest therein belonging to the estate to be

as of the date of the death of the testator or intestate. Hooper v. Bradford, 178 Mass 95, Howe v Howe, 179 Mass 546

If an annuity of a life estate is subject to the tax, the tax is to be paid out of the annuity or out of the income of the life estate, and at the time when payments are first made on account of the annuity or life estate. Minot v Winthrop, 162 Mass 113

The value of an annuity or of a life estate is to be determined according to the "actuaries' combined experience table" and not according to the time that the annuitant or person entitled to the life estate actually lived. Howe v Howe, 179 Mass 546.

[1] The jurisdiction of the probate court under this section does not take away the right of a legatee to sue for his legacy at common law in the superior court and to have the question heard and determined there whether the legacy is subject to a tax. Essex v. Brooks, 164 Mass 79

The probate court has jurisdiction of a petition by the executor of a foreign will proved in this commonwealth for instructions whether he is liable to pay a tax upon the property, real and personal, of the testate found here. Callahan v Woodbridge, 171 Mass. 595.

settled by said account have been paid; and the receipt of the treasurer and receiver-general for such tax shall be the proper voucher for such payment."

"SECT. 20 The treasurer and receiver-general shall commence an action for the recovery of any of said taxes within six months after the same become payable; and also whenever the judge of a probate court certifies to him that the final account of an executor, administrator, or trustee has been filed in such court and that the settlement of the estate is delayed because of the non-payment of said tax. The probate court shall so certify upon the application of any heir, legatee, or other person interested therein, and may extend the payment of said tax whenever the circumstances of the case require."[1]

PRACTICE OF TREASURER'S DEPARTMENT IN DETERMINING AMOUNT OF TAX.

It may be of service to state in a general way the practice of the department of the treasurer of the commonwealth in regard to certain questions which frequently arise in determining the amount upon which the tax is to be paid The law provides that the debts and charges of administration are to be deducted, but there might be certain expenses and charges of an administrator or executor which would be allowed by a probate court, if assented to by the parties in interest, and which would not be allowed

---

[1] The provision that the treasurer of the commonwealth shall within six months after the taxes are due and payable (§ 4 providing that the taxes shall be payable by executors, administrators, and trustees at the expiration of two years from the date of their giving bond), is directory merely, and does not limit the right of recovery by the treasurer of the commonwealth to two years and six months after the giving of bonds by executors and trustees. Howe v Howe, 179 Mass. 546

by the treasurer. For instance, taxes paid by the administrator or executor on real estate, if the taxes were assessed as of a date subsequent to the death of the testate or intestate. Taxes are assessed as of May 1 in each year. If the deceased person died at any time prior to May 1, the tax assessed on his property on May 1 of the year of his death would not be a debt which the treasurer would allow to be deducted. So also of repairs on real estate. Briefly, the treasurer allows to be deducted only the strictly legal debts and charges of administration.

If the testator gives by will a specific legacy to a person not exempt from payment of the legacy tax and directs that the tax thereon shall be paid out of the residue of his estate, the legacy is construed as one of a sum equal to the specific legacy plus the tax thereon; for instance, if the legacy was five thousand dollars, the tax thereon would be two hundred and fifty dollars, and the legacy is construed by the treasurer as if it had been a legacy of five thousand two hundred and fifty dollars and the tax would be collected on this amount.

APPENDIX.

APPENDIX.

PROBATE AND EQUITY RULES

Prepared by the Judges of the Probate Courts for regulating the Practice and conducting the Business in their Courts, and approved by the Supreme Judicial Court, to take effect and be in force throughout the Commonwealth on and after May 15, 1894

PROBATE RULES.

I

Any party may appear in the Probate Court in person, or by an attorney authorized to practice in the courts of this Commonwealth, or by a person authorized by a writing, filed in said court, for that purpose.

Any person appearing for another in the Probate Court shall enter his appearance in writing, giving his name, place of residence or business, the matter in which, and the name or names of the person or persons for whom, he appears. Said writing shall be filed with the register, and the fact entered in the docket

Each petition shall be considered a separate proceeding, and appearance of the attorney entered accordingly.

II.

If a party shall change his attorney, pending any proceeding, the name of the new attorney shall be substituted on the docket for that of the former attorney, and notice thereof given to the adverse party, and until such notice of the change of an attorney, all notices given to or by the attorney first appointed shall be considered in all respects as notice to or from his client, except in cases in which by law the notice is required to be given to the party personally; provided, however, that nothing in these rules shall be construed to prevent any party interested from appearing for himself in the manner provided by law; and in such case, the party so appearing shall be subject to the same rules that are or may be provided for attorneys in like cases, so far as the same are applicable.

III

When the authority of an attorney-at-law to appear for any party shall be demanded, if the attorney shall declare that he has been duly authorized to appear by an application made directly to him by such party, or by some person whom he believes to have been authorized to employ him, such declaration shall be deemed and taken to be evidence of authority to appear and prosecute or defend in any action or proceeding.

IV

In addition to making appointments of guardians *ad litem* in cases required by statute, whenever it shall appear that a minor is interested in any matter pending, a guardian *ad litem* for such minor may be appointed by the court at its discretion, with or without notice.

V.

The court will grant commissions to take the depositions of witnesses without the Commonwealth; and any party may, on application to the Register, obtain a commission, which shall be directed to any commissioner appointed by the governor of the Commonwealth to take depositions in any other of the United States, or the commission may be directed to any justice of the peace, notary public, or other officer legally empowered to take depositions or affidavits in the State or country where the deposition is to be taken. In each case the depositions shall be taken upon interrogatories, to be filed by the party applying for the commission, and upon such cross-interrogatories as shall be filed by the adverse party, — the whole of which interrogatories shall be annexed to the commission The party applying for the commission shall in each case file his interrogatories in the register's office, and give notice thereof to the adverse party, or his attorney, seven days at least before taking out the commission, and fourteen days at least before the taking, if the party or his attorney live out of the Commonwealth But where the adverse party does not appear, such interrogatories need not be exhibited to him, nor notice be given to him of the same. And when a deposition shall be taken and certified by any person as a justice of the peace, or other officer as aforesaid, by force of such commission, if it shall be objected that the person so taking and certifying the same was not such officer, the burden of proof shall be on the party so objecting, and if a like objection shall be made to a deposition taken without such commission, it shall be incumbent on the party producing the deposition to prove that it was taken and certified by a person duly authorized.

VI

In all cases where depositions shall be taken on interrogatories, no party shall be permitted to attend at the taking of such deposition, either himself, or by attorney or agent, nor be permitted to communicate by interrogatories or suggestions with the deponent while giving his deposition It shall be the duty of the commissioner to take such deposition in a place separate and apart from all other persons, and to permit no person to be present during such examination, except the deponent and himself, and such disinterested person, if any, as he may think fit to appoint as a clerk to assist him in reducing the deposition to writing And it shall be the duty of the commissioner to put the several interrogatories and cross-interrogatories to the deponent in their order, and to take the answer of the deponent to each. fully and clearly, before proceeding to the next; and not to read to the deponent, nor permit the deponent to read, a succeeding interrogatory until the answer to the preceding has been fully taken down.

And it shall be the duty of the register, on issuing a commission to take a deposition on interrogatories, to insert the substance of this order therein, or to annex this order, or the substance thereof, to the commission, by way of notice and instruction to the commissioner

VII.

All depositions shall be opened and filed by the register when received. The deposition shall afterwards be in his custody, subject to the order of the court, as other documents in the case; and if not read on the trial by the party taking it, it may be used by any other party, if he sees fit, he paying the costs of taking the same.

VIII.

Whenever, in any case, a notice given in accordance with the general forms of procedure or otherwise is held by the judge to be insufficient, he may order such further notice as the case requires

IX.

No executor or administrator shall receive any compensation by way of a commission upon the estate by him administered, but shall be allowed his reasonable expenses incurred in the execution of his trust, and such compensation for his services as the court in each case may deem just and reasonable. The account shall contain an itemized statement of the nature of the services rendered, and of such other matters as may be necessary to enable the court to determine what compensation is reasonable

X.

Probate accounts should be stated in schedules as follows : —

1. SCHEDULE A. Containing cash items only, beginning with the amount of cash in the inventory, or with the cash balance of the previous account, followed by items of every

sum of money received, whether from the sale of real or personal estate or otherwise.

2 SCHEDULE B Containing every sum of money paid for any purpose

3. SCHEDULE C Containing all items of personal estate (other than cash), whether the same were stated in the inventory, or subsequently came to the possession or knowledge of the accountant, together with the valuation put upon them by inventory or by the accountant.

4. SCHEDULE D. Containing all items of property that have been delivered by order of the court or otherwise without having been converted into cash.

XI.

Notice upon an account not intended as final will be issued only by direction of the judge.

Every such account, when no notice has been ordered, unless accompanied by the assent in writing of all persons interested, will be filed, the footings of its schedules entered upon the docket, and the consideration of its allowance will be postponed till the hearing upon the final account.

EQUITY RULES

I

IN all cases in equity the petition shall begin after the address, by stating the names and known residence of all persons interested, together with any disability of any of them, and then proceed to state fully all facts necessary to be proved to maintain the petitioner's claim It shall describe all property to be affected thereby, with sufficient accuracy for identification, and contain a special prayer for each form of relief desired, as well as one for general relief. No other allegations, charges, or prayers need be included.

(Form of Petition.)

To the Honorable the Judge of the Probate Court in and for the County of   .

Respectfully represents   , petitioners   town   , county   , State   , that   bring this petition against   , respondents   town   , county   , State   , and allege them to be all the parties interested in the matter of said petition, and further represent

II.

The original process to require the appearance of respondents shall be a citation in the following form: —

COMMONWEALTH OF MASSACHUSETTS.

ss.   PROBATE COURT.

To

Whereas,   has presented to said court h   petition, praying   , you are hereby cited to appear at a Probate Court to be holden at   , in said county of   , on the   day of   next, at   o'clock in the forenoon, to show cause, if any you have, against the same.

And said petitioner   is ordered to serve this citation by delivering a copy thereof to each of you who may be found in said Commonwealth, fourteen days at least before said court, or if any of you shall not be so found, either by delivering a copy thereof to you wherever found, or by leaving a copy thereof at your usual place of abode, or by mailing a copy thereof to you at your last known post-office address, fourteen days at least before said court

Witness,   , Esq., judge of said court, this   day of   , in the year one thousand   hundred and   .

Register.

I have served the foregoing citation by

ss.   A. D. 19 .

Personally appeared the above named,   , and made oath to the truth of the above returns by h   subscribed

Before me,

Justice of the Peace.

All processes shall be made returnable at a statute court day within three months after the date of such process. In any case such further notice shall be given as the court may order.

III.

No injunction or other proceeding shall be ordered until the petition is filed, unless for good cause shown. No injunction shall issue, except upon a petition which has been sworn to, or upon verification of the material facts by affidavit.

IV.

The respondent shall answer fully, directly, and specifically to every material allegation or statement in the petition.

V.

The day of appearance shall be the return-day of the citation, unless the court shall otherwise order; and if the respondent shall not appear and file his answer, plea, or demurrer within fourteen days thereafter, the petition shall be taken for confessed, and the matter thereof may be decreed accordingly, unless good cause shall appear to the contrary.

VI.

The respondent may at any time before the citation is taken for confessed, or afterwards by leave of the court, demur, plead, or answer to the petition; and he may demur to part, plead to part, and answer as to the residue; and in any case in which the petition charges fraud or combination, a plea to such part must be accompanied with an answer supporting the plea, and explicitly denying the fraud or combination, and the facts on which the charge is founded.

VII.

The petitioner may set down a plea or demurrer to be argued, or take issue on the plea, within fourteen days from the time when the same is filed; and if he shall fail to do so, a decree dismissing the petition may be entered upon motion unless good cause appear to the contrary.

VIII.

If a plea or demurrer be overruled, no other plea or demurrer shall be received, but the respondent shall proceed to answer the petition; and if he shall fail to do so within fourteen days, the petitioner may enter an order that the same, or so much thereof as is covered by the plea or demurrer, be taken for confessed, and the matter may be decreed accordingly, unless good cause shall appear to the contrary.

IX.

The respondent, instead of filing a formal plea or demurrer, may insist on any special matter in his answer, and have the same benefit therefrom as if he had pleaded the same, or demurred to the petition.

X

The respondent to a cross-petition shall in no case be compelled to answer thereto before the respondent to the original petition shall have answered such original petition

XI.

The form of the general replication shall be that the plaintiff joins issue on the answer. The petitioner shall file exceptions, or set down the case for hearing within fourteen days after the answer is required to be filed, or if the answer be filed before it is required, then within fourteen days after written notice of such filing, and if he fails so to do, a decree may be entered for the dismissal of the petition.

XII.

If the petitioner shall except to an answer as insufficient, he shall file his exceptions, and forthwith give notice thereof to the respondent or his attorney; and if within fourteen days the respondent shall put in a sufficient answer, the same shall be received. But if the respondent insist on the sufficiency of his answer, he shall, within fourteen days, file a statement to that effect, and give notice thereof to the petitioner, and thereupon his exceptions shall be set down to be argued. If the answer shall be adjudged insufficient, a new answer shall be filed within fourteen days.

XIII.

Upon a second answer being adjudged insufficient, the respondent may be examined upon interrogatories, and committed until he shall answer them.

XIV.

The court may in its discretion allow the parties to amend their pleadings, and order or permit the pleadings to be filed, or any proceeding to be had, at other times than are provided in these rules; and may in all cases impose just and reasonable terms upon the parties.

XV.

All notices in a case required to be given to the party may be given to his attorney of record; and if transmitted through the post-office, post paid, shall be deemed to have been received by the person to whom they are addressed, in due course of mail, unless the contrary shall appear by affidavit or otherwise.

XVI.

When the death of any party shall be suggested in writing, and entered on the docket, the register, upon application, may issue process to bring into court the representative of such deceased party.

XVII.

When the circumstances of the case are such as to require a petition of revivor or supplemental petition, or petition in the nature of either or both, or the joinder of additional or different parties, the requisite allegations may be made by way of amendment to the original petition ; and after service on any new parties, as in the case of an original petition, and service of copies of the amendment on all the respondents affected thereby, shall entitle the petitioner to proceed as on an original petition.

XVIII.

In petitions by executors or trustees to obtain the instructions of the court, and in petitions of interpleader, or in the nature of interpleader, no attorney for the petitioner shall appear, or be heard, or act for or in behalf of any or either of the respondents.

XIX.

All facts alleged in a petition, other than for discovery only, which are not denied or put in issue by the answer, shall be deemed to be admitted.

XX.

Testimony taken by depositions shall be taken in the manner required by statute and by the rules of the court in matters of probate

XXI.

When any matter shall be referred to a master, he shall, upon the application of either party, assign a time and place for hearing, which shall not be less than ten days thereafter; and the party obtaining the reference shall serve the adverse party, at least seven days before the time appointed for the hearing, with a summons requiring his attendance at such time and place, and make proof thereof to the master ; and thereupon, if the party summoned shall not appear to show cause to the contrary, the master may proceed *ex parte*, and if the party obtaining the reference shall not appear at the time and place, or show cause why he does not, the master may either proceed *ex parte*, or the party obtaining the reference shall lose the benefit of the same at the election of the adverse party.

XXII.

When the master has prepared a draft copy of his report, he shall notify the parties, or their attorneys, of the time and place when and where they may attend to hear the same, and suggest such alterations, if any, as they may think proper. Upon consideration whereof, the master will finally settle the draft of his report, and give notice thereof to the parties or their attorneys, whereupon, after examining the same, or being furnished with a copy thereof, five days shall be allowed for bringing in written objections thereto, which objections, if any, shall be appended to the report. No exception to a master's report will be allowed without a special order of the court, unless founded upon an objection made before the master, and shown by his report, and unless filed with the register within fourteen days from the filing of the report. Notice of the filing of the master's report shall be forthwith sent by the register to each party or his attorney.

XXIII.

When exceptions shall be taken to the report of the master, they shall be filed with the register, and notice thereof shall forthwith be given to the adverse party; and the exceptions shall then be set down for argument. In every case, the exceptions shall briefly and clearly specify the matter excepted to, and the cause thereof, and the exceptions shall not be valid as to any matter not so specified.

XXIV.

When any party shall desire a hearing in equity, he may apply to the judge to appoint a time and place therefor; and when such time and place shall have been appointed, he shall give notice thereof to the adverse party, or his attorney, through the post-office, post paid, but this rule shall not prevent a party from obtaining a preliminary injunction, or a dissolution of an injunction or other order, upon a shorter notice, or without notice, if the court shall think the same reasonable. Cases may be heard by consent of parties, and the permission of the court, without such notice.

XXV.

The attorney of the party in whose favor a decree or order is passed shall draw the same. All pleadings shall be recorded, unless the court shall otherwise order

(Form of Decree.)

ss.

On the petition in equity of , petitioners, against , respondents, praying it appearing that notice according to the order of the court has been given all parties interested person objecting after hearing and consideration, the court doth order and decree,

XXVI.

Rules I., II., and III in Probate shall apply to proceedings in equity.

PROBATE FORMS.

Petition for Administration — with Sureties.

To the Honorable the Judge of the Probate Court in and for the County of   :

Respectfully represents   , of   , in said County   , that   , who last dwelt in said   , died on the   day of   , in the year of our Lord one thousand nine hundred and   intestate, possessed of goods and estate   remaining to be administered, leaving as widow — husband, h   only heirs-at-law and next of kin the persons whose names, residences, and relationship to the deceased are as follows, viz..

Name	Residence	Relationship.

that your petitioner is

Wherefore your petitioner prays that he, or some other suitable person, be appointed administrat   of the estate of said deceased, and certifies that the statements herein contained are true to the best of h   knowledge and belief.

Dated this   day of   , A. D. 19   .

      , ss.   Subscribed and sworn to this   day of   , A. D. 19   .

Before me,

Justice of the Peace.

The undersigned, being all the persons interested residing in the Commonwealth, who are of full age and legal capacity, hereby assent to the foregoing petition.

<small>Citation by publication once a week for three successive weeks, the last publication to be one day at least before return day, and by mailing a copy of citation to each of next of kin seven days at least before return day</small>

Petition for Administration — without Sureties.

To the Honorable the Judge of the Probate Court in and for the County of   .

Respectfully represents   , of   , in the County of   , that   , who last dwelt in said   , died on the   day of   , in the year of our Lord one thousand nine hundred and   , intestate, possessed of goods and estate   remaining to be administered, leaving as widow — husband, h   only heirs-at-law and next of kin the persons whose names, residences, and relationship to the deceased are as follows, viz.:

Name	Residence.	Relationship.

that your petitioner is

Wherefore your petitioner prays that he may be appointed administrat   of the estate of said deceased without giving a surety on h   bond, and certifies that the statements herein contained are true to the best of h   knowledge and belief.

Dated this   day of   , A D 19   .

          , ss.   Subscribed and sworn to this   day of   , A. D. 19   .

Before me,

Justice of the Peace.

The undersigned, being all the persons interested in the estate, who are of full age and legal capacity, other than creditors, and the guardians of persons interested therein, hereby consent that the above-named petitioner be exempt from giving any surety on h   bond.

Citation by publication once a week for three successive weeks, the last publication to be one day at least before return day.

PETITION FOR ADMINISTRATION DE BONIS NON

To the Honorable the Judge of the Probate Court in and for the County of :

Respectfully represents   , of   , in the County of   , that on the   day of   , A. D 19 ,   was appointed, by this Court, administrat   of the estate of   , late of said   , deceased, that the said   has   without having fully administered said estate, that there are goods and estate of the said   to the amount of twenty dollars remaining to be administered,

that your petitioner is

Wherefore your petitioner prays that he, or some other suitable person, be appointed administrat   of the estate, not already administered, of said   , and certifies that the statements herein contained are true to the best of h   knowledge and belief

Dated this   day of   , A D. 19 .

       , ss   Subscribed and sworn to this   day of   , A. D 19 .
            Before me,
                    Justice of the Peace

The undersigned, being all persons interested, hereby assent to the foregoing petition.

Citation by publication once a week for three successive weeks, the last publication to be one day at least before return day

---

PETITION FOR SPECIAL ADMINISTRATION.

[R L. c 137, § 9.]

[Notice may be ordered at the discretion of the Court]

To the Honorable the Judge of the Probate Court in and for the County of   ·

Respectfully represents   , of   , in said County,

that   , who last dwelt in said   , died on the   day of   , in the year of our Lord one thousand nine hundred and   , possessed of goods and estate remaining to be administered, and that there is delay in granting letters   on h   estate, by reason of

and that your petitioner is

Wherefore your petitioner pray that he   may be appointed special administrat   of the estate of said deceased, and may be authorized to take charge of all the real estate of said deceased,   and to collect rents and make necessary repairs, and certifies that the statements herein contained are true to the best of h   knowledge and belief.

Dated this   day of   , A D, 19   .

           , ss.   Subscribed and sworn to this   day of   , A D 19   .
           Before me,
                                           Justice of the Peace.

The undersigned, being all the persons interested, hereby assent to the foregoing petition.

Citation by publication once a week for three successive weeks, the last publication to be one day at least before return day

---

PETITION FOR PUBLIC ADMINISTRATION.

To the Honorable the Judge of the Probate Court in and for the County of   :

Respectfully represents   of   , in the County of   , public administrator in and for the County of   , that   died intestate, in   , in said County of   , on the   day of   , A D 19   , not leaving a known husband — widow — or heir in this Commonwealth, that said deceased left property in said County of   , to be administered,

that your petitioner is entitled to administer thereon,

Wherefore he prays that letters of administration on the estate of said deceased may be granted to him agreeably to the law in such cases made and provided, and certifies that the statements herein contained are true to the best of his knowledge and belief

Dated this   day of   , A. D. 19 .

      , ss.   Subscribed and sworn to this   day of   , A. D 19 .

Before me,

Justice of the Peace.

Citation by publication once a week for three successive weeks, the last publication to be one day at least before return day

---

Petition for Probate of Will — with Sureties.

[Minors must be so designated, and the names of their guardians, if any, given The heirs-at-law and next-of-kin may be determined by reference to Chapters 133 and 137 of the Revised Laws]

To the Honorable the Judge of the Probate Court in and for the County of   :

Respectfully represents   of   , in the County of   , that   , who last dwelt in said   , died on the   day of   , in the year of our Lord one thousand nine hundred and   , possessed of goods and estate remaining to be administered, leaving as widow — husband — h   only heirs-at-law and next of kin, the persons whose names, residences, and relationship to the deceased are as follows, viz :

| Name | Residence | Relationship. |

That said deceased left a WILL — and   CODICIL — herewith presented, wherein your petitioner   named execut   .

Wherefore your petitioner pray that said will — and codicil — may be proved and allowed and letters testamentary issued to h , and certifies that the statements herein contained are true to the best of h knowledge and belief

Dated this   day of   , A D 19 .

, ss.   Subscribed and sworn to this   day of , A. D. 19 .

Before me,
                              Justice of the Peace.

The undersigned, being all the persons interested, hereby assent to the foregoing petition.

Citation by publication once a week for three successive weeks, the last publication to be one day at least before return day, and by mailing post-paid, or delivering a copy of the citation to all known persons interested in the estate seven days at least before return day

---

PETITION FOR PROBATE OF WILL — WITHOUT SURETIES.

[Minors must be so designated, and the names of their guardians, if any, given. The heirs-at-law and next-of-kin may be determined by reference to Chapters 133 and 137 of the Revised Laws]

To the Honorable the Judge of the Probate Court in and for the County of

Respectfully represents   of   in the County of   , that   , who last dwelt in said   , died on the   day of   in the year of our Lord one thousand nine hundred and   , possessed of goods and estate remaining to be administered, leaving as widow — husband — h only heirs-at-law and next of kin, the persons whose names, residences, and relationship to the deceased are as follows, viz.:

| NAME. | RESIDENCE | RELATIONSHIP |

That said deceased left a WILL — and   CODICIL — herewith presented, wherein your petitioner   named execut , and wherein the testat   has requested that your petitioner be exempt from giving a surety on h   bond.

PROBATE FORMS. 545

Wherefore your petitioner pray that said will — and codicil — may be proved and allowed and letters testamentary issued to h   , without giving a surety on h   official bond , and certifies that the statements herein contained are true to the best of h   knowledge and belief.

Dated this   day of   , A. D. 19   .

     , ss.   Subscribed and sworn to this   day of   , A. D. 19   .
     Before me,
                                    Justice of the Peace.

The undersigned, being all the persons interested in the estate who are of full age and legal capacity, other than creditors, and the guardians of persons interested therein, hereby consent that the above-named petitioner be exempt from giving any surety on h   bond.

Citation by publication once a week for three successive weeks, the last publication to be one day at least before return day, and by mailing post-paid, or delivering a copy of the citation to all known persons interested in the estate seven days at least before return day.

PETITION FOR ALLOWANCE OF FOREIGN WILL AND LETTERS.
[R L c 136, §§ 10, 11, 12]

[The petitioner should state that he is Executor, if he is so, and if not, how he is interested]

To the Honorable the Judge of the Probate Court in and for the County of   :

Respectfully represents   of ·   in the County of   , and State of   , that the last will and testament of   , late of   , in the County of   , and State of   , deceased, testate, has been duly proved and allowed by the   Court in and for the   , according to the laws of said State of   , a copy of which will, and of the probate thereof, duly authenticated, are herewith produced, that said testat   at the time of his decease had estate in said County of   , on which said will may operate, that the same ought to be allowed

35

in this State as the last will and testament of said deceased; that your petitioner is the execut   therein named,

and therefore pray , that the copy of said will may be filed and recorded in the Registry of Probate in said County of   , pursuant to the statute in that case made and provided, and that letters testamentary   may be granted thereon to h   , and certifies that the statements made in the foregoing petition are true to the best of his knowledge and belief

Dated this   day of   , A D. 19   .

, ss.   Subscribed and sworn to this   day of   , A D 19 .

Before me,

Justice of the Peace.

Citation by publication once a week for three successive weeks, the first publication to be thirty days at least before return day

---

PETITION FOR ADMINISTRATION WITH THE WILL ANNEXED.

[Minors must be so designated, and the names of their guardians, if any, given The heirs-at-law and next-of-kin may be determined by reference to Chapters 133 and 137 of the Revised Laws

To the Honorable the Judge of the Probate Court in and for the County of   :

Respectfully represents   , of   , in the County of   , that   , who last dwelt in   , in said County of   , died on the   day of   , in the year of our Lord one thousand nine hundred and   , possessed of goods and estate remaining to be administered, leaving as widow — husband — h   only heirs-at-law and next of kin, the persons whose names, residences, and relationship to the deceased are as follows, viz.

NAME.   RESIDENCE   RELATIONSHIP.

That said deceased left a WILL — and   CODICIL — herewith presented, wherein   w   named execut   and has

Wherefore your petitioner pray that said will — and codicil — may be proved and allowed, and letters of administration with the will annexed, issued to h , or some other suitable person, and certifies that the statements herein contained are true to the best of h knowledge and belief.

Dated this day of , A. D. 19 .

, ss Subscribed and sworn to this day of , A. D. 19 .

Before me,

Justice of the Peace.

The undersigned, being all the persons interested, hereby assent to the foregoing petition.

Citation by publication once a week for three successive weeks, the last publication to be one day at least before return day, and by mailing post-paid, or delivering a copy of the citation to all known persons interested in the estate seven days at least before return day.

Petition for Administration De Bonis Non with the Will Annexed.

To the Honorable the Judge of the Probate Court in and for the County of .

Respectfully represents of in the County of , that the will of , late of , in said County of , deceased, was duly proved and allowed on the day of , A. D. 19 , in said Court, and that appointed execut thereof, and that said execut has without having fully executed said will .

and that your petitioner is

Wherefore your petitioner pray that he, or some other suitable person, be appointed administrat with the will annexed of the estate of said deceased not already administered, and certifies that the statements herein contained are true to the best of h   knowledge and belief.

Dated this   day of   , A D. 19   .

        , ss.   Subscribed and sworn to this   day of   , A D 19   .
        Before me,
                                Justice of the Peace.

The undersigned, being all the persons interested, hereby assent to the foregoing petition.

Citation by publication once a week for three successive weeks, the last publication to be one day at least before return day, and by mailing post-paid, or delivering a copy of the citation to all devisees and legatees named in the will seven days before return day.

ADMINISTRATOR'S BOND — WITHOUT SURETIES

[R L. c 149 § 1, cl 2, § 3]

KNOW ALL MEN BY THESE PRESENTS,

That I,   , of   in the County of   , in the Commonwealth of Massachusetts, am holden and stand firmly bound and obliged unto   , Esquire, Judge of the Probate Court in and for the County of   , in the full and just sum of   dollars, to be paid to said Judge and his successors in said office , to the true payment whereof I bind myself and my heirs, executors, and administrators by these presents. Sealed with my seal, and dated the   day of   , in the year of our Lord one thousand nine hundred and   .

THE CONDITION OF THIS OBLIGATION IS SUCH, that if the above-bounden   , administrat   of the estate of   , late of   , in said County of   , deceased, intestate, shall,

First, make and return to said Probate Court, within three months after h   appointment, a true inventory of all the real and personal estate of said deceased which at the time of the making of such inventory shall have come to the possession or knowledge of said administrat   ;

Second, administer according to law all the personal estate of said deceased which may come to the possession of said administrat   , or of any person for h   , and also the proceeds of any of the real estate of said deceased that may be sold or mortgaged by said administrat   ;

Third, render upon oath a true account of h   administration at least once a year, until h   trust is fulfilled, unless he is excused therefrom in any year by said Court, and also render such account at such other times as said Court may order;

Fourth, pay to such persons as said Court may direct any balance remaining in h   hands upon the settlement of h   accounts, and

Fifth, deliver h   letters of administration into said Court in case any will of said deceased is hereafter duly proved and allowed

Then this obligation to be void, otherwise to remain in full force and virtue.

Signed, sealed, and delivered
   in presence of

    , ss.   19   . Examined and approved.
                     Judge of Probate Court.

I,   , the within-named administrat   , declare that, to the best of my knowledge and belief, the estate and effects of the within-named deceased do not exceed in value the following mentioned sums, viz ·

         Real Estate, $.
         Personal Estate, $.
              [SIGN]

ADMINISTRATOR'S BOND DE BONIS NON — WITH SURETIES.

[R L c 149, § 1]

KNOW ALL MEN BY THESE PRESENTS,

That we,   , of   in the County of   , as principal , and   , of   , in the County of   , and   , of   , in the County of   , as sureties, and all within the Commonwealth of Massachusetts, are holden and stand firmly bound and obliged unto   , Esquire, Judge of the Probate Court in and for the County of   , in the full and just sum of   dollars. to be paid to said Judge and his successors in said office, to the true payment whereof we bind ourselves and each of us, our and each of our heirs, executors, and administrators, jointly and severally, by these presents. Sealed with our seals, and dated the   day of   , in the year of our Lord one thousand nine hundred and   .

THE CONDITION OF THIS OBLIGATION IS SUCH, that if the above-bounden   , administrat   of the estate not already administered of   , late of said   , deceased, intestate, shall,

First, make and return to said Probate Court, within three months after h   appointment, a true inventory of all the real and personal estate of said deceased which at the time of the making of such inventory shall have come to the possession or knowledge of said administrat   ,

Second, administer according to law all the personal estate of said deceased which may come to the possession of said administrat   , or of any person for h   , and also the proceeds of any of the real estate of said deceased that may be sold or mortgaged by said administrat   ,

Third, render upon oath a true account of h   adminirstration at least once a year, until h   trust is fulfilled, unless he is excused therefrom in any year by said Court, and also render such account at such other times as said Court may order;

Fourth, pay to such persons as said Court may direct any balance remaining in h   hands upon the settlement of h   accounts, and

Fifth, deliver h   letters of administration into said Court in case any will of said deceased is hereafter duly proved and allowed

Then this obligation to be void, otherwise to remain in full force and virtue.

Signed, sealed, and delivered
in presence of

ss.   19   .   Examined and approved.
                              Judge of Probate Court.

I,   , the within-named administrat   , declare that, to the best of my knowledge and belief, the estate and effects of the within-named deceased do not exceed in value the following-mentioned sums, viz.

Real Estate, $.
Personal Estate, $.
                [SIGN]

ADMINISTRATOR'S BOND DE BONIS NON — WITHOUT SURETIES.

[R L c 149, §§ 1, 8]

KNOW ALL MEN BY THESE PRESENTS,

That I,   , of   , in the County of   , in the Commonwealth of Massachusetts, am holden and stand firmly bound and obliged unto   , Esquire, Judge of the Probate Court in and for the County of   , in the full and just sum of   dollars, to be paid to said Judge and his successors in said office, to the true payment whereof I bind myself and my heirs, executors, and administrators by these presents. Sealed with my seal, and dated the   day of   , in the year of our Lord one thousand nine hundred and   .

THE CONDITION OF THIS OBLIGATION IS SUCH, that if the above-bounden   , administrat   of the estate not already

552   APPENDIX.

administered of   , late of said   , deceased, intestate, shall,

First, make and return to said Probate Court, within three months after h   appointment, a true inventory of all the real and personal estate of said deceased which at the time of the making of such inventory shall have come to the possession or knowledge of said administrat   ;

Second, administer according to law all the personal estate of said deceased which may come to the possession of said administrat   , or of any person for h   , and also the proceeds of any of the real estate of said deceased that may be sold or mortgaged by said administrat   ,

Third, render upon oath a true account of h   administration at least once a year until h   trust is fulfilled, unless he is excused therefrom in any year by said Court, and also render such account at such other times as said Court may order,

Fourth, pay to such persons as said Court may direct any balance remaining in h   hands upon the settlement of h   accounts, and

Fifth, deliver h   letters of administration into said Court in case any will of said deceased is hereafter duly proved and allowed

Then this obligation to be void, otherwise to remain in full force and virtue.

 Signed, sealed, and delivered
  in presence of

 ss.   19   .   Examined and approved.
          Judge of Probate Court.

I,   , the within-named administrat   , declare that, to the best of my knowledge and belief, the estate and effects of the within-named deceased do not exceed in value the following-mentioned sums, viz.:

   Real Estate, $.
   Personal Estate, $.
    [SIGN]

Special Administrator's Bond.

[R L c 149, § 1.]

Know all Men by these Presents,

That we,   , of   , in the County of   , as principal , and   , of   , in the County of   , and   , of   , in the County of   , as sureties, and all within the Commonwealth of Massachusetts, are holden and stand firmly bound and obliged unto   , Esquire, Judge of the Probate Court in and for the County of   , in the full and just sum of   dollars, to be paid to the said Judge and his successors in said office, to the true payment whereof we bind ourselves and each of us, our and each of our heirs, executors, and administrators, jointly and severally, by these presents. Sealed with our seals, and dated the   day of   , in the year of our Lord one thousand nine hundred and   .

The condition of this obligation is such, that if the above-bounden   , special administrat   of the estate of   , late of said   . , deceased, shall

Make and return to said Probate Court, within three months after h   appointment, said Court having so ordered, a true inventory of all the personal estate of said deceased which at the time of the making of such inventory shall have come to h   possession or knowledge, and, whenever required by said Court, truly account, on oath, for all the estate of said deceased that may be received by h   as such special administrat   , and deliver the same to any person who may be appointed execut   or administrat   of said deceased, or may be otherwise lawfully authorized to receive the same.

Then this obligation to be void, otherwise to remain in full force and virtue.

Signed, sealed, and delivered
in presence of

ss.   19 . Examined and approved.

Judge of Probate Court.

I, , the within-named administrat , declare that, to the best of my knowledge and belief, the estate and effects of the within-named deceased do not exceed in value the following-mentioned sums, viz

        Real Estate, $.
        Personal Estate, $.
            [SIGN]

PUBLIC ADMINISTRATOR'S BOND.

[R L c 138, §§ 6, 7]

KNOW ALL MEN BY THESE PRESENTS,

That we, , of , in the County of , as principal, and , of , in the County of , and of , in the County of , as sureties, and all within the Commonwealth of Massachusetts, are holden and stand firmly bound and obliged unto , Esquire, Judge of the Probate Court in and for the County of , in the full and just sum of dollars, to be paid to said Judge and his successors in said office, to the true payment whereof we bind ourselves and each of us, our and each of our heirs, executors, and administrators, jointly and severally, by these presents. Sealed with our seals, and dated the day of , in the year of our Lord one thousand nine hundred and .

THE CONDITION OF THIS OBLIGATION IS SUCH, that if the above-bounden , public administrator in and for said County of , administrator of the estate of , late of , in said County of , deceased, intestate, shall

First, make and return to said Probate Court, within three months after his appointment, a true inventory of all the real and personal estate of said deceased which at the time of the making of such inventory shall have come to the possession or knowledge of said administrator;

Second, administer according to law all the personal estate of said deceased which may come to the possession of said administrator, or of any person for him, and also the proceeds of any of the real estate of said deceased that may be sold or mortgaged by him,

Third, render upon oath a true account of his administration at least once a year until his trust is fulfilled, unless he is excused therefrom in any year by said Court, and also render such account at such other times as said Court may order,

Fourth, pay the balance of said estate remaining in his hands upon the settlement of his accounts to such persons as said Court may direct; and, when said estate has been fully administered, to deposit with the Treasurer of the Commonwealth the whole amount remaining in his hands,

Fifth, upon the appointment and qualification in any case of an executor or administrator as his successor, to surrender into said Court said letters of administration, with an account under oath of his doings therein, and, upon a just settlement of such account, to pay over and deliver to such successor all sums of money remaining in his hands, and all property, effects, and credits of said deceased not then administered.

Then this obligation to be void, otherwise to remain in full force and virtue.

Signed, sealed, and delivered in presence of } [SEAL] [SEAL] [SEAL]

ss. A. D. 19 Examined and approved.
            Judge of Probate Court.

I,   , the within-named administrat   , declare that, to the best of my   knowledge and belief, the estate and effects of the within-named deceased do not exceed in value the following-mentioned sums, viz:

Real Estate, $.
Personal Estate, $.
[SIGN]

Executor's Bond — with Sureties.

[R L c 149, § 1]

Know all Men by these Presents,

That we,   , of   , in the County of   , as principal , and   , of   , in the County of   , and   , of   , in the County of   , as sureties, and all within the Commonwealth of Massachusetts, are holden and stand firmly bound and obliged unto   , Esquire, Judge of the Probate Court in and for the County of   , in the full and just sum of   dollars, to be paid to said Judge and his successors in said office; to the true payment whereof we bind ourselves and each of us, our and each of our heirs, executors, and administrators, jointly and severally, by these presents. Sealed with our seals, and dated the   day of   , in the year of our Lord one thousand nine hundred and   .

THE CONDITION OF THIS OBLIGATION IS SUCH, that if the above-bounden   , execut   of the last will and testament of   , late of said   , deceased, testate, shall . —

First, make and return to said Probate Court, within three months after h   appointment, a true inventory of all the real and personal estate of said deceased which at the time of the making of such inventory shall have come to the possession or knowledge of said execut   .

Second, administer according to law and to the will of said deceased all the personal estate of said deceased which may come to the possession of said execut   , or of any person for h   , and also the proceeds of any of the real estate of said deceased that may be sold or mortgaged by said execut   , and

Third, render upon oath a true account of h   administration at least once a year until h   trust is fulfilled, unless he is excused therefrom in any year by said Court, and also render such account at such other times as said Court may order.

Then this obligation to be void, otherwise to remain in full force and virtue

Signed, sealed, and delivered
in presence of }

ss.   A. D. 19   . Examined and approved.
                            Judge of Probate Court.

I,   , the within-named execut   , declare that, to the best of my knowledge and belief, the estate and effects of the within-named deceased do not exceed in value the following-mentioned sums, viz.

        Real Estate, $.
        Personal Estate, $.
            [SIGN]

Executor's Bond — without Sureties.

[R L c 149, § 3]

Know all Men by these Presents,

That I,   , of   , in the County of   , in the Commonwealth of Massachusetts, am holden and stand firmly bound and obliged unto   , Esquire, Judge of the Probate Court in and for the County of   , in the full and just sum of   dollars, to be paid to said Judge and his successors in said office; to the true payment whereof I bind myself and my heirs, executors, and administrators by these presents. Sealed with my seal, and dated the   day of   , in the year of our Lord one thousand nine hundred and   .

The condition of this obligation is such, that if the above-bounden   , execut   of the last will and testament of   , late of said   , deceased, testate, shall,

First, make and return to said Probate Court, within three months after h   appointment, a true inventory of all the real and personal estate of said deceased which at the time of the

558   APPENDIX.

making of such inventory shall have come to the possession or knowledge of said execut   ,

Second, administer according to law and to the will of said deceased all the personal estate of said deceased which may come to the possession of said execut   , or of any person for h   , and also the proceeds of any of the real estate of said deceased that may be sold or mortgaged by said execut   ; and

Third, render upon oath a true account of h   administration at least once a year, until h   trust is fulfilled, unless h   is excused therefrom in any year by said Court, and also render such account at such other times as said Court may order,

Then this obligation to be void, otherwise to remain in full force and virtue

Signed, sealed, and delivered
in presence of

ss.   A D 19 . Examined and approved.
                            Judge of Probate Court.

I,   , the within-named execut   , declare that, to the best of my knowledge and belief, the estate and effects of the within-named deceased do not exceed in value the following-mentioned sums, viz

    Real Estate, $.
    Personal Estate, $.
     [SIGN]

EXECUTOR'S BOND TO PAY DEBTS AND LEGACIES — RESIDUARY.

KNOW ALL MEN BY THESE PRESENTS,

That we,   , of   , in the County of   , as principal , and   , of   , in the County of   , and   , of   , in the County of   , as sureties, and all within the Commonwealth of Massachusetts, are holden and stand firmly bound and obliged unto   , Esquire, Judge of the Probate Court in and for the County of   , in the full and just sum of   dollars, to be paid to said Judge and his successors in said office; to the true payment whereof we bind ourselves and each of us, our and each of our heirs, executors, and administrators, jointly and severally, by these presents. Sealed with our seals, and dated the   day of   , in the year of our Lord one thousand nine hundred and   .

THE CONDITION OF THIS OBLIGATION IS SUCH, that if the above-bounden   , execut   of the last will and testament of   , late of   , in said County of   , deceased, testate, being RESIDUARY LEGATEE in said will, shall pay all debts and legacies of said deceased, and such sums as may be allowed by said Probate Court for necessaries to the widow and minor children of said deceased,

Then this obligation to be void, otherwise to remain in full force and virtue

  Signed, sealed, and delivered
   in presence of

 ss. A. D. 19   .   Examined and approved.
           Judge of Probate Court.

I,   , the within-named execut   , declare that, to the best of my knowledge and belief, the estate and effects of the within-named deceased do not exceed in value the following-mentioned sums, viz

    Real Estate, $.
    Personal Estate, $.
      [SIGN]

ADMINISTRATOR'S BOND — WILL ANNEXED — WITH SURETIES.

[R L c 149, § 1]

KNOW ALL MEN BY THESE PRESENTS,

That we,   , of   , in the County of   , as principal , and   , of   , in the County of   , and   , of   , in the County of   , as sureties, and all within

560   APPENDIX

the Commonwealth of Massachusetts, are holden and stand firmly bound and obliged unto   , Esquire, Judge of the Probate Court in and for the County of   , in the full and just sum of   dollars, to be paid to said Judge and his successors in said office, to the true payment whereof we bind ourselves and each of us, our and each of our heirs, executors, and administrators, jointly and severally, by these presents Sealed with our seals, and dated the   day of   , in the year of our Lord one thousand eight hundred and ninety-

THE CONDITION OF THIS OBLIGATION IS SUCH, that if the above-bounden   , administrat   , with the will annexed, of the estate   , of   , late of said   , deceased, testate, shall,

First, make and return to said Probate Court, within three months after h   appointment, a true inventory of all the real and personal estate of said deceased which at the time of the making of such inventory shall have come to the possession or knowledge of said administrat   ,

Second, administer according to law and to the will of said deceased all the personal estate of said deceased which may come to the possession of said administrat   , or of any person for h   , and also the proceeds of any of the real estate of said deceased that may be sold or mortgaged by said administrat   , and

Third, render upon oath a true account of h   administration at least once a year, until h   trust is fulfilled, unless he is excused therefrom in any year by said Court, and also render such account at such other times as said Court may order,

Then this obligation to be void, otherwise to remain in full force and virtue.

Signed, sealed, and delivered
  in presence of   }

    ss.   A. D. 19   .   Examined and approved.
                                    Judge of Probate Court.

I,   , the within-named administrat   , declare that, to the best of my knowledge and belief, the estate and effects of the within-named deceased do not exceed in value the following-mentioned sums, viz.

   Real Estate, $.
   Personal Estate, $.
     [SIGN]

ADMINISTRATOR'S BOND — WILL ANNEXED — WITHOUT SURETIES.

[R L c 149, §§ 1, 3.]

KNOW ALL MEN BY THESE PRESENTS,

That I, , of , in the County of , in the Commonwealth of Massachusetts, am holden and stand firmly bound and obliged unto , Esquire, Judge of the Probate Court in and for the County of , in the full and just sum of dollars, to be paid to said Judge and his successors in said office; to the true payment whereof I bind myself and my heirs, executors, and administrators by these presents. Sealed with my seal, and dated the day of , in the year of our Lord one thousand nine hundred and .

THE CONDITION OF THIS OBLIGATION IS SUCH, that if the above-bounden . administrat , with the will annexed, of the estate , of , late of , in said County of , deceased, testate, shall,

First, make and return to said Probate Court, within three months after h appointment, a true inventory of all the real and personal estate of said deceased which at the time of the making of such inventory shall have come to the possession or knowledge of said administrat ;

Second, administer according to law and to the will of said deceased all the personal estate of said deceased which may come to the possession of said administrat , or of any person for h , and also the proceeds of any of the real estate of said deceased that may be sold or mortgaged by said administrat , and

Third, render upon oath a true account of h administration at least once a year, until h   trust is fulfilled, unless he is excused therefrom in any year by said Court, and also render such account at such other times as said Court may order,

Then this obligation to be void, otherwise to remain in full force and virtue.

Signed, sealed, and delivered
in presence of

 ss. A. D 19 Examined and approved
            Judge of Probate Court.

I, , the within-named administrat , declare that, to the best of my knowledge and belief, the estate and effects of the within-named deceased do not exceed in value the following-mentioned sums, viz

    Real Estate, $.
    Personal Estate, $.
      [SIGN]

ADMINISTRATOR'S BOND — WILL ANNEXED DE BONIS NON — WITH SURETIES.

[R L c 149, § 1]

KNOW ALL MEN BY THESE PRESENTS,

That we, , of, in the County of , as principal , and , of , in the County of , and , of , in the County of , as sureties, and all within the Commonwealth of Massachusetts, are holden and stand firmly bound and obliged unto , Esquire, Judge of the Probate Court in and for the County of , in the full and just sum of dollars, to be paid to said Judge and his successors in said office; to the true payment whereof we bind ourselves and each of us, our and each of our heirs, executors, and administrators, jointly and severally, by these presents.

Sealed with our seals, and dated the   day of   , in the year of our Lord one thousand eight hundred and ninety-

THE CONDITION OF THIS OBLIGATION IS SUCH, that if the above-bounden   , administrat   , with the will annexed, of the estate not already administered,   , of   , late of said   , deceased, testate, shall,

First, make and return to said Probate Court, within three months after h   appointment, a true inventory of all the real and personal estate of said deceased which at the time of the making of such inventory shall have come to the possession or knowledge of said administrat   ,

Second, administer according to law and to the will of said deceased all the personal estate of said deceased not already administered which may come to the possession of said administrat   , or of any person for h   , and also the proceeds of any of the real estate of said deceased that may be sold or mortgaged by said administrat   ; and

Third, render upon oath a true account of h   administration at least once a year, until h   trust is fulfilled, unless he is excused therefrom in any year by said Court, and also render such account at such other times as said Court may order,

Then this obligation to be void, otherwise to remain in full force and virtue.

Signed, sealed, and delivered
in presence of

ss.   A. D 19 .   Examined and approved
                                 Judge of Probate Court.

I,   , the within-named administrat   , declare that, to the best of my knowledge and belief, the estate and effects of the within-named deceased do not exceed in value the following-mentioned sums, viz.

Real Estate, $.
Personal Estate, $.
[SIGN]

Guardian's Bond — with Sureties.

Know all Men by these Presents,

That we,   , of   , in the County of   , as principal , and   , of   , in the County of   , and   , of   , in the County of   , as sureties, and all within the Commonwealth of Massachusetts, are holden and stand firmly bound and obliged unto   , Esquire, Judge of the Probate Court in and for the County of   , in the full and just sum of   dollars, to be paid to said Judge and his successors in said office, to the true payment whereof we bind ourselves and each of us, our and each of our heirs, executors, and administrators, jointly and severally, by these presents. Sealed with our seals, and dated the   day of   , in the year of our Lord one thousand nine hundred and   .

THE CONDITION OF THIS OBLIGATION IS SUCH, that if the above-bounden   , guardian of   , of   , in said County of   , minor , shall,

First, make and return to said Probate Court, at such time as it may order, a true inventory of all the real and personal estate of said ward that at the time of the making of such inventory shall have come to the possession or knowledge of said guardian,

Second, manage and dispose of all such estate according to raw and for the best interests of said ward, and faithfully discharge h   trust in relation to such estate, and to the custody, education, and maintenance of said ward   ;

Third, render upon oath at least once a year, until h   trust is fulfilled, unless h   is excused therefrom in any year by said Court, a true account of the property in h   hands, including the proceeds of all real estate sold or mortgaged by h   , and of the management and disposition thereof, and also render such account at such other times as said Court may order; and

Fourth, at the expiration of h   trust, settle h   account in said Court, or with said ward, or h   legal representatives, and pay over and deliver all the estate remaining in h   hands, or due from h   on such settlement, to the person or persons lawfully entitled thereto;

Then this obligation to be void, otherwise to remain in full force and virtue

    Signed, sealed, and delivered
        in presence of

ss.   A. D. 19 . Examined and approved.
                                Judge of Probate Court.

I,   , the within-named guardian, declare that, to the best of my knowledge and belief, the estate and effects of the within-named ward   do not exceed in value the following-mentioned sums, viz.
        Real Estate, $.
        Personal Estate, $.
           [SIGN]

GUARDIAN'S BOND — WITHOUT SURETIES.

[R. L. c. 149, §§ 1, 4, 5, 6.]

KNOW ALL MEN BY THESE PRESENTS,

That I,   , of   , in the County of   , in the Commonwealth of Massachusetts, am holden and stand firmly bound and obliged unto   , Esquire, Judge of the Probate Court in and for the County of   , in the full and just sum of   dollars, to be paid to said Judge and his successors in said office; to the true payment whereof I bind myself and my heirs, executors, and administrators by these presents. Sealed with my seal, and dated the   day of   , in the year of our Lord one thousand nine hundred and   .

THE CONDITION OF THIS OBLIGATION IS SUCH, that if the above-bounden   , guardian of   , of   , in said County of   , minor , shall,

566   APPENDIX

First, make and return to said Probate Court, at such time as it may order, a true inventory of all the real and personal estate of said ward that at the time of the making of such inventory shall have come to the possession or knowledge of said guardian,

Second, manage and dispose of all such estate according to law and for the best interests of said ward, and faithfully discharge h   trust in relation to such estate, and to the custody, education, and maintenance of said ward,

Third, render upon oath at least once a year, until h   trust is fulfilled, unless h   is excused therefrom in any year by said Court, a true account of the property in h   hands, including the proceeds of all real estate sold or mortgaged by h   , and of the management and disposition thereof, and also render such account at such other times as said Court may order; and

Fourth, at the expiration of h   trust, settle h   account in said Court, or with said ward , or h   legal representatives, and pay over and deliver all the estate remaining in h   hands, or due from h   on such settlement, to the person or persons lawfully entitled thereto,

Then this obligation to be void, otherwise to remain in full force and virtue.

    Signed, sealed, and delivered
      in presence of

    ss.   A D 19   Examined and approved
                                         Judge of Probate Court.

I,   , the within-named guardian, declare that, to the best of my knowledge and belief. the estate and effects of the within-named ward do not exceed in value the following-mentioned sums, viz :

                Real Estate, $.
                Personal Estate, $.
                      [SIGN]

Guardian's Bond — Spendthrift.

[R L. c 145, § 10, c 149, § 1]

Know all Men by these Presents,

That we,   , of   , in the County of   , as principal , and   , of   , in the County of   , and   , of   , in the County of   , as sureties, and all within the Commonwealth of Massachusetts, are holden and stand firmly bound and obliged unto   , Esquire, Judge of the Probate Court in and for the County of   , in the full and just sum of   dollars, to be paid to said Judge and his successors in said office; to the true payment whereof we bind ourselves and each of us, our and each of our heirs, executors, and administrators, jointly and severally, by these presents. Sealed with our seals, and dated the   day of   in the year of our Lord one thousand nine hundred and   .

The condition of this obligation is such, that if the above-bounden   , guardian of   , of   , in said County of   , a spendthrift, shall,

First, make and return to said Probate Court, at such time as it may order, a true inventory of all the real and personal estate of said ward that at the time of the making of such inventory shall have come to the possession or knowledge of said guardian;

Second, manage and dispose of all such estate according to law and for the best interests of said ward, and faithfully discharge h   trust in relation to such estate, and to the custody and maintenance of said ward;

Third, render upon oath at least once a year, until h   trust is fulfilled, unless h   is excused therefrom in any year by said Court, a true account of the property in h   hands, including the proceeds of all real estate sold or mortgaged by h   , and of the management and disposition thereof, and also render such account at such other times as said Court may order; and

Fourth, at the expiration of h   trust, settle h   account in said Court, or with said ward, or h   legal representatives, and pay over and deliver all the estate remaining in h hands, or due from h on such settlement, to the person or persons lawfully entitled thereto,

Then this obligation to be void, otherwise to remain in full force and virtue.

Signed, sealed, and delivered
in presence of

ss.   A. D 19 .   Examined and approved.
Judge of Probate Court.

I,   , the within-named guardian, declare that, to the best of my knowledge and belief, the estate and effects of the within-named ward do not exceed in value the following-mentioned sums, viz.:

   Real Estate, $.
   Personal Estate, $.
     [SIGN]

Trustee's Bond — with Sureties.

[R L c 149, § 1.]

Know all Men by these Presents,

That we,   , of   , in the County of   , as principal , and   , of   , in the County of   , and   , of   , in the County of   , as sureties, and all within the Commonwealth of Massachusetts, are holden and stand firmly bound and obliged unto   , Esquire, Judge of the Probate Court in and for the County of   , in the full and just sum of   dollars, to be paid to said Judge and his successors in said office; to the true payment whereof we bind ourselves and each of us, our and each of our heirs, executors, and administrators, jointly and severally, by these presents. Sealed with our seals, and dated the   day of   , in the year of our Lord one thousand nine hundred and   .

THE CONDITION OF THIS OBLIGATION IS SUCH, that if the above-bounden   , trustee of certain estate given in trust for the benefit of   , under the will of   , late of   , in said County of   , deceased, testate, shall,

First, make and return to said Probate Court, at such time as it may order, a true inventory of all the real and personal estate belonging to h   as such trustee which at the time of the making of such inventory shall have come to h   possession or knowledge,

Second, manage and dispose of all such estate, and faithfully discharge h   trust in relation thereto, according to law and to the will of said testat   ;

Third, render upon oath at least once a year, until h   trust is fulfilled, unless h   is excused therefrom in any year by said Court, a true account of the property in h   hands, and of the management and disposition thereof, and also render such account at such other times as said Court may order,

Fourth, at the expiration of h   trust, settle h   account in said Court, and pay over and deliver all the estate remaining in h   hands, or due from h   on such settlement, to the person or persons entitled thereto,

Then this obligation to be void, otherwise to remain in full force and virtue.

Signed, sealed, and delivered
    in presence of   {

ss.   A. D. 19   .   Examined and approved
                    Judge of Probate Court.

I,   , the within-named trustee, declare that, to the best of my knowledge and belief, the within-named estate does not exceed in value the following-mentioned sums, viz..

    Real Estate, $.
    Personal Estate, $.
            [SIGN]

TRUSTEE'S BOND — WITHOUT SURETIES.

[R L c 149, §§ 1, 4]

KNOW ALL MEN BY THESE PRESENTS,

That I,   , of   , in the County of   , in the Commonwealth of Massachusetts, am holden and stand firmly bound and obliged unto   , Esquire, Judge of the Probate Court in and for the County of   , in the full and just sum of   dollars, to be paid to said Judge and his successors in said office; to the true payment whereof I bind myself and my heirs, executors, and administrators by these presents. Sealed with my seal, and dated the   day of   , in the year of our Lord one thousand nine hundred and   .

THE CONDITION OF THIS OBLIGATION IS SUCH, that if the above-bounden   , trustee of certain estate given in trust for the benefit of   , under the will of   , late of   , in said County of   , deceased, testate, shall,

First, make and return to said Probate Court, at such time as it may order, a true inventory of all the real and personal estate belonging to h   as such trustee which at the time of the making of such inventory shall have come to h   possession or knowledge,

Second, manage and dispose of all such estate, and faithfully discharge h   trust in relation thereto, according to law and to the will of said testat   ;

Third, render upon oath at least once a year, until h   trust is fulfilled, unless h   is excused therefrom in any year by said Court, a true account of the property in h   hands, and of the management and disposition thereof, and also render such account at such other times as said Court may order,

Fourth, at the expiration of h   trust, settle h   account in said Court, and pay over and deliver all the estate remaining in h   hands, or due from h   on such settlement, to the person or persons entitled thereto,

Then this obligation to be void, otherwise to remain in full force and virtue

Signed, sealed, and delivered
in presence of

ss.   A. D. 19 .   Examined and approved.
                                   Judge of Probate Court.

I,   , the within-named trustee, declare that, to the best of my knowledge and belief, the within-named estate does not exceed in value the following-mentioned sums, viz..

Real Estate, $.
Personal Estate, $.
[SIGN]

TRUSTEE'S BOND — INVENTORY NOT REQUIRED — WITH SURETIES.

[R L c 147, § 7.]

KNOW ALL MEN BY THESE PRESENTS,

That we,   , of   , in the County of   , as principal , and   , of   , in the County of   , and   , of   , in the County of   , as sureties, and all within the Commonwealth of Massachusetts, are holden and stand firmly bound and obliged unto   , Esquire, Judge of the Probate Court in and for the County of   , in the full and just sum of   dollars, to be paid to said Judge and his successors in said office, to the true payment whereof we bind ourselves and each of us, our and each of our heirs, executors, and administrators, jointly and severally, by these presents. Sealed with our seals, and dated the   day of   , in the year of our Lord one thousand nine hundred and   .

THE CONDITION OF THIS OBLIGATION IS SUCH, that if the above-bounden   , trustee of certain estate given in trust for the benefit of   , under the will of   , late of   in said County of   , deceased, testate, shall,

First, manage and dispose of all the real and personal estate belonging to h   as such trustee , and faithfully discharge h   trust in relation thereto, according to law and to the will of said testat   ;

Second, render upon oath at least once a year, until h   trust is fulfilled, unless h   is excused therefrom in any year by said Court, a true account of the property in h   hands, and of the management and disposition thereof, and also render such account at such other times as said Court may order,

Third, at the expiration of h   trust, settle h   account in said Court, and pay over and deliver all the estate remaining in   h   hands, or due from h   on such settlement, to the person or persons entitled thereto,

Then this obligation to be void, otherwise to remain in full force and virtue,

Signed, sealed, and delivered
in presence of

ss.   A. D. 19 . Examined and approved
                    Judge of Probate Court.

I,   , the within-named trustee, declare that, to the best of my knowledge and belief, the within-named estate does not exceed in value the following-mentioned sums, viz.

    Real Estate, $.
    Personal Estate, $.
            [SIGN]

TRUSTEE'S BOND — INVENTORY NOT REQUIRED — WITHOUT SURETIES.

[R. L. c. 147, § 7; c. 149, § 4]

KNOW ALL MEN BY THESE PRESENTS,

That I,   , of   , in the County of   , in the Commonwealth of Massachusetts, am holden and stand firmly bound and obliged unto   , Esquire, Judge of the Probate Court in and for the County of   , in the full and just sum of   dollars, to be paid to said Judge and his successors in said office; to the true payment whereof I bind myself and my heirs, executors, and administrators by these presents. Sealed with my seal, and dated the ´ day of   , in the year of our Lord one thousand nine hundred and   .

THE CONDITION OF THIS OBLIGATION IS SUCH, that if the above-bounden   , trustee of certain estate given in trust for the benefit of   , under the will of   , late of   , in said County of   , deceased, testate, shall,

First, manage and dispose of all the real and personal estate belonging to h   as such trustee , and faithfully discharge h   trust in relation thereto, according to law and to the will of said testat   ,

Second, render upon oath at least once a year, until h   trust is fulfilled, unless h   is excused therefrom in any year by said Court, a true account of the property in h   hands, and of the management and disposition thereof, and also render such account at such other times as said Court may order,

Third, at the expiration of h   trust, settle h   account in said Court, and pay over and deliver all the estate remaining in h   hands, or due from h   on such settlement, to the person or persons entitled thereto,

Then this obligation to be void, otherwise to remain in full force and virtue.

Signed, sealed, and delivered
in presence of

ss.   A. D 19 . Examined and approved.
                              Judge of Probate Court.

I,   , the within-named trustee , declare that, to the best of my knowledge and belief, the within-named estate does not exceed in value the following-mentioned sums, viz.:

Real Estate, $.
Personal Estate, $.
[SIGN]

Petition for Guardianship.

[After the name of each minor, state the *exact* date of birth Notice must be given to the parents, if living, or to the survivor of them, or their assent must be obtained]

To the Honorable the Judge of the Probate Court in and for the County of   :

Respectfully represents   , of   , in the County of   , that there is occasion for the appointment of a guardian of

	born	18 ,
	"	18 ,
	"	18 ,

of   , in the County of   , minor and child of   , late of   , in the County of   , deceased, and   , his widow,

and your petitioner prays that he, or some other suitable person may be appointed to that trust.

Dated this   day of   , A. D. 19   .

        ss   A D 19   .
Personally appeared the above-named   , minor , above the age of fourteen years, and nominated said   to be h guardian.
        Before me,
                                Justice of the Peace.

I, the surviving parent   of said minor , hereby assent to the granting of the foregoing petition.

Citation by publication once a week for three successive weeks, the last publication to be one day at least before return day, or by delivering a copy seven days at least before return day.

Petition for Guardianship of Insane.

[This application must be made by two or more of the relations or friends of the insane person, or the selectmen, or Mayor and Aldermen, of the place of which he is an inhabitant or resident, or upon which he is or may become chargeable.]

To the Honorable the Judge of the Probate Court in and for the County of .

Respectfully represent , of , in the County of , that , an inhabitant or resident of , in said County of , is an insane person, and incapable of taking care of h self. Your petitioners therefore pray that , of , or some other suitable person, may be appointed guardian of said , agreeably to the law in such case made and provided

Dated this day of , A. D. 19 .

Citation by delivering a copy to the insane person fourteen days at least before return day

---

Petition for Guardianship of Spendthrift.

[R. L. c. 145, § 7.]

[The complaint may be made by the relations, or Overseers of the Poor of the place of which the spendthrift is an inhabitant or resident.]

To the Honorable the Judge of the Probate Court in and for the County of .

Respectfully complain relation of , overseers of the poor of the city of — town of — selectmen of the town of — in said County, that in h judgment, , an inhabitant or resident of , does, by excessive drinking, gaming, idleness, so spend, waste, and lessen h estate, as to expose h self and family to want or suffering; and does also thereby expose said city of — town of , to charge or expense for h and their support.

Wherefore he pray , that , of , in County of , or some other suitable person, may be appointed guardian of the person and estate of said , agreeably to the law in such case made and provided

Dated this day of A. D. 19 .

Citation by serving spendthrift with copy of order fourteen days at least before return day.

Petition for Guardianship by Foreign Guardian.

To the Honorable the Judge of the Probate Court in and for the County of   :

Respectfully represents   that he is a resident of   , in the State of   , that he is the guardian of   , a minor, who is a resident of   , in said State of   , duly appointed on the   day of   , A. D. 19   , by a Court of competent jurisdiction, to wit the   Court in and for   , and has given a bond and security as such guardian in double the value of the property of such ward, to wit in the sum of   dollars; a full and complete and duly exemplified or authenticated transcript from the records of said   Court in and for said   , are herewith produced That h   appointment is still in full force, that his ward   entitled to property in the said County of   , to wit·

that a removal of the movable property or estate of said ward out of this Commonwealth will not conflict with the terms or limitations attending the right by which the ward owns the same.

Wherefore your petitioner prays that letters of guardianship of the estate of said ward in this Commonwealth be issued to him, which shall authorize him to care for and manage the real estate of said ward, to collect the rents, issues and profits therefrom, and to demand, sue for, and recover any such property, and to remove any of the movable property or estate of said ward out of this Commonwealth.

Petition for Trusteeship — with Sureties

[No notice required for the appointment of a trustee who is designated in a will]

To the Honorable the Judge of the Probate Court in and for the County of   .

Respectfully represents   , of   , in the County of   , that   , late of   , in said County of   , deceased, testate, by h   last will and testament, duly proved and allowed on the   day of   , A. D. 19   , in said

Court, did therein give certain estate in trust for the use and benefit of   , and appointed   , trustee thereof,

and that h   is willing to accept said trust, and give bond according to law for the faithful discharge thereof, he therefore pray that he may be appointed trustee as aforesaid, according to the provisions of the law in such case made and provided.
Dated this   day of   , A. D. 19   .

The undersigned, being all the persons interested, hereby assent to the foregoing petition

<small>Citation by publication once a week for three successive weeks, the last publication to be one day at least before return day.</small>

Petition for Trusteeship — Without Sureties.

[R L c 149, § 4]

To the Honorable the Judge of the Probate Court in and for the County of   :

Respectfully represents   , of   , in the County of   , that   , late of   , in the County of   , deceased, testate, by h   last will and testament, proved and allowed on the   day of   , A. D. 19   , in said Court, did therein give certain estate in trust for the use and benefit of   , and appointed   trustee thereof, and in and by said will requested that said   be exempted from giving a surety on h   bond as such trustee ,   that he   willing to accept said trust, and give bond according to law for the faithful discharge thereof, he therefore pray that he may be appointed trustee as aforesaid, and that he may be exempt from giving a surety on h   bond , according to the provisions of the law in such case made and provided.
Dated this   day of   , A. D. 19   .

Administrator's Bond — with Sureties.

[R L c 149, § 1]

Know all Men by these Presents,

That we,   , of   , in the County of   , as principal , and   , of   , in the County of   , and   , of   , in the County of   , as sureties, and all within the Commonwealth of Massachusetts, are holden and stand firmly bound and obliged unto   , Esquire, Judge of the Probate Court in and for the County of   , in the full and just sum of   dollars, to be paid to said Judge and his successors in said office; to the true payment whereof we bind ourselves and each of us, our and each of our heirs, executors, and administrators, jointly and severally, by these presents. Sealed with our seals, and dated the   day of   , in the year of our Lord one thousand nine hundred and   .

THE CONDITION OF THIS OBLIGATION IS SUCH, that if the above-bounden   , administrat   of the estate of   , late of said   , deceased, intestate, shall,

First, make and return to said Probate Court, within three months after h   appointment, a true inventory of all the real and personal estate of said deceased which at the time of the making of such inventory shall have come to the possession or knowledge of said administrat   ,

Second, administer according to law all the personal estate of said deceased which may come to the possession of said administrat   , or of any person for h   , and also the proceeds of any of the real estate of said deceased that may be sold or mortgaged by said administrat   ,

Third, render upon oath, a true account of h   administration at least once a year, until h   trust is fulfilled, unless he is excused therefrom in any year by said Court, and also render such account at such other times as said Court may order,

Fourth, pay to such persons as said Court may direct any balance remaining in h   hands upon the settlement of h   accounts, and

Fifth, deliver h   letters of administration into said Court in case any will of said deceased is hereafter duly proved and allowed.

Then this obligation to be void, otherwise to remain in full force and virtue.

Signed, sealed, and delivered
in presence of

ss.   19 . Examined and approved.
Judge of Probate Court.

I,   , the within-named administrat   , declare that, to the best of my   knowledge and belief, the estate and effects of the within-named deceased do not exceed in value the following-mentioned sums, viz..

Real Estate, $.
Personal Estate, $.

PETITION FOR NEW BOND.

To the Honorable the Judge of the Probate Court in and for the County of

Respectfully represents   , of   , in the County of   , that he is heir-at-law   , of   , late of said   , deceased,   and is interested in the estate of the said deceased.

that at a Probate Court held at said   , on the   day of   , A. D. 19 ,   of said   , was duly appointed administrat   — execut   of the   estate of said deceased, and gave bond in the sum of   dollars, with   , of   , and   , of   , as sureties, for the faithful discharge of h   trust, that said estate is not fully administered; that said sureties are not sufficient to ensure the faithful discharge of said trust; the said administrat — execut having

Wherefore he prays that said may be required to give a new bond with such sureties and in such sum as the Court may direct.

Dated this   day of   , A. D. 19 .

Personal service on executor, administrator, guardian, or trustee.

Administrator's Letter.

COMMONWEALTH OF MASSACHUSETTS.

, ss.   Probate Court.

To , of , in the County of , and Commonwealth aforesaid.

You are appointed administrat of the estate of , late of , in said County of , deceased, intestate.

And you are required to make and return to said Probate Court, within three months from the date hereof, a true inventory of all the real and personal estate of said deceased which at the time of the making of such inventory shall have come to your possession or knowledge;

To administer according to law all the personal estate of said deceased which may come to your possession, or that of any person for you, and also the proceeds of any of the real estate of said deceased that may be sold or mortgaged by you,

To render upon oath a true account of your administration at least once a year, until your trust is fulfilled, unless excused therefrom in any year by said Court,

To pay any balance remaining in your hands upon the settlement of your accounts to such persons as said Court shall direct,

To deliver these letters of administration into said Court in case any will of said deceased shall be hereafter duly proved and allowed;

PROBATE FORMS. 581

And also, within three months, to cause notice of your appointment to be published once in each week for three successive weeks in the   , a newspaper published in   , and return your affidavit of having given such notice, with a copy thereof, to the Probate Court.

Witness,   , Judge of said Court, at   , this   day of   , in the year of our Lord one thousand nine hundred and   .

              Register.

ADMINISTRATOR'S AFFIDAVIT OF NOTICE OF APPOINTMENT.

[This should be filed in the Registry of Probate immediately after giving the notice.]

I,   , do testify and say that   gave notice of appointment to and acceptance of the trust of administrat   of the estate   , of   , late of   , in the County of   , deceased, within three months from the   day of   , A. D 19 , the time of said appointment,   by publishing a notification thereof once in each week for three successive weeks in the   , a newspaper published in   , commencing on the   day of   , A. D. 19 , and the following is a true copy thereof, viz : —

Notice is hereby given that the subscriber has been duly appointed administrat   of the estate of   , late of   , in the County of   , deceased, intestate, and ha   taken upon h   self that trust by giving bond , as the law directs. All persons having demands upon the estate of said deceased are required to exhibit the same; and all persons indebted to said estate are called upon to make payment to

(*Address*)

   ,   , 19 .

                Adm.

                Adm.

   , ss.   , A. D 19 . Personally appeared   , and made oath that the foregoing affidavit by h   subscribed is true.

   Before me,

             Justice of the Peace.

Administrator's Letter — De Bonis Non.

COMMONWEALTH OF MASSACHUSETTS.

, ss.   Probate Court.

To   , of   , in the County of   , and Commonwealth aforesaid .

You are appointed administrat   of the estate not already administered of   , late of   , in said County of   , deceased, intestate.

And you are required to make and return to said Probate Court, within three months from the date hereof, a true inventory of all the real and personal estate of said deceased which at the time of the making of such inventory shall have come to your possession or knowledge,

To administer according to law all the personal estate of said deceased which may come to your possession, or that of any person for you, and also the proceeds of any of the real estate of said deceased that may be sold or mortgaged by you,

To render upon oath a true account of your administration at least once a year, until your trust is fulfilled, unless excused therefrom in any year by said Court,

To pay any balance remaining in your hands upon the settlement of your accounts to such persons as said Court shall direct,

To deliver these letters of administration into said Court in case any will of said deceased shall be hereafter duly proved and allowed,

And also, within three months, to cause notice of your appointment to be published once in each week for three successive weeks in the   , a newspaper published in   , and return your affidavit of having given such notice, with a copy thereof, to the Probate Court

Witness,   , Judge of said Court, at   , this   day of   , in the year of our Lord one thousand nine hundred and   .

Register.

Administrator's Affidavit of Notice of Appointment — De Bonis Non

[This should be filed in the Registry of Probate immediately after giving the notice]

I,   , do testify and say that   gave notice of appointment to and acceptance of the trust of administrat   of the estate not already administered of   , late of   , in the County of   , deceased, within three months from the   day of   , A. D. 19 , the time of said appointment, by publishing a notification thereof once in each week for three successive weeks in the   , a newspaper published in   , commencing on the   day of   , A. D. 19 , and the following is a true copy thereof, viz. —

Notice is hereby given that the subscriber has been duly appointed administrat   of the estate not already administered of   , late of   , in the County of   , deceased, intestate, and has taken upon h   self that trust by giving bond, as the law directs. All persons having demands upon the estate of said deceased are required to exhibit the same; and all persons indebted to said estate are called upon to make payment to

(*Address*)
   ,   , 19 .

Adm.

Adm.

   , ss.   A. D. 19 . Personally appeared   , and made oath that the foregoing affidavit by h   subscribed is true

Before me,

Justice of the Peace.

Special Administrator's Letter

COMMONWEALTH OF MASSACHUSETTS

, ss.   Probate Court.

To   , of,   , in the County of   , and Commonwealth aforesaid:

You are appointed special administrat   of the estate of   , late of   , in the County of   , deceased.

And you are required to make and return into said Probate Court, within three months from the date hereof, a true inventory of all the goods, chattels, rights, and credits of said deceased which have or shall come to your possession or knowledge, and truly account on oath for all the goods, chattels, debts, and effects of said deceased that shall be received by you as such special administrat   whenever required by the Probate Court, and deliver the same to whomsoever shall be appointed executor or administrator of the estate of said deceased, or to such other person as shall be lawfully authorized to receive the same, and you are authorized to take charge of all real estate of said deceased, collect the rents, and make necessary repairs.

Witness,   , Judge of said Court, at   , this   day of   , in the year of our Lord one thousand nine hundred and   .

Register.

Public Administrator's Letter.

COMMONWEALTH OF MASSACHUSETTS

, ss.   Probate Court.

To   , *Public Administrator in and for said County of   :*

These letters of administration upon the estate of   , late of   , in said County of   , deceased, intestate, are hereby granted unto you.

And you are required to make and return to said Probate Court, within three months from the date hereof, a true inventory of all the real and personal estate of said deceased which at the time of the making of such inventory shall have come to your possession or knowledge;

To administer according to law all the personal estate of said deceased which may come to your possession, or that of any person for you, and also the proceeds of any of the real estate of said deceased that may be sold by you;

To render upon oath a true account of your administration at least once a year, until your trust is fulfilled, unless excused therefrom in any year by said Court;

To pay the balance of said estate remaining in your hands upon the settlement of your accounts to such persons as said Court may direct, and, when said estate has been fully administered, to deposit with the Treasurer of the Commonwealth the whole amount remaining in your hands;

And, upon the appointment and qualification in any case of an executor or administrator as your successor, to surrender into said Court said letters of administration, with an account under oath of your doings therein, and upon a just settlement of such account to pay over and deliver to such successor all sums of money remaining in your hands, and all property, effects, and credits of said deceased not then administered;

And also, within three months, to cause notice of your appointment to be published once in each week for three successive weeks in the   , a newspaper published in said   , and return your affidavit of having given such notice, with a copy thereof, to the Probate Court.

Witness,   , Judge of said Court, at   , this   day of   , in the year of our Lord one thousand nine hundred and   .

Register.

Public Administrator's Affidavit of Notice of Appointment.

[This should be filed in the Registry of Probate immediately after giving the notice]

I,   , do testify and say that I gave notice of my appointment to and acceptance of the trust of public administrator of the estate of   , late of   , in the County of   , deceased, within three months from the   day of   , A. D. 19 , the time of said appointment,   by publishing a notification thereof once in each week for three successive weeks in the   , a newspaper published in   , commencing on the   day of   , A. D. 19 , and the following is a true copy thereof, viz : —

Notice is hereby given that the subscriber has been duly appointed public administrator of the estate   , of   , late of   , in the County of   , deceased, intestate, and has taken upon himself that trust by giving bond as the law directs. All persons having demands upon the estate of said deceased are hereby required to exhibit the same; and all persons indebted to said estate are called upon to make payment to

(*Address*)

    ,   , 19 .

            .   *Public Adm.*

                         Public Adm.

    , ss.   , A D. 19 . Personally appeared   and made oath that the foregoing affidavit by h   subscribed is true

        Before me,

                    Justice of the Peace.

Executor's Letter.

COMMONWEALTH OF MASSACHUSETTS.

, ss.   Probate Court.

To   , of   , in the County of   , and Commonwealth aforesaid.

You are appointed execut   of the last will and testament of   , late of   , in said County of   , deceased, testate, which will was proved and allowed on the   day of   , A. D. 19   , by said Court, and is now of record in this Court

And you are required to make and return into said Probate Court, within three months from the date hereof, a true inventory of all the real and personal estate of said deceased which at the time of the making of such inventory shall have come to your possession or knowledge;

To administer according to law and to the will of said deceased all the personal estate of said deceased which may come to your possession, or that of any person for you, and also the proceeds of any of the real estate of said deceased that may be sold or mortgaged by you;

To render upon oath a true account of your administration at least once a year, until your trust is fulfilled, unless excused therefrom in any year by said Court;

And also, within three months, to cause notice of your appointment to be published once in each week for three successive weeks in the   , a newspaper published in said   , and return your affidavit of having given such notice, with a copy thereof, to the Probate Court

Witness,   , Judge of said Court, at   , this   day of   , in the year of our Lord one thousand nine hundred and   .

Register.

Executor's Affidavit of Notice of Appointment.

[This should be filed in the Registry of Probate immediately after giving the notice.]

I,   , do testify and say that I gave notice of my appointment to and acceptance of the trust of execut   of the will of   , late of   , in the County of   , deceased, testate, within three months from the   day of   , A D. 19 , the time of said appointment,   by publishing a notification thereof once in each week for three successive weeks in the   , a newspaper published in   , commencing on the   day of   , A D. 19 , and the following is a true copy thereof, viz : —

Notice is hereby given that the subscriber ha   been duly appointed execut   of the will of   , late of   , in the County of   , deceased, testate, and ha   taken upon h   se   that trust by giving bond , as the law directs.

All persons having demands upon the estate of said deceased are hereby required to exhibit the same, and all persons indebted to said estate are called upon to make payment to

(*Address*)

   ,   , 19 .

Execut .

Execut .

   , ss.   , A D. **19** . Personally appeared   and made oath that the foregoing affidavit by h   subscribed is true.

Before me,

Justice of the Peace.

Letter on Foreign Will.

COMMONWEALTH OF MASSACHUSETTS.

, ss.   Probate Court.

To   , of   , in the County of   , and Commonwealth aforesaid·

You are appointed execut   of the last will and testament of   , late of   , deceased, testate, which said will was proved and allowed in said State of   , and on the   day of   , A. D. 19   , a copy thereof was required to be filed and recorded in the Registry of Probate of this County, and is now of record in this Court.

And you are required to make and return into said Probate Court, within three months from the date hereof, a true inventory of all the real and personal estate of said deceased which at the time of the making of such inventory shall have come to your possession or knowledge;

To administer according to law and to the will of said deceased all the personal estate of said deceased which may come to your possession, or that of any person for you, and also the proceeds of any of the real estate of said deceased that may be sold or mortgaged by you;

To render upon oath a true account of your administration at least once a year, until your trust is fulfilled, unless excused therefrom in any year by said Court;

And also, within three months, to cause notice of your appointment to be published once in each week for three successive weeks in the   , a newspaper published in said   , and return your affidavit of having given such notice, with a copy thereof, to the Probate Court

Witness,   , Judge of said Court, at   , this   day of   , in the year of our Lord one thousand nine hundred and   .

Register.

Executor's Affidavit of Notice of Appointment — Foreign Will.

[This should be filed in the Registry of Probate immediately after giving the notice]

I,   , do testify and say that   gave notice of appointment to and acceptance of the trust of execut   of the will of   , late of   , in the County of   , deceased, testate, within three months from the   day of   , A D 19   , the time of said appointment,   by publishing a notification thereof once in each week for three successive weeks in the   , a newspaper published in   , commencing on the   day of   , A. D 19   , and the following is a true copy thereof, viz. —

Notice is hereby given that the subscriber ha   been duly appointed execut   of the will of   , late of   , in the County of   , deceased, testate, and ha   taken upon h   self that trust by giving bond , as the law directs.

All persons having demands upon the estate of said deceased are required to exhibit the same; and all persons indebted to said estate are called upon to make payment to

(*Address*)
     ,   , 19 .

Execut .

Execut .

    , ss   , A. D. 19 . Personally appeared   and made oath that the foregoing affidavit by h   subscribed is true.

Before me,

Justice of the Peace.

Executor's Letter — Residuary.

COMMONWEALTH OF MASSACHUSETTS.

, ss.   Probate Court.

To   , of   , in the County of   , and Commonwealth aforesaid

You are appointed execut   of the last will and testament of   , late of   , in the County of   , deceased, testate, which will was proved and allowed on the   day of   , A. D. 19 , by said Court, and is now of record in this Court

And you, being residuary legatee, and having given bond therefor, are required to pay all debts and legacies of said deceased;

And also, within three months, to cause notice of your appointment to be published once in each week for three successive weeks in the   , a newspaper published in   , and return your affidavit of having given such notice, with a copy thereof, to the Probate Court.

Witness,   , Judge of said Court, at   , this   day of   , in the year of our Lord one thousand nine hundred and   .

Register.

Executor's Affidavit of Notice of Appointment.

[This should be filed in the Registry of Probate immediately after giving the notice.]

I,   , do testify and say that I gave notice of my appointment to and acceptance of the trust of execut   of the will of   , late of   , in the County of   , deceased, testate, within three months from the   day of   , A D. 19 . the time of said appointment,   by publishing a notification thereof once in each week for three successive weeks in the   , a newspaper published in   , commencing on the   day of   , A. D. 19 , and the following is a true copy theieof, viz. : —

Notice is hereby given that the subscriber ha   been duly appointed execut   of the will of   , late of   , in the County of   , deceased, testate, and ha   taken upon h   self that trust by giving bond , as the law directs.

All persons having demands upon the estate of said deceased are required to exhibit the same; and all persons indebted to said estate are called upon to make payment to
(*Address*)
    ,   , 19 .

Execut .

Execut .

    , ss.   , A. D. 19 . Personally appeared   and made oath that the foregoing affidavit by h   subscribed is true.
    Before me,
            Justice of the Peace.

LETTER OF ADMINISTRATION WITH WILL ANNEXED.

COMMONWEALTH OF MASSACHUSETTS

    , ss.   PROBATE COURT

To   , of   , in the County of   , and Commonwealth aforesaid ·

You are appointed administrat   with the will annexed of the estate of   , late of   , in the County of   , deceased, testate, which will was proved and allowed on the   day of   , A. D. 19 , by said Court, and is now of record in this Court.

And you are required to make and return to said Probate Court, within three months from the date hereof, a true inventory of all the real and personal estate of said deceased which at the time of the making of such inventory shall have come to your possession or knowledge,

To administer according to law and to the will of said deceased all the personal estate of said deceased which may come to your possession, or that of any person for you, and also the proceeds of any of the real estate of said deceased that may be sold or mortgaged by you;

To render upon oath a true account of your administration at least once a year, until your trust is fulfilled, unless excused therefrom in any year by said Court;

And also, within three months, to cause notice of your appointment to be published once in each week for three successive weeks in the   , a newspaper published in   , and return your affidavit of having given such notice, with a copy thereof, to the Probate Court

Witness,   , Judge of said Court, at   , this   day of   , in the year of our Lord one thousand nine hundred and   .

Register.

Administrator's Affidavit of Notice of Appointment — Will Annexed.

[This should be filed in the Registry of Probate immediately after giving the notice.]

I,   , do testify and say that   gave notice of appointment to and acceptance of the trust of administrat   with the will annexed of the estate of   , late of   , in the County of   , deceased, within three months from the   day of   , A. D. 19 , the time of said appointment, by publishing a notification thereof once in each week for three successive weeks in the   , a newspaper published in   , commencing on the   day of   , A D. 19 , and the following is a true copy thereof, viz.: —

Notice is hereby given that the subscriber has been duly appointed administrat   with the will annexed of the estate of   . late of   , in the County of   , deceased, testate, and has taken upon h   self that trust by giving bond , as the law directs All persons having demands upon the estate of said deceased are required to exhibit the same, and all persons indebted to said estate are called upon to make payment to

   (*Address*)
          ,   , 19 .

                                                    Adm.

                                                    Adm.

      , ss.   , A. D 19 . Personally appeared   and made oath that the foregoing affidavit by h   subscribed is true.
         Before me,
                                          Justice of the Peace.

Guardian's Letter

COMMONWEALTH OF MASSACHUSETTS.

   , ss.   Probate Court.

To   , of   , in the County of   , and Commonwealth aforesaid.

You are appointed guardian of   minor , with full power and authority to take possession of all real and personal estate of said ward ; and

You are required to make and return into said Probate Court, within three months from the date hereof, a true inventory of all the real and personal estate of said ward , which at the time of the making of such inventory shall have come to your possession or knowledge,

To manage and dispose of all such estate according to law and for the best interests of said ward , and faithfully to discharge your trust in relation to such estate, and to the custody, education, and maintenance of said ward ,

To render, upon oath, a true account of the property in your hands, including the proceeds of all real estate sold or mortgaged by you, and of the management and disposition of all such property, at least once a year, until your trust is fulfilled, unless excused therefrom in any year by said Court,

At the expiration of your trust, to settle your accounts in said Court, or with said ward or h legal representative, and to pay over and deliver all the estate and effects remaining in your hands, or due from you on such settlement, to the person or persons lawfully entitled thereto.

Witness, Judge of said Court, at , this day of , in the year of our Lord one thousand eight hundred and ninety-

Register.

Letter of Guardianship to Foreign Guardian.

[R L. c 145, § 19]

COMMONWEALTH OF MASSACHUSETTS.

, ss Probate Court.

To , *appointed guardian of , by the Court for the , in said State of*

You are appointed guardian of the estate of said in this Commonwealth, to wit. with authority to demand, sue for and recover such property, and to remove the same out of said Commonwealth

Witness, , Judge of said Court, at , this day of , in the year of our Lord one thousand nine hundred and .

Register.

Trustee's Letter.

COMMONWEALTH OF MASSACHUSETTS.

, ss. Probate Court.

To

You are appointed trustee of the estate given in trust for the benefit of , under the will of , late of , in the County of , deceased, testate, which will was proved and allowed on the   day of   A. D. 19   , by said Court, and is now of record in this Court,

And you are required to make and return to said Probate Court, within three months from the date hereof, a true inventory of all real and personal estate belonging to you as trustee , which at the time of the making of such inventory shall have come to your possession or knowledge;

To manage and dispose of all such estate, and faithfully to discharge your trust in relation thereto, according to law and the will of said testat   ;

To render, upon oath, a true account of the property in your hands, and of the management and disposition thereof, at least once a year until your trust is fulfilled, unless excused therefrom in any year by said Court; and

At the expiration of your trust to settle your account in said Court, and pay over and deliver all the estate and effects remaining in your hands, or due from you on such settlement, to the person or persons entitled thereto

Witness,   , Judge of said Court, at   , this day of   , in the year of our Lord one thousand nine hundred and   .

Register.

Trustee's Letter, not requiring Inventory.

COMMONWEALTH OF MASSACHUSETTS.

, ss.   Probate Court

To   , of   , in the County of   , and Commonwealth aforesaid.

You are appointed trustee of the estate given in trust for the benefit of   , under the will of   , late of   , in said County of   , deceased, testate,   , which will was proved and allowed on the   day of   , A D 19   , by said Court, and is now of record in this Court,

And you are required to manage and dispose of all real and personal estate belonging to you as trustee , and faithfully to discharge your trust in relation thereto, according to law and to the will of said testat ;

To render, upon oath, a true account of the property in your hands, and of the management and disposition thereof, at least once a year, until your trust is fulfilled, unless excused therefrom in any year by said Court, and

At the expiration of your trust, to settle your account in said Court, and pay over and deliver all the estate and effects remaining in your hands, or due from you on such settlement, to the person or persons entitled thereto.

Witness,   , Judge of said Court, at   , this   day of   , in the year of our Lord one thousand nine hundred and   .

Register.

Notice of the Appointment of an Executor.

Notice is hereby given that the subscriber ha been duly appointed execut   of the will of   , late of   , in the County of   , deceased, testate, and ha taken upon   h sel   that trust by giving bond , as the law directs.

All persons having demands upon the estate of said deceased are required to exhibit the same; and all persons indebted to said estate are called upon to make payment to

(*Address*)

} *Execut* .

,   , 19 .

Notice of the Appointment of a Foreign Executor.

Notice is hereby given that the subscriber ha been duly appointed execut   of the will of   , late of   , in the County of   , deceased, testate, and ha taken upon   h sel   that trust by giving bond , and appointing   , of   , his agent, as the law directs.

598   APPENDIX.

All persons having demands upon the estate of said deceased are required to exhibit the same, and all persons indebted to said estate are called upon to make payment to the subscriber.
   (Address)
                                              } Execut   .

    ,   , 19   .

NOTICE OF THE APPOINTMENT OF AN ADMINISTRATOR.

Notice is hereby given that the subscriber   ha   been duly appointed administrat   of the estate of   , late of   , in the County of   , deceased, intestate, and h   taken upon h   sel   that trust by giving bond , as the law directs.

All persons having demands upon the estate of said deceased are required to exhibit the same, and all persons indebted to said estate are called upon to make payment to
   (Address)
                                                        Adm.
    ,   , 19   .

NOTICE OF APPOINTMENT OF A FOREIGN ADMINISTRATOR

Notice is hereby given that the subscriber   ha   been duly appointed administrat   of the estate of   , late of   , in the County of   , deceased, and ha   taken upon h   sel   that trust by giving bond , and appointing   , of   , his agent, as the law directs.

All persons having demands upon the estate of said deceased are required to exhibit the same, and all persons indebted to said estate are called upon to make payment to the subscriber
   (Address)
                                                        Adm.
    ,   , 19   .

PROBATE FORMS. 599

NOTICE OF APPOINTMENT OF AN ADMINISTRATOR WITH THE WILL ANNEXED.

Notice is hereby given that the subscriber ha been duly appointed administrat with the will annexed of the estate of , late of , in the County of , deceased, testate, and ha taken upon h sel that trust by giving bond, as the law directs.

All persons having demands upon the estate of said deceased are required to exhibit the same, and all persons indebted to said estate are called upon to make payment to

(*Address*)

, , 19 .

Adm.

NOTICE OF APPOINTMENT OF FOREIGN ADMINISTRATOR WITH THE WILL ANNEXED.

Notice is hereby given that the subscriber ha been duly appointed administrat with the will annexed of the estate of , late of , in the County of , deceased, testate, and ha taken upon h sel that trust by giving bond, and appointing , of , his agent, as the law directs.

All persons having demands upon the estate of said deceased are required to exhibit the same; and all persons indebted to said estate are called upon to make payment to the subscriber.

(*Address*)

, , 19 .

Adm.

ADMINISTRATOR'S AFFIDAVIT OF NOTICE OF APPOINTMENT

[This should be filed in the Registry of Probate immediately after giving the notice.]

I, , do testify and say that gave notice of appointment to and acceptance of the trust of administrat of the estate , of , late of , in the County of

600   APPENDIX.

, deceased, within three months from the   day of   , A. D. 19   , the time of said appointment, by publishing a notification thereof once in each week for three successive weeks in the   , a newspaper published in   , commencing on the   day of   , A. D. 19   , and the following is a true copy thereof, viz. —

Notice is hereby given that the subscriber has been duly appointed administrat   of the estate of   , late of   , in the County of   , deceased, intestate, and has taken upon h   self that trust by giving bond , as the law directs. All persons having demands upon the estate of said deceased are required to exhibit the same, and all persons indebted to said estate are called upon to make payment to
   (*Address*)
        ,   , 19 .

                                            Adm.

                                            Adm.

      , ss.   , A D. 19 . Personally appeared   and made oath that the foregoing affidavit by h   subscribed is true.
        Before me,
                               Justice of the Peace.

ADMINISTRATOR'S AFFIDAVIT OF NOTICE OF APPOINTMENT — AGENT.

[This should be filed in the Registry of Probate immediately after giving the notice.]

I,   , do testify and say that   gave notice of appointment to and acceptance of the trust of administrat   of the estate of   , late of   , in the County of   , deceased, within three months from the   day of   , A. D. 19   , the time of said appointment,   by publishing a notification thereof once in each week for three successive weeks, in the   , a newspaper published in   , commencing on the   day of   , A. D. 19   , and the following is a true copy thereof, viz.. —

Notice is hereby given that the subscriber has been duly appointed administrat   of the estate of   , late of   , in the County of   , deceased, and has taken upon h   self that trust by giving bond , and appointing   of   his agent, as the law directs All persons having demands upon the estate of said deceased are required to exhibit the same; and all persons indebted to said estate are called upon to make payment to the subscriber.

(*Address*)

   ,   , 19   .

Adm.

Adm.

   , ss.   A. D. 19   . Personally appeared   and made oath that the foregoing affidavit by h   subscribed is true.

Before me,

Justice of the Peace.

Executor's Affidavit of Notice of Appointment.

[This should be filed in the Registry of Probate immediately after giving the notice]

I,   , do testify and say that I gave notice of my appointment to and acceptance of the trust of execut   of the will of   , late of   , in the County of   , deceased, testate, within three months from the   day of   , A. D. 19   , the time of said appointment,   by publishing a notification thereof once in each week for three successive weeks, in the   , a newspaper published in   , commencing on the   day of   A. D 19   , and the following is a true copy thereof. viz. : —

Notice is hereby given that the subscriber   ha   been duly appointed execut   of the will of   , late of   , in the County of   , deceased, testate, and ha   taken upon h   self that trust by giving bond , as the law directs.

All persons having demands upon the estate of said deceased are required to exhibit the same; and all persons indebted to said estate are called upon to make payment to
(*Address*)
, , 19 .

Execut .

Execut .

, ss.   A. D. 19 . Personally appeared   , and made oath that the foregoing affidavit by h   subscribed is true.

Before me,

Justice of the Peace.

EXECUTORS' AFFIDAVIT OF NOTICE OF APPOINTMENT — AGENT.

[This should be filed in the Registry of Probate immediately after giving the notice]

I,   , do testify and say that I gave notice of my appointment to and acceptance of the trust of execut   of the will of   , late of   , in the County of   , deceased, testate, within three months from the   day of   , A. D. 19 , the time of said appointment,   by publishing a notification thereof once in each week for three successive weeks, in the   , a newspaper published in   , commencing on the   day of   , A. D. 19 , and the following is a true copy thereof, viz.: —

Notice is hereby given that the subscriber   ha   been duly appointed execut   of the will of   , late of   , in the County of   , deceased, testate, and ha   taken upon h   self that trust by giving bond , and appointing   , of   his agent, as the law directs.

All persons having demands upon the estate of said deceased are required to exhibit the same, and all persons indebted to said estate are called upon to make payment to the subscriber.
(*Address*)
　　　　,　　　, 19　　.

　　　　　　　　　　　　　　　　　　Execut 　.

　　　　　　　　　　　　　　　　　　Execut 　.

　　　, ss.　　　, A. D 19　. Personally appeared　　, and made oath that the foregoing affidavit by h　subscribed is true.
　　Before me,
　　　　　　　　　　　　　　　Justice of the Peace.

Administrator's Affidavit of Notice of Appointment — Will annexed.

[This should be filed in the Registry of Probate immediately after giving the notice.]

　I,　　, do testify and say that　　gave notice of appointment to and acceptance of the trust of administrat　with the will annexed of the estate of　　, late of　　, in the County of　　, deceased, within three months from the　　day of　　, A D 19　, the time of said appointment, by publishing a notification thereof once in each week for three successive weeks, in the　　, a newspaper published in　　, commencing on the　　day of　　, A D. 19　, and the following is a true copy thereof, viz. : —

　Notice is hereby given that the subscriber has been duly appointed administrat　with the will annexed of the estate of　　, late of　　, in the County of　　, deceased, testate, and has taken upon h　self that trust by giving bond, as the law directs. All persons having demands upon the estate of said deceased are required to exhibit the same, and all persons indebted to said estate are called upon to make payment to

(*Address*)

   ,   , 19 .

Adm.

Adm.

  , ss. , A. D. 19 . Personally appeared , and made oath that the foregoing affidavit by h subscribed is true.

  Before me,

Justice of the Peace.

Administrator's Affidavit of Notice of Appointment — Will Annexed — Agent.

[This notice should be filed in the Registry of Probate immediately after giving the notice.]

 I, , do testify and say that gave notice of appointment to and acceptance of the trust of administrat with the will annexed of the estate of , late of , in the County of , deceased, within three months from the day of , A. D. 19 , the time of said appointment, by publishing a notification thereof once in each week for three successive weeks in the , a newspaper published in , commencing on the day of , A D. 19 , and the following is a true copy thereof, viz.. —

 Notice is hereby given that the subscriber ha been duly appointed administrat with the will annexed of the estate of , late of , in the County of , deceased, testate, and ha taken upon h self that trust by giving bond , and appointing , of , his agent, as the law directs. All persons having demands upon the estate of said deceased

are required to exhibit the same; and all persons indebted to said estate are called upon to make payment to the subscriber.
    (*Address*)
        ,   , 19 .

                                                                Adm

                                                                Adm.

      , ss.   , A. D. 19 . Personally appeared and made oath that the foregoing affidavit by h subscribed is true.
    Before me,
                               Justice of the Peace.

ADMINISTRATOR'S INVENTORY.

[The administrator must file the inventory in the Registry of Probate within three months after his appointment.]

COMMONWEALTH OF MASSACHUSETTS.

      , ss.   PROBATE COURT.
To
                                                          GREETING:

    You are hereby appointed to appraise on oath the estate and effects of   , late of   , in said County of   , deceased, which may be in said Commonwealth. When you have performed that service, you will deliver this order, with your doings in pursuance thereof, to   , administrat of the estate   , of said deceased, that he may return the same to the Probate Court for said County of   .

    Witness my hand and the seal of said Court this   day of   , in the year of our Lord one thousand nine hundred and   .
                                  Register of Probate Court.

        , ss.   , A. D 19 . Then the above-named appraisers personally appeared and made oath that they would faithfully and impartially discharge the trust reposed in them by the foregoing order.
    Before me,
                               Justice of the Peace.

Pursuant to the foregoing order to us directed we have appraised said estate as follows, to wit

Amount of Personal Estate, as per schedule exhibited, $.
Amount of Real Estate, as per schedule exhibited, $.

$\Big\}$ *Appraisers.*

, ss.   , A. D. 19 . Then personally appeared , the administrat   of said estate, and made oath that the foregoing is a true and perfect inventory of all the estate of said deceased that has come to h possession or knowledge.

Before me,

Justice of the Peace.

Executor's Inventory.

[The executor must file the inventory in the Registry of Probate within three months after his appointment]

COMMONWEALTH OF MASSACHUSETTS.

, ss.   Probate Court.

To

Greeting:

You are hereby appointed to appraise on oath the estate and effects of   , late of   , in said County of   , deceased, which may be in said Commonwealth. When you have performed that service, you will deliver this order, with your doings in pursuance thereof. to   , the execut   of the last will and testament of said deceased, that he may return the same to the Probate Court for said County of   .

Witness my hand and the seal of said Court this   day of   , in the year of our Lord one thousand nine hundred and   .

Register of Probate Court.

, ss.   , A. D. 19 . Then the above-named appraisers personally appeared and made oath that they would faithfully and impartially discharge the trust reposed in them by the foregoing order
   Before me,
Justice of the Peace.

Pursuant to the foregoing order to us directed we have appraised said estate as follows, to wit
 Amount of Personal Estate, as per schedule exhibited, $
 Amount of Real Estate, as per schedule exhibited, $.
} *Appraisers.*

, ss.   , A. D. 19 . Then personally appeared   , the execut   of the will of said deceased, and made oath that the foregoing is a true and perfect inventory of all the estate of said deceased that has come to   h   possession or knowledge.
   Before me,
Justice of the Peace.

GUARDIAN'S INVENTORY.

COMMONWEALTH OF MASSACHUSETTS.

   , ss. PROBATE COURT
To
GREETING:

You are hereby appointed to appraise, on oath, the estate and effects of   , of   , in said County of   , which may be in said Commonwealth   When you have performed that service, you will deliver this order, with your doings in pursuance thereof, to   , guardian of said ward , that he may return the same to the Probate Court for said County of   .

 Witness my hand and the seal of said Court, this   day of   , in the year of our Lord one thousand nine hundred and   .
Register of Probate Court.

608   APPENDIX.

, ss.   , A. D. 19 . Then the above-named appraisers personally appeared and made oath that they would faithfully and impartially discharge the trust reposed in them by the foregoing order.
Before me,
Justice of the Peace.

Pursuant to the foregoing order to us directed. we have appraised said estate as follows, to wit. —
Amount of Personal Estate, as per schedule exhibited, $
Amount of Real Estate, as per schedule exhibited, $

} *Appraisers.*

, ss.   , A D. 19 . Then personally appeared , the guardian of said ward , and made oath that the foregoing is a true and perfect inventory of all the estate of said ward that has come to h   possession or knowledge.
Before me,
Justice of the Peace.

TRUSTEE'S INVENTORY.

COMMONWEALTH OF MASSACHUSETTS.

, ss.   PROBATE COURT.

To
GREETING:
You are hereby appointed to appraise, on oath. the estate and effects of   , late of   , in said County of   , deceased, which may be in said Commonwealth, and which said deceased gave in h   will in trust for the benefit of   .
When you have performed that service you will deliver this order, with your doings in pursuance thereof, to   , the trustee under the will of said deceased, that he may return the same to the Probate Court for said County of   .

Witness my hand and the seal of said Court, this   day of   , in the year of our Lord one thousand nine hundred and   .
Register of Probate Court.

, ss.   , A. D 19 . Then the above-named appraisers personally appeared and made oath that they would faithfully and impartially discharge the trust reposed in them by the foregoing order.

  Before me,
         Justice of the Peace.

 Pursuant to the foregoing order to us directed, we have appraised said estate as follows, to wit —
Amount of Personal Estate, as per schedule exhibited, $
Amount of Real Estate, as per schedule exhibited, $

         } *Appraisers.*

, ss   , A. D 19 . Then personally appeared , the trustee under the will of said deceased, and made oath that the foregoing is a true and perfect inventory of all the estate of said deceased, given and devised as aforesaid, that has come to   possession or knowledge
  Before me,
         Justice of the Peace.

Petition for Revocation of Warrant for Appraisal, and for New Warrant.

To the Honorable the Judge of the Probate Court in and for the County of :

 Respectfully represents   , administrat of the estate of   , late of   , in said County of   , deceased,   , that at a Probate Court holden at   , in and for said county, on the   day of   , A. D. 19 , a warrant was issued for the appraisal of the estate of said deceased, — that said warrant has been lost or mislaid, and prays that said warrant may be revoked and a new warrant issued for the appraisal of said estate.

 Dated this   day of   , A D 19 .

INSOLVENCY.

[The executor or administrator must present with this petition a list of all persons claiming to be creditors of the estate so far as known to him]

To the Honorable the Judge of the Probate Court in and for the County of :

Respectfully represents   , administrat   of the estate   of   , late of   , in said County of   , deceased, appointed on the   day of   A. D 19   , that within three months from his said appointment   he caused notice thereof to be given as ordered by the Court, that the debts claimed as owed by the deceased at the time of his death, according to the list hereto appended, amount to $
The necessary funeral expenses, to $
The allowance by the Court for necessaries to the widow, to $
The charges of administration, including future probable charges, to $
          Amounting in the whole to the sum of $
That all the estate of the deceased known to be chargeable with the payment thereof is as follows, viz ·
Real Estate not exceeding in value, $
Personal Estate not exceeding in value, $
and other Personal Estate not mentioned in the Inventory, $
          Balance, $

And your petitioner believe. that said estate will probably be insolvent, for the reason that   , he   therefore pray that two or more fit persons be appointed commissioners to receive and examine all claims of creditors against the estate, and return a list of all claims laid before them, with the sum allowed on each claim, pursuant to the law in such case made and provided

Dated this   day of   , A D. 19   .

Adm.

, ss   , A. D. 19   . Then personally appeared said   , and made oath that the above is a correct representation of the probable condition of said estate, according to the best of h   knowledge and belief.

Before me,

Justice of the Peace.

ORDER TO ADMINISTRATOR OF INSOLVENT ESTATE TO NOTIFY CREDITORS TO PRESENT CLAIMS.

[R L. c 142, § 5]

COMMONWEALTH OF MASSACHUSETTS

, ss.   PROBATE COURT.

To   , administrat   of the estate of   , late of   , in said County, deceased, intestate, represented insolvent:

You are hereby ordered to notify the creditors of said insolvent estate that the Court will receive, hear, and examine all claims of creditors against said insolvent estate at the Probate Court to be holden at   , in and for said County, on   , the   day of   , A. D. 19   . and on   , the day of   , A D 19   , at   o'clock in the   noon, respectively, that they may then and there present and prove their claims.

Six months from the date hereof are allowed to creditors within which to present and prove their said claims.

And you are ordered to give at least seven days' written notice, by mail or otherwise, to all known creditors of the time and place of each of said hearings, and cause notices to be published in the   , a newspaper published in   , once in each week for three successive weeks before said first hearing

Claims allowed may be adjusted by finding the net amount due   , the date of death of said deceased

You will make return hereof, with your doings hereon, on

or before the date of said first hearing   , day of   ,
A. D. 19
    Witness,   , Esquire, Judge of said Court, at   , this   day of   , in the year of our Lord one thousand nine hundred and   .

Register.

I have served the foregoing order as therein ordered.

    , ss.   , A. D. 19 . Then personally appeared   , and made oath to the truth of the above return by him subscribed.
    Before me,

Justice of the Peace.

Form of Administrator's Notice to Creditors of Insolvent Estate.

Estate of   , late of   , in the County of   , deceased, represented insolvent.

    The Probate Court for said County will receive and examine all claims of creditors against the estate of said   , and notice is hereby given that six months from the   day of   , A D 19 , are allowed to creditors to present and prove their claims against said estate. and that the Court will sit to examine the claims of creditors at   , on the   day of   , A. D. 19 , at   o'clock in the   noon, and at   , on   the   day of   , A D 19 , at   o'clock in the   noon.

Administrat .

Insolvent Estate — Warrant to Commissioners.

COMMONWEALTH OF MASSACHUSETTS.

, ss.   Probate Court.

To

You are appointed commissioners to receive and examine all claims of creditors against the estate of   , late of   , in said County deceased

You are to appoint convenient times and places for your meetings, first being sworn to the faithful discharge of your duties, and by mail or otherwise give the administrat   and all known creditors (whose names and residences he   required to furnish to you fourteen days before your first meeting) at least seven days' written notice of the time and place of each meeting, and cause notice to be published once in each week for three successive weeks in the   , a newspaper published in   , the last publication to be one day at least before your first meeting You may examine any claimant on oath (which either of you may administer), and if he refuses to take such oath, or to answer fully all questions, you may disallow h   claim. If a creditor has security, you will deduct the value thereof from the amount of the claim, and allow the balance only, estimating such value yourselves, unless the same is determined by a sale of the security by agreement between the creditor and administrat   , but if the creditor waives his security, he may prove his whole claim, in either case you will state the facts in your report Six months from the date hereof are allowed to the creditors to present and prove their claims, after which time you will return to said Court, with this commission, a list of all claims presented, whether allowed or not, with the sums you allow on each, computing the net amount due   , A D. 19   , the time of the death of the deceased, with interest on claims expressly bearing interest, and rebate of interest on claims not on interest and not then matured, stating in separate classes: *First*, debts entitled to a preference under the laws of the United States, *Second*, public rates, taxes, and excise duties;

Third, wages or compensation to an amount not exceeding one hundred dollars, due to a clerk, servant, or operative for labor performed within one year next preceding the death of such deceased person, or for such labor so performed for the recovery of payment for which a judgment has been rendered, and *Fourth,* debts due all other persons, — *specifying* in separate lists, also, those due from the deceased individually, and as a member of any partnership

Witness,   , Judge of said Court, at   , this day of   , in the year of our Lord one thousand nine hundred and   .

Register.

    , ss   , A. D. 19   . Then personally appeared the above-named commissioners, and made oath that they would faithfully and impartially execute the duties assigned them by the foregoing warrant.

Before me,

Justice of the Peace.

Insolvent Estate — Report of Commissioners.

To the Honorable the Judge of the Probate Court in and for the County of   :

The subscribers, commissioners appointed by said Court to examine all claims of creditors against the estate of   , late of   , in said County, deceased, respectfully report as follows.

Having first been sworn, and having given notice according to law and the order of Court, we received and examined all such claims presented to us, and the following is a true list thereof, and of the sums allowed on each

Names of Claimants	[State any finding of Fact which may show that a Claim is preferred] Nature of Claims	Sums Claimed	Sums Allowed	Sums Disallowed

Form of Commissioners' Notice to Creditors of Insolvent Estate

Estate of   , late of   , in the County of   , deceased, represented insolvent

The subscribers having been appointed by the Probate Court for said County, commissioners to receive and examine all claims of creditors against the estate of said   , hereby give notice that six months from the   day of   , A. D. 19 , are allowed to creditors to present and prove their claims against said estate, and that they will meet to examine the claims of creditors at   , on the   day of   next, at   o'clock in the   noon.
     ,   , A. D. 19 .

} *Commissioners.*

New Commissioner of Insolvent Estate and Extending Time for Allowing Claims.

[R L c 142, §§ 6, 9]

To the Honorable the Judge of the Probate Court in and for the County of   :

Respectfully represents   , that   were appointed commissioners upon the insolvent estate of   , late of   , in said County of   , deceased,   , testate, on the   day of   A D 19 , and that said   has

Wherefore your petitioner prays that a new commissioner may be appointed in place of said   , and that the time for taking proof of claims and making returns   thereof may be extended.

Dated this   day of   , A. D. 19 .

INSOLVENT ESTATE — ORDER FOR DISTRIBUTION.

COMMONWEALTH OF MASSACHUSETTS.

    , ss.   PROBATE COURT

To   , administrat   of the estate of   , late of   in said County, deceased.

You are ordered to distribute the balance of   dollars, in your hands, according to your account allowed by said Court, on the   day of   A. D 19   , by paying forthwith to the persons and in the amounts hereinafter specified, who, it appears to the Court, are the creditors of said deceased, whose claims have been finally allowed, and are entitled thereto in such proportions, retaining in your hands   dollars thereof for future charges

You are ordered to give written notice by mail or otherwise, to each of said persons of the amount due him or her, and if any of said sums remain for six months unclaimed, you are directed to deposit the same in the   Savings   , in the name of the Judge of said Court, for the time being, to accumulate for the persons entitled thereto.

Within one year after the date hereof, you are required to present to this Court, under oath, a true account of the payments made by you, and of the amounts deposited as aforesaid, together with the original certificates or other evidence of such deposit, and also to return this order and the receipts of the persons whom you have paid

Witness,   , Judge of said Court, at   , this   day of   , in the year of our Lord one thousand nine hundred and   .

                                              Register.

INSOLVENT ESTATE — REPORT ON ORDER FOR DISTRIBUTION.

The names and amounts to be distributed, as aforesaid, are as follows.	We severally acknowledge the receipt of the sums set against our respective names

Names of persons to be paid	Amounts

I hereby certify that I have paid, according to the foregoing order, all the before-named persons the sums to which they are entitled, as appears by their respective receipts or vouchers, except the sums due to   , amounting to   dollars, which I have deposited in the   Savings   , according to the order of Court, and return the evidence thereof herewith
Adm.

RULE TO AUDITOR.

COMMONWEALTH OF MASSACHUSETTS.

, ss.   PROBATE COURT
A. D 19

In the matter of the   account of   , of the of   , late of   , in said County of   , deceased

It is ordered that   , of   , be, and he hereby is, appointed auditor in the above-mentioned matter, to hear the parties interested, examine vouchers and evidence, and report upon the same to this Court.

Judge of Probate Court.

PETITION TO RENDER INVENTORY AND ACCOUNT

To the Honorable the Judge of the Probate Court in and for the County of

Respectfully represents   , of   , in the County of   , that by a decree of said Court made on the   day

of   , A D 19   ,   , of   , in the County of   ,
was appointed   , and gave bond for the due performance of
said trust, and that h   ha   neglected to file an inventory
and to render an account as required by law and the condition
of h   bond

Your petitioner further represents that h   is a party
interested in the due administration of said estate.

Wherefore h   pray that the said   may be ordered to
render to the Court an inventory of said estate and an account
of h   administration thereof.

Dated this   , day of   , A. D. 19   .

Order to Render Inventory or Account.

COMMONWEALTH OF MASSACHUSETTS

   , ss.   Probate Court.

Estate of   , deceased, to   , of said deceased:

You are hereby ordered to render to this Court an inventory
    account of your administration of said estate   , on
or before the   day of   , A D. 19   , and in default
thereof to show cause therefor.

Witness my hand and the seal of said Court this   day of
      , in the year of our Lord one thousand nine hundred
and

Judge of Probate Court.

I have served the foregoing order on the above-named
by giving h   in hand an attested copy thereof.

      , ss.   , A D 19 . Personally appeared   ,
and made oath to the truth of the above return by h
subscribed.

Before me,

Justice of the Peace

DISTRIBUTION — WIDOW — HUSBAND — NEXT OF KIN — WARRANT

COMMONWEALTH OF MASSACHUSETTS.

, ss   PROBATE COURT.

To   , administrat   of the estate of   , late of   ,
in the County of   , deceased ·

You are ordered to distribute the balance of   dollars, in your hands, according to your account allowed by said Court, on the   day of   , A. D. 19   , by paying forthwith to the persons, and in the amounts hereinafter specified, who, it appears to the Court, are the widow — husband — and next of kin   of said deceased, and entitled thereto in such proportions, retaining in your hands   dollars thereof, for future charges

You are ordered to give written notice, by mail or otherwise, to each of said persons of the amount due him or her, and if any of said sums remain for six months unclaimed, you are directed to deposit the same in the   Savings   , in the name of the Judge of said Court, for the time being, to accumulate for the persons entitled thereto.

Within one year after the date hereof, you are required to present to this Court, under oath, a true account of the payments made by you, and of the amounts deposited as aforesaid, together with the original certificates or other evidence of such deposits, and also to return this order and the receipts of the persons whom you have paid

Witness,   , Judge of said Court, at   , this   day of   , in the year of our Lord one thousand nine hundred and   .

Register.

Distribution — Report.

The names and amounts to be distributed, as aforesaid, are as follows.	We severally acknowledge the receipt of the sums set against our respective names
Names of persons to be paid / **Amounts**	

I hereby certify that I have paid, according to the foregoing order, all the before-named persons the sums to which they are entitled, as appears by their respective receipts, except the sums due to   , amounting to   dollars, which I have deposited in the   Savings   , according to the order of Court, and return the evidence thereof herewith

Adm

Distribution — Intestate Estate.

To the Honorable the Judge of the Probate Court in and for the County of   .

Respectfully represents   , that there is a balance of the estate of   , late of   , in said County of   , deceased, intestate, in the hands of h   administrat   , which remains to be distributed among h   widow and next of kin, whose names, places of residence, and relationship to the deceased are supposed, or claimed to be, as follows

Name   Residence   Relationship   Share

Wherefore your petitioner pray that distribution of such balance may be decreed by the Court among such persons as may be proved to be entitled thereto, according to law.

Dated this   day of   , A. D. 19 .

, ss.   , A. D 19 . Then personally appeared
, and made oath to the truth of the above representation,
according to the best of h   knowledge and belief
     Before me,
                              Justice of the Peace.

Citation by publication once a week for three successive weeks, the last publication to be one day at least before return day.

Administrator's Account.

[RULE IX "No executor or administrator shall receive any compensation by way of a commission upon the estate by him administered but shall be allowed his reasonable expenses incurred in the execution of his trust, and such compensation for his services as the Court in each case may deem just and reasonable The account shall contain an itemized statement of the expenses incurred, and shall be accompanied by a statement of the nature of the services rendered, and of such other matters as may be necessary to enable the Court to determine what compensation is reasonable "]

The   account of   , administrat   of the estate of
    , late of   , in the County of   , deceased.
This account is for the period beginning with the   day
of   , A. D. 19 , and ending with the   day of   ,
A. D. 19 .

Said accountant charge h   sel   with the several
    amounts received, as stated in Schedule A, here-
    with exhibited, $
and ask to be allowed for sundry payments and charges,
    as stated in Schedule B, herewith exhibited, $
        Balance, as stated in Schedule C, herewith
          exhibited, $
                                            Administrat

APPENDIX.

The undersigned, being all persons interested, having examined the foregoing account, request that the same may be allowed without further notice.

[Citation by delivering a copy to all persons interested in the estate, fourteen days at least before return day; or by publication once a week for three successive weeks, the last publication to be at least one day before return day, and by mailing, post-paid, a copy to all known persons interested in the estate, seven days at least before return day.]

[Number the items.]

Schedule A.

Number of Item.	Date.		Dolls. Cts.
		Amount of personal property, according to inventory, or Balance of next prior account, Amounts received from income, gain on sale of personal property over appraised value, and from other property, as follows:	

Schedule B.

Number of Item.	Date.		Dolls. Cts.
		Showing payments, charges, losses, and distributions,	

SCHEDULE C.

[This schedule contains all items of personal property now in possession of the accountant, including cash]

, ss , A. D. 19 . Then appeared the within-named and made oath that the within account is just and true.

Before me,

Justice of the Peace.

EXECUTOR'S ACCOUNT.

The account of , execut of the last will and testament of , late of , in the County of deceased.

This account is for the period beginning with the day of , A D. 19 , and ending with the day of , A.D. 19 .

Said accountant charge h sel with the several amounts received, as stated in Schedule A, herewith exhibited, $
and asks to be allowed for sundry payments and charges, as stated in Schedule B, herewith exhibited, $
Balance, as stated in Schedule C, herewith exhibited, $

Executor.

The undersigned, being all persons interested, having examined the foregoing account, request that the same may be allowed without further notice.

[Citation by delivering a copy to all persons interested in the estate, fourteen days at least before return day, or by publication once a week for three successive weeks, the last publication to be one day at least before return day, and by mailing, post-paid, a copy to all known persons interested in the estate, seven days at least before return day]

[Number the items.]

Schedule A.

Number of Item.	Date.		Dolls.	Cts.
		Amount of personal property, according to inventory, or Balance of next prior account, Amounts received from income, gain on sale of personal property over appraised value, and from other property, as follows:		

Schedule B.

Number of Item.	Date.		Dolls.	Cts.
		Showing payments, charges, losses, and distributions,	.	

Schedule C.

[This schedule contains all items of personal property now in possession of the accountant, including cash.]

         , ss.   , A.D. 19 . Then appeared the within-named   and made oath that the within account is just and true.

    Before me,

Justice of the Peace.

Trustee's Account.

The account of , trustee under the will of ,
late of , in the County of , deceased, for the benefit of
This account is for the period beginning with the day of , A.D 19 , and ending with the day of , A.D 19 .

Said accountant charge h sel with the several amounts received, on account of principal, as stated in Schedule A, herewith exhibited, $
and asks to be allowed for sundry payments and charges, on account of principal, as stated in Schedule B, herewith exhibited, $
 Balance of principal invested, as stated in Schedule C, herewith exhibited, $
h also charges h sel with the several amounts received, on account of income, as stated in Schedule D, herewith exhibited, $
and asks to be allowed for sundry payments and charges, on account of income, as stated in Schedule E, herewith exhibited, $
 Balance of income, $

Trustee

The undersigned, being all persons interested, having examined the foregoing account, request that the same may be allowed without further notice.

[Citation by delivering a copy to all persons interested in the estate, fourteen days at least before return day, or by publication once a week, for three successive weeks, the last publication to be one day at least before return day, and by mailing, post-paid, a copy to all known persons interested in the estate, seven days at least before return day]

[Number the items.]

Schedule A.

Number of Item.	Date.		Dolls. Cts.
		Amount of personal property, according to inventory, or Balance of principal, according to next prior account, Amounts received on account of principal, gain on sale of personal property, and from other property, as follows:	

Schedule B.

Number of Item.	Date.		Dolls. Cts.
		Amounts paid out and charges, on account of principal, as follows:	

Schedule C.

[This schedule contains statement showing how principal is invested.]

Schedule D.

Number of Item.	Date.		Dolls. Cts.
		Balance of income according to next prior account, Amounts received on account of income, as follows:	

SCHEDULE E.

Number of Item.	Date.		Dolls. Cts.
		Amounts paid out and charges on account of income, as follows:	

        , ss.   , A. D. 19 . Then appeared the within-named   and made oath that the within account is just and true.

        Before me,

                            Justice of the Peace.

GUARDIAN'S ACCOUNT.

The   account of   , guardian of   , of   , in the County of   , minor.

This account is for the period beginning with the   day of   , A. D. 19 , and ending with the   day of   , A. D. 19 .

Said accountant charge h sel with the several amounts received, as stated in Schedule A, herewith exhibited, $

and asks to be allowed for sundry payments and charges, as stated in Schedule B, herewith exhibited, $

    Balance, as stated in Schedule C, herewith exhibited, $

                                  Guardian.

The undersigned, being   interested, having examined the foregoing account, request   that the same may be allowed without further notice.

[Citation by delivering a copy to all persons interested in the estate, fourteen days at least before return day; or by publication once a week for three successive weeks, the last publication to be one day at least before return day, and by mailing, post-paid, a copy to all known persons interested in the estate seven days at least before return day.]

[Number the items.]

SCHEDULE A.

Number of Item.	Date.		Dolls. Cts.
		Amount of personal property, according to inventory, or Balance of next prior account, Amounts received from income, gain on sale of personal property over appraised value, and from other property, as follows:	

SCHEDULE B.

Number of Item.	Date.		Dolls. Cts.
		Showing payments, charges, losses, and distributions.	

SCHEDULE C.

[This schedule contains all items of personal property now in possession of the accountant, including cash.]

, ss.   , A.D. 19 . Then appeared the within-named   and made oath that the within account is just and true.

Before me,

Justice of the Peace.

Compromise — Arbitration — Petition.

To the Honorable the Judge of the Probate Court in and for the County of

Respectfully represents   , of   , in the County of   , administrat   execut   guardian   trustee   of the estate of   , late of   , in the County of   , deceased,   that there is a demand   the estate represented by h   as such   , of   , described as follows

that it is probable the same can be adjusted by compromise on the following terms·

and it is for the interest of said estate   that it be done, or that it be submitted to arbitration.

Wherefore he prays that he may be authorized to adjust said demand by compromise, or submit it to arbitation.

Dated this   day of   , A D. 19   .

Petition for Sale of Real Estate — Executors — Administrators   [Public.]

[A description of the land to be sold, sufficient to identify it, should be given]

To the Honorable the Judge of the Probate Court in and for the County of

Respectfully represents   , of the   of   , late of   , in said County of   , deceased

That the debts due from the deceased, as nearly as they can now be ascertained, as shown by the list herewith filed, amount to	$
The legacies given in said will to	$
And the charges of administration to	$
Amounting in all to	$
That the value of the personal estate in the hands of the petitioner (exclusive of the widow's allowance) is	$

That the personal estate is, therefore, insufficient to pay the debts — *legacies* — of the deceased and the charges of administration, and it is necessary for that purpose to sell some part of the real estate to raise the sum of $

That the real estate which the petitioner proposes to sell consists of the following parcel   , to wit

and that by a partial sale thereof   the residue would be greatly injured

Wherefore your petitioner prays that he may be licensed to sell the whole of said parcel   at public auction for the payment of said debts — *legacies* — and charges of administration

Dated this   day of   , A. D 19   .

The undersigned, being all the persons interested, hereby assent to the foregoing petition.

Citation by delivering a copy to each person interested in the estate fourteen days at least before return day, or by publishing the same once a week for three successive weeks, the last publication to be one day at least before return day.

COMMONWEALTH OF MASSACHUSETTS.

, ss.   Probate Court.

A list of debts   which appear to be due from the estate of
         , late of   , in said County   . deceased.

Name of Creditor	Residence, or Usual Place of Business	Nature of Debt	Security	Amount

Administrat   .

, ss.   , A. D. 19 .   Then personally appeared   , and made oath that the above statement, by h   subscribed, is true to the best of h   knowledge and belief
        Before me,

Justice of the Peace.

License for Sale of Real Estate — Executors — Administrators [Public.]

COMMONWEALTH OF MASSACHUSETTS.

   , ss   Probate Court.

To   , administrat   of the estate of   , late of   ,
in said County of   , deceased

You are licensed to sell at public auction, at any time within one year from the date hereof, the following-described parcel of real estate of said deceased for the payment of h debts — legacies — and charges of administration, to wit:

You are required to give public notice of the time and place of such sale, by publishing a notification thereof once in each week for three successive weeks in the   , a newspaper published in   , and, within one year after such sale, return your affidavit of having given such notice, with a copy thereof, to the Probate Court.

Witness,   , Judge of said Court, at   , this   day of   , in the year of our Lord one thousand nine hundred and   .

                                                                      Register.

Affidavit of Sale of Real Estate at Public Auction.

[This affidavit should be returned immediately after the sale.]

I do testify and say that, being authorized by the Probate Court, for the County of   , on the   day of   , A. D. 19   , to make sale of the real estate hereinafter described of   , deceased, for the purposes in the license set forth, I gave public notice of the time and place of sale, by publishing a notification thereof once in each week for three successive weeks in the   , a newspaper published in   , commencing on the   day of   , A. D. 19   , and the following is a true copy of said notice:

COMMONWEALTH OF MASSACHUSETTS.

, ss   , A D. 19 . Then personally appeared , and made oath to the truth of the above affidavit by
h   subscribed
    Before me,
                              Justice of the Peace.

PETITION FOR SALE OF REAL ESTATE — EXECUTORS — ADMINISTRATORS   [PRIVATE]

[R L c 146, § 9]
[A description of the land to be sold, sufficient to identify it, should be given]

To the Honorable the Judge of the Probate Court in and for the County of .

Respectfully represents   , administrat   execut   of the   of   , late of   , in said County of   , deceased.

That the debts due from the deceased, as nearly as they can now be ascertained, as shown by the list herewith filed, amount to $
The legacies given in said will to $
And the charges of administration to $
    Amounting in all to $
That the value of the personal estate in the hands of the petitioner (exclusive of the widow's allowance) is $ _____
That the personal estate is, therefore, insufficient to pay the debts — *legacies* — of the deceased and the charges of administration, and it is necessary for that purpose to sell some part of the real estate to raise the sum of $

That an advantageous offer for the purchase of the parcel hereinafter described has been made to your petitioner, to wit, the sum of   dollars,

That the real estate which the petitioner proposes to sell consists of the following parcel, to wit.

And that by a partial sale thereof the residue would be greatly injured, and that the interests of all parties concerned will be best promoted by an acceptance of said offer. Wherefore your petitioner prays that he may be licensed to sell at private sale, in accordance with said offer, or upon such terms as may be adjudged best, the whole of said parcel for the payment of said debts — *legacies* — and charges of administration.
Dated the   day of   , A. D 19   .

The undersigned, being all the persons interested, hereby assent to the foregoing petition.

<small>Citation by delivering a copy to each person interested in the estate fourteen days at least before return day, or by publication once a week for three successive weeks, the last publication to be one day at least before return day</small>

COMMONWEALTH OF MASSACHUSETTS.

, ss.   PROBATE COURT.

Estate of   , deceased.

A list of debts which appear to be due from the estate of   ,
    late of   , in said County   , deceased.

Name of Creditor	Residence, or Usual Place of Business	Nature of Debt.	Security.	Amount.

Administrat   .

    , ss.   , A. D. 19   . Then personally appeared
    , and made oath that the above statement, by h   subscribed, is true to the best of h   knowledge and belief.
        Before me,
                        Justice of the Peace.

634   APPENDIX.

LICENSE FOR SALE OF REAL ESTATE — EXECUTOR OR ADMINISTRATOR. [PRIVATE.]

COMMONWEALTH OF MASSACHUSETTS.

, ss.   PROBATE COURT.

To   , administrat   of the estate of   , late of   , in said County of   , deceased ·

You are licensed to sell and convey, at private sale, at any time within one year from the date hereof, for the sum of   dollars, or for a larger sum, the whole of the parcel hereinafter described of the real estate of said deceased, for the payment of h   debts   and charges of administration, to wit certain parcel   lying in   , in said County of   , and described as follows, to wit.

But if, notwithstanding, you deem it best to sell the same at public auction, you are required to give public notice of the time and place of such sale at auction, by publishing a notification thereof once in each week for three successive weeks in the   , a newspaper published in   . and, within one year after such sale, return your affidavit of having given such notice, with a copy thereof, to the Probate Court.

Witness,   , Judge of said Court, at   , this   day of   , in the year of our Lord one thousand nine hundred and   .

Register.

ADMINISTRATOR'S PETITION FOR SALE OF REAL ESTATE — DISTRIBUTION.

[R L c. 146, § 18]

To the Honorable the Judge of the Probate Court in and for the County of   :

Respectfully represents   , administrat   of the estate of   , late of   , in said County, deceased, intestate, that said   , at the time of his decease, was the owner of certain real estate situate in   , in the County of   , bounded and described as follows, viz.

the same being all the real estate of said deceased.

That the value of the said estate, according to the appraisal now on file in said Court, does not exceed the sum of fifteen hundred dollars, that it is for the advantage of all parties interested   that the same be sold for the purpose of distribution, that an advantageous offer for the purchase thereof, to wit, the sum of   dollars, has been made to your petitioner by   , and that the interest of all parties concerned will be best promoted by an acceptance of such offer.

Therefore your petitioner pray that he may be licensed to sell the said real estate of said deceased at private sale, in accordance with such offer, or in such manner as the Court may direct, for the purpose of distribution

Dated this   day of   , A. D. 19   .

The undersigned, being all persons interested, hereby assent to the foregoing petition.

Citation by delivering a copy to all persons interested who can be found within the Commonwealth fourteen days at least before return day, and if any one cannot so be found, by publication once a week for three successive weeks, the last publication to be one day at least before return day

---

ADMINISTRATOR'S LICENSE FOR SALE OF REAL ESTATE — DISTRIBUTION

COMMONWEALTH OF MASSACHUSETTS.

      , ss.   PROBATE COURT.

To   , administrat   of the estate   of   , late of   , in said County, deceased, intestate

You are licensed to sell and convey, at private sale, for the sum of   dollars, or for a larger sum, at any time within one year from the date hereof, the following-described real estate of said deceased, for the purpose of distribution, namely

But if, notwithstanding, you deem it best to sell said real estate at public auction, you are required to give notice of the time and place of such sale, by publishing a notification thereof once in each week, for three successive weeks, in the   , a newspaper published in   , and, within one year after such sale, return your affidavit of having given such notice, with a copy thereof, to the Probate Court.

Witness,   , Judge of said Court, at   , this   day of   , in the year of our Lord one thousand nine hundred and   .

Register.

Petition for Sale of Real Estate — Guardian — Maintenance. [Public.]

[A description of the real estate, sufficient to identify it, must be given, together with its condition, and the reason why it is necessary to sell it.]

To the Honorable the Judge of the Probate Court in and for the County of

Respectfully represents   guardian of   , of   , in said County of   , minor,   that said ward interested in certain real estate, to wit. —

that it is necessary that said ward's interest therein be sold for h   maintenance, for the reason that the income of h   estate is insufficient to maintain h   , and that

Wherefore said guardian prays that he may be licensed to sell and convey the same, agreeably to the law in such case made and provided.

Dated this   day of   A. D. 19   .

The undersigned, being all the persons interested, hereby assent to the foregoing petition.

[Notice to the overseers of the poor is required only in cases where the ward is insane or a spendthrift.]

The undersigned, overseers of the poor for the , waive notice and assent to the foregoing petition

Citation by delivering a copy to all persons interested fourteen days at least before return day, or by publication once a week for three successive weeks, the last publication being one day at least before return day

NOTICE TO OVERSEERS OF THE POOR OF SALE OF REAL ESTATE

COMMONWEALTH OF MASSACHUSETTS

, ss.   PROBATE COURT.

, , A. D 19 .

In the matter of the petition of , guardian of , an insane person, praying for license to sell real estate of h ward, now pending in said Court.

We, the Overseers of the Poor of , where said ward is an inhabitant or resides, hereby acknowledge due notice of said petition and make no objection to the granting of the prayer thereof

LICENSE FOR SALE OF REAL ESTATE — GUARDIANS — MAINTENANCE. [PUBLIC.]

COMMONWEALTH OF MASSACHUSETTS.

, ss.   PROBATE COURT.

To , *guardian of* , *of* , *in the County of* , *minor*

You are licensed to sell, at any time within one year from the date hereof, the following-described real estate of said ward for h maintenance

And you are required to give public notice of the time and place of such sale, by publishing a notification thereof once in each week, for three successive weeks, in the , a newspaper published in   , and, within one year after such sale, return your affidavit of having given such notice, with a copy thereof, to the Probate Court.

Witness,   , Judge of said Court, at   this   day of   , in the year of our Lord one thousand eight hundred and ninety-   .

Register.

Affidavit of Sale of Real Estate — Guardian — Maintenance.

I do testify and say that, being authorized by the Probate Court, for the County of   , on the   day of   , A D 19   , to make sale of the real estate of   minor , for the purposes in the license set forth, I gave public notice of the time and place of sale, by publishing a notification thereof, once in each week, for three successive weeks, in the   , a newspaper published in   , commencing on the   day of   A. D. 19   , and the following is a true copy of said notice

Guardian

, ss   , A. D. 19   . Then personally appeared   and made oath to the truth of the above affidavit by h   subscribed

Before me,

Justice of the Peace.

Petition for Sale of Real Estate — Guardian's — Maintenance — Private.

[A description of the real estate, sufficient to identify it, must be given, together with its condition, and the reason why it is necessary to sell it]

To the Honorable the Judge of the Probate Court in and for the County of

Respectfully represents   , guardian of   , of   , in said County of   , minor,   that said ward interested in certain real estate, to wit: —

that an advantageous offer has been made to your petitioner for said ward's share, to wit, the sum of   dollars, that the

interest of all parties concerned will be best promoted by an acceptance of said offer, and that it is necessary that said ward's interest therein be sold for h   maintenance,
for the reason that the income of h   estate is insufficient to maintain h   .

Wherefore said guardian prays that he may be licensed to sell and convey the same, at private sale, in accordance with said offer, or upon such terms as may be adjudged best, agreeably to the law in such case made and provided.

Dated this   day of   , A D 19   .

The undersigned, being all the persons interested, hereby assent to the foregoing petition.

[Notice to the overseers of the poor is required only in cases where the ward is insane or a spendthrift]

The undersigned, being overseers of the poor of   , waive notice and assent to the foregoing petition

Citation by delivering a copy to each person interested fourteen days at least before return day, or by publication once a week for three successive weeks, the last publication to be one day at least before return day

---

LICENSE FOR SALE OF REAL ESTATE — GUARDIAN — MAINTENANCE. [PRIVATE.]

COMMONWEALTH OF MASSACHUSETTS

    , ss.   PROBATE COURT.

To   , Guardian of   , of   , in said County of   , minors.

You are licensed to sell, and convey, at private sale for the sum of   dollars, or for a larger sum, at any time within one year from the date hereof, the following-described real estate of said ward for h   maintenance

But if, notwithstanding, you deem it best to sell said real estate at public auction;

You are required to give public notice of the time and place of such sale, by publishing a notification thereof once in each week, for three successive weeks, in the   , a newspaper published in said   , and, within one year after such sale, return your affidavit of having given such notice, with a copy thereof, to the Probate Court.

Witness,   , Judge of said Court, at   , this   day of   , in the year of our Lord one thousand nine hundred and   .

Register.

Petition for Sale of Real Estate — Guardian's — Investment. [Public]

[A description of the real estate, sufficient to identify it, must be given, together with its condition, and the reason why it would be for the interest of the ward to have it sold]

To the Honorable the Judge of the Probate Court in and for the County of   .

Respectfully represents   , guardian of   , of   , in said County of   , minor,   that said ward interested in certain real estate, to wit·

that it will be for the benefit of said ward that h   interest therein be sold and the proceeds thereof put out on interest, or invested in some productive stock, for the reason that

Wherefore said guardian prays that he may be licensed to sell and convey the same, agreeably to the law in such case made and provided

Dated this   day of   , A. D. 19   .

The undersigned, being all the persons interested, hereby assent to the foregoing petition

[Notice to the overseers of the poor is required only in cases where the ward is insane or a spendthrift]

The undersigned, being overseers of the poor of   , waive notice and assent to the foregoing petition.

Citation by delivering a copy to each person interested fourteen days at least before return day, or by publication once a week for three successive weeks, the last publication to be one day at least before return day

LICENSE TO SELL REAL ESTATE — GUARDIANS — INVESTMENT. [PUBLIC]

COMMONWEALTH OF MASSACHUSETTS.

, ss.   PROBATE COURT

To   , guardian of   , of   , in the County of   , minor .

You are licensed to sell, at any time within one year from the date hereof, the following described real estate of said ward and put out the proceeds on interest, or invest the same in some productive stock,

And you are required to give public notice of the time and place of such sale, by publishing a notification thereof once in each week, for three successive weeks, in the   , a newspaper published in   , and, within one year after such sale, return your affidavit of having given such notice, with a copy thereof, to the Probate Court

Witness,   , Judge of said Court, at   , this   day of   , in the year of our Lord one thousand nine hundred and   .

Register.

AFFIDAVIT OF SALE OF REAL ESTATE BY GUARDIAN FOR INVESTMENT.

[This affidavit should be returned immediately after the sale.]

I do testify and say that, being authorized by the Probate Court, for the County of   , on the   day of   , A. D. 19   , to make sale of the real estate of   , minor , for the purposes in the license set forth, I gave public notice of the time and place of sale, by publishing a notification thereof, once in each week, for three successive weeks, in the   , a newspaper published in   , commencing on the   day of   , A. D. 19   , and the following is a true copy of said notice:

Guardian.

ss, .   , A D. 189 . Then personally appeared and made oath to the truth of the above affidavit by h   subscribed.
Before me,

Justice of the Peace.

Petition for Sale of Real Estate—Guardians— Investment. [Private]

[A description of the real estate, sufficient to identify it, must be given, together with its condition, and the reason why it would be for the interest of the ward to have it sold]

To the Honorable the Judge of the Probate Court in and for the County of   .

Respectfully represents   , guardian of   , of   . in said County of   , minor,   that said ward interested in certain real estate, to wit.

that an advantageous offer has been made to your petitioner for said ward   share, to wit. the sum of   dollars, that the interest   of all parties concerned will be best promoted by an acceptance of said offer, and that it will be for the benefit of said ward that h   interest therein be sold, and the proceeds thereof put out on interest, or invested in some productive stock, for the reason that

Wherefore said guardian   pray   that he   may be licensed to sell and convey the same in accordance with such offer   at private sale, or upon such terms as may be adjudged best, agreeably to the law in such case made and provided.

Dated this   day of   , A D 19 .

The undersigned, being all the persons interested, hereby assent to the foregoing petition.

[Notice to the overseers of the poor is required only in cases where the ward is insane or a spendthrift]

The undersigned, being overseers of the poor of   , waive notice and assent to the foregoing petition.

Citation by delivering a copy to each person interested fourteen days at least before return day, or by publication once a week for three successive weeks, the last publication to be one day at least before return day.

License to Sell Real Estate — Guardian — Investment. [Private.]

COMMONWEALTH OF MASSACHUSETTS.

, ss.   Probate Court.

To   , *guardian of*   , *of*   , *in the County of*   , *minor* ·

You are licensed to sell and convey at private sale, for the sum of   dollars, or for a larger sum, at any time within one year from the date hereof, the following-described real estate of said ward, and put out the proceeds on interest, or invest the same in some productive stock;

But if, notwithstanding, you deem it best to sell said real estate at public auction, —

You are required to give public notice of the time and place of such sale, by publishing a notification thereof once in each week for three successive weeks in the   , a newspaper published in   , and within one year after such sale return your affidavit of having given such notice, with a copy thereof, to the Probate Court.

Witness,   , Judge of said Court, at   , this   day of   , in the year of our Lord one thousand nine hundred and

Register.

Petition for Sale of Trust Estate — Real or Personal — Trustee.

[R L c 147, §§ 15, 16]

[A description of the property to be sold, sufficient to identify it, should be given. Minors and insane persons should be so designated.]

To the Honorable the Judge of the Probate Court in and for the County of   .

Respectfully represents   , trustee under the will of   , late of   , in the County of   , deceased, testate, for the benefit of the persons below named, that he holds as such trustee certain   estate, to wit.

that the sale, conveyance, and transfer of said estate is necessary and expedient, for the reason that   , that an offer of
dollars has been made for it, which is its full value, that it is desirable that the proceeds thereof be invested and applied in the following manner

After diligent search, the following are found to be the only persons known to the petitioner who are or may become interested therein.

| Name | Residence. | Nature of Interest. |

that the only persons now ascertained whose issue, not now in being, may become interested are:

| Name | Residence. |

Wherefore your petitioner pray that he may be authorized to make said sale, conveyance, and transfer at private sale or at public auction, and to make the said investment and application of the proceeds thereof

Dated this   day of   , A D. 19 .

The undersigned, being all the persons interested, assent to the above petition

Citation by delivering a copy to each person interested in the estate fourteen days at least before return day, or by publication once a week for three successive weeks, the last publication to be one day at least before return day.

SALE OF TRUST ESTATE — APPOINTMENT OF NEXT FRIEND
    GUARDIAN FOR THE CASE

COMMONWEALTH OF MASSACHUSETTS.

, ss.   PROBATE COURT

*At a Probate Court holden at   , in said County, on the
    day of   , in the year of our Lord one thousand
    nine hundred and*

In the matter of the petition of   , trustee   under the will   , of   , late of   , in the County of   , for the benefit of   , and others.

It appearing to said Court that there is need therefor, it doth appoint   , of   , in the County of   , to appear and act therein as the next friend of all persons not ascertained, or not in being, who are or may become interested in said estate, and it also appearing that   , minor , and interested in said case, and ha   no legal guardian, it doth appoint   , of   , in said County of   , to be guardian for the case, to appear and act for said minor in the above-mentioned matter.

Judge of Probate Court.

I hereby accept the above appointment, and

PETITION FOR SALE OF PERSONAL ESTATE.

[R. L. c. 145, § 35]

*To the Honorable the Judge of the Probate Court in and for
    the County of*

Respectfully represents   , of   , in the County of   , that he is interested as   , in the estate of   , late of   , in said County of   , deceased; and that it will be most for the interest of all concerned in said estate that certain of the personal estate of said deceased, hereinafter named, to wit:

should be sold at private sale or public auction.

Wherefore h pray that the of said estate may be ordered by said Court to sell said personal estate at private sale, for a sum not less than dollars, or at public auction.

Dated this day of , A. D. 19 .

The undersigned, being all the persons interested, hereby assent to the foregoing petition

Citation by delivering a copy to each person interested fourteen days at least before return day, or by publication once a week for three successive weeks, the last publication to be one day at least before return day

---

PETITION FOR SALE OF PERSONAL ESTATE BY FOREIGN ———.

[R L c 148, § 3]

To the Honorable the Judge of the Probate Court in and for the County of

Respectfully represents , of , in the State of , that he is the of the estate of , late of , in the County of , and State of , deceased, duly appointed by the Court in and for said County of , and has been duly qualified and is acting as such . That as such he is entitled to certain personal property situated in said County of , to wit.

which said corporation ha established or usual place of business in said County of . That there is no executor, administrator, guardian, or trustee appointed in this Commonwealth who is authorized to receive and dispose of such shares or estate, and that your petitioner as such will be liable upon and after the receipt or sale of said shares or estate to account for the same or for the proceeds thereof in said State in which he was appointed. That said died on the day of   , A D. 19 , and that six months from the death of said deceased have expired.

And your petitioner prays that he as such   be licensed to receive or to sell by public or private sale, on such terms and to such person or persons as he shall think fit, or otherwise to dispose of, and to transfer and convey said shares and estate.

Dated this   day of   A D 19

Citation by publication once a week for three successive weeks, the last publication to be one day at least before return day, and by delivering a copy of the citation to the treasurer of the Commonwealth fourteen days at least before the return day

Petition for Release of Right of Dower of an Insane Woman.

[R L c 153, § 19]

To the Honorable the Judge of the Probate Court in and for the County of   :

Respectfully represents   , of   , in said County, that he is seized of a certain parcel of real estate situate in   , in said County, and described as follows

that he is desirous of conveying said real estate in fee   but that   his wife, is incompetent, by reason of insanity, to release her right of dower   in the same; that the interests of your petitioner require that such conveyance should be made, and that the right of his said wife in said real estate should be released, that

He therefore prays that   , guardian of said   may be authorized and empowered to join him in a conveyance of said real estate for the purpose of releasing her right of dower therein.

Dated this   day of   , A D 19

Citation by delivering a copy to each person interested   days at least before return day, or by publication once a week for three successive weeks, the last publication to be one day at least before return day

Petition for Mortgage of Real Estate — Executor — Administrator.

[All the heirs of the intestate or their guardians must assent to a mortgage by an administrator.]

[A description of the real estate, sufficient to identify it, must be given, and a sworn list of the debts of the deceased should accompany the petition.]

To the Honorable the Judge of the Probate Court in and for the County of   :

Respectfully represents   , administrat execut of the   of   , late of   , in said County of   , deceased, that said deceased died seized of the following described real estate, viz.·

that he desires to mortgage the same to secure the sum of   dollars, the amount necessary to be raised thereon for the following purposes, viz.·

Wherefore he prays that he may be authorized to mortgage said real estate for said purposes.

Dated this   day of   , A. D. 19   .

The undersigned, being all the persons interested, hereby assent to the foregoing petition.

Citation by delivering a copy to each person interested fourteen days at least before return day, or by publication once a week for three successive weeks, the last publication to be one day at least before return day.

Petition to Mortgage Real Estate — Guardian.

[A description of the real estate, sufficient to identify it, must be given, together with its condition, and the reason why it would be for the interest of the ward to have it mortgaged, and if the object of the mortgage is the payment of debts, a sworn list of debts should accompany the petition.]

To the Honorable the Judge of the Probate Court in and for the County of   ·

Respectfully represents   , guardian of   , of   , in said County, minor   , that said ward   interested in certain real estate, to wit:

that said real estate is valued at   dollars, and said wards
interest therein is   part thereof; that it is necessary to
raise the sum of   dollars for

and that the interests of said wards require that said guardian
shall have power to mortgage said real estate to raise said
sum for the purpose aforesaid.

Wherefore said guardian pray that he may be authorized
to mortgage the same agreeably to the law in such case made
and provided.

Dated this   day of   , A. D. 19   .

The undersigned, being all the persons interested, hereby
assent to the foregoing petition.

[Notice to the overseers of the poor is required only in cases where the ward is insane or a spendthrift.]

The undersigned, being overseers of the poor of   , waive
notice and assent to the foregoing petition.

Citation by delivering a copy to each person interested fourteen days at least before return day, or by publication once a week for three successive weeks, the last publication to be one day at least before return day.

PETITION TO MORTGAGE REAL ESTATE — TRUSTEE.

[R L c 147, § 18]

To the Honorable the Judge of the Probate Court in and for the County of   :

Respectfully represents   , trustee under the will of
late of   , in said County, deceased,

that it will be for the benefit of the trust estate held by h   as such trustee that certain of said trust estate, to wit

be mortgaged to raise the sum of   dollars for the purpose of and that the following-named persons only are interested in said estate, namely·

Wherefore said trustee pray that he may be authorized to mortgage said real estate to the amount aforesaid for the purposes aforesaid, agreeably to the law in such case made and provided.

Dated this   day of   A D. 19   .

The undersigned, being all the persons interested, hereby assent to the foregoing petition.

Citation by publication once a week for three successive weeks, the last publication to be one day at least before return day, and by sending a copy properly mailed, postage prepaid, to each of the persons interested in the trust estate, or their legal representatives known to the petitioner, seven days at least before return day.

Petition for Separate Support.

[The words in *italics* in the prayer of the petition should be stricken out unless that part of the prayer is based upon specifications.]

To the Honorable the Judge of the Probate Court in and for the County of

Respectfully represents   , of   , in the County of   , that she is the lawful wife of   , of said   , that her said husband fails, without just cause, to furnish suitable support for her, and has deserted her, and that she is living apart from her said husband for justifiable cause, and she herein sets forth the following specifications

that there ha been born to them the following children.

Wherefore your petitioner prays that said Court will, — *by its order, prohibit her said husband from imposing any restraint on her personal liberty, and* — make such   order

as it deems expedient concerning her support, and the care, custody, and maintenance of said minor children.
Dated this   day of   , A. D 19   .

Citation by delivering the respondent a copy fourteen days at least before return day, if he may be found within the Commonwealth, or if he shall not be so found, by delivering to him such copy wherever found, or by leaving it at his usual place of abode, or by mailing the same to him at his last known post-office address, fourteen days at least before return day, and also, unless it shall be made to appear to the Court by affidavit that he has had actual notice of the proceedings, by publication once a week, for three successive weeks, the last publication to be one day at least before return day

---

SEPARATE SUPPORT — ORDER OF NOTICE AND ATTACHMENT.
COMMONWEALTH OF MASSACHUSETTS.

       , ss   PROBATE COURT.

On the petition of   , of   , in said County, the wife of   , of said   , representing that her said husband fails without just cause to furnish suitable support for her, and praying that said Court will, *by its order, prohibit her said husband from imposing any restraint on her personal liberty, and* make such   order as it deems expedient concerning her support, and the care, custody and maintenance of the minor children of herself and her said husband, and also praying that an attachment of the goods and estate of her said husband may be made to secure the decree which said petitioner may obtain for such support, and especially his goods and estate in the hands and possession of   , trustee of her said husband, it is ordered that the petitioner give notice to the said   to appear at a Probate Court to be held at   , in said County of   . on the   day of   , A. D. 19   , at ten o'clock in the forenoon, by delivering to him a copy of this order fourteen days at least before said Court, if he may be found within this Commonwealth, that he may then and there show cause, if any he has, why the prayer of said petition should not be granted, or, if he shall not be so found, by delivering to him such copy wherever found, or by leaving such copy at his usual place of abode, or by mailing the same to him at his last known post-office address fourteen days at least before said Court, and also, unless it shall be made to appear to the Court by affidavit that he has had actual notice of the proceedings, by publishing the same once in each week for three successive weeks in   , a newspaper published in   , the last publication to be one day at least before said Court

And in order to secure to the petitioner, and to such children as may be committed to her care and custody, a suitable support and maintenance, the sheriffs of the several counties, or either of their deputies, are hereby directed to attach the real and personal estate of the said   to the amount of   dollars, and especially his goods, effects, and credits in the hands and possession of the said trustee   , and to summon the said trustee if h   be found in his precinct, by serving h   with an attested copy of this order fourteen days at least before said return day, to appear before said Court, to be held as aforesaid, to show cause, if any h   ha   why execution to be issued upon such decree as the said Court may make in favor of said petitioner (if any) should not issue against the goods, effects, and credits of the said   in the hands and possession of the said   supposed trustee   .

Witness,   , Esquire, Judge of said Court, this   day of   , in the year one thousand nine hundred and

Register.

I have served the within citation by

     , ss.   , A D 19   . Personally appeared and made oath to the truth of the above return by h   subscribed

Justice of the Peace.

SEPARATE SUPPORT — EXECUTION

COMMONWEALTH OF MASSACHUSETTS.

, ss.   PROBATE COURT.

To the Sheriffs of our several Counties, or their Deputies, or any Constable of the City of   in said County

GREETING:

Whereas, on the petition of   , of   , in said County of   , wife of   , of said   , said Court, by its decree made on the   day of   , A. D. 19   , ordered said   to pay said   , for the support of herself and the maintenance of minor children, the sum of   dollars, forthwith, and a further sum of   dollars on each and every   thereafter, and whereas, under said decree, there now remains due and unpaid the sum of   dollars, whereof execution is requested to be done, and whereas, on the   day of   , A. D 19   , it was ordered by said Court that execution issue for the sum of   dollars.

You are hereby commanded, therefore, that of the goods, chattels, or lands of the said   , within your precinct, you cause to be paid and satisfied unto the said   , at the value thereof in money, the sum of   dollars, with interest thereon from said   , and thereof also to satisfy yourself for your own fees; and for want of goods, chattels, or lands of the said   , to be by him shown unto you, or found within your precinct, to the acceptance of the said petitioner to satisfy the sums aforesaid, with interest as aforesaid, *you are commanded* to take the *body* of said   , and him commit unto our jail in   , in our County of   , or any jail in your precinct, aforesaid, and him detain in your custody within our said jail until *he* pay the full sum of   dollars, with interest and your fees as aforesaid, or that *he* be discharged by the said petitioner, or otherwise by order of law. Hereof fail not, and make return of this writ, with your doings therein, into the Registry of Probate at   , in said County of   , in sixty days after the date hereof.

Witness,   , at   , the   day of   , in the year of our Lord one thousand nine hundred and   .

Register.

Separate Support — Capias

COMMONWEALTH OF MASSACHUSETTS.

 , ss   Probate Court

To the Sheriff of our County of   , or either of his Deputies, or any Constable of the City of   in said County

GREETING:

Whereas,   , of   , in said County of   , was duly ordered to appear before said Probate Court, on the   day of   , A. D. 19   , at ten o'clock in the forenoon, then and there to show cause, if any he had, why he should not be held to be in contempt of said Court in not obeying its decree dated   , A. D. 19   , wherein he was ordered to pay certain sums for the support and maintenance of his wife and minor child   , from which said   day of   , the consideration of said case was continued from time to time to this   day of   , A. D 19   , and hath neglected to appear, in contempt of said Court   You are hereby commanded to apprehend the body of the said   (if he may be found in your precinct), and bring him before said Court, at   , on the   day of   , A D 19   , at ten o'clock in the forenoon, that he may submit himself to an examination according to law ; and also to answer for his contempt in not obeying the aforesaid decree of said Court, and in not appearing according to a summons served on him agreeably to law   Hereof fail not, and make due return of this precept, with your doings herein.

Witness,   , Esquire, Judge of said Court, at   , this   day of   , in the year of our Lord one thousand nine hundred and   .

Register.

PROBATE FORMS. 655

Separate Support — Mittimus for Contempt.

COMMONWEALTH OF MASSACHUSETTS

  , ss.   Probate Court.

To the Sheriff of our County of   , his Deputies, and the Keeper of the Jail at   , in our County of

                                            Greeting:

Whereas, by the consideration of our Probate Court holden at   , within and for the County of   , on the   day of   , in the year of our Lord one thousand nine hundred and   , now in custody of   , one of said deputies, was ordered to pay certain sums for the support of his wife   , and their minor children intrusted to her care, and for the costs and expenses of his said wife in maintaining her suit therefor, and it appearing that the full and just sum of   dollars has become due and payable under and by virtue of said order, and that the said   neglects and refuses to pay the same, and it further appearing that the said   is guilty of contempt of Court in his said neglect and refusal.

You and each of you, the said sheriff and deputies, are therefore hereby commanded, in the name of the Commonwealth of Massachusetts, forthwith to take the said   , and him carry to the said jail and him deliver to the keeper thereof, together with an attested copy hereof, and thereafterward forthwith to return this warrant, with your doings thereon, into said Court.

And you, the said keeper, are alike commanded to receive said   into your custody in said jail, and him there safely keep until he shall purge himself of his said contempt by payment of the sum of   dollars, and the costs of serving this precept, or until the further order of this Court, or until he be otherwise discharged by due course of law.

Witness,   , Esquire, at   , this   day of   , in the year of our Lord one thousand nine hundred and

                                                Register.

, ss , A D 19 .

Pursuant to the warrant, I have taken and conveyed the above-named   to the jail in   , in said County, and delivered him and a copy of this warrant to the keeper thereof.

Deputy Sheriff.

Petition on Desertion and Living Apart.

[R L c 153, §§ 33, 36]

To the Honorable the Judge of the Probate Court in and for the County of

Respectfully represents   , of   , in the County of   , that she is the lawful wife of   , of said   , that her said husband fails, without just cause, to furnish suitable support for her, and has deserted her, and that your petitioner, for justifiable cause, is actually living apart from her said husband, and that there have been born to them the following children.

She further represents that she has need to be relieved of the disabilities of coverture so far as to be enabled to dispose of her personal and real estate without her husband's written consent, in the same manner and with the same effect as if she were sole.

Wherefore she prays that said Court, after due notice to her said husband and full consideration of the premises, will enter a decree establishing the fact of such desertion, and that such living apart from her husband is on her part for justifiable cause.

Dated this   day of   , A D. 19 .

Citation by delivering the respondent a copy fourteen days at least before return day, if he may be found within the Commonwealth, or, if he shall not be so found, by either leaving such copy at his usual place of abode, or by mailing such copy to his last known post-office address, and also, unless it shall be made to appear to the Court by affidavit that he has had actual notice of the proceedings, by publication once a week for three successive weeks, the last publication to be one day at least before return day.

Petition for Custody of Children.

[R L c. 153, § 37]

To the Honorable the Judge of the Probate Court in and for the County of   :

Respectfully represents   , of   , in the County of   , that he is the lawful wife — husband — of   , of said   , and that your petitioner and said   are actually living apart from each other, that children have been born to them who are now living, and whose names and dates of birth are as follows.

Your petitioner further represents that the happiness and welfare of said children, who are minors, require that he should have custody and possession of them.

Wherefore he prays that said Court will make such order as it deems expedient concerning the care, custody, education, and maintenance of said minor children, and order that they remain with your petitioner.

Dated this   day of   , A D 19   .

Citation by delivering a copy to the respondent   days before return day

---

Petition for Adoption and Change of Name

To the Honorable the Judge of the Probate Court in and for the County of   :

Respectfully represents   , of   , in said County,   and   , his wife, that they are of the age of twenty-one years or upwards, and are desirous of adopting   , of   , a child of   , of   , in the County of   , and   , his wife,   which said child was born in   , on the   day of   , A D 19   , that

Wherefore he pray for leave to adopt said child, and that h   name may be changed to that of   .

Dated this   day of   , A. D. 19 .

The undersigned, being the   of said child, hereby consent to the adoption, as above prayed for.

I, the child above-named, being above the age of fourteen years, hereby consent to the adoption as above prayed for.

Citation by delivering to the parties interested a copy seven days at least before return day, or, if they be not found within the Commonwealth, by publication once a week for three successive weeks, the last publication to be seven days at least before return day.

Petition for Change of Name.

To the Honorable the Judge of the Probate Court in and for the County of   .

Respectfully represents   , of   , in said County, that he was born in   , in the County of   , and State of   , on the   day of   , A D 19 , that he has heretofore resided in the following places only:

that h   occupation is that of a   , and that he wishes to change h   name to that of   , for the reason that

Wherefore your petitioner prays that h   name may be changed, and that he may take the name of   , as aforesaid

Dated this   day of   , A. D 19

Citation by publication once a week for three successive weeks, the last publication to be one day at least before return day.

Change of Name — Copy of Decree.

COMMONWEALTH OF MASSACHUSETTS.

, ss.

*At a Probate Court holden at   in and for said County of
, on the   day of   , in the year of our Lord
one thousand nine hundred and   :*

On the petition of   , of   , in said County, praying that h name may be changed to that of   , public notice having been given, according to the order of Court, that all persons might appear and show cause, if any they had, why the same should not be granted, and it appearing that the reason given therefor   sufficient, and consistent with the public interest, and being satisfactory to the Court, and no objection being made

It is decreed that h name be changed, as prayed for, to that of   , which name h shall hereafter bear, and which shall be h legal name, and that he give public notice of said change by publishing this decree once - in each week for three successive weeks in the   , a newspaper published in said   , and make return to this Court under oath that such notice has been given.

Judge of Probate Court.

I have caused the above to be published as ordered.

, ss.   A D. 19 . Personally appeared
and made oath that the above return by h subscribed is true.
Before me,

Justice of the Peace.

CHANGE OF NAME — CERTIFICATE.

COMMONWEALTH OF MASSACHUSETTS.

, ss.   PROBATE COURT.

By virtue of the power and authority vested in me, I,   ,
Esquire, Judge of the Probate Court in and for said County,
hereby certify that at a Probate Court holden at   , in and
for said County, on the   day of   , A D 19 , on h
application, and after due public notice thereof, and for sufficient reason consistent with the public interest, and satisfactory
to said Court, the name of   , of   , was changed to that
of   , that public notice of such change has been given,
according to the order of Court, and that he shall hereafter
bear said name of   , which shall be h   legal name

In witness whereof, I have hereunto set my hand, and caused
the seal of said Court to be affixed, at   , this   day of
  , in the year of our Lord one thousand nine hundred
and   .

Judge of Probate Court.

Countersigned,

Register.

PETITION FOR ASSIGNMENT OF HOMESTEAD.

[The names of the guardians of minors interested should be stated]

*To the Honorable the Judge of the Probate Court in and for the
County of*

Respectfully represents   , of   , in said County of
  , that   , late of   , in said County of   ,
deceased,   testate, whose estate is settled in this Court, died
seized of certain lands in this Commonwealth, that she is his
widow, and entitled to an estate of homestead in said lands,
that her right is not disputed by the heirs,   and that the

names and residences of all parties now interested therein are as follows

Wherefore she prays that her estate of homestead in said lands may be assigned to her by said Court, as provided by law.
Dated this   day of   , A. D 19   .

The undersigned, being the only persons interested, hereby assent to the foregoing petition.

<small>Citation by delivering a copy to each person interested fourteen days at least before return day, or by publication once a week for three successive weeks, the last publication to be one day at least before return day</small>

ASSIGNMENT OF HOMESTEAD — WARRANT — REPORT.

COMMONWEALTH OF MASSACHUSETTS.

, ss.   PROBATE COURT

To

You are appointed commissioners to set off an estate of homestead to   , widow of   , late of   , in said County, deceased

First, being sworn, you will give notice to all persons interested of the time and place appointed by you for setting off said homestead, and you will set off to said widow, by metes and bounds, an estate of homestead to the extent in value of eight hundred dollars in the lot of land and buildings thereon owned or rightly possessed and occupied as a residence by said deceased

You will cause all persons interested, who are satisfied with your doings, to certify the same on your report, and will return this warrant, with your doings thereon, as soon as may be to said Probate Court.

Witness,   , Judge of said Court, at   , this   day of   , in the year of our Lord one thousand nine hundred and   .

Register.

, ss.   , A. D. 19   Then personally appeared the three commissioners above named, and made oath that they would faithfully and impartially execute the duties assigned them by the foregoing warrant.
Before me,
Justice of the Peace.

To the Honorable the Judge of the Probate Court in and for the County of

Pursuant to your warrant to us directed, dated   , A. D. 19   , we, the commissioners therein named, having been first sworn, according to law, and given notice to all persons interested as therein directed, have appraised and set off to   , widow of   , late of   , deceased,   an estate of homestead to the value of eight hundred dollars, bounded and described as follows:

} *Commissioners.*

The undersigned, being all the persons interested in the foregoing report, hereby assent thereto, and request that the same be confirmed without further notice.

PETITION FOR ASSIGNMENT OF DOWER.

[The names of guardians of minors interested should be stated. If part of the land of the deceased lies in common with others, and the widow wishes her dower set off in *that also*, she must have partition made by like proceedings required by Revised Laws, c 184, § 44 This may be done by annexing to the petition a description of *such land*, the deceased's share therein, and the names of the co-tenants, and by referring thereto in the petition, and varying the prayer accordingly]

To the Honorable the Judge of the Probate Court in and for the County of   .

Respectfully represents   , of   , in said County, that   , late of   , in said County of   , deceased, testate, whose estate is settled in this Court, died seized of certain lands in this Commonwealth; that   she is his widow and entitled to dower in said lands, that her right is not disputed by the heirs;   and that the names and residences of all parties now interested therein are as follows.

NAME.   RESIDENCE.

Wherefore the petitioner prays that her dower   in said land may be assigned to her by said Court, as provided by law.
Dated this   day of   , A. D. 19   .

The undersigned, being all the persons interested, hereby assent to the foregoing petition.

Citation by delivering a copy to each person interested fourteen days at least before return day, or by publication once a week for three successive weeks, the last publication being one day at least before return day

---

ASSIGNMENT OF DOWER — WARRANT — REPORT.

COMMONWEALTH OF MASSACHUSETTS.

   , SS.   PROBATE COURT.

To

You are appointed commissioners to set off the dower of   , widow of   , late of   , in said County, deceased, which she is entitled to in the lands of which he died seized in this Commonwealth.

First, being sworn, you will give notice to all persons interested of the time and place appointed by you for setting off said dower, and

You will set off to said widow, by metes and bounds, her dower in all the real estate of which said deceased died seized in this Commonwealth, if it can be so done without damage to the whole estate,

But if the estate out of which dower is to be assigned, consists of a mill or other tenement which cannot be divided without damage to the whole, you will assign to said widow her dower of the rents, issues or profits thereof, to be had and received by her as tenant-in-common with the other owners of the estate

You will cause all persons interested, who are satisfied with your doings, to certify the same on your report, and will return this warrant, with your doings thereon, as soon as may be, to said Probate Court.

Witness,   , Judge of said Court, at   , this   day of   , in the year of our Lord one thousand nine hundred and   .

Register.

, ss.   A D 19   Then personally appeared the three commissioners above named, and made oath that they would faithfully and impartially execute the duties assigned them by the foregoing warrant.

Before me,

Justice of the Peace.

To the Honorable the Judge of the Probate Court in and for the County of .

Pursuant to your warrant to us directed, dated   , A D. 19   , we, the commissioners therein named, having been first sworn, according to law, and given notice to all persons interested as therein directed, have appraised all the real estate in this Commonwealth of which   , late of   , in said County died seized, as follows:

} *Commissioners.*

The undersigned, being all persons interested in the foregoing report, hereby assent thereto, and request that the same be confirmed without further notice.

Petition for Assignment of Real Estate in Fee.

[Superseded by R. L chapters 132, 135, 140]
[The names of the guardians of minors interested must be stated   If part of the land of the deceased lies in common with others, that fact must be stated, and a description of such land, the deceased's share therein, and the names of the co-tenants inserted in or annexed to the petition.]

To the Honorable the Judge of the Probate Court in and for the County of   :

Respectfully represents   , of   , in said County of   , that   , late of   , in said County of   , deceased, intestate, leaving no issue living, died seized of certain real estate in this Commonwealth, that   is h   widow and entitled to said estate in fee to an amount not exceeding five thousand dollars in value,

and that the names and residences of all other persons now interested therein are as follows.

Name	Residence.

Wherefore he prays that said estate of said deceased to an amount not exceeding five thousand dollars in value may be assigned and set out to h   in fee by said Court, as provided by law.

Dated this   day of   , A. D. 19   .

The undersigned, being all the persons interested, hereby assent to the foregoing petition.

Citation by delivering a copy to each person interested who can be found within the Commonwealth fourteen days at least before return day, and if any one can not so be found, by publication once a week for three successive weeks, the last publication to be one day at least before return day

ASSIGNMENT OF REAL ESTATE IN FEE — WARRANT — REPORT.

COMMONWEALTH OF MASSACHUSETTS.

    , ss.   PROBATE COURT.

To

    You are appointed commissioners to assign and set off in fee, by metes and bounds, to   , widow of   , late of   , in said County, deceased, the real estate of which said died seized in this Commonwealth to an amount not exceeding five thousand dollars in value.

    First, being sworn, you will give notice of the time and place appointed by you for making the assignment to all persons interested who are known and within the Commonwealth, and to the agent of any absent heir,   appointed by the Court, that they may be present   The names and residences of all parties interested are as follows:

    You will appraise all said real estate, and you will make assignment thereof to the amount aforesaid, according to law

    You will cause all parties who are satisfied with your doings to certify the same on your report, and make return of your doings, together with this warrant, as soon as may be to this Court.

    Witness,   , Judge of said Court, at   , this   day of   , in the year of our Lord one thousand nine hundred and   .

    Register.

    , ss.   , A. D 19 . Then personally appeared the three commissioners above named, and made oath that they would faithfully and impartially execute the duties assigned them by the foregoing warrant.

    Before me,

    Justice of the Peace.

[The report will not be confirmed unless all parties interested have assented in writing thereto, or have been duly cited and had an opportunity to be heard thereon, and when confirmed a certified copy should be recorded in the Registry of Deeds.]

To the Honorable the Judge of the Probate Court in and for the County of   :

Pursuant to your warrant to us directed, dated   , A. D. 19   , we, the commissioners therein named, having been first sworn, according to law, and having given notice to all persons interested, as therein directed, have appraised all the real estate in this Commonwealth, of which   , late of   , in the County of   , died seized, as follows:

} *Commissioners.*

The undersigned, being all the persons interested, hereby assent to the foregoing report, and request that the same be confirmed without further notice.

PETITION FOR ASSIGNMENT OF WIDOW'S LIFE ESTATE.

[P. S. 124, § 10.]   [The petitioner's estate of $5,000 in fee must first be set off.] [The names of the guardians of minors interested should be stated. If part of the land of the deceased lies in common with others, and the widow wishes her life estate set off in that also, she must have partition made by like proceedings required by R. L. c. 184, § 44. This may be done by annexing to the petition a description of such land, the deceased's share therein, and the names of the co-tenants, and by referring thereto in the petition, and varying the prayer accordingly.]

To the Honorable the Judge of the Probate Court in and for the County of   ·

Respectfully represents   , of   , in said County, that   , late of   , in said County of   , deceased,   testate, whose estate is settled in this Court, died seized of certain lands   in this Commonwealth, that she is his widow, and entitled during her life to one-half of his real estate other than that taken by her in fee; that her right is not disputed by the heirs or devisees;   and that the names and residences of all persons now interested therein are as follows:

NAME.   RESIDENCE.

Wherefore she prays that her said estate may be assigned to her by said Court, as provided by law.

Dated this   day of   , A. D. 19   .

The undersigned, being all the persons interested, hereby assent to the foregoing petition.

Citation by delivering a copy to each person interested fourteen days at least before return day, or by publication once a week for three successive weeks, the last publication being one day at least before return day.

ASSIGNMENT OF WIDOW'S LIFE ESTATE — WARRANT — REPORT

COMMONWEALTH OF MASSACHUSETTS.

          , ss.   PROBATE COURT.

To

You are appointed commissioners to set off to   , widow of   , late of   , in said County, deceased, during her life, one-half of the real estate of which he died seized in this Commonwealth, other than that taken by her in fee

First, being sworn, you will give notice to all parties interested of the time and place appointed by you for setting off one-half of said estate, and

You will set off to said widow, by metes and bounds, one-half of all the real estate of which said deceased died seized in this Commonwealth, other than that taken by her in fee, if it can be so done without damage to the whole estate.

But if the estate out of which one-half is to be assigned consist of a mill, or other tenement, which cannot be divided without damage to the whole, you will assign to said widow one-half of the rents, issues, or profits thereof, to be had and received by her as a tenant-in-common with the other owners of the estate

You will cause all persons interested, who are satisfied with your doings, to certify the same on your report, and will return this warrant, with your doings thereon, as soon as may be to said Probate Court

Witness,   , Judge of said Court, at   , this   day of   , in the year of our Lord one thousand nine hundred and   .

Register.

      , ss.   , A. D. 19 . Then personally appeared the three commissioners above named, and made oath that they would faithfully and impartially execute the duties assigned them by the foregoing warrant

Before me,

Justice of the Peace.

To the Honorable the Judge of the Probate Court in and for the County of   .

Pursuant to your warrant to us directed, dated   , A D 19 , we, the commissioners therein named, having been first sworn and given notice to all persons interested, as therein directed, have appraised all the real estate of which   , late of   , in said County, died seized in this Commonwealth, as follows:

} *Commissioners.*

The undersigned, being all the persons interested in the foregoing report, hereby assent thereto, and request that the same be confirmed without further notice.

Partition of Real Estate — Among Heirs.

[The names of the guardians of minors, who are interested parties, must be stated, and parties absent from the State must have agents, appointed by the Court to act for them If part of the land of the deceased lies in common with others, and the petitioner wishes *that* divided also, he must follow the directions of Revised Laws, c 184, § 44 This may be done by annexing to the petition a description of *such* land, the deceased's shares therein, and the names of the co-tenants, and by referring thereto in the petition, and varying the prayer accordingly]

To the Honorable the Judge of the Probate Court in and for the County of   .

Respectfully represents   , of   , in the County of   , that h interested in   the real estate lying in this Commonwealth, of   , late of   , in said County of   , deceased,   testate, whose estate is in course of settlement in said Court, claiming to hold as   of said deceased   undivided part or share , which he wish to hold in severalty:

That the names and residences of all the other persons now interested, and their respective shares and proportions thereof, are as follows, and are not in dispute nor uncertain.

Name	Residence	Share

Wherefore your petitioner pray that partition may be made of all the real estate aforesaid, according to law.

Dated this   day of   , A. D 19   .

The undersigned, being all the persons interested, hereby assent to the foregoing petition

Citation by delivering a copy to each person interested who can be found within the Commonwealth fourteen days at least before return day, and if any cannot so be found, by publication once a week for three successive weeks, the last publication being one day at least before return day

Appointment of Agent for Absent Persons.

COMMONWEALTH OF MASSACHUSETTS

, ss.   Probate Court.

To   , of   , in said County.

In the matter of the partition of real estate on the petition of

It appearing that

interested in the premises   absent from this Commonwealth.
You are appointed agent to act for said

in all things relating to said partition.

Dated this   day of   , A. D. 19   .

Judge of Probate Court.

Partition — Notice by Commissioners.

COMMONWEALTH OF MASSACHUSETTS.

, ss   Probate Court.

To all persons interested in the petition of   , of   , in the County of   , now pending in this Court, and to their agents, appointed by this Court.

Whereas the undersigned have been appointed Commissioners by this Court to

You are hereby notified to appear before them at   , in said County of   , on the   day of   , A D 19   , at   o'clock in the   noon, where they will meet to

Dated this   day of   , A. D. 19   .

} *Commissioners.*

I have served the foregoing notice this day by mailing, postpaid, a copy thereof to the following persons, at the following addresses:

   , ss. A. D. 19 . Then personally appeared and made oath to the truth of the above return by h subscribed.

  Before me,

           Justice of the Peace

PARTITION OF REAL ESTATE AMONG HEIRS — WARRANT — REPORT

COMMONWEALTH OF MASSACHUSETTS.

  , ss   PROBATE COURT.

To

  You are appointed commissioners to make partition of all the real estate of , late of , in said County, deceased, lying within this Commonwealth, which any party interested requires to have included in the partition, among the of said deceased, whose names and shares are as follows:

  First, being sworn, you will give notice of the time and place appointed by you for making the partition, to all persons interested who are known and within the Commonwealth, and to the agent of any absent heir appointed by the Court, that they may be present.

  You will appraise all the real estate of which said deceased died seized in this Commonwealth, which any party interested as aforesaid desires to have included in the partition, and you will make partition thereof according to law

  You will cause all parties who are satisfied with your doings to certify the same on your report, and those to whom you have awarded money, to acknowledge the receipt or security thereof, and make return of your doings, together with this warrant, as soon as may be to this Court

  Witness, , Judge of said Court, at , this

day of   , in the year of our Lord one thousand nine hundred and   .

Register.

, ss.   , A D. 19 . Personally appeared the three commissioners above named, and made oath that they would faithfully and impartially execute the duties assigned them by the foregoing warrant

Before me,

Justice of the Peace.

The report will not be confirmed until all money awarded is paid or secured, and when confirmed a certified copy should be recorded in the Registry of Deeds.]

To the Honorable the Judge of the Probate Court in and for the County of   :

Pursuant to the foregoing warrant to us directed, dated   , A D. 19 , we, the commissioners therein named, having been first sworn, according to law, and having given notice to all persons interested as therein directed, have appraised all the real estate lying in this Commonwealth, of which   , late of   , in said County, deceased, died seized, and which was required to be included in the partition, as follows:

Our expenses and charges are as follows:

} *Commissioners.*

The undersigned, being all persons interested in the foregoing report, hereby assent thereto, and request that the same be confirmed without further notice; and we, to whom money is awarded, acknowledge the receipt or security thereof.

Citation by mailing, post-paid, or delivering, a copy to all persons interested or their agents appointed by the Court, seven days at least before return day.

Petition for Partition of Real Estate among Tenants-in-Common.

[The names of the guardians of minors interested should be stated, and persons absent from the State must have agents, appointed by the Court, to act for them.]

To the Honorable the Judge of the Probate Court in and for the County of   .

Respectfully represents   , of   , in the County of   , that h   hold as tenant -in-common   undivided part or share of the following-described real estate, situated in   , in the County of   , which he wish to hold in severalty, to wit

that the names and residences of all the other tenants-in-common and their respective shares and proportions thereof, are as follows, and are not in dispute nor uncertain.

Wherefore your petitioner pray that partition may be made of all the real estate aforesaid, according to law.

Dated this   day of   , A. D. 19   .

The undersigned, being all the persons interested, hereby assent to the foregoing petition

Citation by delivering a copy to each person interested who can be found within the Commonwealth fourteen days at least before return day, and, if any one cannot so be found, by publication once a week for three successive weeks, the last publication to be one day at least before return day

---

Partition of Real Estate among Tenants-in-Common — Warrant — Report.

COMMONWEALTH OF MASSACHUSETTS.

     , ss.   Probate Court.

To

You are appointed commissioners to make partition of the

real estate hereinafter described among the tenants-in-common thereof whose names and shares are as follows, to wit.

Said real estate is situated in   , in said County of   , and is bounded and described as follows, to wit:

First, being sworn, you will give notice of the time and place appointed by you for making the partition, to all persons interested who are known and within the State, and to the agent of any absent person interested in the premises appointed by the Court, that they may be present.

You will appraise all said real estate, and you will make partition thereof according to law. You will cause all parties who are satisfied with your doings to certify the same on your report, and those to whom you have awarded money, to acknowledge the receipt or security thereof, and make return of your doings, together with this warrant, as soon as may be to this Court.

Witness,   , Judge of said Court, at   , this   day of   , in the year of our Lord one thousand nine hundred and   .

Register

          , ss   , A D 19   . Then personally appeared the three commissioners above named, and made oath that they would faithfully and impartially execute the duties assigned them by the foregoing warrant.

Before me,

Justice of the Peace.

[The report will not be confirmed until all money awarded is paid, and when confirmed a certified copy should be recorded in the Registry of Deeds.]

To the Honorable the Judge of the Probate Court in and for the County of   .

Pursuant to the foregoing warrant to us directed, dated   , A. D. 19   , we, the commissioners therein named, having been first sworn, and having given notice to all persons interested, as therein directed, have appraised all the real estate described in said warrant, and which was required to be included in the partition, as follows

Our expenses and charges are as follows:

} Commissioners.

The undersigned, being all persons interested in the foregoing report, hereby assent thereto, and request that the same be confirmed without further notice; and we, to whom money is awarded or distributed, acknowledge the receipt thereof.

PETITION FOR PARTITION AND SALE OF REAL ESTATE AMONG TENANTS-IN-COMMON.

[R L c 184, §§ 31, 33]

[The names of the guardians of minors interested should be stated, and persons absent from the State must have agents, appointed by the Court, to act for them]

To the Honorable the Judge of the Probate Court in and for the County of

Respectfully represents   , of   , in the County of   , that h   hold as tenant -in-common   undivided   part or share of the following-described real estate, which he wish to hold in severalty, to wit.

that the names and residences of all the other tenants-in-common, and their respective shares and proportions thereof, are as follows, and are not in dispute nor uncertain.

NAME.	RESIDENCE	SHARE

and your petitioner further represent that said real estate cannot be advantageously divided.

Wherefore your petitioner pray   that partition may be made of all the real estate aforesaid, according to law, and to that end that the commissioners appointed to make said partition be ordered to make sale and conveyance of said real estate at public auction for cash, and to distribute and pay over the net proceeds of the sale in such a manner as to make the partition just and equal.

Dated this   day of   , A D. 19   .

The undersigned, being all the persons interested, hereby assent to the foregoing petition.

Citation by delivering a copy to each person interested who can be found within the Commonwealth fourteen days at least before return day, and, if any one cannot be so found, by publication once a week for three successive weeks, the last publication being one day at least before return day

---

SALE OF LANDS BY COMMISSIONERS — BOND.

[R L c 184, § 47]

KNOW ALL MEN BY THESE PRESENTS,

That we,   , of   , in the County of   , as principal, and   , of   , in the County of   . and   , of   , in the County of   , as sureties, and all within the Commonwealth of Massachusetts, are holden and stand firmly bound and obliged unto   , Esquire, Judge of the Probate Court in and for the County of   , in the full and just sum of   dollars, to be paid to said Judge and his successors in said office; to the true payment whereof we bind ourselves and each of us, our and each of our heirs, executors, and administrators, jointly and severally, by these presents. Sealed with our seals, and dated the   day of   , in the year of our Lord one thousand nine hundred and   .

THE CONDITION OF THIS OBLIGATION IS SUCH, that if the above-bounden   , commissioners appointed by said Court to make partition of   , who have been ordered by said Court to make sale and conveyance of said   , shall account for and dispose of, according to law and the order of the Court, all proceeds of the sale,

Then this obligation to be void, otherwise to remain in full force and virtue

    Signed, sealed, and delivered   [SEAL.]
        in the presence of   [SEAL]
                                                                           [SEAL]

      ss.   , A. D. 19   . Examined and approved

                                               Judge of Probate Court

---

PARTITION OF REAL ESTATE BY SALE — TENANTS-IN-COMMON — WARRANT — REPORT

COMMONWEALTH OF MASSACHUSETTS.

    , ss.   PROBATE COURT.

To

You are appointed commissioners to make partition of the real estate hereinafter described among the tenants in-common thereof whose names and shares are as follows

Said real estate is situated in   , in said County of   , and is bounded and described as follows, to wit:

and you are ordered to make sale and conveyance, at any time within one year from the date hereof, of the whole of said lands.

And you are required to give public notice of the time and place of such sale, by publishing a notification thereof once in each week for three successive weeks in the   , a newspaper published in   , in said County of   , and, within one year after such sale, return your affidavit of having given such notice, with a copy thereof, to the Probate Court.

You are ordered to distribute and pay over the proceeds of the sale in such manner as to make the partition just and equal; and if any distributive share of the money arising from such sale remains unpaid at the time of confirming the proceedings, or establishing the partition, you are directed to deposit the same in the   Savings Bank   , in the name of the Judge of said Court, for the time being, to accumulate for the persons entitled thereto

Within one year after the date hereof, you are required to present to this Court, under oath, a true account of the payments made by you, and of any amount deposited as aforesaid, together with the original certificate or other evidence of any such deposit, and also to return this order and the receipts of the persons whom you have paid

    Witness,   , Esquire, Judge of said Court, at this   day of   , in the year of our Lord one thousand nine hundred and

                                                   Register.

    , ss.   , A. D. 19   . Then personally appeared the commissioners above named and made oath that they would faithfully and impartially execute the duties assigned them by the foregoing warrant

        Before me,

                            Justice of the Peace

To the Honorable the Judge of the Probate Court in and for the County of

Pursuant to the foregoing warrant to us directed, dated A. D. 19 , we, the commissioners therein named, having been first duly sworn, and having given notice as therein required, as will appear by affidavit hereto annexed, have made sale and conveyance of the lands therein described by public auction to   , for the sum of   dollars, which amount was bid by the said   , and was the highest bid made therefor at said auction.

Our expenses and charges are as follows.

We have distributed and paid over the proceeds of said sale as follows, to wit:

Names of Persons Paid	Amounts	We severally acknowledge the receipt of the sums set against our respective names

The distributive share of   , amounting to   dollars, we have deposited in the   Savings Bank   , as directed in said warrant, and return the evidence thereof herewith.

$\Big\}$ *Commissioners.*

[This should be filed in the Probate Court immediately after the sale.]

We, commissioners appointed to make partition, do testify and say that, being authorized by the Probate Court for the County of   , on the   day of   , A. D. 19   , to make sale of the real estate of   , for the purposes in the commission set forth, we gave public notice of the time and place of sale by publishing a notification thereof once in each week for three successive weeks in the   , a newspaper published in   , commencing on the   day of   , A D. 19   , and the following is a true copy of said notices:

$\Big\}$ *Commissioners.*

     , ss.   , A. D 19   Then personally appeared the above-named commissioners, and made oath to the truth of the above affidavit by them subscribed.

      Before me,

Justice of the Peace.

Petition for Discharge from Guardianship.

To the Honorable the Judge of the Probate Court in and for the County of   .

Respectfully represents   , of   , in the County of   , that by a decree of said Court, dated the   day of   , A. D. 19   , he was adjudged to be a   , and   , of   , in the County of   , was appointed his guardian, that said   accepted the trust, and still continues to have the custody of the person of your petitioner, and the management of his estate,

Your petitioner further represents that he believes that he is now capable of managing h   own estate, and that such guardianship is no longer necessary.

Wherefore your petitioner prays that h   said guardian may be discharged.

Dated this   day of   , A. D. 19   .

The undersigned, relatives, friends, and neighbors of the above-named ward, believing that guardianship of said ward is no longer necessary, hereby concur in his petition for his discharge from said guardianship

Citation by delivering a copy to the guardian   days at least before return day, or by publication once a week for three successive weeks, the last publication to be one day at least before return day.

Petition for Removal.

To the Honorable the Judge of the Probate Court in and for the County of   :

Respectfully represents   , of   , in said County of   , that he   is   , of   , of   , in said County of   , and is   interested in the estate of said

, that by a decree of said Court, dated the   day of
      , A. D 19 ,   of   , in said County of   ,
was appointed   of said   , and letters of   were
issued to him
  That

and is evidently unsuitable for the discharge of said trust.
  Wherefore your petitioner prays that said   may be
removed from his said office and trust
  Dated this   day of   , A D 19 .

  Citation by delivering a copy   days at least before return day

Petition for Discharge of Surety on Bond.

To the Honorable the Judge of the Probate Court in and for the County of ·

  Respectfully represents   , of   , in the County of
      , that by a decree of said Court, dated the   day of
      , A D 19 ,   of   , in the County of   ,
was appointed   of   , and gave bond for the faithful
discharge of said trust, that your petitioner is one of the sureties on said bond, that the other surety on said bond is   ,
of   , in said County of   , that the estate of said deceased is not yet fully administered,   and your petitioner
is unwilling to remain longer liable as surety on said bond, for
the reason that

  Wherefore your petitioner prays that he may be discharged
from all further responsibility as such surety, and that said
      may be ordered to furnish a new bond.
  Dated this   day of   , A D 19 .

  The undersigned, being all the persons interested in the foregoing petition, request that the prayer thereof be granted without further notice

  Citation by delivering a copy to the co surety fourteen days at least before
return day, and by publication once a week for three successive weeks, the
last publication to be one day at least before return day

Resignation.

To the Honorable the Judge of the Probate Court in and for the County of

Respectfully represents   that it is inconvenient for any longer to serve as

he   therefore respectfully resign   said trust, and ask   to have resignation accepted.

Dated this   day of   , A. D. 19   .

Declination.

To the Honorable the Judge of the Probate Court in and for the County of   :

It being inconvenient for   to discharge the duty of execut   trustee   of the last will and testament of   , late of   , in said County of   , deceased,   do hereby decline that trust.

Dated this   day of   , A. D. 19   .

Petition for Notice of Appointment.

To the Honorable the Judge of the Probate Court in and for the County of

Respectfully represents   , of the   , of   , late of   , in said County of   , deceased, testate, that on the   day of   , A D 19   , he gave bond for the faithful discharge of his said trust, and that by accident and mistake the notice of his appointment was not given within three months from said date. wherefore he pray that he may be ordered to give said notice within such further time as the Court may order

Dated this   day of   , 19   .

Petition to take Deposition to Will.

[R L c 175, § 26]

To the Honorable the Judge of the Probate Court in and for the County of .

Respectfully represents , of , that an instrument purporting to be the last will and testament of , late of , deceased, wherein your petitioner is named execut , has been presented to said Court for probate, and that a citation has been issued to all parties interested to appear at a Probate Court, to be held at , on the day of , A D 19 , to show cause, if any they have, why said instrument should not be proved and allowed as the last will and testament of said deceased.

And your petitioner further represents that of the subscribing witnesses to said instrument, to wit

and that
is absent from the Commonwealth, sick, infirm, aged , so as to make it probable that he will not be able to attend in the Probate Court and give h testimony.

Wherefore your petitioner prays that a commission from said Court may issue to take the deposition of the said as a subscribing witness to said instrument.

Dated this day of , A. D 19 .

Let the commission as prayed for be issued.

Judge of Probate Court.

Deposition of Witnesses to Will.

COMMONWEALTH OF MASSACHUSETTS.

, ss.   Probate Court.

To   , or any Commissioner appointed by the Governor of said Commonwealth of Massachusetts, Justice of the Peace, Notary Public, or other officer, legally empowered to take Depositions or Affidavits, in the State of   ,
                                                                    Greeting.

Whereas   , of   , in the County of   , has presented to said Court for probate   instrument   , hereto annexed, purporting to be   the last will and testament of   , late of   , in the County of   , deceased, and has requested that the deposition of   ,

of   , in said State of   , witness   thereto, may be taken

Now, therefore, you are by these presents authorized and empowered to take the deposition of the said

and to this end to cause the said deponent to come before you, and the deponent after having been sworn to testify the truth, the whole truth, and nothing but the truth, relating to the cause for which the deposition is taken, to be examined, and h   testimony taken in writing. And you are to take such deposition separate and apart from all other persons, and to permit no person to be present during such examination except the deponent and yourself. And you are to put the several interrogatories subjoined to the deponent in their order, and to take the answer of the deponent to each fully and clearly before proceeding to the next, and not to read to the deponent nor permit the deponent to read, a succeeding interrogatory until the answer to the preceding has been fully taken down. And when you shall have completed the examination aforesaid, the same so taken and subscribed is to be returned, together with this Commission and your doings herein, enclosed, sealed, and directed to the Register of said Court, at   , in said County of   .

Given under the seal of said Court

Witness,   Esquire, Judge of said Court, at   , this   day of   , in the year of our Lord one thousand nine hundred and

Register.

1st Examine the instrument hereto annexed, and state whether or not you signed your name thereto as a witness.
Answer.

2d State whether or not   therein described as the testat signed h name to said instrument as and for h last will and testament in your presence, and where the same was so signed.
Answer

3d State whether or not you signed your name as a witness thereto in the presence of said testat and at h request.
Answer.

4th State whether or not either of the other witnesses thereto signed his or her name as a witness in presence of said testat and at h request, and give the name of each witness who so signed.
Answer

5th. State whether in your opinion said testat   , at the time of signing said instrument, was of sound or unsound mind and whether he was of the full age of twenty-one years.
Answer

State of   ,   ss.

Pursuant to the foregoing commission, I caused the said   to come before me on the   day of   , A D 19   , and after having sworn the said   to testify the truth, the whole truth, and nothing but the truth, relating to the cause for which the deposition is taken, I examined the said   and reduced h   testimony to writing   In taking the deposition I put the interrogatories to the deponent as directed in the foregoing commission, and in all respects, fully and exactly complied with the directions in said commission. And after said deposition was taken, I carefully read the same to the said   and he   subscribed it in my presence.

Appointment of Agent.

COMMONWEALTH OF MASSACHUSETTS.

, ss.   Probate Court.

Know all men, that I,   , of   , in the State of   , appointed by said Court   executor — administrator — guardian — trustee, of the estate   will of   , late of   , in said County of   , deceased, under and in compliance with the provisions of Chapter 139 of the Revised Laws of said Commonwealth, do hereby appoint   , of   , in the County of   , and Commonwealth aforesaid, as my agent, and I do hereby stipulate and agree that the service of any legal process against me as such executor — administrator — guardian — trustee, if made on said agent, shall be of the same legal effect as if made on me personally within said Commonwealth.

In witness whereof, I have hereunto set my hand and seal this   day of   , in the year of our Lord one thousand nine hundred and   .

Signed, sealed, and delivered
in presence of

I, the above-named   hereby accept the above appointment.

[*Address.*]

Embezzlement — Complaint.

[R L c 102, § 43]

To the Honorable the Judge of the Probate Court in and for the County of :

, of , in said County of , on oath complains that he has good cause to suspect, and does suspect, that , of , in the County of , ha fraudulently received, concealed, embezzled, and conveyed away certain articles of personal property belonging to the estate of , late of , in the County of , deceased, to wit

That your complainant is and is interested in said estate.

Wherefore he prays that said may be cited to appear before said Court, to be examined upon oath upon the matter of this complaint, and that such further proceedings may be had in the premises as the law requires

Dated this day of , A D. 19

, ss. , A D. 19 . Then personally appeared and made oath that the above complaint, by subscribed, is true.

Before me,

Justice of the Peace.

Let citation issue as prayed for.

Judge of Probate Court.

Dated , 19 .

Citation by delivering a copy of the complaint, days at least before return day

APPOINTMENT OF GUARDIAN AD LITEM AND NEXT FRIEND.

COMMONWEALTH OF MASSACHUSETTS.

, ss.   PROBATE COURT.

At a Probate Court holden at   , in said County, on the   day of   , in the year of our Lord one thousand nine hundred and   .

Whereas, in the matter of   , it appears that   is a minor   , and interested in said case, and ha   no legal guardian, therefore   , of   , in the County of   , is hereby appointed to act as guardian *ad litem* or next friend for such person , to represent h   interest in said case.
Judge of Probate Court.

I hereby accept the above appointment

, ss.   , A. D. 19 . Personally appeared   and made oath that he would faithfully and impartially perform the duty reposed in him by the foregoing appointment
Justice of the Peace.

Having fully examined and considered the matter of   , I hereby assent to the

---

PETITION FOR WIDOW'S ALLOWANCE.

To the Honorable the Judge of the Probate Court in and for the County of   :

Respectfully represents   that   , late of   , in said County, whose estate is in course of settlement in said Court, died possessed of personal estate, that she is his widow, and has under her charge a family consisting of

Wherefore, she prays that the Court will allow her part of the personal estate of said deceased as necessaries for herself and family under her care, in addition to the provisions and other articles by law belonging to her.

Dated this   day of   , A. D. 19 .

Claim of Appeal.

To the Honorable the Judge of the Probate Court in and for the County of

Represents   , of   , in the County of   , that he is a   , of   , late of   , in the County of   , deceased, and   interested in the estate of said deceased, that he is aggrieved by a decree of the Probate Court held at   , in said County of   , on the   day of   , A. D. 19 , whereby said Court

And he hereby give notice that he claim an appeal from said decree to the Court.

Dated, this   day of   , 19 .

Petition for Lease of Real Estate by Guardian.

[A description of the real estate, sufficient to enable parties interested to identify it, must be given, and the reason why it would be for the interest of the ward to have it leased.]

To the Honorable the Judge of the Probate Court in and for the County of

Respectfully represents   , guardian of   , of   , in said County of   , minor, that said ward   interested in certain real estate, to wit

that it is necessary, expedient, and for the benefit of said ward that a written lease of said real estate be made for the reason that

a copy of the proposed lease is hereto annexed.

Wherefore said guardian prays that he may be authorized to lease the same as aforesaid, or upon such terms as may be adjudged best.

The undersigned, being all the heirs presumptive of the

minor named in the foregoing petition, hereby consent that the same may be granted

Citation by publication once a week for three successive weeks, the last publication to be one day at least before return day.

Appearance.

, ss.   PROBATE COURT.

No
Estate of
In the matter of

To the Register.

Enter   appearance   for
                                               Attorney.

Address
Filed   , 19 .
                                               Register.

Petition in Equity.

To the Honorable the Judge of the Probate Court in and for the County of .

Respectfully represents   , petitioner   , that he bring this petition against

respondents,   , and allege them to be all the parties interested in the matter of said petition, and further represent

Dated this   day of   , 19 .

The undersigned, being all the persons interested in the subject matter of the above petition, hereby accept service of the same

Citation by serving respondents with copy of citation, or leaving at usual place of abode, or by mailing to last known address, fourteen days at least before return day, and unless respondents have actual notice, citation must be published once a week for three successive weeks, the last publication to be seven days at least before return day

---

Decree in Equity.

COMMONWEALTH OF MASSACHUSETTS.

   , ss.   Probate Court.

                           In Equity,   , 19 .

On the petition in equity of   , petitioners, against

respondents,   praying

it appearing that notice according to the order of the Court has been given all parties interested

person objecting, after hearing and consideration, the Court doth order and decree

---

Petition for Appointment as Conservator of Property of Aged Person.

[R L c 145, § 40]

[This application must be made by the aged person himself, or by one or more of his friends]

To the Honorable the Judge of the Probate Court in and for the County of   :

    Respectfully represent   , of   , in the County of   , that   , a resident of   , in said County of   , has become incapacitated by reason of advanced age and mental weakness to properly care for his property. Your petitioners therefore pray that   , of   , in the County of   , or some other suitable person, may be appointed conservator of the property of said   , agreeably to the law in such case made and provided.

Dated this   day of   A D 19 .

Citation by serving aged or mentally weak person with copy of order, fourteen days at least before return day.

Conservator's Bond.

[R L c 145, §§ 40, 41]

Know all Men by these Presents,

That we,   , of   , in the County of   , as principal , and   , of   , in the County of   , and   , of   , in the County of   , as sureties, and all within the Commonwealth of Massachusetts, are holden and stand firmly bound and obliged unto   , Esquire, Judge of the Probate Court in and for the County of   , in the full and just sum of   dollars, to be paid to said Judge and his successors in said office; to the true payment whereof we bind ourselves and each of us, our and each of our heirs, executors, and administrators, jointly and severally by these presents. Sealed with our seals, and dated the   day of   , in the year of our Lord one thousand nine hundred and   .

The condition of this obligation is such, that if the above bounden conservator of the property of   , of   , in said County of   , a person incapacitated by reason of advanced age or mental weakness to properly care for his property, shall,

First, make and return to said Probate Court, at such time as it may order, a true inventory of all the real and personal estate of said person that at the time of the making of such inventory shall have come to the possession or knowledge of said conservator;

Second, manage and dispose of all such estate according to law and for the best interests of said person, and faithfully discharge h   trust in relation to such estate;

Third, render upon oath, at least once a year, until h trust is fulfilled, unless he   is excused therefrom in any year by said Court, a true account of the property in h   hands, including the proceeds of all real estate sold or mortgaged by h   and of the management and disposition thereof, and also render such account at such other times as said Court may order; and

Fourth, at the expiration of h   trust, settle h   account in said Court, or with said person or h   legal representatives, and pay over and deliver all the estate remaining in h   hands, or due from h   on such settlement, to the person or persons lawfully entitled thereto,

Then this obligation to be void, otherwise to remain in full force and virtue.

Signed, sealed, and delivered
in presence of

, ss.   , A. D. 19 . Examined and approved
Judge of Probate Court.

I,   , the within-named conservator, declare that, to the best of my knowledge and belief, the estate and effects of the within-named   do not exceed in value the following-mentioned sums, viz :

Real Estate, $.
Personal Estate, $.
[SIGN]

CONSERVATOR'S LETTER.

COMMONWEALTH OF MASSACHUSETTS.

, ss.   PROBATE COURT.

To   , of   , in the County of   , and Commonwealth aforesaid

You are appointed conservator of the property of   , a resident of   , in said County of

a person incapacitated by reason of advanced age and mental weakness to properly care for h   property, with full power and authority to take possession of all real and personal estate of said person, and to have the charge and management thereof subject to the direction of said Court, and

You are required to make and return into said Probate Court, within three months from the date hereof, a true inventory of all the real and personal estate of said person which at the time of the making of such inventory shall have come to your possession or knowledge;

To manage and dispose of all such estate according to law and for the best interests of said person, and faithfully to discharge your trust in relation to such estate;

To render, upon oath, a true account of the property in your hands, including the proceeds of all real estate sold or mortgaged by you, and of the management and disposition of all such property, at least once a year, until your trust is fulfilled, unless excused therefrom in any year by said Court;

At the expiration of your trust, to settle your accounts in said Court, or with said person, or h   legal representative, and to pay over and deliver all the estate and effects remaining in your hands, or due from you on such settlement, to the person or persons lawfully entitled thereto.

Witness,   , Esquire, Judge of said Court, at   , this   day of   , in the year of our Lord one thousand nine hundred and   .

Register.

INJUNCTION.

COMMONWEALTH OF MASSACHUSETTS.

, ss.   PROBATE COURT.

To

and all Servants, Agents, Attorneys, and Counsellors, acting for or in behalf of you or either of you,
                                                    GREETING.

Whereas, it has been represented to said Court by   , petitioner , that he   , said petitioner , ha   exhibited a Bill of Complaint in our said Court against you, the said

which said Bill is filed in the office of the Register of said Court at   , in and for our said County of   , wherein said petitioner , among other things, pray for a Writ of Injunction against you, the said respondent , to restrain you and the persons before named from proceeding to do what you are hereinafter enjoined from doing:

We, therefore, in consideration of the premises, do strictly enjoin and command you, the said respondent , and all and every the persons before named, to desist and refrain from

until the further order of said Court

Witness,   , Esquire, Judge of said Court at   , the   day of   , in the year of our Lord one thousand nine hundred and   .

                                                    Register

PETITION FOR LEAVE TO DEPOSIT LEGACY.

To the Honorable the Judge of the Probate Court in and for the County of   :

Respectfully represents   that he is execut   of the will of   , late of   , in said County of   , deceased;   that by the terms of said will a legacy of dollars was bequeathed to

that the residence of said legatee is   unknown to your petitioner, that the said legatee is   minor, and has no legal guardian.

Wherefore your petitioner pray that he may be allowed to deposit said legacy   in the   , in the name of the Judge of said Court, or to invest t in

to accumulate for the benefit of the person entitled thereto.

Dated this   day of   , 19 .

Petition for Payment of Deposit.
[R L c 150, § 23]

To the Honorable the Judge of the Probate Court in and for the County of .

Respectfully represents   , of   , in the County of   , that he is an heir-at-law of — guardian of — legatee under the will of   , late of   , in said County of   , deceased, that by an order of said Court, dated the   day of   , 19 ,   , administrat —execut of the estate — will of said deceased, deposited the sum of   dollars in the   Savings Bank on the   day of   , A. D. 19 , in the name of the Judge of said Court, to accumulate for the benefit of your petitioner;

that your petitioner is the person for whose benefit said deposit was made, and is entitled to said sum of   dollars deposited as aforesaid, and to the accumulations thereon

Wherefore your petitioner prays that said bank be ordered to pay to h said sum of   dollars and the accumulations thereon.

Dated the   day of   , A D. 19 .

, ss. Subscribed and sworn to this   day of A. D 19 .

Before me,

Justice of the Peace.

PETITION BY MINOR FOR LICENSE TO MARRY.

[R L c 151, § 20.]

To the Honorable the Judge of the Probate Court in and for the County of   :

Respectfully represents   that he is a minor of the age of   years, and a resident of   , in said County of   , that he desires to marry   , of   , in the County of   ,   who is   years of age, and that h   father, — mother, — guardian, consents hereto; he therefore prays that an order may be made allowing h   to marry the said   .

Dated at   , the   day of   , A. D. 19   .

I,   , being the father, — mother, — guardian of said minor, consent to granting the order asked for in the above petition.

GUARDIAN AD LITEM AND NEXT FRIEND — ACCOUNT.

[R. L. c. 150, § 22]

COMMONWEALTH OF MASSACHUSETTS.

, SS.   PROBATE COURT.

At a Probate Court holden at   , in said County, on the   day of   , in the year of our Lord one thousand nine hundred and   .

Whereas, in the matter of the settlement of the   account of

it appears that there may be persons unborn or unascertained who are or may become interested in said account; — that   , who   or may become interested in said account   legally incompetent to act in h   own behalf, and h   no legal guardian, other than the accountant, therefore   , of   , in the County of   ,   is hereby appointed to act as guardian *ad litem* or next friend for such persons, to represent h   interest in said account, and to examine said account and the vouchers therefor and the securities, and report to this Court.

Judge of Probate Court.

I hereby accept the above appointment.

, ss.   A. D 19   Personally appeared   , and made oath that he would faithfully and impartially perform the duty reposed in him by the foregoing appointment.

Justice of the Peace.

Having fully examined the above-described account, with the vouchers therefor and the securities, I hereby assent to the allowance of the same

Guardian ad litem and next friend.

Representation of Insolvency — Examination of Claims by Court.

[R L. c 142, §§ 4, 5, 9]

[The executor or administrator must present with this petition a list of all persons claiming to be creditors of the estate so far as known to him.]

To the Honorable the Judge of the Probate Court in and for the County of

Respectfully represents

administrat   of the estate   of   , late of   , in said County of   , deceased, appointed on the   day of   , A. D. 19 , that within three months from h   said appointment   he caused notice thereof to be given as ordered by the Court, that the debts claimed as owed by the

deceased at the time of his death, according to the list hereto
appended, amount to $
The necessary funeral expenses, to $
The allowance by the Court for necessaries to the
    widow, to $
The charges of administration, including future prob-
    able charges, to $
        Amounting in the whole to the sum of $
That all the estate of the deceased known to be charge-
    able with the payment thereof, is as follows,
    viz :
Real Estate not exceeding in value $
Personal Eestate not exceeding in value $
and other Personal Estate not mentioned in
    the inventory $
        Balance $
And your petitioner , believe that said estate will prob-
ably be insolvent, for the reason that

he therefore pray the Court to receive and examine all claims of creditors against the estate. and cause a list of all claims presented for proof, with the amount allowed or disallowed on each claim, to be made and certified by the Register of said Court pursuant to the law in such case made and provided.

    Dated this   day of   A D 19 .

                                    } *Admr.*

, ss   A. D. 19 . Then personally appeared said
    and made oath that the above is a correct representation
of the probable condition of said estate, according to the best of
    h   knowledge and belief.
    Before me,
                          Justice of the Peace

INSOLVENCY — ORDER TO ADMINISTRATOR TO NOTIFY CREDITORS TO PRESENT CLAIMS.

[R. L c.142, § 5]

COMMONWEALTH OF MASSACHUSETTS.

, ss. PROBATE COURT

To , administrat of the estate of , late of , in said County of , deceased, intestate, represented insolvent.

You are hereby ordered to notify all known creditors of said insolvent estate that the Court will receive and examine all claims of creditors against said estate at the Probate Court to be holden at , in and for said County of , on the day of A. D. 19 , and on , the day of A D. 19 , at nine o'clock in the forenoon, respectively, that they may then and there present and prove their claims.

And you are ordered to give to all known creditors at least seven days written notice, by mail or otherwise, of the time and place of each meeting, and cause notices to be published once in each week for three successive weeks in the , a newspaper published in , the last publication to be one day at least before said first meeting

Six months from the date hereof are allowed to creditors within which to present and prove their claims.

You will make return hereof, with your doings hereon, on or before the date of said first meeting , 19 .

Witness, , Esquire, Judge of said Court, at , this day of , in the year of our Lord one thousand eight hundred and ninety- .

I have served the foregoing order as therein directed.

Register.

, ss. 19 . Then personally appeared , and made oath to the truth of the above return by him subscribed.

Before me,

Justice of the Peace.

Form of Administrator's Notice to Creditors of Insolvent Estate.

Estate of   , late of   , in the County of   , deceased, intestate, represented insolvent.

The Probate Court for said County will receive and examine all claims of creditors against the estate of said   , and notice is hereby given that six months from the   day of   , A. D. 19   , are allowed to creditors to present and prove their claims against said estate. and that the Court will receive and examine the claims of creditors at   , on the   day of   , 19   , at nine o'clock in the forenoon, and at   , on the   day of   , 19   , at nine o'clock in the forenoon.

} *Administrat*

Petition by Special Administrator for Leave to pay Debts.

[R. L. c. 137, § 13]

To the Honorable the Judge of the Probate Court in and for the County of   :

Respectfully represents   , of   , that he is special administrator of the estate of   , late of   , in said County of   .

That the value of the personal estate in the hands of the petitioner is $

That the debts due from the deceased, as nearly as they can now be ascertained, amount to $

That it is expedient that he should pay from the personal estate in his hands the debts shown by the list herewith filed, amounting to $

Wherefore he pray that he may be authorized to pay from said personal estate the debts shown by said list.
Dated this   day of   , A. D.   .

Citation by delivering, or mailing postpaid, a copy of citation to all persons interested fourteen days at least before return day, and by publishing once a week for three successive weeks, the last publication to be one day at least before return day

Petition for Perpetual Care of Burial Lot.

[R L c 150, § 13,]

To the Honorable the Judge of the Probate Court in and for the County of   :

Respectfully represents   , of   , in the County of   , that he is the administrat — execut   of the will — estate   of   , late of   , in said County of   , deceased,   that the body of the said   is buried in

Wherefore your petitioner pray that the Court determine the amount of money which he may pay for the perpetual care of the lot in which the body of said   is buried, and to whom the same shall be paid.
Dated this   day of   A. D.

The undersigned, being all the persons interested, hereby waive notice hereof.

Citation by delivering copy of citation to all persons interested fourteen days at least before return day, or by publishing once a week for three successive weeks, the last publication to be one day at least before return day, and by mailing postpaid a copy of citation to all persons interested seven days at least before return day.

PETITION FOR SALE OF REAL ESTATE SUBJECT TO CONTINGENT REMAINDER.

[R L c 127, §§ 28–31.]

[A next friend must be appointed to represent minors and persons not ascertained or not in being]

To the Honoruble the Judge of the Probate Court in and for the County of

Respectfully represents , of , in said County, that , of , in said County of , by his last will, proved in said Court on the day of , A. D. 19 , devised certain real estate in the following words

The said real estate is situated in , in said County of , and described as follows:

And the petitioner having an estate in possession in said real estate represents that it is *necessary* expedient to sell said real estate for the following reasons

And represents that the following named persons, including h sel , are the only persons who or whose issue are or may become interested:

Persons	Residence	Nature and Fractional Amount of Interest

Wherefore the petitioner prays that , of , in the County of , or some other suitable person may be appointed a trustee to sell and convey said real estate at private sale for the sum of dollars, or at public auction, and to hold and apply the proceeds of such sale according to the requirements of law in such case made and provided.

Citation by publishing once a week for three successive weeks, the last publication to be one day at least before return day, and by mailing postpaid or delivering copy of citation to all known persons who or whose issue not now in being are or may become interested, seven days at least before return day

Petition for Sale of Estate Subject to Vested Remainder.

[R L c 127, § 29]

To the Honorable the Judge of the Probate Court in and for the County of   :

Respectfully represents   , of   , in said County, that certain real estate, situated in   , in said County, described as follows:

is subject to a vested remainder or reversion created under the will   of   , of   , in said County

That the following are the only persons interested (including the petitioner).

Persons	Residence	Nature and Fractional Amount of Interest

That it is necessary and expedient to sell said real estate for the following reasons:

Wherefore the petitioner prays that   , of   , in the County of   , or some other suitable person, may be appointed a trustee to sell and convey said real estate at private sale for the sum of   dollars, or at public auction, and to hold and apply the proceeds of such sale according to the requirements of law in such case made and provided.

Citation by publishing once a week for three successive weeks, the last publication to be one day at least before return day, and by mailing postpaid or delivering copy of citation to all known persons interested, seven days at least before return day.

Trustee's Bond for Sale of Real Estate — With Sureties — Vested or Contingent Remainder.

Know all Men by these Presents,

That we   , of   , in the County of   , as principal, and   , of   , in the County of   , and   , of   , in the County of   , as sureties, and all within the Commonwealth of Massachusetts, are holden and stand firmly bound and obliged unto   , Esquire, Judge of the Probate Court in and for the County of   , in the full and just sum of   dollars, to be paid to said Judge and his successors in said office, to the true payment whereof we bind ourselves and each of us, our and each of our heirs, executors and administrators, jointly and severally by these presents. Sealed with our seals, and dated the   day of   , in the year of our Lord one thousand nine hundred and   .

The condition of this obligation is such, that if the above-bounden   trustee appointed by decree of this Court dated   to sell certain real estate and hold the proceeds thereof for the benefit of   and others, shall —

First, manage and dispose of all such estate, and faithfully discharge h   trust in relation thereto, according to law;

Second, render upon oath, at least once a year, until h   trust is fulfilled, unless h   is excused therefrom in any year by said Court, a true account of the property in h   hands, and of the management and disposition thereof, and also render such account at such other times as said Court may order;

Third, at the expiration of h   trust, settle h   account in said Court, and pay over and deliver all the estate remaining in h   hands, or due from h   on such settlement, to the person or persons entitled thereto ;

Then this obligation to be void, otherwise to remain in full force and virtue.

Signed, sealed, and delivered
  in presence of

      , ss.   A. D. 19   .   Examined and approved

Judge of Probate Court

I, , the within-named trustee, declare that, to the best of my knowledge and belief, the value of the within-named estate does not exceed $.

[SIGN]

SALE OF ESTATE SUBJECT TO VESTED OR CONTINGENT REMAINDER — APPOINTMENT OF NEXT FRIEND AND GUARDIAN FOR THE CASE.

COMMONWEALTH OF MASSACHUSETTS

, ss.   PROBATE COURT.

At a Probate Court holden at , in said County, on the day of , in the year of our Lord one thousand nine hundred and

In the matter of the petition of , that or some other suitable person be appointed a trustee to sell and convey certain real estate subject to a contingent — vested remainder or reversion created under the will of , late of , in the County of , for the benefit of and others, and to hold and apply the proceeds of such sale as required by law.

It appearing to said Court that there is need therefor, it doth appoint , of , in the County of , to appear and act therein as the next friend of all persons not ascertained. or not in being, who are or may become interested in said estate , and it also appearing that

minor and interested in said case, and ha no legal guardian it doth appoint , of , in said County of , to be guardian for the case, to appear and act for said minor in the above-mentioned matter.

Judge of Probate Court.

I hereby accept the above appointment and

PETITION FOR SPECIFIC PERFORMANCE.

To the Honorable the Judge of the Probate Court in and for the County of   :

Respectfully represents   . of   , in said County   , that   , late of   , in said County,   deceased, during his lifetime, to wit·   on the   day of   , A D. 1   , entered into an agreement ⁻   in writing with your petitioner, a copy of which agreement is hereto annexed:

whereby said   agreed with your petitioner, to convey to him upon the terms and conditions set forth in said agreement   , certain real estate situated in   , in said County,   and fully described in said agreement   , that said   died without making such conveyance, and that your petitioner is ready to perform all the conditions of said agreement   on his part.

Wherefore your petitioner prays that a specific performance of said agreement may be decreed, and that   administrat of the estate   of said   , may be ordered to convey said real estate to him agreeably to the terms thereof.

Dated this   day of   A.D. 1   .

The undersigned, being all the parties interested in the foregoing petition, desire the same may be granted without further notice.

Citation by delivering copy of citation fourteen days at least before return day, or if not found within the Commonwealth, by leaving copy at usual place of abode, or by mailing copy to last post-office address fourteen days at least before return day, and, unless respondent has actual notice, by publishing once a week for three successive weeks, the last publication to be seven days at least before return day

Petition by Special Administrator for Leave to Carry on Business.

[R L c 137, § 11]

[Notice upon this petition shall be such as the Court may order]

To the Honorable the Judge of the Probate Court in and for the County of

Respectfully represents   , of   , special administrator of the estate of   , late of   , in the County of   , deceased.

That the said deceased was at the time of his death engaged in the business of

That the interest of said business and of said estate require that said business should be continued

Wherefore your petitioner pray that he may be authorized to continue business for the benefit of said estate under the direction of the Court.

Petition for Probate of Will — Presumption of Death.

[Superseded by R L c 144, relating to settlement of estates of absentees See page 726]

To the Honorable the Judge of the Probate Court in and for the County of   :

Respectfully represents

of   , in the County of   , that   , whose last known residence in this Commonwealth was in   , in said County of   , disappeared on the   day of   , in the year of our Lord one thousand nine hundred and   , since which time he has been absent from said   , and his whereabouts are unknown to his family, kindred, business associates

710   APPENDIX.

and intimate friends, and that said absentee was last known to have been in   , in the County of   , and State of   , and the petitioner believes that he is dead, testate, possessed of goods and estate   remaining to be administered, leaving as widow — husband — h   only heirs-at-law and next of kin, the persons whose names, residences and relationship to the absentee are as follows, viz

      Name   Residence.   Relationship.

That said absentee left a will — and   codicil — herewith presented, wherein your petitioner   named execut   .

Wherefore your petitioner   pray   that said will — and codicil — may be proved and allowed and letters testamentary issued to h   , and certifies that the statements herein contained are true to the best of h   knowledge and belief.

Dated this   day of   , A.D. 19   .

, ss. Subscribed and sworn to this   day of   , A.D 19 .

Before me,   *Justice of the Peace.*

The undersigned, being interested, hereby assent to the foregoing petition.

Citation by publishing once a week, for four successive weeks, the last publication to be one day at least before return day, by posting copy of citation not less than thirty days before return day in at least two conspicuous places, and by mailing postpaid or delivering copy of citation to all known persons interested, seven days at least before return day

---

Executor's Bond — Presumption of Death.

[Superseded by R L c 144 See p 730]

Know all Men by these Presents

That we,   , of   , in the County of   , as principal , and   , of   , in the County of   , and   , of   , in the County of   , as sureties, and all

PROBATE FORMS. 711

within the Commonwealth of Massachusetts, are holden and stand firmly bound and obliged unto   , Esquire, Judge of the Probate Court in and for the County of   , in the full and just sum of   dollars, to be paid to said Judge and his successors in said office, to the true payment whereof we bind ourselves and each of us, our and each of our heirs, executors and administrators, jointly and severally by these presents. Sealed with our seals, and dated the   day of   , in the year of our Lord one thousand nine hundred and

THE CONDITION OF THIS OBLIGATION IS SUCH, that if the above-bounden

execut   of the last will and testament of   , late of   , in said County of   , deceased, testate, shall,

First, make and return to said Probate Court, within three months after h   appointment, a true inventory of all the real and personal estate of said deceased which at the time of the making of such inventory shall have come to the possession or knowledge of said execut   :

Second, administer according to law and to the will of said deceased all the personal estate of said deceased which may come to the possession of said execut   , or of any person for h   , and also the proceeds of any of the real estate of said deceased that may be sold, mortgaged, leased or rented by said execut   ,

Third, render upon oath, a true account of h   administration at least once a year, until h   trust is fulfilled, unless he is excused therefrom in any year by said Court, and also render such account at such other times as said Court may order,

Fourth, obey all orders and decrees that may be made by said Court.

Then this obligation to be void, otherwise to remain in full force and virtue.

Signed, sealed, and delivered in presence of

     , ss.   A D 19   . Examined and approved
                              Judge of Probate Court.

I,   , the within-named execut   , declare that, to the

best of my knowledge and belief, the estate and effects of the within-named deceased do not exceed in value the following-mentioned sums, viz :

      Real Estate, $.
      Personal Estate, $.
       [SIGN]

EXECUTOR'S LETTER — PRESUMPTION OF DEATH.

[Superseded by R L c 144, relating to settlement of estates of absentees See p. 730.]

COMMONWEALTH OF MASSACHUSETTS.

   , ss.   PROBATE COURT.

To   *, of*   *, in the County of*   *, and Commonwealth aforesaid.*

You are appointed execut of the last will and testament of   , late of   , in said County of   , deceased, testate, which will was proved and allowed on the   day of A D 19   , by said Court, and is now of record in this Court;

And you are required to make and return into said Probate Court, within three months from the date hereof, a true inventory of all the real and personal estate of said deceased which at the time of the making of such inventory shall have come to your possession or knowledge,

To administer, according to law and to the will of said deceased, all the personal estate of said deceased which may come to your possession, or that of any person for you, and also the proceeds of any of the real estate of said deceased that may be sold, mortgaged, leased, or rented by you,

To render, upon oath, a true account of your administration, at least once a year, until your trust is fulfilled, unless excused therefrom, in any year, by said Court,

To obey all orders and decrees that may be made by said Court,

And also, within three months, to cause notice of your appointment to be posted in two or more public places in the city or town in which said deceased last dwelt in this Commonwealth, or cause the same to be published once in each week for three successive weeks in the

a newspaper published in   , and return your affidavit of having given such notice, with a copy thereof, to the Probate Court

Witness,   , Esquire, Judge of said Court, at   , this   day of   , in the year of our Lord one thousand nine hundred and   .

Register.

PETITION FOR PROBATE OF WILL — PRESUMPTION OF DEATH — LETTERS OF ADMINISTRATION WITH THE WILL ANNEXED.

[Superseded by R. L. c. 144, relating to settlement of estates of absentees. See p 726.]

To the Honorable the Judge of the Probate Court in and for the County of   .

Respectfully represents   , of   , in the County of   , that   , whose last known residence in this Commonwealth was in   , in said County of   , disappeared on the   day of   , in the year of our Lord one thousand nine hundred and   , since which time he has been absent from said   , and his whereabouts are unknown to his family, kindred, business associates and intimate friends, and that said absentee was last known to have been in   , in the County of   , and State of   , and the petitioner believes that he is dead, testate, possessed of goods and estate remaining to be administered, leaving as widow — husband — h   only heirs-at-law and next of kin, the persons whose names, residences, and relationship to the deceased are as follows, viz..

NAME.   RESIDENCE.   RELATIONSHIP

That said deceased left a will — and   codicil   — herewith presented, wherein   w   named execut   , and has

That your petitioner is   of said absentee and interested in his estate

Wherefore your petitioner   pray   that said will — and codicil   — may be proved and allowed, and letters of administration with the will annexed, issued to h   , or some other suitable person, and certifies that the statements herein contained are true to the best of h   knowledge and belief.

Dated this   day of   A.D. 19   .

      , ss.   Subscribed and sworn to this   day of A.D. 19   .

Before me,   *Justice of the Peace.*

The undersigned being interested hereby assent to the foregoing petition

Citation by publishing once a week for four successive weeks, the last publication to be one day at least before return day, by posting a copy of citation not less than thirty days before return day, in at least two conspicuous places, and by mailing postpaid, or delivering copy of citation to all known persons interested, seven days at least before return day

---

ADMINISTRATOR'S BOND — PRESUMPTION OF DEATH — WILL ANNEXED

[Superseded by R L c 144   See p 730]

KNOW ALL MEN BY THESE PRESENTS,

That we,   , of   , in the County of   , as principal and   , of   , in the County of   , and of   , in the County of   , as sureties, and all within the Commonwealth of Massachusetts, are holden and stand firmly bound and obliged unto   , Esquire, Judge of the Probate Court in and for the County of   , in the full and just sum

PROBATE FORMS. 715

of   dollars, to be paid to said Judge and his successors in said office, to the true payment whereof we bind ourselves and each of us, our and each of our heirs, executors, and administrators, jointly and severally by these presents. Sealed with our seals, and dated the   day of   , in the year of our Lord one thousand nine hundred and   .

THE CONDITION OF THIS OBLIGATION IS SUCH, that if the above-bounden   , administrat   with the will annexed, of the estate   of   , late of   , in said County of   , deceased, testate, shall,

First, make and return to said Probate Court, within three months after h   appointment, a true inventory of all the real and personal estate of said deceased which at the time of the making of such inventory shall have come to the possession or knowledge of said administrat   ;

Second, administer according to law and to the will of said deceased all the personal estate of said deceased which may come to the possession of said administrat   or of any person for h   , and also the proceeds of any of the real estate of said deceased that may be sold, mortgaged, leased or rented by said administrat   ;

Third, render upon oath, a true account of h   administration at least once a year, until h   trust is fulfilled, unless he is excused therefrom in any year by said Court, and also render such account at such other times as said Court may order ;

Fourth, obey all orders and decrees that may be made by said Court.

Then this obligation to be void, otherwise to remain in full force and virtue.

Signed, sealed, and delivered
in presence of

    , ss.   A D 19   .   Examined and approved
                                    Judge of Probate Court.

I,   , the within-named administrat   , declare that, to the best of my knowledge and belief, the estate and effects of the within-named deceased do not exceed in value the following mentioned sums, viz

    Real Estate, $.
    Personal Estate, $.
    [SIGN]

LETTER OF ADMINISTRATION WITH WILL ANNEXED — PRESUMPTION OF DEATH.

[Superseded by R. L. c 144, relating to settlement of Estates of absentees.]

COMMONWEALTH OF MASSACHUSETTS

 , ss.   PROBATE COURT.

To , of , in the County of , and Commonwealth aforesaid

You are appointed administrat with the will annexed of the estate of , late of , in the County of , deceased, testate, which will was proved and allowed on the day of , A. D. 19 , by said Court, and is now of record in this Court:

And you are required to make and return to said Probate Court, within three months from the date hereof, a true inventory of all the real and personal estate of said deceased, which at the time of the making of such inventory shall have come to your possession or knowledge ;

To administer according to law, and to the will of said deceased, all the personal estate of said deceased which may come to your possession, or that of any person for you, and also the proceeds of any of the real estate of said deceased that may be sold, mortgaged, leased, or rented by you.

To render, upon oath, a true account of your administration, at least once a year, until your trust is fulfilled, unless excused therefrom, in any year, by said Court,

To obey all orders and decrees that may be made by said Court;

And also, within three months, to cause notice of your appointment to be posted in two or more public places in the city or town in which said deceased last dwelt in this Commonwealth, or cause the same to be published once in each week for three successive weeks in the   , a newspaper published in   , and return your affidavit of having given such notice, with a copy thereof, to the Probate Court

Witness,   , Esquire, Judge of said Court, at   , this   day of   , in the year of our Lord one thousand nine hundred and   .

Register.

Petition for Administration — Presumption of Death

[Superseded by R L c 144, relating to settlement of estates of absentees. See p 726.]

To the Honorable the Judge of the Probate Court in and for the County of

Respectfully represents   , of   , in the County of   , that   , whose last known residence in this Commonwealth was in   , in said County of   , disappeared on the   day of   , in the year of our Lord one thousand nine hundred and   , since which time he has been absent from said   , and his whereabouts are unknown to his family. kindred, business associates, and intimate friends, and that said absentee was last known to have been in   , in the County of   , and State of   , and your petitioner believes that he is dead, intestate, possessed of goods and estate   remaining to be administered, leaving, as the only persons interested in said estate, *a* widow — husband, and h   only heirs-at-law and next of kin, the persons whose names, residences, and relationship to the absentee are as follows, viz .

| Name | Residence | Relationship |

that your petitioner   is a   of said absentee, and interested in his estate.

Wherefore your petitioner   prays that   he , or some other suitable person, be appointed administrat   of the estate of said   , and certifies that the statements herein contained are true to the best of   h   knowledge and belief.

Dated this   day of   , A. D. 19   .

    , ss.   Subscribed and sworn to this   day of   , A. D. 19   .

Before me,

Justice of the Peace.

The undersigned, interested in said estate, hereby assent to the foregoing petition.

Citation by publication once a week for four successive weeks, the last publication to be one day at least before return day, by posting a copy of citation not less than thirty days before return day in at least two conspicuous places, and by mailing postpaid or delivering copy of citation to all known persons interested seven days at least before return day

---

ADMINISTRATOR'S BOND — PRESUMPTION OF DEATH.

[Superseded by R. L. c. 144   See p. 730.]

KNOW ALL MEN BY THESE PRESENTS,

That we,   , of   , in the County of   , as principal , and   , of   , in the County of   , and   , of   , in the County of   , as sureties, and all within the Commonwealth of Massachusetts, are holden and stand firmly bound and obliged unto   , Esquire, Judge of the Probate Court in and for the County of   , in the full and just sum of   dollars, to be paid to said Judge and his successors in said office; to the true payment whereof we bind ourselves and each of us, our and each of our heirs, executors and administrators, jointly and severally by these presents. Sealed with our seals, and dated the   day of   , in the year of our Lord one thousand nine hundred and   .

THE CONDITION OF THIS OBLIGATION IS SUCH, that if the above-bounden   , administrat   of the estate of   , late of   , in said County of   , deceased, intestate, shall,

First, make and return to said Probate Court, within three months after h   appointment, a true inventory of all the real and personal estate of said deceased which at the time of the making of such inventory shall have come to the possession or knowledge of said administrat ,

Second, administer according to law all the personal estate of said deceased which may come to the possession of said administrat   , or of any person for h   , and also the proceeds of any of the real estate of said deceased that may be sold, mortgaged, leased or rented by said administrat ,

Third, render upon oath, a true account of h   administration at least once a year, until h   trust is fulfilled, unless he is   excused therefrom in any year by said Court, and also render such account at such other times as said Court may order;

Fourth, pay to such persons as said Court may direct, any balance remaining in h   hands, upon the settlement of h   accounts,

Fifth, deliver h   letters of administration into said Court in case any will of said deceased is hereafter duly proved and allowed; and

Sixth, obey all orders and decrees that may be made by said Court

Then this obligation to be void. otherwise to remain in full force and virtue

    Signed, sealed, and delivered
        in presence of

, ss.   A. D. 19   .   Examined and approved
                                    Judge of Probate Court.

I,   , the within-named administrat   , declare that, to the best of my   knowledge and belief. the estate and effects of the within-named deceased do not exceed in value the following-mentioned sums viz. .

        Real Estate, $.
        Personal Estate, $.
           [SIGN]

ADMINISTRATOR'S LETTER — PRESUMPTION OF DEATH.

[Superseded by R. L. c 144. See p 729.]

COMMONWEALTH OF MASSACHUSETTS

, ss   PROBATE COURT.

To   , of   , in the County of   , and Commonwealth aforesaid.

You are appointed administrat   of the estate of   , late of   , in said County of   , deceased, intestate.

And you are required to make and return to said Probate Court, within three months from the date hereof, a true inventory of all the real and personal estate of said deceased which at the time of the making of such inventory shall have come to your possession or knowledge;

To administer according to law all the personal estate of said deceased which may come to your possession, or that of any person for you, and also the proceeds of any of the real estate of said deceased that may be sold, mortgaged, leased, or rented by you;

To render, upon oath, a true account of your administration, at least once a year, until your trust is fulfilled, unless excused therefrom, in any year, by said Court;

To pay any balance remaining in your hands upon the settlement of your accounts, to such persons as said Court shall direct; to obey all orders and decrees that may be made by said Court;

To deliver these letters of administration into said Court, in case any will of said deceased shall be hereafter duly proved and allowed;

And, also, within three months, to cause notice of your appointment to be posted in two or more public places in the city or town in which said deceased last dwelt in this Commonwealth, or cause the same to be published once in each week for three successive weeks in the   , a newspaper published in   , and return your affidavit of having given such notice, with a copy thereof, to the Probate Court

Witness,   , Esquire, Judge of said Court, at   , this   day of   , in the year of our Lord one thousand nine hundred and   .

                                                                    Register

---

PETITION FOR DISTRIBUTION — PRESUMPTION OF DEATH — INTESTATE ESTATE

[Superseded by R. L. c. 144, § 11.]

To the Honorable the Judge of the Probate Court in and for the County of   .

Respectfully represents   , of   , in said County, administrat   of the estate of   , late of   , in said County   , deceased, intestate   , that said deceased has been missing and unheard from, and his whereabouts have been unknown to his family, kindred, business associates and friends for fourteen consecutive years prior to the filing of this petition, that he was last known to have been alive on the   day of   , in the year one thousand nine hundred and   , that there is a balance of his estate in the hands of h   administrat   which remains to be distributed among h   widow and next of kin, whose names, places of residence, and relationship to the deceased are supposed, or claimed, to be as follows.

    NAME   RESIDENCE   RELATIONSHIP.   SHARE.

Wherefore your petitioner pray   that distribution of such balance may be decreed by the Court among such persons as may be proved to be entitled thereto, according to law.

Dated this   day of   , A. D. 19   .

           , ss   , A. D. 19   . Then personally appeared   , and made oath to the truth of the above representation, according to the best of h   knowledge and belief.

Before me,

                                          Justice of the Peace.

Citation by publishing once a week for three successive weeks, the last publication to be one day at least before return day, and by mailing postpaid copy of citation to all known persons interested, fourteen days at least before return day

BOND OF HEIR — PRESUMPTION OF DEATH.

[Superseded by R. L. c 144.]

KNOW ALL MEN BY THESE PRESENTS,

That we,   of   , in the County of   , as principal   , and   , of   , in the County of   , and   , of   , in the County of   , as sureties, and all within the Commonwealth of Massachusetts, are holden and stand firmly bound and obliged unto   , Esquire, Judge of the Probate Court in and for the County of   , in the full and just sum of   dollars, to be paid to said Judge and his successors in said office, to the true payment whereof we bind ourselves and each of us, our and each of our heirs, executors and administrators, jointly and severally by these presents. Sealed with our seals, and dated the   day of   , in the year of our Lord one thousand nine hundred and   .

THE CONDITION OF THIS OBLIGATION IS SUCH, that if the above-named principal, who is heir — devisee — legatee — distributee — of a certain estate — share — legacy — received by him from the estate of   , formerly of   , in said County of   , whose estate is in course of administration in this Court, upon presumption of his death, upon the   day of   , 189 , as appears by decree of this Court,   shall restore any share, estate, or legacy received or acquired by him from the estate of said   , or its equivalent in money, without interest, to said   if he shall *return and* claim it within eight years from the date hereof.

Then this obligation to be void, otherwise to remain in full force and virtue

    Signed, sealed, and delivered
        in presence of

    , ss.   A. D. 19 .   Examined and approved.
                                        Judge of Probate Court.

Petition for Trusteeship under Written Instrument.

[The original instrument should be filed]

To the Honorable the Judge of the Probate Court in and for the County of   .

Respectfully represents   , of   , in the County of   , that   , late of   , in the County of   , was trustee under a certain instrument in writing, dated   , and recorded in the Registry of Deeds for the County of   , book   , page   , wherein   ,

gave certain estate in trust to   for the benefit of

which said instrument is filed herewith, and said   has   before the objects of said trust are accomplished, and no adequate provision is made therein for supplying the vacancy, that some of the parties interested in said trust request the appointment of your petitioner in place of said

Wherefore he prays that he may be appointed trustee as aforesaid, according to the provisions of the law in such cases made and provided.

Dated this   day of A. D. 19   .

The undersigned, being all persons interested in said trust, request that the prayer of above petition be granted without further notice

Citation by publishing once a week for three successive weeks, the last publication to be one day at least before return day

---

Trustee's Bond — Under Deed.

Know all Men by these Presents

That we,   , of   , in the County of   , as principal   , and   , of   , in the County of   , and   , of   , in the County of   , as sureties, and all within the

Commonwealth of Massachusetts, are holden and stand firmly bound and obliged unto   , Esquire, Judge of the Probate Court in and for the County of   , in the full and just sum of   dollars, to be paid to said Judge and his successors in said office, to the true payment whereof we bind ourselves and each of us, our and each of our heirs, executors and administrators, jointly and severally by these presents. Sealed with our seals, and dated the   day of   , in the year of our Lord one thousand nine hundred and   .

THE CONDITION OF THIS OBLIGATION IS SUCH, that if the above-bounden   , trustee under a certain instrument in writing, dated   , A. D. 18   , wherein   gave to certain estate in trust for the benefit of   , shall,

First, make and return to said Probate Court, within three months, the Court having so ordered, a true inventory of all the real and personal estate belonging to h   as trustee   , which at the time of the making of such inventory shall have come to   h   possession or knowledge;

Second, manage and dispose of all such estate, and faithfully discharge   h   trust in relation thereto, according to law and the terms of said instrument,

Third, render upon oath, at least once a year, until   h   trust is fulfilled, unless he   is excused therefrom in any year by said Court, a true account of the property in   h   hands, and of the management and disposition thereof, and also to render such account at such other times as said Court may order,

Fourth, at the expiration of   h   trust, settle   h   account in said Court, and pay over and deliver all the estate remaining in   h   hands, or due from   h   on such settlement, to the person or persons entitled thereto;

Then this obligation to be void, otherwise to remain in full force and virtue.

   Signed, sealed, and delivered
      in presence of

   , ss.   A. D. 19 .   Examined and approved.
                              Judge of Probate Court.

I,   , the within named trustee, declare that, to the best of my knowledge and belief, the value of the within-named trust estate does not exceed the following-mentioned sums, viz.:

    Real estate, $.
    Personal Estate, $.
     [SIGN]

Trustee's Letter — Under Deed.

[This should be recorded wherever the trust instrument is recorded.]

COMMONWEALTH OF MASSACHUSETTS

 , ss. Probate Court.

To , of , in the County of , and Commonwealth aforesaid,
         Greeting:

You are appointed trustee in place of   , under a certain instrument in writing, to wit:

To have and exercise the same powers, rights and duties under said instrument as if you had been originally appointed, and the trust estate to vest in you in like manner as it   vested in the trustee aforesaid, in whose place you are substituted.

And you are ordered to make and return to said Probate Court, within three months from the date hereof, a true inventory of all the real and personal estate belonging to you as trustee which at the time of the making of such inventory shall have come to your possession or knowledge;

To manage and dispose of all such estate, and faithfully discharge your trust in relation thereto, according to law and the terms of said instrument;

To render upon oath at least once a year, until your trust is fulfilled, unless excused therefrom in any year by said Court a true account of the property in your hands, and of the management and disposition thereof, and also to render such account at such other times as said Court may order, and

At the expiration of your trust, to settle your account in said Court, and pay over and deliver all the estate remaining in your hands or due from you on such settlement, to the person or persons entitled thereto.

Witness,   , Esquire, Judge of said Court, at   , this   day of   , in the year of our Lord one thousand nine hundred and   .

———————
Register.

PETITION FOR RECEIVERSHIP OF ABSENT PERSON'S ESTATE.

[R L c 144]
[A Surety Company required in all cases]

To the Honorable the Judge of the Probate Court in and for the County of

Respectfully represents   , of   , in the County of   , that   , a resident of   , in this Commonwealth, and having property therein, *disappeared, absconded and* absented himself from this Commonwealth on the   day of   A D 1   , that he has left no agent therein, and his whereabouts are unknown, *known to be out of this Commonwealth, to wit. at*   , that he has a wife and minor children dependent upon him wholly *partly* for support, and that he has disappeared without making sufficient provision for such support, that said absentee was   years of age, a   by occupation, and   in the County of   and Commonwealth of Massachusetts   . was his last known residence and address; that he disappeared on the date above-named under the following circumstances, to wit.

and that the names and residences of the family of the absentee and of other persons of whom inquiry may be made are as follows, viz

NAME   RESIDENCE   RELATIONSHIP

That a schedule of the property of said absentee within this Commonwealth, real and personal, and its location, so far as known, is herein contained, and the same is all the property of said absentee known to your petitioner   to be in this Commonwealth; that your petitioner is *acting in behalf of the wife and child* a   of said absentee, and would be entitled to administer upon his estate if he were dead.

Wherefore your petitioner pray that said property may be taken possession of by this Court; that he , or some other suitable person, be appointed receiver of the same, and that a warrant issue therefor, and certif   that the statements herein contained are true to the best of h   knowledge and belief.

Dated this   day of   A. D. 19 .

, ss.   Subscribed and sworn to this   day of A. D. 19 .

Before me,

Justice of the Peace.

SCHEDULE OF PROPERTY.

SCHEDULE OF PROPERTY of   , formerly of   in said County of   , absentee.

Real Estate.	Location.	Value.

Personal Estate.	Location.	Value.

ABSENTEE — ORDER OF NOTICE.

COMMONWEALTH OF MASSACHUSETTS.

, ss.   PROBATE COURT.

To   an absentee who formerly resided in   , in the County of   , having property in said County; to all per-

sons claiming an interest in the property hereinafter named; and to all whom it may concern

Whereas, a petition has been presented to said Court to appoint   , of   in the County of   or some other suitable person, receiver of the following described property of said absentee, and whereas a warrant to take possession thereof has issued to an officer who has taken and now holds the same, to wit

You are hereby cited to appear at a Probate Court to be held at   , in said County of   , on the   day of A D 19 , at nine o'clock in the forenoon, to show cause, if any you have, why the same should not be granted.

And the petitioner is hereby directed to give public notice thereof, by publishing this notice once in each week, for three successive weeks, in the   a newspaper published in   , the last publication to be seven days at least before said Court; and by posting a copy of this notice, not less than thirty days before said Court, upon each parcel of land named herein, and in two or more conspicuous public places in   , the city — town — in which the absentee was last known to have been, and by mailing, postpaid, at least thirty days before said Court, a copy of this notice to said absentee, addressed to him at   , his last known address.

Witness,   , Esquire, Judge of said Court, this   day of   in the year one thousand nine hundred and   .

Register.

ABSENTEE — RETURN OF SERVICE OF ORDER OF NOTICE.

I certify that I have served the foregoing notice as therein ordered, by publishing the same for three successive weeks in the   the last publication in each newspaper being seven days before said Court, by posting a copy thereof upon each of said parcels of land, and in   conspicuous places in the said   of   and by mailing, postpaid, to the said absentee, on the   day of   , 19 , a copy of the same addressed to him at   , his last known address

, ss.   A.D. 19 . Personally appeared   and made oath to the truth of the above return by h   subscribed.
Before me,
                              Justice of the Peace.

Absentee — Warrant to Sheriff to take Possession of Property.

[R L c 144]

COMMONWEALTH OF MASSACHUSETTS

, ss.   Probate Court.

To the Sheriffs of our several Counties, or their Deputies,
                              Greeting·

You are hereby directed to take possession forthwith of all the following described property and estate, real and personal, of   , formerly of   , in the County of   , absentee, and hold the same safely, subject to the order of the Court, to wit ·

And you are also directed to post a copy of this warrant upon each parcel of land named herein, and cause so much hereof as relates to land to be recorded in the Registry of Deeds for the County and District in which the land is located, and to make return of this warrant forthwith with your doings thereon, and with a schedule of all property taken possession of by virtue hereof, together with your costs and expenses thereon.

In witness whereof, I have hereunto set my hand, and caused the seal of said Court to be affixed, at   , this   day of   in the year one thousand nine hundred and   .
                              Judge of Probate Court.

Absentee — Decree on Petition for Appointment of Receiver

COMMONWEALTH OF MASSACHUSETTS.

, ss

At a Probate Court, holden at   , in and for said County of   , on the   day of   in the year of our Lord one thousand nine hundred and   .

The petition of   of   in the County of   ,
praying that he , or some other suitable person, be appointed
receiver of certain property and estate of   , absentee, lying
in part in   in said County of   , and described in
the return of the officer, and the warrant and return thereon
having been considered, after a hearing, it appearing that said
            disappeared from this Commonwealth on the   day
of   in the year 1   , and that his whereabouts are unknown, and the said absentee and all other persons interested
having been notified according to the order of the Court, to
appear and show cause, if any they have, against the same, and
no party objecting thereto, and it appearing that need for a
receiver exists; it is found by the Court and ordered to be
recorded that the date of the disappearance of said absentee
was the   day of   in the year 1

AND IT IS DECREED that said petitioner   be appointed
receiver of said property and estate described in said return,
first giving bond, according to law, for the due performance of
said trust, and that said officer transfer and deliver unto said
receiver forthwith upon the filing and approval of his bond,
all the property and estate named in the said officer's return,

Judge of Probate Court.

Receiver's Bond

[R L c 144]

Know all Men by these Presents,

That we,   , of   , in the County of   , as principal, and   , of   , in the County of   , and   ,
of   , in the County of   , as sureties, and all within
the Commonwealth of Massachusetts, are holden and stand
firmly bound and obliged unto   , Esquire, Judge of the
Probate Court in and for the County of   , in the full and
just sum of   dollars, to be paid to said Judge and his successors in said office; to the true payment whereof we bind
ourselves and each of us, our and each of our heirs, executors
and administrators, jointly and severally by these presents.

Sealed with our seals, and dated the   day of   , in the year of our Lord one thousand nine hundred and

THE CONDITION OF THIS OBLIGATION IS SUCH, that if the above-bounden   , receiver for all the property of   , lately resident in   , in said County of   , an absentee shall,

First, make and return to said Probate Court forthwith a true inventory of all the real and personal estate of said absentee that at the time of the making of the same shall have come to the possession of said receiver, and, at such time as it may order, a true inventory of such additional property as may come into h   possession hereafter,

Second, manage and dispose of all such estate according to law and for the best interests of said absentee, and also the proceeds of any of the real estate of said absentee that may be sold or mortgaged by said receiver, and faithfully discharge h   trust in relation to such estate and to the support and maintenance of his wife and minor children;

Third, render upon oath, at least once a year, until h   trust is fulfilled, unless he   is   excused therefrom in any year by said Court, a true account of the property in h   hands, including the proceeds of all real estate sold or mortgaged by h   , and of the management and disposition thereof, and also render such account at such other times as said Court may order; and

Fourth, obey all orders and decrees made by said Court,

Fifth, at the expiration of h   trust, settle h   account in said Court, or with said absentee or his legal representatives, and pay over and deliver all the estate remaining in h   hands, or due from h   on such settlement, to the person or persons lawfully entitled thereto

Then this obligation to be void, otherwise to remain in full force and virtue.

Signed, sealed, and delivered
in presence of

, SS.   , A. D. 19   Examined and approved.
Judge of Probate Court.

Receiver's Letter.

COMMONWEALTH OF MASSACHUSETTS.

. ss   Probate Court.

To   , of   , *in County of*   , *and Commonwealth aforesaid.*

You are appointed receiver for certain property and estate of   , formerly a resident of   , in said Commonwealth   , an absentee, which property is described in the following schedule, to wit

And you have full power and authority to take possession of the same, and to have the care, custody, leasing, investing and application of it and its proceeds under the direction of said Court, and likewise of any additional property, of said absentee, and its proceeds, which in future you may be authorized and directed to take possession of.

You are required to manage and dispose of all such estate according to law and the orders of the Court and for the best interests of said absentee, and faithfully to discharge your trust in relation to such estate, and to the support and maintenance of the wife and minor children of said absentee,

To render, upon oath, a true account of the property in your hands, including the proceeds of all real estate sold or mortgaged by you, and of the management and disposition of all such property, at least once a year, until your trust is fulfilled, unless excused therefrom in any year by said Court;

At the expiration of your trust to settle your accounts in said Court, or with said absentee or his legal representative, and to pay over and deliver all the estate and effects remaining in your hands, or due from you on such settlement, to the person or persons lawfully entitled thereto

Witness,   , Esquire, Judge of said Court, at   this   day of   in the year of our Lord one thousand nine hundred and   .

Register.

Petition for Assignment of Real Estate in Fee ($5,000) — By the Court.

[Superseded by R L c 135, § 16, c 140, § 3]

[The names of the guardians of minors interested must be stated. If part of the land of the deceased lies in common with others that fact must be stated, and a description of such land, the deceased's share therein, and the names of the co-tenants inserted in or annexed to the petition]

To the Honorable the Judge of the Probate Court in and for the County of   .

Respectfully represents   , of   , in the County of   , that   , late of   , in said County of   , deceased, intestate, leaving no issue living, died seized of certain real estate in this Commonwealth, that   is h   widow — husband   and entitled to said estate in fee to an amount not exceeding five thousand dollars in value, that the entire real estate of the deceased consists of the following described parcels, namely

and your petitioner further says that the whole of said real estate of the deceased, above described, does not exceed the value of five thousand dollars, as appears by the inventory filed in this Court, being of the value only of   dollars, as your petitioner is prepared to verify, and that the names and residences of all other persons now interested therein are as follows:

Wherefore he   prays that the whole of said estate of said deceased may be assigned and set out to   h   in fee by said Court, as provided by law

Dated this   day of   A.D. 19 .

The undersigned, being all the persons interested, hereby assent to the foregoing petition

Citation by delivering copy of citation to each person interested who can be found within the Commonwealth, fourteen days at least before return day; and if any one cannot be so found, by publishing once a week for three successive weeks, the last publication to be one day at least before return day

PETITION FOR DISTRIBUTION AMONG A CLASS — TRUST ESTATE.

[R L c 147, § 20]

To the Honorable the Judge of the Probate Court in and for the County of .

Respectfully represents   trustee   under the will of   , late of   , in the County of   , for the benefit of the persons named below, that he holds as such trustee certain   estate, to wit.

that by the provisions of said will   the said trust estate is to be distributed in   among the heirs — the next of kin of   in a class of persons, namely, the   of   whose names and places of residence are supposed or claimed to be as follows:

| Name | Residence | Relationship | Share |

Wherefore your petitioner pray   that he may be ordered to convert the said trust estate into cash, and that distribution of the same may be decreed by the Court, among such persons as may be proved to be entitled thereto, according to law.

Dated this   day of   A D 19 .

ss   A D 19 .   Then personally appeared   and made oath to the truth of the above representation, according to the best of h   knowledge and belief

Before me,   *Justice of the Peace.*

Citation by publishing once a week for three successive weeks, the last publication to be one day at least before return day, and by mailing postpaid or delivering copy of citation to all known persons interested, fourteen days at least before return day

---

PETITION FOR DISTRIBUTION OF LEGACY AMONG A CLASS.

[R L c 141, § 22]

To the Honorable the Judge of the Probate Court in and for the County of

Respectfully represents   executor   of the will of —   administrator   with the will annexed of the estate of late of   , in said County of   , deceased, testate, that, by the provision of the will of said deceased, a certain legacy, amounting to the sum of   dollars, remains to be distributed   among the heirs, the next of kin, of   in a class of persons, namely, the   , of   , whose names and places of residence are supposed, or claimed to be, as follows.

NAME   RESIDENCE.   RELATIONSHIP   SHARE.

Wherefore your petitioner pray that distribution of such legacy may be decreed by the Court, among such persons as may be proved to be entitled thereto, according to law.

Dated this   , day of   , A D 19   .

       , ss.   A.D 19   . Then personally appeared and made oath to the truth of the above representation, according to the best of h   knowledge and belief.

Before me,

Justice of the Peace.

Citation by publishing once a week for three successive weeks, the last publication to be one day at least before return day, and by mailing postpaid or delivering copy of citation to all known persons interested fourteen days at least before return day

---

PETITION FOR AMENDMENT OF RECORD.

To the Honorable the Judge of the Probate Court in and for the County of   :

Respectfully represents   of   , in said County, that on the   day of   A D 19   , he was appointed by this Court administrat   of the estate   of   late of   , deceased; that said   was also sometimes called   and sometimes called   .

Wherefore your petitioner prays that the files and records in said case may be amended by inserting after the name   , wherever the same occurs, the words, — sometimes called   and sometimes called

Dated this   day of   A. D 19   .

COMMONWEALTH OF MASSACHUSETTS.

ss.   19 . Personally appeared the above-named
          , and made oath to the truth of the facts by him set
forth in the foregoing petition
    Before me,
                                    Justice of the Peace.

SEPARATE SUPPORT — PETITION FOR EXECUTION — TRUSTEE.

*To the Honorable the Judges of the Probate Court in and for
the County of*   .

Respectfully represents   of   , in said County of   ,
wife of   of said   , that on her petition for separate
support heretofore filed in said Court, an attachment of the
goods and estate of her said husband, *and also of his goods,
effects and credits in the hands and possession of*   *trustee
of her said husband,* was made to secure the decree which she
might obtain for such support   that *said trustee has filed
his answer that, at the time of the service of the Court's order
upon him, he had in his possession*   *dollars of the goods,
effects and credits of her said husband,*   that said Court by
its decree on said petition for separate support made on the
       day of   A. D. 19 , ordered said   to pay your
petitioner, for the support of herself and the maintenance of
minor children, the sum of   dollars, forthwith, and a further
sum of   dollars on each and every   thereafter,
and that there now remains due and unpaid under said decree the
sum of   dollars, and that said   neglects and refuses
to pay the same,

Wherefore your petitioner prays *that said*   *be charged
on his answer as trustee, in the sum of   dollars*, and
that an execution issue in favor of your petitioner, for the sum
of   dollars, against the goods, chattels and lands of said

and against his goods, effects and credits in the hands and possession of   trustee of said   jointly and severally.

Dated this   day of   A. D. 19 .

Citation by delivering a copy to husband, if found in the Commonwealth, at least seven days before return day, and, if not so found, by publication once a week for three successive weeks, the last publication to be one day at least before return day

---

SEPARATE SUPPORT — PETITION TO CHARGE TRUSTEE AND FOR EXECUTION.

To the Honorable the Judges of the Probate Court in and for the County of

Respectfully represents   of   ,   in said County of   ,   , wife of   of said   ,   that on her petition for separate support heretofore filed in said Court, an attachment of the goods and estate of her said husband, *and also of his goods, effects and credits in the hands and possession of   trustee of her said husband*, was made to secure the decree which she might obtain for such support.   *that said trustee has filed his answer that, at the time of the service of the Court's order upon him, he had in his possession   dollars of the goods, effects and credits of her said husband,*   that said Court by its decree on said petition for separate support made on the   day of   A. D. 19 , ordered said   to pay your petitioner, for the support of herself and the maintenance of minor children, the sum of   dollars, forthwith, and a further sum of   dollars on each and every   thereafter,   and that there now remains due and unpaid under said decree the sum of   dollars, and that said   neglects and refuses to pay the same,

Wherefore your petitioner prays *that said   be charged on his answer as trustee, in the sum of   dollars ,   and* that an execution issue in favor of your petitioner, for the sum of   dollars, against the goods, chattels and lands of said *and against his goods, effects and credits in the hands and possession of   trustee of said   jointly and severally.*

Dated this   day of   A D. 19 .

Citation by delivering a copy seven days at least before return day or by publication once a week for three successive weeks, the last publication to be one day at least before return day

---

SEPARATE SUPPORT — EXECUTION — TRUSTEE

COMMONWEALTH OF MASSACHUSETTS.

, ss   PROBATE COURT

To the Sheriffs of our several Counties, or their Deputies, or any Constable of the City of   , in said County,

GREETING

Whereas, on the petition of   , of   , in said County of   , wife of   , of said   , said Court, by its decree made on the   day of   A D 19   , ordered said   to pay said   for the support of herself and the maintenance of their minor children, the sum of   dollars, forthwith, and a further sum of   dollars on the   day of   each and every   thereafter, and whereas, under said decree, there now remains due and unpaid the sum of   dollars, whereof execution is requested to be done, and whereas, on the   day of   A. D 19   , it was ordered by said Court that execution issue for the sum of   dollars against said   , and against the goods, effects, and credits of the said   , in the hands and possession of   , trustee of said   , as appears of record in this Court, whereof execution remains to be done

You are hereby commanded, therefore, that of the goods, chattels, or lands of the said   , in his own hands and possession within your precinct and of the goods, effects, and credits of said   , in the hands and possession of said trustee, jointly and severally, you cause to be paid and satisfied unto the said

, at the value thereof in money, the sum of   dollars, with interest thereon from said   , and thereof also to satisfy yourself for your own fees, and for want of goods, chattels, or lands of the said   , to be by him shown unto you, or found within your precinct, to the acceptance of the said petitioner to satisfy the sums aforesaid, with interest as aforesaid, and for want of goods, effects, and credits of said   , in the hands and possession of the said trustee, to be by him discovered and exposed to you, to satisfy the said sum, with interest as aforesaid, with your own fees, you are commanded to take the body of said   , and him commit unto our jail in   , in our County of   , or any jail in your precinct, aforesaid, and him detain in your custody within our said jail until *he* pay the full sum of   , dollars with interest and your fees as aforesaid, or that *he* be discharged by the said petitioner, or otherwise by order of law. Hereof fail not, and make return of this writ, with your doings therein, into the Registry of Probate at   , in said County of   , in sixty days after the date hereof.

Witness,   , Esquire,   , Judge of said Court, this   day of   , in the year of our Lord one thousand nine hundred and   .

Register.

Petition for Leave to Deposit in Savings Bank

[R. L. c 150, § 25]

To the Honorable the Judge of the Probate Court in and for the County of

Respectfully represents   , that he is execut — trustee under the will — administrator of the estate — guardian of   , late of   , in said County of   , deceased; that it is advisable to deposit the sum of   dollars in a savings bank for the benefit of   , for the reason that h   is of residence unknown to the petitioner   , a minor and has no guardian

Wherefore your petitioner pray that he may be allowed to deposit said sum in the   , in the name of the Judge of said Court, to accumulate for the benefit of the person entitled thereto.

Dated this   day of   , 19   .

Guardian's Bond — Insane Person

Know all Men by these Presents,

That we,   of   in the County of   as principal , and   of   in the County of   and   of   in the County of   as sureties, and all within the Commonwealth of Massachusetts, are holden and stand firmly bound and obliged unto   , Esquire, Judge of the Probate Court in and for the County of   , in the full and just sum of   dollars, to be paid to said Judge and his successors in said office, to the true payment whereof we bind ourselves and each of us, our and each of our heirs, executors and administrators, jointly and severally by these presents. Sealed with our seals, and dated the   day of   in the year of our Lord one thousand nine hundred and   .

The condition of this obligation is such, that if the above-bounden   guardian of   of   , in said County of   , an insane person, shall: —

First, make and return to said Probate Court, at such time as it may order, a true inventory of all the real and personal estate of said ward that at the time of the making of such inventory shall have come to the possession or knowledge of said guardian ,

Second, manage and dispose of all such estate according to law and for the best interests of said ward, and faithfully discharge h   trust in relation to such estate, and to the custody and maintenance of said ward;

Third, render upon oath, at least once a year, until h   trust is fulfilled, unless h   is excused therefrom in any year by said Court, a true account of the property in h   hands, including the proceeds of all real estate sold or mortgaged by h   and of the management and disposition thereof, and also render such account at such other times as said Court may order, and

Fourth, at the expiration of h   trust, settle h   account in said Court, or with said ward, or h   legal representatives, and pay over and deliver all the estate remaining in h   hands, or due from h   on such settlement, to the person or persons lawfully entitled thereto,

Then this obligation to be void, otherwise to remain in full force and virtue

Signed, sealed and delivered
in presence of

, ss.   A D. 19 .   Examined and approved.
                                        Judge of Probate Court.

I,   the within-named guardian, declare that, to the best of my knowledge and belief, the estate and effects of the within-named ward   do not exceed in value the following-mentioned sums, viz :

Real Estate, $.
Personal Estate, $.
        [SIGN]

PETITION BY COMMISSIONERS FOR SALE OF REAL ESTATE.

To the Honorable the Judge of the Probate Court in and for the County of

Respectfully represent   that they are the commissioners appointed by said Court to make partition of certain real estate hereinafter described, among the tenants in common thereof,

Said real estate is situat   , in said County of   , and is bounded and described as follows, to wit

That said real estate cannot be advantageously divided.

Wherefore your petitioners pray that they be ordered by said Court to make sale and conveyance of said real estate at public auction for cash, and to distribute and pay over the net proceeds of the sale in such manner as to make the partition just and equal.

The undersigned, being all the persons interested, hereby assent to the foregoing petition

Citation by delivering a copy to each person interested who can be found in the Commonwealth, fourteen days at least before return day, and, if any one cannot so be found, by publication once a week for three successive weeks, the last publication to be one day at least before return day.

PETITION FOR TRUSTEESHIP TO FILL VACANCY.

To the Honorable the Judge of the Probate Court in and for the County of

Respectfully represents   of   , in the County of   , that   late of   , in said County of   , deceased, testate, by h   last will and testament, duly proved and allowed on the   day of   A D 19   in said Court, did therein give certain estate in trust for the use and benefit of   that   was duly appointed trustee thereof, and has   before the objects of said trust have been accomplished, that there is no adequate provision made in said will for supplying the vacancy caused by said   that your petitioner is   willing to accept said trust, and give bond according to law, for the faithful discharge thereof,   he therefore pray that he, or some other suitable person, be appointed trustee as aforesaid, according to the provisions of the law in such case made and provided.

Dated this   day of   A. D. 19   .

The undersigned, being all the persons interested, hereby assent to the foregoing petition.

Citation by publication once a week for three successive weeks, the last publication to be one day at least before return day

PETITION FOR LEAVE TO BRING SUIT ON BOND.

To the Honorable the Judge of the Probate Court in and for the County of

Respectfully represents   of   , in said County of   , that he is   and is interested in the estate of   late of said   , deceased, that by a decree of said Court, dated the   day of   A D 19   ,   of said   , was duly appointed executor — administrator — of the will — estate of said deceased   , and gave bond with   of   and   of   as sureties, for the faithful performance of the trust of executor — administrator as aforesaid, that, and said   has failed to perform h   duty in the discharge of said trust.

Wherefore your petitioner prays that he may be authorized to bring an action in the Superior Court upon the bond of said executor — administrator — in the name of the Judge of the Probate Court, for the recovery of the damage sustained by such neglect and maladministration of said

Dated this   day of   A D 19   .

WAIVER OF WILL.

[R L c 135, § 16]

[This waiver must be filed in the registry of probate within one year after the probate of the will If curtesy or dower is desired the claim therefor under R L c 132, § 1, must also be filed within one year]

To the Honorable the Judges of the Probate Court in and for the County of

Respectfully represents   of   in the County of   , that he is   the widow — *husband* — of   late of   in the County of   , deceased, that the will of said deceased was admitted to probate in said County by decree of this Court dated   19   , and he doth hereby waive any provisions that may have been made in it for   h   and doth claim such portions of the estate of the deceased as   he   would have taken if the deceased had died intestate.

Dated this   day of   19   .

Claim of Dower or Curtesy and Waiver of Will.

[R L c 132, § 1]

[This claim must be filed within one year from the approval of the bond of the executor or administrator of the deceased If the deceased left no will, the clause below relating thereto should be omitted   If the deceased was *insolvent* or *nearly* so or had in his lifetime conveyed real estate which was a large part of his whole estate, without the claimant herein joining, it may be for the interest of such to claim curtesy or dower in place of the provisions in fee of the above named chapter, as they are subject to the debts of the deceased, while curtesy or dower is not]

To the Honorable the Judges of the Probate Court in and for the County of

Respectfully represents   of   in the County of   that   he is   the widow — *husband* — of   late of   in the County of   , deceased, that on the   day of   19   , the bond of   the executor — administrator — of the estate — will — of the deceased was approved by this Court, and that   he doth hereby elect and claim dower — *curtesy* — in the estate of the deceased, instead of the interest in real property of the deceased given in section three of chapter one hundred and forty of the Revised Laws.

And   he doth also hereby waive any provisions that may have been made in the will of the deceased for h   and doth claim such portions of the estate of the deceased as   h   would have taken if the deceased had died intestate.

Dated this   day   of   19   .

INDEX.

INDEX.

A.

ABANDONED PROPERTY OF NON-RESIDENTS,   PAGE
    appointment of receiver for, when and how 342–346

ABSENTEES, ESTATES OF,
    appointment of receiver for, when 341–346
    distribution of 345, 346
    lease and sale of, by receiver 344, 345
    settlement of 345, 346

ABSENT HEIR,
    presumption of death of, when 357
    no presumption of marriage or issue of 357

ACCOUNTS,
    administrators and executors allowed for,
        assessments paid, if legally laid 296
        charges of administration 299
        certain claims paid, when estate is insolvent . . . 298
        costs and expenses of suits . . . . . 300, note
        debts paid, if legally due . . . 295
        debts due themselves and interest thereon . . . 303, 304
        expenses of last sickness of deceased 298
        funeral expenses 298
        judgments rendered against them . . . 300
        loss on sale of personal property 302
        money paid surety on probate bonds . . . 300, note
        not, for claims barred by statute of limitations . 297
        not, for distributive payments to residuary legatees . . . 304
    chargeable for,
        amount of debts uncollected by their neglect . . . 290
        compound interest, when . . . 293
        debts due from themselves . . . 294
        gain on sale of personal property . . . 286
        interest on funds in their hands, when . . 292
        interest, profit and income of personal property 286

ACCOUNTS (continued)   PAGE
  chargeable for,
    not, for property stolen without their default 289
    proceeds of real estate sold 286
    profits of business of deceased, if continued by them . 290
    rents of real estate, when 293
    value of personal property, whether inventoried or not . . . 286
        of property lost through their negligence 288
  administrators, executors, guardians and trustees,
    to render annual . . 279
    to render, although not legally appointed 280
  auditor may be appointed to examine 312
  citation to render, how issued . 284
    may issue, though executor, etc , has settled with parties and
        taken their receipts . . . 281
  conservator to render 143
  evidence of payment or delivery by administrator, etc , how per-
    petuated . . . . 316, note
  executor, etc , failing to render, may be cited 284
  failure to render, unfaithful administration . . . 162, 230, 284
  final, not to be settled until succession tax paid . 279, 316
  form of . 285
    second and additional 304
  guardian *ad litem*, when appointed 313, 314
  guardians allowed for,
    expenses of guardianship and services . 311
    expenses of ward's support and education, when . . 309
    interest on advances 310
  guardians and trustees chargeable for,
    compound interest, when 307
    gain on sale of personal property 305
    income of real estate 305
    interest received . . 306
    loss of interest from neglect to invest . . . 306
    losses from improper investments 306
    value of personal property as inventoried 305
  notice of presenting for allowance, to be given, unless . 312
    who entitled to . 312
  of joint executors etc , may be allowed on oath of one . 315
  one of two joint executors, etc , dying, survivor to render . 281
  public administrator to render on appointment of successor 282
    on first day of January annually . 283
        neglecting to render, district attorney to act 283
  separate, to be rendered by guardian of several wards jointly
    interested 312
  settled, when may be opened to correct error 316

INDEX. 749

ACCOUNTS (*continued*) PAGE
    sole executor, etc., dying, by whom to be rendered . . . 281
    special administrators to render, when ordered by court . . 280
    trustees allowed for expenses of trust and services . . . 311

ACTIONS (*by and against executors and administrators*),
    barred, when estate exhausted by payment before notice of claim
      or by payment of preferred claims, etc . . 203, 204, 212, 214
    limitation of, against executors and administrators 124, 195, 199, 200,
                                                                                                                  203
      proceedings when creditor's right of action accrues after two
        years 199, 200
      survival of . . . . . . 494, note, 495, note
      set-off, right of . . 205
      tort, liability of executor or administrator in . . . 205, 495
      trustee process against executors and administrators . . 499
        (See *Executor, actions by and against*.)

ADMINISTRATION,
    ancillary 104
    county, in what must be applied for 106
    creditors entitled to administer, when 112
    de bonis non 102, 103, 114
      to whom granted 114
    de bonis non with will annexed 103
    granted, in what cases and where 102
    granted to public administrator, when 109
    kindred, lineal or collateral 109
    next of kin, who are 108
      when entitled to administer 107, 110
    original, to whom granted 107–114
    petition for . . . 115
      notice of, to parties interested 116
      notice of, when dispensed with . . 117
    presumption of death, when . . 118
    proof of death 118
    special, when granted 104
    revoked by proof and allowance of will of deceased 105
    renunciation, by party entitled to administer, to be in writing 117
    time, within what must be applied for . . 106
    widow, right of to administer 107, 110

ADMINISTRATOR,
    account (See *Accounts*)
      settlement of, when good defence to suit on bond 205, note
    actions by and against (See *Executor, actions by and against*)
    affidavit of notice of appointment of 193

750 INDEX

ADMINISTRATOR (continued) PAGE
  appointment of 102-125
    notice of, to be given 192
  authority of, except special administrator, suspended pending
    appeal from decree appointing 123
  bond of 119
    exempt from giving sureties, when 120, 121
  creditor, when may be 107
  de bonis non, when appointed 102, 103, 114
    bond of 120
  de bonis non with will annexed, when appointed 103
    bond of 120
  domestic trust company may be 108
  husband of married woman, right to be 107
  collateral legacies and successions, taxes on to be paid by 204, note,
    208, note
  collection of the effects by 174-176
  complaints by or against for fraudulent concealment, embezzle-
    ment, etc , of property of the estate . . . 175
  corporation stock, liability of administrator, etc , for 502
    right of voting on 502
  delivery of property by or to successor, enforcement of . 13, 165
  distribution 354
  set-off against distributive share of debt due from distributee . . 207
  inventory to be returned within three months from appointment,
    by, except by administrator with will annexed who has given
    bond as residuary legatee 168
    what to include and by whom made . . 171-173
    one only required 174
  liability of, for loss resulting from his unreasonable delay or
    neglect . . . 176
  liability of, under license for sale of real estate . . . 260, 261
  mortgage of real estate by, how authorized . . 272
  non-resident, to appoint agent in this commonwealth . . . 102, 194
  notice of appointment to be given . . . 192
    proof of giving, by affidavit 193
  next of kin, when to be appointed 107, 110
  public, in what cases to act 114
    bond of 121
    sales by 271
  special, when appointed 104
    authority of 123
    bond of 121
    may act pending appeal, unless . . 123
  who entitled to be appointed 107, 108
  widow, when entitled to be 107, 110

INDEX 751

ADMINISTRATOR (*continued*).   PAGE
   release of certain remote interests in real property by, when
     authorized 272
   removal and resignation of 159–166
     decrees making removals, effective, pending appeal, unless 166
   grounds for removal 159, 160, 162
     conflict of interest . . . 159
   insanity or incapacity 159
   neglect to furnish bond or sureties or to render account when
     required 162
   removal from state and failure to appoint agent here . 162
   unfaithful administration 162
   sale of outstanding debts and claims by, when authorized . . 185
     of personal property 184
   sale of personal property by foreign . 186
   sales of real estate by (See *Executor, sale of real estate by*)
   scire facias, writs of, when may issue against 206
     temporary investments by, how authorized 190

ADMISSION OF ASSETS,
   by executor who is residuary legatee and gives bond to pay debts,
     etc, conclusive 98, 215

ADOPTION OF CHILDREN,
   appeal from decree for, when 484
   "child," used in grant, devise, etc, includes adopted child, when 483
   consent to, when required 480
     of child over fourteen years of age 480
     of guardian, if any 480
     of husband, of married woman . . . 480
     of mother of illegitimate child 480
     of parent or parents 480
     of previous adopting parents 480
   consent, except of child and her husband, when not required 480
   decree for, effect of 482, 483
     as to natural rights and duties 482
     as to succession to property 483
     appeal from, when allowed . 484
     determination of legal consequences of former, if child previously adopted 484
     petitions to annul, who may bring, and on what grounds 484, note
       requests for certain rulings at trial of, properly refused . . . 479, note
   distribution of property of adopted person dying intestate . . 483
   guardian *ad litem*, when appointed . 481, 482
   jurisdiction of probate court . . 479, 483
   petition for, by whom and in what county 479

752 INDEX.

ADOPTION OF CHILDREN (*continued*) PAGE
   by non-residents in what county . . 479
   husband or wife to join in . 479
   notice of, what required without written consent of certain
     persons . . 481 and note
     to state board of charity, when . . 481
   state board of charity, certain powers of and notices to 181, 485, 486
   succession of adopted persons to property 483
     of persons adopted in another state to property here 484
   who may be adopted 479

ADVANCEMENTS,
   distribution, in case of 363, 364
   evidence of . . . 361–363
   interests not to be computed on . . 360
   may be made in real or personal estate . . 360
   not to be refunded, though exceeding share 360
   questions concerning to be determined by probate court 361
   value of 363
   widow's share, in case of 363

AFFIDAVIT,
   by administrator, etc , of notice of appointment 193
     effect of 193
   by administrator, etc , of notice of time and place of sale of real
     estate 255
     effect of 255
   by commissioners ordered to sell lands . . 388
   by persons other than administrators, etc , how and when
     made . . 193, note, 255, note
   when not filed, notice proved, how 255

AGENT,
   for absent party in proceedings for partition 382
   non resident executor and administrator to appoint . . . 94, 194
     service of process on . . . 95
   non-resident guardian to appoint . . 142, 194
   non-resident trustee to appoint . . . 154, 194
   neglect to appoint, by administrator, etc , cause for removal 194

AGREEMENT,
   to give legacies 88
   to make wills 88
   written, for conveyance of land, specific performance of . . 448

ALLOWANCES TO WIDOWS AND MINOR CHILDREN,
   amount of, in discretion of court 177, 179
   appeal from decree upon widow's petition for . . 182
   distinct from widow's distributive share 182
   enforced by action 183

INDEX 753

ALLOWANCES TO WIDOWS, ETC *(continued).* PAGE
    made even when estate insolvent 180
    priority of 180
    purpose of 179
    real property may be sold to pay, when 177

ALLOWANCES TO WIVES OF INSANE PERSONS UNDER
    GUARDIANSHIP 183

ANCILLARY ADMINISTRATION,
    granted, when 104
    granted here, although no administrator appointed in place of deceased's domicile . 105
        or although will of deceased not proved at place of his domicile 105
    creditor here, to be first paid from estate 236
        if estate insolvent, to have just proportion 237
    residue of estate, how disposed of 237

APPEAL,
    bond, none required on 468, 469
    claim of 467, 469, 476
    complaint for affirmation of decree, on failure to enter or prosecute 475
    consolidation of separate 468
    decree remaining in force, notwithstanding, unless 472, notes
        appointing special administrator . . . . . . 472, note
        in equity . . . . 472, note
        removing executor, etc. . . . 472, note
    dismissal of, by probate court, when 475
    effect of 471–473
        suspends, ordinarily, but does not vacate decree appealed from 471
    entry of 467, 469, 477
        late, when allowed . . . 470, 477, 478
    from allowance or disallowance of claim against insolvent debtor
        or against insolvent estates of deceased persons 226–228, 476–478
            claim and notice of 226, 476
            costs on 227, 477
            entry of, where and when . . 226, 469, 477
            late entry of, when allowed . . . 228, 478
            proceedings on 477, 478
            statement of claim 477
            waiver and arbitration . . 228, 477
    issues of fact, to be tried by jury, framed when 469, 474
        framing of, discretionary with court in probate cases 474, note
        to be framed on demand of debtor, etc , on appeal from decision granting or refusing discharge of insolvent debtor 469

48

754 INDEX

APPEAL (*continued*).   PAGE
  proceedings on, in appellate court 473
    affirmation or reversal, in whole or in part, of decree appealed
      from . . . 474
    appeal to full court from decision of single justice as to matter
      of fact as well as of law 475
    appellant to file statement of objections 467
    appellant, if creditor, to file statement of claim 469
    issues of fact, for trial by jury, when framed . 469, 474
    judgment of appellate court to be carried into effect by probate
      court . . . 474
    jurisdiction of appellate court, to what limited . 474
  taken to superior court, in what cases 463, 469
    from decrees as to care, custody, and maintenance of minor
      children . . 463
    from decrees as to separate property or separate support of
      married women 463
    from decisions by court of insolvency allowing or disallowing
      claim, and granting or refusing discharge of insolvent debtor 469
    to superior or to supreme judicial court from allowance or disallowance of claims against insolvent estates of deceased
      persons 469
  taken to supreme judicial court, except as otherwise provided 463
  waiver of 472, 477
  who entitled to
    administrator *de bonis non*, from decree allowing account of
      original executor or administrator. . . . 464
    any person "aggrieved," when his rights are affected by decree or order 464
    creditor, when, 464, note, 467, note, 469, 476
    foreign administrator from decree appointing administrator
      here 466
    purchaser of land from heirs or devisees, when . . 466

ANNUITIES,
  tables for ascertaining present value of . . 420, 421

APPRAISAL OF ESTATES (See *Inventory*)

APPRAISERS,
  appointment and authority of . . 172, 173
  fees of . . . 173, note, 385, note, 413, note
  of estates subject to collateral inheritance tax, appointed on application of state treasurer . 173, note, 521
  one appraiser only may be appointed, when 172

ARBITRATION,
  of claim of executor or administrator against estate 303
  of claim of heirs for income of real estate 293

INDEX

ARBITRATION (*continued*)   PAGE
   of claims presented to commissioners of insolvent estates, when
      appeal has been taken and waived . . 228, 477
   of demands generally, court may authorize . . . 449
      proceedings on 449

ASSETS,
   what are . . . . 169, 170, notes
   goods delivered up by administrator, etc, on judgment in replevin,
      not . . . . 296, note, 497
   marshalling of, for payment of debts . . . 252

ASSISTANT REGISTERS OF PROBATE,
   appointed, how and for what counties 23
   bond of 24
   duties of 24
   prohibited from acting as counsel or attorney, from holding certain
      trusts, and from being interested in the fees and emoluments
      thereof . . . 25, 26
   suits on bond of . . . 25
   vacancy in office of, to be reported by register . . 24

ATTESTATION CLAUSE,
   of will 38, 39

ATTESTING WITNESSES TO WILL,
   affidavit of, before register of probate, when sufficient to prove
      will 72
   attestation of, not evidence that witness believed testator to be
      sane, ... 49
   competency of, restored by pardon . . . 41
      not restored by remission of sentence 41
   contradiction of, when allowable . . . 75
   crimes, what disqualify 41
   devise to void, unless 40
   diligence required in search for absence 73
   fees of 505
   failure of recollection of 75
   handwriting of, proof of 73
   incompetency of, by reason of interest, crime, etc . . . 39
      subsequent incompetency of not to prevent probate . . 41
   "mark," may subscribe by . . . 88
   marks of, how proved . . . 74
   must be competent at time of attesting 41
   number necessary . 82
   opinions of, as to testator's sanity, admissible . 47
   presence of testator, what is . 36, 37
   presumptions as to attestations of 38
   subscribing by, in each other's presence, not required 38

ATTESTING WITNESSES TO WILL (continued)   PAGE
    in testator's presence, required 36
    summoned, how 73
    testimony of all of, when required 73
        of one only, when sufficient to prove will 72
ATTORNEY,
    may enter appearance 14, 27
    retained on behalf of insane person may visit client in hospital,
        when 503
    service of notices and processes upon . 14, 27
    when may testify, on probate of will, as to directions given him by
        testator for drafting the will 59
AUDITORS,
    may be appointed to examine probate accounts 312

B

BOARD OF CHARITY,
    to consider applications for children from state institutions for
        adoption 486
    to seek out suitable persons willing to adopt abandoned, etc.,
        children 487
    to supervise infants under two years taken for adoption . 485
BONDS,
    action on, limitation of time for bringing 440
    amount of penalty in 430
    approval of, by judge or register 428, 429
    certificate of value of property, required on . . 430
    condition of . 97, 119, 121, 140, 155
    French spoliation awards, of administrators of 446
        condition of 447
    joint or separate, when 429
    new, when may be required 430
        failure to give, effect of 431
    payable to judge of probate and his successors, except . . . 21, 429
    separate or joint, when . . 429
    suits on, of executors and administrators 432
        continuance of, at request of sureties, when resident principal
            not made defendant 442
        execution in, how awarded . 443
            money received on, is assets of estate 444
        leave of court generally necessary for 432, 437–440
            appeal from decree granting . . 411
            granted only by decree . . . 441
        leave of court unnecessary for, when . . . 434–437

BONDS (*continued*)
  limitation of time for bringing 440
  petition for leave to bring, by any person interested . . 440
   citation to issue on 441
   facts to be shown on hearing on . 441
   register may grant when judge is obligor or surety on
    bond given to former judge . . . 442
  to be brought in superior court 442
  suits on, of trustees and guardians 445
   limitation of, against guardian's sureties 446
   proceedings to authorize . . . 446, 447
  writs in, by whom to be indorsed 442
  sureties on, qualifications of 428
   discharge of, when 431
   liable, when principal gives new bond, for breaches committed
    before approval of new bond 432
   release of, in case of marriage of female principal, when . 431
BROTHERS,
  when entitled to administer as next of kin 110
  when to inherit 321

C.

CEMETERIES,
  rights of husband and widow in family lot in 334
  sale of lots in by executors, etc, how authorized 277
  special trust funds for care, etc, of, who may hold 152, 504
CEMETERY CORPORATIONS,
  may hold in trust funds for certain purposes 152
CHANGE OF NAME,
  annual return and publication of, by whom to be made . 486
  none to be made, except on adoption of a child or marriage or
   divorce of a married woman, unless for sufficient reason, consistent with public interests, and satisfactory to probate court . 485
  probate court, jurisdiction of, to decree . . 485
  register of probate to make annual returns of, to secretary of state 486
CHURCHES,
  may appoint trustees, when 152
CITATIONS,
  may be issued at any time 11
  may be issued by register 18
  service of 71
CITY,
  or town may hold certain funds in trust, when 152

758   INDEX.

CODICIL,   PAGE
   admitted to probate subsequent to probate of will 76, 77
   effect of, by republication 44
      upon unattested will   43
      upon will executed by person under age, etc 43, 44
   execution of   42
   included in term " will "   42
   may not be revoked, though will is 64
   revocation of will by   64
COLLATERAL INHERITANCE TAX,
   action to recover by state treasurer   .   . . 280, 523, 523, note
      penalty for not filing inventory, for   169, 518, 519
   administration state treasurer may apply for   70, note, 113, note, 522
   administration accounts, no final settlement of before payment of
      tax 279, 316, 522
   amount of   513
      practice of state treasurer's department in determining 523
      tax on, when payable   .   517, note
   amount received from, in Massachusetts   .   .   508, note
   annuities, value of, how computed   .   . 173, 419, 521, 522, note
      tables of value of   .   .   420, 421
   appraisal, remainder to collateral heir, of property subject to
      tax   173, note, 479, note, 521, 522, note
   bequests, limit of value of, exempt from tax   507 and note
   constitutionality of, under Acts of Congress   . . 509, note
      under laws of states other than Massachusetts   . 510, note
      under laws of Massachusetts   .   . 512, note
   decisions construing Massachusetts law   513–517, notes, 520, note
   executor, bequest to, taxable when   .   514
      collection by, of tax from heir or legatee . 208, note, 517, 518
      personal liability of a foreign   514, note, 519, 520, note
      sale of land by, for payment of   212, note, 243, 518
   exemptions, bequests under $500   .   507
      bequests to charitable, etc., societies   506, 513, note, 514, note
      to city or town for public purposes   . . . . 506, 507, note
      to certain relations of decedent   506
   history and definition of   .   506–509, notes
   interest payable on overdue   .   517
   inventory of property subject to, when to be filed   169, note, 518
      copy of, to be sent by register to state treasurer .   17, 519
      penalty for neglect to file   . .   .   519
   jurisdiction, probate court to have, subject to appeal . 8, note, 522
                                                                               and note
   liability of administrator, etc, for payment of 506
   lien of   . . . .   204, note, 517

INDEX 759

COLLATERAL INHERITANCE TAX (continued) PAGE
  non-residents, notice required of transfer of assets of deceased . 519.
                                                                                                          520, 521
  notice by executor, etc., to state treasurer of estate liable to . 519
  payment of tax, when and to whom 517
    action for, by state treasurer . . . 523 and note
    corporate stock of deceased non-residents 519, 520 and note
    extension of time for, when . . . . . 513, note, 523
    foreign executor, etc., by, when 519
    legacy charged on real estate 518
    suspension of, when . . 513, note, 517
    voucher, proper, for . . . 523
  probate court, to have jurisdiction, subject to appeal, of questions
    relative to . . . . . 8, note, 522
  property subject to . . 506
    appraisal of 173, 419, note, 521, 522, notes
    administration charges and debts to be deducted from . 514, note
  deceased non-residents, of . . . . 514, note, 519, 520
    legacy tax paid United States to be deducted from 514, note
  pecuniary legacy for limited period . . 518
  real estate charged with legacy 518
  rate of tax 513
  real estate, legacies charged on, as to 518
  sale of, for payment of tax . . . 242, 243, 518
  refunding of tax, when 521
  register to send copy of inventory to state treasurer . 17, 519
    notice by, if inventory not filed 519
  remainder to collateral heir taxable 508–513
  specific legacy, collection of tax on 518
  state treasurer, action to recover, by . . 523, note
    administration, to apply for, when . 522
    amount of tax, how usually determined by . . 523
    party to petition of foreign executor, etc., for license to re-
      ceive and dispose of personal property 521
  trustees, bequests to, when taxable . . 514
  value, of annuities, how computed 173, 419, 521, 522, notes
    of property, subject to tax, how determined 173, note, 419, note
                                                                                              521, 522, notes
    time of ascertaining, date of decedent's death . 515, note

COMMISSION,
  or warrant may be revoked by probate court for cause 12, 385, note,
                                                                                                                 412, note,
  new one may issue . . . . . . 12, 385, note, 412, note

COMMISSIONERS,
  to assign dower (see *Dower*) 412

COMMISSIONERS (*continued*) PAGE
    to examine claims against insolvent estates (see *Insolvent Estates*)   215
    to make partition (see *Partition*) . . 383

COMPLAINT,
    against person concealing will 92
    for embezzling estate of deceased person or ward 14, 175
    for non-entry of appeal . . . 475

COMPROMISE,
    of demands in favor of or against estate, probate court may
        authorize executors to make 449
        proceedings on 449

CONTEMPT,
    power of probate court to punish 12

CONTINGENT RIGHTS,
    in real or personal estate, sale of by executors, etc 186
    notice of petition for leave to sell, what to be given . . 186

CONTRACTS,
    in writing, for sale of land, specific performance of . . 448

CONCEALMENT,
    fraudulent, of estate of deceased person or ward, proceedings for
        discovery . 14, 175
    of will, proceedings for discovery 92

CONFIRMATION,
    of defective acts, etc, of probate courts and of certain acts of
        executors, etc . . 100, 459

CONSERVATORS OF PROPERTY OF AGED PERSONS,
    appointment of . . . 143
    bond of 143
    discharge of . . . 143
    non resident, to appoint agents in this commonwealth 143

CONTRIBUTION AMONG DEVISEES AND LEGATEES,
    child or issue of child omitted in will, liable to, when . . . 461
    estate of devisee taken for payment of debts, loss how borne . 461
    estate of devisee taken for widow's dower, loss how borne 406, 462
    posthumous child, when to make 461
    executors and administrators of deceased devisee or legatee,
        liable for . . . 462
    exemption from, by specific devise or bequest 461
        by provisions of will . 462
    insolvency of person liable to, loss occasioned by, how borne 461
    when to be made to child omitted in will . . 352, 460
        to posthumous child 460

CORPORATION STOCK,
liability of executor, etc, for	502
right of voting on	502

COSTS,
may be awarded in contested cases in discretion of court	15
general rules as to allowance of	15, note
of suit, paid by executor, etc, allowed in his account, unless	300, 301
of executors and trustees in suits for instructions as to will	16, note
of executor in sustaining proof of will, to be paid by special administrator	16, note

COURTS,
police, district and municipal may issue writs of *scire facias* against administrators, etc.	206

CREDITOR,
entitled to administer, when	107, 113
may complain in cases of embezzlement, etc, of estate of deceased person or ward	175
may be witness in support of petition to sell lands to pay debts	249
not to bring action against executors, etc, after two years, except	195
not to bring action against executor, etc, within one year, except	203, 212
proceedings by, when right of action accrues after two years	199, 200
when may appeal from decree of probate court	467, note

of insolvent estates,
allowed six months to prove claim	216
and further time by leave of court	216
claim of, if not presented to commissioners, barred, unless new assets	234
claim of, not barred by lapse of time, when new assets	235
having contingent claim, how may proceed	224
if assets sufficient, to be paid in full	235
otherwise, to be paid ratably	231
if secured, must waive security or prove only balance of claim	221
of deceased copartner, may prove claim	220
of deceased foreigners, claims how paid	236
may appeal	226
may cause commission to be reopened, when new assets	235
may submit claim to arbitration, if appeal waived	228
may sue after eighteen months, if question of insolvency not then determined	236
not to bring actions after representation of insolvency, except	233
preferred, paid in full	231

INDEX.

CREDITOR (*continued*)   PAGE
    preferred, who is 211
    remedy of, when appeal not taken in time . . . 228
    required to refund money paid by executor, etc, when   213, note
    to prove claim before commissioners, or the court . 216
    unclaimed dividends, when divided among . . 233
    unmatured claims of, may be proved 220

CURTESY, ESTATE OF,
    conveyance free from, when 269
    husband's, at common law, abolished 327
        established by Revised Laws 326
        must be claimed 326
    release of, by guardian of insane married man . . 268, 456
    waste by tenant, ground for forfeiture 406

D.

DAMAGES,
    administrator, etc, not liable to exemplary 205, 495

DEATH,
    of absent person presumed after seven years 118, 357
    of several persons, by same calamity, presumed to be simultaneous   358·

DEBTS,
    of deceased set off in action by administrator or executor . . 205
    due from heir to be set off against distributive share . . 359
    due from legatee to be set off against legacy 207
    lands liable for . . . . . 243, note
    outstanding, when may be sold by executors, etc. . . . 185
        proceedings in such case 185

DECLARATIONS OF TESTATOR,
    admissible to show his mental condition . . . 55
    as to manner of disposing of his estate 54
    as to revocation of will . . . 62, 63, note
    when made near time of making will 49
    subsequent, not admissible to prove intoxication at time of execut-
        ing will 53
        or that undue influence was used . . 58

DECREES,
    allowing accounts conclusive, except, when . . 313, note, 315
    allowing will or adjudicating intestacy, conclusive when   29, note
    conclusive, unless appealed from . . 5
    conclusive as to purchasers for value, when . 29, note, 119, note
    enforcement of 12
    entry, if transaction out of court 11

INDEX. 763

DECREES (*continued*) PAGE
    in equity, no stay or suspension pending appeal without special
        order . . . . 472, note
    form of 7
    outside of county, may be made . . . 21
    revocation of . . . . 12, note
    writing, to be in and recorded 12

DEPOSIT OF MONEY OF ESTATE,
    how authorized 13, 14
    limitation of amount to be received by savings banks, etc, not
        applicable to . . 368
    payment of, unclaimed for five years, to state treasurer, when . 368

DESCENT OF REAL ESTATE,
    adopted child, rights of 482
        is "issue" within R L c 140, § 8 . 483, note
    definition of, under Revised Laws 320
    deceased non-residents 341, 353
    devisee or legatee dying in testator's lifetime, issue of, to take
        deceased's share, unless . 352
    general rules of, under Revised Laws . . . 320–322
    homestead estates of widows and minor children . 338
    illegitimate children . . . 341
    husband, action by, for recovery of interest in deceased wife's
        estate, not to be brought after twenty years from her decease 332
        rights of, in wife's property under Public Statutes . 322–324, 326
            under Revised Laws . . 326, 334
            cemeteries, lots in 332–334
            curtesy, assignment of 327
                at common law abolished, except 327, 334
                claim for, necessary, and when to be made 326
                none in land mortgaged by wife to obtain whole or part
                    of purchase money 327
            tenancy by the 326, 334
        share of, if wife dies intestate . . 329, 330
        summary of changes made by Revised Laws, as to rights
            of, in wife's property . . 334–336
        waiver by, of wife's will, when to be made and effect of 330, 331
    kindred, how computed . . . 348
        half blood inherit equally with whole blood 330, note, 349
    next of kin, how ascertained . 347
    "heirs at law" mean, when 349, note
    omission by testator to provide in will for child or issue of deceased
        child, effect of 349
        burden of proof on party opposing child's claim to show inten-
            tional 351

INDEX

DESCENT OF REAL ESTATE (*continued*)   PAGE
  evidence of intentional . 350, 351, and notes
  share of child in case of unintentional . . 351
  posthumous child, share of 352
  rules of, general, under Revised Laws . 320-322
  settlement of estates of deceased non-residents . 341, 353
  what real estate descends . . 320
  wife, action by, for recovery of interest in deceased husband's
    estate not to be brought after twenty years 332
  rights of, in husband's property under Public Statutes 324-326
    under Revised Laws 326-329, 336
    allowances to, as necessaries 323
      real estate to be sold to pay, when 329
    cemeteries, lots in 332-334
    dower, assignment of 327
    claim for necessary, and when to be made 327
    entitled to against all but mortgages, etc, although released
      in mortgage, when 328
    none in wild land, except 328
  husband's house, may occupy for six months rent free 328
  share of, if husband dies intestate 329, 330
  summary of changes by Revised Laws as to rights of, in husband's
    property . . . 336-338
  waiver by, of husband's will, when to be made and effect of . . 331

DEVISE,
  to attesting witness to will void, unless 40

DEVISEES AND LEGATEES,
  contribution among 352, 460
  dying in life time of testator, issue of to take share of deceased,
    unless 352
  liable to suit, when 202
  refund of collateral inheritance tax to, when . 204, note, 356, note, 521

DIPSOMANIACS,
  commitment of . . . . . . 8, note, 492, 493

DISCOVERY,
  of facts and documents, interrogatories for 14
  proceedings for, in case of concealment of will 92
    embezzlement, etc, of property of deceased persons and
      wards 14, 15, 175

DISTRIBUTION,
  advancements of real and personal property 360
    evidence of 361
    method of distribution, in case of 363
    questions concerning, how determined 361
    value of 363

INDEX. 765

DISTRIBUTION (*continued*) PAGE
  widow's share, in case of 363
  among class, of legacy under will, how made . . . 359
  balances in hands of public administrators . 368
  collateral inheritance tax, payable on . 204, note, 358, note, 517
  debts due from heir or distributee to be set off or deducted . . 359
  decree for, and effect of . . . 354
    form of 356
    perpetuation of evidence of payments to under . . . 363
    persons to be included in, how determined . . 357, 358
    presumption of death, when 357
    no presumption of marriage or issue 357
  final discharge of executor, etc., on 365
  final, of money deposited or invested by order of court . . . 369
  foreign guardians and trustees, payments to . . . 372
  partial, when 359
  petition for decree of 355
    notice of 355
  time for making 258

DISTRICT COURT,
  may issue *scire facias* against administrators, etc. 206

DOWER,
  assignment of 327, 397–427
  barred, how 400, 408
  claim of, how and when to be made . . 327, 397, 408
  commissioners, appointment of, to assign 411
    appraisal by 412
    assignment by metes and bounds, except 413
    dwelling-house 414
    mill, etc. 413
  notice to be given by, except 412
  oath of 412
  return of, form, etc. 414
    citation on 415
    confirmation and record of . . 415
  conveyance free from, when 269, 401
  divorce, effect of, on 400
  estate of, at common law . 398
    marriage, seisin of husband during coverture, and death of
    husband, necessary to establish claim to . 399
  lands, what subject to 397, 401–406
    held in common 402
    leased for long term 405
    mines and quarries 402
    mortgages, except as to mortgagee, etc 403

INDEX

DOWER (*continued*)
 taken on execution against husband or his executor or administrator 406
 wild lands, not, except . . 401
 limitation of claim or suit by widow for, and for interest in realty . . 332, 410
 petition for assignment of, or of other interest, form of, etc 410
  citation on, issue and service of 411
  description of land, when necessary . . . 411
 present value of estates of . . 419
  tables showing 420, 421
 proceedings for assignment of 410-416
 proceeds of release of, reserved for wife, when . 400
 tables showing present value of . . 420, 421
 value, present of estates of 419, 420, 421
 waiver by widow of provisions of will . . . 406
 widow, assignment of her undivided life interest other than dower 426
  endowed anew, after eviction, when 415
 writ of, and proceedings under 410-419

E

EMBEZZLEMENT,
 of property of deceased persons or wards 175
 proceedings for discovery 14, 175
 punishment for 502

EQUITY,
 jurisdiction of probate court, in . . 9, 157, 158

ESTATE BY THE CURTESY (See *Curtesy, Estate of.*)

ESTATE IN LIEU OF DOWER (See *Dower*)

EVIDENCE,
 of declarations of testator, how far admissible . . 49, 55, 58, 62
 of handwriting of attesting witness, when admissible . . 73
 of "mark" of attesting witness 74
 parol, admissible, of testator's intentional omission to provide for child 350, 351
 on questions of testator's sanity . 46-55
 perpetuation of, that executor, etc., gave notice of appointment 193
  notice of time and place of sale of lands 255
 of delivery of property by administrator, etc., under decree 316, note
  of payments under order of distribution 232, 233, 366
 presumption as to attestation of witnesses to will . . 36
  of death of absent person . . 118, 357
  of testator's intention to revoke will 63

INDEX 767

EVIDENCE *(continued)*   PAGE
    of testator's knowledge of contents of will . . . 35
    of testator's sanity 46

EXECUTION,
    for costs, may be issued by probate court . . . 15, 16
    Land held on, by executor, etc, deemed personal estate . 245
        may be sold, before foreclosure of right of redemption, in same
            manner as personal property 245
        if not sold or redeemed, to be distributed as personal estate 320, note

EXECUTOR.
    account (See *Accounts*)
    (*Actions by or against*)
    actions against, barred when estate exhausted by payments before
        notice of claim, and by payment of preferred claims 203, 204,
                                                                   212, 214
    costs in 497
    death or removal of executor, etc, pending, proceedings on 498
    death or removal of executor, etc, after judgment, proceedings on 499
    executions in, except for costs only, run against goods and estate
        of deceased in hands of executor, etc . 497
    not held to answer to, commenced within one year from appoint-
        ment, unless . . . 203
    proceedings in, when creditor's right of action accrues after two
        years . . 203
        replevin or tort for goods detained, property or money recov-
            ered in not assets in hands of executor, etc 497
    scire facias, when issued in . 498, 499, 500
    set off, right of, in 205
    survival of . . . . 494, note
        actions which do not survive 495, note
    tort, liability of executor or administrator in 205, 495
    trustee process in, what subject to attachment by 499
        death of person summoned as trustee in his own right, pro-
            ceedings on . 500
        execution against executor, etc, as trustee, runs against goods
            or estate of deceased on his hands . . . 501
    remedy by suit on bond of executor, etc, adjudged trustee, when 501
    writs of attachment or execution in, run against goods or estate
        in hands of executor, etc . . . 497
    writs of *scire facias*, when issued 498, 499, 500
    affidavit of notice of appointment of . 193
    appointment of . . 94
        irregularity in, effect of 99, 100
    bond to be given by 96
        exemption from giving sureties on, when 99

EXECUTOR (continued)

	PAGE
bond when executor is residuary legatee	97
collection of the effects by	174
collateral legacies and successions, taxes on to be paid by	204, note, 208, note
complaints by or against for fraudulent concealment, etc, of property of the estate	175
corporation stock, liability of executor, etc, for	502
right of voting on	502
delivery of property by, to successor, enforcement of	13, 165
inventory to be returned by, within three months after appointment, except when executor has given bond as residuary legatee	168, 169
what to include and by whom made	167–173

legacies,

deposit of	206, note
payment of	206
set-off against, of debts due from legatee	207
liability of, for loss resulting from his unreasonable delay or neglect	176
liability of under license for sale of real estate	260, 261
married woman may be executrix	95
minor cannot be	95
mortgage of real estate by, how authorized	272
notice of appointment of, to be given	192
proof of giving, by affidavit	193
release by, of certain vested, contingent, or possible interests in real property, when authorized	272
removal and resignation of	159–166
decrees making removal, effective, pending appeal, unless	166
grounds for removal	159, 160, 162
conflict of interest	159
insanity or incapacity	159
neglect to furnish bonds, sureties, or to render account when required	162
removal from State and failure to appoint agent here	162
unfaithful administration	162, 230
non-resident, to appoint agent in this Commonwealth	95, 194
removal of, petition for	163
notice of petition to be given	164
right of, to vote at corporation meetings	502
sale of outstanding debts and claims by, when authorized	185
of personal property	184
sale of personal property, by foreign	186
sale of lots in cemeteries by, and by administrators	277
sale of real estate by, and by administrator	239–262
adjournment of	256

INDEX. 769

EXECUTOR (*continued*).   PAGE

    affidavit of notice of . . . 255 and note
    deed under license for, form, etc . . . 260
    executor or administrator not to be purchaser at . . 256, 257
    foreign executors and administrators . . . 262
    license for, granted to pay debts and legacies . . 239, 242
        continues in force for one year only 253
        granted to administrator on consent of all parties interested, unless real estate exceeds $1,500 in value . . . 241
        granted for payment of tax on collateral legacies and successions 242, 243
        must concur with petition . . 251
        not granted to executor who has given bond as residuary legatee 242
        not granted when the only debt is secured by mortgage 240, note
        not ordinarily granted after two years 252
        not granted when parties interested pay executor or administrator amount needed to pay claims against estate 249
        notice to parties interested of petition for 248
            when dispensed with 248
        petition for, form, etc 245
            hearings on, adjudication of probate court as to existence of debts and charges, final . . . 249
            what real estate may be sold under . . 243–245
            will, provisions of, as affecting . . 247
    marshalling assets for payment of debts, as affecting 252
    necessity of, to be shown 248
    notice of time and place of 254
        proof of giving 253
        proceedings when affidavit of, has not been filed . . 255
        proceeds of, balance remaining on settlement of account of executor, administrator, or guardian to be considered as real estate and distributed accordingly 261
        to be by public auction, unless authorized to be by private sale 250, 251, 256
        purchaser at, protected against certain irregularities . 257–259
        registered land 492
        statute requirements as to 258
    of whole or part of real estate, when authorized . . 250, 251
    scire facias, writs of, when may issue against . . . 206, 444
    temporary investment by, how authorized . 190
    who may be 95

EXEMPLARY DAMAGES,
    administrators and executors not liable to 205, 495

EXPERTS,
    evidence of, on questions of sanity 47, 48

F.

FATHER,   PAGE
    administration, entitled to, when 110
    custody of his child, entitled to, although other person is guardian   128
    estate of child descends to, and to mother .   321
    may appoint by will guardians for his children   .   131
    may not appoint by will guardians for other children, though he
        gives them his property 131
    rights of, how affected by adoption of children   482

FEEBLE-MINDED,
    commitment of   .   . .   . . 8, note

FOREIGN EXECUTORS AND ADMINISTRATORS
    (See *Non-Resident Executors and Administrators*)

FOREIGN GUARDIANS   (See *Non-Resident Guardian*)

FOREIGN TRUSTEES   (See *Non-Resident Trustees.*)

FORMS, PROBATE   (See *Index to Probate Forms*)
    authority to prescribe 10, 11

FRAUD,
    will obtained by, void 55, 56

FRAUDULENT CONCEALMENT,
    of estate of deceased persons and wards, proceedings for dis-
      covery 11, 175

FRENCH SPOLIATION AWARDS,
    bond required of administrators of, condition of 446, 447
    jurisdiction of probate court as to . . . . . . 8, note, 9, 446, 447

"FULL AGE,"
    when attained   . . . . 31, note

G.

GRANDCHILDREN,
    when entitled to administer as next of kin 109
    when inherit. 347

GRANDPARENTS,
    when entitled to administer as next of kin 109
    when inherit   347

GUARDIAN,
    account   (See *Accounts*)
    administrator of estate not to be, of heir of same estate . .   131
    appointment of .   .   126-143
    bond of   . .   140

GUARDIAN (*continued*)	PAGE
exempt from giving surety, when	142
complaint by or against, for fraudulent concealment of ward's property	175
delivery of property by, to successor, enforcement of	13, 165
discharge of	137
domestic trust company may be	129
of insane persons	133–137
proceedings on petition for appointment of	133–136
release by, of curtesy, dower, or homestead	136, 137, 457
reservation for insane person of portion of proceeds, when	137, 268, 401, 458
inventory to be returned when directed by court	169
what to include and by whom made	171–173
marriage of female under guardianship deprives guardian of right to her custody and education	166
of married women	139
release by, of ward's dower or homestead estate	140, 260
of minors	126
minor over fourteen years of age, right to nominate	127
power and duties of guardian of minors	128, note, 127–129, 263–265
natural, father and mother, and equally entitled to custody and care of minor child	126, note
natural, has ordinarily custody of child	127, 128, note
non-resident, to appoint agent resident here	194
of persons out of the state	138
petition for appointment of	131
for removal of	163
notice of, to be given	164
purchase of interests in ward's real estate, may be authorized to make	451
release by, of certain vested, contingent, or possible interests in real property, when authorized	272
of damages for land taken by railway companies	502
removal and resignation of	159–166
decrees making removals, effective, pending appeal, unless	166
grounds for removal	159, 161, 162
conflict of interest	159
incapacity or insanity	159
neglect to furnish bond when required	159
unfaithful administration	162
unsuitability	161
sale and investment of personal property by	187
sale of real estate by	263–270
agreement with wife of insane ward as to her release of dower and homestead, upon	267

GUARDIAN (continued)

	PAGE
homestead	264
of minors, for maintenance or investment	264, 265
for payment of debts and charges	263
by foreign	270
of wood, standing or growing	264
private sale, when authorized	270
public sale, unless private authorized	264, note
of whole or part, may be authorized	263
license for, notice of petition for to be given	265
notice of petition, what to be given in case of insane person or spendthrift	266
petition for, form, etc	263, 264, 265
notice of time and place of, what to be given	266
proceeds of, how to be applied or invested	266, 267
of spendthrifts	133–136
proceedings on petition for appointment of	134, 134, note, 135, 136
temporary	133
testamentary	131
bond of	141
exempt from giving sureties, when	141
who are suitable to be	129–131

GUARDIAN AD LITEM,

appointed when	313, 314, 382, 481, 482

GUARDIANSHIP,

support of minor children under	454

H

HABEAS CORPUS,

when probate court may issue writs of	462

HANDWRITING,

of attesting witness to will, when may be proved	73

HEIRS,

who to be, of intestate property	321, 347, 348

HOMESTEAD,

estates of	421
partition may be made of	377, 424
released, how	423
right of, of insolvent persons	425
sale of, by guardian, when by widow, when	424

HUSBAND,

action by, for recovery of interest in deceased wife's estate, not to be brought after twenty years from her decease	332

INDEX. 773

HUSBAND (*continued*)   PAGE
    to administer wife's estate, unless . . 107
    may be prohibited from imposing restraint on personal liberty of
        wife 452
    paying funeral expenses of wife, may recover them from her
        executor . . . . . . 211, note
    rights of in wife's property
        under Public Statutes 322–326
        under Revised Laws 326–336
    summary of changes made by Revised Laws as to rights of, in
        wife's property 334–336
    support of wife living apart from, for justifiable cause . . 452
    waiver by, of wife's will, when to be made and effect of   330, 331

I.

ILLEGITIMATE CHILD,
    heir of mother and of any maternal ancestor . . 341
    intermarriage of parents and acknowledgment by father, renders
        legitimate 341
    mother of, natural guardian . . . . . 126, note
    mother of, to be heir of 341
    omitted in parent's will, not to share in his estate . . . 351
INFANTS,
    cannot administer 95, 112
    cannot dispose of property by will . . 31
    full age, when attained by . . . . 31, note
INHERITANCE,
    by "right of representation," how construed . . . 346, 347
INSANE PERSONS,
    appointment of guardian for 133–138
    commitment of . . . . . 8, note, 492, 493
    privileges and discharge of, after commitment . . 503
    release and sale of property or rights of (See *Guardian*)
    trustee may, in certain cases, convey real estate free from all right
        of curtesy or dower of . . 269
INSANITY,
    attesting witnesses to will, may give opinion as to, of testator . . 47
    contents of will, etc, admissible as to . . . 49
    eccentricity distinguished from 50
    evidence on the question of 47
    experts, testimony of, as to 47, 48
    fact of guardianship as evidence of 49
    hereditary . . . 49, 50
    induced by what diseases 52

INDEX.

INSANITY *(continued)* — PAGE
  intemperance . 53
  life, opinions, and habits of testator reviewed, to test allegations
    of . . . 51
  lucid intervals 53
  partial — monomania 54
  suicide as evidence of 48

INSOLVENT DEBTORS,
  rights of homestead 425

INSOLVENT ESTATES OF DECEASED PERSONS,
  actions against, by creditors, after representation of insolvency . 233
  claims against, contingent, provisions as to 224
    interest on, how computed 222
      order of preference in payment of 211, 231
    proof of 218
    extension of time for proof of 216
    not provable unless suit brought or presentation to commissioners or court for allowance within two years after bond
      given by administrator . 217, 218, note
    not proved before commissioners or court, barred except as
      to new assets . . 234
    secured, not provable until security surrendered or its value
      deducted 221
    time allowed for proof of . 216
    what are provable . . 220 and note, 221, 222, and notes
  commissioners, appeals from decisions of, or of probate court . 226
    allowance of and effect . . . 228
    claim, entry, and notice of . 226
    statement of claim to be filed . . 227
    waiver of and arbitration, ... 228
  commissioners, appointment of to examine claims against . 215
    creditors, list of, to be furnished to by executor or administrator 218
    examination of claimants by 219
    return of . . . . . . 223 and note
  creditors, proof by of claims against 215-226
    secured, to surrender or deduct value of security before proving claim . . . 221
    when required to refund payment . . 213
  deposit of unclaimed dividends on . . . 232 and note
  distribution of 229
    decree or order directing form of, etc . . 232
    evidence of payments under decree of, how perpetuated . . 229
    final, not made until settlement of accounts of executor or
      administrator 230

INDEX. 775

INSOLVENT ESTATES, ETC (*continued*) PAGE
    priority of payment in making 231
    dividends, unclaimed, to be deposited . . . . . . 232 and note
        on deposit, payment of . . . . . . 232, note
        after twenty years, to be distributed 233
    insolvency, representation of 212
        when to be made 214
        where and how to be made 215
    of non-residents, provisions as to 236

INTEREST,
    executors and administrators chargeable with, when . . . 292
        with compound, when 293
    guardians and trustees chargeable with, when . . . 306
        with compound, when 307
    how computed on legacies 209
        on claims against insolvent estates . . . 222
    on claim of executor, etc., against estate of deceased . 304
    on money advanced, when allowed to executors, etc 300

INTERROGATORIES,
    may be filed to be answered by adverse party as in civil actions . 14

INTOXICATION,
    will made by person in state of 53

INVENTORY,
    appraisers, may be appointed by court 172
        may be appointed by justice of the peace, when estate is in
        his county 173
        appointment of, may be revoked 12
        must first be sworn 173
        person employed in probate office not to be 172
        to deliver inventory to executor, etc . 174
    by executors and administrators, to be returned in three months
        after appointment 169
    by guardians and trustees, when ordered by the court . 169
    by special administrators, when ordered by the court . . 121
    copy of, of estate subject to succession tax, to be sent by register
        to state treasurer 17, 519
    not required of executors who have given bond to pay debts and
        legacies . . . 169
        nor of trustees, when court deems it unnecessary . 169
    objects of 171
    of estate subject to succession tax, to be filed under penalty 169, 518
    of partnership and individual estate, to be returned on separate
        schedules . . . 173
    of wards having same guardian, when to be separate schedules 173

INDEX.

INVENTORY (*continued*)   PAGE
  to be sworn to by executor, etc 174
  what to be included in 171

INVESTMENT,
  of personal property, in hands of guardians and trustees, by order
    of court 187
      proceedings in such cases 187
  sale of real estate for 264
  temporary, by executors and administrators 13, 190, 191

J.

JOINTURE,
  to bar dower, what must consist of and when to take effect . . . 408
  wife's assent to, how expressed 409
  when may be waived and dower claimed 409
  widow evicted from land held as, may be endowed anew . . 415
  widow's undivided interest under, may be set off, when . 389, 411

JUDGES OF PROBATE,
  appointment of probate court officers by, in Suffolk and Middlesex counties 493
  assignment of one judge to perform duties of another, when 19
  assistant registers of probate, appointed by, for certain counties . 23
  complaint against master, apprentice, or servant, jurisdiction of, by 492
  compensation of judge when performing duties of another . 20
  contempt, may punish for 26
  decrees of, to be in writing and recorded 12
  deposit or investment in name of 18
  dipsomaniacs, commitment of, by 492
  disqualifications of to act, when . . . . . . 19, 20, notes
  inebriates, commitment of, by 492
  insane persons, commitment of, by 492
  interchange of duties by 18
  judge may act outside of his county . . 21
    may be appointed, in another county, guardian of his minor
    child 26
  juvenile offenders, commitment of, by . . . 491
  marriage of minors, may authorize . . . . 8, note
    may transact business out of court, when . . 21
    not to act as counsel or attorney . . . 26
    not to hold certain trusts or to be interested in fees or emoluments . 25, 26
    shall be a member of board of examiners 491
  number of 17
  oath, authority of to administer 13

INDEX. 777

JUDGES OF PROBATE (*continued*) PAGE
  oaths to be taken by . 17
  probate officers in Middlesex and Suffolk counties, appointment of 493
  rules and forms, to be made and prescribed by 10
  temporary register, may appoint 25

JURISDICTION. (See *Probate Courts*.)

JUSTICE OF THE PEACE,
  may administer oaths required in probate proceedings . 13
  may appoint appraisers, when estate to be appraised is in his
    county 173
  may summon witnesses 73

JUVENILE OFFENDERS,
  probate court has jurisdiction to commit, except . . . 8, note, 941

K

KINDRED,
  collateral 109
  degrees of, computed according to rules of civil law . . . 108
  lineal 109
  of half blood, to inherit equally with those of whole blood . 349
  what, to inherit estates 347, 348

L.

LEGACIES,
  agreements to give 88
  deposit of, when . . . . 206, note
  interest on 209
  issue of legatee to take, when 352
  payment of 206
  recoverable in action at law, when 200
  set off against, of debts due from legatee . . . 207

LOST WILLS,
  admitted to probate if fact of loss and contents proved . 79, 80
  presumed to have been revoked 79
  proof of contents of . . . . . 80, note

LUCID INTERVAL,
  evidence of 53, 54
  wills made in, valid 53

LUNATIC. (See *Insane Person — Insanity*.)

M.

MARINERS AT SEA,   PAGE
   may make nuncupative will 83
   nuncupative will of, how made 85
      how proved 86
   who are, within the statute 86

MARK,
   how identified 74
   will sufficiently signed by 32

MARRIAGE,
   of absent heir, not presumed 357
   of parents of illegitimate children, effect of 341
   works revocation of will 68

MARRIED WOMAN,
   dower and homestead of minor, may be released by her joining
      in conveyance by husband . . . 400, 456
   insane, appointment of guardians for . 133, 140
      dower and homestead of, may be released how . 456
   living apart from husband for justifiable cause, may have order
      prohibiting him from restraining her personal liberty 451
   may make a will 30
   minor, having property, appointment of guardian for . 139
   sale and release of interest of, in lands, when husband under
      guardianship . . . 136, 137, 140, 267, 269, 455
   signature of minor, valid, to conveyance by husband of his
      land 400, 456
   support of, order for, when 451
      attachment of husband's property on petition for 453
   wife of ward under guardianship may join in conveyance with
      guardian and release dower and homestead 267, 269
   proceeds reserved for, in case of such release . . 267

MARSHALLING OF ASSETS,
   for payment of debts 247, 252

MENTAL CAPACITY OF TESTATOR (See *Will*)

MEDICAL WITNESS,
   when may testify on question of sanity . . 47, 48

MINORS,
   care and custody of 126, 128
   care, custody, and maintenance of, orders concerning . . . 452
   cannot act as executor . . 95
      nor as administrator . . 112
   child of deceased person entitled to articles of apparel and orna-
      ment 328

INDEX. 779

MINORS (*continued*)
                            PAGE
  to allowance from estate of father when there is no widow   329
  guardian *ad litem* may be appointed for   314, 383, 481, 482
  guardians may be appointed for, by court   126
    by will of parent   131
  marriage of, probate judge may authorize   8, note
  over fourteen years of age may nominate guardian   127
  property of, may be sold on petition of guardian, when   263–265
    may be sold on petition of friend, when   265
  support of, under guardianship   454
MONOMANIA,
  distinguished from eccentricity   51, 54
MORTGAGE,
  land held in, by executor or administrator, deemed personal
    estate   185, 245
    if not sold or redeemed, how distributed   320, note
    may be sold, before foreclosure, in same manner as personal property   245
    partition of, among parties interested   395
  of real estate, by executors and administrators,   272, 273
    by guardians   273
    by trustees   273, 274
MOTHER,
  entitled to administer as next of kin, when   110
    to custody of child, equally with father   128
    to estate of deceased child, when   321
  guardian by nature of child, if father not living   126
  heir of illegitimate child   341
  may appoint by will guardian of child, when   131

N.

NAMES. (See *Change of Name*)
NEWSPAPER,
  judge may order publication in one other than that selected by
    parties for publishing notice or citation   16
    parties may select, for publication of citation on their petitions   16
  what is a, for insertion of legal notices   16, note, 192, note
NEXT OF KIN,
  how determined   108
  liable to suit, when   202
  " heirs at law " mean, when   349, note
  of adopting parent, may petition to annul decree of adoption,
    when   484, note

780 INDEX.

NON COMPOS. (See *Insane Person — Insanity*)   PAGE
NON-RESIDENT EXECUTORS AND ADMINISTRATORS,
    all proceedings in court to be in county where appointment is first filed . 271
    bond to be given by, when . . 262
    copy of appointment of, to be filed in probate court of any country where land lies . 262
    may be licensed to receive and sell personal property . 186, 187, 520
    may be licensed to sell land of deceased in this state to pay debts, etc 262
    neglect to appoint resident agent, cause for removal . 194
    not entitled to letters of appointment till agent appointed 95, 102
    proceedings of, under license to sell land 263
    resident agent, to appoint in writing 94, 102

NON-RESIDENT GUARDIANS,
    all proceedings in court to be in county where copy of appointment first filed . . . 271
    bond to be given by, when . 271
    copy of appointment of, to be filed in what court . 270
    may be licensed to receive and sell personal property 186
    may be licensed to sell land of ward in this state . . 270
    may remove ward's property from state, when . . 139
    neglect to appoint resident agent, cause for removal 194
    not entitled to letters of appointment till agent appointed . 142, 143
    resident agent, to appoint in writing 142

NON-RESIDENT TRUSTEES,
    neglect to appoint resident agent, cause for removal 194
    resident agent, to appoint in writing 154

NOTICE,
    effect of, served on attorney 14, 27
    evidence that notice was given, how perpetuated 193
    newspaper in which to publish, may be selected by parties . 16
    of their appointment, to be given by executors and administrators
        within three months . . . 192
        unless so given, statute of limitations does not apply . 192
        proof of giving, by affidavit . . 193
        proved otherwise than by affidavit 191, note
    of time and place of sale of lands under license 254
        affidavit that such notice was given to be filed and recorded 255
        effect of such affidavit . . . 255
        may be proved, how, when affidavit not filed . . . 255, 256
        proved otherwise than by affidavit 255, note
    publication of, not essential to appointment of guardian, when . 131, note
    to parties, when dispensed with 16

INDEX. 781

NOTICE (*continued*) PAGE
 rules regarding, by whom to be made 28
 service of, on attorney, effect of 14, 27
NUNCUPATIVE WILL,
 definition of 83
 how made 85
 how proved 86, 87
 no particular number of witnesses necessary to establish . . 86
 soldiers in actual service and mariners at sea may make . . 83
  who are mariners at sea 86
  who are soldiers in actual service 86

O.

OATHS,
 by whom to be administered 13
 certificate of, to be filed 13
 may be required to be before judge in open court . . . 13
 of claimants and witnesses, by commissioners of insolvent estates 219
OLD AGE,
 as affecting testamentary capacity 46
OVERSEERS OF THE POOR,
 notice to be given to, before license granted to guardian of insane
  persons or spendthrifts to sell land 266

P.

PARENTS,
 deprived of legal rights as to adopted child . . . 482
 entitled to administer as next of kin, when . . . 110
  to custody of minor child under guardianship of another
   person when . . 128
  to inherit estate, when 321
 natural guardians of minor child 126
PARKS,
 special trust funds for, who may hold 152, 504
PARTITION OF LAND,
 binding, upon whom 392
 cases where can be had . . . . 374, note
 cases where cannot be had . . . . 375, note
 commissioners, appointment of, to make 383
  acts of majority of, valid, when all present . . . 385
  appraisal by 385
  compensation of, how determined . . . . 385, note

782   INDEX

PARTITION OF LAND (continued).   PAGE
    expenses of, how allowed and paid . 391
    notice to be given by . . . 385
    oath of 385
    order for payments to equalize division, when may make 386
    passageway, may assign right in, when . . . 386 note
    proceedings of, in making . . 384
    return of, form of, etc 388
        decree on, and form of 391
        not to be made until moneys awarded by commis
            sioners to equalize division are paid or secured . 391
        notice on, unless . 389
        parties interested may object to . . 390
        power of court to set aside . . . 390
        proceedings on 388
    sale to be ordered by, when 387
    warrant to, form of, etc 383
        revocation of . . . . 385, note
    conveyances of undivided interest in land subject to, validity
        and effect of . . 393, 394
death of any party in suit or petition for, pending proceedings,
    effect of . 384, 387
entire estate held by petitioner, jointly or in common, to be parti
    tioned, except 378, 386
guardian may petition for, except 378, 381
guardian ad litem, to be appointed when 382
improvements, compensation for, when . . 379, 380
jurisdiction of probate court to make, in what cases . . 374
    concurrent, with superior court, when . . 374
lands held by executor or administrator in mortgage or on exe
    cution . 395
may be made of lands owned by husband in common and in which
    his widow has an undivided interest . 378
may be made notwithstanding existence of lease or homestead or
    dower right 377
mortgage of undivided interest in a separate parcel of lands held
    in common, invalid against co-tenants and disregarded in 393 and note
mortgage of undivided interest in all of lands held in common valid,
    and mortgage lien attaches to parcel set off to mortgagor . 394 and
        note
new, to be made after eviction, when . . . 379
no, if shares uncertain or in dispute . . 376
person interested may petition for, if widow entitled to undivided
    interest does not within one year from husband's death 381
petition for, form of, etc 380
    description of land, when necessary 380

PARTITION OF LAND (*continued*).

 notice of, what and to whom, unless . . 381, 382
  where to be brought 376
 registered land 396
 share of petitioner in entire estate held by him jointly or in common, to be set off to him, but residue may be left for future partition . 378
 share of party, dying pending, to be assigned in his name to his estate 387
 trustee, when to be appointed . . 383
 water rights 394

PERPETUATION OF EVIDENCE,

 by executors and administrators, that notice of their appointment was given 103
 by executors, etc, of payments under decree of court 366
 by executors, etc, selling land under license, that notice of time and place of sale was given . . . 255

PERSONAL ESTATE,

 debts, etc, held by executor, etc, may be sold by order of court 185
 distribution of, among heirs . . 354
 final distribution of money invested or deposited by order of court 367, 368
 foreign administrators, etc, may be licensed to sell . 186
 how to be accounted for . 184
 in hands of guardian or trustee, may be sold by order of court and invested . . . 187, 189
 may be sold by executors, etc, without order of court 184
 mortgages of land, and land taken on execution, in hands of executors, etc, deemed 185
 sale of, may be ordered by court 184
 vested, contingent, or possible interest in, may be sold by executors, etc, under license . . 186

POLICE COURT,

 may issue *scire facias* against administrators, etc. . . . 206

POSTHUMOUS CHILDREN,

 guardian of, may be appointed by father in his will . . . 131
 omitted in father's will, to take share as of intestate estate 352

"PRESENCE OF TESTATOR,"

 what amounts to 36

PRESUMPTIONS,

 as to attestation of witnesses 38
 as to death of absent person 118, 357
 as to marriage and issue of absent heir 357
 as to survivorship, when several persons perish by same calamity 358

PRESUMPTIONS (*continued*).

	PAGE
as to testator's sanity	46
of testator's intention to revoke will	35
of testator's knowledge of contents of his will	35

PROBATE COURTS,

history and origin of,

under colony charter	1
under province charter	2
under state constitution	3

jurisdiction, general and in equity of . . 4–10, 157, 158

abandoned property of non-residents, appointment of receiver for	341–346
absentee's property, appointment of receiver for	341–346
administrators, appointment of	7, 102
adoption of children	8, note, 479
advancements, determination of questions as to	361
agreements of decedents, etc, to convey real estate, enforcement of	8, note, 448
apprenticeship, complaints in cases of	492

change of name	485, 486
charitable funds, removal of trustees of	163, 164
children, adoption of	8, note 479
children, petitions for care, etc, of	9
children, support of under guardianship	8, note, 454, 455
collateral legacy and succession tax	8, note, 522
complaint for concealment of property	14, 175
compromise or arbitration of controversies between claimants under a will and under statutes regulating descent and distribution, no power in probate court to authorize	9, 10, note
compromise of demands by or against estate	449
concurrent, in equity, with supreme judicial and superior courts of matters relative to wills, trusts, administration, etc	9, 157, 158
confirmation of certain defective and irregular acts and proceedings	100, 459
conservators of property of aged and feeble-minded persons, appointment of	8, note, 143
contempt, may punish for	12, 26
contingent remainders, etc, sale of land subject to	276, 277
court first taking jurisdiction to retain it, when case within jurisdiction of probate courts in two or more counties	10
curtesy, assignment of	327
curtesy, release of, of insane husband	136, 268, 269, 456, 457
curtesy, proceeds of, reserved for husband, when	137, 457
defective acts and proceedings, confirmation of	100, 459
delivery of property by executors, etc, to successors, enforcement of	13, 165

INDEX 785

PROBATE COURTS (*continued*) PAGE
deposits or investments . 13, 14, 190, 191, 206, 232, 388
deposits, unclaimed, disposal of . . 232, 367, 368
distribution of intestate estates . . . 354
dipsomaniacs, commitment of . . 8, note, 492, 493
dower, assignment of 327, 397
dower, release of, of insane wife . 136, 140, 268, 269, 456, 457
dower, proceeds of, reserved for wife . 137, 268, 401, 458
enforcement of delivery of property by executors, etc, to successors 13, 165
equity jurisdiction, concurrent with supreme judicial and superior courts as to trusts, wills, and administration of estates of decedents . 9, 157, 158
exclusive and original jurisdiction, when 7, 10, 455
executors, etc, appointment of 7, 8
feeble-minded, commitment of . . 8, note
French spoliation awards . . 8, note, 446, 447
guardians, appointment of . . . . 8, note, 126
    complaints for concealment of property by . . 175
    delivery of ward's property to successor, enforcement of . 13, 165
    leases by, of ward's real estate . . 278
    sales by, of ward's real estate 263
homestead, setting off and sale of . . 264, 423, 425
    release of, by guardian of insane person . . 136, 140, 268, 457
insolvent estates of deceased persons 211-238
inebriates, commitment of . . . . 8, note, 492, 493
insane persons, commitment of . . . 8, note, 492, 493
investments or deposits by executors, etc 13, 190, 232
jointure, assignment of 330
juvenile offenders, commitment of 491, 492
legacies, distribution of 359
liberty, personal, proceedings to obtain when wrongful deprivation of . . 8, note
married women, petitions relative to separate estate of 9
    support of, when living apart from husbands . . 451, 463
minors, appointment of guardians for . 126
    authorization of marriage of, ... 8, note
    petitions for care, etc., of 9, 452, 455, 463
    petition for support of . 8, note, 129, 452, 455
    partition of real estate, concurrent with superior court . 371
    of registered land . . 396
religious societies, removal of trustees of . 163, 164
rules and forms of, to make 11
sales and mortgages of land by conservators 143, 263-270, 273
    by executors, etc . 8, note, 239-263, 272, 273
    by guardians . . 263-270, 273

PROBATE COURTS (*continued*)

 for payment of collateral succession tax . . . 208, note, 518
 by receivers . . . 8, note, 344, 345
 of registered land, by receivers, etc . 492
 by trustees . . . . 8, note, 137, 187, 240, note, 273
 sales of personal property by executors, etc. 184
 specific performance of decedent's or ward's agreement to convey
  real property . . . . . . 8, note, 448
 support of minor child by parents . 8, note, 129
  of children or wife of insane person under guardianship 183, 310
 taxes, apportionment of, on collateral legacy . . . 208, 518
 taxes on collateral legacies and successions, to determine all questions relative to . . . . 8, note, 522
 trustee, appointment of, etc 144–158
 trusts created by will or other written instrument, in equity 9, 157, 158
 (*sessions of*) . . 26, 27, 488–491
  adjournment of 27
  always to be open for hearing, etc 26, 27
  holiday, time of holding when regular term occurs on . 27

PROBATE OF WILL,

 citation on petition for 71
  dispensed with, when 72
  how served 71
 conclusively establishes due execution . . . 29
 facts necessary to be proved for 30, 31
 necessary, to give it effect 30
 not barred by partial revocation 66
 of nuncupative wills . . . 83–87
 of wills accidentally, etc , lost or destroyed . . . 79
 of wills made out of the State 78
 petition for, to be filed with will 71
  certificate to be appended to 71

PUBLIC ADMINISTRATOR,

 accounts to be rendered by . . 279, 282
 appointment of, notice to be given within three months . . 192
  affidavit of notice of appointment to be made by . 193
  proceedings when notice not given 193
 authority of, over estate ceases, if husband, widow, etc, takes
  administration . 114
 bond of . . . 121
 deposit by, of balances with state treasurer . . . 282, 367
 duty of, on appointment of executor or administrator as successor 282
 duties of, how enforced . . . 369, 370
 entitled to administer, when . 114
 not entitled to administer, when husband, widow, or heir claims
  administration, or requests appointment of some suitable person 114

INDEX. 787

PUBLIC ADMINISTRATOR (*continued*) PAGE
    inventory, to be returned by . . . 168
    letters to be revoked, if will of deceased is afterward proved 165
    limitation of actions against . . . 195
    neglect of, to return inventory or perform other duties . . 283
    not liable to actions within one year, except . 202
    notice to, of application of heir, etc., to take administration, what
        required 369
    may adjust claims by arbitration or compromise when authorized
        by court . . 449
    may give separate bond for each estate or general bond . 121
    may be licensed to sell lands for payment of debts . . 239
        after three years may be licensed to sell lands not required for
            payment of debts, when 271
        proceedings in such case . 271
    may represent estate insolvent . . . 212
    sales of property by, how authorized . . . 271
    surrender by, of letters of administration, on appointment of
        executor or administrator 282

R.

REAL ESTATE,
    descent of (See *Descent*)
    held by executors, etc., in mortgage or on execution, deemed per-
        sonal estate . . . 245
    income of, to be accounted for by guardians and trustees 306
        to be accounted for by executors and administrators, when 293
    may be sold for distribution, when . 240
    partition of (See *Partition*)
    specific performance of agreement for sale of, how enforced 448
    surplus of proceeds of land sold by executors, etc., to be deemed
        and disposed of as . . . 261, 330

REGISTER OF PROBATE,
    appraisers, may be appointed by 23
    assistant registers, appointment of 23
    attachment, process of, to issue 23
    bonds, approval of sureties in 428, 429
    bond, to give 22
    care and custody of books and papers 22
    certified copy of will, inventory, etc., to make one without charge
        and deliver to executor, etc 17
    citations, etc., to issue 18
    docket, to keep a 12, 13
    clerk, may be appointed by register of probate of Suffolk county 24
    execution, to issue . . . 23

REGISTER OF PROBATE (continued).

	PAGE
fees, to pay over to state treasurer	23
index, to keep a	13
inspection of doings of, to be made by judge	24
may be appointed, in another county, guardian of his minor child	26
not to act as counsel or attorney	26
not to hold certain trusts, nor to be interested in fees or emoluments	25, 26
oaths to be taken by	21, 22
records, to furnish copies of	23
releases, etc, to record at request of party interested	16, 17
suits on bond of	25
temporary, when appointed	25

REGISTERED LAND,

partition of	306
sale or mortgage of	492

RELIGIOUS SOCIETIES,

may appoint trustees, when	152

REMAINDERS,

belonging to estate of deceased person, may be sold for payment of debts	243, note
land subject to contigent, may be sold by trustee	149
to be inherited	320

REMOVAL OF EXECUTORS, ADMINISTRATORS, GUARDIANS, AND TRUSTEES,

as to appeal from decree making removal	166
decrees making removals, effective, pending appeal, unless	166
grounds for removal	159, 161, 162
conflict of interest	159
incapacity or insanity	159
neglect to furnish bond or to render account when required	159
unfaithful administration	162
unsuitability	161
lawful acts of executors, etc, remain valid, although removed	164
one of two executors removed, other to proceed in the trust	163
petition for, by any person interested	164
proceedings for	163, 164
of trustee holding funds given to a city or town for charitable, etc, purposes, for neglect to make annual exhibit	163
to be on petition of five persons	164
of trustee, when essential to interests of parties concerned	163

REPRESENTATION,

inheritance by right of	346, 347

INDEX 789

RENTS OF REAL ESTATE, PAGE
   belong to heirs or devisees 293
   to be accounted for by executors and administrators, when   293, 294
   to be accounted for by guardians and trustees . . . 305

RESIGNATION OF EXECUTORS, ADMINISTRATORS, GUAR-
   DIANS, AND TRUSTEES,
   accounts first to be settled 165
   allowed by court, when 164

REVERSIONS,
   belonging to estate of deceased persons, may be sold for payment
      of debts . . . . 243, note
   inheritable . . . . 320, note

REVOCATION,
   of decrees of probate court . . . . . . 12, note

REVOCATION OF WILL,
   effect of, on codicil 64
   manner of 59
   express, by burning, tearing, etc 61
      by codicil 64
      declarations, to explain testator's intention 62
      declared intention, without act, not sufficient 62
      dependent on testator's intention . 62
      later inconsistent will 64
      presumptions as to intention . . . 63
      revocatory writing 66
   implied, from alteration of estate 68
      from marriage 67, 68
         exempt, when will makes provisions 67, 68
         not rebutted by parol evidence 67
      not from increase in value of estate . . . 69
      not from insanity of testator 69
      not from partition by tenants in common 69
   partial 64

REVOCATORY WRITING,
   how to be executed 66

"RIGHT OF REPRESENTATION,"
   inheritance by, how construed 346, 347

RULES OF PROBATE COURTS,
   authority to make 10, 11
   equity rules 531–538
   probate rules 527–531

S.

SALE OF LAND,
    by executors and administrators (see *Executor, sale of real estate by*) 239-262
    by foreign executors and administrators (see *Non-Resident Executors and Administrators*) 262, 263
    by guardians (see *Guardian, sale of real estate by*) . . 263-270
    by foreign guardian (see *Non-Resident Guardian*) . . 270-272
    by public administrator (see *Public Administrator*) 271
    by trustees 274, 275
    on petition of friend of a minor
        proceedings on such petition 265
        proceeds of, in such case, how disposed of 265

SCIRE FACIAS,
    issue of writs of, by police, district and municipal courts against administrators, etc 206

SECRETARY OF COMMONWEALTH,
    to publish annually changes of names 486

SESSIONS OF PROBATE COURTS,
    times and places of 488-491

SET-OFF,
    by administrator, etc, when sued, of demands of intestate, etc . 205
    of debt of deceased in action by administrator or executor . 205
    of debt due estate from heir, against distributive share . 359
    of debt due estate from legatee, against legacy . . 207
    probate court to determine validity and amount of debt . 207, 359

SISTERS,
    when entitled to administer as next of kin 110
    when to inherit 321

SIGNATURE OF TESTATOR,
    what is sufficient 32

SOLDIER,
    in actual military service, may make nuncupative will . . . 83
    in actual military service, when 86
    nuncupative will of, how made and proved 86, 87

"SOUND MIND," 44-56

SPECIAL ADMINISTRATOR,
    appointment of 104
    authority of . . . . 123, 242, note
    bond of 121
    certain expenses and debts may be paid by . 299, note
    may act, pending appeal, unless 123
    not liable to action by creditor 199
    who entitled to be appointed 107, 108

SPECIFIC PERFORMANCE,
    of written agreement for conveyance of lands, when party dies or is put under guardianship 448
        conveyance, how ordered 448
            effect of 448

SPENDTHRIFTS,
    guardians of, appointment of . . . 133–136
    sales of property of 266

STANDING WOOD AND TIMBER,
    held in dower, etc, when may be sold 150, 450
    on land of ward, guardian authorized to sell by license of court 264
    trustee may be appointed to sell and invest the proceeds . 150, 450

SUCCESSIONS. (See *Collateral Inheritance Tax*)

SUICIDE,
    as evidence of insanity 48

SUPERIOR COURT,
    appeals from probate court in certain cases . . . . 6, note, 463

SUPREME COURT OF PROBATE,
    supreme judicial court constituted 6
    appeal to, from probate court, by whom may be taken . 463
        when to be claimed and entered . . . 467
        proceedings on 467, 468
    may make rules regulating proceedings in probate court . . . 11
    may re-examine on appeal and affirm or reverse decrees of probate court 6

SURETIES,
    in probate bonds to be inhabitants of this state 428
        and such as the judge or register approves 428
    liable, when principal gives new bond, for all breaches prior to approval of new bond 432
    may be discharged, when court decrees it reasonable and proper 431
    may have suit continued when resident principal not made a party . 442

SURVIVORSHIP,
    not presumed, when all perish in same calamity 358

T.

TABLES,
    for ascertaining present value of life estate and of widow's dower 420, 421

TAX,
    on collateral inheritances, etc (See *Collateral Inheritance Tax.*)

TEMPORARY REGISTER OF PROBATE,
    appointed, when 25
    oath of 25

792 INDEX

TESTATOR (See *Will*)

TOWN,   PAGE
  may be trustee, when 152

TREASURER OF COMMONWEALTH,
  collateral inheritance and succession tax, to be payable to 517
    to apply for appointment of administrator on estates subject
      to, when . 532
    to cause property subject to, to be appraised . 521
      to pay fee of appraisers . 521
    copy of inventory of property subject to, register of probate
      to send to . . 519
    to enforce penalty for failure to file inventory of estate subject to 519
    to be made party to all petitions by foreign executors, etc , for
      license to receive and dispose of personal property 52
    to be notified of real estate subject to . 519
    to represent commonwealth in all court proceedings for deter-
      mining questions relative to . . 522
    to sue in his own name for unpaid tax 280, 523, and note

TRUST COMPANY,
  domestic, may be appointed administrator, executor, guardian, or
    trustee . . 96, 108, 120, 144, note, 153

TRUSTEE,
  accounts of (See *Accounts*)
  appointed by will should petition probate court to confirm appoint-
    ment 153
  appointed in what cases . . 144-153
    under will, when necessary to carry its provisions into effect 144
    under written instrument, to fill vacancy . . . 145
    when tenant for life or years and remainderman or reversioner
      sustain damages in their property by laying out, etc , of
      highway or by the taking of land for public uses, and
      entire damages are assessed . . . 146, 147
    when, in partition of land, an estate for life or years belongs
      to one person and the remainder to another . 148
    when husband or wife waives provision of will and becomes
      entitled to property exceeding $10,000 in value 148
    when probate court authorizes sale of land subject to contin-
      gent or vested remainder 149
    when standing wood or timber on land subject to estate for
      life or years have ceased to improve, to sell 150
    when person seised of real or personal estate upon a trust is
      a minor, insane, out of the state, or not amenable to legal
      process, trustee to convey may be appointed 278
  appointment of 144-157
    notice of petition for, to be given 144, 145, 150

INDEX 793

TRUSTEE (*continued*)
	PAGE
bond of	150, 154
none required of trustees of charitable trust	156
exempt from giving sureties, when	156
cemetery corporation may hold in trust funds for certain purposes	152
city or town may hold in trust funds for care, etc., of cemeteries and burial lots, and for laying out or improving parks	152
churches or religious societies may appoint trustees to hold property given to such churches or societies	152
collateral legacies and successions, taxes on to be paid	204, note, 208 note
delivery of property by, to successor, enforcement of	13, 165
deriving appointment from a court having no jurisdiction in this commonwealth and holding land in this commonwealth for residents here, to take out letters of trust from probate court in county where the land lies	151
embezzlement by, liability for	503
incorporated and unincorporated religious societies and churches may appoint trustees to hold funds given for their benefit	153
inventory to be returned by when directed by court	169
what to include and by whom made	171–173
mortgage of real estate by	273
non resident, to appoint agent in this commonwealth	154, 194
petition for appointment of	153
real estate, when may be conveyed by, free from curtesy or dower of insane person	269
release by, of certain vested, contingent, or possible interests in real property, when authorized	272
sale and mortgage by, of estates subject to remainders	276
trust companies, domestic, may be appointed	108
removal and resignation of	159–166
decrees making removals, effective, pending appeal, unless	166
grounds for removal	159, 162, 163
conflict of interest	159
incapacity or insanity	159
neglect to furnish bond or, when holding funds given to a city or town for charitable and other purposes, neglect to make annual exhibit	159, 163
removal from state and failure to appoint agent here	162
unfaithful administration	163
unsuitability	163
removal of, petition for	163
petition for, when holding funds given to city or town for charitable and other purposes, to be signed by five persons	164
notice of petition to be given	164
sale and investment by, of real or personal property	187

TRUSTEE PROCESS,   PAGE
   against administrators, etc 499
TRUSTEES (See also *Trustee*.)
   general equity jurisdiction of 157
   termination of certain 157

U.

UNDUE INFLUENCE,
   degree of, to invalidate will 56, 57
   evidence of 57
   may be invalidated in part only, by 59
   will obtained by, void 56

V.

VESTED RIGHTS,
   in real or personal estate, may be released by order of probate
   court 186
VOTING AT CORPORATION MEETINGS,
   right of, possessed by executor, etc 502

W.

WARRANTS OR COMMISSIONS OF PROBATE COURT,
   may be revoked 12
WEARING APPAREL,
   of widow, and of minor children of a deceased person, belongs to
   them 177
WIDOW,
   advancements, value of, to be deducted in determining share of,
   in husband's property 363
   entitled to administer husband's estate, when 110
      no right to name administrator, if she renounces administra-
      tion 110
      no right to other than original administration . . . 114
   entitled to allowance for necessaries from husband's estate . 328
   entitled to use of husband's house, free of charge, for six months 329
   rights of, in husband's property (see *Descent of Real Estate, rights
   of wife in husband's property*) 326–336
      (See *Dower* 327, 397–427)
   waiver of will by 330, 331
WIFE. (See *Married Woman*.)

INDEX. 795

WILL, PAGE
  agreements to make, or to give legacies 88
  allowance and probate necessary to make effective . . . 29, 30
  administration revoked upon 165
    decree for, conclusive as to capacity of testator and due execution, unless appealed from . 29
    conclusive, after two years, in favor of purchasers for value, etc . 29, note, 119, note
  attestation of, by three competent witnesses 30
    witnesses must sign in presence of testator and where he can see them subscribe 36
    witnesses need not sign in presence of each other . 38
  children dying before testator, effect upon . . 206, note, 352
    adopted child included in "child," when . . 483, 483, note
    issue to take by right of representation, when 352
    omitted children or issue of deceased child entitled to share as if parent intestate, unless . 319
  contribution by devisees or legatees to omitted or posthumous child . . . 352
  competency of attesting witnesses 39–42
    beneficial devise or legacy to subscribing witness to a will, or to the husband or wife of such witness, void unless three other competent subscribing witnesses 40
    creditor a competent witness . 40
    person convicted of infamous crime not competent witness 40, 41
  competency to be determined as of time of execution of will 41
  compromise of, only supreme judicial court jurisdiction to authorize 89
  concealment of, proceedings on complaints for . . 92
  deposit in registry of probate, if testator desires 91
  delivery of, after such deposit, in testator's lifetime, how obtained 91
    to whom 92
  execution of 31–39
    attestation by witnesses 36–39
    signature by testator 31–36
  facts to be proved in support of 31
  formal proceedings in probate of 70–77
    petition and notice 71
    hearing and evidence 72–76
  foreign will, allowance of 81–83
  incorporation of paper by reference in 77
  invalidated by fraud and undue influence . . 55
    attorney who drafted will may testify as to directions given him by testator . 59
    persuasions and suggestions do not necessarily amount to undue influence 57
    testator's declarations admissible . . . . . . 58, note

WILL (continued)

	PAGE
lucid intervals	53
memory of testator, "disposing" necessary	44, 45
monomania	54
sanity of testator, evidence on question of	46–55
persons competent to give in evidence their opinions as to	48
presumption in favor of	46
what testimony admissible to show insanity	48–55
married woman may make	30
of married woman, deserted by husband or justifiably living apart from him, provisions of cannot be waived by husband	30, note
lost, proof of	79–81
made out of state, proof of	78
nuncupative, proof of	83–87
requirements of	85
persons of full age and sound mind may make	30
posthumous child, to share as if parent died intestate	352
publication of, formal not necessary	34
seal not required	35
revocation of	59–70
express revocation of,	60–67
by burning, tearing, etc	59–64
by execution of new will or codicil	64–67
implied revocation of	67–70
by change in condition and circumstances of testator	67
by marriage	68
not by change in value of property	69
signature by testator	31
where to be made	32
may be by mark	32
may be written by another person by testator's direction and in his presence	32
need not be in presence of witnesses, but must be acknowledged in their presence	33
Sunday, executed on, valid	36
waiver of, by husband or widow	330, 331
what passes under	87, 89
witnesses to (See *Attesting Witnesses*)	

WITNESSES,

fees of	505
to wills	36–42

WRITTEN AGREEMENT,

to sell land, enforcement of, when party dies or is put under guardianship	448

INDEX TO PRÓBATE FORMS.

ABSENTEE,   PAGE
    petition for receivership of estate of 726
    order of notice 727
    return of service of order of notice 728
    warrant 729
    decree 729

ACCOUNTS,
    administrator 621
    executor 623
    trustee 625
    guardian 627
    appointment of guardian *ad litem* and next friend for . . . 638

ADMINISTRATION,
    with sureties, petition 539
    without sureties, petition 540
    de bonis non, petition 541
    special, petition 542
    public, petition 542
    with will annexed, petition 546
    de bonis non, with will annexed, petition . . . 547
    presumption of death, petition 717
    presumption of death, with will annexed, petition 713

ADOPTION AND CHANGE OF NAME,
    petition 657

AFFIDAVIT OF NOTICE OF APPOINTMENT,
    administrator 581, 599
        de bonis non 583
        agent 600
    public administrator 586
    executor 588, 591, 601
        agent 602
        foreign will 590
    administrator, will annexed 593, 603
        agent 604

INDEX

	PAGE
AMENDMENT,	
of record, petition	735
APPEARANCE,	691
APPOINTMENT, &c	627
of agent	686
of guardian *ad litem* and next friend	689
of guardian *ad litem* and next friend, account	698
of next friend and guardian for the case, in sale of real estate subject to vested or contingent remainder	647
APPRAISAL,	
petition for revocation of warrant, and for new warrant	609
ASSIGNMENT OF DOWER,	
petition	662
warrant	663
report	664
ASSIGNMENT OF HOMESTEAD,	
petition	660
warrant	661
report	662
ASSIGNMENT OF REAL ESTATE IN FEE,	
petition	665
warrant	666
report	667
by Court, petition	733
ASSIGNMENT OF WIDOW'S LIFE ESTATE,	
petition	667
warrant	668
report	669
AUDITOR,	
rule to	617
BOND,	
of administrator, with sureties	578
without sureties	548
de bonis non, with sureties	550
without sureties	551
will annexed, with sureties	559
without sureties	561
de bonis non, with sureties	562
presumption of death	718
with will annexed, presumption of death	714
of special administrator	553
of public administrator	554
of executor, with sureties	556

INDEX. 799

BOND (*continued*) PAGE
   of executor without sureties 557
      to pay debts, residuary 558
      presumption of death 710
   of guardian, with sureties 564
      without sureties 565
      of insane person 740
      spendthrift 567
   of conservator 693
   of receiver of absentee's estate . . . 730
   of trustee, with sureties 568
      without sureties 570
      with sureties, inventory not required 571
      without sureties, inventory not required 572
      under deed 723
   of heir, presumption of death . . . 722
   in case of sale of real estate subject to vested or contingent
      remainder . . . 646
   petition for new 579

BURIAL LOT,
   perpetual care of, petition 703

BUSINESS,
   petition of special administrator for leave to carry on 709

CHANGE OF NAME,
   petition 658
   copy of decree 659
   certificate 660

CLAIM OF APPEAL 690
CLAIM OF DOWER OR CURTESY 744

COMPROMISE,
   petition to arbitrate 629

CONSERVATORSHIP,
   of aged person, petition 692

CUSTODY OF CHILDREN,
   petition 657

DEBTS,
   petition by special administrator for leave to pay 702

DECLINATION 683

DEPOSIT,
   of legacy, petition 696
   payment of, petition 697
   in savings bank, petition 739

DESERTION AND LIVING APART,
petition 656
DISCHARGE FROM GUARDIANSHIP,
petition 681
DISCHARGE OF SURETY ON BOND,
petition 682
DISTRIBUTION,
warrant 619
report 620
intestate estate, petition . . . 620
of legacy among a class petition 784
among a class, trust estate, petition 734
presumption of death, petition 721

EMBEZZLEMENT,
complaint 688
EQUITY,
petition 691
decree 692
injunction 696

GUARDIANSHIP,
of minors, petition 574
of insane, petition 575
of spendthrift, petition 575
letter to foreign guardian 576

INJUNCTION 696
INSOLVENCY,
representation 610
representation, claims to be examined by court . . 699
INSOLVENT ESTATE,
order to administrator to notify creditors to present claims 611, 701
form of notice of administrator to creditors 612, 702
warrant to commissioners 613
report 614
form of notice of commissioners to creditors . 615
petition for new commissioner, and extending time for allowing
claims . . . 615
order for distribution . . . 616
report on order for distribution . . 617
INVENTORY,
administrator 605
executor 606
guardian 607

INDEX. 801

INVENTORY (*continued*)   PAGE
   trustee 608
   petition to render, and account 617
   order to render, or account 618

LEASE OF REAL ESTATE BY GUARDIAN,
   petition 690

LETTER,
   of administrator 580
      de bonis non 582
      presumption of death 720
   of special administrator 584
   of public administrator 584
   of executor 587
      residuary 591
      presumption of death 712
      on foreign will 589
   of administrator with will annexed 592
      presumption of death 716
   of guardian 594
   of guardianship to foreign guardian 595
   of conservator 695
   of receiver of absentee's estate 732
   of trustee 595
      not requiring inventory 596
      under deed 725

MARRIAGE,
   of minor, petition for license of 698

MORTGAGE OF REAL ESTATE,
   executor, administrator, petition 648
   guardian, petition 648
   trustee, petition 649

NOTICE OF APPOINTMENT,
   executor 597
      agent 597
   administrator 598
      agent 598
      will annexed 599
      agent 599
   petition for 683

PARTITION OF REAL ESTATE AMONG HEIRS,
   petition 670
   appointment of agent 671

51

802   INDEX.

PARTITION OF REAL ESTATE, ETC (*continued*)   PAGE
    notice by commissioners 671
    warrant 672
    report 673
PARTITION OF REAL ESTATE AMONG TENANTS IN
    COMMON,
    petition 674
    warrant 674
    report 675
PARTITION AND SALE OF REAL ESTATE AMONG
    TENANTS IN COMMON,
    petition 676
        sale of lands by commissioners, bond 677
        warrant 678
        report 679
        petition by commissioners for sale . . . 741
PRESUMPTION OF DEATH,
    probate of will, petition 649
    bond of executor 650
    executor's letter 652
    administration with will annexed, petition 653
    bond of administrator with will annexed 654
    letter of administrator with will annexed . . . 656
    administration, petition 657
    bond of administrator 658
    letter of administrator 660
    petition for distribution 661
    bond of heir 662

RECEIVERSHIP,
    of absent person's estate, petition 666
RELEASE OF RIGHT OF DOWER OF AN INSANE WOMAN,
    petition 647
REMOVAL,
    petition 681
RESIGNATION 683

SALE OF PERSONAL ESTATE,
    petition 645
        by foreign ——, petition 646
SALE OF REAL ESTATE,
    public, executor or administrator, petition 620
        license 631
        affidavit 631

SALE OF REAL ESTATE (*continued*)

	PAGE
private, executor or administrator, petition	632
license	634
administrator, distribution, petition	634
license	635
public, guardian, maintenance, petition	636
notice to overseers of poor of sale	637
license	637
affidavit	638
private, guardian, maintenance, petition	638
license	639
public, guardian, investment, petition	640
license	641
affidavit	641
private, guardian, investment, petition	642
license	643
subject to contingent remainder, petition	704
subject to vested remainder, petition	705
subject to vested or contingent remainder, bond	706
subject to vested or contingent remainder, appointment of next friend and guardian for the case	707

SALE OF TRUST ESTATE,

real, personal, trustee, petition	643
appointment of next friend	645

SEPARATE SUPPORT

petition	650
order of notice and attachment	651
petition to charge trustee and for execution	736, 737
execution	653
execution, trustee	738
capias	654
mittimus for contempt	655

SPECIFIC PERFORMANCE,

petition	708

SUIT ON BOND,

petition for leave to bring	743

TRUSTEESHIP,

to fill vacancy, petition	742
with sureties, petition	576
without sureties, petition	577
under written instrument, petition	723
waiver of will	744

WIDOW'S ALLOWANCE,
 petition 689
WILL,
 petition for probate, with sureties 543
  without sureties 544
 foreign, petition for allowance of 545
 petition to take deposition to 684
 deposition of witnesses to 685
 presumption of death, petition for probate 700